**7**th edition

# ETHICS
## for the information age

**7th edition**

# ETHICS
## for the information age

MICHAEL J. QUINN
Seattle University

**PEARSON**

Boston   Columbus   Indianapolis   New York   San Francisco   Hoboken
Amsterdam   Cape Town   Dubai   London   Madrid   Milan   Munich   Paris   Montreal   Toronto
Delhi   Mexico City   Sao Paulo   Sydney   Hong Kong   Seoul   Singapore   Taipei   Tokyo

*Editorial Director, ECS*   Marcia Horton
*Acquisitions Editor*   Matt Goldstein
*Editorial Assistant*   Kristy Alaura
*Executive Marketing Manager*   Tim Galligan
*Director of Marketing*   Christy Lesko
*Product Marketing Manager*   Bram van Kempen
*Field Marketing Manager*   Demetrius Hall
*Marketing Assistant*   Jon Bryant
*Team Lead Program and Product Management*   Scott Disanno
*Program Manager*   Carole Snyder
*Cover Designer*   Joyce Consentino Wells
*Text Designer*   Sandra Rigney
*Manager, Text Permissions*   Tim Nicholls
*Text Permission Project Manager*   Maya Gomez
*Media Project Manager*   Renata Butera
*Full-Service Project Management*   Cypress Graphics, Paul C. Anagnostopoulos
*Printer/Binder*   LSC Communications/Harrisonburg
*Text Fonts*   Minion and Nofret

Credits and acknowledgments borrowed from other sources and reproduced, with permission, appear on the appropriate page in the text.

Library of Congress Cataloging-in-Publication Data on file

5    18

ISBN 10: 0-13-429654-0
ISBN 13: 978-0-13-429654-8

# Brief Contents

# Contents

# 2  Introduction to Ethics   49

# 5   Information Privacy   227

# *6*    Privacy and the Government    271

## 8    Computer Reliability    365

**9  Professional Ethics**   413

# Appendix A: Plagiarism  503

# Preface

Computers and high-speed communication networks are transforming our world. These technologies have brought us many benefits, but they have also raised many social and ethical concerns. My view is that we ought to approach every new technology in a thoughtful manner, considering not just its short-term benefits, but also how its long-term use will affect our lives. A thoughtful response to information technology requires a basic understanding of its history, an awareness of current information-technology-related issues, and a familiarity with ethics. I have written *Ethics for the Information Age* with these ends in mind.

*Ethics for the Information Age* is suitable for college students at all levels. The only prerequisite is some experience using computers and the Internet. The book is appropriate for a stand-alone "computers and society" or "computer ethics" course offered by a computer science, business, or philosophy department. It can also be used as a supplemental textbook in a technical course that devotes some time to social and ethical issues related to computing.

As students discuss controversial issues related to information technology, they have the opportunity to learn from one other and improve their critical thinking skills. The provocative questions raised at the end of every chapter, together with dozens of in-class exercises, provide many opportunities for students to express their viewpoints. My hope is that they will get better at evaluating complex issues and defending their conclusions with facts, sound values, and rational arguments.

## WHAT'S NEW IN THE SEVENTH EDITION

The most significant change in the seventh edition is the reorganization of Chapter 4, Intellectual Property. The "new, improved" chapter is organized around six important themes:

- Intellectual property is different from tangible property. Trying to apply Locke's theory of property rights to intellectual property is problematic.

- Intellectual property is protected by trade secrets, trademarks, service marks, patents, and copyrights.

- Governments have attempted to find the proper balance between the interests of creators of intellectual property, who wish to maintain control over their creations, and the interests of the public, which wants to be able to use these creations. The concept of "fair use" is an example of such a compromise.

- The digital representation of intellectual property enables perfect copies to be made. Free copies are widely available, thanks to high-speed Internet connections. Together, these two technological developments have made possible an unprecedented amount of illegal copying, forcing companies selling these products to make "doing the right thing"—obtaining a legal copy—as easy as "doing the wrong thing"—obtaining a pirated copy [Christopher Kauffman, private communication].

- The concepts of copyright and patent have been extended to computer software, but issuing software patents has been problematic. The arguments for granting intellectual property protection to software are not strong.

- Some believe that the current system of intellectual property protection actually inhibits creativity. The open-source movement advocates the distribution of source code to programs. Creative Commons has developed licenses that make it easier for artists, musicians, and writers to use the Internet as a vehicle for stimulating creativity and enhancing collaboration.

The seventh edition also adds new coverage of many important recent developments. Among them are

- employers accessing social media to learn more about job candidates
- the growth of the "gig economy"
- the "right to be forgotten" and the European Union court order requiring Google to suppress certain search results
- revenge porn
- fake online reviews and efforts to filter them out
- the debate over whether mashups are a violation of copyright law
- breaches of privacy caused by corporations releasing large data sets that were not correctly anonymized
- the "smartphone patent wars"
- the Open Internet Order released by the Federal Communications Commission to preserve net neutrality
- responses by China and South Korea to the Internet addiction of many of its youth
- the use of darknets by criminals, political dissidents, and others
- recent US Supreme Court rulings that seem to indicate that software, as a class, is worthy of patent protection
- passage of the USA Freedom Act to reform the Patriot Act in light of Edward Snowden's revelations
- the emerging power of data brokers
- the trend away from using direct-recording electronic voting machines in the United States

The seventh edition contains many other improvements. It introduces two new ethical case studies: one in Chapter 4 and the other in Chapter 10. Dozens of new review questions require the reader to apply and analyze material appearing in the chapters, replacing more simplistic review questions. Finally, I have updated a significant number of facts and figures throughout the book.

## ORGANIZATION OF THE BOOK

The book is divided into 10 chapters. Chapter 1 has three objectives: to get the reader thinking about the process of technological change; to present a brief history of computing, networking, and information storage and retrieval; and to provide examples of moral problems brought about by the introduction of information technology.

Chapter 2 is an introduction to ethics. It presents nine different theories of ethical decision making, weighing the pros and cons of each one. Five of these theories—Kantianism, act utilitarianism, rule utilitarianism, social contract theory, and virtue ethics—are deemed the most appropriate "tools" for analyzing moral problems in the remaining chapters.

Chapters 3–10 discuss a wide variety of issues related to the introduction of information technology into society. I think of these chapters as forming concentric rings around a particular computer user.

Chapter 3 is the innermost ring, dealing with what can happen when people communicate over the Internet using the Web, email, and Twitter. Issues such as the increase in spam, easy access to pornography, cyberbullying, and Internet addiction raise important questions related to quality of life, free speech, and censorship.

The next ring, Chapter 4, deals with the creation and exchange of intellectual property. It discusses intellectual property rights; legal safeguards for intellectual property; the definition of fair use; the impact of digital media, peer-to-peer networks, and cyberlockers; the legitimacy of intellectual property protection for software; and the rise of the open-source movement.

Chapter 5 focuses on information privacy. What is privacy exactly? Is there a natural right to privacy? How do others learn so much about us? The chapter examines the electronic trail that people leave behind when they use a cell phone, make credit card purchases, open a bank account, go to a physician, or apply for a loan, and it explains how mining data to predict consumer behavior has become an important industry.

Chapter 6 focuses on privacy and the US government. Using Daniel Solove's taxonomy of privacy as our organizing principle, we look at how the government has steered between the competing interests of personal privacy and public safety. We consider US legislation to restrict information collection and government surveillance; government regulation of private databases and abuses of large government databases; legislation to reduce the dissemination of information and legislation that has had the opposite effect; and finally government actions to prevent the invasion of privacy as well as invasive government actions. Along the way, we discuss the implications of the USA PATRIOT Act and the debate over the REAL ID Act to establish a de facto national identification card.

Chapter 7 focuses on the vulnerabilities of networked computers. A case study focuses on the release of the Firesheep extension to the Firefox Web browser. A section on malware discusses rootkits, spyware, cross-site scripting, and drive-by downloads. We discuss common Internet-based attacks—phishing, spear phishing, SQL injection, denial-of-service attacks, and distributed denial-of-service attacks—and how they are used for cyber crime, cyber espionage, and cyber attacks. We conclude with a discussion of the risks associated with online voting.

Computerized system failures have led to lost business, the destruction of property, human suffering, and even death. Chapter 8 describes some notable software system failures, including the story of the Therac-25 radiation therapy system. It also discusses the reliability of computer simulations, the emergence of software engineering as a distinct discipline, and the validity of software warranties.

Chapter 9 is particularly relevant for those readers who plan to take jobs in the computer industry. The chapter presents a professional code related to computing, the Software Engineering Code of Ethics and Professional Practice, followed by an analysis of the code. Several case studies illustrate how to use the code to evaluate moral problems related to the use of computers. The chapter concludes with an ethical evaluation of whistle-blowing, an extreme example of organizational dissent.

Chapter 10 raises a wide variety of issues related to how information technology has impacted work and wealth. Topics include workplace monitoring, telecommuting, and globalization. Does automation increase unemployment? Is there a "digital divide" separating society into "haves" and "have nots"? Is information technology widening the gap between rich and poor? These are just a few of the important questions the chapter addresses.

## NOTE TO INSTRUCTORS

In December 2013, a joint task force of the Association for Computing Machinery and the IEEE Computer Society released the final draft of *Computer Science Curricula 2013* (www.acm.org/education/CS2013-final-report.pdf). The report recommends that every undergraduate computer science degree program incorporate instruction related to Social Issues and Professional Practice through "a combination of one required course along with short modules in other courses" (*Computer Science Curricula 2013*, p. 193). *Ethics for the Information Age* covers nearly all of the core and elective material described in the report, with the notable exception of Professional Communications. Table 1 shows

| Name | Chapter(s) |
|------|-----------|
| SP/Social Context | 3, 10 |
| SP/Analytical Tools | 2 |
| SP/Professional Ethics | 9 |
| SP/Intellectual Property | 4 |
| SP/Privacy and Civil Liberties | 5, 6 |
| SP/Sustainability | 8, 10 |
| SP/History | 1 |
| SP/Economies of Computing | 10 |
| SP/Security Policies, Laws, and Computer Crimes | 7 |

TABLE 1 Mapping between the conceptual areas of Social and Professional Issues in *Computer Science Curricula 2013* and the chapters of this book.

the mapping between the other conceptual areas within Social Issues and Professional Practice and the chapters of this book.

The organization of the book makes it easy to adapt to your particular needs. If your syllabus does not include the history of information technology, you can skip the middle three sections of Chapter 1 and still expose your students to examples motivating the formal study of ethics in Chapter 2. After Chapter 2, you may cover the remaining chapters in any order you choose, because Chapters 3–10 do not depend on one other.

Many departments choose to incorporate discussions of social and ethical issues throughout the undergraduate curriculum. The independence of Chapters 3–10 makes it convenient to use *Ethics for the Information Age* as a supplementary textbook. You can simply assign readings from the chapters most closely related to the course topic.

## SUPPLEMENTS

The following supplements are available to qualified instructors on Pearson's Instructor Resource Center. Please contact your local Pearson sales representative or visit www .pearsonhighered.com/educator to access this material.

- An instructor's manual provides tips for teaching a course in computer ethics. It also contains answers to all of the review questions.

- A test bank contains more than 300 multiple-choice, fill-in-the-blank, and essay questions that you can use for quizzes, midterms, and final examinations.

- A set of PowerPoint lecture slides outlines the material covered in every chapter.

## FEEDBACK

*Ethics for the Information Age* cites hundreds of sources and includes dozens of ethical analyses. Despite my best efforts and those of many reviewers, the book is bound to contain errors. I appreciate getting comments (both positive and negative), corrections, and suggestions from readers. Please send them to quinnm@seattleu.edu or Michael J. Quinn, Seattle University, College of Science and Engineering, 901 12th Avenue, Seattle, WA 98122.

## ACKNOWLEDGMENTS

I appreciate the continuing support of a great publications team, beginning with editor Matt Goldstein, and including Carole Snyder, Scott Disanno, Kristy Alaura, Joyce Wells, Paul Anagnostopoulos, Jacqui Scarlott, Jennifer McClain, Richard Camp, Laurel Muller, and Ted Laux. I thank them and everyone else who helped produce this edition.

A superb group of reviewers provided me with many helpful suggestions regarding new material to incorporate into the seventh edition. My thanks to Richard Egan, New Jersey Institute of Technology; Fred Geldon, George Mason University; D.C. Grant, Columbia Basin College; Musconda Kapatamoyo, Southern Illinois University, Edwardsville; Christopher Kauggman, George Mason University; James Markulic, New Jersey Institute of Technology; Linda O'Hara, Oregon State University; Dorothy Sunio, Leeward Community College; and Todd Will, New Jersey Institute of Technology.

I am grateful to professors Paulette Kidder and Gregory Silverman of Seattle University, who reviewed the new case studies and provided me with helpful suggestions on how to improve them.

I thank all who participated in the creation of the first six editions or provided useful suggestions for the seventh edition: Paul Anagnostopoulos, Valerie Anctil, Beth Anderson, Bob Baddeley, George Beekman, Brian Breck, Maria Carl, Sherry Clark, Thomas Dietterich, Roger Eastman, Beverly Fusfield, Robert Greene, Peter Harris, Susan Hartman, Michael Hirsch, Michael Johnson, Paulette Kidder, Marilyn Lloyd, Pat McCutcheon, Beth Paquin, Konrad Puczynski, Brandon Quinn, Courtney Quinn, Stuart Quinn, Victoria Quinn, Charley Renn, Gregory Silverman, Lindsey Triebel, Charles Volzka, Shauna Weaver, and Todd Will.

Reviewers of previous editions include Ramprasad Bala, University of Massachusetts at Dartmouth; Phillip Barry, University of Minnesota; Bo Brinkman, Miami University; Diane Cassidy, University of North Carolina at Charlotte; Madhavi M. Chakrabarty, New Jersey Institute of Technology; John Clark, University of Colorado at Denver; Timothy Colburn, University of Minnesota Duluth; Lorrie Faith Cranor, Carnegie Mellon University; Lee D. Cornell, Minnesota State University, Mankato; Donna Maria D'Ambrosio, University of South Florida; Dawit Demissie, The Sage Colleges; J.C. Diaz, University of Tulsa; Richard W. Egan, New Jersey Institute of Technology; Fred Geldon, George Mason University; David Goodall, State University of New York at Albany; Richard E. Gordon, University of Delaware; Mike Gourley, University of Central Oklahoma; Robert Greene, University of Wisconsin-Eau Claire; Fritz H. Grupe, University of Nevada, Reno; Ric Heishman, George Mason University; Gurdeep Hura, University of Maryland Eastern Shore; Evelyn Lulis, DePaul University; Tamara A. Maddox, George Mason University; Aparna Mahadev, Worcester State University; Eric Manley, Drake University; Richard D. Manning, Nova Southeastern University; John G. Messerly, University of Texas at Austin; Joe Oldham, Centre College; Mimi Opkins, California State University, Long Beach; Daniel Palmer, Kent State University; Holly Patterson-McNeill, Lewis-Clark State College; Colin Potts, Georgia Tech; Jason Rogers, George Mason University; Medha S. Sarkar, Middle Tennessee State University; Michael Scanlan, Oregon State University; Robert Sloan, University of Illinois at Chicago; Matthew Stockton, Portland Community College; Leon Tabak, Cornell College; Renée Turban, Arizona State University; Scott Vitz, Indiana University–Purdue University Fort Wayne; David Womack, University of Texas at San Antonio; John Wright, Juniata College; and Matthew Zullo, Wake Technical Community College.

Finally, I am indebted to my wife, Victoria, for her support and encouragement. You are a wonderful helpmate. Thanks for everything.

Michael J. Quinn
*Seattle, Washington*

We never know how high we are
Till we are called to rise;
And then, if we are true to plan,
Our statures touch the skies.

The heroism we recite
Would be a daily thing,
Did not ourselves the cubits warp
For fear to be a king.

—EMILY DICKINSON, *Aspiration*

I dedicate this book to my children *Shauna, Brandon,* and *Courtney.*

Know that my love goes with you, wherever your aspirations may lead you.

# 1

# Catalysts for Change

A tourist came in from Orbitville,
parked in the air, and said:

The creatures of this star
are made of metal and glass.

Through the transparent parts
you can see their guts.

Their feet are round and roll
on diagrams of long

measuring tapes, dark
with white lines.

They have four eyes.
The two in back are red.

Sometimes you can see a five-eyed
one, with a red eye turning

on the top of his head.
He must be special—

the others respect him
and go slow

when he passes, winding
among them from behind.

They all hiss as they glide,
like inches, down the marked

tapes. Those soft shapes,
shadowy inside

the hard bodies—are they
their guts or their brains?

—MAY SWENSON, "Southbound on the Freeway"[1]

**FIGURE 1.1** Low-cost computers and high-speed communication networks make possible the products of the Information Age, such as the Apple iPhone 6. It functions as a phone, email client, Web browser, camera, video recorder, digital compass, and more. (Richard Sharrocks/Alamy)

## 1.1 Introduction

MOST OF US TAKE TECHNOLOGICAL CHANGE FOR GRANTED. In the past two decades alone, we have witnessed the emergence of exciting new technologies, including smartphones, digital photography, automobile navigation systems, and Internet-based music and video streaming. There is good reason to say we are living in the Information Age. Never before have so many people had such easy access to information. The two principal catalysts for the Information Age have been low-cost computers and high-speed communication networks (Figure 1.1). Even in a society accustomed to change, the rate at which computers and communication networks have transformed our lives is breathtaking.

In 1950 there were no more than a handful of electronic digital computers in the world. Today we are surrounded by devices containing embedded computers. We rely upon microprocessors to control our heating and cooling systems, microwaves, smartphones, elevators, and a multitude of other devices we use every day. Thanks to microprocessors, our automobiles get better gas mileage and produce less pollution. On the other hand, the days of the do-it-yourself tune-up are gone. It takes a mechanic with computerized diagnostic equipment to work on a modern engine.

In 1990 few people other than college professors used email. Today more than a billion people around the world have email accounts. Email messages are routed instantaneously for very low cost, which can be both a blessing and a curse. Business communications have never been so efficient, but it's not unusual to hear businesspeople complain that they can never get caught up with their email.

The World Wide Web was still being designed in 1990; today it contains more than a trillion pages and makes possible extraordinarily valuable information retrieval systems. Even grade school children are expected to gather information from the Web when writing their reports. However, many parents worry that their Web-surfing children may be exposed to pornographic images or other inappropriate material.

May Swenson has vividly described our ambivalent feelings toward technology. In her poem "Southbound on the Freeway," an alien hovers above an expressway and watches the cars move along [1]. The alien notes "soft shapes" inside the automobiles and wonders, "are they their guts or their brains?" It's fair to ask: Do we drive technology, or does technology drive us?

Our relationship with technology is complicated. We create technology and choose to adopt it. However, once we have adopted a technological device, it can transform us and how we relate to other people and our environment.

Some of the transformations are physical. The neural pathways and synapses in our brains demonstrate neuroplasticity: literally changing with our experiences. One well-known brain study focused on London taxi drivers. In order to get a license, aspiring London taxi drivers must spend two to four years memorizing the complicated road network of 25,000 streets within 10 kilometers of the Charing Cross train station, as well as the locations of thousands of tourist destinations. The hippocampus is the region of the brain responsible for long-term memory and spatial navigation. Neuroscientists at University College London found that the brains of London taxi drivers have larger-than-average hippocampi and that the hippocampi of aspiring taxi drivers grow as they learn the road network [2].

Stronger longer-term memory and spatial navigation skills are great outcomes of mental exercise, but sometimes the physical effects of our mental exertions are more insidious. For example, studies with macaque monkeys suggest that when we satisfy our hunger for quick access to information through our use of Web browsers, Twitter, and texting, neurons inside our brains release dopamine, producing a desire to seek out additional information, causing further releases of dopamine, and so on, which may explain why we find it difficult to break away from these activities [3, 4].

Adopting a technology can change our perceptions, too. More than 90 percent of cell phone users report that having a cell phone makes them feel safer, but once people get used to carrying a cell phone, losing the phone may make them feel more vulnerable than they ever did before they began carrying one. A Rutgers University professor asked his students to go without their cell phones for 48 hours. Some students couldn't do it. A female student reported to the student newspaper, "I felt like I was going to get raped if I didn't have my cell phone in my hand." Some parents purchase cell phones for their

**FIGURE 1.2** The Amish carefully evaluate new technologies, choosing those that enhance family and community solidarity. (AP photo/*The Indianapolis Star and News*, Mike Fender)

children so that a child may call a family member in an emergency. However, parents who provide a cell phone "lifeline" may be implicitly communicating to their children the idea that people in trouble cannot expect help from strangers [5].

The Amish understand that the adoption of a new technology can affect the way people relate to each other (Figure 1.2). Amish bishops meet twice a year to discuss matters of importance to the church, including whether any new technologies should be allowed. Their discussion about a new technology is driven by the question, "Does it bring us together, or draw us apart?" You can visit an "Old Order" Amish home and find a gas barbecue on the front porch but no telephone inside, because they believe gas barbecues bring people together while telephones interfere with face-to-face conversations [6].

New technologies are adopted to solve problems, but they often create problems, too. The automobile has given people the ability to travel where they want, when they want. On the other hand, millions of people spend an hour or more each day stuck in traffic commuting between home and work. Refrigerators make it possible for us to keep food fresh for long periods of time. We save time because we don't have to go grocery shopping every day. Unfortunately, Freon leaking from refrigerators has contributed to the depletion of the ozone layer that protects us from harmful ultraviolet rays. New communication technologies have made it possible for us to get access to news and entertainment from around the world. However, the same technologies have enabled major software companies to move thousands of jobs to India, China, and Vietnam, putting downward pressure on the salaries of computer programmers in the United States [7].

We may not be able to prevent a new technology from being invented, but we do have control over whether to adopt it. Nuclear power is a case in point. Nuclear power plants create electricity without producing carbon dioxide emissions, but they also produce radioactive waste products that must be safely stored for 100,000 years. Although nuclear power technology is available, no new nuclear power plants were built in the United States for more than 25 years after the accident at Three Mile Island in 1979 [8].

Finally, we *can* influence the rate at which new technologies are developed. Some societies, such as the United States, have a history of nurturing and exploiting new inventions. Congress has passed intellectual property laws that allow people to make money from their creative work, and the federal income tax structure allows individuals to accumulate great wealth.

Most of us appreciate the many beneficial changes that technology has brought into our lives. In health care alone, computed tomography (CT) and magnetic resonance imaging (MRI) scanners have greatly improved our ability to diagnose major illnesses; new vaccines and pharmaceuticals have eradicated some deadly diseases and brought others under control; and pacemakers, hearing aids, and artificial joints have improved the physical well-being of millions.

To sum up, societies develop new technologies to solve problems or make life better, but the use of new technologies changes social conditions and may create new problems. That doesn't mean we should never adopt a new technology, but it does give us a good reason why we should be making informed decisions, weighing the benefits and potential harms associated with the use of new devices. To that end, this book will help you gain a better understanding of contemporary ethical issues related to the use of information technology.

This chapter sets the stage for the remainder of the book. Electronic digital computers and high-performance communication networks are central to contemporary information technology. While the impact of these inventions has been dramatic in the past few decades, their roots go back hundreds of years. Section 1.2 tells the story of the development of computers, showing how they evolved from simple manual calculation aids to complex microprocessors. In Section 1.3 we describe two centuries of progress in networking technology, starting with the semaphore telegraph and culminating in the creation of an email system connecting over a billion users. Section 1.4 shows how information storage and retrieval evolved from the creation of the Greek alphabet to Google. Finally, Section 1.5 discusses some of the moral issues that have arisen from the deployment of information technology.

## 1.2  Milestones in Computing

Calculating devices have supported the development of commercial enterprises, governments, science, and weapons. As you will see in this section, the introduction of new technologies has often had a social impact.

### 1.2.1  Aids to Manual Calculating

Adding and subtracting are as old as commerce and taxes. Fingers and toes are handy calculation aids, but to manipulate numbers above 20, people need more than their own digits. The tablet, the abacus, and mathematical tables are three important aids to manual calculating [9].

Simply having a tablet to write down the numbers being manipulated is a great help. In ancient times, erasable clay and wax tablets served this purpose. By the late Middle Ages, Europeans often used erasable slates. Paper tablets became common in the nineteenth century, and they are still popular today.

An **abacus** is a computing aid in which a person performs arithmetic operations by sliding counters along rods, wires, or lines. The first abacus was probably developed in the Middle East more than 2,000 years ago. In a Chinese, Japanese, or Russian abacus, counters move along rods or wires held in a rectangular frame. Beginning in medieval Europe, merchants performed their calculations by sliding wooden or metal counters along lines drawn in a wooden counting board (Figure 1.3). Eventually, the word "counter" came to mean not only the disk being manipulated but also the place in a store where transactions take place [9].

Mathematical tables have been another important aid to manual computing for about 2,000 years. A great breakthrough occurred in the early seventeenth century, when John Napier and Johannes Kepler published tables of logarithms. These tables were tremendous time savers to anyone doing complicated math because they allowed them to multiply two numbers by simply adding their logarithms. Many other useful tables were created as well. For example, businesspeople consulted tables to compute interest and convert between currencies. Today people who compute their income taxes "by hand" make use of tax tables to determine how much they owe.

Even with tablets, abacuses, and mathematical tables, manual calculating is slow, tedious, and error-prone. To make matters worse, mathematical tables prepared centuries ago usually contained errors. That's because somebody had to compute each table entry and somebody had to typeset each entry, and errors could occur in either of these steps. Advances in science, engineering, and business in the post-Renaissance period motivated European inventors to create new devices to make calculations faster and more reliable and to automate the printing of mathematical tables.

### 1.2.2  Mechanical Calculators

Blaise Pascal had a weak physique but a powerful mind. When he got tired of summing by hand long columns of numbers given him by his father, a French tax collector, he constructed a mechanical calculator to speed the chore. Pascal's calculator, built in 1640, was capable of adding whole numbers containing up to six digits. Inspired by Pascal's invention, the German Gottfried Leibniz constructed a more sophisticated calculator that could add, subtract, multiply, and divide whole numbers. The hand-cranked machine, which he called the Step Reckoner, performed multiplications and divisions through repeated additions and subtractions, respectively. The calculators of Pascal and Leibniz were not reliable, however, and did not enjoy commercial success.

**FIGURE 1.3** This illustration from Gregor Reisch's *Margarita Philosophica*, published in 1503, shows two aids to manual calculating. The person on the left is using a tablet; the person on the right is adding numbers using a counting board, a type of abacus. (Heritage Images/Fine Art/Corbis)

In the nineteenth century, advances in machine tools and mass-production methods, combined with larger markets, made possible the creation of practical calculating machines. Frenchman Charles Thomas de Colmar utilized the stepped drum gear mechanism invented by Leibniz to create the Arithmometer, the first commercially successful calculator. Many insurance companies purchased Arithmometers to help their actuaries compute rate tables more rapidly [9].

Swedish publisher Georg Scheutz was intimately familiar with printing errors associated with the production of mathematical tables. He resolved to build a machine capable of automatically calculating and typesetting table values. Scheutz knew about the earlier work of English mathematician Charles Babbage, who had demonstrated how a machine could compute the values of polynomial functions through the method of differences. Despite promising early results, Babbage's efforts to construct a full-scale difference engine had been unsuccessful. In contrast, Georg Scheutz and his son Edvard, who developed their own designs, completed the world's first printing calculator: a machine capable of calculating mathematical tables and typesetting the values onto molds. The Dudley Observatory in Albany, New York, purchased the Scheutz difference engine in 1856. With support from the US Nautical Almanac Office, astronomers used the machine to help them compute the motion of Mars and the refraction of starlight. Difference engines were never widely used; the technology was eclipsed by the emergence of simpler and less expensive calculating machines [9].

America in the late 1800s was fertile ground for the development of new calculating technologies. This period of American history, commonly known as the Gilded Age, was characterized by rapid industrialization, economic expansion, and a concentration of corporate power. Corporations merged to increase efficiency and profits, but the new, larger corporate organizations had multiple layers of management and multiple locations. In order for middle- and upper-level managers to monitor and improve performance, they needed access to up-to-date, comprehensive, reliable, and affordable information. All these requirements could not be met by bookkeepers and accountants using pen and paper to sum long columns of transactions by hand [10].

To meet this demand, many entrepreneurs began producing adding and calculating machines. One of these inventors was William Burroughs, a former bank clerk who had spent long days adding columns of figures. Burroughs devised a practical adding machine and offered it for sale. He found himself in a cutthroat market; companies competed fiercely to reduce the size of their machines and make them faster and easier to use. Burroughs distinguished himself from his competitors by putting together first-class manufacturing and marketing organizations, and by the 1890s the Burroughs Adding Machine Company led the industry. Calculating machines were entrenched in the offices of large American corporations by the turn of the century [10].

The adoption of mechanical calculators led to the "de-skilling" and "feminization" of bookkeeping (Figure 1.4). Before the introduction of calculating machines, offices were a male bastion, and men who could rapidly compute sums by hand were at a premium. Calculators leveled the playing field, making people of average ability quite productive. In fact, a 1909 Burroughs study concluded that a clerk using a calculator was six times faster than a clerk adding the same column of figures by hand [11]. As managers introduced mechanical calculators into offices, they replaced male bookkeepers with female bookkeepers and lowered wages. In 1880 only 5.7 percent of bookkeepers, cashiers, and accountants were women, but by 1910 the number of women in these jobs had risen to 38.5 percent [12].

## 1.2.3  Cash Register

Store owners in the late 1800s faced challenges related to accounting and embezzlement. Keeping accurate sales records was becoming more difficult as smaller stores evolved

FIGURE 1.4 Mechanical calculators led to the "de-skilling" and "feminization" of book-keeping. (Automatic Data Processing (ADP))

into "department stores" with several departments and many clerks. Preventing embezzlement was tricky when clerks could steal cash simply by not creating receipts for some sales.

While on a European holiday in 1878, Ohio restaurateur James Ritty saw a mechanical counter connected to the propeller shaft of his ship. A year later he and his brother John used that concept to construct the first cash register, essentially an adding machine capable of expressing values in dollars and cents. Enhancements followed rapidly, and by the early 1900s the cash register had become an important information-processing device (Figure 1.5). Cash registers created printed, itemized receipts for customers, maintained printed logs of transactions, and performed other accounting functions that provided store owners with the detailed sales records they needed.

Cash registers also made embezzlement by clerks more difficult. The bell made it impossible for clerks to sneak money from the cash drawer and helped ensure that every sale was "rung up." Printed logs made it easy for department store owners to compare cash on hand against sales receipts [10].

### 1.2.4 Punched–Card Tabulation

As corporations and governmental organizations grew larger in the late 1800s, they needed to handle greater volumes of information. One of these agencies was the US Bureau of the Census, which collected and analyzed information on tens of millions of residents every decade. Aware of the tedium and errors associated with clerks manually copying and tallying figures, several Census Bureau employees developed mechanical tabulating machines. Herman Hollerith created the most successful device. Unlike a predecessor, who chose to record information on rolls of paper, Hollerith decided to record information on punched cards. The use of punched cards to store data was a

**FIGURE 1.5** An NCR cash register in Miller's Shoe Shine Parlor, Dayton, Ohio (1904). (The NCR Archive at Dayton History)

much better approach because cards could be sorted into groups, allowing the computation of subtotals by categories. Hollerith's equipment proved to be a great success when used in the 1890 census. In contrast to the 1880 census, which had required eight years to complete, the 1890 census was finished in only two years. Automating the census saved the Census Bureau five million dollars, about one-third of its annual budget [13].

Other data-intensive organizations found applications for punched cards. Railroads used them to improve their accounting operations and send bills out more frequently. Retail organizations, such as Marshall Field's, used punched cards to perform more sophisticated analyses of information generated by the cash registers at its many stores. The Pennsylvania Steel Company and other heavy industries began to use punched-card technology to do cost accounting on manufacturing processes.

The invention of sorters, tabulators, and other devices to manipulate the data on punched cards created a positive feedback loop. As organizations began using tabulating machines, they thought up new uses of information-processing equipment, stimulating further technological innovations.

International Business Machines (IBM) is the corporate descendant of Hollerith's company. Over a period of several decades, IBM and its principal competitor, Remington Rand, developed sophisticated machines based around punched cards: card punches, card verifiers, card tabulators, card sorters, and alphabetizers. Customers used these devices to create **data-processing systems** that received input data, performed one or more calculations, and produced output data. Within these systems, punched cards stored input data, intermediate results, and output data. In the most complicated systems, punched cards also stored the program—the steps of the computational process to be followed. Early systems relied on human operators to carry cards from one machine to the next. Later systems had electrical connections that allowed the output of one machine to be transmitted to the next machine without the use of punched cards or human intervention.

Organizations with large data-processing needs found punched-card tabulators and calculators to be valuable devices, and they continually clamored for new features that would improve the computational capabilities and speed of their systems [10]. These organizations would become a natural market for commercial electronic digital computers.

Some customers of data-processing equipment used these systems for nefarious purposes. For example, IBM machines played an infamous role in the Holocaust. After Adolf Hitler came to power in Germany in 1933, IBM chief executive Thomas J. Watson overlooked well-publicized accounts of anti-Semitic violence and the opening of concentration camps, focusing instead on a golden business opportunity. The firm expanded the operations of its German subsidiary, Dehomag, built a new factory in Germany, and actively sought business from the German government. Tabulating, sorting, collating, and alphabetizing machines and support services provided by Dehomag allowed the Nazi government to rapidly conduct censuses, identify acknowledged Jews and those with Jewish ancestors, and generate the alphabetical lists of names needed to efficiently seize their assets, confine them to ghettos, and deport them to death camps [13].

### 1.2.5 Precursors of Commercial Computers

Several computing devices developed during and immediately after World War II paved the way for the commercialization of electronic digital computers.

Between 1939 and 1941, Iowa State College professor John Atanasoff and his graduate student Clifford Berry constructed an electronic device for solving systems of linear equations. The Atanasoff-Berry Computer was the first computing device built with vacuum tubes, but it was not programmable.

Dr. John W. Mauchly, a physics professor at the University of Pennsylvania, visited Iowa State College in 1941 to learn more about the Atanasoff-Berry Computer. After he returned to Penn, Mauchly worked with J. Presper Eckert to create a design for an electronic computer to speed the computation of artillery tables for the US Army. They led a team that completed work on the ENIAC (electronic numerical integrator and computer) in 1946. As it turns out, the war ended before the ENIAC could provide the Army with any ballistics tables, but its speed was truly impressive. A person with a desk

FIGURE 1.6  The ENIAC's first six programmers were women. Every instruction was programmed by connecting several wires into plugboards. (Historical/Corbis)

calculator could compute a 60-second trajectory in 20 hours. The ENIAC performed the computation in 30 seconds. In other words, the ENIAC was 2,400 times faster than a person with a desk calculator.

The ENIAC had many features of a modern computer. All of its internal components were electronic, and it could be programmed to perform a variety of computations. However, its program was not stored inside memory. Instead, it was "wired in" from the outside. Reprogramming the computer meant removing and reattaching many wires. This process could take many days (Figure 1.6).

Even before the ENIAC was completed, work began on a follow-on system called the EDVAC (electronic discrete variable automatic computer). The design of the EDVAC incorporated many improvements over the ENIAC. The most important improvement was that the EDVAC stored the program in primary memory, along with the data manipulated by the program. In 1946 Eckert, Mauchly, and several other computer pioneers gave a series of 48 lectures at the Moore School. While some of the lectures discussed lessons learned from the ENIAC, others focused on the design of its successor, the EDVAC. These lectures influenced the design of future machines built in the United States and the United Kingdom.

During World War II, British engineer F. C. Williams was actively involved in the development of cathode ray tubes (CRTs) used in radar systems. After the war, he decided to put his knowledge to use by figuring out how to use a CRT as a storage device for digital information. In early 1948 a team at the University of Manchester set out to build a small computer that would use a CRT storage device, now called the Williams Tube, to store the program and its data. They called their system the Small-Scale Experimental Machine. The computer successfully executed its first program in 1948. The Small-Scale Experimental Machine was the first operational, fully electronic computer system that had both program and data stored in its memory.

### 1.2.6 First Commercial Computers

In 1951 the British corporation Ferranti Ltd. introduced the Ferranti Mark 1, the world's first commercial computer. The computer was the direct descendant of research computers constructed at the University of Manchester. Ferranti delivered nine computers between 1951 and 1957, and later Ferranti models boasted a variety of technological breakthroughs, thanks to the company's close association with research undertaken at the University of Manchester and Cambridge University.

After completing work on the ENIAC, Eckert and Mauchly formed their own company to produce a commercial digital computer. The Eckert-Mauchly Computer Corporation signed a preliminary agreement with the National Bureau of Standards (representing the Census Bureau) in 1946 to develop a commercial computer, which they called the UNIVAC, for "universal automatic computer." The project experienced huge cost overruns, and by 1950 the Eckert-Mauchly Computer Corporation was on the brink of bankruptcy. Remington Rand bought them out and delivered the UNIVAC I to the US Bureau of the Census in 1951 [14].

In a public relations coup, Remington Rand cooperated with CBS to use a UNIVAC computer to predict the outcome of the 1952 presidential election (Figure 1.7). The events of election night illustrate the tough decisions people can face when computers produce unexpected results.

Adlai Stevenson had led Dwight Eisenhower in polls taken before the election, but less than an hour after the polls closed, with just 7 percent of the votes tabulated, the UNIVAC was predicting Dwight Eisenhower would win the election in a landslide. When CBS correspondent Charles Collingwood asked Remington Rand for the computer's prediction, however, he was given the run-around. The computer's engineers were convinced there was a programming error. For one thing, UNIVAC was predicting that Eisenhower would carry several Southern states, and everybody "knew" that Republican presidential candidates never won in the South. Remington Rand's director of advanced research ordered the engineers to change the programming so the outcome would be closer to what the political pundits expected. An hour later, the reprogrammed computer predicted that Eisenhower would win by only nine electoral votes, and that's what CBS announced. As it turns out, the computer was right and the human "experts" were wrong. Before being reprogrammed, UNIVAC had predicted Eisenhower would win 438 electoral votes to 93 for Stevenson. The official result was a 442–89 victory for Eisenhower [14].

In America in the early 1950s, the word "UNIVAC" was synonymous with "computer." Remington Rand sold a total of 46 UNIVACs to government agencies, such as the US Air Force, the US Army Map Service, the Atomic Energy Commission, and the US Navy, as well as to large corporations and public utilities, such as General Electric,

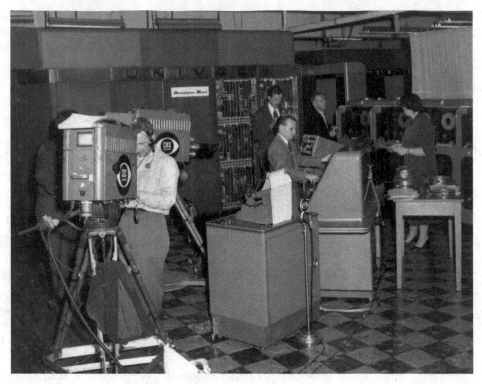

**FIGURE 1.7** CBS news coverage of the 1952 presidential election included predictions made by a UNIVAC computer. When the computer predicted Eisenhower would win in a landslide, consternation followed. (Photo reproduced courtesy of Unisys Corporation)

Metropolitan Life, US Steel, Du Pont, Franklin Life Insurance, Westinghouse, Pacific Mutual Life Insurance, Sylvania Electric, and Consolidated Edison.

Office automation leader IBM did not enter the commercial computer market until 1953, and its initial products were inferior to the UNIVAC. However, IBM quickly turned the tables on Remington Rand, thanks to a larger base of existing customers, a far superior sales and marketing organization, and a much greater investment in research and development. In 1955 IBM held more than half the market, and by the mid-1960s IBM dominated the computer industry with 65 percent of total sales, compared to 12 percent for number two computer maker Sperry Rand (the successor to Remington Rand) [14].

## 1.2.7 Programming Languages and Time–Sharing

In the earliest digital computers, every instruction was coded as a long string of 0s and 1s. People immediately began looking for ways to make coding faster and less error-prone. One early improvement was the creation of assembly language, which allowed programmers to work with symbolic representations of the instruction codes. Still, one assembly language instruction was required for every machine instruction. Programmers wanted fewer, higher-level instructions to generate more machine instructions. In 1951 Frances Holberton, one of the six original ENIAC programmers, created a sort-merge generator for the UNIVAC that took a specification of files to be manipulated and automatically produced the machine program to do the sorting and merging. Building on this work, Grace Murray Hopper, also at Remington Rand, developed the A-0 system that automated the process of linking together subroutines to form the complete machine code [15].

Over at IBM, John Backus convinced his superiors of the need for a higher-level programming language for IBM computers. He led the effort to develop the IBM Mathematical Formula Translating System, or FORTRAN. Designed for scientific applications, the first system was completed in 1957. Many skeptics believed that any "automatic programming" system would generate inefficient machine code compared to hand-coded assembly language, but they were proven wrong: the FORTRAN compiler generated high-quality code. What's more, programmers could write FORTRAN programs 5 to 20 times faster than the equivalent assembly language programs. Most programmers quickly shifted allegiance from assembly language to FORTRAN. Eventually, other computer manufacturers developed their own FORTRAN compilers, and FORTRAN became an international standard [16].

Meanwhile, business-oriented programming languages were also being developed by several computer manufacturers. Grace Murray Hopper specified FLOW-MATIC, an English-like programming language for the UNIVAC. Other manufacturers began to develop their own languages. Customers didn't like incompatible languages, because it meant programs written for one brand of computer had to be rewritten before they could be run on another brand of computer. In 1959 an extremely important customer, the US Department of Defense, brought together a committee to develop a common business-oriented programming language that all manufacturers would support. The committee wrote the specification for COBOL. By requiring manufacturers to support COBOL in order to get defense contracts, the US Department of Defense helped ensure its widespread adoption [17].

In the early 1960s, John Kemeny and Thomas Kurtz at Dartmouth College directed teams of undergraduate students who developed a time-sharing system and an easy-to-learn programming language. The Dartmouth Time-Sharing System (DTSS) gave multiple users the ability to edit and run their programs simultaneously, by dividing the computer's time among all the users. Time-sharing made computers accessible to more people because it allowed the cost of owning and operating a computer system to be divided among a large pool of users who purchased the right to connect to the system [18].

The development of BASIC, a simple, easy-to-learn programming language, was another important step toward making computers accessible to a wider audience. Kemeny and Kurtz saw BASIC as a way to teach programming, and soon many other educational institutions began teaching students how to program using Dartmouth BASIC. The language's popularity led computer manufacturers to develop their own versions of BASIC [18].

## 1.2.8  Transistor and Integrated Circuit

Although the British had radar installations at the beginning of World War II, it became clear during the Battle of Britain that their systems were inadequate. The British and the Americans worked together to develop microwave radar systems capable of locating enemy planes more precisely. Microwave radar required higher-frequency receivers utilizing semiconductors, and in the process of manufacturing microwave radar systems for the war effort, several American companies, including AT&T, greatly improved their ability to create semiconductors [19].

AT&T was on the lookout for a new technology to replace the vacuum tube. Its long-distance network relied on vacuum tubes to amplify signals, but the tubes required a lot of power, generated a lot of heat, and burned out like lightbulbs. After the war, AT&T put together a team of Bell Labs scientists, led by Bill Shockley, to develop a semiconductor substitute for the vacuum tube. In 1948 Bell Labs announced the invention of such a device, which they called the **transistor** [20].

While most electronics companies ignored the invention of the transistor, Bill Shockley understood its potential. He left Bell Labs and moved to Palo Alto, California, where he founded Shockley Semiconductor in 1956. He hired an exceptional team of engineers and physicists, but many disliked his heavy-handed management style [20]. In September 1957, eight of Shockley's most talented employees, including Gordon Moore and Robert Noyce, walked out. The group, soon to be known as the "traitorous eight," founded Fairchild Semiconductor (Figure 1.8). By this time transistors were being used in a wide variety of devices, from transistor radios to computers. While transistors were far superior to vacuum tubes, they were still too big for some applications. Fairchild Semiconductor set out to produce a single semiconductor device containing transistors, capacitors, and resistors; in other words, an **integrated circuit**. Another firm, Texas Instruments, was on the same mission. Today Robert Noyce of Fairchild Semiconductor and Jack Kilby of Texas Instruments are credited for independently inventing the integrated circuit [21].

The Cold War between the United States and the Soviet Union played an important role in advancing integrated circuit technology. American engineers developing the Minuteman II ballistic missile in the early 1960s decided to use integrated circuits to improve the processing speed of its guidance computer. The Minuteman II program was the single largest consumer of integrated circuits in the United States between 1962 and 1965, representing about 20 percent of total sales. During these years companies learned how to make rugged, reliable integrated circuits [9]. They also continued to shrink the components within the integrated circuits, leading to an exponential increase in their power. Gordon Moore noted this trend in a 1965 paper and predicted it would continue. Today **Moore's law** refers to the phenomenon of integrated circuits becoming twice as powerful roughly every two years.

## 1.2.9  IBM System/360

The integrated circuit made possible the construction of much more powerful and reliable computers. The 1960s was the era of mainframe computers—large computers

**FIGURE 1.8** The eight founders of Fairchild Semiconductor on the factory floor. Gordon Moore is second from the left and Robert Noyce is on the right. (Wayne Miller/Magnum Photos, Inc.)

designed to serve the data-processing needs of large businesses. Mainframe computers enabled enterprises to centralize all of their data-processing applications in a single system. As we have seen, by this time IBM dominated the mainframe market in the United States.

In 1964 IBM unveiled the System/360, a series of 19 compatible computers with varying levels of computing speed and memory capacity (Figure 1.9). Because the systems were software compatible, a business could upgrade its computer without having to rewrite its application programs. This feature was important, because by the 1960s companies were making much larger investments in software.

## 1.2.10 Microprocessor

In 1968 Robert Noyce and Gordon Moore left Fairchild Semiconductor to found another semiconductor manufacturing company, which they named Intel. A year later Japanese calculator manufacturer Busicom approached Intel about designing 12 custom chips for use in a new scientific calculator. Intel agreed to provide the chips and assigned responsibility for the project to Marcian "Ted" Hoff. After reviewing the project, Hoff suggested that it was not in Intel's best interest to manufacture a custom chip for every customer. As an alternative, he suggested that Intel create a general-purpose chip that could be programmed to perform a wide variety of tasks. Each customer could program

**FIGURE 1.9** In the 1960s, IBM dominated the mainframe computer market in the United States.  (IBM/AP Photo)

the chip to meet its particular needs. Intel and Busicom agreed to the plan, which reduced the required number of chips for Busicom's calculator from 12 to 4. A year of development by Ted Hoff, Stanley Mazor, and Federico Faggin led to the release of the Intel 4004, the world's first **microprocessor**. Inside the 1/8-inch × 1/6-inch chip were 2,300 transistors, giving the Intel 4004 the same computing power as the ENIAC, which had occupied 3,000 cubic feet.

Microprocessors made it possible to integrate computers into everyday devices. Today we're surrounded by devices containing microprocessors: cell phones, MP3 players, digital cameras, wristwatches, ATM machines, automobiles, microwave ovens, thermostats, traffic lights, and much more. The highest-profile use of microprocessors, however, is in personal computers.

## 1.2.11  Personal Computer

During the Vietnam conflict in the late 1960s and early 1970s, the area around San Francisco was home to a significant counterculture, including a large number of antiwar and antiestablishment activists. The do-it-yourself idealism of the power-to-the-people movement intersected with advances in computer technology in a variety of ways, including the *Whole Earth Catalog*, the People's Computer Company, and the Homebrew Computer Club [22].

The *Whole Earth Catalog*, first published in 1968, was, in the words of Steve Jobs, "sort of like Google in paperback form" [23]—an effort to pull together in a single large volume lists of helpful tools, in this case for the creation of a more just and environmentally sensitive society. The definition of "tools" was broad; the catalog's lists included books, classes, garden tools, camping equipment, and (in later issues) early personal computers. "With the *Whole Earth Catalog*, Stewart Brand offered a generation of computer engineers and programmers an alternative vision of technology as a tool for individual and collective transformation" [24, p. 104].

The People's Computer Company was a not-for-profit corporation dedicated to educating people on how to use computers. One of its activities was publishing a newspaper. The cover of the first issue read: "Computers are mostly used against people instead of for people, used to control people instead of to <u>free</u> them, time to change all that—we need a PEOPLE'S COMPUTER COMPANY" [25]. Typical issues contained programming tips and the source code to programs, particularly educational games written in BASIC. The newspaper's publisher, Bob Albrecht, said, "I was heavily influenced by the *Whole Earth Catalog*. I wanted to give away ideas" [24, p. 114]. The People's Computer Company also set up the People's Computer Center in a strip mall in Menlo Park, California. The center allowed people to rent teletype terminals connected to a time-shared computer. A large number of teenagers were drawn to computing through Friday evening game-playing sessions. Many users wrote their own programs, and the center promoted a culture in which computer enthusiasts freely shared software with each other.

In 1975 the Homebrew Computer Club, an outgrowth of the People's Computer Company, became a meeting place for hobbyists interested in building personal computers out of microprocessors. A company in Albuquerque, New Mexico, called MITS, had recently begun shipping the Altair 8800 personal computer, and during the first few Homebrew Computer Club meetings, members showed off various enhancements to the Altair 8800. Progress was frustratingly slow, however, due to the lack of a higher-level programming language.

Three months after the establishment of the Homebrew Computer Club, MITS representatives visited Palo Alto, California, to demonstrate the Altair 8800 and the BASIC interpreter created by Paul Allen and Bill Gates, who had a tiny company called Micro-Soft. The audience in the hotel conference room was far larger than expected, and during the overcrowded and chaotic meeting somebody acquired a paper tape containing the source code to Altair BASIC. More than 70 copies of the tape were handed out at the next meeting of the Homebrew Computer Club. After that, free copies of the interpreter proliferated. Some hobbyists felt that the asking price of $500 for the BASIC interpreter was too high, considering that the Altair computer itself cost only $395 as a kit or $495 preassembled [22].

Bill Gates responded by writing "An Open Letter to Hobbyists," which was reprinted in a variety of publications. In the letter he asserted that less than 10 percent of all Altair owners had purchased BASIC, even though far more people than that were using it. According to Gates, the royalties Micro-Soft had received from Altair BASIC made the time spent on the software worth less than $2 an hour. He wrote, "Nothing would please me more than being able to hire 10 programmers and deluge the hobby market with good software," but the theft of software created "very little incentive" for his company to release new products [22].

The controversy over Altair BASIC did not slow the pace of innovations. Hobbyists wanted to do more than flip the toggle switches and watch the lights blink on the Altair 8800. Steve Wozniak, a computer engineer at Hewlett-Packard, created a more powerful personal computer that supported keyboard input and television monitor output. Wozniak's goal was to make a machine for himself and to impress other members of the Homebrew Computer Club, but his friend Steve Jobs thought of a few improvements and convinced Wozniak they should go into business (Figure 1.10). They raised $1,300 by selling Jobs's Volkswagen van and Wozniak's Hewlett-Packard scientific calculator, launching Apple Computer. Although the company sold only 200 Apple I computers, its next product, the Apple II, became one of the most popular personal computers of all time.

**FIGURE 1.10** Steve Jobs (right) convinced Steve Wozniak (left) they should go into business selling the personal computer Wozniak designed. They named their company Apple Computer. (Kimberly White/Corbis News/Corbis)

By the end of the 1970s, many companies, including Apple Computer and Tandy, were producing personal computers. While hundreds of thousands of people bought personal computers for home use, businesses were reluctant to move to the new computer platform. However, two significant developments made personal computers more attractive to businesses.

The first development was the computer spreadsheet program. For decades firms had used spreadsheets to perform financial predictions. Manually computing spreadsheets was monotonous and error-prone, since changing a value in a single cell could require updating many other cells. In the fall of 1979, Bob Frankston and Harvard MBA student Dan Bricklin released their program, called VisiCalc, for the Apple II. VisiCalc's labor-saving potential was obvious to businesses. After a slow start, it quickly became one of the most popular application programs for personal computers. Sales of the Apple II computer increased significantly after the introduction of VisiCalc.

The second development was the release of the IBM PC in 1981. The IBM name exuded reliability and respectability, making it easier for companies to make the move to desktop systems for their employees. As the saying went, "Nobody ever got fired for buying from IBM." In contrast to the approach taken by Apple Computer, IBM decided to make its PC an open architecture, meaning the system was built from off-the-shelf parts and other companies could manufacture "clones" with the same functionality. This decision helped to make the IBM PC the dominant personal computer architecture.

The success of IBM-compatible PCs fueled the growth of Microsoft. In 1980 IBM contracted with Microsoft to provide the DOS operating system for the IBM PC. Microsoft let IBM have DOS for practically nothing, but in return IBM gave Microsoft the right to collect royalties from other companies manufacturing PC-compatible computers. Microsoft profited handsomely from this arrangement when PC-compatibles manufactured by other companies gained more than 80 percent of the PC market [26].

# 1.3  Milestones in Networking

In the early nineteenth century, the United States fell far behind Europe in networking technology. The French had begun constructing a network of telegraph towers in the 1790s, and 40 years later there were towers all over the European continent (Figure 1.11). At the top of each tower was a pair of semaphores. Operators raised and lowered the semaphores; each pattern corresponded to a letter or symbol. A message initiated at one tower would be seen by another tower within viewing distance. The receiving tower would then repeat the message for the next tower in the network, and so on. This optical telegraph system could transmit messages at the impressive rate of about 350 miles per hour when skies were clear.

In 1837 Congress asked for proposals to create a telegraph system between New York and New Orleans. It received one proposal based on proven European technology. Samuel Morse submitted a radically different proposal. He suggested constructing a telegraph system that used electricity to communicate the signals. Let's step back and review some of the key discoveries and inventions that enabled Morse to make his dramatic proposal.

**FIGURE 1.11** A semaphore telegraph tower on the first line from Paris to Lille (1794). (Leemage/Universal Images Group/Getty Images)

## 1.3.1  Electricity and Electromagnetism

Amber is a hard, translucent, yellowish-brown fossil resin often used to make beads and other ornamental items. About 2,600 years ago the Greeks discovered that if you rub amber, it becomes charged with a force enabling it to attract light objects such as feathers and dried leaves. The Greek word for amber is ηλεκτρων (electron). Our word "electric" literally means "to be like amber."

For more than 2,000 years amber's ability to attract other materials was seen as a curiosity with no practical value, but in the seventeenth and eighteenth centuries scientists began to study electricity in earnest. Alessandro Volta, a professor of physics at the University of Pavia, made a key breakthrough when he discovered that electricity could be generated chemically. He produced an electric current by submerging two different metals close to each other in an acid. In 1799 Volta used this principle to create the world's first battery. Volta's battery produced an electric charge more than 1,000 times as powerful as that produced by rubbing amber. Scientists soon put this power to practical use.

In 1820 Danish physicist Christian Oersted discovered that an electric current creates a magnetic field. Five years later British electrician William Sturgeon constructed an electromagnet by coiling wire around a horseshoe-shaped piece of iron. When he ran an electric current through the coil, the iron became magnetized. Sturgeon showed how a single battery was capable of producing a charge strong enough to pick up a nine-pound metal object.

In 1830 American professor Joseph Henry rigged up an experiment that showed how a telegraph machine could work. He strung a mile of wire around the walls of his classroom at the Albany Academy. At one end he placed a battery; at the other end he connected an electromagnet, a pivoting metal bar, and a bell. When Henry connected the battery, the electromagnet attracted the metal bar, causing it to ring the bell. Disconnecting the battery allowed the bar to return to its original position. In this way he could produce a series of rings.

## 1.3.2 Telegraph

Samuel Morse, a professor of arts and design at New York University, worked on the idea of a telegraph during most of the 1830s, and in 1838 he patented his design of a telegraph machine. The US Congress did not approve Morse's proposal in 1837 to construct a New York–to–New Orleans telegraph system, but it did not fund any of the other proposals either. Morse persisted with his lobbying, and in 1843 Congress appropriated $30,000 to Morse for the construction of a 40-mile telegraph line between Washington, DC, and Baltimore, Maryland.

On May 1, 1844, the Whig party convention in Baltimore nominated Henry Clay for president. The telegraph line had been completed to Annapolis Junction at that time. A courier hand-carried a message about Clay's nomination from Baltimore to Annapolis Junction, where it was telegraphed to Washington. This was the first news reported via telegraph. The line officially opened on May 24. Morse, seated in the old Supreme Court chamber inside the US Capitol, sent his partner in Baltimore a verse from the Bible: "What hath God wrought?"

The value of the telegraph was immediately apparent, and the number of telegraph lines quickly increased. By 1846 telegraph lines connected Washington, Baltimore, Philadelphia, New York, Buffalo, and Boston. In 1850 twenty different companies operated 12,000 miles of telegraph lines. The first transcontinental telegraph line was completed in 1861, putting the Pony Express out of business (Figure 1.12). The telegraph was the sole method of rapid long-distance communication until 1877. By this time the United States was networked by more than 200,000 miles of telegraph wire [27].

The telegraph was a versatile tool, and people kept finding new applications for it. For example, by 1870 fire alarm telegraphs were in use in 75 major cities in the United States. New York City alone had 600 fire alarm telegraphs. When a person pulled the lever of the alarm box, it automatically transmitted a message identifying its location to a fire station. These devices greatly improved the ability of fire departments to dispatch equipment quickly to the correct location [27].

## 1.3.3 Telephone

Alexander Graham Bell was born in Edinburgh, Scotland, into a family focused on impairments of speech and hearing. His father and grandfather were experts in elocution and the correction of speech. His mother was almost completely deaf. Bell was educated

**FIGURE 1.12** Pony Express riders lost their jobs when the US transcontinental telegraph line was completed in 1861. (© North Wind Picture Archives/Alamy)

to follow in the same career path as his father and grandfather, and he became a teacher of deaf students. Later, he married a deaf woman.

Bell pursued inventing as a means of achieving financial independence. At first he focused on making improvements to the telegraph. A significant problem with early telegraph systems was that a single wire could transmit only one message at a time. If multiple messages could be sent simultaneously along the same wire, communication delays would be reduced, and the value of the entire system would increase.

Bell's solution to this problem was called a harmonic or musical telegraph. If you imagine hearing Morse code, it's obvious that all of the dots and dashes are the same note played for a shorter or longer period of time. The harmonic telegraph assigned a different note (different sound frequency) to each message. At the receiving end, different receivers could be tuned to respond to different notes, as you can tune your radio to hear only what is broadcast by a particular station.

Bell knew that the human voice is made up of sounds at many different frequencies. From his work on the harmonic telegraph, he speculated that it should be possible to capture and transmit human voice over a wire. He and Thomas A. Watson succeeded in transmitting speech electronically in 1876. Soon after, they commercialized their invention.

Nearly all early telephones were installed in businesses. Leasing a telephone was expensive, and most people focused on its commercial value rather than its social value. However, the number of phones placed in homes increased rapidly in the 1890s, after Bell's first patent expired.

Once telephones were placed in the home, the traditional boundaries between private family life and public business life became blurred. People enjoyed being able to conduct business transactions from the privacy of their home, but they also found that a ringing telephone could be an unwelcome interruption [28].

Another consequence of the telephone was that it eroded traditional social hierarchies. An 1897 issue of *Western Electrician* reports that Governor Chauncey Depew of New York was receiving unwanted phone calls from ordinary citizens: "Every time they see anything about him in the newspapers, they call and tell him what a 'fine letter he wrote' or 'what a lovely speech he made,' or ask if this or that report is true; and all this from people who, if they came to his office, would probably never say more than 'Good morning' " [29].

People also worried about the loss of privacy brought about by the telephone. In 1877 the *New York Times* reported that telephone workers responsible for operating an early system in Providence, Rhode Island, overheard many confidential conversations. The writer fretted that telephone eavesdropping would make it dangerous for anyone in Providence to accept a nomination for public office [28].

The telephone enabled the creation of the first "online" communities. In rural areas the most common form of phone service was the party line: a single circuit connecting multiple phones to the telephone exchange. Party lines enabled farmers to gather by their phones every evening to talk about the weather and exchange gossip [30].

The power of this new medium was demonstrated in the Bryan/McKinley presidential election of 1896. For the first time, presidential election returns were transmitted directly into people's homes. "Thousands sat with their ear glued to the receiver the whole night long, hypnotized by the possibilities unfolding to them for the first time" [31].

### 1.3.4  Typewriter and Teletype

For hundreds of years people dreamed of a device that would allow an individual to produce a document that looked as if it had been typeset, but the dream was not realized until 1867, when Americans Christopher Sholes, Carlos Glidden, and Samuel Soule patented the first typewriter. In late 1873 Remington & Sons Company, famous for guns and sewing machines, produced the first commercial typewriter. It was difficult to use and was not well received; Remington & Co. sold only 5,000 machines in the first five years. However, the typewriter did get the attention of Mark Twain, who used it to produce *Tom Sawyer*, which may have been the world's first typewritten manuscript. By 1890 more reliable typewriters were being produced, and the typewriter became a common piece of office equipment [32].

In 1908 Charles and Howard Krum succeeded in testing an experimental machine that allowed a modified Oliver typewriter to print a message transmitted over a telegraph line. They called their invention the teletype. During the 1920s, news organizations began using teletype machines to transmit stories between distant offices, and Wall Street firms began sending records of stock transactions over teletypes.

### 1.3.5 Radio

Earlier we described how the experiments of Oersted, Sturgeon, and Henry led to the development of the electromagnet and the telegraph. The connection between electricity and magnetism remained mysterious, however, until Scottish physicist James Clerk Maxwell published a mathematical theory demonstrating their relationship. This theory predicted the existence of an electromagnetic wave spreading with the velocity of light. It also predicted that light itself was an electromagnetic phenomenon. In 1885 Heinrich Hertz successfully generated electromagnetic waves, proving the correctness of Maxwell's theory.

Guglielmo Marconi put Hertz's discovery to practical use by successfully transmitting radio signals in the hills outside Bologna, Italy, in 1895. Unable to attract the attention of the Italian government, he took his invention to England, where he founded the Marconi Wireless Telegraph Company. The name of the company reflects Marconi's concept of how his invention would be used. To Marconi, radio, or "wireless," was a superior way to transmit telegraph messages.

David Sarnoff emigrated from Russia to the United States with his family when he was nine. When he had completed school, he landed a position with the Marconi Wireless Telegraph Company. In 1912 Sarnoff made a name for himself when his office relayed news about the sinking of the *Titanic*. Four years later, Sarnoff suggested the use of radio as an entertainment device, writing: "I have in mind a plan of development which would make radio a household utility in the same sense as the piano or phonograph. . . . The receiver can be designed in the form of a simple music box . . . [which] can be placed in the parlor or living room" [33]. In two decades, Sarnoff's vision had become a reality.

The power of radio as a medium of mass communication was demonstrated on the evening of October 30, 1938 (the night before Halloween). From CBS Radio Studio One in New York, Orson Welles and the Mercury Theater put on a one-hour dramatization of H. G. Wells's *War of the Worlds*. To increase suspense, the play was performed as a series of news bulletins interrupting a concert of dance music. These bulletins described events occurring on a farm near Grovers Mill, New Jersey. Many listeners panicked. "People packed the roads, hid in cellars, loaded guns, even wrapped their heads in wet towels as protection from Martian poison gas, oblivious to the fact that they were acting out the role of the panic-stricken public that actually belonged in a radio play" [34].

### 1.3.6 Television

Broadcasting video over a wire began in 1884 with the invention of an electromechanical television by Paul Nipkow, but the first completely electronic television transmission was made in 1927 by Philo Farnsworth. Millions of Americans were formally introduced to the television at the 1939 World's Fair held in New York City, which had as its theme "The World of Tomorrow." Since an early retail television set cost about as much as an automobile, televisions remained a rarity in American households until the 1950s, when prices fell dramatically.

Television's ability to send a message around the world was demonstrated in July 1969. Hundreds of millions of people watched on live TV as astronaut Neil Armstrong stepped from the lunar module onto the surface of the Moon (Figure 1.13).

**FIGURE 1.13** On July 20, 1969, television images of Neil Armstrong walking on the Moon were broadcast to hundreds of millions of viewers around the world. (Courtesy of NASA)

Television has created many opportunities for "news junkies" to get their fixes. The major commercial broadcast television networks have been supplemented by Fox, CNN, and other cable news organizations as well as a myriad of Web sites. The various organizations compete with each other to be the first to break news stories. Increasingly, the media have turned to computer technology to help them provide information to the public. Sometimes this has led to embarrassing mistakes, as in the 2000 US presidential election.

At about 7:50 P.M. on the evening of Tuesday, November 7, 2000, before the polls had even closed in the Florida panhandle, the major networks began announcing that Al Gore would be the winner in Florida. Based on the expected result of the Florida election, the networks went on to predict—while people were still voting in the Western states—that Al Gore would be the next president of the United States.

You might be wondering how it is possible to predict the outcome of an election before everyone has voted. In a practice known as exit polling, a company called Voter News Service questions people leaving polling places. It combines the information it collects with early returns to predict the outcome of elections. Since 1988 the television networks have relied upon the Voter News Service to provide them with exit polling results.

As it turns out, Voter News Service's prediction was wrong. More than a month after the election, after a series of recounts and court decisions, George W. Bush was declared the victor in Florida. With Florida's electoral votes in hand, Bush won the presidency.

## 1.3.7  Remote Computing

Working at his kitchen table in 1937, Bell Labs researcher George Stibitz built a binary adder out of telephone relays, batteries, flashlight bulbs, tin strips, and wire. He took his invention back to Bell Labs and enlisted the help of Samuel Williams. Over the next two years they built the Complex Number Calculator, an electromechanical system that would add, subtract, multiply, and divide complex numbers.

Stibitz's next action is what sets him apart from other computer pioneers. He made a teletype machine the input/output device for the Complex Number Calculator. With this innovation, he did not have to be in the same room as the calculator to use it; he could operate it remotely.

In 1940 Stibitz demonstrated remote computing to members of the American Mathematical Society who were meeting at Dartmouth College in New Hampshire. He typed numbers into the teletype, which transmitted the data 250 miles to the calculator in New York City. After the calculator had computed the answer, it transmitted the data back to the teletype, which printed the result.

## 1.3.8  ARPANET

In reaction to the launch of Sputnik by the Soviet Union in 1957, the Department of Defense created the Advanced Research Projects Agency (ARPA). ARPA funded research and development at prominent universities. The agency's first director, J. C .R. Licklider, imagined a "galactic network"—a global computer network that would facilitate the exchange of programs and data.[2] This view of the computer as a device to improve communication was in stark contrast to the mind-set of computer manufacturers, which continued to think of computers as number-crunching machines.

Conventional, circuit-switched telephone networks were not a good foundation upon which to build a global computer network (Figure 1.14a). Between 1961 and 1967, three research teams independently came up with an alternative to circuit-switched networks. These teams were led by Donald Davies and Roger Scantlebury at NPL in England, Paul Baran at RAND, and Leonard Kleinrock at MIT. Eventually, the new design came to be called a packet-switched network (Figure 1.14b).

In 1967 ARPA initiated the design and construction of the ARPANET. Fear of a nuclear attack led to the crucially important design decision that the network should be decentralized. In other words, the loss of any single computer or communication link would not prevent the rest of the network from working. Every computer on the network would have the ability to make decisions about how message traffic should be routed. Packet-switched networks met this condition; circuit-switched networks did not.

BBN in Boston was responsible for the Interface Message Processor (IMP) that connected a computer to the telephone network. In 1969 BBN delivered its first four IMPs to UCLA, the Stanford Research Institute, the University of California at Santa Barbara, and the University of Utah.

## 1.3.9  Email

During the earliest years of ARPANET, the networked computers could transfer programs and data only. ARPANET users still relied upon the telephone for personal communications. In March 1972, Ray Tomlinson at BBN wrote the first software enabling

2. The primary source document for this description of the evolution of the Internet is *A Brief History of the Internet* by Barry M. Leiner et al. [35].

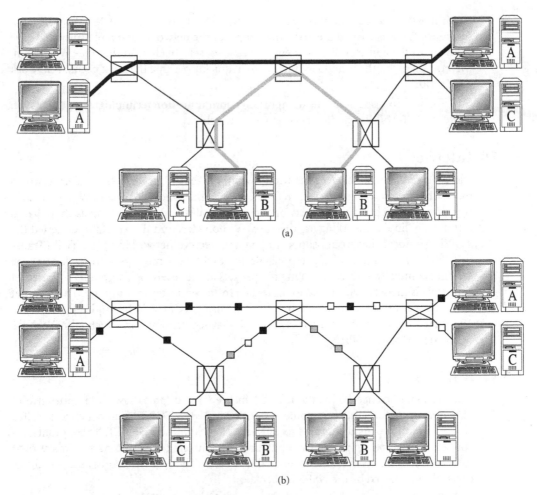

(a)

(b)

FIGURE 1.14 Comparison of circuit-switched networking and packet-switched networking. (a) In a **circuit-switched network**, a single physical connection is established between the two ends. The physical connection cannot be shared. In this illustration, one circuit links the two computers labeled A, and another circuit links the two computers labeled B. The computers labeled C may not communicate at this time, because no circuit can be established. (b) In a **packet-switched network**, a message is divided into small bundles of data called packets. Every packet has the address of the computer where it should be routed. If there is more than one path from the message source to the message destination, different message packets may take different routes. Packets from different messages may share the same wire. In this illustration, three pairs of computers (labeled A, B, and C) are communicating simultaneously over a packet-switched network.

email messages to be sent and received by ARPANET computers. A few months later, Lawrence Roberts created the first "killer app" for the network: an email utility that gave individuals the ability to list their email messages, selectively read them, reply to them, forward them to others, and save them. Email quickly became the most popular network application.

Email is now one of the most important communication technologies on the planet. More than 200 billion email messages are sent each day.

### 1.3.10  Internet

ARPA researchers anticipated the need to connect the ARPANET with other networks based on different designs. Robert Kahn developed the concept of open architecture networking, in which individual networks could be quite different as long as they shared a common "internetworking architecture." Vinton Cerf and Robert Kahn designed the TCP/IP protocol that would support open architecture networking [36]. TCP (Transmission Control Protocol) is responsible for dividing a message into packets at the sending computer and reassembling the packets at the receiving computer. IP (Internet Protocol) is the set of rules used to route data from computer to computer. The **Internet** is the network of networks that communicate using TCP/IP. You could call January 1, 1983, the birth date of the Internet, because that was the date on which all ARPANET hosts converted to TCP/IP.

### 1.3.11  NSFNET

The National Science Foundation (NSF) in the United States saw the importance of networking to the academic community. It created a TCP/IP–based network called NSFNET, and it provided grants to universities to join the NSFNET. These grants encouraged broad participation by stipulating that universities would have to make their Internet connections available to all qualified users. The NSFNET consisted of regional networks connected by the NSFNET backbone.

The NSF encouraged the universities participating in regional networks to reduce their network subscription costs by finding commercial customers for the networks. At the same time, the NSF banned commercial traffic on the NSFNET backbone. These policies stimulated private companies to create commercial, long-distance Internet connections in the United States. In April 1995 the NSF ceased funding the NSFNET backbone. Commercial network providers, well established by this time, took over the task of supplying long-distance Internet connections in the United States.

### 1.3.12  Broadband

The term **broadband** refers to a high-speed Internet connection. Broadband connections make feasible the transfer of large files, such as those containing images, music, and video. The growth of file swapping among Internet users has paralleled the growth of broadband connections.

Typical broadband speeds vary widely among highly developed countries. The world broadband leaders are South Korea, with an average speed of 22.2 megabits per second; Hong Kong, at 16.8 megabits per second; and Japan, at 15.2 megabits per second. The United States ranks sixteenth in the world, with an average broadband speed of 11.1 megabits per second [37].

### 1.3.13 Wireless Networks

**Cell phones,** also known as mobile phones, allow telephone calls to be made over radio links. The first cell phone, demonstrated by Motorola in 1973, was quite large and weighed two and a half pounds. Advances in integrated circuits and other technologies have allowed companies to shrink the size and weight of cell phones substantially while greatly increasing their capabilities. Modern **smartphones,** such as the one shown in Figure 1.1, weigh just a few ounces and support a wide variety of services in addition to voice communication, including text messaging, email, and broadband Internet access.

The social impact of cellular networks has been dramatic, particularly in developing countries. People living in areas never reached by wired telephone service now have the ability to communicate with others and access the Internet. In fact, the total number of cell phone subscriptions worldwide is now roughly equal to the world's population: 7.5 billion. That doesn't mean everyone on Earth has a phone, however. Many people have one cell phone for business use and another one for personal use. In some countries it's common for people who travel a lot to purchase different subscriber identity module (SIM) cards and get different phone numbers for cities they frequent in order to get better phone rates, and each SIM card is considered a subscription. In Russia, for example, there are about 185 cell phone subscriptions per 100 Russians, but only about 70 percent of Russians have a cell phone. Still, about 60 percent of the people in the world now have at least one cell phone [38].

In 1993 Henrik Sjödin proposed the development of public access wireless local area networks. Today wireless Internet access points, or **hotspots,** are commonplace at coffee shops, libraries, airports, university campuses, and other public places where people gather. Computers and other electronic devices within range of the hotspot communicate with the hotspot using radio waves. Most hotspots use a technology known as Wi-Fi.

# 1.4 Milestones in Information Storage and Retrieval

The previous two sections surveyed technological developments related to manipulating and transmitting information, respectively. This section focuses on the development of technologies to store and retrieve information.

### 1.4.1 Greek Alphabet

As civilizations expanded around 6,000 years ago, writing systems were developed to allow the recording and communication of various types of information, such as laws and financial records. There are three general types of writing systems. In a logography each character represents a word, in a syllabary each character represents a syllable, and in an alphabet each character represents a phoneme.

Around 750 BC the Greeks developed the first true alphabet: an alphabet representing vowel sounds as well as consonant sounds. Compared with earlier writing systems developed in Mesopotamia and Egypt, the 24-letter Greek alphabet was a simple, efficient way of transforming the spoken word into written form, and it marked an important milestone on the journey of civilization from an oral culture to a written culture. The English alphabet we use today is a direct descendant of the alphabet used by the ancient Greeks.

## 1.4.2  Codex and Paper

Two thousand years ago, important information was recorded on papyrus scrolls wrapped around wooden rods. Papyrus had to be stored this way to keep from breaking apart. Even so, the ends of papyrus scrolls tended to fall off.

The development of the codex was a significant advance in information storage and retrieval technology. A codex was made up of rectangular pages sewn together on one side. These pages were made out of sheepskin (parchment) or calfskin (vellum). The codex was superior to papyrus in two ways. First, the codex was much more durable than a papyrus roll. Second, since it was divided into pages, the codex made it much easier for readers to find a particular passage: they could simply flip to the desired page.

Between the second and fourth centuries, the codex gradually replaced the scroll as the most popular method of recording important information. The Church accelerated the transition by insisting that all sacred texts be recorded in codices, to distinguish them from Hebrew scriptures kept on scrolls.

After the fall of the Roman Empire, Irish monks preserved Western culture by copying Greco-Roman and Judeo-Christian texts into codices [39]. Centuries later, most codices were produced using a process of wood engraving. A craftsman would take a block of wood and laboriously chisel away the background for a portion of a page, leaving the letters and illustrations raised. When all the wooden blocks for a page were carved, they would be fastened together. After the surface was inked, a blank page would be printed by pressing the blocks down on the inked surface.

In the late Middle Ages, explorers brought back from China the technology for manufacturing paper in mass quantities. By the fifteenth century paper gradually began to replace parchment in less expensive European codices.

## 1.4.3  Gutenberg's Printing Press

In 1436 Johannes Gutenberg began work on a printing press that would imprint pages using movable metal type rather than wood blocks, and in 1455 work was completed on Gutenberg's famous "42 Line Bible." Soon other printers were using the same technology to produce codices. The principal customer of these publishers was the Church. Hence most early publications were religious books and pamphlets.

The printing press proved itself to be a powerful tool for mass communication during the Reformation. Martin Luther did more than nail his 95 theses to the door of a church—he published them. Between 1517 and 1520, more than 300,000 copies of Martin Luther's publications were sold [40]. In the next 50 years, the number of religious tracts produced by Protestant reformers would outnumber those of their Catholic opponents by a factor of 10 to 1.

### 1.4.4 Newspapers

The printing press made possible the establishment of newspapers. Newspapers provided an important new way for private citizens to get their points of view heard. A free press serves as a powerful counterweight to government and its desire to manage the flow of information. It is not surprising, then, that there is a long history of government censorship or suppression of newspapers.

The first English-language newspaper appeared in Great Britain in the 1600s. Throughout most of the seventeenth century the government controlled the press by licensing approved newspapers and suppressing the rest. However, in 1695 Parliament declined to renew the Licensing Act, paving the way for a free press in England.

In America, newspapers helped to unify the colonies. As colonists read newspapers published in other colonies, they came to realize what values and concerns they shared with other colonists up and down the Atlantic seaboard. In this way newspapers played an important role in swaying American public opinion toward favoring independence from Great Britain.

### 1.4.5 Hypertext

The July 1945 issue of the *Atlantic Monthly* contained a visionary paper, "As We May Think," written by Vannevar Bush, who had served as director of the Office of Scientific Research and Development in World War II. In the paper Bush noted, "The world has arrived at an age of cheap complex devices of great reliability; and something is bound to come of it" [41, p. 102]. He described many ways in which technology can solve important problems. One of the problems he focused on was that of information retrieval. He pointed out how difficult it is for scientists to keep up with all the research results that are being published, especially when indexing systems do not lend themselves toward exposing the relationships among documents. Bush noted that the human mind doesn't work by indexing. Instead, our memories are associative. When we think of one thing, other related memories awaken in our minds. He suggested that a machine could simulate, to some degree, the mind's ability to make associations between pieces of information. He gave a description for the Memex, an information retrieval system equipped with "a provision whereby any item may be caused at will to select immediately and automatically another" [41, p. 107].

Ted Nelson was raised by his grandparents in Greenwich Village, New York. He was a graduate student studying sociology at Harvard when he took his first computer class. There he discovered that "everything everyone was saying about computers was a lie. It was up to me to design the literature of the future" [42, p. 134]. In 1965 Nelson coined the word **hypertext**, which refers to a linked network of nodes containing information. The links allow readers to visit the nodes in a nonlinear fashion [43]. The proposed system had much in common with Bush's proposal for Memex. In 1967 Nelson proposed the creation of a system called Xanadu, a worldwide network of connected literature.

Despite decades of work and a $5 million investment from Autodesk, the system was never completed [42].

## 1.4.6 Graphical User Interface

Douglas Engelbart grew up on a dairy farm in Oregon. After graduating from high school, he attended Oregon State College, but his electrical engineering studies were interrupted by World War II. While he was stationed in the Philippines, he worked with radar and read "As We May Think" by Vannevar Bush. These two experiences shaped his views about the potential of computing. When his military service ended, he completed his degree at OSC and took a job at Ames Laboratory, but soon began wondering, "How can my career maximize my contribution to mankind?" [44]. Engelbart decided to return to school and completed a PhD in electrical engineering from the University of California, Berkeley, in 1955. He joined the Stanford Research Institute, where he set out to use the power of the computer to augment human intellect.

In the 1950s and 1960s, people submitted computer jobs in the form of decks of punch cards and often waited hours for them to run. Computer output was typically pages full of numbers that programmers would laboriously examine. Engelbart wondered why people couldn't interact directly with computers and view the output on a CRT, like radar images. He created a research lab called the Augmentation Research Center. This lab developed a hypermedia and groupware system called NLS (oNLine System). Engelbart invented several new input devices, including the computer mouse. In 1968 at the Fall Joint Computer Conference in San Francisco, he gave a 90-minute demonstration of NLS that included a video display divided into windows, email, use of a mouse to direct a cursor, and live videoconferencing with staff members 30 miles away (Figure 1.15). Engelbart's presentation is still called "the mother of all demos." Paul Saffo said, "It was like a UFO landing on the White House lawn." The presentation was so far ahead of its time that some audience members thought it was a hoax [45]. Others thought Engelbart's ideas were completely impractical, noting that he was treating a computer as if it were for his personal use.

Alan Kay saw Engelbart's demo, understood the ramifications of NLS, and was eager to take the next step. In 1970 he became one of the founding members of Xerox Palo Alto Research Center (PARC), a new facility dedicated to performing research into digital technology. The research team created the Alto, a small minicomputer designed to be used by a single person. The Alto incorporated a bitmapped display, a keyboard, and a mouse. Kay played a leading role in developing the Alto's graphical user interface that responded to the point, click, and drag operations of a mouse. In order to link together the Altos, the Xerox PARC team also created **Ethernet**, which became a networking standard throughout the computer industry. Ultimately, however, Xerox failed in its attempt to market a commercial personal computer.

In 1979 Apple Computer sold 10 percent of its stock to Xerox. In return, Xerox let Steve Jobs and some Apple engineers visit Xerox PARC to learn more about its research. Jobs returned from the visit committed to building a computer with a graphical user interface. A few years later Apple released the Lisa, a $10,000 personal computer with a graphical user interface. The price tag was too high, the processor was too slow, and

**FIGURE 1.15** Douglas Engelbart rehearses for his presentation at the 1968 Fall Joint Computer Conference. It is still called "the mother of all demos." (Courtesy of Doug Engelbart)

the Lisa was not commercially successful. However, in January 1984 Apple released the Macintosh, a faster $2,495 computer with a graphical user interface. The Macintosh was an instant hit: Apple sold 300,000 in the first year.

During the 1980s IBM, VisiCorp, and Microsoft all offered graphical user interfaces for IBM PC-compatible computers, but they could not compare in sophistication to the interface of the Apple Macintosh. Finally, in May 1990 Microsoft released Windows 3.0 for IBM PCs. Consumers eagerly bought 10 million copies of Windows, giving Microsoft a near monopoly in the graphical user interface market that it has maintained ever since.

### 1.4.7 Single–Computer Hypertext Systems

In 1982 Peter Brown at the University of Kent at Canterbury started a hypertext research project. He named the software Guide. Later, Office Workstations Ltd. commercialized Guide, releasing versions for both the Apple Macintosh and the IBM PC.

In 1987 Apple Computer released HyperCard, a hypertext system that enabled programmers to create "stacks" of "cards." A card could contain text and images. The HyperCard programmer created links from one card to another with "buttons." Buttons could be visible to the user and labeled, or they could be transparent and associated with an image or an area of the card.

Users typically viewed one card at a time. They jumped from one card to another by using the computer's mouse to move a cursor over a button and then clicking the mouse. The best-selling computer games Myst and Riven were actually HyperCard stacks.

### 1.4.8   Networked Hypertext: World Wide Web

Tim Berners-Lee is the son of two mathematicians, both of whom were programmers for the Ferranti Mark 1 computer in the 1950s. From them, Berners-Lee learned that, "in principle, a person could program a computer to do most anything" [46, p. 3]. He also learned that it is easy to get a computer to keep information in lists or tables, but much more difficult to get it to remember arbitrary relationships.

When Berners-Lee was in high school, his father read some books about the brain; the two of them talked about how a computer might be able to make neural-like connections the way a brain does. This idea stuck with Berners-Lee, and in 1980, while working for CERN in Switzerland, he wrote a program called Enquire that incorporated links between information. Berners-Lee was not familiar with the work of Vannevar Bush, Ted Nelson, or Doug Engelbart, but he was heading in the same direction.

In late 1989 Berners-Lee wrote a memo to a management team at CERN, proposing the development of a networked hypertext system that could be used for documentation purposes. When they didn't respond, he tried again in the spring of 1990. Again, no response. However, an intriguing new personal computer called the NeXT had just been released. Berners-Lee asked his boss if he could purchase a NeXT to check out its operating system and programming environment. His boss okayed the purchase, then puckishly suggested that maybe Berners-Lee ought to test the system's capabilities by implementing his proposed hypertext system on it [46].

Unlike earlier commercial hypertext systems, Berners-Lee's system allowed links between information stored on different computers connected by a network. Because it is built on top of the TCP/IP protocol, links can connect any two computers on the Internet, even if they have different hardware or are running different operating systems.

A **Web browser** is a program that allows a user to view Web pages and traverse hyperlinks between pages. Berners-Lee completed the first Web browser on the NeXT Computer on Christmas Day 1990. He called his browser WorldWideWeb. In March 1991 he released the browser to some computer users at CERN.

The first widely used Web browser was Mosaic, developed at the University of Illinois at Urbana-Champaign. Today the most popular Web browsers are Chrome, Internet Explorer, Firefox, and Safari. These browsers enable Web surfers to retrieve text, still images, movies, songs, computer programs—in theory, anything that can be digitized. The Web has also become a convenient way for organizations to provide access to news updates and dynamically changing information (Figure 1.16).

### 1.4.9   Search Engines

A **search engine** is a program that accepts a list of keywords from a user, searches a database of documents, and returns those documents most closely matching the specified keywords. Today the term is most frequently used to describe programs that search databases of Web pages. Web search engines are the most powerful information retrieval devices ever invented. The most popular Web search engine, Google, has indexed billions of Web pages.

**FIGURE 1.16** Using the Web, you can access up-to-date traffic information from many major cities. (Copyright © 2011 by WSDOT. Reprinted with permission.)

There are two types of Web search engines. Crawler-based search engines, such as Google and AltaVista, automatically create the database of information about Web pages. In a process similar to Web surfing, programs called spiders follow hyperlinks, eventually visiting millions of different Web pages. Summary information about these pages is collected into massive databases. When you perform a query, the search engine consults its database to find the closest matches.

The second type of Web search engine relies upon humans to build the database of information about various Web pages. People who develop a Web site can submit a summary of their site to the keepers of the search engine. Alternatively, those responsible for the search engine may create their own reviews of Web sites. The advantage of this kind of search engine is that humans can create more accurate summaries of a Web page than a spider program. The disadvantage of this approach is that only a small fraction of the Web can be cataloged. The Open Directory Project falls into this category.

## 1.5 Information Technology Issues

**Information technology** (IT) refers to devices used in the creation, storage, manipulation, exchange, and dissemination of data, including text, sound, and images. Computers, telephones, and video cameras are examples of IT. The cost of IT devices continues to fall while their capabilities continue to increase. As a result, people are making greater use of IT in their everyday lives. Some of these uses create new issues that need to be resolved. Let's look at a few of the questions raised by the growth of IT.

For many items of value, making the original copy is expensive, but making copies of the original is inexpensive. For example, entertainment companies spend vast sums producing songs, movies, and television shows, but once they have been digitized, the Internet provides a fast and free way to distribute them. In April 2015 more than a million people in the United States alone illegally downloaded the first episode of the fifth season of *Game of Thrones*, which was leaked online a day before appearing on HBO [47]. Creators of computer software are also affected. About three-quarters of the users of Microsoft products in China do not have properly licensed software. In March 2015 Microsoft announced it would be offering free upgrades to the Windows 10 operating system to all Windows users, regardless of whether they were running genuine or illegally obtained copies of Windows [48]. What are reasonable intellectual property rights in the Information Age? Do the laws need to change? How must businesses adapt?

The convenience of credit cards is undeniable, but when credit card information is stolen, it can be decidedly inconvenient for customers to determine the fraudulent charges, report them to the issuer, fill out the paperwork, and wait for the replacement card to arrive. Sometimes card information is stolen on a massive scale, affecting millions of consumers. In November and December of 2013, hackers broke into computers at Target and stole credit card data, phone numbers, and email addresses of at least 12 million Target customers [49]. Credit card companies credit the accounts of consumers who have fraudulent charges and debit the accounts of merchants who sell goods to thieves using stolen card information. That's good for credit card holders, but bad for small businesses who have no idea the cards are stolen.

The use of credit cards raises privacy concerns, too. When I use a credit card to purchase an item, the credit card company now has information about my spending habits. Who has a right to that information? If I buy a pair of water skis with my credit card, does the credit card company have a right to sell my name, address, and phone number to other companies that may want to sell me related products?

The use of IT has changed the way that banks process loan applications. Rather than using a personal interview to decide my creditworthiness, the bank consults a national credit bureau. What are the advantages and disadvantages of this alternative approach to lending money?

Computers are now embedded in many devices on which we depend, from traffic signals to pacemakers. Software errors have resulted in injury and even death. When bugs result in harm to humans, what should the liability be for the people or corporations that produced the software?

When employees use IT devices in their work, companies can monitor their actions closely. For example, a company can track the number of calls per minute each of its telephone operators is handling. It can document the number of keystrokes per minute of its data entry operators. It can log all of the Web sites its employees visit, and it can read the email they send and receive at work. How does such monitoring affect the workplace? Does it create an unacceptable level of stress among employees?

IT is allowing more people than ever to work from home. What are the advantages and disadvantages of telecommuting?

IT capabilities are leading to changes in the IT industry itself. Silicon Valley used to be the epicenter of the IT industry, but improvements in the speed and reliability of communication networks have led to a more decentralized landscape. Hotspots of innovation now include Seattle, Washington (Amazon, Expedia, and Microsoft); Austin, Texas (Advanced Micro Devices, Cisco Systems, and Dell); Walldorf, Germany (SAP); and Bangalore, India (Infosys and Wipro). US-based software companies are doing more development in countries where salaries are much lower, such as India, China, and Vietnam [7]. Will this trend continue? How many software jobs in the United States will be lost to countries where labor is significantly cheaper?

Human rights organizations have criticized Foxconn, the contract manufacturer that makes electronic devices for Apple, Amazon, Dell, and HP, for placing its Chinese employees in unsafe working conditions and forcing them to work longer than the Chinese legal maximum of 49 hours per week [50]. Should consumers of electronic devices boycott products that are made under unsafe or illegal conditions, or would such boycotts actually make conditions worse for workers in developing nations by depriving them of an income?

The World Wide Web has provided an unprecedented opportunity for individuals and nongovernmental organizations to have their points of view made available to billions. This could bring about new levels of citizen involvement and democratic reform. On the other hand, some countries are making large portions of the Web unavailable to their citizens. Will the Web prove to be a tool for democracy, or will it be muzzled by repressive regimes?

# Summary

We are living in the Information Age, an era characterized by ubiquitous computing and communication devices that have made information much easier to collect, store, retrieve, manipulate, and transmit. These devices are the culmination of centuries of technological progress.

What conclusions can we draw from our study of the development of computers, communication networks, and information storage and retrieval devices? First, revolutionary discoveries are rare. Most innovations represent simply the next step in a long staircase of evolutionary changes. Each inventor, or team of inventors, relies upon prior work. In many cases different inventors come up with the same "original" idea at the same time.

A second conclusion we can draw from these stories is that information technology did not begin with the personal computer and the World Wide Web. Many other inventions, including the telegraph, the telephone, the mechanical calculator, the radio, and the television, led to significant social changes when they were adopted.

Finally, the rapid rate of technological change is causing a number of important new questions to emerge that test our values. Is it right to give your friends copies of songs you have purchased? Is it right for a government to keep track of every telephone call made by its citizens? Is it wrong to contribute to the development of autonomous automobiles that could put hundreds of thousands of taxicab drivers out of work?

The use of a new technology can have a significant impact on a society, but we need to remember that, as societies and as individuals, we have a great deal of control over how we choose to use a technology in order to maintain the values we hold to be fundamentally important. As Seymour Papert observed:

> So we are entering this computer future; but what will it be like? What sort of a world will it be? There is no shortage of experts, futurists, and prophets who are ready to tell us, but they don't agree. The Utopians promise us a new millennium, a wonderful world in which the computer will solve all our problems. The computer critics warn us of the dehumanizing effect of too much exposure to machinery, and of disruption of employment in the workplace and the economy.
>
> Who is right? Well, both are wrong—because they are asking the wrong question. The question is not "What will the computer do to us?" The question is "What will we make of the computer?" The point is not to predict the computer future. The point is to make it. [51]

© Zits Partnership, King Features Syndicate

# Further Reading and Viewing

Nicholar Carr. "Is Google Making Us Stupid?" *Atlantic*, July/August 2008.

Charles Duhigg and David Barboza. "In China, the Human Costs That Are Built into an iPad." *New York Times*, January 26, 2012.

Andrew Keen. "Opinion: Facebook Threatens to 'Zuck Up' the Human Race." CNN.com, May 30, 2012. www.cnn.com.

Kevin Kelly. "We Are the Web." *Wired*, August 2005.

⊙ Erik Kruse. "On the Brink of a Networked Society." *BOLDtalks*, April 1, 2013. 18:36. www.youtube.com/watch?v=iazoyHS5tZ4.

⊙ Randall Maclowry. "Silicon Valley." *American Experience*, February 5, 2013. 1:23:11. video.pbs.org.

Marc Perry. "Scholars Sound the Alert from the 'Dark Side' of Tech Innovation." *Chronicle of Higher Education*, May 8, 2013.

Robert Rosenberger. "Viewpoint: The Problem with Hands-Free Dashboard Cellphones." *Communications of the ACM*, April 2013.

Paul Solman. "How Virtual Reality Games Can Transform Society, Prosperity." *PBS News-Hour*, July 11, 2013. 10:27. video.pbs.org.

John D. Sutter. "Despite Horses and Buggies, Amish Aren't Necessarily 'Low-Tech.'" CNN .com, June 22, 2011. www.cnn.com.

# Review Questions

1. Elements of information technology, such as the alphabet and the abacus, are more than 2,000 years old. What about the present era distinguishes it as the Information Age?

2. How did the popularity of mathematical tables stimulate the development of autonomous calculating machines?

3. Compare and contrast the social conditions in the United States that stimulated the growth of the mechanical calculator market in the latter half of the nineteenth century with the social conditions that stimulated the growth of the personal computer market in the latter half of the twentieth century.

4. The Burroughs Adding Machine Company dominated the mechanical calculator market in the 1890s, and IBM dominated the electronic computer industry in the 1960s. What did these companies have in common that led them to the number one position in their respective markets?

5. Name three ways the development of radar in World War II stimulated advances in computing.

6. In what way did the Cold War help bring about the personal computer?

7. Can you think of a practical reason why the semaphore telegraph was adopted more rapidly on the continent of Europe than in the British Isles?

8. Compare and contrast the social impact of these three information technologies: the telegraph, the telephone, and wireless networks.

9. In what important ways did the hypertext system of Berners-Lee differ from earlier hypertext systems?

10. Give four examples from this chapter of how a social condition influenced the development of a new information technology.

11. Give four examples from this chapter of a social change brought about by the adoption of a new information technology.

# Discussion Questions

12. Think about the last piece of consumer electronics you purchased. How did you first learn about it? What factors (features, price, ease of use, etc.) did you weigh before you purchased it? Which of these factors were most influential in your purchase decision? Are you still happy with your purchase?

13. Do you tend to acquire new technological devices before or after the majority of your friends? What are the advantages of being an early adopter of a new technology? What are the advantages of being a late adopter of a new technology?

14. Have you ever gone camping or had another experience where you went for at least a few days without access to a phone, radio, television, or computer? (In other words, there was no communication between you and the outside world.) What did you learn from your experience?

15. Are there any information technologies that you wish had never been adopted? If so, which ones?

16. Some say that no technology is inherently good or evil; rather, any technology can be used for either good or evil purposes. Do you share this view?

17. The telephone eroded traditional social hierarchies. Has email had the same effect within colleges and universities? Do students send emails to people they would be uncomfortable talking with personally? Are these emails effective?

18. Is the cell phone changing our views about polite and impolite behavior? For example, is it polite for someone to be talking on their cell phone while ordering a drink at Starbucks?

19. Martin Carnoy writes, "Thanks to a communications and software revolution, we are more 'connected' than ever before—by cell phone, email, and video conferencing—yet more disconnected than in the past from social interaction" [52]. Do you agree?

20. Was it wrong for Altair 8800 owners to use Altair BASIC on their computers without paying Micro-Soft?

21. The story of Altair BASIC highlights a clash between those who see software as something to be developed and freely shared among computer enthusiasts and those who see software development as an entrepreneurial activity. Give some contemporary examples that illustrate these contrasting views of software.

22. More than 90 percent of personal computers run a version of the Microsoft Windows operating system. In what ways is this situation beneficial to computer users? In what ways does this situation harm computer users?

23. Angelo says, "When I'm trying to have a face-to-face conversation with someone, and that person repeatedly interrupts the conversation to answer their cell phone or exchange text messages, they are basically telling me that I'm not worth all of their attention." Do you agree with Angelo?

## In–Class Exercises

24. Use four different search engines (www.altavista.com, www.bing.com, www.google.com, www.yahoo.com) to perform a search on the phrase "Information Technology." Create a table that compares the top 10 Web pages returned by each search engine. Which engines were the most similar?

25. Managers of health clubs are concerned that people in locker rooms may be secretly photographed by other members carrying smartphones.

Debate the following proposition: "Health clubs should ban all smartphone use within their premises."

26. In the 1984 presidential election, all the major television networks used computers to predict that Republican Ronald Reagan would defeat Democrat Walter Mondale, even before the polls closed on the West Coast. When they heard this news, some Mondale supporters who had been waiting in line to vote simply went home without voting. Although the national election was already settled, the TV networks may have influenced the results of some statewide and local elections.

Debate the following proposition: "In presidential elections polls should close at the same time everywhere in the United States."

27. Ford, Honda, Mercedes-Benz, Subaru, Toyota, Volvo, and other automobile manufacturers are currently offering collision mitigation systems on some of their vehicles. A collision mitigation system uses radar to sense when the distance between the car and the vehicle in front of it is rapidly decreasing. The system provides audio and visual warnings to the driver when dangerous situations are detected. It also pretightens the seat belts. If the driver fails to respond, the system brakes the car and tightens the seat belt further to reduce the impact of the collision.

Debate the following proposition: "Every new car should be equipped with a collision mitigation system."

28. Read about "Star Wars Kid" and "The Bus Uncle" on Wikipedia, then debate the following proposition: "It is wrong to post a photo or video of someone else on the Internet without their permission."

# References

[1]   May Swenson. "Southbound on the Freeway." *New Yorker*, February 16, 1963.

[2]   Ferris Jabr. "Cache Cab: Taxi Drivers' Brains Grow to Navigate London's Streets." *Scientific American*, December 8, 2011.

[3]   Ethan S. Bromberg-Martin and Okihide Hikosaka. "Midbrain Dopamine Neurons Signal Preference for Advance Information about Upcoming Rewards," *Neuron*, Vol. 26, pp. 119–126, July 16, 2009.

[4]   Susan Weinschenk. "100 Things You Should Know about People: #8—Dopamine Makes You Addicted to Seeking Information." *What Makes Them Click: Applying Psychology to Understand How People Think, Work, and Relate* (blog), November 7, 2009. www.whatmakesthemclick.net.

[5]   Christine Rosen. "Our Cell Phones, Ourselves." *New Atlantis: A Journal of Technology & Society*, Summer 2004.

[6]   Howard Rheingold. "Look Who's Talking." *Wired* (7.01), January 1999.

[7]   "The New Geography of the IT Industry." *The Economist*, pp. 47–49, July 19, 2003.

[8]   D'Arcy Jenish and Catherine Roberts. "Heating Up Nuclear Power." *Maclean's* 113(24): 19, June 11, 2001.

[9]   Peggy A. Kidwell and Paul E. Ceruzzi. *Landmarks in Digital Computing: A Smithsonian Pictorial History.* Smithsonian Institution Press, Washington, DC, 1994.

[10]   James Cortada. *Before the Computer: IBM, NCR, Burroughs, & Remington Rand & the Industry They Created, 1865–1956*. Princeton University Press, Princeton, NJ, 2000.

[11]   "A Better Day's Work at Less Cost of Time, Work, and Worry to the Man at the Desk: In Three Parts Illustrated," 3d ed. Burroughs Adding Machine Company, Detroit, MI, 1909.

[12]   Sharon H. Strom. " 'Machines Instead of Clerks': Technology and the Feminization of Bookkeeping, 1910–1950." In *Computer Chips and Paper Clips: Technology and Women's Employment, Volume II: Case Studies and Policy Perspectives,* edited by Heidi I. Hartmann, Robert E. Kraut, and Louise A. Tilly. National Academies Press, Washington, DC, 1987.

[13]   Edwin Black. *IBM and the Holocaust: The Strategic Alliance between Nazi Germany and America's Most Powerful Corporation*. Dialog Press, Washington, DC, 2011.

[14]   Joel Shurkin. *Engines of the Mind: The Evolution of the Computer from Mainframes to Microprocessors*. W.W. Norton & Company, New York, NY, 1996.

[15]   Grace Murray Hopper. "Keynote Address." In *History of Programming Languages*, edited by Richard L. Wexelblat. Academic Press, New York, NY, 1981.

[16]   John Backus. "The History of FORTRAN I, II, and III." In *History of Programming Languages*, edited by Richard L. Wexelblat. Academic Press, New York, NY, 1981.

[17]   Jean E. Sammet. "The Early History of COBOL." In *History of Programming Languages*, edited by Richard L. Wexelblat. Academic Press, New York, NY, 1981.

[18]   Thomas E. Kurtz. "Basic." In *History of Programming Languages*, edited by Richard L. Wexelblat. Academic Press, New York, NY, 1981.

[19]   Robert Buderi. *The Invention That Changed the World: How a Small Group of Radar Pioneers Won the Second World War and Launched a Technological Revolution*. Simon and Schuster, New York, NY, 1996.

[20]   Michael Riordan and Lillian Hoddeson. *Crystal Fire: The Birth of the Information Age*. W. W. Norton & Company, New York, NY, 1997.

[21]   Frederick Seitz and Norman G. Einspruch. *Electronic Genie: The Tangled History of Silicon*. University of Illinois Press, Urbana, IL, 1998.

[22]   John Markoff. *What the Dormouse Said: How the Sixties Counterculture Shaped the Personal Computer Industry*. Penguin Books, New York, NY, 2005.

[23]   Steve Jobs. "You've Got to Find What You Love." Commencement speech, Stanford University, June 12, 2005.

[24]   Fred Turner. *From Counterculture to Cyberculture: Stewart Brand, the Whole Earth Network, and the Rise of Digital Utopianism*. University of Chicago Press, Chicago, IL, 2006.

[25]   *The People's Computer Company*, Issue 1, cover, October 1972.

[26]   Paul Carroll. *Big Blues: The Unmaking of IBM*. Crown Publishers, New York, NY, 1993.

[27]   Sidney H. Aronson. "Bell's Electrical Toy." In *The Social Impact of the Telephone*, edited by Ithiel de Sola Pool. MIT Press, Cambridge, MA, 1977.

[28]   Carolyn Marvin. *When Old Technologies Were New: Thinking about Electric Communications in the Late Nineteenth Century*. Oxford University Press, New York, NY, 1988.

[29]   "Telephone Cranks." *Western Electrician* (Chicago), p. 37, July 17, 1897.

[30]   Ithiel de Sola Pool. Introduction. In *The Social Impact of the Telephone*, edited by Ithiel de Sola Pool. MIT Press, Cambridge, MA, 1977.

[31]  Asa Briggs. "The Pleasure Telephone." In *The Social Impact of the Telephone*, edited by Ithiel de Sola Pool. MIT Press, Cambridge, MA, 1977.

[32]  Martin Campbell-Kelly and William Aspray. *Computer: A History of the Information Machine*. BasicBooks, New York, NY, 1996.

[33]  James Wood. *History of International Broadcasting*. Peter Peregrinus, London, United Kingdom, 1992, p. 12.

[34]  "War of the Worlds, Orson Welles, and the Invasion from Mars." Transparency (Web site). www.transparencynow.com.

[35]  Barry M. Leiner, Vinton G. Cerf, David D. Clark, Robert E. Kahn, Leonard Kleinrock, Daniel C. Lynch, Jon Postel, Larry G. Roberts, and Stephen Wolff. *A Brief History of the Internet, Version 3.32*, December 10, 2003. www.isoc.org/internet/history/brief.shtml.

[36]  Vinton G. Cerf and Robert E. Kahn. "A Protocol for Packet Network Intercommunication." *IEEE Transactions on Communications*, COM-22(5), May 1974.

[37]  Akamai Technologies. "Akamai's State of the Internet Q4 2014 Report," Vol. 7, No. 4, 2014.

[38]  "Worldwide Cellphone Subscriptions Forecast to Exceed Worldwide Population in 2015!" IC Insights, November 12, 2014. www.icinsights.com.

[39]  Thomas Cahill. *How the Irish Saved Civilization: The Untold Story of Ireland's Role from the Fall of Rome to the Rise of Medieval Europe*. Anchor Books, New York, NY, 1995.

[40]  Elizabeth L. Eisenstein. *The Printing Press as an Agent of Change*. Volume 1. Cambridge University Press, Cambridge, England, 1979.

[41]  Vannevar Bush. "As We May Think." *Atlantic Monthly*, 176(1):101–108, August 1945.

[42]  Owen Edwards. "Ted Nelson." *Forbes ASAP*, August 25, 1997.

[43]  Lauren Wedeles. "Prof. Nelson Talk Analyzes P.R.I.D.E." *Vassar Miscellany News*, February 3, 1965.

[44]  Tia O'Brien. "From the Archives: Douglas Engelbart's Lasting Legacy, 1999." *San Jose Mercury News*, July 3, 2013.

[45]  "Internet Pioneers: Doug Engelbart." ibiblio (Web site) accessed September 23, 2013. www.ibiblio.org/pioneers/engelbart.html.

[46]  Tim Berners-Lee. *Weaving the Web*. HarperCollins Publishers, New York, NY, 1999.

[47]  *Game of Thrones* Season 5 Infographic. *Tru Optik*, April 2015. www.truoptik.com.

[48]  Bill Rigby and Paul Carsten. "Microsoft Tackles China Piracy with Free Upgrade to Windows 10." *Reuters*, March 18, 2015. www.reuters.com.

[49]  Ben Elgin. "Three New Details from Target's Credit Card Breach." *Bloomberg*, March 26, 2014. www.bloomberg.com.

[50]  Vindu Goel. "Foxconn Audit Finds a Workweek Still Too Long." *New York Times*, May 16, 2013.

[51]  Seymour Papert. "A Critique of Technocentrism in Thinking about the School of the Future." Technical report, MIT Media Lab, September 1990. Epistemology and Learning Memo No. 2.

[52]  Martin Carnoy. *Sustaining the New Economy: Work, Family, and the Community in the Information Age*, p. x. Russell Sage Foundation/Harvard University Press, New York, NY/Cambridge, MA, 2000.

# Dalton Conley

Dalton Conley is dean for the social sciences, as well as university professor, at New York University. In 2005 he became the first sociologist (and second social scientist) to win the Alan T. Waterman Award from the National Science Foundation for best young researcher in any field of science, math, or engineering. Conley's research focuses on how socioeconomic status is transmitted across generations and on the public policies that affect that process.

He has written six books, including *Elsewhere, U.S.A.: How We Got from the Company Man, Family Dinners and the Age of Affluence to the Home Office, BlackBerry Moms and Economic Anxiety* (2009, New York: Pantheon). In addition to writing books, he is a frequent contributor to the *New York Times, Los Angeles Times, Salon, Slate, Fortune,* and the *Chronicle of Higher Education.* He also lectures frequently and has appeared on *Today, The O'Reilly Factor, PBS NewsHour, Fresh Air,* and *20/20.* He has been named one of nine "innovative minds" by *SEED* magazine.

---

### What do you mean by your term the "Elsewhere Ethic"?

I argue that whereas once the ethical imperative in American life—as embodied in the culture of individualism—was to "find oneself," that ethic has morphed into one in which we need to "manage one's selves." That is, with constant connectivity and the concomitant decline in solitude, we no longer have the space or opportunity to find a true, single, authentic self. With Facebook, Twitter, email logs, and so on, there is hardly a private social space anymore—what sociologist Erving Goffman called the "backstage." Instead, the imperative is to be able to manage these multiple data streams and impulses and avatars in different media of communication.

### What are the phenomena that have given rise to the Elsewhere Ethic?

Communications technology, of course, but also rising income inequality and economic anxiety as well as increased work–life tension due to the rapid rise in working mothers (combined with a lack of decline in fathers' work hours that might have compensated).

### Are you saying that teenagers texting at the dinner table are just following the lead of adults?

I am saying that the entire culture has shifted, and often youth—the so-called digital natives—have been completely reared and socialized within the new normative context. Older folks like myself are caught between the old ethic of individualism and the new fragmented intravidualism.

### How has social change driven the development of new information technologies, such as cell phones, text messaging, and movie-recommendation software?

A Marxist would say that technology drives social change. Some others might say that technology merely embodies or reacts to social change. Most of the rest of us social scientists would say that there is a feedback loop. Yes, the Internet revolution and other telecommunications technologies have fundamentally altered the social landscape by, for example, erasing boundaries between home and office, work and leisure, friends and colleagues, public and private. But the development and spread of those technologies is also reactive to social changes such as the increase in two-working-parent families, which, in a sense, necessitate an increased level of connectivity to manage work and home responsibilities. Likewise, rising work hours and inequality have also adopted the work-always ethos of the current epoch, which is both facilitated by and drives demand for ever-faster telecommunications technologies.

### Is it possible or even desirable to return to a less connected lifestyle in which people really give each other their undivided attention?

Desirable is in the eye of the beholder. We can always make a conscious choice to drop out, tune in, and so on. And you can already see a backlash in the popular culture in the form of the slow-food, slow-living movement. However, you can never go home again, as the saying goes, because even if you make efforts to regulate your own attention and usage of technologies, you are doing so on a shifted playing field, fighting intense forces that didn't exist to the same degree in earlier times.

### Okay, so there's no going back. What's the best way to move forward?

There are many great aspects of this networked world of "weisure" (a portmanteau that combines work and leisure in this blurred lifestyle). If we are lucky enough to be a member of the Elsewhere Class, we can telecommute when our kids are home sick. We can use our iPhone to locate a farmers' market in a strange city in which we find ourselves on a business trip. And work has become more fun for this class. More and more of us find not just our calling—our identity—from our work; many of us also find pleasure and joy in the rhythm of our weisurely lives where we are needed and connected. So my advice is not to pine for a nostalgic past of uninterrupted family dinners and beach vacations. The most successful (and fulfilled) firms and individuals are going to be the ones who bend and blend rather than erect rigid modernist boundaries between the spheres of life. That might mean de-emphasizing "face time" if tasks can be done on Skype. Or it could mean providing on-site day care. Or laundry rooms and gyms at the office (as Google does). Employees find that more convenient, and employers get more productive workers whose other tasks don't get in the way of their work in the knowledge economy.

# 2

# Introduction to Ethics

No man is an island, entire of itself; every man is a piece of the continent, a part of the main. If a clod be washed away by the sea, Europe is the less, as well as if a promontory were, as well as if a manor of thy friend's or of thine own were. Any man's death diminishes me, because I am involved in mankind; and therefore never send to know for whom the bell tolls; it tolls for thee.

—JOHN DONNE, *Meditation XVII*

## 2.1 Introduction

IMAGINE HOVERING ABOVE THE EARTH in a spacecraft on a cloudless night. Looking down upon our planet, you see beautiful constellations of artificial light (Figure 2.1). The stars in these incandescent galaxies are our communities.

Communities provide many benefits to the people who live in them. They make people more secure against external dangers, and they facilitate the exchange of goods and services. Instead of each family assuming responsibility for all of its needs, such as food, housing, clothing, education, and health care, individuals can focus on particular activities. Specialization results in higher productivity that increases the average standard of living. In addition, communities foster the development of fulfilling personal relationships.

There is a price associated with being part of a community. Communities prohibit certain actions and make other actions obligatory. Those who do not conform to these

**FIGURE 2.1**  Looking down on London, England, at night from space.  (Courtesy of NASA)

prohibitions and obligations can be punished. Still, the fact that almost everyone *does* live in a community is strong evidence that the advantages of community life outweigh the disadvantages.

Responsible community members take the needs and desires of other people into account when they make decisions. They recognize that virtually everybody shares the "core values" of life, happiness, and the ability to accomplish goals. People who respect only their own needs and desires are taking the selfish point of view. Moving to the "ethical point of view" requires a decision that other people and their core values are also worthy of respect [1].

People who take the ethical point of view may still disagree over what is the proper course of action to take in a particular situation. Sometimes the facts of the matters are disputable. At other times, different value judgments arising from competing ethical theories lead people to opposite conclusions. For this reason, it is worthwhile to have a basic understanding of some of the most popular ethical theories. In this chapter we describe the difference between morality and ethics, discuss a variety of ethical theories, evaluate their pros and cons, and show how to use the more viable ethical theories to solve moral problems.

### 2.1.1  Defining Terms

A **society** is an association of people organized under a system of rules designed to advance the good of its members over time [2]. Cooperation among individuals helps promote the common good. However, people in a society also compete with each other;

for example, when deciding how to divide limited benefits among themselves. Sometimes the competition is relatively trivial, such as when many people vie for tickets to a concert. At other times the competition is much more significant, such as when two start-up companies seek dominance of an emerging market. Every society has rules of conduct describing what people ought and ought not to do in various situations. We call these rules **morality**.

A person may simultaneously belong to multiple societies, which can lead to moral dilemmas. For example, what happens when a pacifist (according to the rules of his religion) is drafted to serve in the armed forces (according to the laws of his nation)?

**Ethics** is the philosophical study of morality, a rational examination into people's moral beliefs and behavior. Consider the following analogy (Figure 2.2). Society is like a town full of people driving cars. Morality is the road network within the town. People ought to keep their cars on the roads. Those who choose to "do ethics" are in balloons floating above the town. From this perspective, an observer can evaluate individual roads (particular moral guidelines) as well as the quality of the entire road network (moral system). The observer can also judge whether individual drivers are staying on the roads (acting morally) or taking shortcuts (acting immorally). Finally, the observer can propose and evaluate various ways of constructing road networks (alternative moral

**FIGURE 2.2** An analogy explaining the difference between ethics and morality. Imagine society as a town. Morality is the road network within the town. People doing ethics are in balloons floating above the town.

systems). While there may in fact be a definite answer regarding the best way to construct and operate a road network, it may be difficult for the observers to identify and agree upon this answer, because each observer has a different viewpoint.

The study of ethics is particularly important right now. Our society is changing rapidly as it incorporates the latest advances in information technology. Just think about how smartphones and social apps have changed how we spend our time and interact with others! New products and services have brought us many benefits. However, some people selfishly exploit new technologies for personal gain, even if that reduces their overall benefit for the rest of us. Here are two examples. While most of us are happy to have the ability to send email to people all over the world, others engage in phishing to steal financial information. Access to the World Wide Web provides libraries with an important new information resource for their patrons, but should children be allowed to follow links leading to pornographic Web sites?

When we encounter new problems such as phishing or pornographic Web sites, we need to decide which activities are morally "good," which are morally "neutral," and which are morally "bad." Unfortunately, existing moral guidelines sometimes seem old-fashioned or unclear. If we can't always count on "common wisdom" to help us answer these questions, we need to learn how to work through these problems ourselves.

## 2.1.2 Four Scenarios

As an initiation into the study of ethics, carefully read each of the following scenarios. After reflection, come up with your own answer to each of the questions.

### ∼ SCENARIO 1

Alexis, a gifted high school student, wants to become a doctor. Because she comes from a poor family, she will need a scholarship in order to attend college. Some of her classes require students to do extra research projects in order to get an A. Her high school has a few older PCs, but there are always long lines of students waiting to use them during the school day. After school, she usually works at a part-time job to help support her family.

One evening Alexis visits the library of a private college a few miles from her family's apartment, and she finds plenty of unused PCs connected to the Internet. She surreptitiously looks over the shoulder of another student to learn a valid login/password combination. Alexis returns to the library several times a week, and by using its PCs and printers she efficiently completes the extra research projects, graduates from high school with straight A's, and gets a full-ride scholarship to attend a prestigious university.

### Questions
1. Did Alexis do anything wrong?
2. Who benefited from Alexis's course of action?
3. Who was hurt by Alexis's course of action?
4. Did Alexis have an unfair advantage over her high school classmates?

5. Would any of your answers change if it turns out Alexis did not win a college scholarship after all and is now working at the Burger Barn?

6. Are there better ways Alexis could have accomplished her objective?

7. What additional information, if any, would help you answer the previous questions?                                                                          ∽

## ∽ SCENARIO 2

An organization dedicated to reducing spam tries to get Internet service providers (ISPs) in an East Asian country to stop the spammers by protecting their email servers. When this effort is unsuccessful, the antispam organization puts the addresses of these ISPs on its blacklist. Many ISPs in the United States consult the blacklist and refuse to accept email from the blacklisted ISPs. This action has two results. First, the amount of spam received by the typical email user in the United States drops by 25 percent. Second, tens of thousands of innocent computer users in the East Asian country are unable to send email to friends and business associates in the United States.

### Questions

1. Did the antispam organization do anything wrong?

2. Did the ISPs that refused to accept email from the blacklisted ISPs do anything wrong?

3. Who benefited from the organization's action?

4. Who was hurt by the organization's action?

5. Could the organization have achieved its goals through a better course of action?

6. What additional information, if any, would help you answer the previous questions?                                                                          ∽

## ∽ SCENARIO 3

In an attempt to deter speeders, the East Dakota State Police (EDSP) installs video cameras on all of its freeway overpasses. The cameras are connected to computers that can reliably detect cars traveling more than five miles per hour above the speed limit. These computers have sophisticated image recognition software that enables them to read license plate numbers and capture high-resolution pictures of vehicle drivers. If the picture of the driver matches the driver's license photo of one of the registered owners of the car, the system issues a speeding ticket to the driver, complete with photo evidence. Six months after the system is put into operation, the number of people speeding on East Dakota freeways is reduced by 90 percent.

The FBI asks the EDSP for real-time access to the information collected by the video cameras. The EDSP complies with this request. Three months later, the FBI uses this information to arrest five members of a terrorist organization.

## Questions

1. Did the East Dakota State Police do anything wrong?

2. Who benefited from the actions of the EDSP?

3. Who was harmed by the actions of the EDSP?

4. What other courses of action could the EDSP have taken to achieve its objectives? Examine the advantages and disadvantages of these alternative courses of action.

5. What additional information, if any, would help you answer the previous questions?  ∼

## ∼ SCENARIO 4

You are the senior software engineer at a start-up company developing an exciting new mobile app that will allow salespeople to generate and email sales quotes and customer invoices from their smartphones.

Your company's sales force has led a major corporation to believe your product will be available next week. Unfortunately, at this point the software still contains quite a few bugs. The leader of the testing group has reported that all of the known bugs appear to be minor, but it will take another month of testing for his team to be confident the product contains no catastrophic errors.

Because of the fierce competition in the mobile app industry, it is critical that your company be "first to market." To the best of your knowledge, a well-established company will release a similar product in a few weeks. If its product appears first, your start-up company will probably go out of business.

## Questions

1. Should you recommend release of the product next week?

2. Who will benefit if the company follows your recommendation?

3. Who will be harmed if the company follows your recommendation?

4. Do you have an obligation to any group of people that may be affected by your decision?

5. What additional information, if any, would help you answer the previous questions?  ∼

Reflect on the process you used in each scenario to come up with your answers. How did you decide if particular actions or decisions were right or wrong? Were your reasons consistent from one case to the next? Did you use the same methodology in more than one scenario? If someone disagreed with you on the answer to one of these questions, how would you try to convince that person that your position makes more sense?

Ethics is the rational, systematic analysis of conduct that can cause benefit or harm to other people. Because ethics is based in reason, people are required to explain *why* they hold the opinions they do. This gives us the opportunity to compare ethical evaluations. When two people reach different conclusions, we can weigh the facts and the reasoning process behind their conclusions to determine the stronger line of thinking.

It's important to note that ethics is focused on the *voluntary, moral* choices people make because they have decided they ought to take one course of action rather than an alternative. Ethics is not concerned about involuntary choices or choices outside the moral realm.

For example, if I am ordering a new car, I may get to choose whether it is red, white, green, or blue. This choice is not in the moral realm, because it does not involve benefit or harm to other people.

Now, suppose I'm driving my new red car down a city street. A pedestrian, obscured from my view by a parked car, runs out into traffic. In an attempt to miss the pedestrian, I swerve, lose control of my car, and kill another pedestrian walking along the sidewalk. While my action caused harm to another person, this is not an example of ethical decision making, because my decision was a reflex action rather than a reasoned choice.

However, suppose I did not have full control of the car because I had been driving while intoxicated. In that case the consequences of my voluntary choice to drink alcohol before driving affected another moral being (the innocent pedestrian). Now the problem has entered the realm of ethics.

### 2.1.3 Overview of Ethical Theories

The formal study of ethics goes back at least 2,400 years, to the Greek philosopher Socrates. Socrates did not put any of his philosophy in writing, but his student Plato did. In Plato's dialogue called the *Crito*, imprisoned Socrates uses ethical reasoning to explain why he ought to face an unjust death penalty rather than take advantage of an opportunity to flee into exile with his family [3].

In the past two millennia, philosophers have proposed many ethical theories. In this chapter we review some of them. How do we decide if a particular theory is useful? A useful theory allows its proponents to examine moral problems, reach conclusions, and defend those conclusions in front of a skeptical, yet open-minded audience (Figure 2.3).

FIGURE 2.3 A good ethical theory should enable you to make a persuasive, logical argument to a diverse audience.

Suppose you and I are debating a moral problem in front of a nonpartisan crowd. You have concluded that a particular course of action is right, while I believe it is wrong. It is only natural for me to ask you, "Why do you think doing such-and-such is right?" If you are unable to give any logical reasons why your position is correct, you are unlikely to persuade anyone. On the other hand, if you can explain the chain of reasoning that led you to your conclusion, you will be more likely to convince the audience that your position is correct. At the very least you will help reveal where there are disputed facts or values. Therefore, we will reject proposed ethical theories that are not based on reasoning from facts or commonly accepted values.

In the following sections we consider nine ethical theories—nine frameworks for moral decision making. We present the motivation or insight underlying each theory, explain how it can be used to determine whether an action is right or wrong, and give the "case for" and the "case against" the theory. The workable theories will be those that both respect the ethical point of view and make it possible for a person to present a persuasive, logical argument to a diverse audience of skeptical, yet open-minded people.

## 2.2  Subjective Relativism

**Ethical relativism** is the theory that there are no universal moral norms of right and wrong. According to this theory, different individuals or groups of people can have completely opposite views of a moral problem, and both can be right. Two particular kinds of ethical relativism we'll discuss are subjective relativism and cultural relativism.

**Subjective relativism** holds that each person decides right and wrong for himself or herself. This notion is captured in the popular expression, "What's right for you may not be right for me."

### 2.2.1  The Case for Subjective Relativism

1. *Well-meaning and intelligent people can have totally opposite opinions about moral issues.*

   For example, consider the issue of legalized abortion in the United States. There are a significant number of rational people on each side of the issue. Subjective relativists would contend that the reason people cannot reach the same conclusion is that morality is not like gravity; it is not something "out there" that rational people can discover and try to understand. Instead, each of us creates his or her own morality.

2. *Ethical debates are disagreeable and pointless.*

   Going back to the example of abortion, the debate in the United States has been going on for more than 40 years. An agreement about whether abortion is right or wrong may never be reached. Nobody is all-knowing. When faced with a difficult moral problem, who is to say which side is correct? If morality is relative, we do not have to try to reconcile opposing views. Both sides are right.

### 2.2.2 The Case against Subjective Relativism

1. *With subjective relativism the line between doing what you think is right and doing what you want to do is not sharply drawn.*

   People are good at rationalizing their bad behavior. Subjective relativism provides an ideal last line of defense for someone whose conduct is being questioned. When pressed to explain a decision or action, a subjective relativist can reply, "Who are *you* to tell *me* what I should and should not do?" If morality means doing whatever you want to do, it doesn't mean much, if it means anything at all.

2. *By allowing each person to decide right and wrong for himself or herself, subjective relativism makes no moral distinction between the actions of different people.*

   The fact is that some people have caused millions to suffer, while others have led lives of great service to humanity. Suppose both Adolf Hitler and Mother Teresa spent their entire lives doing what they thought was the right thing to do. Do you want to give both of them credit for living good lives?

   A modification of the original formulation of subjective relativism might be, "I can decide what's right for me, as long as my actions don't hurt anybody else." That solves the problem of Adolf Hitler versus Mother Teresa. However, as soon as you introduce the idea that you shouldn't harm others, you must come to an agreement with others about what it means to harm someone. At this point the process is no longer subjective or completely up to the individual. In other words, a statement of the form, "I can decide what's right for me, as long as my actions don't hurt anyone else," is inconsistent with subjective relativism.

3. *Subjective relativism and tolerance are two different things.*

   Some people may be attracted to ethical relativism because they believe in tolerance. There is a lot to be said for tolerance. It allows individuals in a pluralistic society like the United States to live in harmony. However, tolerance is not the same thing as subjective relativism. Subjective relativism holds that individuals decide for themselves what is right and what is wrong. If you are a tolerant person, is it okay with you if some people decide they want to be intolerant? What if a person decides that he will only deal fairly with people of his own racial group? You can't say that racial bigotry is wrong without undermining the foundation of subjective relativism, because any statement of the form, "People ought to be tolerant," is an example of a universal moral **norm**, or rule. Relativism is based on the idea that there are *no* universal moral norms, so a blanket statement about the need for tolerance is incompatible with subjective relativism.

4. *We should not give legitimacy to an ethical theory that allows people to make decisions based on something other than reason.*

   If individuals decide for themselves what is right and what is wrong, they can reach their conclusions by any means they see fit. They may choose to base their decisions on something other than logic and reason, such as the rolling of dice or the turning of tarot cards. This path is contrary to using logic and reason.

   If your goal is to persuade others that your solutions to actual moral problems are correct, adopting subjective relativism is self-defeating because it is based on the idea that each person decides for himself or herself what is right and what is wrong. According to subjective relativism, nobody's conclusions are any more valid that anyone else's, no matter how these conclusions are drawn. Therefore, we reject subjective relativism as a workable ethical theory.

## 2.3 Cultural Relativism

If subjective relativism is unworkable, what about different views of right and wrong held by different societies at the same point in time, or those held by the same society at different points in time?

In the modern era, anthropologists have collected evidence of societies with moral codes markedly different from those of the societies of Europe and North America. William Graham Sumner described the evolution of "folkways," which he argues eventually become institutionalized into the moral guidelines of a society:

> The first task of life is to live. . . . The struggle to maintain existence was not carried on individually but in groups. Each profited by the other's experience; hence there was concurrence towards that which proved to be the most expedient. All at last adopted the same way for the same purpose; hence the ways turned into customs and became mass phenomena. Instincts were learned in connection with them. In this way folkways arise. The young learn by tradition, imitation, and authority. The folkways, at a time, provide for all the needs of life then and there. They are uniform, universal in the group, imperative, and invariable. As time goes on, the folkways become more and more arbitrary, positive, and imperative. If asked why they act in a certain way in certain cases, primitive people always answer that it is because they and their ancestors always have done so. . . . The morality of a group at a time is the sum of the taboos and prescriptions in the folkways by which right conduct is defined. . . . "Good" mores are those which are well adapted to the situation. "Bad" mores are those which are not so well adapted. [4]

**Cultural relativism** is the ethical theory that the meaning of "right" and "wrong" rests with a society's actual moral guidelines. These guidelines vary from place to place and from time to time.

### 2.3.1 The Case for Cultural Relativism

1. *Different social contexts demand different moral guidelines.*

It's unrealistic to assume that the same set of moral guidelines can be expected to work for all human societies in every part of the world for all ages. Just think about how our relationship with our environment has changed. For most of the past 10,000 years, human beings have spent most of their time trying to produce enough food to survive. Thanks to science and technology, the human population of the Earth has increased exponentially in the past century. The struggle for survival has shifted away from people to the rest of Nature. Overpopulation has created a host of environmental problems, such as the extinction of many species, the destruction of fisheries in the world's oceans, and the accumulation of greenhouse gases. People must change their ideas about what is acceptable conduct and what is not, or they will destroy the planet.

2. *It is arrogant for one society to judge another.*

Anthropologists have documented many important differences among societies with respect to what they consider proper and improper moral conduct. We may have more technology than people in other societies, but we are no more intelligent than they are. It is arrogant for a person living in twenty-first-century Italy to judge the actions of another person who lived in the Inca Empire in the fifteenth century.

### 2.3.2 The Case against Cultural Relativism

1. *Just because two societies do have different views about right and wrong doesn't imply that they ought to have different views.*

Perhaps one society has good guidelines and another has bad guidelines. Perhaps neither society has good guidelines.

Suppose two societies are suffering from a severe drought. The first society constructs an aqueduct to carry water to the affected cities. The second society makes human sacrifices to appease the rain god. Are both "solutions" equally acceptable? No, they are not. Yet, if we accept cultural relativism, we cannot speak out against this wrongdoing, because no person in one society can make any statements about the morality of another society.

2. *Cultural relativism does not explain how an individual determines the moral guidelines of a particular society.*

Suppose I am new to a society and I understand I am supposed to abide by its moral guidelines. How do I determine what those guidelines are?

One approach would be to poll other people, but this begs the question. Here's why. Suppose I ask other people whether the society considers a particular action to be morally acceptable. I'm not interested in knowing whether they feel personally that the action is right or wrong. I want them to tell me whether the society as a whole thinks the action is moral. That puts the people I poll in the same position I'm in—trying to determine the moral guidelines of a society. How are they to know whether the action is right or wrong?

Perhaps the guidelines are summarized in the society's laws, but laws take time to enact. Hence the legal code reflects at best the moral guidelines of the same society at some point in the past, but that's not the same society I am living in today, because the morals of any society change over time. That leads us to our next objection.

3. *Cultural relativism does not explain how to determine right from wrong when there are no cultural norms.*

Sometimes different groups within a society disagree about whether a particular action is right or wrong. This situation often occurs when a new technology emerges.

For example, the Internet has made possible massive exchanges of digitized information. Millions of Americans seem to think sharing copyrighted music is okay, but other groups insist this activity is nothing more than stealing. Who is correct?

4. *Cultural relativism does not do a good job of characterizing actions when moral guidelines evolve.*

   Until the 1960s many southern American states had segregated universities. Today these universities are integrated. This cultural shift was accelerated by the actions of a few brave people of color who challenged the status quo and enrolled in universities that had been the exclusive preserve of white students. At the time these students were doing what they "ought not" to have done; they were doing something wrong according to the dominant culture of those states at that time. By today's standards they did nothing wrong, and many people view them as heroic figures. Doesn't it make more sense to believe that their actions were the right thing to do all along?

5. *Cultural relativism provides no framework for reconciliation between cultures in conflict.*

   Think about the culture of the Palestinians who have been crowded into refugee camps in the Gaza Strip for more than 60 years. Some of these people are completely committed to an armed struggle against Israel. Meanwhile, some people in Israel believe the Jewish state ought to be larger and are completely committed to the expansion of settlements into the Gaza Strip. The values of each society lead to actions that harm the other, yet cultural relativism says each society's moral guidelines are right. Cultural relativism provides no way out—no way for the two sides to find common ground.

6. *The existence of many acceptable cultural practices does not imply that any cultural practice would be acceptable.*

   Judging many options to be acceptable and then reaching the conclusion that any option is acceptable is called the **many/any fallacy**. To illustrate this fallacy, consider documentation styles for computer programs. There are many good ways to add comments to a program; that does not mean that any commenting style is good.

   It is false that all possible cultural practices have equal legitimacy. Certain practices must be forbidden and others must be mandated if a society is to survive [1]. This observation leads us directly to our next point.

7. *Societies do, in fact, share certain core values.*

   While a superficial observation of the cultural practices of different societies may lead you to believe they are quite different, a closer examination often reveals similar values underlying these practices. James Rachels argues that all societies, in order to maintain their existence, must have a set of core values [5]. For example, newborn babies are helpless. A society must care for its infants if it wishes to continue. Hence a core value of every society is that babies must be cared for. Communities rely upon people being able to believe each other. Hence telling the truth is another core value. Finally, in order to live together, people must not constantly be on guard against attack from their community members. For this reason a prohibition against murder is a core value of any society.

The existence of common values among all societies is a powerful response to the contention that different social contexts demand different moral guidelines, which is at the heart of the argument in favor of cultural relativism. Because societies do share certain core values, there is reason to believe we could use these values as a starting point in the creation of a universal ethical theory that would not have the deficiencies of cultural relativism.

8. *Cultural relativism is only indirectly based on reason.*

As Sumner observed, many moral guidelines are a result of tradition. Traditions develop because they meet a need, but once a tradition has been established, people behave in a certain way because it's what they're supposed to do, not because they understand the rationality deeply embedded within the tradition.

Cultural relativism has significant weaknesses as a tool for ethical persuasion. According to cultural relativism, the ethical evaluation of a moral problem made by a person in one society may be meaningless when applied to the same moral problem in another society. Cultural relativism suggests there are no universal moral guidelines. It gives tradition more weight in ethical evaluations than facts and reason. For these reasons, cultural relativism is not a powerful tool for constructing ethical evaluations persuasive to a diverse audience, and we consider it no further.

## 2.4 Divine Command Theory

The three great religious traditions that arose in the Middle East—Judaism, Christianity, and Islam—teach that a single God is the creator of the universe and that human beings are part of God's creation. Each of these religions has sacred writings containing God's revelation.

Jews, Christians, and Muslims all believe that God inspired the Torah. Here is a selection of verses from Chapter 19 of the third book of the Torah, called Leviticus:

> You shall each revere his mother and his father, and keep My sabbaths. When you reap the harvest of your land, you shall not reap all the way to the edges of your field, or gather the gleanings of your harvest. You shall not pick your vineyard bare, or gather the fallen fruit of your vineyard; you shall leave them for the poor and the stranger. You shall not steal; you shall not deal deceitfully or falsely with one another. You shall not swear falsely by My name. You shall not defraud your neighbor. You shall not commit robbery. The wages of a laborer shall not remain with you until morning. You shall not insult the deaf, or place a stumbling block before the blind. You shall not take vengeance or bear a grudge against your kinsfolk. Love your neighbor as yourself. [6]

The **divine command theory** is based on the idea that good actions are those aligned with the will of God and bad actions are those contrary to the will of God. Since the holy books contain God's directions, we can use the holy books as moral decision-making guides. God says we should revere our mothers and fathers, so revering our parents is good. God says do not lie or steal, so lying and stealing are bad (Figure 2.4).

**FIGURE 2.4** The divine command theory of ethics is based on two premises: good actions are those actions aligned with the will of God, and God's will has been revealed to us.

It is important to note that the divine command theory is subscribed to by some, but not all, Jews, Christians, and Muslims. Fundamentalists are more likely to consider holy books authentic and authoritative. Most sects within these religious traditions augment holy books with other sources when developing their moral codes.

## 2.4.1 The Case for the Divine Command Theory

1. *We owe obedience to our Creator.*

   God is the creator of the universe. God created each one of us. We are dependent upon God for our lives. For this reason, we are obligated to follow God's rules.

2. *God is all-good and all-knowing.*

   God loves us and wants the best for us. God is omniscient; we are not. Because God knows better than we do what we must do to be happy, we should align ourselves with the will of God.

3. *God is the ultimate authority.*

   Since most people are religious, they are more likely to submit to God's law than to a law made by people. Our goal is to create a society where everyone obeys the moral laws. Therefore, our moral laws should be based on God's directions to us.

## 2.4.2 The Case against the Divine Command Theory

1. *There are many holy books, and some of their teachings disagree with each other.*

   There is no single holy book that is recognized by people of all faiths, and it is unrealistic to assume everyone in a society will adopt the same religion. Even among Christians there are different versions of the Bible. The Catholic Bible has six books not found in the Protestant Bible. Some Protestant denominations rely upon the King James version, but others use more modern translations. Every translation has significant differences. Even when people read the same translation, they often interpret the same verse in different ways.

2. *It is unrealistic to assume a multicultural society will adopt a religion-based morality.*

   An obvious example is the United States. In the past two centuries, immigrants representing virtually every race, creed, and culture have made America their home. Some Americans are atheists. When a society is made up of people with different religious beliefs, the society's moral guidelines should emerge from a secular authority, not a religious authority.

3. *Some moral problems are not addressed directly in scripture.*

   For example, there are no verses in the Bible mentioning the Internet. When we discuss moral problems arising from information technology, a proponent of the divine command theory must resort to analogy. At this point the conclusion is based not simply on what appears in the sacred text but also on the insight of the person who invented the analogy. The holy book alone is not sufficient to solve the moral problem.

4. *It is fallacious to equate "the good" with "God."*

   Religious people are likely to agree with the statement "God is good." That does not mean, however, that God and "the good" are exactly the same thing. Trying to equate two related but distinct things is called the **equivalence fallacy**. Instead, the statement "God is good" means there is an objective standard of goodness that God meets perfectly.

   Here's another way to put the question. Is an action good because God commands it, or does God command it because it's good? This is an ancient question: Plato raised it about 2,400 years ago in the Socratic dialogue *Euthyphro*. In this dialogue, Socrates concludes, "The gods love piety because it is pious, and it is not pious because they love it" [7]. In other words, "the good" is something that exists outside of God and was not created by God.

   We can reason our way to the same conclusion. If good means "commanded by God," then good is arbitrary. Why should we praise God for being good if good is whatever God wills? According to this view of the good, it doesn't matter whether God commanded, "Thou shalt not commit adultery," or "Thou shalt commit adultery." Either way, the command would have been good by definition. If you object that there is no way God would command us to commit adultery because marital fidelity is good and adultery is bad, then you are proving our point: there is an objective standard of right and wrong separate from God. That means we can talk about the good without talking about God; we can have a nontheological discussion of the good.

5. *The divine command theory is based on obedience, not reason.*

If good means "willed by God," and if religious texts contain everything we need to know about what God wills, then there is no room left for collecting and analyzing facts. Hence the divine command theory is not based on reaching sound conclusions from premises through logical reasoning. There is no need for a person to question a commandment. The instruction is right because it's commanded by God, period.

Consider the story of Abraham in the book of Genesis. God commands Abraham to take his only son, Isaac, up on a mountain, kill him, and make of him a burnt offering. Abraham obeys God's command and is ready to kill Isaac with his knife when an angel calls down and tells him not to harm the boy. Because he does not withhold his only son from God, God blesses Abraham [8]. However, earlier in Genesis God condemns Cain for killing Abel [9]. How, then, can Abraham's sacrifice of Isaac be considered good? To devout readers, the logic of God's command is irrelevant to this story. Abraham is a good person, a heroic model of faith, because he demonstrated his obedience to the will of God.

In the divine command theory, moral guidelines are not the result of a logical progression from a set of underlying principles, and this is a significant problem. While you may choose to live your life so that your actions are aligned with God's will, the divine command theory often fails to produce arguments that can persuade skeptical listeners whose religious beliefs are different. For the purposes of this book, it is not a workable theory.

## 2.5 Ethical Egoism

In sharp contrast to the divine command theory, which promotes a concern for others with scriptural injunctions such as "Love your neighbor as yourself," ethical egoism is the philosophy that each person should focus exclusively on his or her self-interest. In other words, according to ethical egoism, the morally right action for a person to take in a particular situation is the action that will provide that person with the maximum long-term benefit.

This idea may sound familiar to you if you have read *The Fountainhead* or *Atlas Shrugged*. The author of these novels, Ayn Rand, espoused a philosophy akin to ethical egoism (although you should not view this section's description of ethical egoism as a summary of her thinking). Rand's moral philosophy "holds man's life as the *standard* of value—and *his own life* as the ethical *purpose* of every individual man" [10, p. 27]. With respect to human relationships, she wrote, "The principle of *trade* is the only rational ethical principle for all human relationships, personal and social, private and public, spiritual and material" [10, p. 34].

Ethical egoism does not prohibit acting to help someone else, but assisting another is the right thing to do if and only if it is in the helper's own long-term best interest.

For example, suppose I depend upon a friend to give me a ride to work every day. If my friend's car breaks down and she doesn't have $100 to fix it, I ought to loan her the money. Although I'm out $100 until she pays me back, I'm better off giving her the loan because I'm still able to travel to work and make money. If I don't lend her the money, I'll lose my income. Lending $100 to my friend is the right thing to do because it provides me the maximum overall benefit [11].

### 2.5.1 The Case for Ethical Egoism

1. *Ethical egoism is a practical moral philosophy.*

   We are naturally inclined to do what's best for ourselves because each of us has only one life to live, and we want to make the best of it. Unlike other moral codes that ask us to sacrifice our own well-being for the good of other people, ethical egoism recognizes that we should focus on our own well-being.

2. *It's better to let other people take care of themselves.*

   We can't know for sure what is good for someone else. All too often, a "good deed" backfires and actually does more harm than good. Even when people appreciate something done on their behalf, it's not healthy. Dependence upon the charity of others leads to a loss of self-esteem. In contrast, people who accomplish things through their own efforts have higher self-esteem and are able to interact with other successful people as equals.

3. *The community can benefit when individuals put their well-being first.*

   When individuals act in their own self-interest, they often benefit not only themselves but others as well. For example, successful entrepreneurs may make a lot of money for themselves, but they also create jobs that strengthen the economy.

4. *Other moral principles are rooted in the principle of self-interest.*

   Ethical egoism is a rational philosophy. Any rational person will figure out that it doesn't make sense to go around breaking promises, because eventually people will realize that the promise breaker cannot be trusted, and they will refuse to cooperate with that person. Therefore, it's not in a person's long-term self-interest to break promises. Likewise, it's a bad idea to lie to other people or cheat other people because the long-term consequences of lying and cheating are detrimental to the person doing these things. For this reason, it can be seen that other well-known moral principles are actually rooted in the principle of self-interest.

### 2.5.2 The Case against Ethical Egoism

1. *An easy moral philosophy may not be the best moral philosophy.*

   The fact that it may be easier to live by a particular moral philosophy is no proof that it is the best moral philosophy to live by. Besides, the statement that ethical egoism aligns with our natural inclination to do what's best for ourselves ignores the fact that our natural inclinations often do not align with our own best interests. For example, some students find it difficult to pass up short-term pleasures (such as partying) in order achieve goals that will most likely result in long-term benefits (such as passing the classes needed to earn a college degree).

2. *We do, in fact, know a lot about what is good for someone else.*

   As we noted at the beginning of the chapter, practically everyone shares the "core values" of life, happiness, and the ability to accomplish goals. It's not that hard to figure out what would help another. The question is, how are we going to respond to that person's need? Charity usually doesn't lead to dependence; rather, it gives someone the opportunity to become more independent. Consider, for example, how a scholarship can provide a promising high school student from a poor family with a path to a university degree, a well-paying job, and economic self-sufficiency.

3. *A self-interested focus can lead to blatantly immoral behavior.*

   Here is a true story related by James Rachels [12]. An affluent doctor in a small Southern town in the 1970s was visited by a poor, uneducated African American woman, who had a variety of minor complaints. The doctor quickly determined that the woman was suffering from malnutrition. He knew that she worked a variety of menial jobs, but earned very little money to support herself or her children. After spending no more than five minutes with her, and doing nothing for her, the doctor told her the charge would be $25. The woman had only $12 to her name, so the doctor took the $12 as payment, leaving the woman with no money to buy food. There were no negative consequences to the doctor as a result of his action. According to the theory of ethical egoism, the doctor did the right thing: he was only supposed to take his own interest into account, and receiving $12 from the woman was to his advantage. This answer, however, is incorrect; what the doctor did was morally reprehensible.

4. *Other moral principles are superior to the principle of self-interest.*

   Suppose you have the opportunity to save a drowning person at the cost of getting one of your shirtsleeves wet [11]. According to the theory of ethical egoism, saving a life is the right thing to do if and only if that action will provide you with the maximum benefit. Possible benefits from saving a drowning person include earning that person's undying gratitude and gaining favorable publicity. But isn't this a backward and degrading way of evaluating the action? Doesn't it make a lot more sense to consider the action in light of the value of a human life? If you have the opportunity to save a human life with no signficant negative consequences to yourself, you should do it, even if your action is not rewarded. This example demonstrates that the principle of preserving life is superior to the principle of self-interest.

5. *People who take the good of others into account live happier lives.*

   In the Framingham Heart Study, which followed 5,000 individuals over a 20-year period, scientists discovered that happiness spreads through close relationships with family members, friends, and neighbors [13]. In order to create and maintain close relationships with other people, it is necessary to consider what is good for them.

Ethical egoism does not respect the ethical point of view: it does not recognize that in order to reap the benefits of living in a community, individuals must consider the good of other community members. For this reason we reject ethical egoism as a workable ethical theory.

# 2.6 Kantianism

Kantianism is the name given to the ethical theory of the German philosopher Immanuel Kant (1724–1804). Kant spent his entire life in or near Königsberg in East Prussia, where he was a professor at the university. Kant believed that people's actions ought to be guided by moral laws, and that these moral laws were universal. He held that in order to apply to all rational beings, any supreme principle of morality must itself be based on reason. While many of the moral laws Kant describes can also be found in the Bible, Kant's methodology allows these laws to be derived through a reasoning process. A Kantian is able to go beyond simply stating that an action is right or wrong by citing chapter and verse; a Kantian can explain *why* it is right or wrong.

## 2.6.1 Good Will and the Categorical Imperative

Kant begins his inquiry by asking, "What is always good without qualification?" Many things, such as intelligence and courage, can be good, but they can also be used in a way that is harmful. For example, a group of gangsters may use intelligence and courage to rob a bank. Kant's conclusion is that the only thing in the world that can be called good without qualification is a good will. People with good will often accomplish good deeds, but producing beneficial outcomes is not what makes a good will good. A good will is good in and of itself. Even if a person's best efforts at doing good should fall short and cause harm, the good will behind the efforts is still good. Since a good will is the only thing that is universally good, the proper function of reason is to cultivate a will that is good in itself.

Most of us have probably had many experiences when we've been torn between what we want to do and what we ought to do. According to Kant, what we want to do is of no importance. Our focus should be on what we ought to do. Our sense of "ought to" is called **dutifulness** [14]. A dutiful person feels compelled to act in a certain way out of respect for some moral rule. Our will, then, should be grounded in a conception of moral rules. The moral value of an action depends upon the underlying moral rule. It is critical, therefore, that we be able to determine if our actions are grounded in an appropriate moral rule.

For Kant, an **imperative** is a way in which reason commands the will. There are two kinds of imperatives: hypothetical and categorical. A **hypothetical imperative** is a conditional rule of the form, "If you want X then do Y" [15]. It explains the means you should take to achieve a particular end. An example of a hypothetical imperative would be, "If you want to lose weight then eat less." A **categorical imperative** is an unconditional rule: a rule that always applies, regardless of the circumstances. For Kant, only a categorical imperative can be a moral imperative.

What is the Categorical Imperative, the rule that all humans should obey unconditionally, regardless of their particular circumstances and goals? Kant proposes several formulations of the Categorical Imperative, which he believes communicate the same concept in different ways. We will cover the first two formulations. Here is the first.

∾

## Categorical Imperative (First Formulation)

Act only from moral rules that you can at the same time will to be
universal moral laws.

∾

In other words, you should act only on moral rules that you can imagine everyone else following without deriving a logical contradiction [15].

To illustrate the Categorical Imperative, Kant poses the problem of an individual in a difficult situation who must decide if he will make a promise with the intention of later breaking it. The translation of this moral rule could be as follows: "A person may make a false promise when that is the only way to escape a difficult situation."

To evaluate this moral rule, we universalize it. What would happen if everybody in extreme circumstances made false promises? If that were the case, nobody would believe promises, and it would be impossible for our individual in distress to make a promise that anyone believed. The moral rule self-destructs when we try to make it a universal law. Therefore, it is wrong for a person in distress to make a promise with the intention of breaking it.

It is important to see that Kant is *not* arguing that the harmful consequences of everybody breaking promises is why we cannot imagine turning our hypothetical moral rule into a universal law. Rather, Kant is saying that simply willing that our moral rule become a universal law produces a logical contradiction.

Let's see how. Suppose I am the person who can escape from a difficult situation by making a promise I intend to break later on. On the one hand, it is my will that I be able to make a promise that is believed. After all, that's what promises are for. If my promise isn't believed, I won't be able to get out of the difficult situation I am in. But when I universalize the moral rule, I am willing that everybody be able to break promises. If that were a reality, then promises would not be believable, which means there would be no such thing as a promise [16]. If there were no such thing as a promise, I would not be able to make a promise to get myself out of a difficult situation. Trying to universalize our proposed moral rule leads to a contradiction.

Here's another way to see why the proposed moral rule cannot be made a universal moral law. In order for my false promise to be believed, I want everyone *except* myself to be truthful all the time. In other words, I want to privilege my own needs and desires over those of everyone else [15]. Because there is a contradiction between what I wish to do and how I expect others in a similar situation to act, I know that what I am considering doing is wrong.

If you are wondering whether or not it is morally acceptable under Kantianism to do something to someone else, mentally reverse roles. What would you think if that person did the same thing to you? If you cannot wish to be treated that way by another, you have evidence that the action you are contemplating privileges your own needs and desires and violates the Categorical Imperative.

FIGURE 2.5 The second formulation of the Categorical Imperative states that it is wrong for one person to use himself or another person solely as a means to an end.

Kant also presents a second formulation of the Categorical Imperative, which many people find easier to work with when doing ethical analyses.

~

## CATEGORICAL IMPERATIVE (SECOND FORMULATION)

Act so that you always treat both yourself and other people as ends in themselves, and never only as a means to an end.

~

To use popular terminology, the second formulation of the Categorical Imperative says it is wrong for one person to "use" another (Figure 2.5). Instead, every interaction with other people must give them the dignity and respect they deserve as autonomous, rational beings.

Here is an example that illustrates how we can apply the second formulation. Suppose I manage a semiconductor fabrication plant for a large corporation. The plant manufactures integrated circuits on 8-inch wafers. I know that in one year the corporation is going to shut down the plant and move all of its production to other sites capable of producing 12-inch wafers. In the meantime, I need new employees to work in the clean room. Many of the best applicants are from out of state. I am afraid that if they knew the plant was going to shut down next year, they would not want to go through the hassle and expense of moving to this area. If that happens, I'll have to hire less qualified local workers. Should I disclose this information to the job applicants?

According to the second formulation of the Categorical Imperative, I have an obligation to inform the applicants, since I know this information is likely to influence their decision. If I deny them this information, I am treating them as a means to an end (a way to get wafers produced), not as ends in themselves (rational beings).

## 2.6.2  Evaluating a Scenario Using Kantianism

### ∼ SCENARIO

Carla is a single mother who is working hard to complete her college education while taking care of her daughter. Carla has a full-time job and is taking two evening courses per semester. If she can pass both courses this semester, she will graduate. She knows her child will benefit if she can spend more time at home.

One of her required classes is modern European history. In addition to the midterm and final examinations, the professor assigns four lengthy reports, which is far more than the usual amount of work required for a single class. Students must submit all four reports in order to pass the class.

Carla earns an A on each of her first three reports. At the end of the term, she is required to put in a lot of overtime where she works. She simply does not have time to research and write the final report. Carla uses the Web to identify a company that sells term papers. She purchases a report from the company and submits it as her own work.

Was Carla's action morally justifiable?

### Analysis

Many times it is easier to use the second formulation of the Categorical Imperative to analyze a moral problem from a Kantian point of view, so that's where we begin. By submitting another person's work as her own, Carla treated her professor as a means to an end. She deceived her professor with the goal of getting credit for someone else's work. It was wrong for Carla to treat the professor as a grade-generating machine rather than a rational agent with whom she could have communicated her unusual circumstances.

We can also look at this problem using the first formulation of the Categorical Imperative. Carla wants to be able to get credit for turning in a report she has purchased. A proposed moral rule might be, "I may claim academic credit for a report written by someone else." However, if everyone followed this rule, reports would cease to be credible indicators of the students' knowledge, and professors would not give academic credit for reports. Her proposed moral rule is self-defeating. Therefore, it is wrong for Carla to purchase a report and turn it in as her own work.

### Commentary

Note that the Kantian analysis of the moral problem focuses on the will behind the action. It asks the question, "What was Carla trying to do when she submitted under her own name a term paper written by someone else?" The analysis ignores extenuating circumstances that non-Kantians may cite to justify her action.  ∼

## 2.6.3  The Case for Kantianism

1. *It treats all persons as moral equals.*

   A popular belief is that "all people are created equal." Because it holds that people in similar situations should be treated in similar ways, Kantianism provides an ethical framework to combat discrimination.

2. *It gives all persons moral worth by considering them as rational, autonomous beings.*

Every human being has an inherent dignity and deserves respect [15]. That is why, according to Kant, other persons should always be treated as ends in themselves, not merely as the means to an end. This perspective aligns with the commonly held view that it is wrong for one person to manipulate another.

3. *Everyone is held to the same standard.*

According to Kantianism, it is wrong for you to grant yourself an exception to a principle you expect everyone else to abide by. For example, it would be wrong to break a legal contract and also desire that everyone else in a similar circumstance would honor the contract. This basic principle of justice is a natural corollary of Kant's view that all persons are moral equals, and it is reflected in the proverb, "What's good for the goose is good for the gander."

4. *Kantianism produces universal moral guidelines.*

Kantianism aligns with the intuition of many people that the same morality ought to apply to all people for all of history. These guidelines allow us to make clear moral judgments. For example, one such judgment might be the following: "Sacrificing living human beings to appease the gods is wrong." It is wrong in Europe in the twenty-first century, and it was wrong in South America in the fifteenth century.

### 2.6.4 The Case against Kantianism

1. *Sometimes no single rule fully characterizes an action.*

Kant holds that every action is motivated from a rule. The appropriate rule depends upon how we characterize the action. Once we know the rule, we can test its value using the Categorical Imperative. What happens when no single rule fully explains the situation? Suppose I'm considering stealing food from a grocery store to feed my starving children [11]. How should I characterize this action? Am I stealing? Am I caring for my children? Am I trying to save the lives of innocent people? Until I characterize my action, I cannot determine the rule and test it against the Categorical Imperative. Yet no single one of these ways of characterizing the action seems to capture the ethical problem in its fullness.

2. *Sometimes there is no way to resolve a conflict between rules.*

One way to address the previous problem is to allow multiple rules to be relevant to a particular action. In the previous example, we might say that the relevant rules are (1) you should not steal and (2) you should try to save the lives of innocent persons. Now the question becomes, if we have a conflict between two rules, which one should we follow?

Kant distinguished between **perfect duties**, duties we are obliged to fulfill in every instance, and **imperfect duties**, duties we are obliged to fulfill in general but not in every instance. For example, you have a perfect duty to tell the truth. That means you must always tell the truth without exception. On the other hand, you have an imperfect duty to develop your talents. If you happen to have a talent for music, you ought to find a way to develop it, but you do not have to take up every instrument in the orchestra.

If we have a conflict between a perfect duty and an imperfect duty, the perfect duty must prevail. Returning to our example, we have a perfect duty not to steal. In contrast, we have only an imperfect duty to help others. Therefore, according to Kant, it is wrong to steal bread to feed my starving children.

In this case we were fortunate because the conflict was between a perfect duty and an imperfect duty. (Whether the children are fortunate is debatable.) In those cases where there is a conflict between perfect duties, Kantianism does not provide us a way to choose between them.

3. *Kantianism allows no exceptions to perfect duties.*

Common sense tells us that sometimes we ought to "bend" the rules a bit if we want to get along with other people. For example, suppose your mother asks you if you like her new haircut, and you think it is the ugliest haircut you have ever seen. What should you say? Common sense dictates that there is no point in criticizing your mother's hair. She certainly isn't going to get her hair uncut, no matter what you say. If you compliment her, she will be happy, and if you criticize her looks, she will be angry and hurt. She expects you to say something complimentary, even if you don't mean it. There just seems to be no downside to lying. Yet a Kantian would argue that lying is always wrong because we have a perfect duty to tell the truth. Any ethical theory so unbending is not going to be useful for solving "real-world" problems.

While these objections point out weaknesses with Kantianism, the theory does support moral decision making based on logical reasoning from facts and commonly held values. It is culture-neutral and treats all humans as equals. Hence it meets our criteria for a workable ethical theory, and we will use it as a way of evaluating moral problems in the rest of the book..

# 2.7 Act Utilitarianism

The English philosophers Jeremy Bentham (1748–1832) and John Stuart Mill (1806–1873) proposed a theory that is in sharp contrast to Kantianism. According to Bentham and Mill, an action is good if its benefits exceed its harms, and an action is bad if its harms exceed its benefits. Their ethical theory, called **utilitarianism,** is based upon the principle of utility, also called the Greatest Happiness Principle.

## 2.7.1 Principle of Utility

**Utility** is the tendency of an object to produce happiness or prevent unhappiness for an individual or a community. Depending on the circumstances, you may think of "happiness" as advantage, benefit, good, or pleasure, and "unhappiness" as disadvantage, cost, evil, or pain.

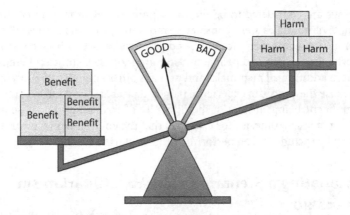

**FIGURE 2.6** Utilitarianism is based on the principle of utility, which states that an action is good (or bad) to the extent that it increases (or decreases) the total happiness of the affected parties.

~

### PRINCIPLE OF UTILITY (GREATEST HAPPINESS PRINCIPLE)

An action is right (or wrong) to the extent that it increases (or decreases) the total happiness of the affected parties.

~

We can use the principle of utility as a yardstick to judge all actions in the moral realm. Suppose in a particular situation we have a set of possible actions. For each possible action, we must determine, for each affected person, the increase or decrease in that person's happiness and then add up all of these values to reach a grand total: the overall increase or decrease in happiness caused by that particular action (Figure 2.6). We repeat this procedure for every action in the set of possible actions. The moral action is the one that produces the maximum increase in happiness. (If every possible action results in a decrease in happiness, then the moral action is the one that minimizes the decrease in happiness.)

Note that the morality of an action has nothing to do with the attitude behind the action. Bentham writes, "There is no such thing as any sort of motive that is in itself a bad one. If [motives] are good or bad, it is only on account of their effects" [17]. We call utilitarianism a **consequentialist** theory, because the focus is on the consequences of an action.

**Act utilitarianism** is the ethical theory that an action is good if its net effect (over all affected beings) is to produce more happiness than unhappiness. Suppose we measure pleasure as a positive number and pain as a negative number. To make a moral evaluation of an action, we simply add up, over all affected beings, the change in their happiness. If the sum is positive, the action is good. If the sum is negative, the action is bad.

Did you notice that I used the word "beings" rather than "persons" in the previous paragraph? An important decision an act utilitarian must make is determining which beings are considered to be morally significant. Bentham noted that at one time only adult white males were considered morally significant beings. Bentham felt that any being that can experience pain and pleasure ought to be seen as morally significant. Certainly, women and people of color are morally significant beings by this definition, but in addition all mammals (and perhaps other animals) are morally significant beings, because they, too, can experience pain and pleasure. Of course, as the number of morally significant beings increases, the difficulty of evaluating the consequences of an action also increases. It means, for example, that the environmental impacts of decisions must often be included when performing the utilitarian calculus.

## 2.7.2  Evaluating a Scenario Using Act Utilitarianism

### ∼ SCENARIO

A state is considering replacing a curvy stretch of highway that passes along the outskirts of a large city. Would building the highway be a good action?

### Analysis

To perform the analysis of this problem, we must determine who is affected and the effects of the highway construction on them. Our analysis is in terms of dollars and cents. For this reason we'll use the terms "benefit" and "cost" instead of "happiness" and "unhappiness."

About 150 houses lie on or very near the proposed path of the new, straighter section of highway. Using its power of eminent domain, the state can condemn these properties. It would cost the state $20 million to provide fair compensation to the homeowners. Constructing the new highway, which is three miles long, would cost the taxpayers of the state another $10 million. Suppose the environmental impact of the new highway in terms of lost habitat for morally significant animal species is valued at $1 million.

Every weekday, 15,000 cars are expected to travel on this section of highway, which is one mile shorter than the curvy highway it replaces. Assuming it costs 40 cents per mile to operate a motor vehicle, construction of the new highway will save drivers $6,000 per weekday in operating costs. The highway has an expected operating lifetime of 25 years. Over a 25-year period, the expected total savings to drivers will be $39 million.

We'll assume the highway project will have no positive or negative effects on any other people. Since the overall cost of the new highway is $31 million and the benefit of the new highway is $39 million, building the highway would be a good action.

### Commentary

Performing the benefit/cost (or happiness/unhappiness) calculations is crucial to the utilitarian approach, yet it can be controversial. In our example, we translated everything into dollars and cents. Was that reasonable? Neighborhoods are the site of many important relationships. We did not assign a value to the harm the proposed highway would do to these neighborhoods. There is a good chance that many of the homeowners would be angry about being forced out of their houses, even if they were paid a fair price for their properties. How do we put a dollar value on their emotional distress? On the other hand, we can't add apples and oranges. Translating everything into dollars and cents is one way to put everything into common units.                                                    ∼

Bentham acknowledged that a complete analysis must look beyond simple benefits and harms. Not all benefits have equal weight. To measure them, he proposed seven attributes that can be used to increase or decrease the weight of a particular pleasure or pain:

- *Intensity:* magnitude of the experience
- *Duration:* how long the experience lasts
- *Certainty:* probability it will actually happen
- *Propinquity:* how close the experience is in space and time
- *Fecundity:* its ability to produce more experiences of the same kind
- *Purity:* extent to which pleasure is not diluted by pain or vice versa
- *Extent:* number of people affected

As you can see, performing a complete calculation for a particular moral problem can be a daunting prospect!

### 2.7.3 The Case for Act Utilitarianism

1. *It focuses on happiness.*

   By relying upon the Greatest Happiness Principle as the yardstick for measuring moral behavior, utilitarianism fits the intuition of many people that the purpose of life is to be happy.

2. *It is practical.*

   The utilitarian calculus provides a straightforward way to determine the right course of action to take. Start by identifying the set of possible alternatives. Next, consider each of the alternatives in turn. For each alternative, total up the anticipated positive and negative consequences to all of the affected parties resulting from the action. Finally, identify the alternative with the maximum total. That alternative is the right action to take. This process, conducted in an open manner in which all the information is made available to all the key stakeholders, is a good way for a diverse group of people to come to a collective decision about a controversial topic.

   For example, suppose your state needs to build a new prison because the number of prisoners is growing. Everybody understands the prison must be built somewhere in the state, but nobody wants the prison in their neighborhood. A panel of trusted citizens considers a variety of siting options and, after a series of public hearings to gather evidence, weighs the pluses and minuses of each location. At the end of the process, the panel makes public the individual scores and grand totals and recommends the site with the highest grand total. While some will be unhappy at the prospect of a prison being built near their homes, an open and impartial process can speed their acceptance of the decision.

3. *It is comprehensive.*

Act utilitarianism allows the moral agent to take into account all the elements of a particular situation. Do you remember the problem of having to decide what to say about your mother's awful haircut? Utilitarianism allows you to take into account the emotional distress that telling the truth would cause to you and your mother. That harm could tilt the balance toward telling your mother what she wants to hear.

## 2.7.4 The Case against Act Utilitarianism

1. *When performing the utilitarian calculus, it is not clear where to draw the line, yet where we draw the line can change the outcome of our evaluation.*

In order to perform our calculation of total net happiness produced by an action, we must determine whom to include in our calculation and how far into the future to consider the consequences. In our highway example, we counted the people who lost their homes and the people who would travel the new highway in the next 25 years. The proposed highway may cut neighborhoods in two, making it more difficult for some children to get to school, but we did not factor in consequences for neighbors. The highway may cause people to change their commutes, increasing traffic congestion in other parts of town, but we did not count those people either. The highway may be in existence for more than 25 years, but we didn't look beyond that date. We cannot include all morally relevant beings for all time into the future. We must draw the line somewhere. Deciding where to draw the line can be a difficult problem.

2. *It is not practical to put so much energy into every moral decision.*

Correctly performing the utilitarian calculus requires a great deal of time and effort. It seems unrealistic that everyone would go to so much trouble every time they were faced with a moral problem.

A response to this criticism is that act utilitarians are free to come up with moral "rules of thumb." For example, a moral rule of thumb might be, "It is wrong to lie." In most situations it will be obvious this is the right thing to do, even without performing the complete utilitarian calculus. However, an act utilitarian always reserves the right to go against the rule of thumb if particular circumstances should warrant it. In these cases, the act utilitarian will perform a detailed analysis of the consequences to determine the best course of action.

3. *Act utilitarianism ignores our innate sense of duty.*

Utilitarianism seems to be at odds with how ordinary people make moral decisions. People often act out of a sense of duty or obligation, yet the act utilitarian theory gives no weight to these notions. Instead, all that matters are the consequences of the action.

W. D. Ross gives the following example [18]. Suppose I've made a promise to A. If I keep my word, I will perform an action that produces 1,000 units of good for him. If I break my promise, I will be able to perform an action that produces 1,001 units of good for B. According to act utilitarianism, I ought to break my promise to A and produce 1,001 units of good for B. Yet most people would say the right thing for me to do is keep my word.

Note that it does no good for an act utilitarian to come back and say that the hard feelings caused by breaking my word to A will have a negative impact on total happiness of $-N$ units, because all I have to do is change the scenario so that breaking my promise to A enables me to produce $1,001 + N$ units of good for B. We've arrived at the same result: breaking my promise results in 1 more unit of good than keeping my word. The real issue is that utilitarianism forces us to reduce all consequences to a positive or negative number. "Doing the right thing" has a value that is difficult to quantify.

4. *We cannot predict with certainty the consequences of an action.*

In doing the utilitarian calculus, we can identify possible consequences of an action, but we may misjudge the certainty, intensity, and duration of these consequences. The action may have other unforeseen consequences that we forget to include in our calculation. These errors may cause us to choose the wrong course of action.

5. *Act utilitarianism is susceptible to the problem of moral luck.*

As we noted in the previous point, sometimes actions have unforeseen consequences. Is it right for the moral worth of an action to depend solely on its consequences when these consequences are not fully under the control of the moral agent? This is called the **problem of moral luck.**

Suppose I hear that one of my aunts is in the hospital, and I send her a bouquet of flowers. After the bouquet is delivered, she suffers a violent allergic reaction to one of the exotic flowers in the floral arrangement, extending her stay in the hospital. My gift gave my aunt a bad case of hives and a much larger hospital bill. Since my action had far more negative consequences than positive consequences, an act utilitarian would say my action was bad. That doesn't seem fair.

Two additional arguments have been raised against utilitarianism in general. We'll save these arguments for the end of the section on rule utilitarianism.

While it is not perfect, act utilitarianism is an objective, rational ethical theory that allows a person to explain why a particular action is right or wrong. It joins Kantianism on our list of workable ethical theories we can use to evaluate moral problems.

## 2.8 Rule Utilitarianism

The weaknesses of act utilitarianism have led some philosophers to develop another ethical theory based on the principle of utility. This theory is called rule utilitarianism. Some philosophers have concluded that John Stuart Mill was actually a rule utilitarian, but others disagree.

### 2.8.1  Basis of Rule Utilitarianism

**Rule utilitarianism** is the ethical theory that holds that we ought to adopt those moral rules that, if followed by everyone, lead to the greatest increase in total happiness over all affected parties. Hence a rule utilitarian applies the principle of utility to moral rules, while an act utilitarian applies the principle of utility to individual moral actions.

Both rule utilitarianism and Kantianism are focused on rules, and the rules these two ethical theories derive may have significant overlap. However, the two ethical theories derive moral rules in completely different ways. A rule utilitarian chooses to follow a moral rule because its universal adoption would result in the greatest net increase in happiness. A Kantian follows a moral rule because it is in accord with the Categorical Imperative: all human beings are to be treated as ends in themselves, not merely as means to an end. In other words, the rule utilitarian is looking at the consequences of the action, while the Kantian is looking at the will motivating the action.

### 2.8.2  Evaluating a Scenario Using Rule Utilitarianism

#### ∽ SCENARIO

A worm is a self-contained program that spreads through a computer network by taking advantage of security holes in the computers connected to the network. In August 2003, the Blaster worm infected many computers running the Windows 2000, Windows NT, and Windows XP operating systems. The Blaster worm caused computers it infected to reboot every few minutes.

Soon another worm was exploiting the same security hole in Windows to spread through the Internet. However, the purpose of the new worm, named Nachi, was benevolent. Since Nachi took advantage of the same security hole as Blaster, it could not infect computers that were immune to the Blaster worm. Once Nachi gained access to a computer with the security hole, it located and destroyed copies of the Blaster worm. It also automatically downloaded from Microsoft a patch to the operating system software that would fix the security problem. Finally, it used the computer as a launching pad to seek out other Windows PCs with the security hole.

Was the action of the person who released the Nachi worm morally right or wrong?

#### Analysis

To analyze this moral problem from a rule utilitarian point of view, we must think of an appropriate moral rule and determine if its universal adoption would increase the happiness of the affected parties. In this case, an appropriate moral rule might be the following: "If I can write and release a helpful worm that improves the security of the computers it infects, I should do so."

What would be the benefits if everyone followed the proposed moral rule? Many people do not keep their computers up to date with the latest patches to the operating system. They would benefit from a worm that automatically removed their network vulnerabilities.

What harm would be caused by the universal adoption of the rule? If everyone followed this rule, the appearance of every new harmful worm would be followed by the release of many other worms designed to eradicate the harmful worm. Worms make networks less usable by creating a lot of extra network traffic. For example, the Nachi worm disabled networks of Diebold ATM machines at two financial institutions [19]. The universal adoption of the moral rule would reduce the usefulness of the Internet while the various "helpful" worms were circulating.

Another negative consequence would be potential harm done to computers by the supposedly helpful worms. Even worms designed to be benevolent may contain bugs. If many people are releasing worms, there is a good chance some of the worms may accidentally harm data or programs on the computers they infect.

A third harmful consequence would be the extra work placed on system administrators. When system administrators detect a new worm, it is not immediately obvious whether the worm is harmful or beneficial. Hence the prudent response of system administrators is to combat every new worm that attacks their computers. If the proposed moral rule were adopted, more worms would be released, forcing system administrators to spend more of their time fighting worms [20].

In conclusion, the harms caused by the universal adoption of this moral rule appear to outweigh the benefits. Therefore, the action of the person who released the Nachi worm is morally wrong.          ∾

### 2.8.3  The Case for Rule Utilitarianism

1. *Not every moral decision requires performing the utilitarian calculus.*

   A person who relies on rules of behavior does not have to spend a lot of time and effort analyzing every particular moral action in order to determine if it is right or wrong.

2. *Exceptional situations do not overthrow moral rules.*

   Remember the problem of choosing between keeping a promise to A and producing 1,000 units of good for A, or breaking the promise to A and producing 1,001 units of good for B? A rule utilitarian would not be trapped on the horns of this dilemma. A rule utilitarian would reason that the long-term consequences of everyone keeping their promises produce more good than giving everyone the liberty to break their promises, so in this situation a rule utilitarian would conclude the right thing to do is to keep the promise to A.

3. *Rule utilitarianism solves the problem of moral luck.*

   Since it is interested in the typical result of an action, the highly unusual result does not affect the goodness of an action. A rule utilitarian would conclude that sending flowers to people in the hospital is a good action.

4. *Rule utilitarianism reduces the problem of bias.*

   A weakness of act utilitarianism is that it creates the temptation to perform a biased analysis. By asking, "Is it okay for me to do this?" an act utilitarian may conclude the action is acceptable by consciously or unconsciously inflating the personal benefits and/or deflating the anticipated harms to others. In contrast, a rule utilitarian must ask the question, "Is it okay for everyone in a similar circumstance to do this?" The person who answers the latter question is more likely to place appropriate weights on the benefits and harms of the action.

5. *It appeals to a wide cross section of society.*

Bernard Gert points out that utilitarianism is "paradoxically, the kind of moral theory usually held by people who claim that they have no moral theory. Their view is often expressed in phrases like the following: 'It is all right to do anything as long as no one gets hurt,' 'It is the actual consequences that count, not some silly rules,' or 'What is important is that things turn out for the best, not how one goes about making that happen.' On the moral system, it is not the consequences of the particular violation that are decisive in determining its justifiability, but rather the consequences of such a violation being publicly allowed" [21]. In other words, an action is justifiable if allowing that action would, as a rule, bring about greater net happiness than forbidding that action.

## 2.8.4  The Case against Utilitarianism in General

As we have just seen, rule utilitarianism seems to solve several problems associated with act utilitarianism. However, two criticisms have been leveled at utilitarian theories in general. These problems are shared by both act utilitarianism and rule utilitarianism.

1. *Utilitarianism forces us to use a single scale or measure to evaluate completely different kinds of consequences.*

In order to perform the utilitarian calculus, all consequences must be put into the same units. Otherwise we cannot add them up. For example, if we are going to determine the total amount of happiness resulting from the construction of a new highway, many of the costs and benefits (such as construction costs and the gas expenses of car drivers) are easily expressed in dollars. Other costs and benefits are intangible, but we must express them in terms of dollars in order to find the total amount of happiness created or destroyed as a result of the project. Suppose a sociologist informs the state that if it condemns 150 homes, it is likely to cause five divorces among the families being displaced. How do we assign a dollar value to that unfortunate consequence? In certain circumstances utilitarians must quantify the value of a human life. How can the value of a human life be reduced to an amount of money?

2. *Utilitarianism ignores the problem of an unjust distribution of good consequences.*

The second, and far more significant, criticism of utilitarianism is that the utilitarian calculus is solely interested in the total amount of happiness produced. Suppose one course of action results in every member of a society receiving 100 units of good, while another course of action results in half the members of society receiving 201 units of good each, with the other half receiving nothing. According to the calculus of utility, the second course of action is superior because the total amount of good is higher. That doesn't seem right to many people.

A possible response to this criticism is that our goal should be to promote the greatest good to the greatest number. In fact, that is how utilitarianism is often described. A person subscribing to this philosophy might say that we ought to use two principles to guide our conduct: (1) we should act so that the greatest amount of good is produced, and (2) we should distribute the good as widely as possible. The first of these principles is the principle of utility, but the second is a principle of distributive justice. In other words, to "act so as to promote the greatest good to the greatest number" is not pure utilitarianism. The proposed philosophy is not internally consistent, because there are times when the two principles conflict. In order to be useful, the theory also needs a procedure to resolve conflicts between the two principles. We'll talk more about the principle of distributive justice in the next section.

The criticisms leveled at utilitarianism point out circumstances in which it seems to produce the "wrong" answer to a moral problem. However, rule utilitarianism treats all persons as equals and provides its adherents with the ability to give the reasons why a particular action is right or wrong. Hence we consider it a third workable theory for evaluating moral problems, joining Kantianism and act utilitarianism.

## 2.9 Social Contract Theory

In the spring of 2003, a coalition of military forces led by the United States invaded Iraq and removed the government of Saddam Hussein. When the police disappeared, thousands of Baghdad residents looted government ministries [22]. Sidewalk arms merchants did a thriving business selling AK-47 assault rifles to homeowners needing protection against thieves. Are Iraqis much different from residents of other countries, or should we view the events in Baghdad as the typical response of people to a lack of governmental authority and control?

### 2.9.1 The Social Contract

Philosopher Thomas Hobbes (1588–1679) lived during the English civil war and saw firsthand the terrible consequences of social anarchy. In his book *Leviathan*, he argues that without rules and a means of enforcing them, people would not bother to create anything of value, because nobody could be sure of keeping what they created. Instead, people would be consumed with taking what they needed and defending themselves against the attacks of others. They would live in "continuall feare, and danger of violent death," and their lives would be "solitary, poore, nasty, brutish, and short" [23].

To avoid this miserable condition, which Hobbes calls the "state of nature," rational people understand that cooperation is essential. However, cooperation is possible only when people mutually agree to follow certain guidelines. Hence moral rules are "simply the rules that are necessary if we are to gain the benefits of social living" [5, p. 141]. Hobbes argues that everybody living in a civilized society has implicitly agreed to two things: (1) the establishment of such a set of moral rules to govern relations among citizens and (2) a government capable of enforcing these rules. He calls this arrangement the **social contract**.

The Franco-Swiss philosopher Jean-Jacques Rousseau (1712–1778) continued the evolution of social contract theory. In his book *The Social Contract,* he writes, "Since no man has any natural authority over his fellows, and since force alone bestows no right, all legitimate authority among men must be based on covenants" [24, p. 53]. Rousseau states that the critical problem facing society is finding a form of association that guarantees everybody their safety and property, yet enables each person to remain free. The answer, according to Rousseau, is for everybody to give themselves and their rights to the whole community. The community will determine the rules for its members, and each of its members will be obliged to obey the rules. What prevents the community from enacting bad rules is that no one is above the rules. Since everyone is in the same situation, no community members will want to put unfair burdens on others because that would mean putting unfair burdens on themselves.

Social contract theory must deal with the reality that it's easy for an individual to rationalize selfish behavior. How do we prevent people from shirking their duties to the group? Suppose Bill owes the government $10,000 in taxes, but he discovers a way to cheat on his taxes so it appears he owes only $8,000. Bill thinks to himself, "The government gets billions of dollars a year in taxes. So to the government another $2,000 is just a drop in the bucket. But to me, $2,000 is a lot of money." What restrains Bill from acting selfishly and cheating on his taxes is the knowledge that if he is caught, he will be punished. In order for the social contract to function, society must provide not only a system of laws but a system of enforcing the laws as well.

According to Rousseau, living in a civil society gives a person's actions a moral quality they would not have if that person lived in a state of nature. "It is only then, when the voice of duty has taken the place of physical impulse, and right that of desire, that man, who has hitherto thought only of himself, finds himself compelled to act on other principles, and to consult his reason rather than study his inclinations" [24, p. 64].

James Rachels summarizes these ideas in an elegant definition of social contract theory.

∾

## SOCIAL CONTRACT THEORY

Morality consists in the set of rules, governing how people are to treat one another, that rational people will agree to accept, for their mutual benefit, on the condition that others follow those rules as well. [5, p. 145]

∾

Hobbes, Locke, and many other philosophers of the seventeenth and eighteenth centuries held that all morally significant beings have certain rights, such as the right to life, liberty, and property. Some modern philosophers would add other rights to this list, such as the right to privacy.

There is a close correspondence between rights and duties. If you have the right to life, then others have the duty or obligation not to kill you. If you have a right to free health care when you are ill, then others have the duty to make sure you receive it. Rights can be classified according to the duties they put on others. A **negative right** is a right that another can guarantee by leaving you alone to exercise your right. For example, the right of free expression is a negative right. In order for you to have that right, all others have to do is not interfere with you when you express yourself. A **positive right** is a right that obligates others to do something on your behalf. The right to a free education is a positive right. In order for you to have that right, the rest of society must allocate resources so that you may attend school.

Another way to view rights is to consider whether they are absolute or limited. An **absolute right** is a right that is guaranteed without exception. Negative rights, such as the right to life, are usually considered absolute rights. A **limited right** is a right that may be restricted based on the circumstances. Typically, positive rights are considered to be limited rights. For example, American states guarantee their citizens the right to an education. However, because states do not have unlimited budgets, they typically provide a free education for everyone up through the 12th grade but require people to pay for at least some of the costs of their higher education.

Proponents of social contract theory evaluate moral problems from the point of view of moral rights. In contrast, Kantians evaluate moral problems from duties or obligations, since Kant argued that rights follow from duties.

## 2.9.2  Rawls's Theory of Justice

John Rawls (1921–2002) did much to revive interest in social contract theory in the twentieth century. Rawls notes that both cooperative and competitive behavior can be found in every society. People form societies because social cooperation produces more benefits than a situation in which individuals are completely on their own. On the other hand, there is competition regarding how the benefits are divided among the members of society, since everyone would rather have more than less benefits. To be well-ordered, a society must establish the rights and duties of its members and also determine a just way of distributing "the benefits and burdens of social cooperation" [2, p. 4].

How can people agree on what these principles of justice should be, when the natural inclination for each person would be to propose principles that would benefit himself or herself? To prevent people from selfishly promoting their own interests, Rawls proposes a thought experiment: the principles are determined from an original position in which each person is hidden behind a **veil of ignorance**. People must agree to the principles before they know what place they will hold in society; they are ignorant of their sex, race, ethnicity, wealth, intellectual capacity, physical abilities or disabilities, and so on. Rawls claims that agreements reached from this initial condition would be fair because peple would not choose principles that would harm them if they turned out to be in a disadvantaged position in society relative to others. He proposes that rational people put behind a veil of ignorance would agree upon the following two principles of justice.

Just                                    Unjust

FIGURE 2.7 Rawls's first principle of justice states that each person may have a "fully adequate" number of rights and liberties as long as they are consistent with everyone else having the same rights and liberties.

## JOHN RAWLS'S PRINCIPLES OF JUSTICE

1. Each person may claim a "fully adequate" number of basic rights and liberties, such as freedom of thought and speech, freedom of association, the right to be safe from harm, and the right to own property, so long as these claims are consistent with everyone else having a claim to the same rights and liberties.

2. Any social and economic inequalities must satisfy two conditions: first, they are associated with positions in society that everyone has a fair and equal opportunity to assume; and second, they are "to be to the greatest benefit of the least-advantaged members of society (the difference principle)" [25, pp. 42–43].

Rawls's first principle of justice, illustrated in Figure 2.7, is quite close to our original definition of social contract theory, except that it is stated from the point of view of rights and liberties rather than moral rules. The second principle of justice, however, focuses on the question of social and economic inequalities. It is hard to imagine a society in which every person has equal standing. For example, it is unrealistic to expect every person to be involved in every civic decision. Instead, we elect representatives who vote in our place and officials who act on our behalf. Likewise, it is hard to imagine everybody in a society having equal wealth. If we allow people to hold private property, we should expect that some people will acquire more than others. According to Rawls, social and economic inequalities are acceptable if they meet two conditions.

First, every person in the society should have an equal chance to assume a position of higher social or economic standing. That means that two people born with equal

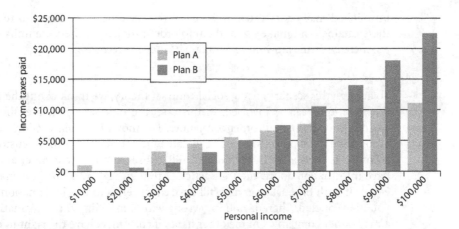

**FIGURE 2.8** Suppose both of these income tax structures will produce the same income to the government. Plan A is a flat tax in which every citizen pays the same percentage of his or her income; plan B is a progressive tax in which the income tax rate gradually rises as a citizen's income increases. Plan B does not treat every citizen equally, but the inequality is justified under Rawls's difference principle because it is of greatest benefit to the most disadvantaged.

intelligence, equal talents, and equal motivation to use them wisely should have the same probability of reaching an advantaged position, regardless of the social or economic class to which they were born. For example, the fact that someone's last name is Bush or Clinton should not give that person a greater probability of being elected president of the United States than any other American born with equal intelligence, talent, and determination.

The second condition, called the **difference principle**, states that social and economic inequalities must be justified. The only way to justify a social or economic inequality is to show that its overall effect is to provide the most benefit to the least advantaged. The purpose of this principle is to help maintain a society composed of free *and equal* citizens. An example of the difference principle in action is a graduated income tax system in which people with higher incomes pay a higher percentage of their income in taxes (Figure 2.8). An example of a violation of the difference principle would be a military draft system in which poor people had a higher probability of being drafted than wealthy people.

### 2.9.3  Evaluating a Scenario Using Social Contract Theory

#### ∽ SCENARIO

Bill, the owner of a chain of DVD rental stores in a major metropolitan area, uses a computer to keep track of the DVDs rented by each customer. Using this information, he is able to construct profiles of the customers. For example, a customer who rents a large number of Disney titles is likely to have children. Bill sells these profiles to mail-order companies. The customers begin receiving many unsolicited mail-order catalogs. Some of the customers are happy to receive these catalogs and make use of them to order products. Others are unhappy at the increase in the amount of "junk mail" they are receiving.

*Analysis*

To analyze this scenario using social contract theory, we think about the rights of the rational agents involved. In this case, the rational agents are Bill, his customers, and the mail-order companies. The morality of Bill's actions revolve around the question of whether he violated the privacy rights of his customers. If someone rents a DVD from one of Bill's stores, both the customer and Bill have information about the transaction. Are their rights to this information equal? If both the customer and Bill have equal rights to this information, then you may conclude there is nothing wrong with him selling this information to a mail-order company. On the other hand, if customers have the right to expect transactions to be confidential, you may conclude that Bill was wrong to sell this information without gaining the permission of the customer.    ∽

## 2.9.4  The Case for Social Contract Theory

1. *It is framed in the language of rights.*

   The cultures of many modern countries, particularly Western-style democracies, promote individualism. For people raised in these cultures, the concept of individual rights is powerful and attractive.

2. *It is based on a solid understanding of human nature, recognizing that rational people act out of self-interest in the absence of a common agreement.*

   The **tragedy of the commons** is a modern term used to describe a situation in which individuals benefit from exploiting a resource, while the costs of the exploitation are shared by a community. The term comes from a paper written in England in the 1830s. In medieval England many villages had commons on which herders were allowed to graze their cattle. Sometimes shepherds grazed their sheep on the commons, which was problematic because sheep can overgraze pastures much quicker than cattle. Since an individual shepherd profits from allowing his sheep to overgraze the commons, and no shepherd can save the commons from overgrazing by restraining his sheep if other shepherds allowed their own sheep to overgraze, the rational economic decision for every shepherd is to become a **free rider** and allow his sheep to overgraze the commons. Unfortunately, too many free riders destroy the shared resource and harm the entire community. The way to prevent this consequence is for the community to establish a law against overgrazing, a punishment associated with breaking the law, and a system of law enforcement. Each shepherd will be restrained from acting selfishly by the knowledge that if he is caught, he will be punished.

   Social contract theory is based on the idea that morality is the result of an implicit agreement among rational beings who understand that there is a tension between self-interest and the common good. The common good is best realized when everyone cooperates. Cooperation occurs when those acting selfishly suffer negative consequences.

You might ask, "If everyone has a right to liberty, how can we put in prison someone who has committed a crime?" The social contract is based on the notion that everyone benefits when everyone bears the burden of following certain rules. Knowledge that those who do not follow the rules will be punished restrains individuals from selfishly flouting their obligations. People will have this knowledge only if society punishes those who commit crimes.

3. *It explains why under certain circumstances civil disobedience can be the morally right decision.*

Consider the lunch counter sit-ins of the 1960s. On February 1, 1960, four African American students from North Carolina A&T walked into the Woolworth's store on South Elm Street in Greensboro, sat down at a whites-only lunch counter, and asked for service. When they were denied service, they refused to leave, sitting at their stools until the store closed. Two days later, eighty-five students participated in the sit-in at Woolworth's. All of these students were breaking segregation laws, but according to social contract theory, their actions could be considered morally justified. As we have said, the social contract is based on the idea that everyone receives certain benefits in return for bearing certain burdens. The segregation laws were designed to give people of color greater burdens and fewer benefits than white people. Therefore, they were unjust.

## 2.9.5 The Case against Social Contract Theory

1. *None of us signed the social contract.*

The social contract is not a real contract. Since none of us have actually agreed to the obligations of citizens set forth in our society, why should we be bound by them?

Defenders of social contract theory point out that the social contract is a theoretical notion that is supposed to explain the rational process through which communities adopt moral guidelines. As John Rawls puts it, social contract agreements are hypothetical and nonhistorical. They are hypothetical in the sense that they are what reasonable people "could, or would, agree to, not what they have agreed to" [25, p. 16]. They are nonhistorical because they "do not suppose the agreement has ever, or indeed ever could actually be entered into" [25, pp. 16–17]. Furthermore, even if it could be entered into, that would make no difference. The reason it would make no difference is because the moral guidelines are supposed to be the result of analysis (facts and values plus logical reasoning), not history. Social contract theory is *not* cultural relativism in disguise.

2. *Some actions can be characterized in multiple ways.*

This is a problem social contract theory shares with Kantianism. Some situations are complicated and can be described in more than one way. Our characterization of a situation can affect the rules or rights we determine to be relevant to our analysis.

3. *Social contract theory does not explain how to solve a moral problem when the analysis reveals conflicting rights.*

This is another problem social contract theory shares with Kantianism. Consider the knotty moral problem of abortion, in which the mother's right to privacy is pitted against the fetus's right to life. As long as each of these rights is embraced by one side in the controversy, the issue cannot be resolved. What typically happens in debates is that advocates on one side of the issue "solve" the problem by discounting or denying the right invoked by their adversaries.

4. *Social contract theory may be unjust to those people who are incapable of upholding their side of the contract.*

Social contract theory provides every person with certain rights in return for that person bearing certain burdens. When a person does not follow the moral rules, he or she is punished. What about human beings who, through no fault of their own, are unable to follow the moral rules?

A response to this objection is that there is a difference between someone who deliberately chooses to break a moral rule and someone who is incapable of understanding a rule. Society must distinguish between these two groups of people. People who deliberately break moral rules should be punished, but people who cannot understand a rule must be cared for.

However, this response overlooks the fact that distinguishing between these two groups of people can be difficult. For example, how should we treat drug addicts who steal to feed their addiction? Some countries treat them as criminals and put them in a prison. Other countries treat them as mentally ill people and put them in a hospital.

These criticisms demonstrate some of the weaknesses of social contract theory. Nevertheless, social contract theory is logical and analytical. It allows people to explain why a particular action is moral or immoral. According to our criteria, it is a workable ethical theory, joining Kantianism, act utilitarianism, and rule utilitarianism as a way of evaluating moral problems.

# 2.10 Virtue Ethics

Some moral philosophers criticize Kantianism, utilitarianism, and social contract theory because they ignore what these philosophers consider to be important aspects of living a moral life, including moral education, moral wisdom, family and social relationships, and the role of emotions [26]. Over the past several decades there has been a resurgence of interest in virtue ethics, an ethical theory that accounts for all of these factors.

Unlike Kantianism, utilitarianism, and social contract theory, which grew out of the Enlightenment, virtue ethics can be traced all the way back to ancient Greece. The notion of *arete*, usually translated as **virtue** or excellence, refers to reaching one's highest potential. The most influential treatment of virtue appears in Aristotle's *Nicomachean Ethics*, written in the fourth century BC. In this book Aristotle expresses the opinion that the path to true happiness and genuine flourishing as a human being lies in living a life of virtue [27].

## 2.10.1 Virtues and Vices

According to Aristotle, there are two kinds of virtues: intellectual virtues and moral virtues. **Intellectual virtues** are those virtues associated with reasoning and truth. **Moral**

**FIGURE 2.9** According to Aristotle, happiness derives from living a life of virtue. You acquire moral virtues by repeating the appropriate acts.

**virtues**, often called virtues of character by today's writers, are habits or dispositions formed through the repetition of the relevant virtuous actions (Figure 2.9). For example, you can develop the moral virtue of honesty by habitually telling the truth or performing other honest actions. In this section our primary focus is on the moral virtues.

A moral virtue is a deep-seated character trait. Consider someone who possesses the virtue of honesty, for example. An honest person will tell the truth as a matter of course, will be uncomfortable with even the thought of doing something deceitful, and will not appreciate being invited by others to join in a dishonest activity. Morally good people consistently do what is right; it becomes second nature to them.

Note, then, that a moral virtue is not simply a disposition to *act* in a particular way, it is also a disposition to *feel* in a particular way. According to Aristotle, you can tell a lot about someone's character by observing what pleases them and what bothers them. He wrote, "We may even go so far as to state that the man who does not enjoy performing noble actions is not a good man at all. Nobody would call a man just who does not enjoy acting justly, nor generous who does not enjoy generous actions, and so on" [27, p. 16].

Of course, some moral virtues have a more direct connection to the emotions than others. Courage is a good example of a virtue that has a close connection with the emotions. In order to be courageous, you must be able to moderate your fear.

As noted earlier, a moral virtue is a deep-seated character trait, and character traits take time to become deep-seated. Consider a young Boy Scout who is encouraged by his scoutmaster to take the Boy Scout slogan seriously and "do a good turn daily." The scout initially responds to this encouragement by actively looking for opportunities to help someone each day, not so much because he is interested in being helpful, but because he looks up to his scoutmaster and seeks his praise and approval. The young scout continues doing daily good deeds for family members, friends, and even strangers for a significant period of time. Eventually, he realizes that he has persisted in his practice of doing a good turn daily so that it has become a habit—something so ingrained that he no longer relies upon the compliments of his scoutmaster for motivation. His daily efforts give him a sense of genuine satisfaction. At this point being helpful to others has become second nature to the scout; he has become benevolent.

When someone possessing a virtue does not exercise the virtue, we know there is a good explanation. Suppose Shirley is known for her reliability. She does what she says she will do, and she shows up on time for meetings. Everybody knows they can count on Shirley. One morning Shirley does not show up for a meeting she had promised to attend. When the others notice her absence, they say, "Something must have happened." They understand that there must have been an extenuating circumstance that prevented Shirley from showing up for the meeting on time.

～

## Summary of Virtue Ethics

A right action is an action that a virtuous person, acting in character, would do in the same circumstances. A virtuous person is a person who possesses and lives out the virtues. The virtues are those character traits human beings need in order to flourish and be truly happy.

～

Which virtues are those humans need in order to flourish and be truly happy? To some extent that depends on the culture. In Homeric Greece physical courage was prized; pioneers to the American West put a high value on self-reliance; in today's multicultural society tolerance is important. However, certain core virtues, such as honesty, justice, and loyalty, seem to be of universal importance.

A **vice** is a character trait that prevents a human being from flourishing or being truly happy. Vices, then, are the opposite of virtues. Aristotle noticed that in many cases two different vices can be associated with a virtue: one corresponding to an excess and the other corresponding to a deficiency. For example, the virtue of courage can be seen occupying a middle ground between cowardice (having an excess of fear) and rashness (having a deficiency of fear). The virtue of friendliness is somewhere in between quarrelsomeness (being too critical of what others like or what they want to do) and obsequiousness (giving in too easily and not being critical enough of what others like or what they want to do).

Virtue ethics pays particular attention to the agent (the person performing the action) as well as the action (as in Kantianism and social contract theory) and the consequences of the action (as in utilitarianism). A good person does "the right thing at the right time for the right reason" [28].

According to the theory of virtue ethics, moral decision making cannot be reduced to the routine application of a set of rules. That is not to say there is no place for "rules of thumb." In order to develop the virtue of trustworthiness, for example, it is a good idea to follow the rule of thumb "Keep confidences." However, under certain circumstances keeping a confidence may not be the right course of action. Moral wisdom or discernment takes precedence over any rule [26].

## 2.10.2  Making a Decision Using Virtue Ethics

### ∼ SCENARIO

Josh is a senior majoring in computer science at a small university. All the seniors in computer science are friends because they have taken most of their computer science courses together. Josh is particularly close to Matt. Josh and Matt are from the same city about 200 miles from campus, and Matt has given Josh rides to and from home a half dozen times at the start and end of school holidays. Notably, Matt never asked Josh to help pay for the gas on any of these trips, and Josh never offered to do so.

When it is time for seniors to choose partners for their capstone project, no one is surprised when Josh and Matt end up on the same team. Unfortunately, Josh and the other teammates soon regret inviting Matt onto their team. Everyone has known Matt to be hard-working, trustworthy, and reliable, but his father just died in a car accident, and he has lost all interest in school. To make matters worse, Matt is drinking too much. He doesn't show up for a lot of the team meetings, and the code he produces doesn't meet the specifications. Josh and the other teammates can't persuade Matt to take the project more seriously, and since they don't have any real control over his behavior, they decide it's easier simply to rewrite Matt's part of the system themselves. Matt does contribute his share of the PowerPoint slides, and during the oral presentation he stands up and talks about "his" portion of the code, never mentioning that it was all rewritten by his teammates.

Everyone in the class is supposed to send the professor an email grading the performance of their teammates. The department prides itself on graduating students who have proven they can work well on software development teams, and students getting poor or failing performance reviews from all of their teammates may be forced to repeat the class. Matt comes to Josh, tells him that he really needs to pass this class because he can't afford to stay in college any longer, and pleads for a good performance review. What should Josh do?

### Decision

Josh must decide whether or not to disclose to the professor that Matt did not even come close to doing his share of the team project, fully aware that a poor or failing performance evaluation may prevent Matt from graduating. Josh is an honest person, and he has a hard time imagining that he could tell the professor that Matt did a good job when that is far from the truth. However, Josh is also a just person, and he feels indebted toward Matt, who has done him a lot of favors over the past four years—particularly those free rides to and from his hometown. Josh also feels compassion toward Matt, who lost his father. It's bad enough to lose a parent, but because of the sudden nature of his father's death, Matt didn't even have the chance to say goodbye to him.

As he ponders his dilemma, Josh begins to realize that he finds himself in this difficult spot because at several points in the past he didn't step up and do the right thing. He took advantage of Matt's generosity (and gave in to his own greedy impulses) by taking all those free rides to and from his hometown. If he had paid his share of the gas money, he wouldn't be feeling so obligated toward Matt. Josh also knows he wasn't a very good friend when he failed to talk with Matt about how he was feeling about his father's death and how that was affecting his performance on the senior project. Matt's lack of attention to his schoolwork was definitely out of character, a sign that he was suffering a lot. Josh now understands that he and the other teammates should have had a conversation with the professor in charge of the senior projects when it first became apparent that Matt was not participating fully as a teammate. An early intervention could have resulted in a completely different outcome.

After reflecting on what he should do, Josh concludes he must be truthful with the professor. However, he will not simply tell the professor that Matt's performance was poor. Josh decides he will also take responsibility for his role in the fiasco by providing a full account to the professor of how his own failure to respond to the situation earlier in the year contributed to the unsatisfactory outcome.

### 2.10.3  The Case for Virtue Ethics

1. *In many situations it makes more sense to focus on virtues than on obligations, rights, or consequences.* Consider, for example, why it is wrong to steal to satisfy a selfish desire. According to Kantianism, the act is wrong because the person doing the stealing is not treating his or her victims as ends in themselves. According to rule utilitarianism, stealing is wrong because the long-term consequences of everybody stealing all the time would produce more harm than good. The explanation from the perspective of virtue ethics is much simpler: stealing to satisfy a selfish desire is wrong because it disrupts one's acquisition of the virtue of honesty.

2. *Personal relationships can be morally relevant to decision making.* Recall that utilitarianism, Kantianism, and social contract theory require us to be completely impartial and treat all human beings as equal. This assumption leads to conclusions that are hard for most people to accept. For example, when a couple is faced with the choice between using $5,000 to take their children to Disneyland for a week or feeding 1,000 starving refugees for a month, the calculus of utility would conclude saving 1,000 lives was the better option. When evaluating the same choice from the perspective of virtue ethics, the relationship the couple has with their children is morally relevant. Parents are supposed to be partial toward their own children, and this can be taken into account when determining the best action to take.

3. *Virtue ethics recognizes that our moral decision-making skills develop over time.* People develop moral virtues by making habits of the appropriate acts. It takes time for a person's character to develop. Moral wisdom is an intellectual virtue that also takes

time to develop. Each of us is on the journey from the-person-I-am to the-person-I-am-meant-to-be, and if I am confused about the right action to take in a particular circumstance, I can go ask someone who is further along in the journey. In this way virtue ethics aligns with our everyday experience. People commonly ask someone "older and wiser" when they truly want to do the right thing and feel uncertain about the best course of action.

4. *There are no irresolvable moral dilemmas.* Recall that a weakness of Kantianism is that if there is conflict between perfect duties, there is no way to choose between them. Virtue ethics does not have this defect. Different virtues may tug a person in different directions, but the right action can always be determined by a person with sufficient moral wisdom. This is not to say that there are no dilemmas. Bad things can happen to good people, and sometimes people face tragic dilemmas, where every conceivable alternative is bad. The emotional consequences of making decisions under these circumstances is addressed in the next point.

5. *Virtue ethics recognizes the important role that emotions play in living a moral life.* Virtue ethics recognizes that humans are not dispassionate calculating machines. They are flesh-and-blood creatures with feelings, and when things are going right, their feelings and thoughts are in alignment. As noted before, virtuous people do the right things at the right times for the right reasons. They feel satisfied doing good. When faced with difficult decisions, they are deeply affected.

## 2.10.4  The Case against Virtue Ethics

1. *Different people may have quite different conceptions of human flourishing.* According to virtue ethics, virtues are character traits that humans need in order to flourish. We do not live in a homogeneous society, and there are a wide variety of perspectives about what character traits lead to the most fulfilling life. If we cannot agree on which character traits are virtues, then we will not be able to agree on what a virtuous person would do in a particular situation. Therefore, the virtue ethics approach is not as powerful as Kantianism, rule utilitarianism, and social contract theory, which identify moral norms that are universally true.

2. *Virtue ethics cannot be used to guide government policy.* Virtue ethics focuses on the agent, a virtuous human being, more than the act or the consequences of the act. Government policy is typically set by government agencies or groups of officials, not individuals. Consider the case brought up in Section 2.7.2, in which a state must decide whether or not to replace a section of highway. An act utilitarian can determine the monetary costs and benefits of the proposal and reach a conclusion about the better option. Virtue ethics has something to say about the officials involved in the decision—they should be honest, diligent, and prudent, for example—but it has nothing more to contribute to the analysis.

3. *Virtue ethics undermines attempts to hold people responsible for their bad actions.* According to virtue ethics, people are not born virtuous. Instead, intellectual and moral virtues must be acquired over time. To a great extent, the virtues a person attains depends upon how she is raised by her parents, the education she receives, and the community she grows up in. All of these things are outside the control of a

child. In that case, how can we hold a person responsible if she acquires vices instead of virtues [29]?

These criticisms show that virtue ethics is not perfect. However, virtue ethics does provide a framework for people to analyze moral situations, to reach a conclusion about the right course of action, and to justify the conclusion using logical arguments. Therefore, we determine that virtue ethics is a workable ethical theory, along with Kantianism, act utilitarianism, rule utilitarianism, and social contract theory.

## 2.11 Comparing Workable Ethical Theories

The divine command theory, ethical egoism, Kantianism, act utilitarianism, rule utilitarianism, social contract theory, and virtue ethics share the viewpoint that moral good and moral precepts are objective. In other words, morality has an existence outside the human mind. Philosophers call this view **ethical objectivism**.

What distinguishes ethical egoism, Kantianism, utilitarianism, social contract theory, and virtue ethics from the divine command theory is the assumption that ethical decision making is a rational process by which people can discover objective moral principles with the use of logical reasoning based on facts and commonly held values. Kantianism, utilitarianism, social contract theory, and virtue ethics explicitly take other people into consideration when defining what makes an action morally correct, which sets these theories apart from ethical egoism. Of all the theories we have considered, we conclude that Kantianism, act utilitarianism, rule utilitarianism, social contract theory, and virtue ethics are the most workable.

An act utilitarian considers the consequences of the action, computing the total change in utility to determine if an action is right or wrong. Kantianism, rule utilitarianism, and social contract theory are rule based. According to these theories, an action is morally right if it is in accord with a correct moral rule.

Each of the rule-based theories has a different way of determining if a moral rule is correct. A Kantian relies upon the Categorical Imperative. A rule utilitarian considers what the long-term consequences of everyone following the rule would be for the total good. An adherent of social contract theory considers whether rational people would agree to accept the rule, for everyone's mutual benefit, provided that everyone else agreed to follow the rule as well.

Unlike the other theories, which focus on the act itself or the consequences of the action, virtue ethics focuses on the agent. The purpose of the analysis is to carefully examine the action taken by an agent in a particular situation to determine if that action is characteristic of a virtuous person.

These differences among the theories are presented graphically in Figure 2.10.

## 2.12 Morality of Breaking the Law

What is moral and what is legal are not identical. Certain actions may be wrong, even if there are no laws forbidding these actions. For example, most American states do

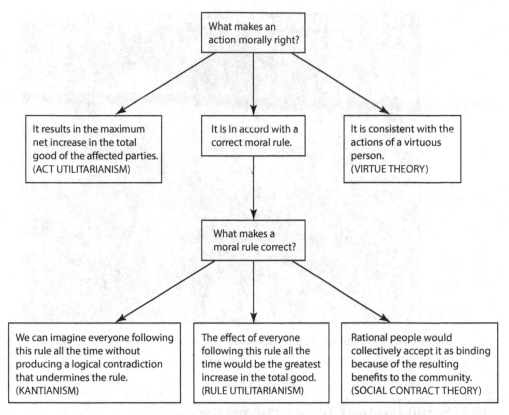

FIGURE 2.10 Comparison of the five workable ethical theories. All of these theories explicitly take people other than the decision maker into consideration, assume that moral good and moral precepts are objective, and rely upon reasoning from facts and commonly held values.

not have laws prohibiting texting while driving, but drivers are still morally responsible for traffic accidents they cause because they are distracted by texting. What about the opposite situation? Is it possible that an action may be the right thing to do, even if it is illegal?

In our discussion of social contract theory, we talked about the morality of civil disobedience, and we concluded that from the perspective of this theory the lunch counter sit-ins were morally acceptable because the segregation laws being violated were unjust. Here we are considering a different situation. We are assuming the law is just. When this is the case, is it possible that an illegal action may be the right action?

To ground our analysis, we will consider a particular illegal action: violating a licensing agreement by copying a CD containing copyrighted music and giving it to a friend.[1]

---

1. This action is illegal in the United States and many other countries, but it is not illegal in every country.

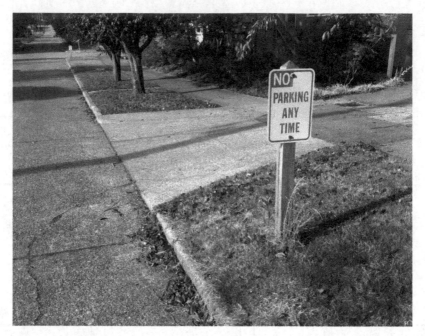

FIGURE 2.11 According to social contract theory, we have a prima facie obligation to obey the law.

## 2.12.1  Social Contract Theory Perspective

Social contract theory is based on the assumption that everyone in society ought to bear certain burdens in order to receive certain benefits. The legal system is instituted to guarantee that people's rights are protected. It guarantees people will not choose their selfish interests over the common good. For this reason we have a prima facie obligation to obey the law (Figure 2.11). That means, everything else being equal, we should be law abiding. In return, our own legal rights will be respected. Our obligation to obey the law should be broken only if we are compelled to follow a higher-order moral obligation.

From the point of view of social contract theory, then, it is wrong to give a friend a copy of a CD containing copyrighted music, because that action violates the legal rights of the person or organization owning the copyright. The desire to do something nice for a friend is not an overriding moral concern.

## 2.12.2  Kantian Perspective

The Kantian perspective is quite similar to that of social contract theory. People need to be able to possess objects in order to freely use them for their own purposes. According to Kant, property rights are made possible through an implicit common agreement. When you declare that an object is yours, you are stating that everyone else is obliged to refrain from using that object. Justice demands that in order for you to make such a claim, you must also respect the similar claims of everyone else. The state ensures that everyone meets the obligation of respecting everyone else's property rights.

If you were to copy a CD containing copyrighted material, you would be violating the property rights of the copyright owner—you would be failing to fulfill your obligations to others as a member of civil society. Therefore, it is wrong to copy the CD.

### 2.12.3   Rule Utilitarian Perspective

What would be the consequences of people ignoring laws whenever they chose? A beneficial consequence would be the immediate happiness of the people who are doing what they please rather than obeying the law. However, there would be numerous harmful consequences. The people directly affected by lawless actions would be harmed. People in general would have less respect for the law, which would encourage more people to break the law. Assuming increased lawlessness puts an additional burden on the criminal justice system, society as a whole would have to pay for having additional police officers, prosecutors, judges, and prisons. If the lawlessness is not controlled by the criminal justice system, criminal behavior could get out of hand, causing great harm to the victims of these criminals. Hence, from a rule utilitarian viewpoint, breaking the law has more harms than benefits and is wrong. We should adopt the moral rule "Obey the law."

### 2.12.4   Act Utilitarian Perspective

It is possible to conceive of situations where the benefits of breaking a law are greater than the harms. Suppose I purchase a copyrighted music CD. I play it, and I think it is great. A friend of mine is in a terrible automobile accident. While he recovers, he will need to stay quiet for a month. I know he has no money to spend on music. In fact, people are doing fund-raisers simply to help his family pay the medical bills. I don't have money to contribute to a fund-raiser, but I think of another way I could help him out. I can give my friend a copy of the CD. He will be grateful for having a diversion during his time of bed rest.

What would be the consequences of my action? The benefit to my friend is at least $15, the price of the CD. I will be very happy to have been able to do something that pleased him so much. We assign the value $10 to that beneficial consequence. As far as I can tell, there is no lost sale, because even if I do not give my friend a copy of the CD, he is unlikely to purchase it. In fact, giving a copy of the CD to my friend may actually increase the sales of the CD if my friend likes it and recommends it to other people who do have money to spend on CDs. So there are no negative consequences to the record label and may even be some positive consequences. We assign a value of $0 as the consequence to the record label. I am not likely to be prosecuted for what I did. Therefore, there will be no impact on the criminal justice system. No extra police detectives, prosecutors, or judges will need to be hired as a result of my action. The calculated consequence of my action on the legal system has a value of $0. Adding up all the consequences, the total is $25 worth of benefit. If I do not give my friend a copy of the CD (i.e., do nothing), there are no consequences, so the total benefit is $0. Therefore, making a copy of the CD and giving it to my hospitalized friend is the right thing to do.

### 2.12.5  Conclusion

There is nothing intrinsically immoral about copying a CD. However, our society has chosen to enact laws that grant intellectual property rights to people who do creative work and distribute it on CDs. From the perspective of social contract theory and Kantianism, we have a prima facie obligation to obey the law and respect everyone's property rights. From the viewpoint of rule utilitarianism, the beneficial consequences of following the moral rule "Obey the law" greatly exceed the harmful consequences. From the point of view of all of these theories, the law should be obeyed unless there is a strong overriding moral obligation. Copying a disc to save a few dollars or help a friend does not fall into that category.

From an act utilitarian viewpoint, it is possible to come up with a circumstance where making a copy of a copyrighted CD is the right action. However, it would be wrong to extrapolate from this particular case and conclude that an act utilitarian analysis would always determine CD copying to be morally acceptable.

## Summary

We live together in communities for our mutual benefit. Every society has guidelines indicating what people are supposed to do in various circumstances. We call these guidelines morality. Ethics, also called moral philosophy, is a rational examination of people's moral beliefs and behaviors. In this chapter we have considered a variety of ethical theories, with the purpose of identifying those that will be of most use to us as we consider the effects of information technology on society.

Ethical relativism is the idea that people *invent* morality. An ethical relativist claims there are no universal moral principles. Subjective relativism is the theory that morality is an individual creation. Cultural relativism is the idea that each society determines its own morality. If morality is invented, and no set of moral guidelines is any better than another, then there are no objective criteria that can be used to determine if one set of guidelines is better than another. Under these circumstances, the study of ethics is extremely difficult, if not impossible.

In contrast, ethical objectivism is based on the idea that morality has an existence outside the human mind. It is the responsibility of people to *discover* morality. An objectivist claims there are certain universal moral principles that are true for all people, regardless of their historical or cultural situation. All the other theories discussed in this chapter are based on ethical objectivism, including the five most practical theories that we will be using throughout the rest of the book: Kantianism, act utilitarianism, rule utilitarianism, social contract theory, and virtue ethics.

Our discussion of the strengths and weaknesses of these practical theories revealed that each of them contains a valuable insight. According to Kant, every human being is equally valuable, and every interaction with another person should respect that person's rationality and autonomy. Utilitarians understand that it's helpful to consider the consequences of an action when deciding whether it is right or wrong. Social contract theory focuses on the individual and collective benefits of protecting certain human rights, such as the right to life, liberty, and property. Virtue ethics is based on the idea that you can count on a good person to do the right thing at the right time in the right way.

Our discussion of these theories also revealed that none of them is perfect. In practice, however, there is no reason why you should not consider virtues *and* duties *and* rights *and* consequences when making moral decisions. If analyses from all of these perspectives result in a consensus on the right course of action, you can make the decision with confidence. For more challenging cases, however, you will find it impossible to come up with a virtuous course of action that respects everyone's rights absolutely and maximizes the total increase in happiness. That's when things get interesting! Most of the scenarios discussed in the rest of the book fall into the latter category.

In the chapters that follow, we'll use Kantianism, act utilitarianism, rule utilitarianism, social contract theory, and virtue ethics to evaluate a variety of situations arising from the introduction of information technology into society. Every analysis will be based on one of the theories, so that you may come to a better understanding of how to apply each theory to different situations. As you ponder these cases and discuss them with others, you will learn more about your own values, what kind of person you want to be, and what kind of world you want to live in.

## Further Reading and Viewing

Jonathan Haidt. "The Moral Roots of Liberals and Conservatives." *TEDTalks*, September 2008. 18:40. www.ted.com/talks/jonathan_haidt_on_the_moral_mind.html.

Christopher Shea. "Rule Breaker." *Chronicle of Higher Education*, June 12, 2011. chronicle.com.

Paul Solman. "Finding the Connection between Prosperity and Happiness." *PBS NewsHour*, June 20, 2013. 9:44. video.pbs.org.

Paul Solman. "'Pernicious' Effects of Economic Inequality." *PBS NewsHour*, June 21, 2013. 9:24. video.pbs.org.

Thomas Sowell. "The Fallacy of 'Fairness.'" Creators.com, February 9, 2010. www.creators.com.

## Review Questions

1. Define in your own words what "the ethical point of view" means.

2. What is the difference between morality and ethics?

3. What is the difference between ethical relativism and ethical objectivism?

4. Two people are debating the morality of a particular action. Person A explains why he believes the action is wrong. Person B disagrees with person A. Her response to him is, "That's your opinion." Person B has not made a strong ethical argument. Why not?

5. What do we mean when we say an ethical theory is rational?

6. What is the many/any fallacy? Invent your own example of this fallacy.

7. What is the equivalence fallacy? Invent your own example of this fallacy.

8. Come up with your own example of a moral rule that would violate the Categorical Imperative.

9. What is plagiarism? Describe four different ways that a person can commit plagiarism. (See Appendix A.)

10. What is the difference between plagiarism and misuse of sources?

11. What is the difference between a consequentialist theory and a nonconsequentialist theory?

12. Give three examples of a situation in which your action would be primarily motivated by a sense of duty or obligation. Give three examples of a situation in which your action would be primarily motivated by its expected consequences.

13. Create your own example that demonstrates the problem of moral luck.

14. Why do businesses and governments often use utilitarian thinking to determine the proper course of action?

15. Think of a real-life law or policy that violates the difference principle.

16. Is social contract theory as first presented a consequentialist theory or a nonconsequentialist theory? Is social contract theory as articulated in Rawls's two principles of justice a consequentialist theory or a nonconsequentialist theory?

17. Come up with a list of 20 virtues not mentioned in Section 2.10.

18. Describe similarities and differences between subjective relativism and ethical egoism.

19. Describe similarities and differences between divine command theory and Kantianism.

20. Describe similarities and differences between subjective relativism and act utilitarianism.

21. Describe similarities and differences between Kantianism and rule utilitarianism.

22. Describe similarities and differences between act utilitarianism and rule utilitarianism.

23. Describe similarities and differences between cultural relativism and social contract theory.

24. Describe similarities and differences between Kantianism and social contract theory.

25. Describe similarities and differences between cultural relativism and virtue ethics.

26. Evaluate the four scenarios presented in Section 2.1.2 from a Kantian perspective.

27. Evaluate the four scenarios presented in Section 2.1.2 from an act utilitarian perspective.

28. Evaluate the four scenarios presented in Section 2.1.2 from a rule utilitarian perspective.

29. Evaluate the four scenarios presented in Section 2.1.2 from the perspective of social contract theory.

30. Evaluate the four scenarios presented in Section 2.1.2 from the perspective of virtue ethics.

# Discussion Questions

31. If everyone agreed to take the ethical point of view by respecting others and their core values, would there be any need for a rigorous study of ethics?

32. If you had to choose only one of the ethical theories presented in this chapter and use it for all of your personal ethical decision making, which theory would you choose? Why? How would you respond to the arguments raised against the theory you have chosen?

33. Most ethical theories agree on a large number of moral guidelines. For example, it is nearly universally held that it is wrong to steal. What difference, then, does it make whether someone subscribes to the divine command theory, Kantianism, utilitarianism, or one of the other ethical theories?

34. Suppose a spaceship lands in your neighborhood. Friendly aliens emerge and invite humans to enter the galactic community. You learn that this race of aliens has colonized virtually the entire galaxy; Earth is one of the few inhabitable planets to host a different intelligent species. The aliens seem to be remarkably open-minded. They ask you to outline the ethical theory that should guide the interactions between our two species. Which ethical theory would you describe? Why?

35. The Silver Rule states, "Do not do unto others what you do not want them to do unto you." Which of the five workable ethical theories is closest to the Silver Rule?

36. According to the Golden Rule, you should do unto others as you would want them to do unto you. Which of the five workable ethical theories is closest to the Golden Rule?

37. Are there any ethical theories described in this chapter that would allow someone to use the argument, "Everybody is doing it," to show that an activity is not wrong?

38. How well does Moor's theory of just consequentialism (described in the interview at the end of this chapter) solve the problems associated with Kantianism and rule utilitarianism?

39. Can moral decisions be made on a completely codified, algorithmic basis, or are there fundamental weaknesses to this approach to moral decision making?

40. What are some examples of contemporary information technology issues for which our society's moral guidelines seem to be nonexistent or unclear? (Hint: Think about issues that are generating a lot of media coverage.)

41. People give a variety of reasons for copying a music CD from a friend instead of buying it [30]. Refute each of the reasons given below, using one of the viable theories described in this chapter. (You don't have to use the same theory each time.)

    a. I don't have enough money to buy it.
    b. The retail price is too high. The company is gouging customers.
    c. Since I wouldn't have bought it anyway, the company didn't lose a sale.
    d. I'm giving my friend the opportunity to do a good deed.
    e. Everyone else is doing it. Why should I be the only person to buy it when everyone else is getting it for free?
    f. This is a drop in the bucket compared to Chinese pirates who sell billions of dollars worth of copied music.
    g. This is insignificant compared to the billions of dollars worth of music being exchanged over the Internet.

42. Students in a history class are asked to take a quiz posted on the course Web site. The instructor has explained the following rules to the students: First, they are supposed to do their own work. Second, they are free to consult their lecture notes and the textbook while taking the quiz. Third, in order to get credit for the quiz, they must correctly answer at least 80 percent of the questions. If they do not get a score of 80 percent, they may retake the quiz as many times as they wish.

Mary and John are both taking the quiz. They are sitting next to each other in the computer room. John asks Mary for help in answering one of the questions. He says, "What's the difference if you tell me the answer, I look it up in the book, or I find out from the computer that my answer is wrong and retake the quiz? In any case, I'll end up getting credit for the right answer." Mary tells John the correct answer to the question.

Discuss the morality of Mary's decision.

43. Suppose a society holds that it is wrong for one individual to eavesdrop on the telephone conversations of another citizen. Should that society also prohibit the government from listening in on its citizens' telephone conversations?

## In-Class Exercises

44. In Plato's dialogue *The Republic*, Glaucon argues that people do not voluntarily do what is right [31]. According to Glaucon, anyone who has the means to do something unjust and get away with it will do so. Glaucon illustrates his point by telling the story of Gyges.

Gyges, a shepherd, finds a magic ring. He accidentally discovers that wearing this ring renders him invisible. He uses the power of the ring to seduce the queen, kill the king, and take over the kingdom.

Divide the class into two groups (pro and con) to debate the following proposition: Whenever people have the opportunity to act unjustly without any fear of getting caught or anyone thinking the worse of them, they do so.

45. For one of the following issues divide the class into two groups (pro and con) to argue whether the right should be considered a legitimate positive right by our society:
   a. The right to a higher education
   b. The right to housing
   c. The right to health care
   d. The right of a presidential candidate to receive time on television

46. Is the right to life a negative right or a positive right? In other words, when we say someone has the right to life, are we simply saying we have an obligation not to harm that person, or are we saying we have an obligation to provide that person with what he or she needs in order to live, such as food and shelter?

Divide the class into two groups. One group should argue that the right to life is a negative right; the other should argue that the right to life is a positive right.

47. Divide the class into two groups (pro and con) to debate this proposition: The citizens of a representative democracy are morally responsible for the actions of their government.

48. Divide the class into two groups (pro and con) to debate this proposition: The moral guidelines for individuals should apply to interactions among nation-states.

# References

[1]   James H. Moor. "Reason, Relativity, and Responsibility in Computer Ethics." In *Readings in CyberEthics*. 2nd ed. Edited by Richard A. Spinello and Herman T. Tavani. Jones and Bartlett, Sudbury, MA, 2004.

[2]   John Rawls. *A Theory of Justice, Revised Edition*. Belknap Press of Harvard University Press, Cambridge, MA, 1999.

[3]   Plato. *Portrait of Socrates: Being the Apology, Crito and Phaedo of Plato in an English Translation*. Translated by Sir R. W. Livingstone. Clarendon Press, Oxford, England, 1961.

[4]   William Graham Sumner. *Folkways: A Study of the Sociological Importance of Usages, Manners, Customs, Mores, and Morals*. Ginn and Company, Boston, MA, 1934.

[5]   James Rachels. *The Elements of Moral Philosophy*. 4th ed. McGraw-Hill, Boston, MA, 2003.

[6]   *The Torah: A Modern Commentary*. Union of American Hebrew Congregations, New York, NY, 1981.

[7]   Plato. *Plato's Euthyphro: With Introduction and Notes and Pseudo-Platonica*. Arno Press, New York, NY, 1976.

[8]   *The Holy Bible, New Revised Standard Version*. Genesis, Chapter 22. Oxford University Press, Oxford, England, 1995.

[9]   *The Holy Bible, New Revised Standard Version*. Genesis, Chapter 4. Oxford University Press, Oxford, England, 1995.

[10]  Ayn Rand. "The Objectivist Ethics." In *The Virtue of Selfishness*. Signet Books, New York, NY, 1964.

[11]  Douglas Birsch. *Ethical Insights: A Brief Introduction*. 2nd ed. McGraw-Hill, Boston, MA, 2002.

[12]  James Rachels. "Two Arguments against Ethical Egoism." *Philosophia*, Vol. 4, Nos. 2–3, pp. 297–314, April–July 1974.

[13]  James H. Fowler and Nicholar A. Christakis. "Dynamic Spread of Happiness in a Large Social Network: Longitudinal Analysis over 20 Years in the Framingham Heart Study." *British Medical Journal*, December 4, 2008.

[14]  Lewis White Beck. "Translator's Introduction." In *Foundations of the Metaphysics of Morals*. 2nd ed. Library of Liberal Arts/Prentice Hall, Upper Saddle River, NJ, 1997.

[15]  Michael J. Sandel. *Justice: What's the Right Thing to Do*. Farrar, Straus and Giroux, New York, NY, 2009.

[16]  William K. Frankena. *Ethics*. 2nd ed. Prentice Hall, Englewood Cliffs, NJ, 1973.

[17]  Jeremy Bentham. *An Introduction to the Principles of Morals and Legislation*, p. 48. Clarendon Press, Oxford, England, 1823.

[18]  W. D. Ross. *The Right and the Good*. 2nd ed. Oxford University Press, Oxford, England, 2003.

[19]  Kevin Poulsen. "Nachi Worm Infected Diebold ATMs." *Register*, November 25, 2003. www.theregister.co.uk.

[20]  Florence Olsen. "Attacks Threaten Computer Networks as Students Arrive for the Fall Semester." *Chronicle of Higher Education*, September 5, 2003.

[21]   Bernard Gert. "Common Morality and Computing." In *Readings in CyberEthics*. 2nd ed., p. 106. Edited by Richard A. Spinello and Herman T. Tavani. Jones and Bartlett, Sudbury, MA, 2004.

[22]   John Daniszewski and Tony Perry. "War with Iraq; U.S. in Control; Baghdad in U.S. Hands; Symbols of Regime Fall as Troops Take Control." *Los Angeles Times*, April 10, 2003.

[23]   Thomas Hobbes. *Leviathan*, p. 186. Penguin Books, London, England, 1985.

[24]   Jean-Jacques Rousseau. *The Social Contract*. Translated by Maurice Cranston. Penguin Books, London, England, 1968.

[25]   John Rawls. *Justice as Fairness: A Restatement*. Belknap Press of Harvard University Press, Cambridge, MA, 2001.

[26]   Rosalind Hursthouse. *On Virtue Ethics*, pp. 2–3. Oxford University Press, Oxford, England, 1999.

[27]   Aristotle. *The Nicomachean Ethics*. Translated by F. H. Peters and M. Ostwald. Oxford University Press, Oxford, England, 1998.

[28]   John Bradshaw. *Reclaiming Virtue: How We Can Develop the Moral Intelligence to Do the Right Thing at the Right Time for the Right Reason*. Piatkus, 2010.

[29]   Nafsika Athanassoulis. "Virtue Ethics." In *The Internet Encyclopedia of Philosophy*, July 7, 2010. www.iep.utm.edu.

[30]   Sara Baase. *A Gift of Fire*. 2nd ed. Prentice Hall, Upper Saddle River, NJ, 2003.

[31]   Plato. *The Republic of Plato*. Translated by F. M. Cornford. Oxford University Press, London, England, 1941.

# James Moor

James Moor is the Daniel P. Stone Professor in Intellectual and Moral Philosophy at Dartmouth College. He is also the editor-in-chief of the philosophical journal *Minds and Machines*, and he has served as president of the International Society for Ethics and Information Technology.

Professor Moor has written extensively on computer ethics, the philosophy of artificial intelligence, the philosophy of mind, the philosophy of science, and logic. His publications include "Why We Need Better Ethics for Emerging Technologies," *Ethics and Information Technology*, Vol. 7, No. 3 (2005), pp. 111–119. He and Terrell Bynum coedited *The Digital Phoenix: How Computers Are Changing Philosophy* (Oxford: Basil Blackwell Publishers, 1998, and revised edition, 2000) and *Cyberphilosophy: The Intersection of Computing and Philosophy* (Oxford: Basil Blackwell Publishers, 2002).

In 2003 Dr. Moor received the Making a Difference Award from the Association for Computing Machinery's Special Interest Group on Computers and Society. In 2006 he received the Barwise Prize for his work in philosophy and computing from the American Philosophical Association. He holds a PhD in history and philosophy of science from Indiana University.

---

### What stimulated your interest in studying the philosophy of technology?

My interest developed initially through a fascination with computing. The philosophy of computing is a combination of logic, epistemology, metaphysics, and value theory—the complete philosophical package wrapped up in a very practical and influential technological form. Who wouldn't be interested in that? Many standard philosophical issues are brought to life in a computer setting. Consider a simple example: In *The Republic*, Plato tells a story about the ring of Gyges in which a shepherd finds a ring that, when he wears it and turns it, makes him invisible. Being a clever but rather unethical shepherd, he uses the power of the ring to take over the kingdom, including killing the king and marrying the queen. Through this story Plato raises a deep and important philosophical question: Why be just if one can get away with being unjust? Today the Internet offers each of us our own ring of Gyges. Agents on the Internet can be largely invisible. The question for us, echoing Plato, is why be just while using the Internet if one can get away with being unjust?

### What distinguishes ethical problems in computing from ethical problems in other fields?

Some have argued that the ethical problems in the field are unique. This is difficult to show, because the problems involving computing usually connect with our ordinary ethical problems in some way. Nevertheless, what makes the field of computer ethics special and important, though probably not unique, is the technology itself—the computer. Computers are logically malleable machines in that they can be shaped to do any task that one can design, train, or evolve them to do. Computers are universal tools, and this explains why they are so commonplace and culturally transforming. Because they are used in so many ways, new situations continually arise for which we do not have clear policies to guide actions. The use of computing creates policy vacuums. For instance, when wireless technology first appeared, there were questions about whether one should be allowed to access someone else's wireless system, for example, when driving down the street. Should such access be considered trespassing? Ethical rights and duties of novel situations are not always clear. Because computers are universal tools and can be applied in so many diverse ways, they tend to create many more policy vacuums than other technologies. This is one respect in which the ethical problems in computing are different from other fields, at least in degree if not in kind. This makes computer ethics an extraordinarily important discipline for all of us.

### How has information technology affected the field of ethics in the past two decades?

Twenty years ago, I had to search newspapers and magazines to find stories on computer/information ethics. Such stories were uncommon. Now many such stories appear daily. They are so common that the fact that computing is involved is unremarkable. Stories about body parts being sold on eBay or identity theft over the Internet or spam legislation all presuppose computing, but computing has so permeated our culture that it is not something uncommon, but something almost everybody uses. In a sense, much of ethics has become computer ethics!

### Why do you believe it is helpful to view computer ethics issues in terms of policies?

When we act ethically, we are acting such that anyone in a similar situation would be allowed to do the same kind of action. I am not allowed to have my own set of ethical policies that allow me to do things that others in a relevantly similar situation cannot do. Ethical policies are public policies. An act utilitarian, by contrast, would consider each situation individually. On this view, cheating would not only be justified but required if the individual doing the cheating benefited and others were not harmed because they did not know about it. This seems to me to be a paradigm of unethical behavior, and hence I advocate a public policy approach. If cheating is allowed for some, then everyone should be allowed to cheat in similar situations.

Rather than using "policies" I could use "rules." But ethical rules are sometimes regarded as binding without exceptions. A system of exceptionless rules will never work as an ethical theory, for rules can conflict and sometimes exceptions must be made because of extraordinary consequences. One might be justified in lying to save a life, for example. I prefer using the word "policy" because I want to suggest modification may be necessary in cases of conflict or in extraordinary circumstances. Notice that the policies involving exceptions must themselves be treated as public policy. If it is justifiable for someone to lie to save a life, it will be justified for others to lie to save a life in similar circumstances.

### Please explain the process of resolving an ethical issue using your theory of just consequentialism.

The view is somewhat like rule utilitarianism and somewhat like Kantian ethics but differs crucially from both of them. Rule utilitarians wish to maximize the good but typically without concern for justice. Just consequentialism does not require maximization of the good, which is in general unknowable, and does not sanction unjust policies simply because they have good consequences. Kant's theory requires us to act only on those maxims that we can will to be a universal law. But Kant's theory does not allow for exceptions. Kant thought one ought never lie. Moreover, the typical Kantian test question of what would happen if everyone did a certain kind of action is not the right question, for this test rules out far too much, for example, becoming a computer programmer (what if everyone were to become a computer programmer?). For just consequentialism, the test question is what would happen if everyone were *allowed* to do a certain kind of action. We need to consider both the consequences and the justice of our public policies.

In ethics we are concerned about rights and duties, and consequences of actions. Just consequentialism is a mixed system in that it is part deontological and part consequential. Rights and duties can be challenged if they are unfair or cause significant harm, but usually are properly taken as normative guides. One's rights as a citizen and one's duties as a parent are examples. In evaluating consequences we need to consider values that all people share, because we want to develop a policy that we can impartially publicly advocate. Everyone in similar circumstances should be allowed to follow it. At least some of these universal values to be considered are happiness, life, ability, security, knowledge, freedom, opportunity, and resources. Notice that these are core goods that any sane human wants regardless of which society the human is in.

In the ethical decision process, step one is to consider a set of policies for acting in the kind of situation under consideration. Step two is to consider the relevant duties, rights, and consequences involved with each policy. Step three is to decide whether the policy can be impartially advocated as a public policy, that is, anyone should be allowed to act in a similar way in similar circumstances. Many policies may be readily acceptable. Many may be easily rejected. And some may be in dispute, as people may weigh the relevant values differently or disagree about the factual outcomes.

In general, rights and duties carry prima facie weight in ethical decision making and, in general, cannot be overridden lightly. But if the consequences of following certain rights and duties are bad enough, then overriding them may be acceptable as long as this kind of exception can be an acceptable public policy. In controversial cases, there will be rational disagreements. Just consequentialism does not require complete agreement on every issue. Note that we have disagreements in ordinary nonethical decision making as well. But just consequentialism does guide us in determining where and why the disagreements occur so that further discussion and resolution may be possible.

*You have also studied the field of artificial intelligence from a philosophical point of view. Do you believe it is possible to create a truly intelligent machine capable of ethical decision making? If so, how far are we from making such a machine a reality?*

Nobody has shown that it is impossible, but I think we are very far away from such a possibility. The problem may have less to do with ethics than with epistemology. Computers (expert systems) sometimes possess considerable knowledge about special topics, but they lack commonsense knowledge. Without even the ability to understand simple things that any normal child can grasp, computers will not be able to make considered ethical decisions in any robust sense.

*Can an inanimate object have intrinsic moral worth, or is the value of an object strictly determined by its utility to one or more humans?*

I take values or moral worth to be a judgment based on standards. The standards that count for us are human. We judge other objects using our standards. This may go beyond utility, however, as we might judge a nonuseful object to be aesthetically pleasing. Our human standards might be challenged sometime in the future if robots developed consciousness or if we become cyborgs with a different set of standards. Stay tuned.

# 3 Networked Communications

Lo, soul, seest thou not God's purpose from the first?
The earth to be spann'd, connected by network,
The races, neighbors, to marry and be given in marriage,
The oceans to be cross'd, the distant brought near,
The lands to be welded together.

—WALT WHITMAN, "Passage to India"

## 3.1 Introduction

DURING GOVERNMENT MEETINGS IN WASHINGTON, DC, it's common for those sitting around the conference table to bow their heads. They're not praying—they're using their smartphones. "You'll have half the participants [texting] each other as a submeeting, with a running commentary on the primary meeting," reports Philippe Reines, who served as senior adviser to former Secretary of State Hillary Clinton [1].

Musician Ken Stringfellow of the Posies uses the Web to interact with his fans. "I log in to Facebook, and in like 30 seconds, I have like 50 people in my chat windows. And I answer their questions: 'Oh, yeah, you wanna get that record? I've got a couple of those in stock.' That kind of stuff" [2].

As busy as they are, adults continue to be hungry for news, but their sources are evolving. According to a 2014 survey, 78 percent of American adults who own smartphones use them to get news at least once a week, and 40 percent of adults get

**FIGURE 3.1** Far more people in the world have access to cell phones than have access to electricity or clean water. (Charles Sturge/Alamy)

some of their news from social media. The survey also revealed that people who own more information technology are more likely to say "they enjoy keeping up with the news" [3].

The Internet has opened up new opportunities for politicians to attract donations. During his successful run for the presidency in 2008, Barack Obama raised $500 million from three million donors who contributed over the Internet [4]. A grassroots movement supporting long-shot presidential candidate Ron Paul raised $4 million for him in a single day in 2007 [5]. Eight years later, his son Rand Paul became the first presidential candidate in history to accept donations in the form of bitcoins [6].

These stories illustrate how networked communications have become integrated into our lives. The Internet and cellular networks efficiently support our desire to interact with other people and accomplish a wide variety of everyday tasks (Figure 3.1). On the other hand, some people use these technologies to lower the quality of our lives through such activities as trying to sell us products we don't want to buy, harassing us, or luring us into wasting our time with frivolous or counterproductive activities.

In this chapter we explore how people use and abuse the Internet and cellular networks. We discuss how people communicate with one another and how they organize and find information. Some governments are threatened by the way in which modern networks have supported these activities; we detail various kinds of censorship and consider appropriate limits to the freedom of expression. We also discuss and evaluate new behaviors that have emerged with the growth of these networks, such as sexting, cyberbullying, and Internet addiction.

# 3.2 Spam

The growth of email has been phenomenal—about 2.5 billion people now have email accounts [7]. Every day about 200 billion email messages are sent. Unfortunately, a significant percentage of this traffic consists of unsolicited bulk email, or **spam**.

Why is spam called spam? Brad Templeton, chairman of the board of the Electronic Frontier Foundation, traces the term back to the SPAM sketch from *The Final Rip Off* by Monty Python's Flying Circus, in which a group of Vikings drown out a cafe conversation by loudly and obnoxiously repeating the word "spam" [8]. In a similar way, legitimate email messages can get "drowned out" by spam.

## 3.2.1 The Spam Epidemic

The rise of spam corresponds with the transformation of the Internet from a noncommercial academic and research enterprise into a commercial global network. Early spam messages provoked Internet users and generated big headlines. For example, in 1994 Phoenix lawyers Laurence Canter and Martha Siegel sent an email advertising their immigration services to more than 9,000 electronic newsgroups. Canter and Siegel received tens of thousands of responses from outraged newsgroup users who did not appreciate seeing an off-topic, commercial message. The *New York Times* reported the incident with the tongue-in-cheek headline, "An Ad (Gasp!) in Cyberspace." Canter and Siegel were undeterred. Their ad was successful in bringing them new clients. "We will definitely advertise on the Web again," Canter said. "I'm sure other businesses will be advertising on the network in the very near future" [9].

As recently as the year 2000, spam accounted for only about 8 percent of all email. It was still viewed as a problem for individuals to handle as they managed their mailboxes. By 2009 about 90 percent of all emails were spam (Figure 3.2) [10]. Today spam consumes a large percentage of the Internet's bandwidth and huge amounts of storage space on mail servers and individual computers. An entire industry has grown up developing software designed to filter out spam. Even with spam filters in place, the cost to businesses from spam that gets through is estimated at billions of dollars per year in wasted productivity.

The volume of spam is so large because spam is effective. The principal advantage of spam is its low cost compared to other forms of advertising. For about $10, a company can send an advertisement to a million different email addresses [11]. Sending the same advertisement to a million addresses using the US Postal Service costs at least $40,000 for the mailing list and $280,000 for bulk-rate postage. And that doesn't include the cost of the brochures! In other words, an email advertisement is more than 30,000 times cheaper than a traditional flyer sent out in the mail.

Where do spammers get email lists with millions of addresses? The Internet provides a variety of sources of email addresses that can be harvested and sold to spammers. For example, email addresses often appear in Web sites, in chat-room conversations, and newsgroups. Some computer viruses gather email addresses stored in the address books of PCs and transmit these addresses to spammers.

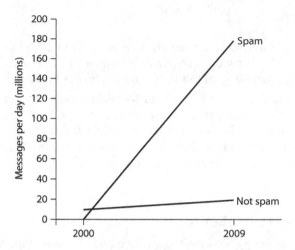

**FIGURE 3.2** The increase in spam between 2000 and 2009. In 2000 spam accounted for 8 percent of all email. By 2009 the volume of email had increased 20-fold, and about 90 percent of email messages were spam.

Another way to garner email addresses is through dictionary attacks (also called directory harvest attacks). Spammers bombard Internet service providers (ISPs) with millions of emails containing made-up addresses, such as AdamA@isprovider.com, AdamB@isprovider.com, AdamC@isprovider.com, and so on. Of course, most of these emails will bounce back, because the addresses are no good. However, if an email doesn't bounce, the spammer knows there is a user with that email address and adds it to its mailing list.

Sometimes people voluntarily reveal their email address. Have you ever entered a contest on the Web? There is a good chance the fine print on the entry form said you agree to receive "occasional offers of products you might find valuable" from the company's marketing partners; in other words, spam [12]. Sign-ups for email lists often contain this fine print, too.

How can spammers send out so many email messages? About 90 percent of spam is sent out by bot herders: people who are able to take control of huge networks of computers. Bot herders create these networks by launching programs that search the Internet for computers with inadequate security and install software robot programs, called bots, on these vulnerable systems. A computer with the bot program installed on it is called a zombie because it can be directed by a remote computer to perform certain tasks. Bot herders can send out billions of email messages every day by dividing the address lists among hundreds of thousands of zombies they control [13].

To deal with this deluge, ISPs install spam filters to block spam from reaching users' mailboxes. These filters look for a large number of messages coming from the same email address, messages with suspicious subject lines, or messages with spamlike content.

### 3.2.2 Need for Social–Technical Solutions

As we saw in Chapter 1, new technologies sometimes cause new social situations to emerge. The spam epidemic is an example of this phenomenon. The Internet allows people to send email messages for virtually no cost. Because a spammer's profits increase as the number of sent messages increases, every spammer has an incentive to send as many messages as possible.

The spam problem arose because the Internet and email technology developed without taking social expectations into account. The design of the Internet allows sophisticated users to disguise their own email addresses. Spammers take advantage of this loophole to send out millions of messages, knowing that unhappy recipients will not be able to respond. This is contrary to a fundamental social expectation: fairness. In order to be fair, communications should be two-way, not one-way [14].

### 3.2.3 Case Study: Ann the Acme Accountant

Ann is an accountant at Acme Corporation, a medium-sized firm with 50 employees. All the employees work in the same building, and Ann knows all of them on a first-name basis. In fact, Ann distributes paychecks to Acme's employees at the end of every month.

Ann's 10-year-old daughter is a Girl Scout. During the annual Girl Scout cookie sale, Ann sent an email to all the other Acme employees, inviting them to stop by her desk during a break and place orders. (There is no company rule prohibiting the use of the email system for personal emails.) Nine of the recipients were happy to get Ann's email, and they ordered an average of four boxes of cookies, but the other 40 recipients did not appreciate having to take the time to read and delete an unwanted message; half of them complained to a coworker about Ann's action.

Did Ann do anything wrong?

#### KANTIAN ANALYSIS

According to the second formulation of the Categorical Imperative, we should always respect the autonomy of other people, treating them as ends in themselves and never only as the means to an end. The story provides evidence that Ann was not simply "using" her coworkers as the means to her end of making money for the Girl Scouts. She didn't misrepresent what she was doing. She didn't force anyone to buy the cookies or even read the entire email; employees not interested in Girl Scout cookies could simply delete Ann's message as soon as they read the subject line. Some people who received the email freely chose to buy some cookies. Therefore, what Ann did wasn't strictly wrong.

On the other hand, if Ann had found a way for those people interested in hearing about the Girl Scout cookie drive to "opt in" to her announcement, those people not interested in purchasing Girl Scout cookies would not have been bothered by her email. An "opt in" approach would have been better because it would have shown more respect for the time of Ann's coworkers.

## ACT UTILITARIAN ANALYSIS

We will do our evaluation in terms of dollars and cents, quantifying the benefits and costs of Ann's action. Let's begin with the benefits. A box of cookies costs $4 and provides $3 of profit to the Girl Scouts. Someone who buys a box of Girl Scout cookies understands it is a fund-raising activity and is happy with what he receives for $4. Since the cost of $4 is matched with $4 of benefit, they cancel each other out in our analysis, and we do not have to worry about this factor anymore. The average employee who participated in the sale purchased four boxes of cookies. Nine employees participated, which means Ann sold 36 boxes of cookies and provided $108 of benefit to the Girl Scouts.

Now let's look at the harms. The principal harm is going to be the time wasted by Acme's employees. Ann took orders and made deliveries during coffee or lunch breaks, rather than on company time, so our focus is on the 40 employees who did not appreciate getting Ann's solicitation. It's reasonable to assume that they spent an average of 15 seconds reading and deleting the message. That adds up to 10 minutes of lost productivity.

Half of the employees spent 5 minutes complaining about what Ann did with a coworker. You can imagine the typical conversation. "What makes her so special?" "How does she get away with this kind of thing?" "If I did this for my kid, I'd get in trouble." Taking both the employee's time and the coworker's time into account, Acme loses 10 minutes of productivity for each conversation. Multiplying 10 minutes by 20 conversations gives us 200 minutes.

The total time wasted equals 210 minutes or 3.5 hours. Assume the average Acme employee makes $20 per hour. The cost of the lost productivity is 3.5 hours times $20 per hour or $70.

The benefit of $108 exceeds the cost of $70, so we may conclude that Ann's action was good. We should note, however, that all the benefit went to the Girls Scouts and all the cost was borne by Acme Corporation. It would be perfectly reasonable if the owners of Acme Corporation concluded that this kind of activity was not in the best interests of the company and created a new policy forbidding the use of company email for cookie drives and other fund-raisers.

## RULE UTILITARIAN ANALYSIS

What would the consequences be if everyone used the company email system to solicit donations to their favorite causes? All the employees would receive many more messages unrelated to business. There would be plenty of grumbling among employees, lowering morale. Reading and deleting these solicitations would waste people's time, a definite harm. It's unlikely that any one cause would do well if everyone was trying to raise money for his or her own charity. There is a good chance the owner would become aware of this problem, and a logical response would be to ban employees from sending out this kind of solicitation. Because the harms are much greater than the benefits, it is wrong to use the company email system to solicit donations to a charity.

## SOCIAL CONTRACT THEORY ANALYSIS

Acme Corporation does not have a prohibition against using the company's email system for personal business. You could say that by sending out her email solicitation, Ann was exercising her right to free speech. Of course, she did it in a way that many people might find obnoxious, because even if they did not choose to read her entire message, they had to take the time to scan the subject line and delete it. Unlike spammers, however, Ann did not disguise her identity as the sender, thereby providing unhappy recipients with the opportunity to respond to her email and voice their disapproval of her solicitation. If many of the 40 people who did not appreciate receiving her email sent a reply communicating their displeasure, then Ann got a taste of her own medicine by having to wade through a bunch of unwanted email messages, and she may choose a better method of advertising the Girl Scout cookie drive next year. From a social contract theory point of view, Ann did nothing wrong.

## VIRTUE ETHICS ANALYSIS

Good coworkers exhibit many virtues, including honesty, dependability, fairness, friendliness, and respect for coworkers. Three that seem particularly important for this case study are honesty, fairness, and respect. Ann demonstrated honesty by being completely straightforward about the Girl Scout cookie drive with her fellow employees. However, it wasn't fair or respectful for Ann to use the email system to promote her own daughter's fund-raiser when other employees have not used email for similar solicitations for their children. Ann clearly exercised poor judgment when she sent the email, since half of the company's employees felt the need to complain about it.

Looking at this scenario from a completely different angle, we consider Ann in her role as a parent. Good parents want what is best for their children, and Ann was undoubtedly thinking of her daughter's welfare when she decided to sell the Girl Scout cookies at her workplace. Perhaps her daughter has a quota to meet, or perhaps nice prizes are given to those who sell enough boxes of cookies. Viewed in this light, Ann's actions seem consistent with those of a loving parent. However, parents are also supposed to teach their children how to develop into capable and independent adults. Ann could have used the cookie sale as an opportunity to teach her daughter some of those lessons. After all, her daughter is 10 years old, certainly old enough to handle many of the tasks. Instead, Ann ran the entire cookie sale operation herself and simply handed her daughter the proceeds.

We conclude Ann demonstrated many, but not all, of the characteristics of a good coworker and a good parent in this episode. If Ann wanted to help her 10-year-old daughter sell cookies, fine, but she should have found a way for her daughter to play a more active role in the cookie sale at Acme Corporation. For example, her daughter could have come in after school one day to deliver the cookies to the people who ordered them and collect their payments. In this way Ann's daughter could have gained the satisfaction of knowing she had contributed a good portion of the time and effort needed to achieve the desired result. Furthermore, Ann should have found another way to advertise the sale that respected her workplace's culture of keeping the email system free from solicitations.

## SUMMARY

Although the analyses of Ann's action from the perspectives of these five ethical theories reached different conclusions, it is clear she could have taken another course of action that would have been much less controversial. Since Ann has only 49 coworkers, it would not have been too difficult for her to find out who wanted to be notified the next time the Girl Scouts were selling cookies. She could have put a sign-up sheet on her desk or the company bulletin board, for example. By notifying only those people who signed up, Ann's emails would have been solicited and personal. She could still take advantage of the efficiency of the email system without anyone objecting that she was "using" coworkers or contributing to lost productivity, meaning there would be much less chance of the company instituting a policy forbidding the use of its email system for fund-raising activities. Finally, Ann could have found a way to share the work with her daughter.

# 3.3 Internet Interactions

The Internet mediates communications and commerce among more than two billion people. In this section we review just a few of the myriad number of ways people are using the Internet to interact with others and gain access to information.

## 3.3.1 The World Wide Web

The creation of the World Wide Web stimulated a tremendous growth in the popularity of the Internet. Its creator, Tim Berners-Lee, initially proposed the Web as a documentation system for CERN, the Swiss research center for particle physics, but the creation of easy-to-use Web browsers made the Web accessible to "ordinary" computer users as well [15]. The Web is a hypertext system: a flexible database of information that allows Web pages to be linked to each other in arbitrary fashion. Web browsers such as Chrome, Internet Explorer, Firefox, and Safari allow people to traverse this hypertext system with ease.

Two attributes enabled the Web to become a global tool for information exchange. First, it is decentralized. An individual or organization can add new information to the Web without asking for permission from a central authority. Second, every object on the Web has a unique address. Any object can link to any other object by referencing its address. A Web object's address is called a **URL** (uniform resource locator).

## 3.3.2 Mobile Apps

People are spending more time on smartphones and tablets and less time on laptop or desktop computers. Using Web browsers on mobile devices can be awkward, and for this reason organizations are developing **mobile apps**: software programs that are loaded onto mobile devices. Some mobile apps are stand-alone programs, but others connect to the Internet, allowing people to download and upload data. Mobile apps are becoming an increasingly popular way to access the Internet because they can be optimized to make the best use of a mobile device's resources (limited screen size, touch interface, etc.) [16].

### 3.3.3  How We Use the Internet

Intuitive Web browsers and mobile apps have made the Internet accessible to people with little or no formal computer training. Today millions of people access the Internet for a wide variety of purposes. Here are just a few examples of how people are using the Internet.

1. *We shop.*

   Shopping sites enable us to view and order merchandise from the comfort of our homes. According to the US Census Bureau, ecommerce represented 7 percent of all retail sales in the United States in the first quarter of 2015 [17].

2. *We socialize.*

   The Internet has become a popular way for friends to keep in touch with each other. The most popular social network is Facebook, with more than 1.4 billion active users in March 2015. Another well-known social network is LinkedIn, which serves people looking for professional contacts.

   In 2012 the Dutch airline KLM launched a program that allows ticketed passengers who have uploaded information from their Facebook or LinkedIn profiles to select seatmates based on the profiles provided by other passengers [18].

3. *We contribute content.*

   Popular apps allow people to upload videos, photos, podcasts, or other digital content. Instagram, with more than 300 million subscribers, allows its users to upload photos and videos and share them on social networking services, such as Facebook.

   A **wiki** is a Web site that allows multiple people to contribute and edit its content. The most famous wiki is *Wikipedia*, an online encyclopedia. Relying on the submissions of hundreds of thousands of volunteers, *Wikipedia* has become by far the largest encyclopedia in the world. Fifty languages are represented by at least 100,000 articles, but by far the most popular language is English, with nearly five million articles written as of 2015. However, critics wonder about the quality of a reference work that allows anyone with a Web browser to contribute [19].

4. *We blog.*

   A **blog** (short for "Web log") is a personal journal or diary kept on the Web. Used as a verb, the word blog means to maintain such a journal. Blogs may contain plain text, images, audio clips, or video clips [20].

   Some commentators use the term **Web 2.0** to refer to a change in the way people use the Web. Social networking services, wikis, Flickr, Reddit, and blogs illustrate that hundreds of millions of people are now using the Web not simply to access content but to build communities and upload and share content they have created.

5. *We visit secret Web sites.*

   A **darknet** is a network of Web sites that can only be accessed through special software that encrypts messages and provides users with anonymity. Darknets are popular with people who have something to hide: pedophiles, drug dealers, illegal arms traffickers, and the like. However, Edward Snowden's disclosure of surveillance by the National Security Agency has prompted some people to ponder whether everybody should be using darknets on the principle that the government should not be spying on law-abiding citizens [21].

6. *We crowdsource information.*

   **Crowdsourcing** is an online method of getting information or ideas from a large group of people. The Waze app is an example of crowdsourcing. People use Waze to find the quickest way to drive from one place to another. If they allow the app to run while they are driving, it sends their car's GPS coordinates to Waze, which computes vehicle speeds and then uses this information about traffic congestion to help other Waze users find the best route [22].

7. *We learn.*

   In 2001 the Massachusetts Institute of Technology launched its OpenCourseWare initiative. Since then, the quantity and quality of freely available classes posted online has increased steadily. The potential for **massive open online courses** (**MOOCs**) provided by edX, Coursera, and Udacity to disrupt traditional university education is being widely debated [23].

8. *We explore our roots.*

   In the past, genealogists interested in accessing American immigration and census records had the choice between mailing in their requests and waiting for them to be processed or visiting the National Archives and examining the documents by hand. Now FamilySearch.org offers free access to indexes to US census information from 1790 to 1940, allowing genealogical research to be performed remotely—and much more quickly—over the Internet.

9. *We enter virtual worlds.*

   An **online game** is a game played on a computer network that supports the simultaneous participation of multiple players. Over 700 million people play online games [24]. The Internet enables people to play games with total strangers and makes it possible for aficionados of obscure games to find opponents.

   A **persistent online game** is an online game in which each player assumes the role of a character in a virtual world and the attributes of the character and the world persist beyond a single gaming session. The most popular persistent online game is World of Warcraft, with 7 million subscribers [25]. At times, the number of simultaneous players in China alone has reached one million [26].

   Another hub of persistent online gaming is South Korea. Cybercafes (called **PC bangs** in South Korea) have large-screen monitors enabling spectators to watch the gameplay, which is full of virtual violence and mayhem. Some children spend up to 10 hours a day playing games, hoping to turn professional. Kim Hyun Soo, chairman of the Net Addiction Treatment Center, complains that "young people are losing their ability to relate to each other, except through games" [27]. We discuss the topic of Internet addiction in Section 3.9.

   The phenomenon of global online gaming has created a real economy based on virtual worlds. Some people are making a living playing persistent online games. Chinese "gold farmers" who work 12 hours a day, 7 days a week can earn $3,000 a year killing monsters, harvesting virtual gold coins and artifacts, creating powerful avatars, and selling them over the Internet [28].

10. *We control the Internet of Things.*

An increasing number of non-IT devices—thermostats, appliances, lights, motion sensors, door locks, garage door openers, and baby monitors, to name just a few examples—are being equipped with wireless connections to the Internet, forming an **Internet of Things**. These devices can be controlled from a Web browser, allowing people to control them even when they are not at home.

More significantly, some Internet-connected devices can be programmed to interact with each other without human intervention. Imagine devices at home that can monitor the GPS coordinates of your smartphone. You're driving home after a long, hot day at work. When your car is 15 minutes away from home, the air conditioning in your home turns on. You turn onto your street, and your porch lights turn on. As you pull into your driveway, the garage door opens automatically [29].

11. *We pay our taxes.*

About 122 million Americans filed their federal income tax returns online in 2013 [30].

12. *We gamble.*

Internet gambling is a $32-billion-a-year global business [31]. Running an Internet-based casino is illegal in most states. As a result, many American émigrés are operating gambling sites from the Caribbean or Central America [32].

13. *We take humanitarian action.*

Kiva is a Web site supporting person-to-person microlending. Kiva works with microfinance institutions to identify entrepreneurs from poor communities, and it posts information about these entrepreneurs on its Web site. People who wish to make an interest-free loan are able to identify the particular person to whom they would like to lend money. Lenders have the ability to communicate with the entrepreneurs and see the impact their loans are having on the recipients, their families, and their communities [33].

# 3.4 Text Messaging

Text messaging greatly increases the versatility of cell phones as information-sharing platforms. Some of the most impressive uses of text messaging are in developing countries, where people do not have easy access to the Internet, banks, and other services taken for granted by people in more developed countries.

## 3.4.1 Transforming Lives in Developing Countries

Text-message-based services such as M-PESA in Kenya allow people in developing countries to save money and pay bills using their cell phones, bypassing traditional banks. To pay a bill or transfer funds to a friend, the user simply types a text message that the recipient is able to turn into cash at any M-PESA office.

For the past decade, Kenya's Agricultural Commodities Exchange has partnered with Safaricom to provide information about crop prices to farmers via a text messaging service. Another service, iCow, uses voice and text messaging to help dairy farmers keep track of the gestation of their cows [34].

Counterfeit medicine is a serious problem in many African and Asian countries. Ghanian Bright Simons came up with the idea of putting scratch cards with unique codes on packages of medicine. After scratching the package to reveal the code, a customer can text the code to a designated number to learn if the drug is genuine [34].

### 3.4.2 Twitter

Twitter is a Web-based social networking service that allows its users to send out text messages known as **tweets**. Tweets are limited to 140 characters because that's the maximum length of a cell phone text message. The service is popular because people who want their friends to know what they are doing find it more convenient to post a single tweet than to type a bunch of text messages. Many people also use Twitter as a blogging tool; they make their tweets public so that anyone can read them. Other Twitter members never post tweets, but they sign up to follow the tweets posted by other people they are interested in.

More than 300 million people use Twitter regularly, making it one of the most popular Web services in the world [35]. Users posted a record 580,166 tweets per minute during the World Cup Final soccer match between Germany and Brazil in 2014 [36].

### 3.4.3 Business Promotion

When carpenter Curtis Kimball started a part-time business running a crème brûlée cart in San Francisco, he used Twitter to let people know the cart's location and the flavors of the day. Before long, he had attracted 5,400 followers. Business became so good he quit his day job in order to keep up with demand. Many tiny businesses with no money for advertising rely upon Twitter as their only marketing tool [37].

### 3.4.4 Political Activism

Text messaging played an important role in the ouster of Philippine president Joseph Estrada in 2001. During his impeachment trial, his political allies in the Philippine Congress voted to keep some evidence against him from being revealed. Filipinos who hoped to see President Estrada convicted used text messaging to organize a demonstration on Epifanio de los Santos Avenue in Manila. Over the next couple of days, millions more text messages were sent and forwarded—many reading "Go 2 EDSA. Wear blk."—and the crowd rose to more than one million people. Intimidated by the size of the protest, Estrada's supporters in the Philippine Congress changed their votes and allowed the incriminating evidence against President Estrada to be released. Within hours, Estrada's presidency was over [38].

Ten years later, Twitter and Facebook played a highly visible role in the "Arab Spring" demonstrations that led to revolutions in Tunisia and Egypt, a civil war in Libya, and protests in many other Arab countries. In the midst of the protests in Cairo in 2011 that led to the resignation of President Hosni Mubarak, one protester tweeted, "We use Facebook to schedule the protests, Twitter to coordinate, and YouTube to tell the world" [39]. Arab news organization Al Jazeera created a "Twitter Dashboard" indicating the level of tweeting activity in many Arab nations where there was unrest [40].

Scholars of the Arab Spring uprisings point to an interesting phenomenon: People started using online social networks such as Twitter in order to keep up with their friends, but these interactions caused them to become politicized. Through these networks, bloggers met new people, became exposed to new ideas, and developed an interest in human rights [41].

Others think the role of social media in catalyzing social change has been overblown. They argue that social networks like Twitter and Facebook are great at building networks of people with weak connections to each other, but high-risk activism requires strong ties among the members of a hierarchical organization [42].

# 3.5 Censorship

**Censorship** is the attempt to suppress or regulate public access to material considered offensive or harmful. Historically, most censorship has been exercised by governments and religious institutions. For example, Roman censors banished the poets Ovid and Juvenal for their writings. During the Middle Ages the Inquisition suppressed the publication of many books, including the work of Galileo Galilei.

Censorship became a much more complicated issue with the invention of the printing press. The printing press broke the virtual monopoly held by governments and religious institutions on distributing material to a large audience, and the increase in printed material resulted in a greater number of literate people. For the first time, private individuals could broadcast their ideas to others on a wide scale.

In Western democracies, the gradual separation of church and state left the government as the sole institution responsible for censorship. In other parts of the world, such as the Middle East, religious institutions continue to play a significant role in determining what material should be accessible to the public.

## 3.5.1 Direct Censorship

Direct censorship has three forms: government monopolization, prepublication review, and licensing and registration.

The first form of direct censorship is government monopolization. In the former Soviet Union, for example, the government owned all the television stations, radio stations, and newspapers. Private organizations could not even own a photocopy machine. Government monopolization is an effective way to suppress the flow of information. Modern computer and communication technology makes government monopolization much more difficult than in the past.

Prepublication review is the second form of direct censorship. This form of censorship is essential for material the government wishes to keep secret, such as information about its nuclear weapons program. Most governments have laws restricting the publication of information that would harm national security. In addition, autocratic governments typically block publication of material deemed injurious to the reputations of their rulers.

The third form of direct censorship is licensing and registration. This form of censorship is typically used to control media with limited bandwidth. For example, there are a limited number of radio and television stations that can be accommodated on the electromagnetic spectrum. Hence a radio or television station must obtain a license to broadcast at a particular frequency. Licensing invites censorship. For example, the US Federal Communications Commission has banned the use of certain four-letter words. This led to a challenge that went all the way to the US Supreme Court, as we see in Section 3.6.3.

### 3.5.2 Self–Censorship

Perhaps the most common form of censorship is self-censorship: a group deciding for itself not to publish material. In some countries a publisher may censor itself in order to avoid persecution. For example, after US-led forces toppled the regime of Saddam Hussein in April 2003, CNN's chief news executive, Eason Jordan, admitted that CNN had suppressed negative information about the actions of the Iraqi government for more than a decade in order to keep CNN's Baghdad bureau open and protect Iraqi employees of CNN [43].

In other countries, publishers may want to maintain good relations with government officials. Publications compete with each other for access to information. Often this information is available only from government sources. Publishers know that if they offend the government, their reporters may not be given access to as much information as reporters for rival publications, putting them at a competitive disadvantage. This knowledge can lead a "free" press to censor itself.

Publishers have adopted ratings systems as a way of helping people decide if they (or their children) should access particular offerings. For example, television stations in the United States broadcast shows with "mature content" late in the evening. Voluntary ratings systems help people decide if they (or their children) will see a movie, watch a television show, or listen to a CD.

The Web does not have a universally accepted ratings system. Some Web sites practice a form of labeling. For example, the home page may warn the user that the site contains nudity and require the user to click on an "I agree" button to enter the site. However, other sites have no such warnings. People who stumble onto these sites are immediately confronted with images and text they may find offensive.

### 3.5.3 Challenges Posed by the Internet

Five characteristics of the Internet make censorship more difficult:

1. *Unlike traditional one-to-many broadcast media, the Internet supports many-to-many communications.*

   While it is relatively easy for a government to shut down a newspaper or a radio station, it is very difficult for a government to prevent an idea from being published on the Internet, where millions of people have the ability to post Web pages.

2. *The Internet is dynamic.*

   Millions of new devices are being connected to the Internet each year.

3. *The Internet is huge.*

   There is simply no way for a team of human censors to keep track of everything that is posted on the Web. While automated tools are available, they are fallible. Hence any attempt to control access to material stored on the Internet cannot be 100 percent effective.

4. *The Internet is global.*

   National governments have limited authority to restrict activities happening outside their borders.

5. *It is hard to distinguish between children and adults on the Internet.*

   How can an "adult" Web site verify the age of someone attempting to enter the site?

### 3.5.4 Government Filtering and Surveillance of Internet Content

Despite the difficulties facing those who would seek to censor Internet content, studies reveal that governments around the globe are in fact limiting access to the Internet in a variety of ways [44].

One approach is to make the Internet virtually inaccessible. In North Korea, for example, only 4 percent of the population has access to the Internet [45].

In other countries, Internet access is easier but still carefully controlled. Saudi Arabians gained access to the Internet in 1999, after the government installed a centralized control center outside Riyadh. Virtually all Internet traffic flows through this control center, which blocks pornography sites, gambling sites, and many other pages deemed to be offensive to Islam or the government of Saudi Arabia [46]. Blocked sites and pages are from such diverse categories as Christian evangelism, women's health and sexuality issues, music and movies, gay rights, Middle Eastern politics, and information about ways to circumvent Web filtering.

The Chinese government has blocked access to the Internet during times of social unrest. For example, in July 2009, China responded to ethnic riots in the autonomous region of Xinjiang by turning off Internet service to the entire region for 10 months [47, 48].

China has also built one of the world's most sophisticated Web filtering systems [49]. The Great Firewall of China prevents Chinese citizens from accessing certain Internet content by blocking messages coming from blacklisted sites. The government employs human censors to identify sites that should be blacklisted [50]. Among the Web sites blacklisted by the government include those containing pornography, those associated with the Dalai Lama or the Falun Gong, those referring to the 1989 military crackdown, and those run by certain news organizations, such as Voice of America and BBC News. Before the 2008 Summer Olympics, the International Olympic Committee assured journalists that they would have unfettered access to the Internet during their stay in Beijing, but once the journalists arrived in Beijing, they discovered that many sites were blocked. The International Olympic Committee admitted that it had agreed to allow to be blocked sensitive sites "not considered Games related" [51]. Some contend that blogs and nongovernmental Web sites are eroding the Chinese government's ability to restrict the communications of its citizens [50], but the government has not given up. The government continues to shut down Web sites and censor blogs that it finds contrary to the interests of the state.

Meanwhile, Western nations have different standards about what is acceptable and what is not. For example, Germany forbids access to any neo-Nazi Web site, but Web surfers in the United States can access many such sites.

Political satire and pornography are easily available through American ISPs. Americans are used to political satire, but many citizens are concerned about the corrupting influence of pornography, particularly with respect to minors. Since 1996 the US Congress has passed three laws aimed at restricting children's access to sexually explicit material on the Web: the Communications Decency Act, the Child Online Protection Act, and the Children's Internet Protection Act. The first two laws were ruled unconstitutional by the US Supreme Court; the third was upheld by the Supreme Court in June 2003.

### 3.5.5 Ethical Perspectives on Censorship

It is interesting that Immanuel Kant and John Stuart Mill, who had quite different ethical theories, had similar views regarding censorship.

#### KANT'S VIEWS ON CENSORSHIP

As a thinker in the tradition of the Enlightenment, Kant's motto was, "Have courage to use your own reason" [52]. Kant asks the rhetorical question, "Why don't people think for themselves?" and answers it: "Laziness and cowardice are the reasons why so great a portion of mankind, after nature has long since discharged them from external direction, nevertheless remain under lifelong tutelage, and why it is so easy for others to set themselves up as their guardians. It is so easy not to be of age. If I have a book which understands for me, a pastor who has a conscience for me, a physician who decides my diet, and so forth, I need not trouble myself. I need not think, if I can only pay—others will readily undertake the irksome work for me" [52, p. 85].

The Enlightenment was a reaction to the institutional control over thought held by the aristocracy and the Church. Kant believed he was living in a time in which the obstacles preventing people from exercising their own reason were being removed. He opposed censorship as a backward step.

## MILL'S VIEWS ON CENSORSHIP

John Stuart Mill also championed freedom of expression. He gave four reasons why freedom of opinion, and freedom of expression of opinion, were necessary.

First, none of us is infallible. All of us are capable of error. If we prevent someone from voicing their opinion, we may actually be silencing the voice of truth.

Second, while the opinion expressed by someone may be erroneous, it may yet contain a kernel of truth. In general, the majority opinion is not the whole truth. We ought to let all opinions be voiced so that all parts of the truth are heard.

Third, even if the majority opinion should happen to be the whole truth, it is in the clash of ideas that this truth is rationally tested and validated. The whole truth left untested is simply a prejudice.

Fourth, an opinion that has been tested in the fire of a free and open discourse is more likely to have a "vital effect on the character and conduct" [53, p. 61].

Therefore, Mill, like Kant, fundamentally supported the free exchange of ideas, with the conviction that good ideas would prevail over bad ones. Applying their philosophy to the World Wide Web, it seems they would support the free exchange of opinions and oppose any kind of government censorship of opinions.

## MILL'S PRINCIPLE OF HARM

However, a lack of government censorship can also lead to harm. Under what circumstances should the government intervene? Mill proposed the principle of harm as a way of deciding when an institution should intervene in the conduct of an individual.

~

### PRINCIPLE OF HARM

The only purpose for which power can be rightfully exercised over any member of a civilized community, against his will, is to prevent harm to others. His own good, either physical or moral, is not a sufficient warrant. [53, p. 12]

~

In other words, the government should not get involved in the private activities of individuals, even if the individuals are doing something to harm themselves. Only if individuals' activities are harming other people should the government step in.

The principle of harm can be used to explain the position of most Western democratic governments with respect to censoring pornographic material depicting adults. Some ethicists conclude it is not wrong for adults to view pornography depicting adults. Others hold that this activity is immoral. If the activity is immoral, it is more certain the harm is being done to the individual consumer; less certain is how much harm is being done to other people. Hence the principle of harm can be used as an argument why the government should not be trying to prevent adults from using pornography depicting adults.

# 3.6 Freedom of Expression

In the United States, freedom of expression is one of the most cherished—and most controversial—rights. In this section we explain the history behind the adoption of the First Amendment to the United States Constitution. We also explore why the freedom of expression has not been treated as an absolute right.

## 3.6.1 History

At the time of the American Revolution, any criticism of government was seen as a threat to public order and could result in fines and/or imprisonment. Restrictions on freedom of speech in England date back to 1275 and a law called De Scandalis Magnatum. According to this law, a person could be imprisoned for spreading stories about the King that could have the effect of weakening the loyalty of his subjects. The scope of the law became much broader through numerous revisions over the next two centuries. Eventually, it encompassed seditious words and words spoken against a wide variety of government officials, including justices [54].

De Scandalis Magnatum was administered by the Court of Star Chamber, or "Star Chamber" for short. The Star Chamber reported directly to the King, and it did not have to obey traditional rules of evidence. Rulings of the Star Chamber demonstrated that a person could be convicted for making a verbal insult or for something written in a private letter. The Star Chamber was abolished in 1641, but the law continued to be enforced through Common Law courts [54].

At the end of the eighteenth century, freedom of the press in England and its colonies meant freedom to print without a license. In other words, there were no **prior restraints** on publication. People could publish what they pleased. However, those who published material found to be seditious or libelous would face severe consequences [54].

The law against libel simply considered if the material printed was harmful; arguing that the information was true was not relevant to the proceedings and could not be used in a publisher's defense. Between 1760 and the end of the American Revolution, about 50 people were successfully prosecuted for libel. To prevent such prosecutions from continuing, most states adopted bills of rights after gaining independence from England [54].

In May 1787, delegates from the thirteen states gathered in Philadelphia to revise the Articles of Confederation. Soon they were drafting a completely new Constitution. Delegate George Mason, author of the Virginia Declaration of Rights, strongly opposed the proposed Constitution because it contained no declaration of the rights of the citizens. Patrick Henry and other political leaders shared Mason's objections [54].

While the proposed Constitution was ratified by all thirteen states, most state legislatures adopted the Constitution with the expectation that Congress would offer amendments addressing the human rights concerns brought up by the opponents of the Constitution. During the first Congress, James Madison proposed 12 such amendments. All 12 of these amendments were sent to the states for ratification. Of these 12 amendments, 10 were quickly ratified. Today these 10 amendments are commonly known as the Bill of

**FIGURE 3.3** Jeremy Jaynes was convicted under Virginia law for sending millions of spam messages. His conviction was overturned by the Supreme Court of Virginia because the antispam law was too broad and also prohibited the anonymous transmission of unsolicited bulk emails "containing political, religious or other speech protected by the First Amendment to the United States Constitution" [57]. (The News & Observer/AP Images)

Rights. The first of these amendments, the one Madison considered most essential, was the one guaranteeing freedom of speech and freedom of the press [54].

## FIRST AMENDMENT TO THE UNITED STATES CONSTITUTION

Congress shall make no law respecting an establishment of religion, or prohibiting the free exercise thereof; or abridging the freedom of speech, or of the press; or the right of the people peaceably to assemble, and to petition the government for a redress of grievances.

### 3.6.2 Freedom of Expression Not an Absolute Right

The primary purpose of the First Amendment's free speech guarantee is political. Free speech allows an open discussion of public issues. It helps make government responsive to the will of the people [55].

However, the First Amendment right to free expression is not limited to political speech. Nonpolitical speech is also covered (Figure 3.3). There are good reasons for protecting nonpolitical as well as political speech. First, it is sometimes hard to draw the line between the two. Asking a judge to make the distinction turns it into a political decision. Second, society can benefit from nonpolitical as well as political speech. Hence the free speech guarantee of the First Amendment also promotes scientific and artistic expression. For the same reason, the definition of "speech" encompasses more than words. Protected "speech" includes art and certain kinds of conduct, such as burning an American flag [56].

Decisions by the US Supreme Court have made clear that freedom of expression is not an absolute right. Instead, the private right to freedom of expression must be balanced against the public good. Those who abuse this freedom and harm the public may be punished. For example, protection is not given to "libel, reckless or calculated lies, slander, misrepresentation, perjury, false advertising, obscenity and profanity, solicitation of crime, and personal abuse or 'fighting' words," because these actions do not serve the ends of the First Amendment [55].

Various restrictions on freedom of speech are justified because of the greater public good that results. For example, US law prohibits cigarette advertising on television because cigarette smoking has detrimental effects on public health. Some cities use zoning laws to concentrate adult bookstores in a single part of town because the presence of adult bookstores lowers property values and increases crime.

### 3.6.3  FCC v. Pacifica Foundation

To illustrate limits to First Amendment protections, we consider the decision of the US Supreme Court in the case of *Federal Communications Commission v. Pacifica Foundation et al.*

In 1973 George Carlin recorded a performance made in front of a live audience in California. One track on the resulting record is a 12-minute monologue called "Filthy Words." In the monologue Carlin lists seven words that "you couldn't say on the public, ah, airwaves, um, the ones you definitely wouldn't say, ever" [58]. The audience laughs as Carlin spends the rest of the monologue creating colloquialisms from the list of banned words.

On the afternoon of October 30, 1973, counterculture radio station WBAI in New York aired "Filthy Words" after warning listeners the monologue contained "sensitive language which might be regarded as offensive to some" [59]. A few weeks after the broadcast, the Federal Communications Commission (FCC) received a complaint from a man who had heard the broadcast on his car radio in the presence of his son. In response to this complaint, the FCC issued a declaratory order and informed Pacifica Foundation (the operator of WBAI) that the order would be placed in the station's license file. The FCC warned Pacifica Foundation that further complaints could lead to sanctions.

Pacifica sued the FCC, and the resulting legal battle reached the US Supreme Court. In 1978 the Supreme Court ruled, in a 5–4 decision, that the FCC did not violate the First Amendment [59]. The majority opinion states, "Of all forms of communication, it is broadcasting that has received the most limited First Amendment protection." There are two reasons why broadcasters have less protection than booksellers or theater owners:

1. *"Broadcast media have a uniquely pervasive presence in the lives of all Americans."* [59]

   Offensive, indecent material is broadcast into the privacy of citizens' homes. Since people can change stations or turn their radios on or off at any time, prior warnings cannot completely protect people from being exposed to offensive material. While someone may turn off the radio after hearing something indecent, that does not undo a harm that has already occurred.

2. *"Broadcasting is uniquely accessible to children, even those too young to read."* [59]

   In contrast, restricting children's access to offensive or indecent material is possible in bookstores and movie theaters.

The majority emphasized that its ruling was a narrow one and that the context of the broadcast was all-important. The time of day at which the broadcast occurred (2 p.m.) was an important consideration, because that affected the composition of the listening audience.

### 3.6.4 Case Study: Kate's Blog

Kate is a journalism major who maintains a popular blog focusing on campus life. Kate attends a private birthday party in someone's apartment for her friend Jerry, a college student active in the Whig Party on campus. Someone gives Jerry a Tory Party T-shirt as a gag gift, and Jerry puts it on. Kate uses her cell phone to get a picture of Jerry wearing the T-shirt when he is looking the other way. Jerry gives Kate a ride home after the party, but she does not tell him about the photo. When she is back in her apartment, she posts the photo on her blog. In the blog she identifies Jerry and explains the context in which the photo was taken.

The story is read by many people both on and off campus. The next day Jerry confronts Kate, yells at her for posting the photo, and demands that she remove it from her Web site. Kate complies with Jerry's request by removing the photo, and the two of them remain friends. As a result of the incident, Jerry becomes more popular on campus, and the number of people who read Kate's blog increases.

Was it wrong for Kate to post the picture of Jerry on her blog without first getting his permission?

#### KANTIAN ANALYSIS

By uploading Jerry's photo to her blog without first asking his permission, Kate didn't respect Jerry's autonomy. Instead, she treated him as a means to her end of increasing the readership of her Web site. Therefore, her action was wrong according to the second formulation of the Categorical Imperative.

#### SOCIAL CONTRACT THEORY ANALYSIS

The birthday party was held in the apartment of one of Jerry's friends. In this private setting and among friends Jerry had a legitimate expectation that what happened during the party would not be broadcast to the world. By secretly taking a photo of Jerry doing something out of character and posting that photo on her blog, Kate violated Jerry's right to privacy. For this reason Kate's action was wrong.

## ACT UTILITARIAN ANALYSIS

We need to determine the positive and negative consequences of Kate's action on the two people involved. Kate increased the popularity of her blog, which is precisely the positive outcome she wanted (+10). Jerry's anger at Kate shows that he was hurt and upset by what she did, but after he confronted her, she removed the photo from her Web site and they reconciled. Therefore, while the intensity of this negative consequence to Jerry was significant, its duration was brief (−5). As a result of the posting, Jerry became more popular on campus, a very good thing for someone active in campus politics (+10). Jerry had Kate to thank for this boost in his popularity, further quenching the unhappiness he initially felt when he learned what she had done (+2). We conclude that the short-term consequences for both Kate and Jerry were positive (totaling +17).

The long-term consequences are difficult to determine. It is possible that the photo could land in the wrong hands and be used to discredit Jerry someday in the future (−100), but this would depend on many factors. Jerry is currently politically active. Is he going to stay active in Whig politics after he graduates from college (50%)? The photo was only on the Web for a day. Did anyone download it (20%)? If so, what is the chance that someday the photo will fall into the hands of someone who wants to make Jerry look bad (10%)?

An important part of a utilitarian analysis is looking at the certainty of each consequence: in other words, the probability that it will happen. The short-term consequences of Kate's action are certainly positive for both Kate and Jerry (+17 × 100% = +17). The long-term negative consequences, if any, are not certain at all (−100 × 50% × 20% × 10% = −1). Adding the calculated short-term benefits (+17) to the calculated long-term harms (−1) yields a total benefit of 16, and we conclude her action had a good outcome.

## RULE UTILITARIAN ANALYSIS

Let's consider what would happen if everyone were constantly taking photos of everyone they bumped into and posting them on the Web. There would be some positive consequences. It would be easier for people to see what their friends were up to. People might be more reluctant to engage in illegal activities if they thought photo or video evidence might appear on the Web. There would also be a variety of negative consequences. Once people started to feel as if they were always being photographed, they would become self-conscious, making it more difficult for them to simply be themselves. People would be less free to take off their public persona and express their true feelings. Inevitably, people would post photos that caused hard feelings and led to strained relationships. Ultimately, the negative consequences seem to be more weighty than the positive consequences, and we conclude Kate's action was wrong.

## VIRTUE ETHICS ANALYSIS

Kate and Jerry are friends. Aristotle recognized that people are social beings and that friendship plays an important role in *eudaimonia*, or human flourishing. True friends trust each other and seek each other's good. Reciprocity and an equality of interest are fundamental elements of friendship. There was no reciprocity when Kate sneakily took Jerry's photo without his knowledge; she exploited him by taking something from him without giving him anything in return. She did not act as a friend when she put her own interest above that of Jerry. After the party, Kate had another opportunity to be honest with Jerry. Unfortunately, she did not trust Jerry enough to admit she had taken the picture and ask his permission before posting the photo. Instead, she said nothing to Jerry and simply posted the photo to her blog. Overall, Kate's actions at several points in the story do not seem to be characteristic of a good friend.

### SUMMARY

The analyses from the perspectives of Kantianism, social contract theory, rule utilitarianism, and virtue ethics do not support Kate posting the photo without asking Jerry's permission, though each analysis uses a different line of reasoning to reach that conclusion. Kate imagined (correctly, as it turns out) that Jerry would be angry if she took a photo of him wearing the Tory Party T-shirt, and that is why she took the photo when he wasn't looking. Kate figured it would be better to beg for forgiveness than ask for permission, but what she did was cut Jerry out of a decision that affected both of them. This is no way to treat anybody, much less a friend. Kate would have been better off trying to persuade Jerry that putting the photo on her blog would be to their mutual advantage, posting the image only after obtaining his consent.

## 3.7  Children and Inappropriate Content

Many parents and guardians believe they ought to protect their children from exposure to pornographic and violent materials. A few years ago the center of concern was the Web, and a large software industry sprang up to provide browsers with the ability to block inappropriate images. Now smartphones are ubiquitous, and some parents are being forced to confront the unpleasant reality that their children have emailed sexually provocative images of themselves to friends or even strangers.

### 3.7.1  Web Filters

A **Web filter** is a piece of software that prevents certain Web pages from being displayed by your browser. While you are running your browser, the filter runs as a background process, checking every page your browser attempts to load. If the filter determines that the page is objectionable, it prevents the browser from displaying it.

Filters can be installed on individual computers, or an ISP may provide filtering services for its customers. Programs designed to be installed on individual computers, such as CyberSentinel, eBlaster, and Spector Pro, can be set up to email parents as soon as they detect an inappropriate Web page [60]. AOL Parental Controls enables parents to set the level of filtering on their children's accounts. It also allows parents to look at logs showing the pages their children have visited.

Typical filters use two different methods to determine if a page should be blocked. The first method is to check the URL of the page against a blacklist of objectionable sites. If the Web page comes from a blacklisted site, it is not displayed. The second method is to look for combinations of letters or words that may indicate a site has objectionable content.

Neither of these methods is foolproof. The Web contains millions of pages containing pornography, and new sites continue to be created at a high rate, so any blacklist of pornographic sites will be incomplete by definition. Some filters sponsored by conservative groups have blacklisted sites associated with liberal political causes, such as those sponsored by the National Organization for Women and gay and lesbian groups. The algorithms used to identify objectionable words and phrases can cause Web filters to block out legitimate Web pages.

### 3.7.2 Child Internet Protection Act

In March 2003, the Supreme Court weighed testimony in the case of *United States v. American Library Association*. The question: Can the government require libraries to install antipornography filters in return for receiving federal funds for Internet access?

More than 14 million people access the Internet through public library computers. About one-sixth of the libraries in the United States have already installed filtering software on at least some of their computers. The Child Internet Protection Act requires that libraries receiving federal funds to provide Internet access to its patrons must prevent children from getting access to visual depictions of obscenity and child pornography. The law allows adults who desire access to a blocked page to ask a librarian to remove the filter.

In his testimony before the Supreme Court, Solicitor General Theodore Olson argued that since libraries don't offer patrons X-rated magazines or movies, they should not be obliged to give them access to pornography over the Internet.

Paul Smith, representing the American Library Association and the American Civil Liberties Union, argued that in their attempt to screen out pornography, filters block tens of thousands of inoffensive pages. He added that requiring adults to leave the workstation, find a librarian, and ask for the filter to be turned off would be disruptive to their research and would stigmatize them.

In June 2003, the US Supreme Court upheld CIPA, ruling 6–3 that antipornography filters do not violate First Amendment guarantees [61]. Chief Justice William Rehnquist wrote, "A public library does not acquire Internet terminals in order to create a public forum for Web publishers to express themselves, any more than it collects books in order to provide a public forum for the authors of books to speak . . . Most libraries already exclude pornography from their print collections because they deem it inappropriate for inclusion" [62].

### 3.7.3 Ethical Evaluations of CIPA

In this section we evaluate CIPA from the perspectives of Kantianism, act utilitarianism, and social contract theory.

#### KANTIAN EVALUATION

We have already covered Kant's philosophical position against censorship. He believed that allowing people to use their own reason would lead to society's gradual enlightenment. In this case, however, the focus is narrower. Rather than talking about censorship in general, let's look at CIPA in particular.

The goal of CIPA is to protect children from the harm caused by exposure to pornography. The way the goal is being implemented is through Web filters. Studies have demonstrated that Web filters do not block all pornographic material but do block some nonpornographic Web pages. Some nonpornographic information posted on the Web is not easily accessible at libraries implementing government-mandated Web filters. The people posting this information did not consent to their ideas being blocked. Hence the decision to require the use of Web filters treats the creators of nonoffensive but blocked Web pages solely as means to the end of restricting children's access to pornographic materials. This analysis leads us to conclude that CIPA is wrong.

## ACT UTILITARIAN EVALUATION

Our second evaluation of CIPA is from an act utilitarian point of view. What are the consequences of passing CIPA?

1. While not all children access the Web in public libraries, and while Web filtering software is imperfect, it is probable that enacting CIPA results in fewer children being exposed to pornography, which is good.

2. Because Web filters are imperfect, people are unable to access some legitimate Web sites. As a result, Web browsers in libraries are less useful as research tools, a harmful consequence.

3. Adult patrons who ask for filters to be removed may be stigmatized (rightfully or not) as people who want to view pornography, a harm to them.

4. Some blocked sites may be associated with minority political views, reducing freedom of thought and expression, which is harmful.

Whenever we perform the utilitarian calculus and find some benefits and some harms, we must decide how to weigh them. This is a good time to think about utilitarian philosopher Jeremy Bentham's seven attributes. In particular, how many people are in each affected group? What is the probability the good or bad event will actually happen? How soon is the event likely to occur? How intense will the experience be? To what extent is the pain not diluted by pleasure or vice versa? How long will it last? How likely is the experience to lead to a similar experience? Actually performing the calculus for CIPA is up to each person's judgment. Different people could reach opposite conclusions about whether enacting CIPA is the right thing for the US government to do.

## SOCIAL CONTRACT THEORY EVALUATION

In social contract theory, morally binding rules are those rules mutually agreed to in order to allow social living [63]. Freedom of thought and expression is prized. According to John Rawls, "liberty of conscience is to be limited only when there is a reasonable expectation that not doing so will damage the public order which the government should maintain" [64].

It would be difficult to gain consensus around the idea that the private viewing of pornography makes social living no longer possible. For this reason, the private use of pornography is considered to be outside the social contract and nobody else's business.

However, when we think about the availability of pornography in public libraries, the issue gets thornier.

Some argue that allowing people to view pornography in a public place demeans women, denying them dignity as equal persons [65]. On the other hand, we know that filtering software is imperfect. In the past it has been used to promote a conservative political agenda by blocking sites associated with other viewpoints [66, 67]. Hence it reduces the free exchange of ideas, limiting the freedoms of thought and expression. For some adults, public libraries represent their only opportunity to access the Web for no cost. In order to be treated as free and equal citizens, they should have the same Web access as people who have Internet access from their homes. If Web filters are in place, their access is not equal because they must ask for permission to have the filters disabled. Finally, while most people would agree that children should not be exposed to pornographic material, it would be harder to convince reasonable people that social living would no longer be possible if children happened to see pornography in a library.

Our analysis from the point of view of social contract theory has produced arguments both supporting and opposing the Children's Internet Protection Act. However, installing filters does not seem to be necessary to preserve the public order. For this reason, the issue is outside the social contract and freedom of conscience should be given precedence.

### 3.7.4 Sexting

**Sexting** refers to sending sexually suggestive text messages or emails containing nude or nearly nude photographs [68]. Sexting has drawn a lot of media attention, but early reports on this phenomenon may have overstated the rates at which teenagers are sexting. More recent surveys indicate that between 3 and 7 percent of teens are sexting, and only 1 percent of teens have actually sent photos showing their bare breasts, genitals, or "bottoms" [69].

Whatever its frequency, sexting has had a serious impact on some people's lives. Here are three incidents.

Ohio high school student Jesse Logan sent nude pictures of herself to her boyfriend. When they broke up, the ex-boyfriend distributed the photos to other girls in her high school. Jesse endured months of harassment from her high school classmates and began skipping classes on a daily basis. After attending the funeral of another classmate who committed suicide, Jesse went home and hanged herself [70].

Ting-Yi Oei, a 59-year-old assistant principal at Freedom High School in South Riding, Virginia, was asked to investigate rumors that students were distributing nude photographs on their cell phones. His investigation led to a 16-year-old boy, who admitted to having a provocative photo on his cell phone. The photo showed the torso of a 17-year-old girl wearing panties, with her arms mostly covering her breasts. Oei showed the image to the principal, who told him to keep a copy on his computer as evidence. Two weeks later the same boy got in trouble again, and Oei suspended him for two weeks. When Oei met with the boy's mother, he told her about the earlier photo incident. The boy's mother was upset that Oei hadn't immediately told her about the photo, and she demanded that Oei revoke her son's suspension. When Oei refused, the mother went to the police and told them about the photo. Sheriff's investigators came to the school and found the photo of the girl on Oei's computer. County prosecutor James Plowman gave Oei an ultimatum: resign or face felony charges for possession of child pornography. Plowman's assistant told the press, "We just feel very strongly that this is not someone who should be in the Loudoun County school system." Oei refused to resign, and in August 2008, a grand jury indicted him for possession of child pornography. The school district removed him from his position as vice principal and reassigned him to a job at a testing center. Oei had to take out a second mortgage on his house to pay legal expenses. In April 2009, Loudoun Circuit Court Judge Thomas Horne dismissed the charges, noting that nudity alone is not sufficient to categorize an image of a minor as child pornography. Though never convicted, Oei ended up deeply in debt and with a tarnished reputation, unsure if he would ever return to his former position at the high school [71].

After Phillip Alpert got into an argument with his 16-year-old girlfriend, he emailed a nude photo of her to dozens of her friends and family members. "It was a stupid thing I did because I was upset and tired and it was the middle of the night and I was an immature kid," Alpert said upon reflection. The Orlando, Florida, police arrested Alpert, who had just turned 18, charging him with sending child pornography, a felony. It didn't matter that Alpert's girlfriend was 16, that they had dated for two and a half years, and that she was the one who had originally sent the photo to him. Alpert was sentenced to five years' probation and required to register with the state of Florida as a sex offender. He will remain a registered sex offender until he is 43 years old [72].

There appears to be a widespread sentiment that child pornography laws should not be used to prosecute teenagers who are caught sexting. As of January 2015, 20 states in the United States had passed legislation reducing penalties for minors convicted of engaging in sexting [73].

## 3.8 Breaking Trust

Identity thieves and sexual predators have used the Internet to find new victims. Companies and individuals have used fake online reviews to drum up business. Many people have been humiliated by the widespread dissemination of photos or videos they expected to be kept private.

### 3.8.1 Identity Theft

Dorothy Denning defines **identity theft** as "the misuse of another person's identity, such as name, Social Security number, driver's license, credit card numbers, and bank account numbers. The objective is to take actions permitted to the owner of the identity, such as withdraw funds, transfer money, charge purchases, get access to information, or issue documents and letters under the victim's identity" [74].

By far the leading form of identity theft in the United States involves the fraudulent use of an existing credit card account or bank account. In 2012 about 7 percent of adults in the United States reported being the victims of identity theft, and 50 percent of them noted fraudulent charges of more than $100 [75]. Fortunately, US law says that a consumer's liability for losses due to credit card fraud are limited to $50 if reported promptly. Most victims end up paying nothing out of pocket because their banks and credit card companies offer zero-liability fraud protection.

Identity thieves are much more likely to use low-tech methods rather than sophisticated online attacks to gain access to the account information they need. A 2008 survey of identity theft victims revealed that in 43 percent of the cases, the theft was the result of a lost or stolen wallet, credit card, checkbook, or another physical document [76]. Some identity thieves engage in **dumpster diving**—looking for personal information in garbage cans or recycling bins. Old bills, bank statements, and credit card statements contain a wealth of personal information, including names, addresses, and account numbers. Another simple way to get information is through **shoulder surfing**—looking over the shoulders of people filling out forms.

In 19 percent of the cases surveyed in 2008, someone at a business obtained a credit card number when the owner was making a purchase [76]. Waiters or store clerks match each legal swipe through a cash register with an illegal swipe through a **skimmer**, a small, battery-powered credit card reader. Identity theft rings use numbers collected this way to manufacture counterfeit credit cards.

Surprisingly, 14 percent of the cases of identity theft identified in 2010 were "friendly thefts" in which family members, friends, or in-house employees made purchases without the account holder's consent [77].

Still, a significant number of people are victims of identity theft through their online activities. Gathering financial information via spam is called **phishing** (pronounced "fishing"). Thieves send out spam messages designed to look like they originated from PayPal, eBay, or another well-known Internet-active business. Through these messages they hope to con unsuspecting recipients into connecting with authentic-looking Web sites and revealing their credit card numbers or other personal information. For example, a victim might receive an email message purportedly from PayPal, asking the person to go to the PayPal Web site to confirm a transaction. The email message contains a hypertext link. When the victim clicks on the link, he is connected to the counterfeit PayPal site.

Phishing, spyware, and other online methods resulted in more than a million cases of identity theft in the United States in 2008 [76].

College students are five times more likely to be victims of identity theft than average adults, for a variety of reasons. They use a lot of digital devices, and many do not secure them properly with strong passwords. They tend to post a lot of personal information on social media sites. College students are particularly vulnerable to low-tech methods of identity theft. A high percentage of them live in close quarters with others, and some do not take care to secure sensitive information. Dorm rooms are often left wide open, with checkbooks and financial documents kept in unlocked desk drawers. Students may throw documents containing personal financial information into the trash, where they can be retrieved by dumpster divers [78].

The Identity Theft and Assumption Act of 1998 makes identity theft a federal crime. In 2004 Congress passed the Identity Theft Penalty Enhancement Act, which lengthened prison sentences for identity thieves [79]. A variety of law enforcement agencies investigate alleged violations of this law: the US Secret Service, the FBI, the US Postal Inspection Service, and the Office of the Inspector General of the Social Security Administration [80]. Unfortunately, the probability that a particular case of identity theft will result in an arrest is about 1 in 700 [81].

### 3.8.2 Fake Reviews

A 2014 survey of North Americans by BrightLocal revealed that 88 percent had used online reviews in the past 12 months to gauge the quality of a local business, and 39 percent read reviews regularly. Restaurants, hotels, doctors and dentists, and beauty salons were the business types most frequently searched by consumers [82].

About three-quarters of consumers (72 percent) told surveyers that "positive reviews make them trust a local business more" [82]. Unfortunately, a significant percentage of online reviews are fraudulent. Some businesses try to boost sales by posting fake positive reviews of their enterprises or posting fake negative reviews of their competitors. Alternatively, they may hire third parties to do these things.

One study estimated that 16 percent of restaurant reviews on Yelp were fraudulent [83]. Another researcher concluded that one-third of all Internet reviews were fake [83]. Fake reviews undermine the credibility of the information consumers are using to make purchasing decisions.

In some instances consumers can identify suspect reviews. For example, by tracing through the reviewer's alias, a consumer can see how many reviews that reviewer has written. An alias that has posted only a single review is suspicious [83]. Another way to screen reviews is to look at the number of stars. "Pretty much all fake reviews are 5-star or 1-star reviews. Nobody leaves a fake 3-star review. What would be the point?" says Nicholas White of the *Daily Dot* [84].

Online review provider Yelp invests millions of dollars annually attempting to identify fake reviews posted to its site. About 10 percent of its employees are on the hunt for fraudulent reviews, and it has also developed sophisticated software to detect suspicious reviews. About 25 percent of the reviews submitted to Yelp don't make it past the screening and are not recommended [84].

### 3.8.3 Online Predators

**Instant messaging** refers to a system allowing two people to "chat" via typing in real time over the Internet. Instant messaging is popular among young adults because it allows them to communicate without paying SMS text messaging charges. Kik Messenger is a popular instant messaging app for smartphones; as of January 2015, it had 200 million users, including 40 percent of the teens and young adults in the United States [85]. In addition to text messages, Kik Messenger also allows users to send images and videos.

In August 2013, police began to issue warnings about child predators using Kik Messenger to find victims [86]. A few months later, 39-year-old Manuel Salto pleaded guilty to third-degree criminal sexual conduct after using Kik Messenger to meet a 13-year-old girl whom he later lured to his home for sexual relations [87].

Other social apps have been used by pedophiles as well. According to detectives, 21-year-old Ron Peterson used the Whisper app to meet a 12-year-old girl, communicate with her, and get her to send nude photos of herself to him. He later encouraged her to sneak out of her house to meet him at a motel. According to police, Whisper is particularly dangerous because it allows users to post their location, making it easier for predators to find local targets [88].

For more than 15 years, police have launched sting operations to arrest people seeking sex with minors. Sometimes these sting operations have resulted in dozens of arrests. For example, the Osceola County sheriff's department in Florida conducted a one-week-long sting operation in January 2012 that resulted in the arrest of 40 adults, including a professional golfer, a teacher, and a swim coach. Deputies arrested the suspects as they arrived at an undercover house, thinking they were going to have sex with a minor. According to the sheriff's department, before the suspects arrived at the rendezvous, most of them had already sent sexually explicit images to the "children" they were chatting with [89]. A similar sting operation in Lincolnton, North Carolina, in May 2015 led to 17 arrests [90]. Another sting operation in Galveston, Texas, in June 2015 led to the arrest of 11 men and women hoping to have sex with children [91].

In 2014 WTSP-TV aired an exposé critical of the sting operations in Polk County, Florida, alleging that detectives were resorting to more extreme methods to keep up their arrest rates. For example, an officer responds to an ad on an adult dating site, pretending to be an adult woman, but once an online relationship begins to develop, the detective suggests the man might be interested in having sex with "her" child. Some police tactics have resulted in cases being thrown out of court, with judges making comments such as these:

- "It was the agent who repeatedly steered the conversation back to sexual activity with a minor."
- "The government made a concerted effort to lure him into committing a crime."
- "The law does not tolerate government action to provoke a law-abiding citizen to commit a crime" [92].

### 3.8.4 Ethical Evaluations of Police Sting Operations

Is it morally right for police detectives to entrap pedophiles by posing as children on the Internet and agreeing to meet with them?

#### UTILITARIAN ANALYSIS

Let's consider the various consequences of such a sting operation. A person allegedly interested in having sex with an underage minor is arrested and charged with attempted child rape. Suppose the person is found guilty and must serve time in prison. The direct effects of the sting operation are the denial of one person's freedom (a harm) and an increase in public safety (a benefit). Since the entire public is safer and only a single person is harmed, this is a net good.

The sting operation also has indirect effects. Publicity about the sting operation may deter other pedophiles. This, too, is a beneficial result. It is harder to gauge how knowledge of sting operations influences innocent citizens. First, it may reduce citizens' trust in the police. Many people believe that if they are doing nothing wrong, they have nothing to fear. Others may become less inclined to provide information to the police when requested. Second, sting operations can affect everyone's online experiences. They demonstrate that people are not always who they claim to be. This knowledge may make people less vulnerable to being taken advantage of, but it may also reduce the amount of trust people have in others. Sting operations prove that supposedly private conversations can actually be made public. If instant messaging conversations lack honesty and privacy, people will be less willing to engage in serious conversations. As a result, instant messaging loses some of its utility as a communications system. How much weight you give to the various consequences of police sting operations using instant messaging determines whether the net consequences are positive or negative.

## KANTIAN ANALYSIS

A Kantian focuses on the will leading to the action rather than the results of the action. The police are responsible for maintaining public safety. Pedophiles endanger innocent children. Therefore, it is the duty of police to try to prevent pedophiles from accomplishing what they intend to do. The will of the police detective is to put a pedophile in prison. This seems straightforward enough.

If we dig a level deeper, however, we run into trouble. In order to put a pedophile in prison, the police must identify this person. Since a pedophile is unlikely to confess on the spot if asked a question by a police officer, the police lay a trap. In other words, the will of the police detective is to deceive a pedophile in order to catch him. To a Kantian, lying is wrong, no matter how noble the objective. By collecting evidence of instant messaging conversations, the police detective also violates the presumed privacy of this medium. While police officers have a duty to protect the public safety, it is wrong for them to break other moral laws in order to accomplish this purpose. From a Kantian point of view, the sting operation is morally wrong.

## SOCIAL CONTRACT THEORY ANALYSIS

An adherent of social contract theory could argue that in order to benefit everyone, there are certain moral rules that people communicating online ought to follow. For example, people ought to be honest, and conversations ought to be kept confidential. By misrepresenting identity and/or intentions, the pedophile has broken a moral rule and ought to be punished. In conducting sting operations, however, police detectives also misrepresent their identities and record everything typed by suspected pedophiles. The upholders of the law have broken the rules, too. Furthermore, we have the presumption of innocence until proof of guilt. What if the police detective, through miscommunication or bad judgment, actually entraps someone who is not a pedophile? In this case, an innocent person has not broken any rules. He was simply in the wrong place at the wrong time. Yet society, represented by the police detective, did not provide the benefits instant messaging users expect to receive (honest communications and privacy). In short, there is a conflict between society's need to punish a wrongdoer and its expectation that everyone (including the agents of the government) abide by its moral rules.

SUMMARY OF ETHICAL ANALYSES

To summarize our ethical evaluation of police sting operations, the actions of the police seem immoral from a Kantian point of view. Evaluations using the other ethical theories do not yield a clear-cut endorsement or condemnation of the stings. While the goals of the police are laudable, they accomplish their goals through deception and by revealing details of conversations thought to be private. Sting operations are more likely to be viewed as morally acceptable by someone who is more focused on the results of an action than the methods used; in other words, a consequentialist.

## 3.8.5  False Information

The Web is a more open communication medium than newspapers, radio stations, or television stations. Individuals or groups whose points of view may never be published in a newspaper or broadcast on a television or radio show may create an attractive Web site. The ease with which people may get information out via the Web is one of the reasons the Web contains billions of pages. However, the fact that no one has to review a Web page before it is published means the quality of information available on the Web varies widely.

You can find many Web sites devoted to the American manned space program. You can also find many Web sites that provide evidence the Moon landings were a hoax by NASA. Many Web sites describe the Holocaust committed by the Nazis before and during World War II. Other sites explain why the Holocaust could not have happened.

Disputes about commonly held assumptions did not begin with the Web. Some television networks and newspapers are well known for giving a forum to people who question information provided through government agencies. Twice in 2001, the Fox TV network aired a program called "Conspiracy Theory: Did We Land on the Moon?" The program concludes NASA faked the Moon landing in the Nevada desert. Supermarket tabloids are notorious for their provocative, misleading headlines. Experienced consumers take into account the source of the information.

Most people would agree that *60 Minutes* on CBS is a more reliable source of information than the *Conspiracy Theory* series Similarly, people expect information they find in the *New York Times* to be more reliable than the stories they read in a tabloid.

In traditional publishing, various mechanisms are put in place to improve the quality of the final product. For example, before Addison-Wesley published the first edition of this book, an editor sent draft copies of the manuscript to a dozen reviewers who checked it for errors, omissions, or misleading statements. The author revised the manuscript to respond to the reviewers' suggestions. After the author submitted a revised manuscript, a copy editor made final changes to improve the readability of the text, and a proofreader corrected typographical errors. Every subsequent edition has benefited from the feedback of about a dozen college professors reviewing the proposed changes.

Web pages, on the other hand, can be published without any review. As you're undoubtedly well aware, the quality of Web pages varies dramatically. Fortunately, search engines can help people identify those Web pages that are most relevant and of the highest quality. Let's take a look at how the Google search engine does this.

The Google search engine keeps a database of many billions of Web pages. A software algorithm ranks the quality of these pages. The algorithm invokes a kind of voting mechanism. If Web page A links to Web page B, then page B gets a vote. However, all votes do not have the same weight. If Web page A is itself getting a lot of votes, then page A's link to page B gives its vote more weight than a link to B from an unpopular page.

When a user makes a query to Google, the search engine first finds the pages that closely match the query. It then considers their quality (as measured by the voting algorithm) to determine how to rank the relevant pages.

### 3.8.6 Cyberbullying

In November 2002, Ghyslain Raza, a chubby high school student living in Quebec, Canada, borrowed a videotape and used one of the high school's video cameras to film himself swinging a golf ball retriever like a light saber, à la Darth Maul in *Star Wars Episode I*. A few months later, the owner of the videotape discovered the content and shared it with some friends. After one of them digitized the scene and made it available on the Internet, millions of people downloaded the file in the first two weeks [93]. Ghyslain was nicknamed "the Star Wars kid," endured prolonged harassment from other students, and eventually dropped out of school [94]. By 2006 the video had been viewed more than 900 million times [95].

**Cyberbullying** is the use of the Internet or the phone system to inflict psychological harm on another person. Frequently, a group of persons gangs up to cyberbully the victim. Examples of cyberbullying include the following:

- Repeatedly texting or emailing hurtful messages to another person
- Spreading lies about another person
- Tricking someone into revealing highly personal information
- "Outing" or revealing someone's secrets online
- Posting embarrassing photographs or videos of other people without their consent
- Impersonating someone else online in order to damage that person's reputation
- Threatening or creating significant fear in another person

Surveys have revealed that cyberbullying is common among teenagers. Cox Communications surveyed 655 American teenagers in 2009, and 19 percent reported that they had been cyberbullied online, via cell phone, or through both media. Ten percent of the teenagers admitted to cyberbullying someone else. When asked why they had cyberbullied someone else, the most common responses were "they deserved it" and "to get back at someone" [68].

In some instances cyberbullying has led to the suicide of the victim, as in the case of 13-year-old Megan Meier. According to her mother, "Megan had a lifelong struggle with weight and self-esteem" [96]. She had talked about suicide in third grade, and ever since then she had been seeing a therapist [96]. Megan's spirits soared when she met a 16-year-old boy named Josh Evans on MySpace. They flirted online for four weeks but never met in person. Then Josh seemed to sour on their relationship. One day he let her know that he didn't know if he wanted to be friends with her anymore. The next day he posted the following [96, 97]:

```
You are a bad person and everybody hates you.
Have a shitty rest of your life.
The world would be a better place without you.
```

When Megan angrily responded to this post, others ganged up on her: "Megan Meier is a slut"; "Megan Meier is fat" [96]. Later that afternoon, Megan hanged herself in her bedroom.

Eventually, the community learned that "Josh Evans" did not exist. The MySpace account had been created just a couple of houses away from the Meier home by 18-year-old Ashley Grills, 13-year-old Sarah Drew, and Lori Drew, Sarah's mother. Sarah had a falling out with Megan, and Ashley suggested creating the MySpace account to find out what Megan might be saying about Sarah. Lori Drew had approved the plan. Most of the messages from "Josh" had been written by Sarah or Ashley, but Lori Drew had been aware of what they were doing [98].

The county's district attorney declined to prosecute Lori Drew because there was no Missouri law against cyberbullying [99]. The FBI investigated the case, however, and in 2008 federal prosecutors charged Drew with four felony counts under the Computer Fraud and Abuse Act for violating the MySpace terms of service. A jury found her not guilty of these crimes but did convict her of three misdemeanors [100]. In 2009 a US district judge overturned these convictions, stating that criminal charges should not have been brought against Drew for breaking a contract with an Internet service provider [101].

In April 2009, the Megan Meier Cyberbullying Prevention Act was introduced in the US House of Representatives. The purpose of the proposed law was to "impose criminal penalties on anyone who transmits in interstate or foreign commerce a communication intended to coerce, intimidate, harass, or cause substantial emotional distress to another person, using electronic means to support severe, repeated, and hostile behavior" [102]. Some civil libertarians objected to the proposed legislation, arguing that it would take away free speech rights guaranteed under the First Amendment to the US Constitution. The law did not win approval by the House of Representatives.

### 3.8.7 Revenge Porn

The *Collins English Dictionary* defines **revenge porn** to be "a pornographic image or film which is published, posted (e.g., on the Internet), or otherwise circulated without the consent of one or more of the participants, usually with malicious and vindictive intent, such as following a break-up" [103]. Revenge porn is a special case of cyberbullying.

The Web site Is Anyone Up?, launched in 2010 by Hunter Moore, quickly became a magnet for revenge porn submissions, significantly raising the visibility of this issue. Moore appeared on the talk show *Anderson*, along with two women whose images had appeared on the site without their permission. When asked by Anderson Cooper whether he felt bad about what he had done "to these two women," Moore replied to the women, "No one put a gun to your head and made you take these pictures. It's 2011; everything's on the Internet" [104]. One of the women responded, "If we're choosing to send them to someone we trust, that doesn't mean we expect them to show up on the Internet" [104].

Posting revenge porn has been criminalized in Germany, Israel, the United Kingdom, and about half of the states in the United States. In 2011, after Noe Iniguez broke up with his girlfriend, he posted topless photos of her on her employer's Facebook page. Three years later Iniguez became the first person to be convicted under California's law criminalizing the unauthorized posting of nude images [105].

In the first six months of 2015, three corporations took action to protect victims of revenge porn. Reddit announced it was banning the posting of sexually explicit images without the consent of the people in the images [106]. Twitter updated its rules to include, "You may not post intimate photos or videos that were taken or distributed without the subject's consent," and it promised to remove links to such content [107]. Google announced that it would create an online form enabling victims to request that nude or sexually explicit images of themselves posted without their consent be withheld from Google search results [108].

## 3.9 Internet Addiction

Many people spend a great deal of time staring at screens. You probably know someone who is constantly texting or instant messaging. Perhaps you have a friend who plays computer games for hours on end and doesn't have a social life. Why do people get so attached to their devices? Is it possible to become addicted to these activities?

According to psychiatrist Edward Hallowell, the brains of heavy users of digital devices crave newness, and every text or email message results in a release of the neurotransmitter dopamine that feeds the craving [109]. That's why we find it difficult to break away from these activities [110].

### 3.9.1  Is Internet Addiction Real?

According to neuroscientist Richard Davidson, "the kind of feedback that we get from our devices is immediate and highly reinforcing, so it becomes like a drug. And, in fact, it co-opts the same brain systems that are indicated in addiction" [111].

Psychiatrist Jerald Block argues that Internet addiction is a common disorder with at least three variants: "excessive gaming, sexual preoccupations, and e-mail/text messaging" [112]. Block states that four characteristics are common to these variants: "1) *excessive use*, often associated with a loss of sense of time or a neglect of basic drives, 2) *withdrawal*, includng feelings of anger, tension, and/or depression when the computer is inaccessible, 3) *tolerance*, including the need for better computer equipment, more software, or more hours of use, and 4) *negative repurcussions*, including arguments, lying, poor achievement, social isolation, and fatigue" [112].

Citing insufficient research data, the American Psychiatric Association did not include Internet addiction in its most recent *Diagnostic and Statistical Manual of Mental Disorders* [113]. On the other hand, Internet addiction has been recognized and taken seriously in both South Korea and China since 2007.

**FIGURE 3.4** Many South Koreans play persistent online games in centers called PC bangs. In 2005 a 28-year-old South Korean man died after playing one game practically nonstop for 50 hours. (Kim-Jae Hwan/Newscom)

The average South Korean high school student spends 23 hours per week gaming [114]. After 10 cardiopulmonary-related deaths in Internet cafés (Figure 3.4), South Korea began training mental health counselors in how to treat Internet addiction [115, 116]. In 2011 the South Korean government passed a law prohibiting children under the age of 16 from accessing online games between midnight and 6 a.m. [117].

In 2007 the Chinese government issued a regulation requiring online game providers to implement an "anti-online game addiction system" discouraging players under 18 from playing more than three hours a day. The system requires online players to register using their real identity and tracks the number of hours each player spends online. Online games give players full points for the first three hours they play each day. For the next two hours, players receive only half points, and after five hours, players receive no points [118].

Our concern in this section is excessive use of digital devices that causes harm. We will use the term "Internet addiction" to describe this behavior because it is the term most widely used by the press, even as we recognize that experts disagree about whether excessive use is a genuine addiction.

### 3.9.2 Contributing Factors to Addiction

According to Stanton Peele, social, situational, and individual factors can increase a person's susceptibility to addiction. For example, peer groups play an important role in determining how individuals use alcohol and other drugs. People in stressful situations are more likely to become addicted, as are those who lack social support and intimacy, and those who have limited opportunities for "rewarding, productive activity" [119]. Individual factors that make a person more susceptible to addiction include a tendency to pursue an activity to excess, a lack of achievement, a fear of failure, and feelings of alienation.

Kimberly Young's studies led her to "believe that behaviors related to the Internet have the same ability to provide emotional relief, mental escape, and ways to avoid problems as do alcohol, drugs, food, or gambling" [120]. She noted that the typical Internet addict is addicted to a single application.

### 3.9.3 Ethical Evaluation of Internet Addiction

People who use digital devices excessively can harm themselves and others for whom they are responsible. For this reason, excessive use of digital devices is a moral issue.

Kantianism, utilitarianism, and social contract theory all share the Enlightenment view that individuals, as rational beings, have the capacity and the obligation to use their critical judgment to govern their lives [121]. Kant held that addiction is a vice, because it's wrong to allow your bodily desires to dominate your mind [122]. Mill maintained that some pleasures are more valuable than others and that people have the obligation to help each other distinguish better pleasures from worse ones [53].

Ultimately, people are responsible for the choices they make. Even if an addict is "hooked," the addict is responsible for choosing to engage in the activity the first time. This view assumes that people are capable of controlling their compulsions. According to Jeffrey Reiman, vices are "dispositions that undermine the sovereignty of practical reason. Dispositions, like habits, are hard but not impossible to overcome, and undermining something weakens it without necessarily destroying it entirely" [121, p. 89].

Reiman's view is supported by Peele, who believes addicts can choose to recover from their addictions. "People recover to the extent that they (1) believe an addiction is hurting them and wish to overcome it, (2) feel enough efficacy to manage their withdrawal and life without the addiction, and (3) find sufficient alternative rewards to make life without the addiction worthwhile" [119, p. 156].

While our analysis to this point has concluded that individual addicts are morally responsible for their addictions, it's also possible for a society to bear some collective moral responsibility for the addictions of some of its members. We have already discussed how social conditions can increase a person's susceptibility to addiction, and Peele states an addict will not recover unless life without the addiction has sufficient rewards. Some people use digital devices as a way to escape into their own world, because in the "real world" they suffer from social isolation [123]. Perhaps we should reflect on whether any of our actions or inactions make certain members of our community feel excluded.

# Summary

The Internet and cellular networks are powerful and flexible technologies that have revolutionized communication by making it possible for billions of people to communicate with each other. Never before have so many people around the globe been able to interact: sharing information, engaging in commercial transactions, organizing political movements, competing in online games, helping those in need, and much more. At the same time, those who seek to exploit others have found new ways to do so using these same technologies.

The Web provides a remarkably simple way for people to post and access information, and it now contains trillions of pages. The Web has replaced printed encyclopedias and is giving books, journals, and newspapers a run for their money. It contains images of sublime beauty and shocking cruelty, uplifting poetry and expletive-ridden hate speech, well-organized encyclopedias and figments of paranoid imaginations, useful software and hidden computer viruses. In short, it is a reflection of the best and the worst of humanity.

Texting has supported myriad activities, from the social to the deadly serious. It allows friends and family members to check in on each other and set up social encounters, it is an important way for people to make international money transfers without banks, and it has also been used to organize mass protests and overthrow governments.

Governments have responded to the latent power of these new technologies in a variety of ways. The most repressive governments have made the Internet inaccessible to the masses. Other governments have instituted controls that prevent certain sites from being accessed. To promote social and political stability, the Chinese government prohibits access to certain Internet sites and sometimes restricts cell phone service. On one occasion it shut down the Internet in an entire region for months. In an effort to ensure children are not exposed to online pornography, the United States government requires libraries to install antipornography filters. Given the focus in the United States on preventing children from being exposed to pornography, it is ironic that many minors have voluntarily created and transmitted explicit images of themselves.

Those who wish to exploit other people have found ways to use these new communication technologies to achieve their ends. Spammers are sending out hundreds of billions of spam emails every day. Others make a living selling stolen credit card information. Millions of people every year are the victims of identity theft.

The challenge for each of us is to reflect on our own actions and ponder whether there are times we may have stepped over the line and put ourselves first, privileging our own needs and desires over those of other people. Cyberbullying and posting revenge porn are the result of decisions made by individuals.

Finally, these new communication technologies have provided new opportunities for people to harm themselves. A good example is the phenomenon commonly referred to as Internet addiction. Some people become so engaged with their digital devices that they spend too much time with their eyes glued to their screens and too little time taking care of their responsibilities to themselves and to others.

What is the proper governmental response to the Internet addiction crisis? The governments of South Korea and China have put limits on the number of hours per day that children can play online games, and an educational campaign in South Korean schools informs children of the dangers of Internet addiction and encourages healthy alternative activities, such as listening to music. The US government has not yet taken these kinds of steps.

## Further Reading and Viewing

Chris Anderson and Michael Wolff. "The Web Is Dead. Long Live the Internet." *Wired*, September 2010. www.wired.com.

Anand Giridharadas. "Where a Cellphone Is Still Cutting Edge." *New York Times*, April 9, 2010. www.nytimes.com.

Malcolm Gladwell. "Small Change: Why the Revolution Will Not Be Tweeted." *New Yorker*, October 4, 2010.

Ted Greenwald. "Under the Influence: How Facebook and Twitter and Candy Crush Get Us Addicted to Swiping and Clicking and Posting." *Wired*, January 2015, pp. 76–77.

Judith Horstman. "Internet Addiction: A Clinical Disorder?" *ForaTv*, November 9, 2009. 3:04. www.youtube.com/watch?v=acvkkwySZ20.

Steven Levy. "How Early Twitter Decisions Led to Anthony Weiner's Dickish Demise." *Wired Epicenter*, June 13, 2011. www.wired.com/epicenter/.

Steven Levy. "Mob Rule! How Users Took Over Twitter." *Wired*, November 2009. www.wired.com.

Brian Proffitt. "What's Holding Up the Internet of Things." *ReadWrite*, June 14, 2013. readwrite.com.

Mike Rugnetta. "Are Virtual Video Game Economies Becoming Real?" *Idea Channel*, September 19, 2012. 5:26. video.pbs.org.

Allen Salkin. "Party On, But No Tweets." *New York Times*, August 9, 2009. www.nytimes.com.

Jeanette Thomas. "M-PESA Mobile Money." Consultative Group to Assist the Poor, 2009. 3:30. blip.tv/play/AYHxux0C.html.

Bill Wasik. "Welcome to the Programmable World." *Wired*, June 2013.

Gary Wolf. "The Tragedy of Craigslist." *Wired*, September 2009. www.wired.com.

Judy Woodruff. "Google's Schmidt and Cohen Discuss the Digital Future." *PBS NewsHour*, May 2, 2013. 9:38. video.pbs.org.

⊙ Judy Woodruff. "Spotting the Fakes among the Five-Star Reviews." *PBS NewsHour*, January 19, 2015. 9:30. video.pbs.org.

# Review Questions

1. Nearly all spam is blocked by spam filters. Why does sending spam continue to be so popular?

2. What is the difference between the Web and the Internet?

3. What are the similarities and the differences between texting and instant messaging?

4. Define censorship in your own words.

5. What characteristics of the Internet make the censorship of Internet content difficult?

6. Why do broadcasters in the United States have more limited First Amendment rights than book publishers?

7. How has sexting by teens created new legal challenges for US states?

8. What is the leading form of identity theft in the United States?

9. Why are college students particularly vulnerable to identity theft?

10. Give two examples of high-tech methods of identity theft and two examples of low-tech methods of identity theft.

11. Define cyberbullying in your own words.

12. What physiological reason has been given for the difficulty some people experience detaching themselves from their digital devices?

13. What is the Enlightenment view regarding responsibility for addiction?

# Discussion Questions

14. Why is instant messaging or texting more popular among young adults than making phone calls?

15. Why is "cold calling" considered to be an acceptable sales practice, but spamming isn't?

16. Internet service providers monitor their chat rooms and expel users who violate their codes of conduct. For example, users can be kicked off for insulting a person or a group of people based on their race, religion, or sexual orientation. Is it wrong for an ISP to expel someone for hate speech?

17. Stockbrokers are now required to save all their instant messaging communications. Is having a record of everything you type good or bad? Do you think this requirement will change the behavior of brokers?

18. There is a thriving "real-world" market for gold, artifacts, and avatars from virtual worlds such as World of Warcraft. In effect, rich Westerners are offshoring game playing to China. Do you find this image disturbing?

19. What are the benefits and harms of Internet censorship?

20. Should the tax dollars of citizens of democratic nations be used to help people in authoritarian nations get around the Web censorship of their repressive governments?

21. Should people publishing accusations against others on their blogs or Facebook pages be held responsible if they disseminate false information?

22. Should a college or university have the right to suspend students who brag about breaking its rules on their Facebook pages?

23. In September 2012, Joseph Aziz, a graduate student at Montclair State University in New Jersey, posted a YouTube video in which he said that a fellow student's legs look like "a pair of bleached hams." The university disciplined Aziz for violating the university's code of conduct, ordered him to avoid all contact with the other student, and forbade him from posting anything else about the other student on social media. After being disciplined, Aziz complained about the gag order in a private group on Facebook and made a joke about escaping the other student's "tyrannical ham lock." A member of the Facebook group copied Aziz's comments to university administrators, who then gave Aziz a one-semester suspension that appears on his official college transcript [124]. Was the response of Montclair State University appropriate?

24. Discuss similarities and differences between the Web and each of these other ways that we communicate: the telephone system, physical mail, bookstores, movie theaters, newspapers, broadcast and cable TV. Should governments ignore the Web, or should they regulate it somehow? If governments should regulate the Web, should the regulations be similar to the regulations for one of the aforementioned communication systems, or should they be unique in significant ways?

25. The convenience of *Wikipedia* makes it a popular reference for students. After several instances in which students cited incorrect information, however, the history department at Middlebury College prohibited references to *Wikipedia* articles in papers or exams. Did the Middlebury history department go too far? What is the proper role, if any, for *Wikipedia* in academic research?

26. Should bloggers be given the same rights as newspaper, magazine, or television journalists?

27. Should children be prevented from accessing some Web sites? Who should be responsible for the actions of children surfing the Web?

28. Are there any circumstances under which sexting is morally acceptable?

29. What is the age at which a parent or guardian should provide a child with a cell phone? Should younger children be provided with cell phones having fewer features?

30. Review the exchange in Section 3.8.7 between Hunter Moore, creator of a Web site featuring revenge porn, and one of the women whose image had appeared on the site without her permission. Who has the more compelling argument? Why? If you could ask Hunter Moore a follow-up question, what would it be? If you could ask the woman a follow-up question, what would it be?

31. Discuss the morality of Google's page-ranking algorithm. Does it systematically exclude Web pages containing opinions held only by a small segment of the population? Should every opinion on the Web be given equal consideration?

32. What is the longest amount of time you have ever spent in a single game session on a smartphone, tablet, or computer? Have you ever been so engrossed in a game that you ignored bodily needs, such as eating or going to the bathroom?

33. Should Grand Theft Auto or Call of Duty be pulled off store shelves and not marketed to children?

34. In the United States television commercials for cigarettes are banned. Should there be a ban on commercials for violent video games?

35. The income of companies providing persistent online games depends on the number of subscribers they attract. Since consumers have a choice of many products, each company is motivated to create the best possible experience for its customers. Role-playing adventures have no set length. When playing one of these games, it's easy to spend more time on the computer than originally planned. Some subscribers cause harm to themselves and others by spending too much time playing these games. Should the designers of persistent online games bear some moral responsibility for this problem?

36. The governments of South Korea and China have taken action to restrict the number of hours per day children can access online games. Should the United States government take similar action?

37. A school district forbids students from using their cell phones on school buses, but many students ignore this rule. A frustrated bus driver installs a cell phone jammer on his bus. When the jammer is turned on, cell phones within 40 feet stop working. (The use of jammers is against the law.) The bus driver says, "The kids think they are sneaky by hiding low in their seats and using their phones. Now the kids can't figure out why their phones don't work, but can't ask because they will get in trouble! It's fun to watch them try to get a signal" [125].

    Discuss the morality of the bus driver's use of the jammer.

38. According to some commentators, Facebook and Twitter played a vital role in the Arab Spring uprising because they made it possible for activists to organize large protests in a short amount of time. Others argue that Facebook and Twitter were simply tools used by activists and that genuine social grievances led to the revolutions in Tunisia and Egypt. What is your view?

39. After popular uprisings in Tunisia and Egypt in 2011, the US government said it would spend $30 million to fund the development of new services and technologies designed to allow activists in other countries to get around Internet restrictions imposed by their governments.

    Announcing this initiative, Secretary of State Hillary Clinton said, "We are convinced that an open Internet fosters long-term peace, progress and prosperity. The reverse is also true. An Internet that is closed and fractured, where different governments can block activity or change the rules on a whim—where speech is censored or punished, and privacy does not exist—that is an Internet that can cut off opportunities for peace and progress and discourage innovation and entrepreneurship" [126].

    Should the US government provide activists in other countries the tools to get around Internet restrictions imposed by authoritarian governments?

40. In July 2011, activists shut down a San Francisco subway station as a way of protesting the death of a drunk man shot by a Bay Area Rapid Transit (BART) police officer [127].

A month later, the subway system blocked cell phone service at several stations in an effort to prevent another protest. According to BART officials, protesters had said they "would use mobile devices to coordinate their disruptive activities and communicate about the location and number of BART Police" [128]. The agency said, "A civil disturbance during commute times at busy downtown San Francisco stations could lead to platform overcrowding and unsafe conditions for BART customers, employees and demonstrators" [128].

Was BART justified in blocking cell phone service?

41. What role do online reviews play in your life as a consumer? Do you find online reviews to be more reliable or less reliable than reviews from friends and family members?

42. Should the US government follow the lead of China and South Korea and legislate daily limits to online game playing by children under the age of 18?

# In-Class Exercises

43. Divide the class into groups. Each group should come up with a variant of the case study "Ann the Acme Accountant," in which both a Kantian evaluation and an act utilitarian evaluation would conclude Ann did something wrong.

44. Divide the class into groups. Each group should come up with a variant of the case study "Kate's Blog," in which the analysis from the perspective of social contract theory would conclude Kate did nothing wrong, but an act utilitarian evaluation would conclude Kate did something wrong.

45. Divide the class into teams representing each of the following groups:
   - Small, struggling business
   - Large, established corporation
   - Internet service provider
   - Consumer

   Discuss the value of direct email versus other forms of advertising, such as direct mail, television advertising, radio advertising, the Yellow Pages, and setting up a Web site.

46. A company uses pop-up advertising to market its software product, which blocks pop-ups from appearing when someone is surfing the Web. Debate the morality of the company's marketing strategy.

47. Ad-blocking software attachments to Web browsers enable a Web surfer to visit Web sites without having to view the pop-up advertisements associated with these Web pages. Debate this proposition: "People who use ad-blocking software are violating an implicit 'social contract' with companies that use advertising revenues as a means of providing free access to Web pages."

48. In 2000 the Estonian parliament passed a law declaring Internet access to be a fundamental human right of its citizens. Divide the class into two groups (pro and con) to debate the following proposition: Internet access should be a fundamental human right, along with such other fundamental human rights as the right to life and the right to free speech.

**49.** How do you determine the credibility of information you get from the Web? How would you rank the reliability of information provided by each of the following sources of Web pages? Does the type of information you're seeking affect your ranking?
- Establishment newspaper
- Counterculture newspaper
- Television network
- Corporation
- Nonprofit organization
- Individual

**50.** Martin Dula has suggested that parents should not provide their children with phones capable of taking photos and videos because these phones tempt children to participate in sexting [72].

Debate the following proposition: Parents and legal guardians should not allow their children under the age of 18 to own cell phones capable of taking, transmitting, or receiving photographs or videos.

# References

[1]    Alex Williams. "Mind Your BlackBerry or Mind Your Manners." *New York Times*, June 22, 2009. www.nytimes.com.

[2]    Neda Ulaby. "The Posies: How Do Bands Make Money Now?" *All Things Considered*, National Public Radio, July 29, 2009. www.npr.org.

[3]    "The Personal News Cycle: How Americans Choose to Get Their News." American Press Institute, March 17, 2014. www.americanpressinstitute.org.

[4]    Jose Antonio Vargas. "Obama Raised Half a Billion Online." *WashingtonPost.com*, November 20, 2008.

[5]    "Paul Sets One-Day GOP Fundraising Record." MSNBC, November 6, 2007. www.msnbc.msn.com.

[6]    Jose Pagliery. "Rand Paul Is First Presidential Candidate to Accept Donations in Bitcoin." *CNN Money*, April 7, 2015. money.cnn.com.

[7]    "The Radicati Group, Inc. Releases 'Email Statistics Report, 2015–19.'" Radicati Group, March 2, 2015. www.radicati.com.

[8]    Brad Templeton. "Origin of the Term 'Spam' to Mean Net Abuse," Templetons.com, July 8, 2005. www.templetons.com/brad/spamterm.html.

[9]    Peter H. Lewis. "An Ad (Gasp!) in Cyberspace." *New York Times*, April 19, 1994.

[10]   "Filters Getting Better at Blocking Spam." *Boston Globe*, May 12, 2009.

[11]   Henry Dalziel. "Costs of Nefarious Services from the Underground Cybercriminal World." November 15, 2012. www.concise-courses.com.

[12]   Saul Hansell. "Internet Is Losing Ground in Battle against Spam." *New York Times*, April 22, 2003.

[13]   Joe Stewart. "Top Spam Botnets Exposed." Dell SecureWorks, April 8, 2008. www.secureworks.com/research/threats/topbotnets.

[14]   Brian Whitworth and Elizabeth Whitworth. "Spam and the Social-Technical Gap." *Computer* 37(10):38–45, October 2004.

[15]   Tim Berners-Lee. *Weaving the Web*. HarperCollins Publishers, New York, NY, 1999.

[16]   Gianni Catlfamo. "The Death of the Browser." *KetchumBlog*, February 19, 2011. blog .ketchum.com.

[17]   U.S. Census Bureau News. "Quarterly Retail E-commerce Sales" (press release). U.S. Department of Commerce, May 15, 2015. www.census.gov.

[18]   Nicola Clark. "Selecting a Seatmate to Make Skies Friendlier." *New York Times*, February 24, 2012.

[19]   Daniel H. Pink. "The Book Stops Here." *Wired*, page 125, March 2005.

[20]   Paul Festa. "Dialing for Bloggers." *New York Times*, February 25, 2003.

[21]   Clive Thompson. "Spooked: Using Darknets to Foil the NSA." *Wired*, November 2013.

[22]   "Get the Best Route, Every Day, with Real-Time Help from Other Drivers." Waze, Inc., June 17, 2013. www.waze.com.

[23]   Laura Pappano. "The Year of the MOOC." *New York Times*, November 2, 2012. www .nytimes.com.

[24]   Oscar Diele. "State of Online Gaming Report 2013." Spiel Games Technology, November 25, 2013. www.spilgames.com.

[25]   Heather Newman. "World of Warcraft Lead Designer on Why 7M Players Stuck Around—and Why 3M Left." *GamesBeat*, May 14, 2015. venturebeat.com.

[26]   Tim Ingham. "CHINA: Warcraft Hits One Million Unique Users." MCV, April 14, 2008. www.mcvuk.com.

[27]   Jimmy Yap. "Power Up!" *Internet Magazine*, February 2003.

[28]   David Barboza. "Ogre to Slay? Outsource It to China." *New York Times*, December 9, 2005.

[29]   "Experience Smart Home Awesomation." Revolv, June 14, 2013. revolv.com.

[30]   Internal Revenue Service. "More Than 122 Million Returns e-Filed in 2013." IRS.gov, December 4, 2013. www.irs.gov.

[31]   David Streitfeld. "Tech Industry Sets Its Sights on Gambling." *New York Times*, February 17, 2013. www.nytimes.com.

[32]   Bob Tedeschi. "Gambling Sites Adjust to Scrutiny." *New York Times*, March 31, 2003.

[33]   Kiva (Web site). Accessed October 4, 2013. www.kiva.org.

[34]   Tolu Oguniesi and Stephanie Busari. "Seven Ways Mobile Phones Have Changed Lives in Africa." CNN, September 12, 2012. www.cnn.com.

[35]   Eugene Kim. "This Chart Shows One Major Reason Why Investors Are So Worried about Twitter." *Business Insider*, April 30, 2015. www.businessinsider.com.

[36]   Chris Chase. "Germany's World Cup Rout of Brazil Was the Most Tweeted Event in History." *USA Today*, July 9, 2014. ftw.usatoday.com.

[37]   Claire Cain Miller. "Mom-and-Pop Operators Turn to Social Media." *New York Times*, July 23, 2009.

[38]   Clay Shirky. "The Political Power of Social Media." *Foreign Affairs*, January/February 2011.

[39]   Philip N. Howard. "The Arab Spring's Cascading Effects." *Pacific Standard,* February 23, 2011, www.psmag.com.

[40]   "Region in Turmoil." Al Jazeera. Accessed August 8, 2011. blogs.aljazeera.net/twitter-dashboard.

[41]   William Saletan. "Springtime for Twitter." *Slate*, July 18, 2011, www.slate.com.

[42] Malcolm Gladwell. "Small Change: Why the Revolution Will Not Be Tweeted." *New Yorker*, October 4, 2011.

[43] Eason Jordan. "News We Kept to Ourselves." *New York Times*, April 11, 2003.

[44] "About Filtering." OpenNet Initiative, August 1, 2007. opennet.net/about-filtering.

[45] "Top 10 Internet-Censored Countries." *USA Today*, February 5, 2014. www.usatoday.com.

[46] Jonathan Zittrain and Benjamin Edelman. "Documentation of Internet Filtering in Saudi Arabia." Technical report, Harvard Law School, Cambridge, MA, September 12, 2002.

[47] Rebekah Heacock. "China Shuts Down Internet in Xinjiang Region after Riots." Open-Net Initiative, July 6, 2009. opennet.org.

[48] Asher Moses. "Censoring Mobiles and the Net: How the West Is Clamping Down." *Sydney Morning Herald*, August 15, 2011. www.smh.com.au.

[49] "Internet Filtering in China." OpenNet Initiative, June 15, 2009. opennet.net.

[50] Oliver August. "Staring Down the Censors." *Wired*, November 2007.

[51] "IOC Agrees to Internet Blocking at the Games." *New York Times*, July 30, 2008.

[52] Immanuel Kant. "What Is Enlightenment?" In *Foundations of the Metaphysics of Morals*, Library of Liberal Arts, Upper Saddle River, NJ, 1997.

[53] John Stuart Mill. "On Liberty." In *On Liberty and Utilitarianism*, Bantam Books, New York, NY, 1993.

[54] Edward G. Hudon. *Freedom of Speech and Press in America*. Public Affairs Press, Washington, DC, 1963.

[55] Francis Canavan. *Freedom of Expression: Purpose as Limit*. Carolina Academic Press, Durham, NC, 1984.

[56] Cass R. Sunstein. *Democracy and the Problem of Free Speech*. Free Press, New York, NY, 1993.

[57] Supreme Court of Virginia. Jeremy Jaynes v. Commonwealth of Virginia, Record No. 062388, September 12, 2008.

[58] George Carlin. "Filthy Words." On *Occupation: Foole*, Atlantic Records, 1973.

[59] Supreme Court of the United States. Federal Communications Commission v. Pacifica Foundation et al., 438 US 726 (1978).

[60] "Parent-Controlled Filtering Software." Irvine Unified School District, Orange County, California. Accessed October 5, 2013. www.iusd.org.

[61] Associated Press. "Justices Uphold Use of Internet Filters in Public Libraries." *NYTimes.com*, June 23, 2003.

[62] Jeffrey Kosseff. "Libraries Should Bar Web Porn, Court Rules." *Oregonian* (Portland, OR), June 24, 2003.

[63] James Rachels. *The Elements of Moral Philosophy*. 4th ed. McGraw-Hill, Boston, MA, 2003.

[64] John Rawls. *A Theory of Justice, Revised Edition*, p. 187. Belknap Press of Harvard University Press, Cambridge, MA, 1999.

[65] Lorenne Clark. "Sexual Equality and the Problem of an Adequate Moral Theory: The Poverty of Liberalism." In *Contemporary Moral Issues*, McGraw-Hill Ryerson, Toronto, Ontario, Canada, 1997.

[66] Langdon Winner. "Electronically Implanted 'Values.'" *Technology Review*, 100(2), February/March 1997.

[67] Doug Johnson. "Internet Filters: Censorship by Any Other Name?" *Emergency Librarian*, 25(5), May/June 1998.

[68] "Teen Online & Wireless Safety Survey: Cyberbullying, Sexting, and Parental Controls." Cox Communications, May 2009.

[69] Michele Ybarra. "How Many Teens Are Actually Sexting? Why Teen Sexting Rates Are Overreported in the Media." *Psychology Today*, January 19, 2015. www.psychology today.com.

[70] Mike Celizic. "Her Teen Committed Suicide over 'Sexting.'" *TodayShow.com*, March 6, 2009. www.msnbc.msn.com.

[71] Kim Zetter. "'Sexting' Hysteria Falsely Brands Educator as Child Pornographer." *Wired*, April 3, 2009. www.wired.com.

[72] Martin Dula. "Sexting: The Convergence of Two Revolutions." *Pop Culture History* (blog), June 25, 2009. www.greathistory.com.

[73] Sameer Hinduja and Justin Patchin. "State Sexting Laws: A Brief Review of State Sexting Laws and Policies." Cyberbullying Research Center, January 2015. cyberbullying .us.

[74] Dorothy E. Denning. *Information Warfare and Security*, p. 241. Addison-Wesley, Boston, MA, 1999.

[75] FBI. "Victims of Identity Theft." *FBI Law Enforcement Bulletin*, March 5, 2014. leb.fbi .gov.

[76] Javelin Strategy & Research. "2009 Identity Fraud Survey Report: Consumer Version." February 2009. www.javelinstrategy.com.

[77] Javelin Strategy & Research. "2011 Identity Fraud Survey Report: Consumer Version." February 2011. www.javelinstrategy.com.

[78] Steve Weisman. "Why College Students Are at High Risk of Identity Theft." *FTPress*, October 3, 2013. www.ftpress.com.

[79] David McGuire. "Bush Signs Identity Theft Bill." *WashingtonPost.com*, July 15, 2004.

[80] Federal Trade Commission. "Take Charge: Fighting Back against Identity Theft." FTC.gov, February 2005. www.ftc.gov/bcp/conline.pubs.

[81] "Gartner Says Identity Theft Is Up Nearly 80 Percent." Gartner, Inc., July 21, 2003. www.gartner.com.

[82] Myles Anderson. "Local Consumer Review Survey 2014." July 1, 2014. www.bright local.com.

[83] Logan Kugler. "Keeping Online Reviews Honest." *Communications of the ACM*, November 2014, pp. 20–23.

[84] Judy Woodruff. "Spotting the Fakes among the Five-Star Reviews." *PBS NewsHour*, January 19, 2015. 9:30. video.pbs.org.

[85] Craig Smith. "By the Numbers: 14 Important Kik Messenger Stats." Digital Marketing Stats/Strategy/Gadgets, May 23, 2015. expandedramblings.com.

[86] Steve Jefferson and Emma Koch. "Police Issue Warning about Child Predators Using Kik App." *NBC33 News*, August 22, 2013. www.21alive.com.

[87] Dave Spencer. "Police: Kik App Used by Sexual Predator to Lure West Michigan Teen to Home." *Fox17 News*, January 14, 2014. fox17online.com.

[88]   Howard Koplowitz. "Whisper App Rape: Ronald Peterson III Arrested for Allegedly Raping 12-Year-Old Washington Girl He Met through Secrets App." *International Business Times*, October 22, 2013. www.ibtimes.com.

[89]   Colleen Curry. "Underage Sex Sting Nabs 40 Would-Be Pedophiles." *20/20*, January 18, 2012. abcnews.go.com.

[90]   Phil Perry. "Lincolnton PD Nabs 17 in Child Predator Sting Operation." *Lincoln Times-News*, May 22, 2015. www.lincolntimesnews.com.

[91]   Mark Boyle. "Galveston Task Force Agents Arrest Child Sexual Predators in Sting Operation." Click2Houston (Web site). Accessed June 22, 2015. www.click2houston .com.

[92]   Noah Pransky. "Officers Accused of Bending Rules on Sex Sting Arrests." *USA Today*, August 8, 2014. www.usatoday.com.

[93]   Andy Baio. "Finding the Star Wars Kid." *Waxy.org* (blog), May 13, 2003. waxy.org.

[94]   Tu Thanh Ha. "Parents File Lawsuit over Star Wars Video." *Globe and Mail*, Toronto, Ontario, Canada, July 23, 2003.

[95]   "Star Wars Kid Is Top Viral Video." *BBC News*, November 27, 2006. www.bbc.co.uk.

[96]   Steve Pokin. "'MySpace' Hoax Ends with Suicide of Dardenne Prairie Teen." *Suburban Journals*, November 11, 2007. suburbanjournals.stltoday.com.

[97]   "Parents Want Jail Time for MySpace Hoax Mom." *ABC News*, November 29, 2007. abcnews.go.com.

[98]   Kim Zetter. "Government's Star Witness Stumbles: MySpace Hoax Was Her Idea, Not Drew's." *Wired*, November 20, 2008. www.wired.com.

[99]   "Missouri Begins Prosecuting under Cyberbullying Law." *Fox News*, December 20, 2008. www.foxnews.com.

[100]  Kim Zetter. "Lori Drew Not Guilty of Felonies in Landmark Cyberbullying Trial." *Wired*, November 26, 2008. www.wired.com.

[101]  Kim Zetter. "Judge Acquits Lori Drew in Cyberbullying Case, Overrules Jury." *Wired*, July 2, 2009. www.wired.com.

[102]  Congressional Research Service. "H. R. 1966: Megan Meier Cyberbullying Prevention Act (Summary)." April 2, 2009. www.govtrack.us.

[103]  "revenge porn" (entry). *Collins English Dictionary*. www.collinsdictionary.com.

[104]  "Exposed Women Confront Website Owner: 'What Is Your Motive?'" *Anderson*, November 21, 2011. 1:28. www.youtube.com/watch?v=GAcXjjD3nYg.

[105]  "'Revenge Porn' Conviction Is a First under California Law." *LA Times*, December 4, 2014. www.latimes.com.

[106]  Abby Ohlheiser. "Reddit's New Privacy Policy Bans Sharing Nude Images without Consent." *Washington Post*, February 24, 2015. www.washingtonpost.com.

[107]  "The Twitter Rules." Twitter (Web site). Accessed July 12, 2015. support.twitter.com/ entries/18311.

[108]  Amit Singhal. "'Revenge Porn' and Search." June 19, 2015. googlepublicpolicy .blogspot.com.

[109]  Jacky Lynne A. Oiga. "Is Technology Driving You Crazy?" *Mania Bulletin*, August 20, 2013. www.mb.com.ph.

[110]  Susan Weinschenk. "100 Things You Should Know about People: #8—Dopamine Makes You Addicted to Seeking Information." *What Makes Them Click: Applying Psy-*

*chology to Understand How People Think, Work, and Relate* (blog), November 7, 2009. www.whatmakesthemclick.net.

[111] Carolyn Gregoire. "Our Digital Device Addiction Is Causing 'A National Attention Deficit.'" *Huffington Post*, October 7, 2014. www.huffingtonpost.com.

[112] Jerald J. Block. "Issues for DSM-V: Internet Addiction." *American Journal of Psychiatry*, March 2008. psychiatryonline.org.

[113] American Psychiatric Association. "DSM-5 Proposed Revisions Include New Category of Addiction and Related Disorders; New Category of Behavioral Addictions Also Proposed" (press release). February 10, 2010.

[114] B. N. Kim. "From Internet to 'Family-Net': Internet Addict vs. Digital Leader." 2007 International Symposium on the Counseling and Treatment of Youth Internet Addiction, Seoul, Korea, 2007.

[115] Y. H. Choi. "Advancement of IT and Seriousness of Youth Internet Addiction." 2007 International Symposium on the Counseling and Treatment of Youth Internet Addiction, Seoul, Korea, 2007.

[116] D. H. Ahn. "Korean Policy on Treatment and Rehabilitation for Adolescents' Internet Addiction." 2007 International Symposium on the Counseling and Treatment of Youth Internet Addiction, Seoul, Korea, 2007.

[117] Melia Robinson. "Korea's Internet Addiction Crisis Is Getting Worse, as Teens Spend Up to 88 Hours a Week Gaming." *Business Insider*, March 25, 2015. www.business insider.com.

[118] "The More They Play, the More They Lose." *People's Daily Online*, April 6, 2007. en .people.cn.

[119] Stanton Peele. *The Meaning of Addiction: An Unconventional View.* Jossey-Bass, San Francisco, CA 1998.

[120] Kimberly S. Young. "Internet Addiction: Symptoms, Evaluation, and Treatment." In *Innovations in Clinical Practice*, volume 17, edited by L. VandeCreek and T. L. Jackson. Professional Resource Press, Sarasota, FL, 1999.

[121] Jeffrey Reiman. *Critical Moral Liberalism: Theory and Practice.* Rowman & Littlefield Publishers, Lanham, MD, 1997.

[122] Immanuel Kant. *Lectures on Ethics.* Cambridge University Press, Cambridge, England, 2001.

[123] Mark Griffiths. "Does Internet and Computer 'Addiction' Exist? Some Case Study Evidence." *CyberPsychology and Behavior*, 3(2), 2000.

[124] John Del Signore. "NJ Student Suspended for 'Trolling' on YouTube, Facebook." *Gothamist* (blog), January 16, 2013. gothamist.com.

[125] Matt Richtel. "Devices Enforce Silence of Cellphones, Illegally." *New York Times*, November 4, 2007. www.nytimes.com.

[126] US Department of State. "Internet Freedom." Fact sheet, February 15, 2011. www.state .gov.

[127] "Protesters Angry about Police Shooting Shut Down S.F. Subway Stop." CNN, July 12, 2011. www.cnn.com.

[128] "S.F. Subway System Admits Cutting Cellphone Service to Stop Planned Protest." CNN, August 13, 2011. news.blocks.cnn.com.

# Michael Liebhold

Mike Liebhold is a senior researcher at the Institute for the Future, focusing on the mobile and abundant computation, immersive media, and geospatial Web foundations for context-aware and ubiquitous computing. Previously, Mike was a visiting researcher at Intel Labs, working on a pattern language based on semantic Web frameworks for ubiquitous computing. Before that, during the late 1990s, Mike worked on start-ups building large-scale international public IT services and IP networks for rural and remote regions and for GPS-enhanced precision agriculture, a complete IT architecture for schools in Shandong Province, China, and satellite networks in India, Europe, and Latin America. He was the principal investigator for a National Science Foundation project to bring Internet2 broadband IP networks to 70 rural low-income communities in the United States.

Mike is a frequent speaker on the topic of the geospatial Web and has authored a number of papers, including one recently published in a special edition of the IEEE *Journal on Pervasive Computing*, "Data Management in the World-Wide Sensor Web."

---

***You've said the Apple iPhone represents one of the most important inflection points in the history of technology. What makes the iPhone so significant?***

I've been working in technology since 1977. My iPhone is the most profoundly impressive device that I've ever been around. What it represents is a mobile computer that everyone can afford. It's a device that can compute. It can give you Web access to all kinds of media information. It's a global library. And that's the way to think about the Web—as a global library for humanity. It supports rich video and audio, so you can actually imagine a spoken interactive interface to the global library that would let you gain access to information without being literate. It has position sensing. The device knows where it is, so very precise contextual information can become available to people.

Our forecast is that between 2015 and 2020 every human on Earth will be able to afford a device that's equivalent to an iPhone. Now that's not to say that the cost of network and data connectivity is going to drop commensurately, but over time there will be improved and lower-cost networks for every human on Earth. And so I think we're at the dawning of a new wave of global literacy and connectivity.

***In your answer you alluded to computers being able to provide information to people based on their location. How is geographical information being introduced into the Web?***

The geospatial Web has four components. The first is Web information that is identified by URL and its location: by latitude and longitude and increasingly by elevation. We now have Web standards that allow you to publish a piece of information by location that's viewable in a variety of Web browsers. The second component is a collection of Web-enabled maps of many varieties. Environmental maps, infrastructure maps, commercial maps, historical maps, cultural maps—many types of free and malleable maps are coming online. When I say malleable, I mean you can import the data that work with the map. The third component is real-time sensor data, such as temperature data, humidity data, and video feeds from cameras. Finally, the component of the geospatial Web that's not quite here yet is embedded information. I've seen a computer chip that's as tiny as a mote of dust that has a CPU, a memory, and a radio. There's a group at Carnegie Mellon that has made a Web server that's about as big as your fingernail on your little finger. So you can begin to imagine the physical things and physical places that are going to incorporate data.

### What are people going to do with all this information?

There's a thought exercise that I do regularly, and I encourage people to think of it this way. I imagine I can see the invisible information. As I walk by a tree, I pretend I can see a label that identifies not only the species of the tree but whether it's been watered or pruned lately—its maintenance record. I look at a building, and I imagine I can see the architectural drawings behind the facade. As I look at a historical building, I imagine I can see the tags that describe the historical significance of the place. As I see someone down the street, I imagine they've got a digital cloak on and that they're a game player in a physical space. As I walk by a restaurant or a store, I can see a listing of the things that are in the store. As I walk down the street, I can see traffic indicators—arrows pointing the direction for me.

And in fact these things are all practical now. It's now possible for the viewfinder in your phone to be a Web browser, so you can hold up the viewfinder of your phone and see data attached to a place. Many applications are already available for the iPhone and Android, and there are more to come. There are restaurant menus that you can see as you walk down the street. There are applications that show you the health risk or danger of a place. There are applications that show you if it's safe to park your car. There are applications that guide you to real estate listings, and on and on and on.

### You've been talking about using computers to augment reality, to give people more information about where they are and what they are looking at in the real world. What about the tens of millions of people who use computers to escape to virtual worlds through games like World of Warcraft or Halo?

I have to say that World of Warcraft and many other games are coming. Point-and-shoot video games are immensely popular among young men. So, yes, we do see that in their homes people are going to put on glasses and enjoy all kinds of immersive 3-D experiences, games, virtual travel, and lots of other kinds of things. That's fairly legitimate, but I don't think people are going to be gone or lost any more than they are watching television today. People will get up and go outside. The world is an exciting place.

### On the other hand, if I "travel" in a virtual world, I don't have to worry about the long lines at airport security or the big crowd waiting to see David in Florence.

Telepresence might attract a lot of people, and it's going to help global literacy. There will be very compelling experiences with 3-D, and I think people are going to have a much richer understanding of the world. But telepresence will never equal walking on the streets of Rome.

### Tell me more about how people will use telepresence to enhance their lives in the "real world."

We see really remarkable things happening with applications like Skype videoconferencing. Distant relatives turn on Skype and leave it on all day because it's essentially free. I heard a story about two elderly sisters who use Skype voice calls. They turn it on, sit down, knit, chat, feed the cat, and enjoy each other's companionship. I met a guy who bought a flat-screen television for his parents in France. They put it in their dining area, and he's got one in his kitchen. So when he sits down to have brunch on Sunday mornings his parents have dinner in France. And they can just leave it on and have a family meal together.

I think this is another great trend. I think that modern technology is actually bringing families and friends closer together instead of alienating or isolating people.

# Intellectual Property

Friends share all things.

—PYTHAGORAS

Today's pirates operate not on the high seas but on the Internet.

—RECORDING INDUSTRY ASSOCIATION OF AMERICA

## 4.1 Introduction

*Game of Thrones* is the most frequently pirated television show in the world. In an effort to reduce piracy, HBO simulcast the premiere episode of season 5 in 170 countries and introduced a new video streaming service for $14.99 a month with a 30-day free trial. A record 8 million viewers watched the first episode on HBO. However, a day before it aired, the first four episodes became available on pirate networks, and in a single week were downloaded more than 32 million times worldwide [1]. Is it fair for some people to watch shows for free when others are paying to view them?

At a Bowling for Soup concert, the band made up a song onstage. Singer Jaret Reddick says, "That thing was on YouTube before I even got back home from the show" [2]. Do entertainers have the right to control who sees and hears a performance of their music?

Several years ago a survey of digital music collections of young American adults aged 18–29 revealed that on average 22 percent of the files were downloaded for free and another 22 percent were copied from friends or family members [3]. The Recording

Industry Association of America (RIAA) once went about identifying egregious file sharers, sending each of them a letter warning of an impending lawsuit, and giving them the opportunity to settle out of court, usually by paying between $3,000 and $5,000 [4]. Boston University graduate student Joel Tenenbaum refused to settle out of court, was found guilty of violating copyright law by downloading and sharing 30 songs, and ordered by the jury to pay record companies $675,000 [5]. (A judge later reduced the penalty to $67,500 [6].) Viewing the position of the RIAA as unreasonable, the Electronic Frontier Foundation has urged Americans to put pressure on Congress to change copyright laws (Figure 4.1) [7].

As a society we benefit from access to high-quality television shows, music, movies, computer programs, and other products of the human intellect. The value of these intellectual properties is much higher than the cost of the media on which they are distributed, tempting people to make unauthorized copies. When this happens, producers of intellectual property do not receive all the payments the law says they are entitled to. The legal system has responded by giving more rights to the creators of intellectual property. Are these changes in the best interests of our society, or are politicians catering to special interest groups?

In this chapter we discuss how information technology is affecting our notions of intellectual property. We consider what makes intellectual property different from tangible property and how governments have created a variety of mechanisms to guarantee intellectual property rights. We examine what has been considered "fair use" of intellectual property created by others, and how new copy protection technologies are eroding the notions of fair use. Meanwhile, peer-to-peer networks are making it easier than ever for consumers to get access to music and movies without purchasing them, putting pressure on companies selling these products to make obtaining a legal copy at least as easy as obtaining an illegal copy. We also explore the evolution of intellectual property protection for computer software and the rise of the open-source movement, which advocates the distribution of source code to programs. Finally, we take a look at one organization's efforts to make it easier for artists, musicians, and writers to use the Internet as a vehicle for stimulating creativity and enhancing collaboration.

## 4.2 Intellectual Property Rights

**Intellectual property** is any unique product of the human intellect that has commercial value [8]. Examples of intellectual property are books, songs, movies, paintings, inventions, chemical formulas, and computer programs.

It is important to distinguish between intellectual property and its physical manifestation in some medium. If a poet composes a new poem, for example, the poem itself is the intellectual property, not the piece of paper on which the poem is printed.

In most of the world there is a widely accepted notion that people have the right to own property. Does this right extend to intellectual property as well? To answer this question, we need to examine the philosophical justification for a natural right to property.

FIGURE 4.1 The Electronic Frontier Foundation is advocating a reform of the copyright laws in the United States. (Advertisement from the Electronic Frontier Foundation. Copyright © 2011 by Electronic Frontier Foundation [Creative Commons]. Reprinted with permission.)

### 4.2.1 Property Rights

The English philosopher John Locke (1632–1704) developed an influential theory of property rights. In *The Second Treatise of Government*, Locke makes the following case for a natural right to property. First, people have a right to property in their own person. Nobody has a right to the person of anybody else. Second, people have a right to their

FIGURE 4.2 According to John Locke, people have a natural right to the things they have removed from Nature through their own labor.

own labor. The work that people perform should be to their own benefit. Third, people have a right to those things that they have removed from Nature through their own labor [9].

For example, suppose you are living in a village, in the middle of woods that are held in common. One day you walk into the woods, chop down a tree, saw it into logs, and split the logs into firewood (Figure 4.2). Before you cut down the tree, everyone had a common right to it. By the time you have finished splitting the logs, you have mixed your labor with the wood, and at that point it has become your property. Whether you burn the wood in your stove, sell it to someone else, pile it up for the winter, or give it away, the choice of what to do with the wood is yours.

Locke uses the same reasoning to explain how a person can gain the right to a piece of land. Taking a parcel out of the state of Nature by clearing the trees, tilling the soil, and planting and harvesting crops gives people who performed these labors the right to call the land their property.

To Locke, this definition of property makes sense as long as two conditions hold. First, no person claims more property than he or she can use. In the case of harvesting a natural resource, it is wrong for someone to take so much that some of it is wasted. For example, people should not appropriate more land than they can tend. Second, when people remove something from the common state in order to make it their own property, there is still plenty left over for others to claim through their labor. If the woods are full of trees, I can chop a tree into firewood without denying you or anyone else the opportunity to do the same thing.

Locke's description of a natural right to property is most useful at explaining how virtually unlimited resources are initially appropriated. It is not as useful in situations where there are limited resources left for appropriation.

### 4.2.2  Extending the Argument to Intellectual Property

Is there a natural right to intellectual property?

We can try to demonstrate that such a right exists by extending Locke's theory of property rights to intellectual property. However, since Locke was talking about the ownership of physical objects and we are talking about the ownership of ideas, we must resort to an analogy. We'll compare writing a play to making a belt buckle [10]. In order to make a belt buckle, a person must mine ore, smelt it down, and cast it. To write a play, a playwright "mines" words from the English language, "smelts" them into stirring prose, and "casts" them into a finished play.

Attempting to treat intellectual property the same as ordinary property leads to certain paradoxes, as Michael Scanlan has observed [10]. We consider two of Scanlan's scenarios illustrating problems that arise when we extend Locke's natural rights argument to intellectual property.

### ∼ Scenario A, Act 1

> After a day of rehearsals at the Globe Theatre, William Shakespeare decides to have supper at a pub across the street. The pub is full of gossip about royal intrigue in Denmark. After his second pint of beer, Shakespeare is visited by the muse, and in an astonishing burst of energy, he writes *Hamlet* in one fell swoop.
> ∼

If we apply Locke's theory of property to this situation, clearly Shakespeare has the right to own *Hamlet*. He mixed his labor with the raw resources of the English language and produced a play. Remember, we're not talking about the piece of paper upon which the words of the play are written. We're talking about the sequence of words comprising the play. The paper is simply a way of conveying them.

What should Shakespeare get from his ownership of *Hamlet?* Here are two ideas (you can probably think of more): He should have the right to decide who will perform the play. He should have the right to require others who are performing the play to pay him a fee.

So far, so good. But let's hear the end of the story.

### ∼ Scenario A, Act 2

> On the very same night, Ben Jonson, at a pub on the opposite side of London, hears the same gossip, is struck by the same muse, and writes *Hamlet*—exactly the same play!
> ∼

Ben Jonson has mixed his intellectual labor with the English language to produce a play. According to Locke's theory of natural rights to property, he ought to own it. Is it possible for both Ben Jonson and William Shakespeare to own the same play (Figure 4.3)? No, not as we have defined ownership rights. It is impossible for both of them to have the exclusive right to decide who will perform the play. Both of them cannot have an exclusive claim to royalties collected when *Hamlet* is performed. We've uncovered a paradox: two people labored independently and produced only a single artifact.

**FIGURE 4.3** Suppose both Ben Jonson and William Shakespeare simultaneously write down *Hamlet*. Who owns it? (Ben Jonson, Walker Art Library/Alamy; Shakespeare, Classic Image/Alamy)

We ended up with this paradox because our analogy is imperfect. If two people go to the same iron mine, dig ore, smelt it, and cast it into belt buckles, there are two belt buckles, one for each person. Even if the belt buckles look identical, they are distinct, and we can give each person ownership of one of them. This is not the case with *Hamlet*. Even though Jonson and Shakespeare worked independently, there is only one *Hamlet*: the sequence of words that constitute the play. Whether we give one person complete ownership or divide the ownership among the two men, both cannot get full ownership of the play, which is what they ought to have if the analogy were perfect. Therefore, the uniqueness of intellectual properties is the first way in which they differ from physical objects.

A second paradox has to do with the copying of intellectual property. Consider a slightly different version of our story.

## ⤳ SCENARIO B

One evening William Shakespeare stays up all night in a pub writing *Hamlet* while Ben Jonson goes to a party. The next morning Shakespeare returns to the Globe Theatre, but he carelessly leaves a copy of *Hamlet* in the pub. Jonson stops by for breakfast, sees the manuscript, transcribes it, and walks out the door with a copy of the play in his possession, leaving the original copy where it was.   ⤳

Did Jonson steal *Hamlet*? Shakespeare still has his physical copy of the play, but he has lost exclusive control over who will read, perform, or hear the play. If you want to call this stealing, then stealing in the sense of intellectual property is quite different from stealing a physical object. When you steal someone's car, they can't drive it anymore. When you steal someone's joke, both of you can tell it.

Certainly, any creator of a piece of intellectual property has the right to keep his ideas a secret. After Shakespeare wrote *Hamlet*, he could have locked it in a trunk to prevent others from seeing it. Ben Jonson would not have had the right to break into Shakespeare's trunk to get access to the play. Hence we can argue that there is a natural right to keep an idea confidential. Unfortunately, this is a weak right, because Shakespeare cannot perform the play while he is keeping it confidential. He must give up the confidentiality in order to put his creation to good use.

We began this section with the following question: Is there a natural right to intellectual property? We have found no right other than the weak right to keep an idea confidential. In our quest for stronger rights, we have uncovered two important differences between tangible property and intellectual property. First, every intellectual property is one-of-a-kind. Second, copying a piece of intellectual property is different from stealing a physical object.

### 4.2.3 Benefits of Intellectual Property Protection

New ideas in the form of inventions and artistic works can improve the quality of life for the members of a society. Some people are altruistic and will gladly share their creative energies. For example, Benjamin Franklin (1706–1790) invented many useful items, including an improved wood stove, the lightning rod, the odometer, and bifocals. He did not patent any of them. Franklin said, "As we enjoy great advantages from the invention of others, we should be glad of an opportunity to serve others by any invention of ours; and this we should do freely and generously" [11, p. 28]. However, most people find the allure of money to be a strong inducement for laboring long hours in the hope of creating something useful. So even if there are no natural rights to intellectual property, a society may choose to grant intellectual property rights to people because of the beneficial consequences.

The authors of the Constitution of the United States recognized the benefits society reaps by encouraging creativity. Article I, Section 8, of the US Constitution gives Congress the power to "promote the Progress of Science and useful Arts by securing for limited Times to Authors and Inventors the exclusive Right to their respective Writings and Discoveries."

If a person has the right to control the distribution and use of a piece of intellectual property, there are many opportunities for that person to make money. For example, suppose you build a better mousetrap and the government gives you ownership of this design. You may choose to manufacture the mousetrap yourself. Anyone who wants the better mousetrap must buy it from you, because no other mousetrap manufacturer has the right to copy your design. Alternatively, you may choose to license your design to other manufacturers, who will pay you for the right to build mousetraps according to your design. It is also possible for you to be rewarded for your creativity without the new device ever reaching the public. Suppose you sell an exclusive license for your better mousetrap to the company that dominates the mousetrap market. The company chooses not to manufacture the new mousetrap because—for whatever reason—it can make more money selling the existing technology. In this situation you and the company benefit, but society is deprived access to the new, improved technology.

### 4.2.4 Limits to Intellectual Property Protection

Society benefits the most when inventions are in the public domain and anyone can take advantage of them. Going back to the mousetrap example, we would like everyone in society who needs a mousetrap to get the best possible trap. If someone invents a superior mousetrap, the maximum benefit would result if all mousetrap manufacturers were able to use the better design. On the other hand, if the inventor of the superior mousetrap did not have any expectation of profiting from her new design, she may not have bothered to invent it. Hence there is a tension between the need to reward the creators of intellectual property by giving them exclusive rights to their ideas and the need to disseminate these ideas as widely as possible.

The way Congress has traditionally addressed this tension is through a compromise. It has granted authors and inventors exclusive rights to their writings and discoveries but only for a limited period of time. (Note: Rights to a piece of intellectual property produced by an employee in the normal course of his or her duties belong to the employer.) At the end of that time period, the intellectual property enters the public domain. While creators have control over the distribution of their properties, use of the properties is more expensive, and the creators are rewarded. After properties enter the public domain, using them becomes less expensive, and everyone has the opportunity to produce derivative works from them.

Consider a community orchestra that wishes to perform a piece of classical music. It may purchase a piece of music from the public domain for far less money than it cost simply to rent the same piece of music while it was still protected by copyright (Table 4.1).

The question is, what is a reasonable length of time to grant authors and inventors exclusive rights to their creative works? Supreme Court justice Stephen Breyer [13],

| Artist | Work | Previous Rental Fee | Year Became Public Domain | Purchase Price |
|---|---|---|---|---|
| Ravel | Daphnis et Chloe Suite no. 1 | $450.00 | 1987 | $155.00 |
| Ravel | Mother Goose Suite | 540.00 | 1988 | 70.00 |
| Ravel | Daphnis et Chloe Suite no. 2 | 540.00 | 1989 | 265.00 |
| Griffes | The White Peacock | 335.00 | 1993 | 42.00 |
| Puccini | O Mio Babbino Caro | 252.00 | 1994 | 26.00 |
| Respighi | Fountains of Rome | 441.00 | 1994 | 140.00 |
| Ravel | Le Tombeau de Couperin | 510.00 | 1995 | 86.00 |
| Respighi | Ancient Aires and Dances Suite no. 1 | 441.00 | 1996 | 85.00 |
| Elgar | Cello Concerto | 550.00 | 1997 | 140.00 |
| Holst | The Planets | 815.00 | 1997 | 300.00 |
| Ravel | Alborada Del Gracioso | 360.00 | 1999 | 105.00 |

TABLE 4.1 Once a piece of classical music enters the public domain, it may be purchased for much less than it cost simply to rent the same piece of music for two performances when it was still under copyright protection. These prices assume the orchestra has an annual budget of $150,000 or less [12]. (Table from "Letter to The Honorable Senator Spencer Abraham," by Randolph P. Luck from Luck's Music Library. Copyright © 1996 by Randolph P. Luck. Reprinted with permission.)

Kembrew McLeod [14], and Lawrence Lessig [15] have used "Happy Birthday to You" as evidence that copyright protections are excessive.

"Happy Birthday to You" is the most popular song in the world. Have you ever wondered why you almost never hear it sung on television? The reason is that the music publisher Clayton F. Summy Company (now a subsidiary of Warner Music Group) copyrighted the song in 1935, and television networks must pay Warner Music Group to air it. Warner Music Group collects about $2 million in royalties each year for public performances of "Happy Birthday to You" [16]. Under the Copyright Term Extension Act of 1998, the song will remain copyrighted until at least 2030.

More recently, George Washington University law professor Robert Brauneis has objected that "Happy Birthday to You" should not be used as an example of the "overly generous protection of copyright law." In a meticulously researched article, he concludes that the song "is almost certainly no longer under copyright, due to a lack of evidence about who wrote the words; defective copyright notice; and a failure to file a proper renewal application" [17]. In 2015 the US District Court for the Central District of California ruled that Warner Music Group does not own a valid copyright to the lyrics of "Happy Birthday to You." If the ruling is not overturned, the song will enter the public domain.

## 4.3 Protecting Intellectual Property

While the US Constitution gives Congress the right to grant authors and inventors exclusive rights to their creations, it does not elaborate on how these rights will be protected. Today there are four different ways in which individuals and organizations protect their intellectual property: trade secrets, trademarks/service marks, patents, and copyrights.

### 4.3.1 Trade Secrets

A **trade secret** is a confidential piece of intellectual property that provides a company with a competitive advantage. Examples of trade secrets include formulas, processes, proprietary designs, strategic plans, customer lists, and other collections of information. The right of a company to protect its trade secrets is widely recognized by governments around the world. In order to maintain its rights to a trade secret, a company must take active measures to keep it from being discovered. For example, companies typically require employees with access to a trade secret to execute a confidentiality agreement.

A famous trade secret is the formula for Coca-Cola syrup. The formula, known inside the company as "Merchandise 7X," is locked in a bank vault in Atlanta, Georgia. Only a few people within the company know the entire formula, and they have signed nondisclosure agreements. The task of making the syrup is divided among different groups of employees. Each group makes only one part of the final mixture, so that nobody in these groups learns the complete recipe.

An advantage of trade secrets is that they do not expire. A company never has to disclose a trade secret. Coca-Cola has kept its formula secret for more than 100 years.

The value of trade secrets is in their confidentiality. Hence trade secrets are not an appropriate way to protect many forms of intellectual property. For example, it makes no sense for a company to make a movie a trade secret, because a company can only profit from a movie by allowing it to be viewed, which makes it no longer confidential. On the other hand, it is appropriate for a company to make the idea for a movie a trade secret. Art Buchwald pitched Paramount Pictures a story called *King for a Day*, about an African prince who visits the United States. After the studio produced the movie *Coming to America*, starring Eddie Murphy, Buchwald successfully sued Paramount for breach of contract, because he had made the studio sign a confidentiality agreement before he gave them the plot [18].

While it is illegal to steal a trade secret, there are other ways in which confidentiality may be broken. **Reverse engineering** is one way in which a competing firm can legally gain access to information contained in a trade secret. If another company can purchase a can of Coca-Cola and figure out the formula, it is free to manufacture a soft drink that looks and tastes just like Coke.

Another way in which a competing firm can gain access to information contained in another company's trade secret is by hiring its employees. While a firm can require its employees to sign confidentiality agreements, it cannot erase the memories of an employee who starts working for a competing firm. Hence some "leakage" of confidential information may be inevitable when employees move from one company to another.

## 4.3.2  Trademarks and Service Marks

A **trademark** is a word, symbol, picture, sound, or color used by a business to identify goods. A **service mark** is a mark identifying a service [19]. By granting a trademark or service mark, a government gives a company the right to use it and the right to prevent other companies from using it. Through the use of a trademark, a company can establish a "brand name." Society benefits from branding because branding allows consumers to have more confidence in the quality of the products they purchase.

When a company is the first to market a distinctive product, it runs the risk that its brand name will become a common noun used to describe any similar product. When this happens, the company may lose its right to exclusive use of the brand name. Some trademarks that have become common nouns are yo yo, aspirin, escalator, thermos, and brassiere.

Companies strive to ensure their marks are used as adjectives rather than nouns or verbs. One way they do this is through advertising (Figure 4.4). Kimberly-Clark's advertisements refer to "Kleenex *brand* facial tissue." Remember Johnson & Johnson's jingle, "I am stuck on Band-Aid *brand* 'cause Band-Aid's stuck on me"?

Another way companies protect their trademarks is by contacting those who are misusing them. For example, Adobe has responded to Web posts about "photoshopping images" by posting this follow-up message: "The Photoshop trademark must never be used as a common verb or as a noun. The Photoshop trademark should always be capitalized and should never be used in possessive form, or as a slang term" [20].

FIGURE 4.4 Xerox Corporation ran this advertisement as part of its campaign to protect its trademark. (Screenshot by Xerox. Copyright © 2012 by Xerox Corporation. All rights reserved. Reprinted with permission.)

### 4.3.3 Patents

A **patent** is a way the US government provides an inventor with an exclusive right to a piece of intellectual property. A patent is quite different from a trade secret because a patent is a public document that provides a detailed description of the invention. The owner of the patent can prevent others from making, using, or selling the invention for the lifetime of the patent, which is currently 20 years. After the patent expires, anyone has the right to make use of its ideas.

#### *POLAROID v. KODAK*

Dr. Edwin Land invented "instant" photography. The company he founded, Polaroid Corporation, had 10 patents protecting the invention of film that developed in 60 seconds. Polaroid did not license these patents to other firms, and for many years it was the only company to sell cameras and film allowing photographs to be developed in a minute.

When Kodak introduced its first instant camera in 1976, Polaroid sued Kodak [21]. In 1985 a court ruled that Kodak had infringed on seven of Polaroid's original 10 patents; six years later Kodak paid Polaroid a $925 million settlement [22, 23].

#### CLEARTYPE

Sometimes companies see an advantage in licensing their inventions. For example, Microsoft invented a software technology called ClearType that improves the clarity of text displayed on liquid crystal displays (LCDs), the screens typically used in smartphones, tablets, laptops, and computer monitors. The ClearType technology is protected by 10 US patents. In 2003 Microsoft announced it would begin licensing more of its inventions to other companies, and Agfa Monotype Corp. in Belgium became the first company to license ClearType [24, 25]. The royalty rate was $1 per unit for personal digital assistants, $2 per unit for personal computers, and $3 per unit for tablets. The total amount of revenue Microsoft expected to make from the technology was not enough to have a significant impact on the company's balance sheet, leading some observers to conclude Microsoft was opening up its patent portfolio to other companies to reduce pressure from antitrust regulators in the United States and the European Union [24].

## 4.3.4 Copyrights

A **copyright** is how the US government provides authors with certain rights to original works that they have written. The owner of a copyright has five principal rights:

1. The right to reproduce the copyrighted work
2. The right to distribute copies of the work to the public
3. The right to display copies of the work in public
4. The right to perform the work in public
5. The right to produce new works derived from the copyrighted work

Copyright owners have the right to authorize others to exercise these five rights with respect to their works. Here are two examples. The owner of a copyright to a play may sell a license to a high school drama club that wishes to perform it. After a radio station broadcasts a song, it must pay the songwriter(s) and the composer(s) through a performance rights organization such as ASCAP, BMI, or SESAC. Copyright owners also have the right to prevent others from infringing on their rights to control the reproduction, distribution, display, performance, and production of works derived from their copyrighted work.

Several important industries in the United States, including the motion picture, music, software, and book publishing industries, rely on copyright law for protection. "Copyright industries" account for over 6 percent of the US gross domestic product, with over $900 billion in sales. About five million US citizens work in these industries, which are growing at a much faster rate than the rest of the US economy. With foreign sales and exports of $134 billion, copyright industries were the leading export sector in the United States in 2010 [26].

In this section we examine court cases and legislation that have helped define the limits of copyright in the United States.

### GERSHWIN PUBLISHING v. COLUMBIA ARTISTS

Columbia Artists Management, Inc. (CAMI) managed concert artists, and it sponsored hundreds of local, nonprofit community concert associations that arranged concert series featuring CAMI artists. CAMI helped the associations prepare budgets, select artists, and sell tickets. CAMI printed the programs and sold them to the community concert associations. In addition, all musicians performing at these concerts paid CAMI a portion of their fees.

On January 9, 1965, the CAMI-sponsored Port Washington (NY) Community Concert Association put on a concert that included Gershwin's "Bess, You Is My Woman Now" without obtaining copyright clearance from Gershwin Publishing Corporation. The American Society of Composers, Authors, and Publishers (ASCAP) sued CAMI for infringement of copyright.

CAMI argued that it was not responsible for the copyright infringement, since the concert was put on by the Port Washington Community Concert Association. However, the US District Court for the Southern District of New York ruled that CAMI could be held liable because it was aware that the community concert associations it supported were not obtaining proper copyright clearances. In 1971 the US Court of Appeals for the Second Circuit upheld the ruling of the district court [27].

### DAVEY JONES LOCKER

Richard Kenadek ran a computer bulletin board system (BBS) called Davey Jones Locker. Subscribers paid $99 a year for access to the BBS, which contained copies of more than 200 commercial programs. In 1994 Kenadek was indicted for infringing on the copyrights of the owners of the software. He pleaded guilty and was sentenced to six months' home confinement and two years' probation [28].

### NO ELECTRONIC THEFT ACT

Another incident in 1994 led to further legislation protecting copyrights. David LaMacchia, an MIT student, posted copyrighted software on a public bulletin board he created on a university computer. According to prosecutors, bulletin board users downloaded more than a million dollars' worth of software in less than two months. However, the prosecutors were forced to drop charges against LaMacchia because he had made the programs available for free. Since he had not profited from his actions, he had not violated copyright law. To close this legal loophole, Congress passed the No Electronic Theft Act of 1997, which made it a criminal offense simply to reproduce or distribute more than a thousand dollars' worth of copyrighted material in a six-month period.

### COPYRIGHT CREEP

As a result of the Sonny Bono Copyright Term Extension Act of 1998, works created and published before January 1, 1978, are protected for 95 years. Works created on or after January 1, 1978, are protected for the author's lifetime plus 70 years after the author's death. If the work is a work made for hire, the length of protection is 95 years from the date of publication or 120 years from the date of creation, whichever is less.

According to Siva Vaidhyanathan, "in the early republic and the first century of American legal history, copyright was a Madisonian compromise, a necessary evil, a limited, artificial monopoly, not to be granted or expanded lightly" [29, p. 24]. Over time, however, Congress has gradually increased both the term of copyright protection and the kind of intellectual properties that are protected by copyright (Figure 4.5). One reason has been the desire to have international copyright agreements. In order to complete these agreements, Congress has had to reconcile American copyright law with European

**Figure 4.5** Since the first Copyright Act was passed in 1790, both the length of copyright protection and the kinds of intellectual property that can be copyrighted have grown dramatically.

law, which in general has had much stronger protections for the producers of intellectual property [29]. Another reason for "copyright creep" has been the introduction of new technologies, such as photography, audio recording, and video recording.

For example, since 1831 music publishers have been able to copyright sheet music and collect royalties from musicians performing this music in public. In 1899 Melville Clark introduced the Apollo player piano, which played songs recorded on rolls of heavy paper. Apollo manufactured and sold piano rolls of copyrighted songs. White-Smith Music Company sued Apollo for infringing on its copyrights. In 1908 the Supreme Court ruled that Apollo had not infringed on White-Smith Music's copyrights. The court suggested that Congress ought to change copyright law if it wanted owners of copyrights to have control over recordings such as piano rolls and phonograph records. Congress responded by revising the Copyright Act in 1909. The new copyright law recognized that player piano rolls and phonograph records could be copyrighted.

Some people believe the expansion of the scope of copyright protection has tilted the balance of private versus public rights too far toward the copyright holders. They say it is no coincidence that copyright terms were extended just before Mickey Mouse was to enter the public domain. The Walt Disney Corporation lobbied Congress to pass the Sonny Bono Copyright Term Extension Act (CTEA) of 1998, protecting its profits derived from Mickey Mouse, Donald Duck, and its other famous characters [30]. Some critics suggest that since Walt Disney made a great deal of money on *Snow White and the Seven Dwarfs*, *Cinderella*, *Pinocchio*, *The Hunchback of Notre Dame*, *Alice in Wonderland*, and *The Jungle Book*, all based on stories taken from the public domain, it's only fair that at some point Walt Disney characters become part of the public domain, available for others to use in new creative works [31].

Eric Eldred, who digitizes old books and makes them freely available over the Web, led a group of petitioners who challenged the CTEA. They argued that the US Constitution gives Congress the power to grant exclusive rights to authors for "limited times," and that the writers of the Constitution expected copyright durations to be short. By extending the terms of existing copyrights 11 times in 40 years, they said, Congress had exceeded its constitutional power [32].

The government and groups representing the entertainment industry, including the Walt Disney Co., the Motion Picture Association of America, and the Recording Industry Association of America, argued that Congress does have the constitutional authority to extend the terms of existing copyrights [33].

In a 7–2 decision the US Supreme Court ruled in favor of the government and the entertainment industry, stating that the petitioners did not demonstrate how the CTEA had crossed "a constitutionally significant threshold." In the opinion of the Court, "Those earlier Acts did not create perpetual copyrights, and neither does the CTEA" [34].

### 4.3.5 Case Study: The Database Guru

Arjun worked for five years as a software engineer at Felicity Software, a company that sells database systems to consumers and small businesses. During his time at Felicity, Arjun implemented some clever software optimizations that significantly improved the performance of the database systems sold by Felicity. The company treated the optimizations as trade secrets. It labeled the software as confidential information and took measures to restrict access to the source code to Arjun and a few other software engineers who helped Arjun implement and test the system.

On his first day with Felicity, Arjun had signed an employee confidentiality and proprietary rights agreement. Signing this agreement was a condition of his employment. In this agreement Arjun had indicated that he understood and acknowledged the following:

1. He would have access to confidential, secret, and proprietary information related to Felicity's business.

2. Felicity placed "great competitive importance and commercial value" on its ability to reserve confidential information for its exclusive use.

3. Confidential information he developed would be covered by this agreement.

4. He would not "directly or indirectly disclose, publish, communicate or make available" confidential information to anyone outside of the company.

5. His obligations under the agreement would "continue during and after his employment" by Felicity [35].

After completing the database project at Felicity, Arjun began looking for the opportunity to join a software start-up. With a good reputation in the tight-knit local tech community and strong references from coworkers and managers who praised his talent, work ethic, honesty, and teamwork skills, Arjun quickly found employment at Unrelated.com, a start-up company in a nearby office park.

Unrelated.com plans to support people doing genealogical research. It is developing a proprietary database system that will be used to store genealogical information.

Unrelated.com has no plans to sell the database software. Instead, its income will be derived from the monthly fee users pay in order to access the company's database through the Web or a mobile app. Unrelated.com hopes to acquire hundreds of thousands of subscribers. That means its database system must be capable of quickly responding to queries from 10,000 or more users accessing the system simultaneously.

Arjun's title at Unrelated.com is vice president of software. He supervises several teams of software developers. One of these teams is responsible for implementing the genealogical database system and optimizing its performance. As the project progresses, Arjun realizes that some of the technical solutions proposed by the members of his team are not as good as the solutions he developed for Felicity's database product. The team's preliminary software implementation is unlikely to result in a database system with satisfactory performance when it is being accessed by more than about 5,000 users. In Arjun's judgment significant optimizations are needed before the system is ready to deploy.

Arjun believes he has two viable alternatives. The first option is to follow a "clean room" strategy. He would isolate himself from the team's work product, but he would provide the team with publicly available information on database optimization strategies—in other words, the books, journal articles, and conference papers he benefited from when he implemented the database system optimizations at Felicity. Based on his expertise, Arjun would also provide the team with realistic performance targets that the various components of the database system should be able to meet.

The second option is to become personally involved in making the necessary performance improvements. Arjun believes that if he asks the right questions, in fairly short order he can get the team to rediscover the optimizations he developed for Felicity's database product without actually telling them how to do it.

Which option should Arjun take?

## KANTIAN EVALUATIONS

The first option is innocuous. Arjun is sharing his expertise with the development team without disclosing any confidential information. He is not violating the employee confidentiality and proprietary rights agreement he signed with Felicity. The moral rule, "You should share your expertise with others," can be universalized without contradiction. From a Kantian perspective, this option is morally right.

In the second option, Arjun's will is to get the team to know what he knows without directly communicating the information. Presumably, if he asks questions in a general way, akin to a college professor posing questions for a homework assignment, the members of the team will be able to discover ways of improving the performance of the database software. However, by taking this course of action, Arjun runs the risk of asking the team leading questions—more specifically, propositions disguised as questions that require simply a yes or no answer. Communicating confidential information, even phrased as questions, is prohibited by the confidentiality agreement Arjun signed with Felicity. In this agreement Arjun stated that his obligation not to reveal confidential information outside the company would continue after his employment with Felicity ended. Breaking this contract is equivalent to breaking a promise, and as we saw in Section 2.6.1, it is wrong to break a promise. From a Kantian point of view, this option is morally acceptable only if Arjun can get through the entire line of questioning without asking a leading question. If anywhere in the process he asks a leading question that reveals optimizations he developed by Felicity, this option would be morally wrong. Given the complexity of the system to be implemented, Arjun's desire to help the team discover the optimizations, and the fact that he may feel pressed for time because he is helping the team in addition to his normal job responsibilities, it seems unlikely he would be able to avoid asking leading questions. From a Kantian perspective, this option is morally dubious.

## SOCIAL CONTRACT THEORY EVALUATIONS

Both evaluations from the perspective of social contract theory are similar to the Kantian evaluations. In the first option, Arjun is helping the team without violating any agreements. The action is morally right.

The morality of the second option hinges on whether Arjun can avoid communicating confidential information he acquired while at Felicity. As a condition of his employment at Felicity, Arjun signed a confidentiality and proprietary rights agreement, and there is no overriding moral concern in this situation that would justify his breaking this agreement. If Arjun can engage with the team and avoid asking leading questions, his actions would be morally acceptable, but if he asks any leading questions, that would be wrong.

## ACT UTILITARIAN EVALUATIONS

The affected parties are Arjun, Unrelated.com (its employees and investors), and the future customers of the genealogical research system. We will evaluate the expected consequences of each option on Arjun's standing and reputation within the company. For Unrelated.com's employees and investors, we will estimate the consequences of each option with regard to the time and cost of implementing the database and the risk of litigation from Felicity. With respect to the customers, we will estimate the consequences of each option on the ultimate performance of the system they will be using. The magnitude of the benefits calculated for Unrelated.com will be much larger than the magnitude of the benefits calculated for Arjun because the company has many employees and investors, so benefits and harms to Unrelated.com are much more significant than benefits and harms to Arjun alone. The magnitude of the benefits calculated for Unrelated.com and the customers of Unrelated.com will be roughly the same. While the number of potential customers is much greater than the number of employees and investors of Unrelated.com, the performance of this particular Web site is much less important to each customer than the importance of the company's success is to its investors and employees.

In the first option, Arjun sets up a "clean room" environment for the database team to develop its optimizations. Arjun provides a valuable service to Unrelated.com by providing the team with relevant information in the form of books, journal papers, and conference articles, as well as realistic performance targets. As a result, Arjun's standing and reputation within Unrelated.com should increase (+2). The project is delayed, increasing the time and cost of implementing the database, a negative result (−20). Arjun is not working with the team developing the software, so there is no risk that he would communicate confidential information he acquired while working at Felicity.

Therefore, there is no risk of litigation from Felicity (0). Arjun's decision to send the team back to the drawing board will enable the team to improve the performance of the software, yielding a higher-performing system that will be a positive benefit to the potential customers (+40).

In the second option, Arjun works with the team, asking the members open-ended questions that enable them to discover for themselves the database optimizations. The project is still delayed, but with Arjun's help, the team should be able to come up with the solutions more rapidly than in the previous option. The expected time and cost of implementation is slightly negative (−10). We can expect Arjun to keep at it until the team has developed optimizations that result in a significantly higher level of performance. There is a chance that Arjun may become impatient and ask the team leading questions in order to help the team move in the right direction. That would create the possibility of legal action by Felicity, which would be a strongly negative outcome for Unrelated.com. The chance that this would actually occur is equal to the probability that Arjun would divulge confidential information *and* Felicity would discover what he has done *and* the legal department at Felicity would conclude there is a legal case *and* Felicity would choose to litigate against a company that is not a direct competitor. We conclude the probability of all these events happening is very low, and we set the expected outcome for Unrelated.com with regard to its risk of litigation to be only slightly negative (−5). By demonstrating his technical prowess in the area of database design, Arjun's reputation and standing at Unrelated.com is likely to increase, but in the unlikely event Felicity sues Unrelated.com, he will be in serious trouble. Adding these two terms, we determine the expected consequence to Arjun to be slightly positive (+1). Arjun's decision to work with the team to improve the performance of the software will result in a higher-performing system, a positive benefit to the potential customers (+40).

The anticipated consequences of the two courses of action are summarized in Table 4.2. Which plan is preferable? From an act utilitarian perspective, the overall benefit of option 1 is 22, and the overall benefit of option 2 is 26. The overall expected benefits of option 2 are higher, making it the better option.

| | Course of Action | |
| | (a) Set Up | (b) Ask Team |
| Affected Parties | Clean Room | "Right Questions" |
|---|---|---|
| Arjun | +2 | +1 |
| Employees and shareholders of Unrelated.com | | |
|  Development cost and time to market | −20 | −10 |
|  Litigation risk | 0 | −5 |
| Customers | +40 | +40 |
| *Overall benefit* | +22 | +26 |

TABLE 4.2  Summary of an act utilitarian evaluation of the two options facing Arjun.

## VIRTUE ETHICS EVALUATION

Arjun holds a position of responsibility at Unrelated.com. He is responsible for recruiting, developing, and retaining high-quality employees who can create value for the company. Through his supervision of the software development teams, he must do all he can to ensure that they produce systems that work well and contribute to the company's financial success. As an officer of the company, he must avoid doing anything that puts its future in jeopardy.

Setting up a "clean room" development environment to help the team create a database system with higher performance is consistent with his responsibilities as a manager and company officer.

In the second option, Arjun would become personally engaged with the team, asking the questions that would help the programmers to quickly identify crucial database optimizations. Arjun would have to spend extra time at work, because he would also have to keep up with his other responsibilities. The willingness to work hard for the benefit of their employees and their company is a characteristic of good managers. Sharing expertise is another laudable characteristic of good managers. However, in this option Arjun is running the risk of putting himself in a situation where he gets impatient, reveals an optimization he developed at Felicity, and violates the confidentiality agreement he signed. That would be dishonest, and dishonesty is not a characteristic of a good employee or a good manager.

The prudent choice for Arjun is option 1.

## CONCLUSION

From the perspectives of Kantianism, social contract theory, and virtue ethics, the right thing for Arjun to do is to set up a clean room development environment for his software team and supply the team with publicly available information about database optimizations. Our act utilitarian analysis has reached the conclusion that the other option is preferable; Arjun should engage the members of the software development team and ask them open-ended questions until it rediscovers the optimizations he discovered while working for Felicity Software. Note, however, that a more risk-averse act utilitarian analysis would have assigned a negative number of greater magnitude to the term corresponding to the risk of litigation. If the harm of litigation in option 2 were increased from $-5$ to $-10$ or more, the overall benefit of option 2 would be lower than the overall benefit of option 1, and option 1 would be the preferred choice.

# 4.4 Fair Use

The right given to a copyright owner to reproduce a work is a limited right. Under some circumstances, called **fair use**, it is legal to reproduce a copyrighted work without the permission of the copyright holder. Examples of fair use include citing short excerpts from copyrighted works for the purpose of teaching, scholarship, research, criticism, commentary, and news reporting.

The United States Copyright Act does not precisely list the kinds of copying that are fair use. Instead, what is considered to be fair use has been determined by the judicial system. The courts have relied on Section 107 of the Copyright Act, which lists four factors that need to be considered [36]:

1. *What is the purpose and character of the use?*

   The purposes of criticism, commentary, news reporting, teaching, scholarship, and research are more likely to be permissible than a commercial purpose.

   When judging the character of the use, the most important consideration is the extent to which the author has transformed the original copyrighted work. The more the author has added new expression or meaning to the work, the more likely the work will be judged to be fair use [37].

2. *What is the nature of the work being copied?*

   Use of nonfiction is more likely to be permissible than use of fiction. Published works are preferred over unpublished works.

3. *How much of the copyrighted work is being used?*

   Brief excerpts are more likely to be permissible than entire chapters.

4. *How will this use affect the market for the copyrighted work?*

   Use of out-of-print material is more likely to be permissible than use of a readily available work. A spontaneously chosen selection is better than an assigned reading in the course syllabus.

Let's consider two scenarios in which copyrighted works are duplicated and determine if they made fair use of the material. These scenarios are closely modeled after situations presented on the Web site of CETUS, the Consortium for Educational Technology in University Systems (www.cetus.org).

## ∾ Fair Use Example #1

A professor puts a few journal articles on reserve in the library and makes them assigned reading for the class. Some students in the class complain that they cannot get access to the articles because other students always seem to have them checked out. The professor scans them and posts them on his Web site. The professor gives the students in the class the password they need to access the articles.                                                                                    ∾

The first factor to consider is the purpose of the use. In this case the purpose is strictly educational. This factor weighs in favor of fair use.

The second factor is the nature of the work being copied. The journal articles are nonfiction. Again this weighs in favor of fair use.

The third factor is the amount of material being copied. The fact that the professor is copying entire articles rather than brief excerpts weighs against a ruling of fair use.

The fourth factor is the effect the copying will have on the market for journal sales. If the journal issues containing these articles are no longer for sale, then the professor's actions cannot affect the market. The professor took care to prevent people outside the class from accessing the articles. Overall, this factor appears to weigh in favor of fair use.

Three of the four factors weigh in favor of fair use. The professor's actions probably constitute fair use of the copyrighted material.

∼ FAIR USE EXAMPLE #2

An art professor takes photographs of a number of paintings reproduced in a book about Renaissance artists. She incorporates the photos into PowerPoint lectures for her class. ∼

The first factor to consider is the purpose of the copying. The professor's purpose is strictly educational. Hence the first factor weighs in favor of fair use.

The second factor is the type of material being copied. The material is art. Hence this factor weighs against a ruling of fair use.

The third factor is the amount of material copied. In this case the professor is displaying copies of the paintings in their entirety. Fair use almost never allows a work to be copied in its entirety. Note that even if the original painting is in the public domain, the photograph of the painting appearing in the art book is probably copyrighted.

The final factor is the effect the copying will have on the market. The determination of this factor would depend on how many images the professor took from any one book and whether the publisher is in the business of selling slides of individual images appearing in its book.

Overall, this professor's actions are less likely to be considered fair use than the actions of the professor in the first example.

### 4.4.1 *Sony v. Universal City Studios*

In 1975 Sony introduced its Betamax system, the first consumer VCR. People used these systems to record television shows for viewing later, a practice called **time shifting**. Some customers recorded entire movies onto videotape.

A year later, Universal City Studios and Walt Disney Productions sued Sony, saying it was responsible for copyright infringements performed by those who had purchased VCRs. The movie studios sought monetary damages from Sony and an injunction against the manufacturing and marketing of VCRs. The legal battle went all the way to the US Supreme Court. The Supreme Court evaluated the case in light of the four fair use factors.

The first factor is the intended purpose of the copying. Since the purpose is private, not commercial, time shifting should be seen as fair use with respect to the first factor.

The second factor is the nature of the copied work. Consumers who are time shifting are copying creative work. This would tend to weigh against a ruling of fair use.

The third factor is the amount of material copied. Since a consumer copies the entire work, this weighs against a ruling of fair use.

The final factor is the effect time shifting will have on the market for the work. The Court determined that the studios were unable to demonstrate that time shifting had eroded the commercial value of their copyrights. The movie studios receive large fees from television stations in return for allowing their movies to be broadcast. Television

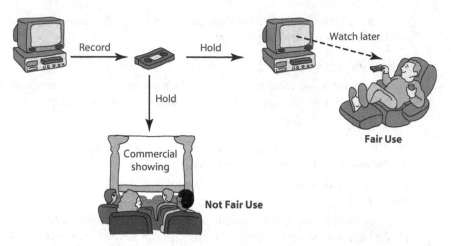

**FIGURE 4.6** The Supreme Court ruled that videotaping television broadcasts for private viewing at a later time is fair use of the copyrighted material. This practice is called time shifting. Using videotaped material for a commercial purpose is not considered fair use.

stations can pay these large fees to the studios because they receive income from advertisers. Advertising rates depend on the size of the audience; the larger the audience, the more a television station can charge an advertiser to broadcast a commercial. Time shifting allows people who would not ordinarily be able to watch a show to view it later. Hence it can be argued that VCRs actually increase the size of the audience, and since audience size determines the fees studios receive to have their movies broadcast on television, it is not at all clear whether the copying of these programs harms the studios.

The Supreme Court ruled, in a 5–4 decision, that time shifting television programs is a fair use of the copyrighted materials [38]. It said that the private, noncommercial use of copyrighted materials ought to be presumed fair use unless it could be shown that the copyright holder would be likely to suffer economic harm from the consumer's actions (Figure 4.6). Importantly, the Court also noted that the Sony Betamax VCR could be used to copy both copyrighted and noncopyrighted material, and that Sony should not be held accountable if some of the people who buy a VCR choose to use it to infringe on copyrights.

### 4.4.2 Audio Home Recording Act of 1992

The Audio Home Recording Act represents a compromise between the desires of the recording industry, the electronics industry, and consumers. The Act protects the right of consumers to make copies of analog or digital recordings for personal, noncommercial use. For example, a consumer may copy a recording to put in another music player, to give to another family member, or to use as a backup.

To reduce the problem of unauthorized copying, the Audio Home Recording Act requires manufacturers of digital audio recorders to incorporate the Serial Copyright

Management System (SCMS). The SCMS allows a consumer to make a digital copy from the original recording, but it prevents someone from making a copy of the copy.

To compensate artists and recording companies for the loss of sales due to copying, the Audio Home Recording Act requires a royalty to be paid on the sale of all digital audio recording devices and blank digital audio recording media. The royalties are divided among songwriters, music publishers, musicians, and recording companies, based on the popularity of their music. As it turns out, these royalty payments have never been a significant source of income for any of these groups.

### 4.4.3 *RIAA v. Diamond Multimedia*

A **compression algorithm** reduces the number of bits needed to store a picture or sound. The most popular compression algorithm for music is MP3, which was developed by a team of European scientists. An MP3 music file is typically less than 10 percent the size of the original file, but it is difficult to hear the difference between the original and the compressed versions. The availability of MP3 encoders and decoders in the mid-1990s helped speed the development of portable music players.

Diamond Multimedia Systems introduced the Rio MP3 portable music player in 1998. About the size of an audiocassette, the Rio stored an hour of digitized music. The Recording Industry Association of America (RIAA) asked for an injunction preventing Diamond Multimedia from manufacturing and distributing the Rio. The RIAA alleged that the Rio did not meet the requirements of the Audio Home Recording Act of 1992 because it did not employ the Serial Copyright Management System to prevent unauthorized copying of copyrighted material.

The US Court of Appeals, Ninth Circuit, upheld the ruling of a lower court that the Rio was not a digital audio recording device as defined by the Audio Home Recording Act. It denied the injunction on these technical grounds. In addition, the Court affirmed that **space shifting**, or copying a recording in order to make it portable, is fair use and entirely consistent with copyright law (Figure 4.7).

### 4.4.4 *Kelly v. Arriba Soft*

Leslie Kelly was a photographer who maintained a Web site containing many of his copyrighted photos. Arriba Soft Corporation created an Internet-based search engine that responded to user queries by displaying thumbnail images. Arriba Soft created the thumbnail images by copying images from other Web sites. When Kelly discovered that the Arriba Soft search engine was displaying thumbnail images of his photographs, he sued Arriba Soft for copyright infringement.

The US Court of Appeals, Ninth Circuit, upheld the ruling of a lower court that Arriba Soft's use of the images was a fair use of the work [39]. Two factors heavily favored Arriba Soft's claim of fair use. First, the character of Arriba Soft's use of the images was "significantly transformative" [39]. Kelly's original images were artistic creations designed to provide the viewer with an aesthetic experience. Arriba Soft's use of the thumbnails was to create a searchable index that would make it easier for people to find images on the Internet. The thumbnail images had such low resolution that enlarging

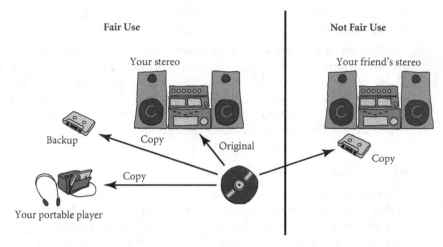

FIGURE 4.7  Space shifting is the creation of a copy for backup purposes or for use in a portable device, and it is considered fair use. Making a copy for a friend is not considered fair use.

them resulted in a blurry image with little aesthetic appeal. Second, Arriba Soft's use of Kelly's images did not harm the value of the original images or the market for these images. If anything, the search engine's display of Kelly's images "would guide users to Kelly's web site rather than away from it," increasing the demand for his photographs [39].

### 4.4.5  *Authors Guild v. Google*

In December 2004, Google announced a plan to scan millions of books held by Harvard University, the University of Michigan, the New York Public Library, Oxford University, and Stanford University, creating a database containing the words contained in all of these books [40]. This database is much more powerful than traditional library card catalogs because it allows users to search for words or phrases appearing anywhere in the cataloged books. The system responds to a user query by returning the books that match the query most closely. If the book is in the public domain, the user can view and download a PDF file containing the scanned images of the book's pages. If the book is still under copyright, the user can see a few sentences from the book that show the search term in context, and the search engine provides links to libraries holding the book and online bookstores selling the book.

In September 2005, the Authors Guild filed a lawsuit in the US District Court for the Southern District of New York, claiming that "by reproducing for itself a copy of those works that are not in the public domain, Google is engaging in massive copyright infringement" [41]. A month later a group of five major publishers sued Google for copyright infringement. The publishers claimed that Google was infringing their rights under the Copyright Act because Google's intent was "purely commercial," and in order to create its database, Google was systematically copying entire books still protected by copyright [42]. Google's defense was that its book scanning project should be considered fair use under Section 107 of the Copyright Act.

After a long and complicated legal battle, in November 2013 Judge Denny Chin found in favor of Google and dismissed the lawsuit. Using the four factors listed in Section 107 of the Copyright Act as his guide, he explained why he determined that Google Books was a fair use of copyrighted books:

- The first factor concerns the purpose and character of the use. Chin noted that the purpose of the Google Books project is to create a massive index from the words appearing in the books, and the character of "Google's use of the copyrighted works is highly transformative" [43, p. 19]. The index Google has created is a powerful tool for librarians, scholars, and researchers. The judge cited the precedent of *Kelly v. Arriba Soft Corporation*. Google's display of small portions of the text of a book is similar to Arriba Soft's display of thumbnail images of photographs. The Google Books project has also been transformative by making possible entirely new kinds of research, such as exploring how the usage of words changes over time. Chin concluded, "the first factor strongly favors a finding of fair use" [43, p. 22].

- The second factor is the nature of the work being copied. Most of the books Google is scanning are nonfiction, and all of the scanned books are published. These factors "favor a finding of fair use" [43, p. 23].

- The third factor has to do with how much of the copyrighted work is being used. In order to index a book, Google must scan the entire book. Even though Google limits the amount of text displayed in response to a query, this factor "weighs slightly against a finding a fair use" [43, p. 24].

- The fourth factor to consider is the effect of Google's use of the copyrighted work on the market for that work. Chin rejected the plaintiffs' argument that the Google Books project would reduce book sales, determining that the Google Books project is actually stimulating book sales by helping people discover books. The judge concluded the fourth factor "weighs strongly in favor of a finding of fair use" [43, p. 25].

The Electronic Frontier Foundation praised the ruling, calling it "a good day for fair use and sane copyright law" [44], but the saga is not over. The Authors Guild has appealed the ruling to the US Second Circuit Court.

### 4.4.6 Mashups

In music, a **mashup** is a composition that incorporates elements taken from preexisting songs. In the simplest form of a mashup, called A vs. B, an artist overlays the instrumental track from one song with the vocal track from another song. An example of an A vs. B mashup is "A Stroke of Geni-Us" by Freelance Hellraiser, which overlays the instrumental track from "Hard to Explain" by the Strokes with Christina Aguilera's voice track from "Genie in a Bottle." In a sophisticated mashup, called an audio collage, the artist creates a new composition from dozens of audio fragments. DJ Danger Mouse created

an audio collage consisting of vocal samples from Jay Z's *The Black Album* and instrumental samples from the Beatles' *White Album*, creating completely new songs that he
issued as *The Grey Album* (naturally).

After Danger Mouse distributed 3,000 promotional copies of *The Grey Album* in
2004, he received a cease-and-desist order from EMI, the publisher owning the copyright
to the Beatles. Danger Mouse complied with the order and never sold the album, but in
an act of civil disobedience others made copies available over the Internet.

Is a mashup an example of fair use? Courts have not yet ruled on this issue, but
Elina Lae has argued that the answer should depend on the type of mashup. In Lae's
view, an audio collage is highly transformative and should receive protection under the
fair use provision of the Copyright Act. In contrast, an artist creating an A vs. B mashup
is not creating a transformative work and should be required to obtain licenses from the
owners of the copyrighted sources. Regardless of whether the artist is creating an audio
collage or an A vs. B, if the purpose of the mashup is "criticism, satire, or parody," the
mashup should be entitled to fair use protection, suggests Lae [37].

# 4.5 Digital Media

CDs and DVDs store sounds and images in digital form. When information is stored
digitally, anyone with the right equipment can make perfect copies, making copyright
infringement easier.

The increase in the number of people with broadband Internet connections has
stimulated digital copying. The number of illegal downloads soared when more people
gained broadband access to the Internet [45]. As a result, the music industry has lost
sales. Total revenue from music sales and licensing in the United States dropped from
$14.6 billion in 1999 to $6.3 billion in 2009 [46].

Governments and recording companies have responded to the threat of illegal copying of copyrighted materials by introducing new legal and technological restrictions on
copying. Sometimes that makes it impossible for consumers to make copies even for purposes that are considered fair use, such as making a backup. Larry Kenswil of Universal
Music Group says, "What we really want to do is not to stop copying, simply to stop
redistributing. But the technology available doesn't distinguish between the two" [47].

## 4.5.1 Digital Rights Management

Digital rights management (DRM) refers to any of a variety of actions owners of intellectual property may take to protect their rights. As Christopher May puts it, "All DRM
technologies are aimed at tracking and controlling the use of content once it has entered
the market" [48]. DRM technologies may be incorporated into a computer's operating
system, a program, or a piece of hardware.

One approach to DRM is to encrypt the digital content so that only authorized users
can access it. Another approach is to place a digital mark on the content so that a device
accessing the content can identify the content as copy protected.

### 4.5.2  Digital Millennium Copyright Act

The Digital Millennium Copyright Act (DMCA), passed by Congress in 1998, was the first major revision of US copyright law since 1976. The primary purpose of the DMCA was to bring the United States into compliance with international copyright agreements it had signed [36]. Provisions in the DMCA significantly curtail fair use of copyrighted material. The DMCA makes it illegal for consumers to circumvent encryption schemes placed on digital media, and it is illegal to sell (or even discuss online) a software program designed to circumvent copy controls [49].

Online service providers that misuse copyrighted materials face severe penalties [49]. That means, for example, a university that knows students are exchanging MP3 files on the campus network and does nothing to stop them can be sued [50].

The DMCA requires Internet radio stations to make royalty payments to the copyright holders of music they broadcast. The rates paid by Internet radio stations are set by the Copyright Royalty Board.

### 4.5.3  Secure Digital Music Initiative

The Secure Digital Music Initiative (SDMI) was an effort to create copy-protected CDs and secure digital music downloads that would play only on SDMI-compliant devices. About 200 entertainment and technology companies joined the consortium, which worked for three years to develop "digital watermarks" that would make unauthorized copying of audio files impossible. The SDMI was unsuccessful for three reasons. First, before any copy protection technologies could be put in place, the number of music files being copied on the Internet mushroomed. Second, some of the sponsors of the SDMI—consumer electronics companies—started making a lot of money selling devices that became more attractive to customers as access to free MP3 files got easier. Their sales could be hurt by restrictions on copying. Third, the digital watermarking scheme was cracked [51]. Here's how that happened.

In September 2000, SDMI issued a "Hack SDMI" challenge. It released some digitally watermarked audio files and offered a $10,000 prize to the first person to crack them. Princeton computer science professor Edward Felten and eight colleagues picked up the gauntlet. Three weeks later the team had successfully read the audio files. The team declined to accept the cash prize. Instead, they wrote a paper describing how they broke the encryption scheme. They prepared to present the paper at the Fourth Annual Information Hiding Workshop at Carnegie Mellon University in April 2001 [52]. At this point, the Recording Industry Association of America sent Dr. Felten a letter stating, "Any disclosure of information gained from participating in the public challenge would be outside the scope of activities permitted by the agreement and could subject you and your research team to actions under the Digital Millennium Copyright Act" [53]. Fearing litigation, Dr. Felten agreed to withdraw the paper from the conference. However, that did not prevent the information from being leaked. Even before the conference, copies of the research paper and the letter from the RIAA were placed on a freedom-of-speech Web site [53]. Four months later Felten's group published the paper [54].

### 4.5.4 Sony BMG Music Entertainment Rootkit

In the summer and fall of 2005, Sony BMG Music Entertainment shipped millions of audio CDs with Extended Copy Protection, a DRM system. Extended Copy Protection prevented users from ripping audio tracks into MP3 format or making more than three backup copies of the CD. It also monitored the user's listening habits and reported back to Sony via the Internet. Extended Copy Protection did this by secretly installing a rootkit on Windows computers when the CD was played for the first time. A **rootkit** is a way of hiding files and processes from users; rootkits are commonly associated with computer hackers. The installation of the rootkit also compromised the security of the user's computer, making it vulnerable to "Trojan horse" programs (see Section 7.3.8) [55].

A computer expert discovered the Sony rootkit on his computer and publicized its existence, resulting in a huge public outcry and a class action lawsuit. Without admitting any wrongdoing, Sony BMG agreed to do the following [56]:

- Cease production of CDs with Extended Copy Protection
- Provide financial incentives to retailers to return unsold audio CDs with Extended Copy Protection
- Make freely available the software patch needed to uninstall the rootkit
- Allow customers to exchange CDs with Extended Copy Protection for identical CDs with no DRM
- Give consumers $7.50 or three free album downloads for every CD with Extended Copy Protection they exchange

### 4.5.5 Criticisms of Digital Rights Management

The introduction of DRM technologies has been controversial. Here are some criticisms that have been raised against DRM.

Many experts suggest that any technological "fix" to the problem of copyright abuse is bound to fail. All prior attempts to create encryption or anticopying schemes have been abandoned or circumvented.

Others argue that DRM undermines the well-established principle of fair use. Under DRM, a consumer may not be able to make a private copy of a DRM-protected work without making an extra payment, even if he has the right to do so under traditional fair use standards. Selena Kim writes:

> In the analogue world, people go ahead and use the work if they believe themselves entitled to do so. It is only if users are sued for infringement that they invoke the relevant copyright exceptions as defence. In a digital world encapsulated by access control and embedded with copy control, a potential user of a work may have to ask for permission twice: once to access a work, and again to copy an excerpt. The exception to copyright is not being put forward as a defence; it is put forward to show entitlement to use the work. [57, p. 112]

DRM restrictions sometimes prevent libraries from reformatting materials to make them more accessible to persons with disabilities. In addition, DRM protections, unlike copyrights, never expire [58].

Finally, some DRM schemes prevent people from anonymously accessing content. Microsoft's Windows Media Player has an embedded globally unique identifier (GUID). The Media Player keeps track of all the content the user views. When the Media Player contacts Microsoft's central server to obtain titles, it can upload information about the user's viewing habits.

### 4.5.6 Online Music Stores Drop Digital Rights Management

When Apple began selling music through the iTunes Music Store in 2003, all of the songs were protected with a DRM scheme called FairPlay. FairPlay blocked users from freely exchanging music they had purchased by preventing songs from being played on more than five computers or being copied onto CDs more than seven times. FairPlay had two other "features" that were strong incentives for consumers to stick with the Apple brand: music purchased from the iTunes store couldn't be played on portable devices other than the Apple iPod, and DRM-protected music purchased from other online retailers couldn't be played on the iPod [59].

Consumers complained about the restrictions associated with DRM, and eventually music retailers responded. In 2007 EMI announced it would begin offering all of its songs without DRM through the iTunes store for $1.29, 30 cents more than the previous price [60]. A year later Amazon became the first online music store to reach an agreement with all four major labels to sell music free of DRM restrictions [61]. Apple followed suit in 2009 with an announcement that it, too, had reached an agreement with all the major music labels to sell music without DRM restrictions [62].

### 4.5.7 Microsoft Xbox One

In June 2013, Microsoft announced that it was creating a cloud-based gaming experience to coincide with the launch of Xbox One. In the new environment people would be able to play their games from any Xbox One without the disc being in the tray, and every Xbox One would automatically be kept current with the latest system and application updates [63].

Consumers soon learned about the restrictions accompanying these benefits, and their reactions were overwhelmingly negative. Three features of the proposed licensing arrangement were particularly controversial: a disc owner would be allowed to share a disc only once, freedom to sell discs and buy secondhand titles was restricted, and Xbox consoles would have to check in online every 24 hours to ensure that the authorized software was up-to-date and that there was no unauthorized software [64]. In the midst of the controversy, Amazon ran a Facebook poll to see which new gaming console consumers were more interested in purchasing: the Microsoft Xbox One or the Sony PlayStation 4. The PlayStation 4 was capturing 95 percent of the votes when Amazon decided to shut down the poll early [65].

Microsoft did not waste time changing course. Thanking consumers for their "assistance in helping us to reshape the future of Xbox One," Microsoft's Don Mattrick announced that the controversial features of the licensing agreement were being dropped [66]. In particular, he indicated consumers would be able to play Xbox One games without being connected to the Internet, the Xbox One would not need to connect to the Internet once every 24 hours, and consumers would be free to lend, rent, or sell their discs. This reversal also meant that people would no longer have the ability to play their games from any Xbox One console without the disc being in the tray.

# 4.6 Peer–to–Peer Networks and Cyberlockers

On the Internet, the term **peer-to-peer** refers to a transient network allowing computers running the same networking program to connect with each other and access files stored on each other's hard drives. Peer-to-peer networks stimulate the exchange of data in three ways. First, they give each user access to data stored in many other computers. Second, they support simultaneous file transfers among arbitrary pairs of computers. Third, they allow users to identify those systems that will be able to deliver the desired data more rapidly, perhaps because they have a faster Internet connection or are fewer routing hops away.

**Cyberlockers** (also called **file-hosting services** or **cloud storage services**) are Internet-based file-sharing services that allow users to upload password-protected files. Users can give other people access to the files they have uploaded by sharing passwords. People who wish to collaborate on a project often find sharing large files through cyberlockers more convenient than sending them back and forth as attachments to email messages. However, cyberlockers also make it easy for people to share copyrighted material, such as songs and movies. In addition, cyberlocker use is much more difficult for government officials to track than peer-to-peer file sharing.

## 4.6.1 RIAA Lawsuits against Napster, Grokster, and Kazaa

Napster, Grokster, and Kazaa were peer-to-peer networks that facilitated the exchange of music files. Napster used a central computer to maintain a global index of all files available for sharing. In contrast, Grokster and Kazaa used a software technology called FastTrack to distribute the index of available files among a large number of computers.

In December 1999, the RIAA sued Napster for copyright infringement, asking for damages of $100,000 each time a Napster user copied a copyrighted song. In June 2000, the RIAA asked for a preliminary injunction to block Napster from trading any copyrighted content from major record labels. In February 2001, a federal appeals court ruled that Napster must stop its users from trading copyrighted material. Napster put in place file-filtering software that was 99 percent effective in blocking the transfer of copyrighted material. In June 2001, a district court judge ruled that unless Napster could block 100 percent of attempted transfers of copyrighted material, it must disable file transfers. This court order effectively killed Napster, which went offline in July 2001 and officially shut down in September 2002 [67, 68, 69]. (The following year Napster reemerged as an online subscription music service and music store.)

In April 2003, the RIAA warned Grokster and Kazaa users that they could face legal penalties for swapping files containing copyrighted music. The message read, in part:

> It appears that you are offering copyrighted music to others from your computer . . . . When you break the law, you risk legal penalties. There is a simple way to avoid that risk: DON'T STEAL MUSIC, either by offering it to others to copy or downloading it on a "file-sharing" system like this. When you offer music on these systems, you are not anonymous and you can easily be identified. [70]

The RIAA identified the IP addresses of the most active Kazaa supernodes, leading it to the ISPs of users who had stored large numbers of copyrighted files on their computers. Under the terms of the Digital Millennium Copyright Act, the RIAA subpoenaed Verizon, asking it to identify the names of customers suspected of running these Kazaa supernodes. Verizon resisted responding to the subpoenas, claiming that responding to the subpoenas would violate the privacy of its customers. In June 2003, a judge in Washington, DC, ruled that Verizon had to release the names of the customers [71].

In September 2003, the RIAA sued 261 individuals for distributing copyrighted music over the Internet [72]. A month later the RIAA sent letters to 204 people who had downloaded at least 1,000 music files, giving them an opportunity to settle before being sued by the RIAA [73].

In December 2003, the RIAA suffered a setback when the US Court of Appeals for the District of Columbia Circuit ruled that Verizon did not have to respond to the subpoenas of the RIAA and identify its customers [74]. Still, there is some evidence the RIAA lawsuits reduced illegal file swapping across the Internet. A survey from ComScore reported activity on Kazaa declined by 15 percent between November 2002 and November 2003 [75]. The Pew Internet & American Life Project reported that the percentage of Internet users who said they download music dropped from 32 percent in October 2002 to 22 percent in January 2005, and more than half of the January 2005 downloaders said that they purchased their music from an online service, such as iTunes. However, the report cautioned that because of the stigma associated with illegal downloading, fewer people may have been willing to admit they do it. Interestingly, about half of music downloaders said they had gotten music from email, instant messages, or someone else's MP3 player or iPod [76].

The RIAA's campaign to impose severe penalties on file sharers has been successful in the courtroom, but huge jury judgments against file sharers have been overruled by judges. In June 2009, a federal jury in Minnesota ordered Jammie Thomas-Rassert, a single mother of four, to pay $1.92 million—$80,000 a song—for violating the copyrights of 24 songs [77]. (The RIAA accused her of making 1,700 songs available on Kazaa, but they only tried to prove 24 copyright infringements.) In July 2011, Judge Michael Davis reduced the damage award against Thomas-Rassett to $54,000. Judge Davis called the original award "appalling," and said it was "so severe and oppressive as to be wholly disproportioned to the offense and obviously unreasonable" [78].

Another verdict went the RIAA's way in July 2009. The RIAA had accused Joel Tenenbaum of copyright infringement for using Kazaa to share 31 music files. The jury awarded the music companies $675,000, or $22,500 per song [5]. In July 2010, Judge

Nancy Gertner reduced the jury's award to $67,500. In her ruling, Judge Gertner wrote: "There is substantial evidence indicating that Congress did not contemplate that the Copyright Act's broad statutory damages provision would be applied to college students like Tenenbaum who file-shared without any pecuniary gain. . . . There is no question that this reduced award is still severe, even harsh. It not only adequately compensates the plaintiffs for the relatively minor harm that Tenenbaum caused them; it sends a strong message that those who exploit peer-to-peer networks to unlawfully download and distribute copyrighted works run the risk of incurring substantial damages awards" [6, p. 3].

During these trials the RIAA did not prove that people had actually downloaded songs from the defendants' computers. Instead, they contended that simply making the music files available to others was a violation of copyright law. In other words, making it possible for someone to download a music file from you means you've violated copyright law, even if no one ever does it. In April 2008, a federal court judge in New York agreed with the position of the RIAA, but judges in Massachusetts and Arizona reached the opposite conclusion, holding that simply making music files available for copying is not copyright infringement [79, 80, 81].

### 4.6.2 *MGM v. Grokster*

A group of movie studios, recording companies, music publishers, and songwriters sued Grokster and StreamCast for the copyright infringements of their users. The plaintiffs (henceforth referred to as MGM) sought damages and an injunction against the defendants.

During the discovery phase of the litigation, the following facts were revealed:

- The defendants' networks were used to transfer billions of files every month.
- About 90 percent of the files available on Grokster's FastTrack network were copyrighted.
- Grokster and StreamCast promoted their networks to investors and potential customers as replacements for Napster.
- An internal StreamCast document revealed that StreamCast's executives wanted to have more copyrighted songs available on their network than on competing networks.
- Grokster sent its users a newsletter touting its ability to deliver popular copyrighted songs.
- Grokster and StreamCast provided technical support to users who were having difficulty locating or playing copyrighted content.

A US District Court granted Grokster and StreamCast a summary judgment; that is, it made its decision without a trial based on the facts and evidence collected. According to the judge, "The defendants distribute and support software, the users of which can and do choose to employ it for both lawful and unlawful ends. Grokster and StreamCast are not significantly different from companies that sell home video recorders or copy machines, both of which can be and are used to infringe copyrights" [82]. The judge referred to *Sony v. Universal City Studios*, the Supreme Court's 1984 ruling on the legality of Sony's Betamax VCR. MGM appealed to the US Court of Appeals for the Ninth Circuit, which upheld the ruling.

After another appeal, the US Supreme Court unanimously reversed the decision of the lower courts in June 2005. Justice Souter wrote: "The question is under what circumstances the distributor of a product capable of both lawful and unlawful use is liable for acts of copyright infringement by third parties using the software. We hold that one who distributes a device with the object of promoting its use to infringe copyright, as shown by clear expression or other affirmative steps taken to foster infringement, is liable for the resulting acts of infringement by third parties" [83].

The Supreme Court made clear it was not reversing the Sony Betamax decision. Instead, it ruled that the "safe harbor" provided to Sony did not apply to Grokster and StreamCast. The Sony Betamax VCR was primarily used for time-shifting television shows, which the Court found to be a fair use. There was no evidence Sony had done anything to increase sales of its VCRs by promoting illegal uses. Therefore, Sony could not be found liable simply for selling VCRs.

The situation for Grokster and StreamCast was quite different. Both companies gave away their software but made money by streaming advertisements to users. Advertising rates are higher when the number of users is greater. Hence both companies wanted to increase their user base. They realized the way to do this was to make sure their networks had the content people were interested in downloading. The opinion notes dryly, "Users seeking Top 40 songs, for example, or the latest release by Modest Mouse, are certain to be far more numerous than those seeking a free Decameron, and Grokster and StreamCast translated that demand into dollars. . . . The unlawful objective is unmistakable" [83].

According to the Supreme Court, the Ninth Circuit Court of Appeals erred when it cited *Sony v. Universal City Studios*. The more relevant precedent was *Gershwin Publishing Corporation v. Columbia Artists Management, Inc.* The Supreme Court remanded the case to the Court of Appeals, suggesting that a summary judgment in favor of MGM would be in order. Grokster shut down its peer-to-peer network in November 2005 and paid $50 million to "movie studios, record labels and music publishers" [84].

### 4.6.3   BitTorrent

For a computer with a broadband connection to the Internet, downloading a file from the network is about 10 times faster than uploading a file to the network. A problem with FastTrack and some other peer-to-peer networking protocols is that when one peer computer shares a file with another peer computer, the file is transferred at the slower upload speed rather than the faster download speed. To solve this problem, Bram Cohen developed BitTorrent [85].

BitTorrent divides a file into pieces about a quarter megabyte in length. Different pieces of a file can be downloaded simultaneously from different computers, avoiding the uploading bottleneck (Figure 4.8). As soon as a user has a piece of a file, the user can share this piece with other users. Since BitTorrent gives a priority for downloads to those users who allow uploading from their machines, users tend to be generous. As a

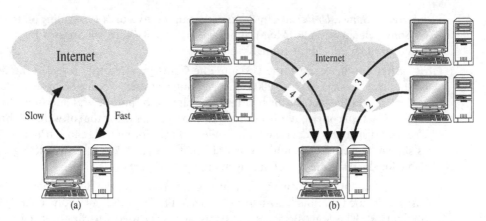

**FIGURE 4.8** (a) Broadband Internet connections provide higher speeds for downloading than for uploading. (b) BitTorrent reduces downloading times by enabling a computer to download different pieces of a file simultaneously from many different peers.

result, downloading speeds increase as more peers get a copy of the file. Put another way, downloading speeds increase with the popularity of a title.

With its markedly higher downloading rates, BitTorrent has made practical the exchange of files hundreds of megabytes long. People are using BitTorrent to download copies of computer programs, television shows, and movies. Linspire, a Linux operating system developer, reduces demand on its servers (and saves money) by using BitTorrent to distribute its software [86]. BitTorrent was also the vehicle by which *Revenge of the Sith* became available on the Internet before it appeared in movie theaters [87].

### 4.6.4 Legal Action against the Pirate Bay

The Pirate Bay, based in Stockholm, Sweden, is one of the biggest file-sharing Web sites in the world, with an estimated 25 million users [88]. People use the Pirate Bay to search for songs, movies, TV shows, or computer programs they can download for free. These items of intellectual property are broken into BitTorrent fragments stored in thousands of different computers scattered across the globe. Established in 2003, the Pirate Bay has been called "the most visible member of a burgeoning international anti-copyright—or pro-piracy—movement" [89].

The movie industry pressured the Swedish government to do something about the Pirate Bay, and in 2006 Swedish police raided its offices and confiscated 186 servers, but the site was offline for only three days [89, 90]. After the site was reactivated, the number of people accessing it increased significantly, perhaps because of the international publicity the Pirate Bay received as a result of the raid [89].

In 2008 the International Federation of the Phonographic Industry sued four individuals connected with the Pirate Bay for making available 33 copyrighted works: twenty songs, nine films, and four computer games [88]. The defendants argued that the Pirate Bay is simply a search engine and does not host any copyrighted content [91]. In April

2009, a District Court in Stockholm found Carl Lundström, Fredrik Neij, Peter Sunde, and Gottfrid Svartholm Warg guilty of aiding and abetting copyright infringement. All four were sentenced to one year in prison, and altogether were fined 30 million Swedish kronor (about $3.6 million). In November 2010, an appeals court in Sweden upheld the convictions but shortened the sentences and increased the fine to 46 million kronor ($6.5 million) [92].

Meanwhile, the Pirate Bay Web site is still operational and enormously popular. Originally, it had the domain name thepiratebay.org. Fearing that their .org domain would be seized by American officials, the site moved to the Swedish domain .se in 2012. When Sweden sought the seizure of the domain name thepiratebay.se in 2013, the Pirate Bay moved to thepiratebay.sx, registered in the tiny Caribbean country of Sint Maarten [93].

In many countries the Pirate Bay's official URL is blocked by Internet service providers. People in these countries are still able to access the Pirate Bay by connecting to one of more than 150 proxy sites hosted in countries that do not block access to the Pirate Bay.

### 4.6.5  PRO–IP Act

In 2008 the US Congress passed the Prioritizing Resources and Organization for Intellectual Property (PRO-IP) Act. The PRO-IP Act gives federal law enforcement agencies the authority to seize the domain names of Web sites that are allegedly facilitating copyright infringement or trafficking in counterfeit goods.

In June 2010, the US Department of Immigration and Customs Enforcement launched Operation In Our Sites, seizing the domain names of 10 Web sites that were making available first-run movies "often within hours of their theatrical release" [94]. Over the next year and a half, several hundred more domain names were seized, including sites that were streaming live broadcasts of the National Football League, the National Basketball Association, the National Hockey League, World Wrestling Entertainment, and the Ultimate Fighting Championship [95].

### 4.6.6  Megaupload Shutdown

Megaupload Limited, based in Hong Kong, was a prominent cyberlocker. It had more than 180 million registered users, and at one point it was the world's 13th most popular Web site, accounting for "approximately four percent of the total traffic on the Internet" [96]. A substantial percentage of the network traffic to and from the cyberlocker was associated with the sharing of copyrighted movies, television programs, songs, and computer games. The founder of Megaupload, Kim Dotcom, lived in Auckland, New Zealand.

In January 2012, the FBI worked with police in New Zealand and Hong Kong to shut down the Megaupload cyberlocker and arrest Kim Dotcom and three associates for violating the PRO-IP Act [97]. According to the grand jury indictment, Kim Dotcom and his codefendants were part of "a worldwide criminal organization whose members engaged in criminal copyright infringement and money laundering on a massive scale with estimated harm to copyright holders well in excess of $500,000,000 and reported income in excess of $175,000,000" [96]. The indictment claimed that the defendants had paid millions of dollars to its premium subscribers for uploading popular copyrighted works to the cyberlocker, as a way of increasing the number of paid subscribers.

Other cyberlockers responded quickly to the news. A few days after the shutdown of Megaupload, FileSonic posted the following announcement on its Web site: "All sharing functionality on FileSonic is now disabled. Our service can only be used to upload and retrieve files that you have uploaded personally" [98]. The FileServe site posted a similar message [99].

## 4.6.7  Legal Online Access to Entertainment

The widespread piracy of music, television shows, and movies on the Internet has put pressure on companies selling these products to make "doing the right thing"— obtaining a legal copy—as easy as "doing the wrong thing" [100]. Industry has risen to the challenge.

A good example is the continued evolution of online music services. As we saw in Section 4.5.6, when Apple launched the iTunes Music Store, it included a digital rights management system called FairPlay with the songs that were downloaded. Consumers were unhappy with the FairPlay restrictions. Meanwhile, Amazon reached an agreement with all four major labels to sell music without digital rights management restrictions. Responding to these consumer and competitive pressures, Apple dropped FairPlay and began selling music free of digital rights management.

A half dozen years later, the popularity of downloading has started to decline, as consumers shift from music ownership toward anytime-anywhere access offered by music streaming services. Globally, there are more than 400 licensed music services, including Spotify, Rdio, Deezer, Pandora, and Apple Music. These providers offer two streaming service models. In the ad-supported model, listeners can have music and advertisements streamed to their devices for free; the services earn income and pay royalties to artists from advertising revenue. In the subscription services model, listeners pay a monthly fee to receive music free from commercial interruptions. Globally, about 100 million people listen to music under the ad-supported model, and about 40 million people subscribe to a streaming music service [101].

In the video streaming arena, a variety of subscription services, including Netflix, Hulu Plus, Amazon Prime Instant Video, and Sling.TV, provide convenient access to television shows, movies, and original programming. About 40 percent of US homes now subscribe to a video streaming service [102].

The rapid growth in the number of subscribers to licensed music and video services demonstrates that consumers are willing to pay for "anytime, anywhere access" to copyrighted content, as long as they judge the cost to be reasonable. That's the good news. The bad news is that the music industry is not making nearly as much money from its share of streaming revenues as it made selling CDs. According to the RIAA, sales of music in the United States are less than half of what they used to be, falling from $14.6 billion in 1999 to $7.0 billion in 2013 [103].

# 4.7 Protections for Software

In the early days of the computer industry, there was no strong demand for intellectual property protection for software. Most commercial software was produced by the same companies manufacturing computer hardware. They sold complete systems to customers, and the licensing agreements covered use of the software as well as the hardware. Interest in copyrighting software grew with the emergence of an independent software industry in the 1960s.

## 4.7.1 Software Copyrights

The first software copyrights were applied for in 1964. The Copyright Office allowed the submitted computer programs to be registered, reasoning that a computer program is like a "how-to" book. The Copyright Act of 1976 explicitly recognizes that software can be copyrighted.

When a piece of software gets copyright protection, what exactly is copyrighted? First, copyright protects the expression of an idea, not the idea itself. For example, suppose you develop a program for a relational database management system. You may be able to copyright your implementation of a relational database management system, but you cannot copyright the concept of using relational databases to store information.

Second, copyright usually protects the object (executable) program, not the source program. Typically, the source code to a program is confidential; in other words, a trade secret of the enterprise that developed it. The company only distributes the object program to its customers. The copyright also protects the screen displays produced by the program as it executes. This is particularly valuable for the developers of video games.

## 4.7.2 Violations of Software Copyrights

The holder of a copyright has a right to control the distribution of the copyrighted material. Obviously, this includes making copies of the program. The definition of what it means to make a copy of a program is broad. Suppose you purchase a program stored on a CD. If you transfer a copy of the program from the CD to a hard disk, you are making a copy of it. If you execute the program, it is copied from the hard disk of the computer into its random access memory (RAM). This, too, is considered making a copy of the program. The standard licensing agreement that comes with a piece of commercial software allows the purchaser of the product to do both of the above-mentioned copying operations.

However, doing any of the following actions without the authorization of the copyright holder is a violation of copyright law:

1. Copying a program onto a CD to give or sell to someone else

2. Preloading a program onto the hard disk of a computer being sold

3. Distributing a program over the Internet

Another kind of copyright violation can occur when a company attempts to create software that competes with an existing product. Two court cases illustrate a copyright infringement and fair use of another company's product.

### APPLE COMPUTER v. FRANKLIN COMPUTER

In the early 1980s, Franklin Computer Corp. manufactured the Franklin ACE to compete with the Apple II. The Franklin ACE was Apple II compatible, meaning that programs sold for the Apple II would run on the Franklin ACE without modification. In order to ensure compatibility, the Franklin ACE contained operating systems functions directly copied from a ROM on the Apple II. Apple Computer sued Franklin for infringing on its copyright. The US Court of Appeals for the Third Circuit ruled in favor of Apple Computer, establishing that object programs are copyrightable.

### SEGA v. ACCOLADE

Video game maker Accolade wanted to port some of its games to the Sega Genesis console. Sega did not make available a technical specification for the Genesis console, so Accolade disassembled the object code of a Sega game in order to determine how to interface a video game with the game console. Sega sued Accolade for infringing on its copyright. In 1992 the US Court of Appeals for the Ninth Circuit ruled in favor of Accolade, judging that Accolade's actions constituted fair use of the software. It noted that Accolade had no other way of discerning the hardware interface and that the public would benefit from additional video games being available on the Genesis console.

## 4.7.3  Safe Software Development

An organization must be careful not to violate the copyrights held by its competitors. Even unconscious copying can have serious consequences. Years after hearing the song "He's So Fine," George Harrison wrote "My Sweet Lord." The owner of "He's So Fine" sued Harrison for copyright infringement and prevailed after a lengthy legal battle. Unconscious copying is a real concern in the software industry because programmers frequently move from one firm to another.

Suppose a company needs to develop a software product that duplicates the functionality of a competitor's product without violating the competitor's copyright. For example, in the 1980s companies developing IBM-compatible computers needed to develop their own implementations of the BIOS (basic input/output system). A "clean room" software development strategy helps ensure a company's software program does not duplicate any code in another company's product.

In this strategy two independent teams work on the project. The first team is responsible for determining how the competitor's program works. It may access the program's source code, if it is available. If it cannot get access to the source, it may disassemble the object code of the competitor's product. It also reads the product's user manuals and technical documentation. The first team produces a technical specification for the software product. The specification simply states how the product is supposed to function. It says nothing about how to implement the functionality.

|                                      | *Software Copyright*           | *Software Patent*               |
| ------------------------------------ | ------------------------------ | ------------------------------- |
| What is protected?                   | Object program, screen displays | Software process with practical utility |
| Is getting protection expensive?     | No                             | Yes                             |
| Is getting protection time consuming? | No                            | Yes                             |
| Is reverse engineering allowed?      | Yes                            | No                              |

**TABLE 4.3** The key differences between the copyright and patent software protection systems.

The second team is isolated from the first team. Members of this team have never seen any code or documentation from the competitor's product. They rely solely on the technical specification to develop, code, and debug the software meeting the specification. By isolating the code developers from the competitor's product, the company developing the competing product can demonstrate that its employees have not copied code, even unconsciously.

### 4.7.4 Software Patents

Both copyrights and patents are used to provide intellectual property protection to software. Table 4.3 shows the primary differences between the two.

#### ORIGINS OF SOFTWARE PATENTS

Until the early 1980s, the US Patent and Trademark Office refused to grant patents for computer software. Its position was that a computer program is a mathematical algorithm, not a process or a machine.

However, a US Supreme Court decision in 1981 forced the Patent and Trademark Office to begin considering software patents. In the case of *Diamond v. Diehr*, the Supreme Court ruled that an invention related to curing rubber could be patented. Even though the company's principal innovation was the use of a computer to control the heating of the rubber, the invention was a new process for rubber molding, and hence patentable.

Further court rulings compelled the Patent and Trademark Office to begin issuing patents for a much broader range of software. In 1992 the Court of Appeals for the Federal Circuit considered a patent application from a company that had developed a computerized monitoring device that analyzed signals from an electrocardiograph to determine whether a heart attack victim was at risk of a dangerous arrhythmia. The court ruled that the software was patentable because the numbers being manipulated by the computer program represented concrete values in the real world. Further court rulings reinforced the idea that computer software and data structures could be patented in the United States [104].

Since then, hundreds of thousands of software patents have been granted [105]. Microsoft alone files about 3,000 patent applications every year [106]. Companies generate revenue by licensing their software patents to other companies. It's also common for several technology companies to hold patents that cover different but essential components of a commercial product. By signing an agreement to cross-license each other's patents, all of the companies are free to bring their own versions of the product to market.

## PATENT-HOLDING COMPANIES

Given the value of software patents, it's not surprising that a secondary market for them has arisen. When a company holding patents goes bankrupt, it is typical for its patents to be sold to another company [107]. Some companies specialize in holding patents and licensing the rights to use these patents. Patent-holding companies aggressively use the courts to enforce their patent rights; these companies are sometimes referred to as **patent trolls**. Because defending against a patent infringement lawsuit can easily exceed a million dollars, companies that get sued have a strong motivation to simply settle out of court, putting patent trolls "in a position to negotiate licensing fees that are grossly out of alignment with their contribution to the alleged infringer's product or services" [108].

In 1992 inventor Thomas Campana and lawyer Donald Stout formed New Technologies Products (NTP), a patent-holding company. The purpose of the company was never to make anything but was to protect valuable intellectual property. About half of the company's 50 patents were originally held by Telefind Corporation, which went out of business. In 2000 NTP sent letters to several companies, warning them that they were infringing on NTP wireless email patents and inviting them to negotiate licensing rights. One of these letters went to Research In Motion (RIM), maker of the BlackBerry, but RIM did not respond to the letter. The next year NTP sued RIM for patent infringement. Instead of settling out of court for a few million dollars, RIM took the case to trial and lost. After more unsuccessful legal maneuvering, RIM in 2006 agreed to pay NTP $612.5 million to settle the patent infringement dispute [109, 110].

## HARMS FROM TOO MANY SOFTWARE PATENTS

Critics of software patents argue that too many software patents have been granted. A problem faced by patent examiners in the Patent and Trademark Office is knowing what the existing technical knowledge (prior art) in computer programming is. Patent examiners typically look at patents already issued to determine prior art. This works fine for other kinds of inventions, but it doesn't work well for software patents because a significant amount of software was written before software patents were first granted. The consequence is that patent examiners have issued many "bad patents"—patents that would not have been issued if the examiner knew about all the prior art. The Patent Office has also been criticized for granting patents for trivial inventions that would be obvious to any skilled computer programmer.

As a consequence of the sheer volume of software patents, the large number of bad patents, and the number of obvious software inventions that are patented, any company releasing a new product that includes software runs a significant risk of being sued for infringing a software patent owned by someone else. Thousands of patent lawsuits are filed in the United States every year [111]. Large corporations are resorting to building stockpiles of their own patents, so that if they are sued for infringing another company's patent, they can retaliate with their own patent infringement countersuit. The use of software patents as legal weapons is a perversion of their original purpose [112].

### SMARTPHONE PATENT WARS

In 2009 Nokia filed a lawsuit against Apple, alleging that Apple had violated 10 patents owned by Nokia related to wireless communication, and demanding royalty payments [113]. Apple responded by suing Nokia for violating 13 patents owned by Apple [114].

Apple also took action against several makers of Android smartphones [111]. Of these lawsuits, the dispute between Apple and Samsung is particularly notable. Apple filed a lawsuit in 2011 accusing Samsung of both patent and trademark infringement, claiming Samsung's Galaxy phones and tablets copied the "look and feel" of Apple iPhones and iPads, including rounded corners, tapered edges, use of a home button, slide-to-unlock, and the bounce-back visual effect when a user overscrolls [115]. Samsung countersued, claiming Apple had violated Samsung patents on mobile communication technologies. The two corporations filed more suits and countersuits around the globe; by the middle of 2012 the companies were involved in more than 50 lawsuits worldwide [116]. Their legal fees exceeded $1 billion [117]. Some of the lawsuits were won by Apple, Samsung prevailed in other cases, and some of the cases were dismissed. Even before the lawsuits were resolved, Android makers began changing portions of their user interfaces to avoid infringing on Apple's patents [118].

Eventually, Sony, Google, Samsung, Microsoft, Motorola, Xiamoni, and HTC were drawn into the fray, which acquired the nickname "the smartphone patent wars." More than 100 lawsuits and countersuits were filed by smartphone manufacturers claiming patent violations by their competitors. By the end of 2014, the legal action was winding down, with the smartphone makers agreeing to cross-license each other's patents [119].

### US SUPREME COURT DECISIONS

According to some critics of the current system, the smartphone patent wars are a good example of how software patents have hampered innovation. Some have been looking to the US Supreme Court to clearly indicate whether software patents are authorized under the Patent Act [120]. In three decisions between 2010 and 2014 (*Bilski v. Kappos*, *Mayo v. Prometheus Laboratories*, and *Alice Corporation v. CLS Bank*), the Court ruled that the particular computer-implemented inventions in question were not patent eligible, but for the reason that they were solely based on laws of nature, natural processes, and/or abstract ideas [121, 122, 123]. Through these rulings the Court seemed to be indicating that "software, as a class, is every bit as worthy of patent protection as any other medium in which innovation can be practiced" [124]. However, there is still confusion among litigants and lower-court judges regarding exactly what makes a software innovation eligible for a patent [125].

# 4.8 Legitimacy of Intellectual Property Protection for Software

Licenses for proprietary software usually forbid you from making copies of the software to give or sell to someone else. These licenses are legal agreements. If you violate the license, you are breaking the law. In this section we are *not* discussing the morality of breaking the law. Rather, we are considering whether as a society we ought to give the producers of software the right to prevent others from copying the software they produce. In other words, should we give copyright and/or patent protection to software?

Rights-based and consequentialist arguments have been given for granting intellectual property protection to those who create software. Let's review and test the strength of these arguments. To simplify the discussion, we'll assume that a piece of software is written by a person. In reality, most software is created by teams, and the company employing the team owns the rights to the software the team produces. However, the logic is the same whether the software creator is an individual or a corporation.

## 4.8.1 Rights-Based Analysis

Not everyone can write good computer programs, and programming is hard work. Programmers who write useful programs that are widely used by others should be rewarded for their labor. That means they should own the programs they write. Ownership implies control. If somebody creates a piece of software, he or she has the right to decide who gets to use it. Software owners ought to be able to charge others for using their programs. Everybody ought to respect these intellectual property rights.

This line of reasoning is a variation of Locke's natural rights argument that we discussed at the beginning of the chapter. It is based on the Lockean notion that mixing your labor with something gives you an ownership right in it.

Here are two criticisms of the "just deserts"[1] argument. First, why does mixing your labor with something mean that you own it? Doesn't it make just as much sense to believe that if you mix your labor with something you lose your labor? Robert Nozick gives this example: If you own a can of tomato juice and pour it in the ocean, mixing the tomato juice with the salt water, you do not own the ocean. Instead, you have lost your can of tomato juice. Certainly, it would be unjust if someone else could claim ownership of something you labored to produce, but if there were no notion of property ownership and everybody understood when they mixed their labor with something they lost their labor, it would be just.

Of course, we do live in a society that has the notion of ownership of tangible property. How can we justify giving a farmer the right to the crop he labors to produce while failing to give a programmer the right to the accounting program he produces for the benefit of the farmer?

Still, if we do want to give ownership rights to those who produce intellectual property, we run into the problem we discussed at the beginning of the chapter. Locke's natural rights argument for owning property does not hold up well when extended to the realm of intellectual property. There are two crucial differences between intellectual property and tangible property. Each piece of intellectual property is unique, and copying intellectual property is different from stealing something physical.

---

1. Pronounced with the accent on the second syllable. Think of the related word "deserve."

**FIGURE 4.9** The chain of reasoning of a consequentialist argument for why copying software is bad. (Beth Anderson)

## 4.8.2  Utilitarian Analysis

Another argument posits that failing to provide intellectual property protection for software producers would have harmful consequences overall. The argument goes like this [126]: When software is copied, it reduces software purchases. If less software is purchased, less money flows to the producers of software. As a result, less new software is produced. As a whole, new software titles benefit society. When the number of new titles drops, society is harmed. Therefore, when software is copied, society is harmed, and copying software is wrong.

You can view this argument as a chain of consequences (Figure 4.9). Copying software causes software sales to drop, which causes the software industry to decline and, subsequently, fewer products to be released, which causes society to be harmed. Logically, all the links in the chain must be strong in order for the argument to be convincing. Let's look at each of the links in turn.

The first claim is that copying software results in reduced sales of software. When talking about software piracy, the computer industry cites the dollar value of the copied software as if each instance of copying represents a lost sale. Obviously, this is an exaggeration. Not everyone who gets a free copy of a computer game has the money or the desire to purchase the game. In fact, sometimes software copying may lead to a sale. A person may not have been interested in buying a particular program. After trying it out for free, the person may decide it is so useful she is willing to buy a copy of the program in order to get access to all the documentation, the technical support line, or another service provided to registered users of the program. It is fair to say that copying software sometimes results in reduced sales of software, but it is not always the case. Hence it is incorrect to make a universal statement.

The second claim is that reduced sales of software result in a decline in the software industry. An argument against this claim is the continued success of Microsoft, despite the fact that software counterfeiting is prevalent in some countries. A better argument against the claim is that it makes a strong cause-and-effect connection between the creation of software and financial remuneration. However, the open-source movement demonstrates many people are willing to create software without being rewarded financially. Some people write programs because they find it fun. Others are motivated by the desire to gain a good reputation by writing a program many people find useful. Advocates of open-source software, including Richard Stallman, suggest that the best way to stimulate innovation is to allow a free exchange of ideas and source code. From this point of view, allowing software producers to control the distribution of their code stifles, rather than promotes, innovation in the software industry.

Furthermore, the second claim assumes that software customers are solely responsible for the health of the software industry. In reality, other groups want to ensure that there are plenty of new software titles released. Intel, for example, makes its money from selling CPU chips. Every year the chips are faster. If a person owns a computer fast enough to run his current programs, he has little motivation to upgrade the hardware. However, if that same person purchases a new program that requires additional CPU cycles, he may be motivated to upgrade his computer. Hence it is in Intel's interest to encourage the development of ever more computationally intensive computer programs. Software customers are not solely responsible for promoting the growth of the software industry.

The third claim is that new software packages benefit society. This is a difficult claim to prove. Certainly, some programs benefit society more than others. Hence it's not the number of different programs that matters; it's what they can be used for. The utility of new software titles must be weighed against the utility of letting people give away copies of programs that would help their friends.

### 4.8.3 Conclusion

We have examined two arguments for why society ought to provide intellectual property protection to software creators. The first argument is based on the notion of just deserts. It is a variation of the natural rights argument we discussed at the beginning of the chapter. This argument is weak; it rests on the faulty assumption that a natural right to own property extends cleanly to intellectual property.

The second argument is based on consequences. It holds that denying intellectual property protection for software would have harmful consequences. It relies upon a chain of cause-and-effect relationships: copying leads to a loss of revenue, which leads to a decline in software production, which harms society. The strength of each of the links in the chain is debatable; taken as a whole, the argument is not strong.

Our conclusion is that the arguments for granting intellectual property protection for software are not strong. Nevertheless, our society *has* granted copyright protection to owners of computer programs. If you violate a licensing agreement by copying a CD containing a computer program and giving it to a friend, you are breaking the law. As we discovered in Chapter 2, from the viewpoint of Kantianism, rule utilitarianism, and social contract theory, breaking the law is wrong unless there is a strong overriding moral obligation to do so.

## 4.9 Open-Source Software

In the early years of commercial computing, there was no independent software industry. Computer manufacturers such as IBM produced both the hardware and the software needed for the system to be usable. Well into the 1960s, software distributions included the source code. Customers who wanted to fix bugs in the programs or add new features could do so by modifying the source code and generating a new executable version of the program.

In the 1970s the number of computer applications expanded, and organizations recognized the increasing value of software. To protect their investments in software development, most companies decided to make their programs proprietary.

Today companies developing proprietary software tightly control the distribution of their intellectual property. Typically, they do this by treating source code as a trade secret and distributing only the object code, which is not in human-readable form. In addition, they do not sell the object code. Instead, when people "purchase" the program, what they are actually buying is a license allowing them to run the program. Their rights to do other things with the code, such as make backup copies, are limited.

## 4.9.1  Consequences of Proprietary Software

Governments have given ownership rights to those who produce computer software because of the perceived beneficial consequences. A key benefit is the ability to profit from the licensing of the software. The assumption is that people will work harder and be more creative if they must compete with others to produce the best product. Those who produce the best products will have the opportunity to make money from them.

While most people point to the benefits of a system encouraging the development of proprietary software, some people have noted the harms caused by such a system. A well-known critic of proprietary software is Richard Stallman. According to Stallman, granting intellectual property rights to creators of computer software has numerous harmful consequences [127]:

- The copyright system was designed for an era in which it was difficult to create copies. Digital technology has made copying trivial. In order to enforce copyrights in the digital age, increasingly harsh measures are being taken. These measures infringe on our liberties.

- The purpose of the copyright system is to promote progress, not to make authors wealthy. Copyrights are not promoting progress in the computer software field.

- It is wrong to allow someone to "own" a piece of intellectual property. Granting someone this ownership forces the users of a piece of intellectual property to choose between respecting ownership rights and helping their friends. When this happens, the correct action is clear. If a friend asks you for a copy of a proprietary program, you would be wrong to refuse your friend. "Cooperation is more important than copyright."

The **open-source movement** is the philosophical position that source code to software ought to be freely distributed and that people should be encouraged to examine and improve each other's code. The open-source software movement promotes a cooperative model of software development.

### 4.9.2 "Open Source" Definition

**Open source** is an alternative way of distributing software. Licenses for open-source programs have the following key characteristics (there are others) [128]:

1. There are no restrictions preventing others from selling or giving away the software.

2. The source code to the program must be included in the distribution or easily available by other means (such as downloadable from the Internet).

3. There are no restrictions preventing people from modifying the source code, and derived works can be distributed according to the same license terms as the original program.

4. There are no restrictions regarding how people can use the software.

5. These rights apply to everyone receiving redistributions of the software without the need for additional licensing agreements.

6. The license cannot put restrictions on other software that is part of the same distribution. For example, a program's open-source license cannot require all the other programs on the CD to be open source.

Note that there is nothing in these guidelines that says an open-source program must be given away for free. While people may freely exchange open-source programs, a company has the right to sell an open-source program. However, a company cannot stop others from selling it either. In order for a company to be successful selling open-source software that people can find for free on the Internet, it must add some value to the software. Perhaps it packages the software so that it is particularly easy to install. It may provide great manuals, or it may provide support after the sale.

The Open Source Initiative (www.opensource.org) is a nonprofit corporation that promotes a common definition of open source. In July 2015, its Web site listed the names of 72 software licenses that met its definition of open source.

### 4.9.3 Beneficial Consequences of Open–Source Software

Advocates of open-source software describe five beneficial consequences of open-source licensing.

The first benefit of open source is that it gives everyone using a program the opportunity to improve it. People can fix bugs, add enhancements, or adapt the program for entirely new uses. Software evolves more quickly when more people are working on it.

Rapid evolution of open-source software leads to the second benefit: new versions of open-source programs appear much more frequently than new versions of commercial programs. Users of open-source programs do not have to wait as long for bug fixes and patches [129].

A third benefit of open source is that it eliminates the tension between obeying copyright law and helping others. Suppose you legally purchased a traditional license to use a program and your friend asks you for a copy. You must choose between helping your friend and conforming to the license agreement. If the program had an open-source license, you would be free to distribute copies of it to anyone who wanted it.

The fourth benefit is that open-source programs are the property of the entire user community, not just a single vendor. If a vendor selling a proprietary program decides not to invest in further improvements to it, the user community is stuck. In contrast, a user community with access to the source code of a program may continue its development indefinitely [129].

The fifth benefit of open source is that it shifts the focus from manufacturing to service, which can result in customers getting better support for their software [129]. If source code were distributed freely, companies would make money by providing support, and the companies that provided the best support would be rewarded in the marketplace [130].

### 4.9.4 Examples of Open–Source Software

Open-source software is a key part of the Internet's infrastructure, and an increasing number of open-source applications are reaching the desktop. Here are a few examples of highly successful programs distributed under open-source licenses:

- BIND provides DNS (domain name service) for the entire Internet.
- Apache runs about half of the world's Web servers.
- The most widely used program for moving email about the Internet is the open-source program sendmail.
- The Android operating system is the world's best-selling smartphone platform [131].
- Chrome is the world's most popular Web browser, and Firefox is the number three browser, according to StatCounter [132].
- OpenOffice.org is an office application suite supporting word processing, spreadsheets, databases, and presentations (Figure 4.10).
- Perl is the most popular Web programming language.
- Other popular open-source programming languages and tools are Python, Ruby, TCL/TK, PHP, and Zope.
- Programmers have long recognized the high quality of the GNU compilers for C, C++, Objective-C, Fortran, Java, and Ada.

Surveys indicate that the quality and dependability of open-source software is about the same as the quality of commercial software [133].

### 4.9.5 The GNU Project and Linux

The GNU Project and Linux are important success stories in the history of the open-source movement. (GNU is pronounced "guh-new" with the accent on the second syllable. It's a tradition among hackers to invent recursive acronyms; GNU stands for "GNU's Not Unix.") Richard Stallman began the GNU Project in 1984. The goal of the project was ambitious: to develop a complete Unix-like operating system consisting entirely of open-source software.

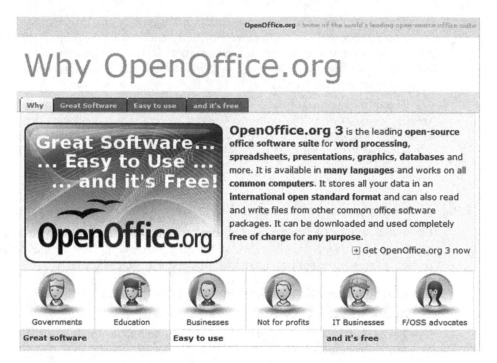

**Figure 4.10** OpenOffice.org is an open-source office application suite that competes with the commercial product Microsoft Office. (Screenshot from OpenOffice.org, a registered trademark of Apache Software Foundation. Copyright © 2012 by Apache Software Foundation. Reprinted with permission.)

In order to be fully functional, a modern operating system must include text editors, command processors, assemblers, compilers, debuggers, device drivers, mail servers, and many other programs. During the late 1980s, Stallman and others developed most of the necessary components. The GNU Project also benefited from open-source software previously developed by others, notably Donald Knuth's TEX typesetting system (used to typeset this book) and MIT's X Window System. Most of the software developed as part of the GNU Project is distributed under the GNU Public License, an example of an open-source license. (For technical reasons some programs have been distributed as open-source software under other licenses.)

In 1991 Linus Torvalds began work on a Unix-like kernel he named Linux. (The kernel is the software at the very heart of an operating system.) He released version 1.0 of the kernel in 1994. Because the other major components of a Unix-like operating system had already been created through the GNU Project, Torvalds was able to combine all the software into a complete, open-source, Unix-like operating system. To the obvious chagrin of Stallman, Linux has become the commonly accepted name for the open-source operating system based on the Linux kernel. (Stallman urges people to refer to the entire system as GNU/Linux [134].)

### 4.9.6  Impact of Open–Source Software

In 1998 Andrew Leonard summarized the impact of Linux this way: "Linux is subversive. Who could have thought even five years ago that a world-class operating system could coalesce as if by magic out of part-time hacking by several thousand developers scattered all over the planet, connected only by the tenuous strands of the Internet?" [130].

Linux has become a viable alternative to proprietary versions of Unix. Many companies adopted Linux as a way to cut costs during the recession of 2008–2009 [135]. A survey conducted in June 2014 revealed that 97 percent of the world's 500 fastest supercomputers were running the Linux operating system [136].

## 4.10  Creative Commons

As we saw earlier in this chapter, some believe strong intellectual property protection stimulates creativity by dangling the prospect of financial reward in front of artists and inventors. Others believe that creativity is suppressed in such an environment. They argue that people are more creative when they are free to build on the work of others. Consider music, for example. It's not just rap musicians who sample the works of others to create new songs. Listen to the classical piece *Appalachian Spring* by Aaron Copland and you'll find that he used the Shaker hymn "Simple Gifts."

Information technology has created an environment in which an unprecedented amount of creativity could be unleashed. Never before has it been so inexpensive to record and mix music, combine photographs and computer-generated images, or tape and edit movies. Wouldn't it be great to take what others have done and add your own talents to produce even better works of art for everyone's enjoyment? Quoting the movie *Get Creative* on the Creative Commons Web site: "Collaboration across space and time. Creative co-authorship with people you've never met. Standing on the shoulders of your peers. It's what the Internet is all about" [137].

Strong intellectual property protection, however, stands in the way of this vision. Under current US copyright law, works of intellectual property are copyrighted the moment they are made, even if the creator does not attach a copyright symbol © to the work. Since copyright is implicit, permission is required before use. The current system discourages people from building on the work of others.

Imagine the difficulty an art professor has trying to put together a Web site of images for an online course! She needs to request permission for every image she wishes to display on the Web site. Suppose there are three suitable images of Michelangelo's *Pieta*. It may be impossible for her to tell in advance which, if any, of the photographers would be willing to let her use the image. It would be better if there were an official way for a photographer to say, "It's fine if you use this photograph, as long as you give me credit for taking it."

Stanford law professor Lawrence Lessig realized there was a need for a system that would allow producers of intellectual property to indicate to the world the rights they wanted to keep. Lessig asks us to think about instances of the **commons**, a "resource to which anyone within the relevant community has a right without obtaining the permission of anyone else" [138, pp. 19–20]. Examples of the commons include public streets, parks, beaches, the theory of relativity, and the works of Shakespeare. Lessig says that "there is a benefit to resources held in common and the Internet is the best evidence of that benefit. . . . The Internet forms an *innovation commons*" [138, p. 23]. The reason Lessig calls the Internet an innovation commons is because its control is decentralized: one person can introduce a new application or new content without getting anyone else's permission.

Lessig joined with Hal Abelson, James Boyle, Eric Eldred, and Eric Saltzman to found the nonprofit corporation Creative Commons in 2001. Creative Commons provides standard copyright licenses free of charge. Every license comes in three forms: human-readable, lawyer-readable, and computer-readable. With a Creative Commons license, you can retain the copyright while allowing some uses of your intellectual property under certain circumstances. Because you have published the circumstances under which your work may be used, others do not have to ask for permission before using your work [137].

How does the system work? Suppose you have taken a photograph and wish to post it on your Web site accompanied by a Creative Commons license. You visit the Creative Commons Web site (www.creativecommons.org), which allows you to choose between six different licenses, depending upon your responses to two questions (quoted verbatim):

- Allow commercial uses of your work?
  - Yes
  - No
- Allow modifications of your work?
  - Yes
  - Yes, as long as others share alike
  - No

After you answer these two questions, the Web site creates HTML code containing the appropriate Creative Commons license. You can copy the HTML code and paste it into the appropriate Web page along with your photograph. Visitors to your Web site will be able to see a human-readable summary of the license you have chosen (Figure 4.11).

Commercial artists may choose to use Creative Commons licenses to increase exposure to their work. For example, suppose you take a great photograph of the Golden Gate Bridge. You post it on your Web site with a Creative Commons license indicating the photograph may be used for noncommercial purposes as long as the user gives attribution to you. People from around the world think the image is stunning, and they copy it to their own personal Web sites, giving you credit for the photo. A travel agent in a foreign country sees the image and wants to put it on a travel poster. Since this is a commercial purpose, she must gain your permission before using the image. At that time you can negotiate a fair price for its use. Without the widespread distribution of the image through a Creative Commons license, the travel agent might never have seen it.

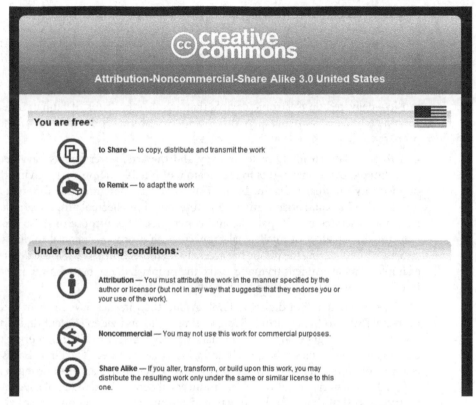

**FIGURE 4.11** A portion of the human-readable summary of a Creative Commons license as it appears to a Web site visitor. (Screenshot from Creative Commons. Copyright © 2011 by Creative Commons. Reprinted with permission.)

The computer-readable versions of the licenses are designed to make it easier for search engines to identify content based upon the particular criteria. For example, a history professor might use a search engine hoping to find an image of the Coliseum in Rome that he could include on his Web site. His purpose is noncommercial, and he is happy to credit the photographer, but he does not want to have to pay to display the image or write a letter asking for the photographer's permission. A search engine could return only those images that meet these criteria.

By 2008 about 130 million different pieces of intellectual property had been distributed using Creative Commons licenses. In 2009 the Creative Commons Attribution-ShareAlike license became the principal content license for *Wikipedia*.

John Buckman has used Creative Commons licenses to create an online record label called Magnatune [139]. Members who pay $15 a month can stream music from the site and make unlimited downloads, with half of the proceeds going to the artists [140].

# Summary

At the beginning of Chapter 2 we noted how forming communities allows us to enjoy better lives than if we lived in isolation. One of the advantages of community life is being able to enjoy the fruits of other people's creativity, and we do in fact spend much of our time enjoying entertainment created by others—television shows, movies, and music—delivered on electronic devices that are also the fruits of human ingenuity. It should come as no surprise, then, that our society promotes the creation of intellectual property.

To stimulate creativity in technology and the arts, governments have decided to grant limited ownership rights to the creators of intellectual property, giving them the opportunity for financial gain. In the United States, there are four different ways in which individuals and organizations can protect their intellectual property: trade secrets, trademarks/service marks, patents, and copyrights. The purpose of these protections is to provide creators of intellectual property with a proper financial reward for their efforts, while ensuring the public has access to their creations. The fair use doctrine is an example of a government trying to strike the proper balance between the rights of the intellectual property creator and the common good.

The introduction of digital technology and the Internet have brought intellectual property issues to the forefront. Representing audio and video content digitally means anyone with the right equipment can make perfect copies. Broadband Internet technology enables these copies to be quickly and widely disseminated. The Pirate Bay is a prime example of an organization leveraging these two technological breakthroughs to make copyrighted material freely available. Producers of copyrighted material have responded by trying to shut down the Pirate Bay and putting new restrictions on copying, even though sometimes these restrictions have made it impossible for consumers to make copies that were previously considered fair use. To a large extent, these efforts have been unsuccessful. Companies trying to sell access to movies, television shows, and songs now understand that they need to make "doing the right thing"—obtaining a legal copy—as easy as "doing the wrong thing." It is now more convenient to get paid content through NetFlix, Hulu Plus, or the Apple iTunes store than it is to get illegal copies through the Pirate Bay.

Until the mid-1960s, there was no intellectual property protection for computer software other than trade secrets. Now, both copyrights and patents are used to protect software. The area of software patents is highly controversial. There are a large number of bad software patents, and many software patents have been issued for obvious inventions. Large corporations are stockpiling software patents, so that if they are sued for infringing another company's patent, they can retaliate with their own patent infringement countersuit.

There are both rights-based and utilitarian arguments as to why we ought to give intellectual property protection to software; neither of these arguments is particularly strong, suggesting that there should be an alternative to a conventional, proprietary model of software development. The open-source movement is such an alternative. A great deal of the software that keeps the Internet running is open-source software.

Other open-source success stories include the Linux and Android operating systems, the Firefox browser, and OpenOffice productivity software.

The story of the GNU Project and Linux demonstrates how thousands of volunteers can work together to produce high-quality, industrial-strength software. Why can't the success of GNU/Linux be replicated in the arts? Imagine a culture that encouraged the production of new creative works from existing works, a culture in which songs would rapidly evolve, different versions of movies were exchanged and compared, and hypertext novels accumulated links to fan sites. Today's intellectual property laws make it difficult to achieve this vision in the entertainment field. Little can be done with a copyrighted work without first asking for permission, a labor-intensive process that puts a drag on innovation. Creative Commons is an effort to streamline the process by allowing copyright holders to indicate up front the conditions under which they are willing to let other people use their work.

# Further Reading and Viewing

Kornhaber Brown. "F.A.T. Lab." *Off Book*, September 13, 2011. 8:38. video.pbs.org.

Charles Duhigg and Steve Lohr. "The Patent, Used as a Sword." *New York Times*, October 7, 2012.

Charles Graeber. "Inside the Mansion—and Mind—of Kim Dotcom, the Most Wanted Man on the Net." *Wired*, October 12, 2012. www.wired.com.

C. G. P. Grey. "Copyright: Forever Less One Day." 6:28. www.youtube.com/watch ?v=tk862BbjWx4.

"Has Fan Culture Changed Society?" *Off Book*, September 7, 2012. 6:49. video.pbs.org.

Leah Hoffmann. "Open for Business." *Communications of the ACM*, Vol. 55, No. 4, April 2012.

Gwen Ifill. "How Effective Is Justice Department Crackdown on Online Sale of Counterfeit Goods?" *PBS NewsHour*, November 29, 2011. 9:13. video.pbs.org.

Steven Levy. "The Patent Problem." *Wired*, December 4, 2012. www.wired.com.

Peter S. Menell. "Design for Symbiosis." *Communications of the ACM*, Vol. 55, No. 5, May 2012.

Nilay Patel. "Slide to Unlock: How Apple's Patents Are Changing Android." *Verge*, March 6, 2012. 1:56. theverge.com/2012/3/6/2849051/slide-to-unlock-patent-apple-android-google.

Randal C. Picker. "The Yin and Yang of Copyright and Technology." *Communications of the ACM*, Vol. 55, No. 1, January 2012.

Ray Suarez. "Big Stakes on Small Devices: Apple and Samsung Square Off in Federal Court." *PBS NewsHour*, July 30, 2012. 7:22. www.pbs.org/newshour.

Zach Weissmueller. "Too Much Copyright." ReasonTV (Web site), April 19, 2012. 8:57. www .youtube.com/watch?v=rFMl0stqai0.

Joel Woldfogel. "Digitization and Copyright: Some Recent Evidence from Music." *Communications of the ACM*, Vol. 55, No. 5, May 2012.

Judy Woodruff. "Supreme Court Unanimously Rules Genes Cannot Be Patented." *PBS NewsHour*, July 8, 2013. 9:39. video.pbs.org.

# Review Questions

1. What features of intellectual property make it more difficult to protect than physical property?

2. What paradoxes arise when we attempt to extend Locke's notion of a natural right to property into the realm of intellectual property?

3. What are the ways in which individuals or firms in the United States may protect their intellectual property?

4. What are the relative advantages and disadvantages of patents versus trade secrets?

5. The case study in Section 4.3.5 evaluates two possible actions by Arjun. Perform act utilitarian evaluations of two other actions Arjun could take:

   Option 3: Arjun does not ask the team of software developers to improve the design of the database system. He allows the team to proceed with the implementation based on the current design.

   Option 4: Arjun meets the team of software developers implementing the database system, shares with them the optimizations he developed at Felicity Software, and asks the team to incorporate his optimizations into the system.

6. When referring to copyrighted materials, what is meant by the term "fair use"?

7. Explain how advances in information technology have made it easier for consumers to violate copyright law.

8. How has the Digital Millennium Copyright Act affected fair use of copyrighted material by consumers?

9. How does BitTorrent provide an order-of-magnitude increase in downloading speed compared to earlier peer-to-peer networks?

10. The US Supreme Court ruled that Sony was not responsible for the copyright infringements of Betamax customers, but Grokster and StreamCast were responsible for the copyright infringements of those who used their peer-to-peer networks. Explain the differences in the two situations that led the Supreme Court to reach opposite conclusions.

11. Briefly describe the most significant changes in the recorded music business in the United States over the past 15 years.

12. Suppose company A wants to develop a program that duplicates the functionality of a program made by company B. Describe how company A may do this without violating the copyrights held by company B.

13. When describing a software license, what does the phrase "open source" mean?

# Discussion Questions

14. Benjamin Franklin created many useful inventions without any desire to receive financial reward. Is intellectual property protection needed in order to promote innovation?

15. Any original piece of intellectual property you have created, such as a poem, term paper, or photograph, is automatically copyrighted, even if you did not label it with a

copyright notice. Think about the most valuable piece of intellectual property you have ever created. Describe in detail the ownership rights you would like to claim on it.

16. Do you support the aims of the Google Books project? Does this initiative give Google too much power?

17. How does the debate over digital music illuminate the differences between ethics, morality, and law?

18. Is the concept of digital rights management doomed to failure?

19. What does the US Supreme Court decision in *MGM v. Grokster* mean for the development of future peer-to-peer network technologies?

20. The current legal system allows both proprietary software and open-source software to be distributed. What are the pros and cons of maintaining the status quo?

21. Examine the analyses of Section 4.8 regarding the legitimacy of providing intellectual property protection for software. Do these arguments apply equally well to the question of providing intellectual property protection for music? Why or why not?

22. Should copyright laws protect musical compositions? Should copyright laws protect recordings of musical performances?

23. Is it hopeless to try to protect intellectual property in digital media?

# In-Class Exercises

24. A plane makes an emergency crash landing on a deserted tropical island. Two dozen survivors must fend for themselves until help arrives. All of them are from large cities, and none of them has camping experience. The survivors find it impossible to gather enough food, and everyone begins losing weight. One person spends a lot of time by himself and figures out how to catch fish. He brings fish back to camp. Others ask him to teach them how to catch fish. He refuses, but offers to share the fish he has caught with the other passengers as long as they take care of the other camp chores, such as hauling fresh water, gathering firewood, and cooking.

    Debate the morality of the bargain proposed by the fisherman. One group should explain why the fisherman's position is morally wrong. The other group should explain why the fisherman's position is morally acceptable.

25. Survey 10 of your peers with these questions. How many tracks do they have in their digital music collection? How many of these tracks did they download for free? How many of these tracks did they get from friends or family members? How many of these tracks did they rip from a CD they purchased? How many of these tracks did they purchase online? After computing the averages, share the results with your classmates.

26. Research your university's policy on bandwidth abuse and file sharing. What kinds of activities are explicitly forbidden? Is the policy sensible?

# References

[1]  Jess Denham. "Game of Thrones Season 5 Breaks Piracy Record with 32M Illegal Downloads." *Independent*, April 23, 2015. independent.co.uk.

[2]  "Cell Phones Taking Center Stage at Concerts." RedOrbit Inc., May 16, 2008. www.redorbit.com.

[3]  Joe Karaganis. "Where Do Music Collections Come From?" American Assembly, October 15, 2012. piracy.americanassembly.org.

[4]  Thomas Mennecke. "RIAA Announces New Campus Lawsuit Strategy." *Slyck News*, February 27, 2007. www.slyck.com.

[5]  Denise Lavoie. "Joel Tenenbaum: Jury Awards $675,000 in Boston Music Downloading Case." *Huffington Post*, July 31, 2009. www.huffingtonpost.com.

[6]  United States District Court for the District of Massachusetts. Sony BMG Music Entertainment; Warner Bros. Records Inc.; Atlantic Recording Corp.; Arista Records LLC; and UMG Recordings, Inc. v. Joel Tenenbaum, 07cv11446-NG (July 9, 2010).

[7]  Adamson Rust. "'RIAA Hit by 'EFFing' Music Campaign." *Inquirer IT*, June 30, 2003.

[8]  University of Texas at Arlington, Office of Technology Transfer. "Intellectual Properties." Accessed October 5, 2013. www.uta.edu/tto/ip-defs.htm.

[9]  John Locke. *Two Treatises of Government*. Cambridge University Press, Cambridge, England, 1988.

[10] Michael J. Scanlan. "Locke and Intellectual Property Rights." In *Intellectual Property Rights in a Networked World*, edited by Richard A. Spinello and Herman T. Tavani. Information Science Publishing, Hershey, PA, 2005, pp. 83–98.

[11] Edmund S. Morgan. *Benjamin Franklin*. Yale University Press, New Haven, CT, 2002.

[12] Randolph P. Luck. "Letter to The Honorable Senator Spencer Abraham." Luck's Music Library, June 28, 1996.

[13] Justice Breyer, dissenting. Supreme Court of the United States. Eric Eldred, et al. v. John D. Ashcroft, No. 01-618 (January 15, 2003).

[14] Kembrew McLeod. *Freedom of Expression(R): Overzealous Copyright Bozos and Other Enemies of Creativity*. Doubleday, New York, NY, 2005.

[15] Lawrence Lessig. "The Same Old Song." *Wired*, July 2005.

[16] "Happy Birthday, We'll Sue." Snopes.com (Web site). Urban legends reference pages, April 27, 2007. www.snopes.com.

[17] Robert Brauneis. "Copyright and the World's Most Popular Song." GWU Legal Studies Research Paper No. 1111624, George Washington University Law School, Washington, DC, March 21, 2008.

[18] Neill A. Levy. "The Rights and Wrongs of Copyright." *CINAHL News*. 15(1), Spring 1996.

[19] "What Is a Trademark?" Free Advice (Web site). Accessed October 5, 2013. www.freeadvice.com.

[20] "General Trademark Guidelines." Adobe Systems Inc. Accessed October 5, 2013. www.adobe.com/misc/trade.html.

[21] John Case. "Snapshots in Legal Drama: Polaroid Inventor vs. Kodak." *Christian Science Monitor*, October 21, 1981.

[22] David E. Sanger. "Kodak Infringed on Polaroid Patents." *New York Times*, September 14, 1985.

[23]   Lawrence Edelman. "Kodak Pays Polaroid $925M; Part of a Surprise Out-of-Court Settlement Ends 15-Year Legal Hassle." *Boston Globe*, July 16, 1991.

[24]   Kim Peterson. "Microsoft Eases Its Rules for Access to Technology." *Seattle Times*, December 4, 2003.

[25]   Agfa Monotype Corp. "Agfa Monotype Licenses ClearType from Microsoft" (press release). December 12, 2003. whattheythink.com/news/20333-agfa-monotype-licenses-cleartype-microsoft/.

[26]   International Intellectual Property Alliance. "Copyright Industries in the US Economy: The 2011 Report." Washington, DC, November 2011. www.iipa.com.

[27]   United States Court of Appeals for the Second Circuit. Gershwin Publishing Corporation, Plaintiff-Appelle, v. Columbia Artists Management, Inc., Defendant-Appellant, and Community Concerts, Inc., Defendant, 443 F.2d 1159 (May 24, 1971).

[28]   "Millbury Man Pleads Guilty in 'Davey Jones' Computer Case." *Worcester Telegram & Gazette*, December 16, 1994.

[29]   Siva Vaidhyanathan. *Copyrights and Copywrongs: The Rise of Intellectual Property and How It Threatens Creativity*. New York University Press, New York, NY, 2001.

[30]   Suzanne Fields. "Free Mickey Mouse (and Robert Frost)." *Jewish World Review*, January 24, 2003.

[31]   Chris Sprigman. "The Mouse That Ate the Public Domain: Disney, the Copyright Term Extension Act, and Eldred v. Ashcroft." FindLaw Legal News and Commentary, March 5, 2002. writ.news.findlaw.com.

[32]   "Brief for Petitioners." Supreme Court of the United States. Eric Eldred et al. v. John D. Ashcroft, in his official capacity as Attorney General. 2002.

[33]   "Eldred v. Ashcroft: A Primer." *WashingtonPost.com*, January 15, 2003.

[34]   Supreme Court of the United States. Eldred et al. v. Ashcroft, Attorney General, 239 F.3d 372, affirmed (January 15, 2003).

[35]   "Employee Confidentiality and Proprietary Rights Agreement (CA)." Practical Law (Web site). Accessed August 7, 2015. practicallaw.com/3-518-4653.

[36]   Kathleen Amen, Tish Keogh, and Necia Wolff. "Digital Copyright." *Computers in Libraries*, May 2002.

[37]   Elina M. Lae. "Mashups—a Protected Form of Appropriation Art or a Blatant Copyright Infringement?" SSRN (Web site), December 2011. papers.ssrn.com.

[38]   Supreme Court of the United States. Sony Corporation of America et al. v. Universal City Studios, Inc., et al., 464 US 417 (January 17, 1984).

[39]   United States Court of Appeals for the Ninth Circuit. Leslie A. Kelly v. Arriba Soft Corporation, 336 F.3d 811 (July 7, 2003).

[40]   "About Google Books." Accessed August 13, 2009. books.google.com/intl/en/google books/about.html.

[41]   US District Court, Southern District of New York. Authors Guild et al. v. Google Inc., 05 CIV 8136 (September 20, 2005).

[42]   US District Court, Southern District of New York. McGraw-Hill Companies et al. v. Google Inc., 05 CV 8881 (October 19, 2005).

[43]   US District Court, Southern District of New York. Authors Guild, Inc., et al. v. Google Inc., 1:05-cv-08136-DC, November 14, 2013.

[44] Corynne McSherry. "Court Upholds Legality of Google Books: Tremendous Victory for Fair Use and the Public Interest" (press release). Electronic Frontier Foundation, November 14, 2013. www.eff.org.

[45] Steven Andersen. "How Piracy, Culture and High-Tech Hackers Brought the Recording Industry to Its Knees." *Corporate Legal Times*, November 2002.

[46] David Goldman. "Music's Lost Decade: Sales Cut in Half." *CNNMoney*, February 3, 2010. money.cnn.com.

[47] "The Copyright Wars." *IEEE Spectrum*, pp. 21–23, May 2003.

[48] Christopher May. "Digital Rights Management and the Breakdown of Social Norms." *First Monday* 8(11), November 2003.

[49] Royal Van Horn. "The Digital Millennium Copyright Act and Other Egregious Laws." *Phi Delta Kappan*, November 2002.

[50] Kelly McCollum and Peter Schmidt. "How Forcefully Should Universities Enforce Copyright Law on Audio Files?" *Chronicle of Higher Education*, November 11, 1999.

[51] Ron Harris. "Where's SDMI? Digital Music Protection Effort Flames Out." *Associated Press*, April 29, 2002.

[52] Kevin Coughlin. "Cyber Music Makers Seek to Gag Code-Breakers." Newhouse News Service, April 24, 2001.

[53] John Markoff. "Scientists Drop Plan to Present Music-Copying Study That Record Industry Opposed." *New York Times*, April 27, 2001.

[54] "A Speed Bump vs. Music Copying: Master Cryptographer—and Code Cracker—Edward Felten Says Technology Isn't the Answer to Digital Copyright Violations." *Business Week Online*, January 9, 2002.

[55] "FAQ: Sony's 'Rootkit' CDs." CNet News (Web site), November 21, 2005. news.cnet .com.

[56] "Sony BMG Settlement FAQ." Electronic Frontier Foundation. Accessed September 29, 2015. www.eff.org/IP/DRM/Sony-BMG.

[57] Selena Kim. "The Reinforcement of International Copyright for the Digital Age." *Intellectual Property Journal*, 16:93–122, 2003.

[58] Tom Espiner. "British Library Calls for Digital Copyright Action." CNet News (Web site), September 25, 2006. news.cnet.com.

[59] Ali Matin. "Digital Rights Management (DRM) in Online Music Stores: DRM-Encumbered Music Downloads' Inevitable Demise as a Result of the Negative Effects of Heavy-Handed Copyright Law." *Entertainment Law Review*, Vol. 28, Loyola Law School, Los Angeles, CA, 2008.

[60] Michael Arrington. "EMI, Apple to Sell DRM-Free Music for $1.29/Song." TechCrunch, April 2, 2007. techcrunch.com.

[61] Jacqui Cheng. "Amazon Rounds Out DRM-Free Music Offering with Sony BMG." Ars Technica (Web site), January 10, 2008. arstechnica.com.

[62] "iTunes Store and DRM-Free Music: What You Need to Know." *MacWorld*, January 7, 2009. www.macworld.com.

[63] Marc Whitten. Letter to Xbox Live members, June 10, 2013. news.xbox.com.

[64] Michael Rundle. "Microsoft Unveils Xbox One Privacy and Digital Rights Details Ahead of E3." *Huffington Post UK*, June 7, 2013. www.huffingtonpost.co.uk.

[65] William Usher. "PS4 Grabs 95 Percent of Consumer Votes after Amazon Ends Poll Early." CinemaBlend (Web site), June 16, 2013. www.cinemablend.com.

[66]  Don Mattrick. "Your Feedback Matters—Update on Xbox One." *Xbox Wire*, June 19, 2013. news.xbox.com.

[67]  Danielle Roy. "Napster Timeline." IDG News Service, Boston Bureau, April 2, 2001.

[68]  Nathan Ruegger. "Napster Withers Away, but Peer-to-Peer Legacy Remains." *Dartmouth*, October 3, 2002.

[69]  Ron Harris. "Bankruptcy Judge Blocks Sale of Napster to Bertelsmann." Associated Press, September 4, 2002.

[70]  Reuters. "Music Industry Sends Warnings to Song Swappers." *NYTimes.com*, April 29, 2003.

[71]  Phil Hardy. "Verizon Agrees to Give the RIAA the Names of Four Subscribers Alleged to Be File-Sharing Copyrighted Works." *Music & Copyright*, June 11, 2003.

[72]  Sara Calabro. "RIAA Lawsuits—Music Industry Mistakes Its Lawsuits for a PR Maneuver." *PR Week*, September 22, 2003.

[73]  Phil Hardy. "Media Reaction to RIAA's New Round of Lawsuits Less Hostile but Grassroots Opposition Grows." *Music & Copyright*, October 29, 2003.

[74]  John Schwartz. "Record Industry May Not Subpoena Online Providers." *NYTimes.com*, December 19, 2003.

[75]  Kevin Fitchard. "Verizon Gains Upper Hand in RIAA Subpoena Ruling." *Telephony*, January 12, 2004.

[76]  Mary Madden and Lee Rainie. "Music and Video Downloading Moves beyond P2P." Report, Pew Internet & American Life Project, March 23, 2005. www.pewinternet.org/reports.

[77]  Mike Harvey. "Single-Mother Digital Pirate Jammie Thomas-Rasset Must Pay $80,000 per Song." *Sunday Times*, June 19, 2009. www.thesundaytimes.co.uk.

[78]  United States District Court, District of Minnesota. Capitol Records, Inc., et al. v. Jammie Thomas-Rasset, 06-1497 (MJD/LIB) (July 22, 2011).

[79]  Fred von Lohmann. "Offering to Distribute = Distribution, Says Court in Elektra v. Barker." Electronic Frontier Foundation, April 1, 2008. www.eff.org.

[80]  Fred von Lohmann. "Making Available Is Not Distribution, Says Court in London-Shire v. Doe." Electronic Frontier Foundation, April 2, 2008. www.eff.org.

[81]  Fred von Lohmann. "Big Victory in Atlantic v. Howell: Court Rejects RIAA 'Making Available' Theory." Electronic Frontier Foundation, April 29, 2008. www.eff.org.

[82]  John Borland. "Judge: File-Swapping Tools Are Legal." CNet News (Web site), April 25, 2003. news.cnet.com.

[83]  Supreme Court of the United States. Metro-Goldwyn-Mayer Studios Inc. et al. v. Grokster, Ltd., et al., 545 US (June 27, 2005).

[84]  John Borland. "Last Waltz for Grokster." CNet News (Web site), November 7, 2005. news.cnet.com.

[85]  Clive Thompson. "The BitTorrent Effect." *Wired*, p. 150, January 2005.

[86]  Krysten Crawford. "BitTorrent as Friend, Not Foe." CNN.com, April 30, 2005.

[87]  "Authorities Strike Back at 'Star Wars' Pirates." Associated Press, May 25, 2005.

[88]  Jenny Stiernstedt, Astrid E. Johansson, and Fredrik Söderling. Translated by Oliver Grassman. "The Pirate Bay Sentenced to One Year in Prison." *Kultur & Nöje* (Sweden), April 17, 2009. www.dn.se.

[89]  David Sarno. "The Internet Sure Loves Its Outlaws." *Los Angeles Times*, April 29, 2007.

[90]  "Police Cleared of Wrongdoing in Pirate Bay Raid." *Local* (Sweden), April 2, 2007. www.thelocal.se.

[91]  Nate Anderson. "Pirate Bay on IFPI Lawsuit: Labels Can 'Go Screw Themselves.'" Ars Technica(Web site), April 1, 2008. arstechnica.com.

[92]  Associated Press. "Swedish Court Upholds Convictions in File-Sharing Case." *New York Times*, November 26, 2010. www.nytimes.com.

[93]  Trace Hagan. "The Pirate Bay Acquires Caribbean Domain Name thepiratebay.sx." TweakTown (Web site), May 1, 2013. www.tweaktown.com.

[94]  "'Operation In Our Sites' Targets Internet Movie Pirates." US Department of Homeland Security, June 30, 2010. www.ice.gov.

[95]  "Operation In Our Sites Protects American Online Shoppers, Cracks Down on Counterfeiters." US Department of Homeland Security, November 28, 2011. www.ice.gov.

[96]  United States District Court for the Eastern District of Virginia. United States of America v. Kim Dotcom et al., [2012] NZHC 2076 (January 5, 2012).

[97]  Geoffrey A. Fowler, Devlin Barrett, and Sam Schechner. "US Shuts Offshore File-Share 'Locker.'" *Wall Street Journal*, January 20, 2012.

[98]  Chloe Albanesius. "After Megaupload, FileSonic Disables File Sharing." *PC Magazine*, January 23, 2012.

[99]  Nate Lanxon. "FileSonic, FileServe Pull Fire-Sharing Services Following Megaupload Arrests." *Wired.co.uk*, January 23, 2012. wired.co.uk.

[100]  Christopher Kauffman. Private communication, March 2015.

[101]  IFPI. "IFPI Publishes Digital Music Report 2015" (press release). April 14, 2015. www.ifpi.org.

[102]  "Stream Engines: Subscription Video Services Give Options to Consumers Looking to Spend on Content." Nielsen, March 11, 2015. www.nielsen.com.

[103]  RIAA. "Scope of the Problem." RIAA (Web site). Accessed July 23, 2015. www.riaa.com/physicalpiracy.php?content_selector=piracy-online-scope-of-the-problem.

[104]  Daniel A. Tysver. "The History of Software Patents: From Benson and Diehr to State Street and Bilski." BitLaw (Web site). Accessed August 14, 2011. www.bitlaw.com.

[105]  Rob Tiller. "The PTO Addresses Bilski and Software Patents." Opensource.com, September 30, 2010. opensource.com.

[106]  "Microsoft Patent Portfolio Tops IT Industry Scorecards." Microsoft News Center, January 28, 2008. www.microsoft.com.

[107]  Michael Kanellos. "Patent Auctions: Lawyer's Dream or Way of the Future?" *ZDNet News*, March 3, 2006. web.archive.org.

[108]  Matthew Sag and Kurt Rohde. "Patent Reform and Differential Policy." Northwestern Law & Econ Research Paper No. 925722, Chicago, IL, August 21, 2006. papers.ssrn.com.

[109]  Barrie McKenna, Paul Waldie, and Simon Avery. "Patently Absurd." *Globel and Mail*, February 21, 2006. www.theglobeandmail.com.

[110]  Rob Kelley. "BlackBerry Maker, NTP Ink $612 Million Settlement." *CNNMoney*, March 3, 2006. money.cnn.com.

[111]  Charles Duhigg and Steve Lohr. "The Patent, Used as a Sword." *New York Times*, October 7, 2012. www.nytimes.com.

[112]  Larry Downes. "The Bilski Case and the Future of Software Patents." Center for Internet and Society, November 11, 2009. cyberlaw.stanford.edu.

[113] Nilay Patel. "Nokia vs. Apple: The In-Depth Analysis." *Engadget* (blog), October 29, 2009. www.engadget.com.

[114] Nilay Patel. "Apple Countersues Nokia for Infringing 13 Patents." *Engadget* (blog), December 11, 2009. www.engadget.com.

[115] US District Court, Northern District of California. Apple Inc. v. Samsung Electronics Co. et al., CV 11 1846 LB, April 15, 2011.

[116] Florian Mueller. "Apple Seeks $2.5 Billion in Damages from Samsung, Offers Half a Cent per Standard-Essential Patent." *Foss Patents* (blog), July 24, 2012. www.foss patents.com.

[117] Kurt Eichenwald. "The Great Smartphone War." *Vanity Fair*, June 2014.

[118] Nilay Patel. "Slide to Unlock: How Apple's Patents Are Changing Android." *Verge*, March 6, 2012. www.theverge.com.

[119] Matt Rosoff. "The Smartphone Patent Wars Are Finally Coming to an End." *Business Insider*, December 23, 2014. www.businessinsider.com.

[120] Ronald Mann. "Argument Preview: Justices Have Chance to Provide Final Solution to Quandary About Patenting Software." *SCOTUSblog*, March 20, 2014.

[121] Supreme Court of the United States. Bernard L. Bilski and Rand A. Warson, Petitioners, v. David J. Kappos, Under Secretary of Commerce for Intellectual Property and Director, Patent and Trademark Office, 561 US 593 (June 28, 2010).

[122] Supreme Court of the United States. Mayo Collaborative Services, DBA Mayo Medical Laboratories et al. v. Prometheus Laboratories, Inc., 566 US ___, Docket No. 10-1150 (March 20, 2012).

[123] Supreme Court of the United States. Alice Corporation Pty. Ltd. v. CLS Bank International, 573 US ___, Docket No. 13-298 (June 19, 2014).

[124] David Kappos. "Symposium: Supreme Court Leaves Patent Protection for Software Innovation Intact." *SCOTUSblog*, June 20, 2014.

[125] Justin Nelson. "Symposium: For Patent Litigants, Court Affirms Status Quo." *SCOTUSblog*, June 20, 2014.

[126] Helen Nissenbaum. "Should I Copy My Neighbor's Software?" In *Computers, Ethics, & Social Values*, edited by Deborah G. Johnson and Helen Nissenbaum. Prentice Hall, Englewood Cliffs, NJ, 1995.

[127] Richard P. Stallman. "Why Software Should Not Have Owners." GNU Project Web server, June 17, 2003. www.gnu.org/philosophy/why-free.html.

[128] "The Open Source Definition." Open Source Initiative, 2003. www.opensource.org/docs/definition.php.

[129] Carolyn A. Kenwood. "A Business Case Study of Open Source Software." Technical report, MITRE Corporation, Bedford, MA, July 2001.

[130] Andrew Leonard. "Let My Software Go!" *Salon* (Web site), April 14, 1998. www.salon.com.

[131] Tarmo Virki and Sinead Carew. "Google Topples Nokia from Smartphones Top Spot." Reuters, January 31, 2011. uk.reuters.com.

[132] "GlobalStats." StatCounter. Accessed June 29, 2015. gs.statcounter.com.

[133] Stephen Shankland. "Study Lauds Open-Source Code Quality." CNet News (Web site), February 19, 2003. news.cnet.com.

[134] Richard P. Stallman. "Linux and the GNU Project." GNU Project Web server, December 14, 2002. www.gnu.org/gnu/linux-and-gnu.html.

[135] Sean Michael Kerner. "LinuxCon Analysts: Linux Is Winning." *Datamation*, August 12, 2010. www.datamation.com.

[136] Katherine Noyes. "Linux Nears Total Domination of the Top 500 Supercomputers." June 25, 2014. www.linux.com.

[137] Creative Commons, Stanford Law School. *Get Creative* (movie), 2002. www.creative commons.org.

[138] Lawrence Lessig. *The Future of Ideas: The Fate of the Commons in a Connected World.* Random House, New York, NY, 2001.

[139] Ariana Eunjung Cha. "Creative Commons Is Rewriting Rules of Copyright." *Washington Post*, March 15, 2005.

[140] "What Is 'Open Music'?" Magnatune (Web site), July 7, 2005. magnatune.com.

# June Besek

June Besek is the executive director of the Kernochan Center for Law, Media and the Arts and a lecturer in law at Columbia Law School in New York City, where she teaches "Current Issues in Copyright" and a seminar that focuses on the rights of individual authors and artists. Previously, she was a partner in a New York City law firm where she specialized in copyright law. She is a former chair of the Copyright Division of the American Bar Association's Intellectual Property Law Section. She is a frequent speaker on copyright issues and the author of many articles on copyright law, particularly as it relates to new technologies.

---

*I read that Bob Dylan, Charlie Daniels, Loretta Lynn, Don Henley from the Eagles, and other recording artists have notified the US Copyright Office that they intend to exercise their termination rights and recover the copyrights to their music. What are termination rights?*

Section 203 of the Copyright Act gives authors or their heirs the right to terminate any grant of copyrights like a license or assignment 35 years after the grant was made. That particular termination right applies only to grants made by the author on or after January 1, 1978. When I say "authors," I mean any kind of creators: book authors, composers, sound-recording artists, and so on. The effect of termination is that all the rights that were transferred or licensed under the grant revert back to the authors or their heirs.

### Why do we have termination rights?

The point of termination is that authors and artists often have very little bargaining power when they negotiate contracts, and frequently neither the author nor the publisher has any realistic idea of how popular or how lucrative their work might become. So this termination provision lets an author renegotiate the agreement or even take the work to a new publisher and maybe get more money or perhaps more control over how the work is marketed.

### Why is this specifically an issue in the sound-recording context?

Federal copyright law didn't protect sound recordings until 1972, and then there was a major revision of the copyright law that went into effect six years later. A lot of the recordings created under the old law were done as "works made for hire," and therefore under the law the grants weren't eligible for termination. The work-made-for-hire rules were changed in 1978, but there haven't yet been any terminations under the revised copyright law, so the effect of the revised work-made-for-hire rules on artists' ability to terminate is uncertain. That's why this is a new issue.

### Must recording artists give notice to reclaim ownership?

Yes, in order to reclaim their rights they have to give notice. If you signed a grant the first day of the new Copyright Act, January 1, 1978, the earliest you could terminate would be January 1, 2013. In order to terminate, you have to serve a notice on the party whose grant you're terminating, and you have to file it in the Copyright Office. That notice can be served anywhere from ten years out to two years out. So if you wanted to terminate at the beginning of 2013, you could have served that notice as early as the beginning of 2003 and as late as the beginning of 2011. But there's a five-year window for terminating. So if you didn't serve the notice in 2011, you can't terminate in 2013. But you have until January 1, 2018, to actually terminate the grant.

It's important to note that even if you terminate the grant to a copyright, you can't cut off the rights to derivative works that have already been made. Suppose the record company licensed your recording to be used in some sort of combination recording, where one track is run over the other to create a new recording. If that was done with authorization, you can't cut off the rights to that. It could still be marketed, and you would continue to be paid for it. But you can prevent new derivative works from being made from your recording.

### Is there any reason why sound-recording artists wouldn't want to reclaim copyright ownership of their work?

Some recording artists own the label. If they own their own label, then they wouldn't have any particular interest in termination. If they're very happy with their relationship with their label, maybe they wouldn't want to terminate. A lot of people wouldn't want to be the test case, so they might kind of drag their heels until they see what's happening with other people.

### What's the problem with being the test case?

Litigation is very expensive. You could spend as much in litigation as you could ever hope to gain on your recordings. So the people who are the test cases will likely be the artists who are making a fair amount of money from their older recordings and are willing to spend money and time and effort to get out from under their record company.

### Which side do you think has the stronger argument?

This is a very complicated issue. It all revolves around whether or not these works are works made for hire, because you can terminate the copyright grant if the work was created in your individual capacity, but you can't terminate if it is a work made for hire.

There are two ways a work can be a work made for hire. One is if it was created by an employee in the course of his or her employment. That usually is not the case with sound recordings. For the most part, the artists are not employees of the label. But the other way it can be a work made for hire is if it's a specially commissioned work. For a commissioned work to be a work made for hire, there has to be an agreement signed by both parties that the work will be work made for hire, and the work has to fall within one of nine specified categories of works. If it doesn't fit into one of these categories, it doesn't matter what you said in your agreement; it's not a work made for hire.

Most of these categories aren't ones that sound recordings would likely fall into. But there are three categories that sound recordings might fit into: a contribution to a collective work, part of a motion picture or other audiovisual work, or a compilation. Most of the time the label's money is going to be on a contribution to a collective work. They'll say, "We have a signed agreement, and we hired you recording artists to create your sound recording as part of a collective work—specifically, an album. Therefore, it is a work made for hire, and you are not entitled under the law to terminate it."

It's not clear to me whether the labels will succeed. I think these cases are going to be very fact based. So to answer your question, I think it's going to depend upon the circumstances under which the sound recording was created. If the recording was created and marketed as a single, I don't think you have a contribution to a collective work. Also, some courts have held that a work-made-for-hire agreement must be signed before the song is recorded. So if the case were to go to one of those courts, then the success of the artist could depend on when the contract was signed. And there are some other more complicated arguments that might be made with regard to whether a particular recording is a work made for hire. But everybody is going to be watching those first cases very carefully.

***Does it matter that artists typically get an advance for making an album, but then they end up having to pay all the costs of producing the album, and that has to come out of their future royalties?***

That's very relevant because it suggests that they're not employees, they're outside contractors. But because the statute allows in some cases for outside contractors to create works made for hire, I don't think the fact that the artists have to pick up these expenses necessarily indicates that it's a not a work for hire. It more likely depends on whether you can shoehorn the particular recording into one of these commissioned-work categories.

As I mentioned, the cases are somewhat fact based. That means the label may win in one case and the artist in another because the facts are different. For example, there are sound recordings that were created as a contribution to a motion picture or other audiovisual work. That's one of the categories. And if that's the case, then it will be a work for hire, assuming there was a signed agreement. But most sound recordings were not created that way. So even if one case comes out one way, it doesn't mean they all will.

***Are the stakes in this so high that the losing party would want to keep appealing all the way to the US Supreme Court?***

Probably. I would be surprised if this would get resolved before you get to that level. If the record labels are not successful in claiming that these are works made for hire, it definitely will diminish an important income stream. So I don't think they will just accept a negative decision. This is true of the artists as well.

# 5

# Information Privacy

With your permission, you give us more information. If you give us information about who some of your friends are, we can probably use some of that information, again, with your permission, to improve the quality of our searches. We don't need you to type at all, because we know where you are, with your permission. We know where you've been, with your permission. We can more or less guess what you're thinking about. [1]

—ERIC SCHMIDT, FORMER CEO OF GOOGLE

## 5.1 Introduction

DO YOU WANT TO KNOW WHERE I LIVE? If you visit the WhitePages.com Web site and type my phone number into the Reverse Phone field, it returns a page giving my name and address and a map of the neighborhood around my house.

Spend a few seconds more, and you can learn a lot about my standard of living. Go to Zillow.com and enter the address that you just learned from WhitePages.com. Zillow dutifully returns the estimated value of my house, based on public records that document its size, its assessed value, and information about recent sales of other homes in my neighborhood. And if you'd like to see what the outside of my house looks like, you can check out the Street View from Google Maps.

If you become a friend of one of my friends on Facebook, you can get even more glimpses into my personal life by viewing photos of me that other people have posted and tagged. You can see me lounging by a swimming pool at a family reunion, juggling croquet balls, unwrapping a Christmas present, and walking my daughter Shauna down the aisle on her wedding day.

Scott McNealy, former CEO of Sun Microsystems, caused quite a stir when he said, "You have zero privacy anyway. Get over it" [2]. You can't deny that computers, databases, and the Internet have made it easier than ever to get lots of information about total strangers. Still, many of us would like to think that we can keep some things private. Is it possible to maintain privacy in the Information Age?

The cartoon planned for this space could not be included because a licensing agreement was not reached with the copyright holder.

In this chapter we focus on privacy issues related to the introduction of information technology. We begin by taking a philosophical look at privacy. What is privacy exactly? Do we have a natural right to privacy in the same way that we have the right to own property and the right to liberty? What about our need to know enough about others so that we can trust them? How do we handle conflicts between the right to privacy and the right to free expression?

We then survey some of the ways that we leave an "electronic trail" of information behind us as we go about our daily lives. Both private organizations and governments construct databases documenting our activities.

Next, we take a look at data mining, an important tool for building profiles of individuals and communities. Companies use data mining to improve service and target product marketing to the right consumers. Data brokers collect massive amounts of information about individuals and produce mailing lists for direct marketers.

Sometimes corporations push on the borders of personal privacy a little too hard; we look at a few examples where they have had to retreat because of a consumer backlash.

# 5.2 Perspectives on Privacy

In this section we explore what the word "privacy" means, survey some positive and negative consequences of granting people privacy, and discuss whether privacy is a natural right, like the right to life.

## 5.2.1 Defining Privacy

Philosophers struggle to define privacy. Discussions about privacy revolve around the notion of *access*, where access means either physical proximity to a person or knowledge about that person. There is a tug-of-war between the desires, rights, and responsibilities of a person who wants to restrict access to himself, and the desires, rights, and responsibilities of outsiders to gain access.

From the point of view of an individual seeking to restrict access, privacy is a "zone of inaccessibility" that surrounds a person [3]. You have privacy to the extent that you can control who is allowed into your zone of inaccessibility. For example, you exercise your privacy when you lock the door behind you when using the toilet. You also exercise your privacy when you choose not to tell the clerk at the health club your Social Security number. However, privacy is not the same thing as being alone. Two people can have a private relationship. It might be a physical relationship, in which each person lets the other person become physically close while excluding others, or it might be an intellectual relationship, in which they exchange letters containing private thoughts.

When we look at privacy from the point of view of outsiders seeking access, the discussion revolves around where to draw the line between what is private and what is public (known to all). Stepping over this line and violating someone's privacy is an affront to that person's dignity [4]. You violate someone's privacy when you treat him or her as a means to an end. Put another way, some things ought not to be known. Suppose a friend invites you to see a cool movie trailer available on the Web. You follow him into the computer lab. He sits down at an available computer and begins to type in his login name and password. While it is his responsibility to keep his password confidential, it is also generally accepted that you ought to avert your eyes when someone is typing in their password. Another person's password is not something that you should know.

On the other hand, society can be harmed if individuals have too much privacy. Suppose a group of wealthy people of the same racial, ethnic, and religious background forms a private club. The members of the club share information with each other that is not available to the general public. If the club facilitates business deals among its members, it may give them an unfair advantage over others in the community who are just as capable of fulfilling the contracts. In this way, privacy can encourage social and economic inequities, and the public at large may benefit if the group had less privacy (or its membership were more diverse).

Here is another example of a public/private conflict, but this one focuses on the privacy of an individual. Most of us distinguish between a person's "private life" (what they do at home) and their "public life" (what they do at work). In general, we may agree that people have the right to keep outsiders from knowing what they do away from work. However, suppose a journalist learns that a wealthy candidate for high public office has lost millions of dollars gambling in Las Vegas. Does the public interest outweigh the politician's desire for privacy in this case?

In summary, privacy is a social arrangement that allows individuals to have some level of control over who is able to gain access to their physical selves and their personal information.

## 5.2.2 Harms and Benefits of Privacy

A little reflection reveals that privacy can have both harmful and beneficial consequences.

### HARMS OF PRIVACY

Giving people privacy can result in harm to society. Some people take advantage of privacy to plan and carry out illegal or immoral activities. Most wrongdoing takes place under the cover of privacy [5].

Some commentators suggest that increasing privacy has caused unhappiness by putting too great a burden on the nuclear family to care for all of its members. In the past people received moral support not just from their immediate family but also from other relatives and neighbors. Today, by contrast, families are expected to solve their own problems, which puts a great strain on some individuals [6].

On a related note, family violence leads to much pain and suffering in our society. Often, outsiders do not even acknowledge that a family is dysfunctional until one of its members is seriously injured. One reason dysfunctional families can maintain the pretense of normality as long as they do is because our culture respects the privacy of each family [7].

Humans are social beings. Most of us seek some engagement with others. The poor, the mentally ill, and others living on the fringes of society may have no problem maintaining a "zone of inaccessibility," because nobody is paying any attention to them. For outcasts, an abundance of privacy may be a curse, not a blessing.

### BENEFITS OF PRIVACY

Socialization and individuation are both necessary steps for a person to reach maturity. Privacy is necessary for a person to blossom as an individual [8].

Privacy is the way in which a social group recognizes and communicates to the individual that he is responsible for his development as a unique person, a separate moral agent [9]. Privacy is a recognition of each person's true freedom [10].

Privacy is valuable because it lets us be ourselves. Consider the following example. Imagine you are in a park playing with your child. How would your behavior be different if you knew someone was carefully watching you, perhaps even videotaping you, so that he or she could tell others about your parenting skills? You might well become self-conscious about your behavior. Few people would be able to carry on without any change to their emotional state or physical actions [11].

On a similar note, privacy lets us remove our public persona [12]. Imagine a businesswoman who is having a hard time with one of her company's important clients. At work, she must be polite to the client and scrupulously avoid saying anything negative about the client in front of any coworkers, lest she demoralize them, or even worse, lose her job. In the privacy of her home, she can "blow off steam" by confiding in her husband, who lends her a sympathetic ear and helps motivate her to get through the tough time at work. If people did not have privacy, they would have to wear their public face at all times, which could be damaging to their psychological health.

Privacy can foster intellectual activities. It allows us to shut out the rest of the world so that we can focus our thoughts without interruption, be creative, and grow spiritually [13, 14, 15].

Some maintain that privacy is the only way in which people can develop relationships involving respect, love, friendship, and trust. You can think of privacy as "moral capital" [16]. People use this capital to build intimate relationships. Taking away people's privacy means taking away their moral capital. Without moral capital, they have no means to develop close personal relationships.

In order to have different kinds of social relationships with different people, we need to have some kind of control over who knows what about us [17]. You can imagine everyone having a "ladder" of privacy [11]. At the top of the ladder is the person we share the most information with. For many people, this person is their spouse. As we work our way down the ladder, we encounter people we would share progressively less information with. Here is an example of what someone's ladder of privacy might look like:

    spouse

    priest/minister/rabbi/imam

    brothers and sisters

    parents

    children

    friends

    in-laws

    coworkers

    neighbors

    marketers

    employers

    government

    news media

    ex-spouses

    potential rivals/enemies

Others are critical of suggestions that tie intimacy too closely to sharing information [9]. A woman might tell her psychoanalyst things she would not even reveal to her
husband, but that does not imply that she experiences deeper intimacy with her psychoanalyst than with her husband. Intimacy is not just about sharing information; it's also
about caring. The mutual caring that characterizes a healthy marriage results in a greater
level of intimacy than can be gained simply by sharing personal information.

### SUMMARY

To summarize our discussion, allowing people to have some privacy has a variety of
beneficial effects. Granting people privacy is one way that society recognizes them as
adults and indicates they are responsible for their own moral behavior. Privacy helps
people to develop as individuals and to truly be themselves. It provides people the
opportunity to shut out the world, be more creative, and develop spiritually. It allows
each of us to create different kinds of relationships with different people.

Privacy also has numerous harmful effects. It provides people with a way of covering
up actions that are immoral or illegal. If a society sends a message that certain kinds
of information must be kept private, some people caught in abusive or dysfunctional
relationships may feel trapped and unable to ask others for help.

Weighing these benefits and harms, we conclude that granting people at least some
privacy is better than denying people any privacy at all. That leads us to our next question: Is privacy a natural right, like the right to life?

## 5.2.3  Is There a Natural Right to Privacy?

Most of us agree that every person has certain natural rights, such as the right to life, the
right to liberty, and the right to own property. Many people also talk about our right to
privacy. Is this a natural right as well?

### PRIVACY RIGHTS EVOLVE FROM PROPERTY RIGHTS

Our belief in a right to privacy may have grown out of our property rights [8]. Historically, Europeans have viewed the home as a sanctuary. The English common law
tradition has been that "a man's home is his castle." No one—not even the king—can
enter without permission, unless there is probable cause of criminal activity.

In 1765 the British Parliament passed the Quartering Act, which required American colonies to provide British soldiers with accommodations in taverns, inns, and
unoccupied buildings. After the Boston Tea Party of 1773, the British Parliament attempted to restore order in the colonies by passing the Coercive Acts. One of these acts
amended the Quartering Act to allow the billeting of soldiers in private homes, breaking
the centuries-old common law tradition and infuriating many colonists. It's not surprising, then, that Americans restored the principle of home as sanctuary in the Bill of
Rights.

∿

# THIRD AMENDMENT TO THE UNITED STATES CONSTITUTION

No Soldier shall, in time of peace be quartered in any house, without the consent of the Owner, nor in time of war, but in a manner to be prescribed by law.

∿

In certain villages in the Basque region of Spain, each house is named after the person who originally constructed it. Villagers refer to people by their house names, even if the family living in the house has no relation to the family originally dwelling there.

These examples show a strong link between a person and their property. From this viewpoint, privacy is seen in terms of control over personal territory, and privacy rights evolve out of property rights.

## WARREN AND BRANDEIS: CLEARLY, PEOPLE HAVE A RIGHT TO PRIVACY

We can see this evolution laid out in a highly influential paper, published in 1890, by Samuel Warren and Louis Brandeis. Samuel Warren was a Harvard-educated lawyer who became a businessman when he inherited a paper manufacturing business. His wife was the daughter of a US senator and a leading socialite in Boston. Her parties attracted the upper crust of Boston society. They also attracted the attention of the *Saturday Evening Gazette*, a tabloid that delighted in shocking its readers with lurid details about the lives of the Boston Brahmins.[1] Fuming at the paper's coverage of his daughter's wedding, Warren enlisted the aid of Harvard classmate Louis Brandeis, a highly successful Boston attorney (and future US Supreme Court justice). Together Warren and Brandeis published an article in the *Harvard Law Review* called "The Right to Privacy" [18]. In their highly influential paper, Warren and Brandeis argue that political, social, and economic changes demand recognition for new kinds of legal rights. In particular, they write that it is clear that people in modern society have a right to privacy and that this right ought to be respected. To make their case, they focus on—as you might have guessed—abuses of newspapers.

According to Warren and Brandeis:

The press is overstepping in every direction the obvious bounds of propriety and of decency. Gossip is no longer the resource of the idle and of the vicious, but has become a trade, which is pursued with industry as well as effrontery. To satisfy the prurient taste the details of sexual relations are spread broadcast in the columns of the daily papers. . . . The intensity and complexity of life, attendant upon advancing civilization, have rendered necessary some retreat from the world, and man, under the refining influence of culture, has become more sensitive to publicity, so

1. To learn more about the Boston Brahmins, consult *Wikipedia* (www.wikipedia.org).

**FIGURE 5.1** Warren and Brandeis argued that the legal system should protect people's "right to be let alone." (PhamousFotos/Splash News/Newscom)

that solitude and privacy have become more essential to the individual; but modern enterprise and invention have, through invasions upon his privacy, subjected him to mental pain and distress, far greater than could be inflicted by mere bodily injury. [18, p. 196]

Meanwhile, Warren and Brandeis argue, there are no adequate legal remedies available to the victims. Laws against libel and slander are not sufficient because they do not address the situation where malicious but true stories about someone are circulated. Laws addressing property rights also fall short because they assume people have control over the ways in which information about them is revealed. However, cameras and other devices are capable of capturing information about a person without that person's consent (Figure 5.1).

Warren and Brandeis pointed out that the right to privacy had already been recognized by French law. They urged the American legal system to recognize the right to privacy, which they called "the right to be let alone" [18]. Their reasoning was highly influential. Though it took decades, the right to privacy is now recognized in courts across America [19].

### THOMSON: EVERY "PRIVACY RIGHT" VIOLATION IS A VIOLATION OF ANOTHER RIGHT

Judith Jarvis Thomson has a completely different view about a right to privacy. She writes: "Perhaps the most striking thing about the right to privacy is that nobody seems to have any very clear idea what it is" [20]. Thomson points out problems with defining privacy as "the right to be let alone," as Warren and Brandeis have done. In some respects, this definition of privacy is too narrow. Suppose the police use an X-ray device and supersensitive microphones to monitor the movements and conversations of Smith in her home. The police have not touched Smith or even come close to her. She has no knowledge they are monitoring her. The police have let Smith alone, yet people who believe in a right to privacy would surely argue that they have violated Smith's privacy. In other respects, the definition of privacy as "the right to be let alone" is too broad. If I hit Jones on the head with a brick, I have not let him alone, but it is not his right of privacy I have violated—it is his right to be secure in his own person.

Thomson argues that whenever the right to privacy is violated, another right is violated as well. For example, suppose a man owns a pornographic picture. He doesn't want anyone else to know he owns it, so he keeps it in a wall safe. He only takes it out of his safe when he has taken pains to prevent others from looking into his home. Suppose we use an X-ray machine to look into his home safe and view the picture. We have violated his privacy, but we have also violated one of his property rights—the right to decide who (if anybody) sees the picture.

Here is another example. Suppose a Saudi Arabian woman wishes to keep her face covered for religious reasons. When she goes out in public, she puts a veil over her face. If I should walk up and pull away her veil to see her face, I have violated her privacy. But I have also violated one of her rights over her person—to decide who should touch her.

According to Thomson, there is a cluster of rights associated with privacy, just as there is a cluster of rights associated with property and a cluster of rights associated with our physical selves. In Thomson's view, every violation of a privacy right is also a violation of a right in some other cluster. Since this is the case, there is no need to define privacy precisely or to decide exactly where to draw the line between violations of privacy and acceptable conduct.

## AUTONOMOUS MORAL AGENTS NEED SOME PRIVACY

Thomson is not alone in disputing that privacy is a natural right. Many philosophers think privacy principles should be based on the more fundamental principle that each person is worthy of respect [10]. We give each other privacy because we recognize privacy is needed if people are to be autonomous moral agents able to develop healthy personal relationships and act as free citizens in a democratic society.

Jeffrey Reiman supports this view:

> The right to privacy protects the individual's interest in becoming, being, and remaining a person. It is thus a right which *all* human individuals possess—even those in solitary confinement. It does not assert a right never to be seen even on a crowded street. It is sufficient that I can control whether and by whom my body is experienced in some significant places and that I have the real possibility of repairing to those places. It is a right which protects my capacity to enter into intimate relations, not because it protects my reserve of generally withheld information,

but because it enables me to make the commitment that underlies caring as *my* commitment uniquely conveyed by *my* thoughts and witnessed by *my* actions. [9, p. 314]

Note Reiman's fairly restricted view of privacy. He carefully points out areas where privacy is necessary. He does not argue that privacy is a natural right, nor does he suggest that a person has complete control over what is held private.

### CONCLUSION: PRIVACY IS A PRUDENTIAL RIGHT

In conclusion, philosophers disagree whether there is a natural right to privacy, but most commentators can agree that privacy is a **prudential right**. That means rational agents would agree to recognize some privacy rights because granting these rights is to the benefit of society [21].

## 5.2.4 Privacy and Trust

While many people complain about threats to privacy, it is clear upon reflection that in some important ways we have more privacy than our ancestors did [22]. Only a couple of centuries ago, our society was agrarian. People lived with their extended families in small homes. The nearest community center was the village, where everyone knew everyone else and people took a keen interest in each other's business. Organized religion played an important role in everyday life. In this kind of society, there was a strong pressure to conform [12]. There was greater emphasis on the community and lesser emphasis on the individual.

Modern culture fosters much greater privacy. Prosperity, the single-family home, the automobile, television, and computers have contributed to our privacy. The single-family home gives us physical separation from other people. The automobile allows us to travel alone instead of on a bus or train in the presence of others. The television brings entertainment to us inside the comfort of our homes, taking us out of the neighborhood movie theater. With a computer and an Internet connection, we can access information at home rather than visit the public library [11]. These are just a few examples of ways in which modern conveniences allow us to spend time by ourselves or in the company of a few family members or friends.

In the past, young people typically lived at home with their parents until they were married. Today many young unmarried adults live autonomously. This lifestyle provides them with previously unthought-of freedom and privacy [22].

The consequence of all this privacy is that we live among strangers. Many people know little more about their neighbors than their names (if that). Yet when we live in a society with others, we must be able to trust them to some extent. How do we know that the taxi driver will get us where we want to go without hurting us or overcharging us? How do parents know that their children's teachers are not child molesters? How does the bank know that, if it loans someone money, it will be repaid?

In order to trust others, we must rely on their reputations. This was easier in the past, when people didn't move around so much and everyone knew everyone else's history. Today society must get information out of people to establish reputations. One way of getting information from a person is through an **ordeal**, such as a lie detector test or a drug test. The other way to learn more about individuals is to issue (and request) **credentials**, such as a driver's license, key, employee badge, credit card, or college degree [22].

### 5.2.5 Case Study: The New Parents

Jim and Peggy Sullivan are the proud parents of a baby girl. As soon as Peggy became pregnant, they had begun exploring options for child care because both of them have full-time and highly satisfying careers in the computer field. They visited numerous day care facilities, but the ones they liked the best had no openings. For this reason they decided to hire a personal nanny, even though it was more expensive. After their daughter was born, Peggy spent three months at home on maternity leave. During this time she interviewed a half dozen nannies and hired one after carefully checking her references and giving Jim the opportunity to interview her as well.

Just before the end of Peggy's maternity leave, she has coffee with a few of her friends who are all mothers of young children. The friends tell Peggy horror stories about abusive nannies, and they all recommend a software program called LiveSecurityWatch. Jim and Peggy purchase LiveSecurityWatch and install it on a laptop computer placed in the family room. With the system in place, Jim and Peggy can use their workplace computers to see and hear how the nanny interacts with their baby. The nanny has no idea that the Sullivans' computer is being used as a surveillance system.

Is it wrong for Jim and Peggy Sullivan to secretly monitor the behavior of their baby's nanny?

#### RULE UTILITARIAN EVALUATION

If all parents monitored their nannies or child care providers and took actions when warranted, such as firing nannies who did not perform well, it is unlikely such monitoring would remain a secret for long. Under these circumstances, nannies would be much more careful to be on their best behavior. This would potentially have the long-term effects of reducing the instances of child abuse and increasing the peace of mind of parents. On the other hand, the harms of the monitoring would be significant in terms of increasing the stress and reducing the job satisfaction of nannies and child care providers. After all, who wants to be monitored constantly? These negative aspects of the job could lead to an increased turnover rate of nannies. Less experienced nannies might well provide lower-quality care to the babies they tend. The harms of having all parents monitoring their nannies or child care providers appear to be greater than the benefits. Hence we conclude it is wrong for the Sullivans to secretly monitor their nanny.

#### SOCIAL CONTRACT THEORY EVALUATION

Social contract theory emphasizes the adoption of rules that rational people would agree to accept because they are to everyone's mutual benefit, as long as everyone else follows the rules as well. As we discussed earlier in this section, privacy is a prudential right. It is reasonable for society to give privacy to people in their own homes, and it is also reasonable for family members within each home to give each other some privacy as well. The nanny wouldn't expect her interactions with the baby in a park or a grocery store to be private, but it is reasonable for her to expect privacy when taking care of the baby inside the Sullivans' home. Hence the Sullivans' decision to secretly monitor the nanny was wrong because it violated her right to privacy.

## KANTIAN EVALUATION

Let's consider the morality of acting according to the following rule: "An employer may secretly monitor the work of an employee who works with vulnerable people." To evaluate the rule using the first formulation of the Categorical Imperative, we universalize it. What would happen if every employer secretly monitored the work of employees who worked with vulnerable people? If that were the case, then employees who worked with vulnerable populations would have no expectation of privacy, and it would be impossible for employers to secretly monitor their work. Hence the proposed rule is self-defeating, and it would be wrong to act according to this rule.

We can also evaluate this situation using the second formulation of the Categorical Imperative. As parents, the Sullivans are responsible for the well-being of their baby. In order to be more confident that their baby is safe in the care of the nanny, they choose to secretly observe the behavior of the nanny. The observation is the means to their desired end of having their baby well cared for. The nanny naturally assumes that her interactions with the baby in the Sullivan residence are private. By not disclosing to the nanny the fact that she is being watched remotely, the Sullivans have treated the nanny as a means to an end. Hence the action of the Sullivans is wrong.

## VIRTUE ETHICS EVALUATION

As parents, the Sullivans are ultimately responsible for the well-being of their daughter. Rather than put their daughter in a day care facility they considered to be second-rate, they decided to spend more money and hire a personal nanny to care for her. That action is characteristic of good parents who put their children's needs before their own. When the Sullivans heard about abusive nannies, it is only natural that they would become worried about their daughter's welfare, particularly because as a baby she is truly defenseless and unable to communicate with them. According to virtue theory, parents should be partial toward their children. We can view the Sullivans' decision to use the webcam as an action characteristic of good parents. However, we would also expect that once the Sullivans are reassured they hired a fine nanny who is taking good care of their infant daughter, they would trust the nanny and discontinue the secret monitoring.

## SUMMARY

From the points of view of rule utilitarianism, social contract theory, and Kantianism, we have concluded that it is wrong for the Sullivans to secretly monitor how well their nanny takes care of their baby. However, from the perspective of virtue ethics, the action of the Sullivans is morally acceptable because it is consistent with parents of good character.

# 5.3 Information Disclosures

As we go about our lives, we leave behind an electronic trail of our activities, thanks to computerized databases. Some events result in the creation of public records. A **public record** contains information about an incident or action reported to a government agency for the purpose of informing the public [23]. Examples of public records are birth certificates, marriage licenses, motor vehicle records, criminal records, deeds to property, and the salaries of state employees (including your professor, if you are studying at a public institution). Making government records public is one way to hold government agencies accountable for their actions and help ensure that all citizens are being treated fairly.

When public records were written on paper and kept in county courthouse basements, they were relatively hard to retrieve. Computerized databases and the Internet have made accessing many public records quick and inexpensive, and there are a lot of good purposes to which we can put all that information. Before a school hires a teacher, it can check the candidate's criminal record to ensure there are no convictions for child abuse. Before a transit system hires a bus driver, it can check the applicant's driving record. Before moving to a new city, you can check out the crime rate of the neighborhood you're interested in.

Other uses of public records may not be as laudable. Thanks to information technology, it's easier than ever to learn a lot about someone's wealth. For most people, their home is their principal asset. Anyone with Internet access can visit Zillow.com, type in the address of someone's house, and quickly learn Zillow's estimate of the house's worth, based on information about the size of the house (a public record), the selling price of the house (a public record), and recent sales of similar houses in the neighborhood (also public records).

Private organizations, too, maintain extensive records of our activities. Databases store information about the purchases we make with our credit cards, the groceries we buy at a discount with our loyalty cards, the calls we make with our cell phones, and much more. The companies collecting this information use it to bill us. They may also use this information to serve us better. For example, Amazon uses information about book purchases to build profiles of its customers. With a customer profile, Amazon can recommend other books the customer may be interested in buying. On the other hand, companies may share information about our purchases with other companies that then send us junk mail for products we have no interest in buying.

Often people voluntarily disclose information to private organizations. Product registration forms and contest entries often ask consumers to reveal a great deal of personal information. I once received a product preference survey from Procter & Gamble; it said, in part:

> Your opinions matter to us. That's why we've selected you to participate in one of the most important consumer research surveys we'll do this year. Whether or not you have completed one of our surveys in the past, you can help us continue to create the products that meet your needs. Simply answer the following questions,

provide your name and address, and mail it back to us. That way, we will be able to contact you if there are any special offers that might be of interest to you.

The questionnaire asked about my family's use of nasal inhalants, coffee, peanut butter, orange juice, laundry detergent, fabric softener, household cleaner, deodorant, toothpaste, detergents, skin care and hair care products, cosmetics, mouthwash, diapers, laxatives, and disposable briefs. It provided a list of 60 leisure activities, ranging from various sports to travel to gambling, and asked me to choose the three activities most important to my family. It also asked my date of birth, the sex and age of everyone living in my home, my occupation, the credit cards we used, and our annual family income. If I had returned the questionnaire (which I didn't), Procter & Gamble would have been free to use this information any way it wished.

Many of us voluntarily share information about our activities by posting messages and uploading photos to social network sites like Facebook. These sites make it easy to communicate with many friends and acquaintances at once, but this information can be put to other purposes as well [24]. Social Intelligence Corporation provides employers with background checks on potential employees by searching the Internet for posts and photos by the job candidates that reveal negative activities specified by the employer, such as "racist remarks or activities, sexually explicit photos or videos, and illegal activity such as drug use" [25].

Recall the perspective that privacy is a "zone of inaccessability." Using this definition, we can say that our personal information is private to the extent that we can control who has access to it. In some settings we expect to have much more control over our personal information than in other venues. For example, we have much more control over who takes our picture when we're at home than when we're at a football game. Hence our expectations about the privacy of our personal information depend on the situation. In the rest of this section, we survey a variety of ways in which private organizations collect and use personal information, starting with situations in which most of us would assume to have less privacy and finishing with situations in which we would expect to have much more privacy.

## 5.3.1 Facebook Tags

In the Facebook social network, a **tag** is a label identifying a person in a photo. When you post a photo to Facebook, you can tag the people in the photo who are on your list of Facebook friends. In a similar way, any of your Facebook friends can tag you in photos they post to the site. People tag photos in Facebook an average of 100 million times per day [26].

In December 2010, Facebook introduced a new time-saving feature called Tag Suggestions. When a Facebook user adds a new photo, Facebook uses facial recognition software to suggest the name of the friend appearing in the photo. In June 2011, the Electronic Privacy Information Center (EPIC) filed a complaint about Facebook Tag Suggestions with the Federal Trade Commission [27]. EPIC claimed that in order to develop its facial recognition technology, Facebook gathered facial data from users' photos without their consent. Others raised the concern that the introduction of an automatic tagging feature would increase the chance that photos would be improperly tagged, which could cause a problem if the photos were not complimentary [28].

### 5.3.2 Enhanced 911 Services

All cell phone providers in the United States are required by law to be able to track the locations of active cell phone users to within 100 meters. The safety benefit of this capability is obvious. Emergency response teams can reach people in distress who have dialed 911, even if they are unable to speak or do not know exactly where they are.

The ability to identify the location of active cell phone users has other benefits. For example, it makes it easier for cell phone companies to identify where signal strength is weak and coverage needs to be improved.

The downside of enhanced 911 service is a potential loss of privacy. Because it is possible to track the location of active cell phone users, what happens if information is sold or shared? Suppose you call your employer and tell him you are too sick to come into work. Your boss is suspicious, since this is the third Friday this winter you've called in sick. Your employer pays your cell phone provider and discovers that you made your call from a ski resort [29].

### 5.3.3 Rewards or Loyalty Programs

Rewards or loyalty programs for shoppers have been around for more than 100 years. Your grandparents may remember using S&H Green Stamps, the most popular rewards program in the United States from the 1950s through the 1970s. Shoppers would collect Green Stamps with purchases, paste them into booklets, and redeem the booklets by shopping in the Sperry & Hutchinson catalog for household items.

Today many shoppers take advantage of rewards programs sponsored by grocery stores. Card-carrying members of the store's "club" save money on many of their purchases, either through coupons or instant discounts at the cash register. The most significant difference between the Green Stamps program and a contemporary shopper's club is that today's rewards programs are run by computers that record every purchase. Companies can use information about the buying habits of particular customers to provide them with individualized service.

For example, ShopRite grocery stores have computerized shopping carts. The shopping cart has a card reader and an LCD screen. Customers identify themselves by swiping their loyalty card through the card reader. A computer taps into a database with the customer's buying history and uses this information to guide the customer to frequently purchased products. As the cart passes through the aisles, pop-up ads display items the computer predicts the customer may be interested in purchasing [30].

Critics of grocery club cards say that the problem is not that card users pay less for their groceries but that those who don't use cards pay more. They give examples of club-member prices being equivalent to the regular product price at stores without customer loyalty programs [31].

FIGURE 5.2  A computer takes a customer's measurements.  (AP photo/Richard Drew)

Some consumers respond to the potential loss of privacy by giving phony personal information when they apply for these cards. Others take it a step further by regularly exchanging their cards with those held by other people [32].

Other consumers have learned how to "game" the system. One shopper noticed that by alternating her ground coffee purchases between Starbucks brand and Dunkin' Donuts brand, she got better prices than when she just bought Starbucks [33].

### 5.3.4  Body Scanners

(This section describes scanners designed to take a person's measurements. Advanced imaging technology scanners used at airport security checkpoints are discussed in Section 6.11.4.)

Looking good is important to many, if not most, of us. Computer technology is making it possible for us to save time shopping and find clothes that fit us better (Figure 5.2).

In some stores in the United Kingdom, you can enter a booth, strip to your undergarments, and be scanned by a computer, which produces a three-dimensional model of your body. The computer uses this information to recommend which pairs of jeans ought to fit you the best. You can then sit in front of a computer screen and preview what various pairs of jeans will look like on you. When you have narrowed down your search to a few particular brands and sizes, you can actually try on the jeans.

**FIGURE 5.3** Employees take inventory more quickly and make fewer errors when items are marked with RFID tags.  (© Marc F. Henning/Alamy)

Body scans are also being used to produce custom-made clothing. At Brooks Brothers stores in the United States, customers who have been scanned can purchase suits tailored to their particular physiques [34].

### 5.3.5  RFID Tags

Imagine getting up in the morning, walking into the bathroom, and seeing a message on the medicine cabinet's computer screen warning you that your bottle of aspirin is close to its expiration date. Later that day you are shopping for a new pair of pants. As you try them on, a screen in the dressing room displays other pieces of clothing that would complement your selection.

These scenarios are possible today thanks to a technology called RFID, short for radio frequency identification. An RFID is a tiny wireless transmitter. Manufacturers are replacing bar codes with RFIDs, because they give more information about the product and are easier to scan. An RFID can contain specific information about the particular item to which it is attached (or embedded), and a scanner can read an RFID from six feet away. When bar codes are replaced by RFIDs, checkouts are quicker and companies track their inventory more accurately (Figure 5.3).

However, because RFIDs are not turned off when an item is purchased, the new technology has raised privacy concerns. Imagine a workplace full of RFID scanners. A scanner in your cubicle enables a monitoring system to associate you with the tags in your clothes. Another scanner picks up your presence at the water cooler. The next thing you know, your boss has called you in for a heart-to-heart talk about how many breaks you're taking. Some privacy advocates say consumers should have a way to remove or disable RFIDs in the products they purchase [35, 36].

### 5.3.6 Implanted Chips

In Taiwan, every domesticated dog must contain a microchip implant identifying its owner and residence [37]. The microchip, about the size of a grain of rice, is implanted into the dog's ear using a syringe. When a dog gets lost, the authorities can easily retrieve the address and return the pet to its owner.

Verichip Corporation created an RFID tag approved for use in humans. The company claimed that 2,000 people worldwide had a Verichip implant. The most common reason for getting an implanted RFID chip was to allow doctors to learn about the medical conditions of unconscious patients [38]. However, in some trendy European nightclubs, patrons have used their implanted RFID chips as in-house "debit cards" for purchasing food and drinks [39]. After some highly publicized incidents of abducted or missing children, the media have reported parents ruminating on the idea of implanting microchip tracking devices in their kids [40, 41].

### 5.3.7 Mobile Apps

It's obvious that Google Maps needs to know your location, but did you know that when you play Angry Birds or use Brightest Flashlight, information about your location is being collected and sold to advertisers and data brokers? These apps are not unusual. Flurry, a company specializing in analyzing data collected from mobile apps, has access to data from more than a half million apps running on most iPhones and Android smartphones [42].

### 5.3.8 OnStar

OnStar Corporation manufactures a communication system incorporated into an automobile's rearview mirror. OnStar provides emergency, security, navigation, and diagnostics services to its subscribers. For example, a driver who runs out of gas can push the Blue OnStar button to initiate a conversation with an OnStar representative. The driver does not have to know his or her exact location, because the system automatically sends the GPS location of the automobile to OnStar, which can send help. The driver does not always need to initiate the communication with OnStar representatives. For example, whenever the air bags deploy on an OnStar-equipped vehicle, the system automatically communicates the location of the vehicle to an OnStar center, which can initiate a 911 call.

The capabilities of the OnStar system were dramatically revealed in Visalia, California, in October 2009, when a man with a sawed-off shotgun ordered two occupants of a 2009 Chevrolet Tahoe to get out of their vehicle. He took their money and drove off in the SUV. After the police got the victim's permission to track down the stolen vehicle, OnStar provided the police with its current location. When police cars began to tail the Tahoe, its driver sped up. At this point the OnStar service center issued a command to the SUV that electronically disabled the gas pedal, causing the Tahoe to gradually slow to a halt and allowing the police to apprehend the carjacker. Visalia Police Chief Colleen Mestas complimented the new technology for preventing a potentially dangerous high-speed car chase [43].

Because OnStar has the ability to track the location of OnStar-equipped vehicles and listen to conversations happening within them, some privacy advocates have expressed concerns about possible abuses that could occur if this information were shared with law enforcement agencies. For example, suppose the police were looking for suspects in an unsolved crime. Should they have the right to gather information from OnStar about all OnStar-equipped vehicles that were in the area at the time of the crime?

In an hour-long Web chat on the General Motors FastLane site in November 2009, OnStar's Jane Speelman responded to these concerns. According to Speelman, OnStar does not continuously monitor the location of OnStar-equipped vehicles, OnStar does not provide information about the speed of vehicles to law enforcement agencies, and OnStar representatives cannot listen to conversations inside a vehicle without alerting the vehicle's occupants [44].

### 5.3.9 Automobile "Black Boxes"

You probably know about airplane flight data recorders, also called "black boxes," which provide information useful in postcrash investigations. Did you know that modern automobiles also come equipped with a "black box"? A microprocessor attached to the car's air bag records information about the speed of the car, the amount of pressure being put on the brake pedal, and whether the seat belts are connected. After a collision, investigators can retrieve the microprocessor from the automobile and view data collected in the five seconds before the accident [45].

### 5.3.10 Medical Records

The change from paper-based to electronic medical records has the potential to lower the costs and improve the quality of medical care by making it quicker and cheaper for information about patients to be shared among nurses, physicians, and other caregivers. The US government has been promoting the conversion to electronic medical records as one way to rein in the rapid increase in health care costs. The Health Information Technology for Economic and Clinical Health (HITECH) Act required doctors and hospitals to move from paper records to electronic records by 2015 or face financial penalties.

However, once an individual's entire medical history is consolidated in a database accessible by many, it can be more difficult to control how that information is disseminated, with potentially significant consequences. An employer may choose to pass over a job candidate who has had serious medical problems [46]. A woman who has successfully completed a treatment program for drug addiction may be discriminated against if information about her former drug use is revealed.

In November 2003, Florida state law enforcement officials seized the medical records of radio commentator Rush Limbaugh, as part of an investigation to determine whether Limbaugh had illegally obtained prescription pain medications from several doctors. The American Civil Liberties Union filed a friend-of-the-court brief in partial support of Limbaugh, arguing that law enforcement officials acted improperly in obtaining a warrant that allowed them to seize all of Limbaugh's medical records, not just those relevant to the criminal investigation [47].

### 5.3.11 Digital Video Recorders

TiVo, Inc. is a well-known manufacturer of digital video recorders. TiVo provides a service that allows its subscribers to more easily record programs they are interested in watching later. For example, with a single command a subscriber can instruct the TiVo to record every episode of a TV series. TiVo collects detailed information about the viewing habits of its users. Because the system monitors the activities of the users second by second, its data are more valuable than those provided by other services. For example, TiVo's records show that 66 percent of the ads shown during primetime on broadcast networks are skipped [48].

### 5.3.12 Cookies and Flash Cookies

A **cookie** is a file placed on your computer's hard drive by a Web server. The file contains information about your visits to a Web site. Cookies can contain login names and passwords, product preferences, and the contents of virtual shopping carts. Web sites use cookies to provide you with personalized services, such as custom Web pages. Instead of asking you to type in the same information multiple times, a Web site can retrieve that information from a cookie. Most Web sites do not ask for permission before creating a cookie on your hard drive. You can configure your Web browser to alert you when a cookie is being placed on your computer, or you can set your Web browser to refuse to accept any cookies. However, some Web sites cannot be accessed by browsers that block cookies.

In recent years Web sites have begun using another kind of cookie called a **flash cookie**, which is a file placed on your computer's hard drive by a Web server running the Adobe Flash Player. Two attributes of flash cookies have raised privacy concerns. First, a flash cookie can hold 25 times as much information as a browser cookie. Second, flash cookies are not controlled by the browser's privacy controls. Some Web sites take advantage of this loophole and use flash cookies as a way of backing up ordinary cookies. That way, if you delete the browser cookie associated with a Web site, it can be "respawned" from the flash cookie. A survey by researchers at the University of California, Berkeley, revealed that more than half of the 100 most popular Web sites use flash cookies, but only four of them mention flash cookies in their privacy policies [49].

## 5.4 Data Mining

In the previous section we surveyed a few of the many ways that companies collect information on people's daily activities. In this section we look at how this information has itself become a commodity that companies buy and sell in order to provide more personalized services to their existing customers and to target potential customers more accurately.

### 5.4.1 Data Mining Defined

Before you use a grocery store's loyalty card, you have to spend some time filling out an application that asks for a lot of personal information, such as your name, address, and phone number. After the store has processed your application, using your loyalty card is easy. You just swipe your card or type in your phone number, and the register recognizes you as a customer and gives you the appropriate discounts on your food purchases. At the same time, information about your purchases is entered into a database.

A record in a database records a single transaction, such as a particular item you purchased at the grocery store. A database record is like a single snapshot of a person. It tells you something about the person, but in isolation its value is limited. **Data mining** is the process of searching through many records in one or more databases looking for patterns or relationships. Data mining is a way to generate new information by combining facts found in multiple transactions, and it can also be a way to predict future events. By drawing upon large numbers of records, data mining allows an organization to build an accurate profile of an individual from a myriad of snapshots.

Google's personalized search and collaborative filtering are two examples of how companies are using data mining to create more personal relationships with their customers [50].

### GOOGLE'S PERSONALIZED SEARCH

Google keeps track of your search queries and the Web pages you have clicked. When you type in a new query, it can use this information to infer what you are interested in and return pages more likely to be what you are seeking. For example, the word "bass" has multiple meanings, but if you have a history of queries and page clicks related to fishing, but not music, that can help the search engine return the most appropriate pages.

Google is able to personalize search results whether or not you have a Google account. If you are signed in to Google, the search engine examines your Web history to personalize the search results. This information is held indefinitely, unless you delete your Web history. If you are not signed in, Google creates a cookie linked to your computer's browser, and it stores records of all queries associated with that cookie, as well as results that have been clicked, for up to 180 days [51].

### COLLABORATIVE FILTERING

**Collaborative filtering** algorithms draw upon information about the preferences of a large number of people to predict what an individual may enjoy. An organization performing collaborative filtering may determine people's preferences explicitly, through rankings, or implicitly, by tracking their purchases. The filtering algorithm looks for patterns in the data. Perhaps many people who purchase peanut butter also purchase jam. If a new customer buys a jar of peanut butter, the software may instruct the register to print out a discount coupon for a particular brand of jam along with the sales receipt. Collaborative filtering software is also used by online retailers and movie sites to make recommendations [52].

## 5.4.2 Opt–In versus Opt–Out Policies

We have just examined a few ways in which a company that collects information about its customers' activities can use this information to provide its customers with a more personalized service. It only makes sense that if several companies pooled the information they had on the same person, they could construct a more complete electronic profile that would lead to new insights into products or services that person might wish to purchase. What rules should govern the sharing of information collected by organizations selling products or services? Two fundamentally different policies are called opt-in and opt-out.

The **opt-in** policy requires the consumer to explicitly give permission for the organization to share the information with another organization. Opt-in policies are preferred by privacy advocates.

The **opt-out** policy requires the consumer to explicitly forbid an organization from sharing information with other organizations. Direct marketing associations prefer the opt-out policy because opt-in is a barrier for new businesses. New businesses do not have the resources to go out and collect all the information they need to target their mailings to the correct individuals. In an opt-out environment, most people will not go through the effort required to actually remove themselves from mailing lists. Hence it is easier for new businesses to get access to the mailing lists they need to succeed [53]. Another argument for opt-out is that companies have the right to control information about the transactions they have made. Information is a valuable commodity. An opt-in policy takes this commodity away from companies.

At this time opt-out policies are far more common than opt-in policies. Information about customers has *itself* become a commodity. Organizations sell or exchange information with other organizations (Figure 5.4). This is a common way for organizations to gather large databases of information they can mine.

For example, a company selling time-share condominiums purchases from a hotel chain the names and addresses of people who have vacationed in a resort area in the past two years. From another organization it purchases a database that gives the approximate annual household income of a family, based on that family's nine-digit ZIP code. Combining these lists allows the time-share agency to target people most likely to have both the interest and the financial resources to purchase a share of a vacation condominium. It uses direct mail to send brochures to these people.

Data mining can be surprisingly powerful. Suppose a government agency managing tollbooths were to sell information records of the following form:

⟨transponder number⟩ ⟨date⟩ ⟨time⟩ ⟨location⟩ ⟨charge⟩

The agency does not reveal the names of the owners of the cars, so it believes it is protecting their anonymity. However, many people have an account set up so that their tollbooth payments are automatically charged to their credit cards. If a credit card company buys these records from the tollbooth agency, it can match the date, time, and amount of the tollbooth payments with the date, time, and charge on its credit cards to determine the identity of the person driving a vehicle with a particular transponder number. Once this has been done, the credit card company can figure out which customers are driving the most miles and are likely to purchase new cars more frequently. It can then sell this information to banks interested in soliciting automobile loan applications [29].

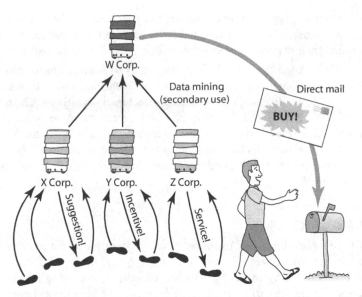

**FIGURE 5.4** Companies use computers to record information about their customers and their buying habits. They analyze this information to suggest additional purchases, provide incentives, and deliver better service. They may also sell this information to other companies. By combining information from various sources, a company can build sophisticated profiles of individuals and target its direct mail advertising to those people most likely to be interested in its products.

### 5.4.3 Examples of Data Mining

Data mining is put to a wide variety of uses in modern society. Here are a few examples.

#### TARGETING PREGNANT WOMEN

The power of data mining was demonstrated in Target's efforts to identify which of its customers were pregnant women. Retailers know that the habits of shoppers—where they buy certain goods and the brands they select—are difficult to change. However, when people graduate from college or move to a new town or get married, their shopping habits are more malleable. New parents are particularly open to changes in their shopping habits. For that reason Target asked its statisticians to find ways to predict which of Target's women customers were in their second trimester of pregnancy. The company's goal was to use direct mail offers to get these women into the habit of buying a wide variety of items at Target stores.

Target's statisticians found customers who had set up baby-shower registries at Target, then looked back in time to discover what products those women had bought when they were in their second trimester. The analysts found about two dozen predictors that a woman is three to six months' pregnant. Tip-offs included purchasing large amounts of unscented lotion, buying extra-large bags of cotton balls, and spending money on nutritional supplements, such as zinc and magnesium. The statisticians determined that they could predict with high confidence whether or not a woman was in her second trimester of pregnancy by examining her purchases of these "predictor" products. For those women who were predicted to be pregnant, the statisticians showed they could predict their expected delivery date within a relatively small window of time.

Target used the algorithms developed by its statisticians to mine its extensive databases of customer purchases. The company identified tens of thousands of women who were probably pregnant and sent them direct mail advertising. The marketing executives were savvy enough to know that the women receiving these promotions might be upset if they discovered Target knew they were pregnant. In order not to tip the women off, Target made sure that the mailings to the women included offers on wineglasses, lawn mowers, and other unrelated items mixed in with the offers for diapers, baby clothes, and cribs [54].

## CREDIT REPORTS

Credit reports are a great example of how information about customers has itself become a commodity. A credit bureau is a company that keeps track of an individual's assets, debts, and history of paying bills and repaying loans, using this information to determine the creditworthiness of that person. Credit bureaus sell credit reports to banks, credit card companies, and other potential lenders.

Thanks to the national credit bureau system, you can get a credit card from a bank or store that you've never done business with. When you want to borrow money to purchase a home, you don't have to go to your local bank. You can get the money from a bank across the country that trusts you to repay the loan because of your high credit score. Competition among banks leads to lower interest rates, a definite advantage for consumers.

Of course, if you have a poor record of paying bills on time and repaying loans, your credit score will be low. People with low credit scores have a harder time getting loans and pay higher interest rates on the loans they do get.

A poor credit report can come back to haunt people in ways they might not have anticipated. Many employers conduct a credit check late in the job interview process as a way of double-checking a candidate before making a job offer. A credit report received by an employer doesn't give the applicant's credit score, but it does list the applicant's debts. Critics of the use of credit reports when making hiring decisions have stated that these reports can cause employers to shy away from minorities and those who are currently out of work. "I think the assumption that is made is, if somebody is behind on their bills, then it tells something about their integrity or responsibility, but in many cases that assumption is flawed," said Sarah Crawford of the Lawyers' Committee for Civil Rights Under Law [55].

## TARGETED DIRECT MAIL AND DATA BROKERS

Years ago direct mail marketing meant mass mailings of advertisements. Today the trend is toward targeted direct mail, in which businesses mail their advertisements only to the leads most likely to be interested in purchasing their products. Customized mailing lists are available from **data brokers**: companies that combine information gathered online with offline information, such as magazine subscriptions, loyalty cards, and government records, to create comprehensive profiles of consumers [56].

Edith Ramirez, head of the US Federal Trade Commission, writes: "You may not know them, but data brokers know you. They know where you live, what you buy, your income, your ethnicity, how old your kids are, your health conditions, and your interests and hobbies" [57].

Have you ever had a store clerk ask you for your ZIP code after you've made a purchase? It turns out that the clerk doesn't need your address to identify you. Your name (taken from your credit or debit card), combined with your ZIP code, is 90 percent accurate at identifying you and allowing your purchase to become another piece of information for data brokers [58].

Two of the most prominent data brokers are Experian (one of the three largest credit report companies in the United States) and Acxiom. Experian has a database of more than 200 million consumers. Acxiom is even larger. It has collected information on 500 million consumers, with an average of 1,500 pieces of information per consumer [58]. Both of these data brokers can provide specialized lists to direct marketers. For example, Acxiom has divided US households into 70 segments based on their demographics and their spending habits. These segments include one for affluent baby boomers, another for young singles, and another one for retirees of modest means.

Besides Experian and Acxiom, there are thousands of other data brokers, and many of them have created highly focused lists. For example, it is possible to purchase mailing lists of gay and lesbian adults, people likely to have bipolar disorder, and people who have purchased sex toys [59].

Did you know that two shoppers visiting the same online retailer may have quite different experiences? Data brokers sell profiles of consumers to some online merchants, who use this information to determine which advertisements to display [57]. Retailers even use customer profiles to determine who should be offered a discount and who should be charged full price and offered more expensive options [60].

When Blue Chip Marketing Worldwide needed to identify candidates for an obesity drug trial, it looked for evidence that a person might be obese, including a pattern of shopping for clothes online, frequent fast-food dining, and subscribing to premium cable TV packages [61]. Privacy experts warn that the success of these efforts demonstrates that the amount of data being collected has reached a point where companies can make accurate inferences about the medical conditions of individuals, even without accessing their private medical records.

## MICROTARGETING

Since 2004 direct marketing based on data mining has become part of US presidential campaigns [62]. In a technique called **microtargeting**, a campaign combines data about voter registration, voting frequency, and contributions with consumer data and information available from a geographic information system to gain insights into which candidate the voter is likely to favor. The campaign then uses direct mailings, email, text messages, or home visits to encourage likely supporters to vote.

### 5.4.4 Social Network Analysis

A relatively new area in data mining is the incorporation of information collected from social networks. Here are a few examples of how organizations are using social network analysis to further their objectives.

About two in five employers in the United States include analysis of social network sites in their background checks of job candidates, and half of these employers report they have found information that has caused them not to hire certain candidates. The most common reasons for rejecting candidates were the discovery of posts containing sexually provocative or inappropriate photos, information about drinking or drug use, criticisms of former employers or coworkers, evidence of poor communication skills, and discriminatory remarks about other people. Interestingly, one-quarter of employers conducting social media background checks reported they had also discovered positive information about a job candidate that led to an immediate job offer [63].

Banks are combining data collected from social networks with credit card statements and other information to evaluate the riskiness of loans. For example, someone applying for a loan to start a new business may be a bad risk if the proposed business has no connection with their social network, educational background, travel history, or previous business dealings [64].

In ultracompetitive cell phone markets, it's crucial that companies keep their subscribers from defecting to rival firms. Bharti Airtel, India's largest cell phone company, uses software to analyze phone records and identify "influencers," those subscribers most likely to be able to persuade their friends and family members to follow them when they switch carriers. It then offers the influencers special promotions to keep them loyal. How can Bharti Airtel identify influencers from their phone records? They are the ones whose calls are quickly returned, who call other people late at night more frequently, and who get more calls on Friday afternoons when parties are often organized [64].

Speaking of parties, police in Richmond, Virginia, monitor Facebook and Twitter messages to determine where parties are happening. Data-mining software identifies the party locations mentioned most frequently. By deploying officers more strategically on big party nights, the department saves about $15,000 on overtime pay, and the community has seen a big drop in criminal activity [64].

### 5.4.5 Release of "Anonymized" Datasets

On at least two occasions, corporations have released large datasets from which they had attempted to strip away personally identifiable information in order to preserve the anonymity of the people creating the data. In neither case were the datasets truly anonymized.

#### NETFLIX PRIZE

Netflix is a popular subscription service for movies and television shows. An important feature of Netflix is its movie recommendation service. After a subscriber has rated several movies, Netflix uses a collaborative filtering algorithm to predict how well the subscriber will like other movies in its collection. It then recommends to the subscriber movies the subscriber is likely to enjoy.

In 2006 Netflix offered a $1 million prize to any group that could come up with a collaborative filtering algorithm that was at least 10 percent better than Netflix's own algorithm at predicting user ratings for movies. Netflix released more than 100 million movie ratings from nearly half a million customers, stripped of private information in an attempt to make the records anonymous. Each movie rating consisted of four pieces of information—subscriber, movie, date of grade, and grade—where each subscriber was represented by an integer.

However, a group of researchers at the University of Texas at Austin demonstrated how it was possible, with just a little information about movies seen by an individual, to identify the movie rating records associated with that person, revealing potentially sensitive information, such as their political leanings or sexual orientation [65]. The revelation that the release of "anonymous" movie ratings information could compromise the privacy of Netflix subscribers led to a complaint by the US Federal Trade Commission and a lawsuit. On March 12, 2010, Netflix announced that it was canceling a Netflix Prize sequel [66].

## AOL SEARCH DATASET

In 2006 an AOL research team led by Dr. Abdur Chowdhury posted to the Web a file containing three months' worth of search queries from about 650,000 AOL users. The purpose of releasing the information was to support university research, but the dataset was downloadable by anybody with a Web browser and a fast enough Internet connection [67].

In an attempt to anonymize the dataset, which consisted of about 20 million queries, the AOL team used a random integer identifier, rather than a name or other personal identifier, to label all the queries submitted by the same user [67]. However, researchers who studied the dataset determined almost immediately that examining a set of queries with the same integer identifier often provided enough information to identify the user. For example, many people apparently performed searches on their names, presumably to see which Web links were returned. Addresses and social security numbers also appeared in queries [68]. Within days, reporters from the *New York Times* identified several of the people whose search results had been posted. Thelma Arnold from Liburn, Georgia, agreed to be identified by the newspaper as user #4417749 [69].

Responding to a storm of negative publicity, AOL took down the dataset three days after posting it, but by then it was too late: copies had already been downloaded and reposted on other Web sites [68]. As the public outcry continued, AOL fired Dr. Chowdhury and his supervisor. Maureen Govern, the chief technology officer of AOL, resigned [67].

According to Kurt Opsahl of the Electronic Frontier Foundation, AOL made two mistakes. The first mistake was failing to get the consent of AOL users before making their queries available to third parties. The second mistake was posting the dataset to the Web, rather than making it available only to university researchers who had agreed to follow reasonable privacy protections [70].

# 5.5 Examples of Consumer Backlash

Advances in information technology have led to a drop in the cost of acquiring information. Meanwhile, the value of information continues to rise, as organizations refine their data-mining techniques. The result of these trends is that corporations have an incentive to acquire more information, making it more difficult for individuals to protect their privacy [21]. Still, people can and do fight back when they feel a corporation has gone too far.

## 5.5.1 Marketplace: Households

Lotus Development Corporation teamed up with credit reporting company Equifax to develop a database on 120 million people and a program in CD format that would allow the user to produce direct mailing lists based on various criteria, such as household income. Lotus hoped to sell the package, which it called "Marketplace: Households," to small businesses. Soon after the product was announced in the spring of 1990, there was a considerable backlash. Consumers complained loudly and vigorously, with more than 30,000 letters, phone calls, and emails. Lotus dropped plans to sell the CD [71].

How times have changed! A little more than two decades later, data brokers Acxiom and Experian are selling direct mailing lists based on much more detailed information about consumers (as you read in the discussion of targeted direct mail in Section 5.4.3).

## 5.5.2 Facebook Beacon

In November 2007, Facebook announced Beacon, "a core element of the Facebook Ads system for connecting businesses with users and targeting advertising to the audiences they want" [72]. Beacon promised to be an important way for Facebook to earn advertising revenue. Fandango, eBay, and 42 other online businesses paid Facebook to do "word-of-mouth" advertising of their products and services through Beacon. For example, after a Facebook user bought movie tickets on Fandango, Fandango would send this information to Facebook so that Facebook could broadcast it to that user's friends.

Beacon was based on an opt-out policy, meaning that it was in effect unless a user explicitly asked to be excluded. That decision was good for Facebook because advertising revenue depends on the size of the audience. However, the decision to make the system opt-out upset many Facebook users, who were unaware of Beacon until it revealed information they thought was private. For example, after Sean Lane purchased what was supposed to be a surprise Christmas gift, the following news headline was broadcast to his wife and more than 700 other people in his Facebook network: "Sean Lane bought 14K White Gold 1/5 ct Diamond Eternity Flower Ring from overstock.com" [73].

Beacon soon attracted strong criticism from a variety of sources. A spokesperson for MoveOn.org said, "Sites like Facebook are revolutionizing how we communicate with one another and organize around issues together in a 21st century democracy. The question is: Will corporate advertisers get to write the rules of the Internet or will these new social networks protect our basic rights, like privacy?" [73]. MoveOn.org created an online group calling for Beacon to require an explicit opt-in from users, and it attracted the support of more than 50,000 Facebook users. A few weeks later, Facebook decided to switch to an opt-in policy for Beacon. "I'm not proud of the way we've handled this situation, and I know we can do better," said Mark Zuckerberg, CEO of Facebook [74].

### 5.5.3 Malls Track Shoppers' Cell Phones

On Black Friday, 2011, two malls in the United States—the Promenade Temecula in California and the Short Pump Town Center in Virginia—began recording the movement of shoppers through the stores by tracking the locations of their cell phones. The malls hoped to be able to answer such questions as these:

- How much time do people spend in store X?
- How many people who shop at store Y also shop at store Z?
- Are there unpopular areas of the mall that do not attract enough shoppers?

Small signs posted throughout the malls informed shoppers of the study. It let them know that the data were being collected anonymously; the mall assigned an ID code to each phone and tracked the movements of the phone without knowing anything about the person carrying the phone. To prevent data about their movements from being collected, shoppers had to turn off their cell phones.

The malls had planned to continue their study through the Christmas buying season, but an intervention by Senator Charles Schumer of New York prompted them to stop collecting data after only three days. The senator issued a statement that said, in part, "Personal cell phones are just that—personal. If retailers want to tap into your phone to see what your shopping patterns are, they can ask you for your permission to do so" [75].

Sharon Biggar, CEO of Path Intelligence, the British firm that made the cell phone tracking equipment, responded to the senator's statements by pointing out that online retailers track far more information about their customers' shopping habits without asking them for permission. "We are simply seeking to create a level playing field for offline retailers," she said [75].

### 5.5.4 iPhone Apps Uploading Address Books

In February 2012, programmer Arun Thampi in Singapore discovered that the app for the social networking site Path was uploading his iPhone's address book without first getting his permission. Thampi wrote on his blog, "I'm not insinuating that Path is doing something nefarious with my address book but I feel quite violated that my address book is being held remotely on a third-party service" [76].

David Morin, the CEO of Path, initially replied to Thampi's post by saying that the purpose of collecting the information was to make it easier for people to connect with family and friends on Path and to let them know when people in their address book join Path. Morin's statement also labeled Path's actions as an "industry best practice." However, it didn't take long for the Internet community to weigh in and point out that Apple's guidelines require apps to ask for permission before uploading information from address books. Facing a storm of negative publicity, Morin issued another statement in which he apologized for what Path had done, promised that the company would destroy the data it had collected, and announced that the app would be changed so that it would no longer upload address books without permission [77].

As the Path controversy erupted, the media pointed out that other popular iPhone apps, including Twitter, Foursquare, and Instagram, were also gathering information from address books without asking for permission. All the aforementioned companies responded by announcing that they, too, would release new versions of their apps that explicitly asked users for permission before uploading contact information from address books [78].

### 5.5.5 Instagram's Proposed Change to Terms of Service

In December 2012, the popular photo-sharing service Instagram announced an upcoming change in its privacy policy and terms-of-service agreement. The terms-of-service agreement appeared to change how Instagram and its parent company, Facebook, could use photographs uploaded by Instagram users. The proposed agreement included the following statement:

> You agree that a business or other entity may pay us to display your username, likeness, photos (along with any associated metadata), and/or actions you take, in connection with paid or sponsored content or promotions, without any compensation to you. [79]

After some legal experts said that the new terms-of-service agreement would allow Instagram or Facebook to use photos on the Instagram site in advertisements without compensating or even getting the permission of the person who uploaded them, the reaction was swift. The hashtag #Boycottinstagram began trending on Twitter, and many Instagram users downloaded alternative photo-sharing apps. The number of people using Pheed and Flickr increased significantly, though the total number of users of these services remained far below the 100-plus million using Instagram [80].

Responding to the uproar, Instagram cofounder Kevin Systrom issued a statement saying that the new privacy policy and terms of service had been misunderstood. He also announced that the advertising section in the terms-of-service agreement was being changed back to its original version [81].

## Summary

This chapter has focused on privacy issues brought to the forefront by the introduction of modern information technology. The issues of privacy and intellectual property are similar in the sense that both issues relate to how information ought to be controlled. Modern information technology makes it much easier to collect and transmit information, whether it be a song, a Social Security number, or a shopping list. Privacy can be seen as a balancing act between the desires of the individual, the profit motive of companies, and the common good. The individual seeks to restrict access to personal information. Companies seek to gather information and sell it to those who want access to it. The common good dictates that some information should be widely known.

Society must decide which information ought to be private, which information can be gathered and sold, and which information should be public.

Sometimes the communities we live in require information disclosures. A public record is a piece of information collected by a government agency. Certain activities, such as getting arrested, buying a house, and having a child, result in the creation of a public record.

Often we voluntarily share information with others in order to get something else we want. For example, there is a tension between privacy and trust. We desire privacy, but we also want others to trust us. In some situations we must reveal some personal information in order to win the trust of others.

We participate in many activities in which private organizations collect information about us. Data mining is a way for organizations to create a complex profile of a person from a large collection of individual facts. Companies use data mining to direct advertising to the most promising customers. Data mining is possible because organizations handling transactions have the right to sell information about these transactions to other organizations. Whether to provide customers with better service, increase their revenues, or both, companies frequently push the boundaries of what consumers are willing to tolerate.

## Further Reading and Viewing

Elizabeth Alex and Mark Clegg. "Smartphone Pictures Pose Privacy Risks." *KSHB/NBC Action News*, November 9, 2010. 3:56. www.youtube.com/watch?v=N2vARzvWxwY.

Maria Bartiromo. "Inside the Mind of Google." CNBC, December 3, 2009. 43:09. video.cnbc.com/gallery/?video=3000021036.

Robby Bryant and Bryan Horling. "Personalized Search." Google, December 4, 2009. 1:32. www.youtube.com/watch?v=N2vARzvWxwY.

Charles Duhigg. "How Companies Learn Your Secrets." *New York Times Magazine*, February 16, 2012.

Poppy Harlow. "My Private Life Revealed on the Web." *CNNMoney Reports*, May 26, 2011. 2:39. money.cnn.com/video/.

Steve Kroft. "The Data Brokers: Selling Your Personal Information." *60 Minutes*, March 9, 2014. 14:22. www.cbs.news.com.

Evan Ratliff. "Shedding Your Identity in the Digital Age." *Wired*, December 2009.

Jeffrey Rosen. "The Web Means the End of Forgetting." *New York Times*, July 21, 2010. www.nytimes.com.

## Review Questions

1. What is the difference between having privacy and being alone? Provide examples.

2. How can an excess of privacy cause harm? How can a lack of privacy cause harm?

3. What does it mean to say privacy is a prudential right?

4. Is privacy a negative right or a positive right?

5. Why is it important that some information be made available to everyone through public records?

6. Provide an example (not already given in the book) of a situation where people must disclose personal information to a private organization in order to obtain a product or service.

7. How do retailers use loyalty cards to improve their sales?

8. What are the advantages of consolidating a patient's medical records into a single database accessible by many? What are the risks associated with this consolidation?

9. How could "cookies" created by a Web server affect a computer user's privacy?

10. What is the difference between data mining and collaborative filtering?

11. Explain the difference between an opt-in policy and an opt-out policy. Which policy is favored by privacy advocates?

12. What lesson should we draw from the release of large datasets in which personal identifiers were replaced by integers?

## Discussion Questions

13. Do you agree with Scott McNealy's statement that people have "zero privacy" and should just get over it?

14. If people value privacy so much, why do they put so much personal information on their Facebook pages and in their blogs?

15. MIT computer science professor Harold Abelson has said, "In today's online world, what your mother told you is true, only more so: people really can judge you by your friends" [82]. Have you ever been upset or embarrassed by what your friends posted on Facebook? Are you concerned that people are going to judge you based on what your friends are posting?

16. Should mobile apps be allowed to collect information about your location and transmit this information to data brokers?

17. Warren and Brandeis argued that it is a violation of a person's privacy to take their photograph without their consent.
    a. Do you agree with their position? Why or why not?
    b. If someone takes your photo, should you just assume it's going to be posted on the Web?

18. What is the difference between privacy and anonymity?

19. Do you agree with the author that it is more difficult to know whom to trust in modern society than it was in a small village of a few centuries ago? Why or why not?

20. Critics of grocery club cards give examples of card-member prices being equal to the regular product price at stores without customer loyalty programs. In other words, customers who want to get food at the regular price must use the card. Customers pay extra if they don't want to use the card. Is it fair for a store to charge us more if we don't want to use its loyalty card? Explain your reasoning.

21. Some consumers give phony personal information when they apply for rewards or loyalty cards at stores. Others take it a step further by regularly exchanging their cards with those held by other people. Are these people doing anything wrong? Why or why not?

22. If you voluntarily have your body scanned at a department store, who should own that information, you or the store? Should the store have the right to sell your body measurements to other businesses? Explain your reasoning.

23. TiVo keeps detailed information about the television viewing habits of customers who subscribe to its service.
    a. Should your television viewing habits be private information?
    b. Do you care if anyone else knows what television shows or pay-per-view movies you have watched in the past year?
    c. Do voters have the right to know the viewing habits of people running for elected office?

24. Enhanced 911 service allows cell phone companies to track the locations of active cell phone users within 100 meters.
    a. Who should have access to location information collected by cell phone companies?
    b. How long should this information be kept?
    c. If this information could be used to help you establish an alibi, would you want the cell phone company to be able to release it to the police?
    d. How would you feel about the cell phone company releasing compromising information about your whereabouts to the police?
    e. Should the police be able to get from the cell phone company the names of all subscribers using their phones close to a crime scene around the time of the crime?

25. Should parents implant microchips in their children to make them easier to identify in case they are lost or kidnapped? Why or why not?

26. Before offering a job candidate a position, some potential employers do a criminal background check of the candidate. What are the pros and cons of this policy?

27. You are setting up an account at a local store that rents outdoor equipment (tents, backpacks, ski gear, etc.). The clerk asks you to fill out the application form completely. One of the fields asks for your Social Security number. You leave that field blank. The clerk refuses to accept your application without the field filled in. You ask to speak to the manager, and the clerk says the manager is not available. Would it be wrong in this situation to fill in a fake Social Security number?

28. A company discovers that some of its proprietary information has been revealed in Internet chat rooms. The disclosure of this information results in a substantial drop in the price of the company's shares. The company provides Internet service providers with the screen names of the people who posted the confidential information. It asks the ISPs to disclose the actual identities of these people. Should the ISPs comply with this request? Explain your reasoning. (This scenario is adapted from an actual event [83].)

29. Music files downloaded from Apple's iTunes Store have the purchaser's name and email address embedded in them [84]. Conceivably, Apple could use this information to learn how much file sharing goes on (e.g., it could find out that a month after Ann purchases a song there are 10 computers that have a copy of Ann's music file).

By including personal information in music files it sells, has Apple violated the privacy rights of its customers?

30. Google Glass provides an information display in eyeglass frames, making it easier for people to view information while on the go. Instead of having to look at the screen of a tablet or smartphone, Google Glass users can see text and images displayed in their field of vision. Google Glass also contains a camera and a microphone, enabling users to take photos and shoot videos from a first-person perspective. Do you believe Google Glass represents a significant new threat to privacy? Under what circumstances, if any, is it inappropriate for someone to wear Google Glass?

31. Homer Gaines used Google Glass while making a marriage proposal to his girlfriend, Tami Stillwell. "I would not have been able to pull off that level of spontaneity with any other device and instantly share it with the world. Glass gave me the ability to share with everyone that special moment from my point of view—the surprise on her face, the way she jumped around, the ring on her finger and the tears of joy in her eyes" [85]. What are your reactions to this episode?

32. What special responsibilities do computer professionals have with respect to understanding and protecting the privacy rights of their fellow citizens?

## In-Class Exercises

33. What does your "ladder of privacy" look like? How does it compare to those of your classmates?

34. Give an example of a piece of information that a person should not have to reveal to anyone else. Give an example of a piece of information that society should be able to demand that a person reveal.

35. Divide the class into two groups. The first group should come up with evidence supporting the proposition "We live in a global village." The second group should come up with evidence supporting the proposition "We live in a world of strangers."

36. When you purchase a product or service using a credit card, the merchant has information linking you to the transaction. Divide the class into two groups (pro and con) to debate the proposition that merchants should be required to follow an opt-in policy. Such a policy would require the consumer to explicitly give permission before a merchant could share information about that consumer with another organization.

37. While the cost of automobile insurance varies from person to person, based on the driving record of each individual, health insurance premiums are typically uniform across groups of people, such as all the employees of a company. However, a majority of health care costs are incurred by a minority of the population.

Today it is possible to take a blood sample from a person and to extract a genetic profile that reveals the person's disposition to certain diseases. Debate the proposition that health insurance rates should be tailored to reflect each individual's propensity to illness.

38. Joe Herzenberg was a historian and politician, as well as the first openly gay elected official in North Carolina. After he died in 2007, his papers, including correspondence,

photographs, diaries, and other materials, were donated to the Southern Historical Collection (SHC). Herzenberg kept a record of his personal and professional accomplishments and struggles in a series of diaries spanning more than 50 years. In the diaries, "Herzenberg documents his sexual encounters and alludes to his friends' sexual relationships and illegal activities" [86].

According to Laura Clark Brown, "Most SHC collections are unrestricted for both research and duplication in the SHC's search room. In that relatively controlled environment, [the SHC transfers] the responsibilities for the use of sensitive materials to the researcher" [86]. SHC librarians must decide whether they should digitize the contents of Joe Herzenberg's diaries and make them available on the Web.

Debate the following proposition: The SHC librarians should not digitize the contents of Joe Herzenberg's diaries until everyone mentioned in the diaries has either given permission or died.

39. Research the case *Google Spain v. AEPD and Mario Costeja González*. This case pits a particular kind of privacy—the right for certain information not to show up in a search result—against the right to free expression.

Debate the following proposition: An individual should have the right to force a search engine to delete links to pages containing information that is correct but no longer relevant.

# References

[1]    Derek Thompson. "Google's CEO: 'The Laws Are Written by Lobbyists.'" *Atlantic*, October 1, 2010. (Quote begins at 15:50 of video.)

[2]    Polly Sprenger. "Sun on Privacy: 'Get Over It.'" *Wired*, January 26, 1999. www.wired .com.

[3]    Edmund F. Byrne. "Privacy." In *Encyclopedia of Applied Ethics*, Ruth F. Chadwick, ed., volume 3, pp. 649–659. Academic Press, Waltham, MA, 1998.

[4]    Edward J. Bloustein. "Privacy as an Aspect of Human Dignity: An Answer to Dean Prossera." In *Philosophical Dimensions of Privacy: An Anthology*, edited by Ferdinand David Schoeman, pp. 156–202, Cambridge University Press, Cambridge, England, 1984.

[5]    Ferdinand Schoeman. "Privacy: Philosophical Dimensions of the Literature." In *Philosophical Dimensions of Privacy: An Anthology*, edited by Ferdinand David Schoeman, pp. 1–33, Cambridge University Press, Cambridge, England, 1984.

[6]    Edmund Ronald Leach. *A Runaway World?* British Broadcasting Corporation, London, England, 1967.

[7]    Marie Hartwell-Walker. "Why Dysfunctional Families Stay That Way." *Amherst Bulletin*, January 28, 1994.

[8]    Morton H. Levine. "Privacy in the Tradition of the Western World." In *Privacy: A Vanishing Value?*, edited by William C. Bier, SJ, pp. 3–21, Fordham University Press, New York, NY, 1980.

[9]    Jeffrey H. Reiman. "Privacy, Intimacy, and Personhood." *Philosophy & Public Affairs* 6(1):26–44, 1976. Reprinted in *Philosophical Dimensions of Privacy: An Anthology*,

edited by Ferdinand David Schoeman, Cambridge University Press, Cambridge, England, 1984.

[10]    Stanley I. Benn. "Privacy, Freedom, and Respect for Persons." In *Philosophical Dimensions of Privacy: An Anthology*, edited by Ferdinand David Schoeman, pp. 223–244, Cambridge University Press, Cambridge, England, 1984.

[11]    Charles J. Sykes. *The End of Privacy*. St. Martin's Press, New York, NY, 1999.

[12]    Gini Graham Scott. *Mind Your Own Business: The Battle for Personal Privacy*. Insight Books/Plenum Press, New York, NY, 1995.

[13]    Constance T. Fischer. "Privacy and Human Development." In *Privacy: A Vanishing Value?*, edited by William C. Bier, SJ, pp. 37–45, Fordham University Press, New York, NY, 1980.

[14]    Robert C. Neville. "Various Meanings of Privacy: A Philosophical Analysis." In *Privacy: A Vanishing Value?*, edited by William C. Bier, SJ, pp. 22–33, Fordham University Press, New York, NY, 1980.

[15]    Joseph G. Keegan, SJ. "Privacy and Spiritual Growth." In *Privacy: A Vanishing Value?*, edited by William C. Bier, SJ, pp. 67–87, Fordham University Press, New York, NY, 1980.

[16]    Charles Fried. "Privacy: A Moral Analysis." *Yale Law Review* 77:475–493, 1968. Reprinted in *Philosophical Dimensions of Privacy: An Anthology*, edited by Ferdinand David Schoeman, Cambridge University Press, Cambridge, England, 1984.

[17]    James Rachels. "Why Privacy Is Important." *Philosophy & Public Affairs* 4(4):323–333, 1975. Reprinted in *Philosophical Dimensions of Privacy: An Anthology*, edited by Ferdinand David Schoeman, Cambridge University Press, Cambridge, England, 1984.

[18]    Samuel D. Warren and Louis D. Brandeis. "The Right to Privacy." *Harvard Law Review* 4(5), December 15, 1890.

[19]    William L. Prosser. "Privacy: A Legal Analysis." *California Law Review* 48:338–423, 1960. Reprinted in *Philosophical Dimensions of Privacy: An Anthology*, edited by Ferdinand David Schoeman, Cambridge University Press, Cambridge, England, 1984.

[20]    Judith Jarvis Thomson. "The Right to Privacy." *Philosophy & Public Affairs* 4(4):295–314, 1975. Reprinted in *Philosophical Dimensions of Privacy: An Anthology*, edited by Ferdinand David Schoeman, Cambridge University Press, Cambridge, England, 1984.

[21]    Alexander Rosenberg. "Privacy as a Matter of Taste and Right." In *The Right to Privacy*, edited by Ellen Frankel Paul, Fred D. Miller Jr., and Jeffrey Paul, pp. 68–90. Cambridge University Press, Cambridge, England, 2000.

[22]    Steven L. Nock. *The Costs of Privacy: Surveillance and Reputation in America*. Aldine de Gruyter, New York, NY, 1993.

[23]    Michael L. Sankey and Peter J. Weber, editors. *Public Records Online: The National Guide to Private & Government Online Sources of Public Records*. 4th ed. Facts on Demand Press, Tempe, AZ, 2003.

[24]    Ben Popken. "New Service Adds Your Drunken Facebook Photos to Employer Background Checks, for Up to Seven Years." *Consumerist*, June 21, 2011. www.consumerist.com.

[25]    Social Intelligence (Web site). Accessed October 15, 2013. www.socialintel.com.

[26]    Justin Mitchell. "Making Photo Tagging Easier." *The Facebook Blog*, December 15, 2010. blog.facebook.com.

[27]  "EPIC Complaint in Re: Facebook and the Facial Identification of Users." Federal Trade Commission, June 10, 2011.

[28]  Rachel King. "Facebook Photo Tag Suggestions: What's So Bad about Them Anyway?" *Between the Lines* (blog), June 9, 2011. www.zdnet.com.

[29]  Jay Warrior, Eric McHenry, and Kenneth McGee. "They Know Where You Are." *IEEE Spectrum*, pp. 20–25, July 2003.

[30]  Elizabeth Montalbano. "Microsoft Helps Put Ads on Computerized Shopping Carts." IDG News, January 16, 2008. www.pcworld.com.

[31]  John Vanderlippe. "Supermarket Cards: An Overview of the Pricing Issues." Consumers against Supermarket Privacy Invasion and Numbering, 2003. www.nocards .org/overview.

[32]  Elizabeth Weise. "Identity Swapping Makes Privacy Relative." *USA Today*, June 6, 2000.

[33]  Stephanie Clifford. "Shopper Alert: Price May Drop for You Alone." *New York Times*, August 10, 2012.

[34]  Amy Tsao. "So, We'll Take It In. . . ." *Retail Traffic*, May 1, 2003.

[35]  Charles J. Murray. "Privacy Concerns Mount over Retail Use of RFID Technology." *Electronic Engineering Times* (1298), December 1, 2003.

[36]  Meg McGinty. "RFID: Is This Game of Tag Fair Play?" *Communications of the ACM* 47(1):15–18, January 2004.

[37]  "Owners of Dogs Lacking Implants Face Fines." *China Post*, September 1, 2000.

[38]  Amal Graafstra. "How Radio-Frequency Identification and I Got Personal." *IEEE Spectrum*, March 2007.

[39]  Duncan Graham-Rowe. "Clubbers Choose Chip Implants to Jump Queues." *New Scientist*, May 21, 2004. www.newscientist.com.

[40]  "Parents Look to Microchip Children." CNN.com/World, September 3, 2002. archives .cnn.com.

[41]  Lylah M. Alphonse. "In the Parenthood." Boston.com Moms, June 9, 2010. www .boston.com.

[42]  Andrew Leonard. "Angry Birds, Tracking Device?" *Salon* (Web site), January 18, 2013. www.salon.com.

[43]  Tom Krisher. "OnStar Halts Stolen SUV in Visalia Police Chase." BakersfieldNow.com, Bakersfield, California, October 19, 2009. www.bakersfieldnow.com.

[44]  "OnStar Takes on Conspiracy Theorists." *Edmunds InsideLine*, November 13, 2009. www.insideline.com.

[45]  Ian Austen. "Your Brake Pads May Have Something to Say (by E-mail)." NYtimes.com, March 27, 2003.

[46]  Editorial. "Your E-Health Records." *New York Times*, January 31, 2009.

[47]  American Civil Liberties Union. "Seizure of Rush Limbaugh's Medical Records Violates Florida's Constitutional Right of Privacy, ACLU Tells Court" (press release). February 17, 2004. www.aclu.org.

[48]  "TiVo: Viewers Skip Fewer 'Relevant Ads.'" *Adweek*, July 30, 2008. www.adweek.com.

[49]  Ashkan Soltani, Shannon Canty, Quentin Mayo, Lauren Thomas, and Chris Jay Hoofnagle. "Flash Cookies and Privacy." University of California, Berkeley, School of Law, Berkeley Center for Law & Technology, August 10, 2009.

[50] L. A. Lorek. "Data Mining Extracts Online Gold; Stores Collect Information about Web Customers to Target Future Sales Pitches." *San Antonio Express-News*, December 15, 2002.

[51] "Personalized Search: Basics." Google Web site. Accessed September 2, 2011. www .google.com/support.

[52] "United We Find." *Economist*, March 10, 2005.

[53] Carolyn Hirschman. "Congress Sticks Its Nose into Online Privacy." *Telephony* 241(7), August 13, 2001.

[54] Charles Duhigg. "How Companies Learn Your Secrets." *New York Times Magazine*, February 16, 2012.

[55] Katie Leslie and Marcus K. Gamer. "Poor Credit Prevents Some from Scoring a Job." *Chicago Tribune*, November 12, 2010. articles.chicagotribune.com.

[56] Craig Timberg. "Brokers Use 'Billions' of Data Points to Profile Americans." *Washington Post*, May 27, 2014. www.washingtonpost.com.

[57] Gary Anthes. "Data Brokers Are Watching You." *Communications of the ACM*, January 2015, pp. 28–30.

[58] Natasha Singer. "Mapping, and Sharing, the Consumer Genome." *New York Times*, June 16, 2012. www.nytimes.com.

[59] Steve Kroft. "The Data Brokers: Selling Your Personal Information." *60 Minutes*, March 9, 2014. 14:22. www.cbsnews.com.

[60] "How Deep Are Your Pockets?" *Economist*, June 30, 2012.

[61] Joseph Walker. "Data Mining to Recruit Sick People." *Wall Street Journal*, December 17, 2013. www.wsj.com.

[62] Jeanne Cummings. "Rove's Patented Strategies Will Endure." *Politico*, August 13, 2007. www.politico.com.

[63] "Number of Employers Passing on Applicants Due to Social Media Posts Continues to Rise, According to New CareerBuilder Survey" (press release). CareerBuilder, June 26, 2014. www.careerbuilder.com.

[64] "Untangling the Social Web." *Economist Technology Quarterly*, pp. 16–17, September 4, 2010.

[65] Arvind Narayanan and Vitaly Shmatikov. "Robust De-anonymization of Large Sparse Datasets." *2008 IEEE Symposium on Security and Privacy*, May 18–21, 2008.

[66] Neil Hunt. "NetFlix Prize Update." *The Official Netflix Blog*, March 12, 2010. blog .netflix.com.

[67] Tom Zeller Jr. "AOL Executive Quits after Posting of Search Data—Technology— International Herald Tribune." *New York Times*, August 22, 2006. www.nytimes.com.

[68] Michael Arrington. "AOL Proudly Releases Massive Amounts of Private Data." TechCrunch, August 6, 2006. techcrunch.com.

[69] Michael Barbaro and Tom Zeller Jr. "A Face Is Exposed for AOL Searcher No. 4417749." *New York Times*, August 9, 2006.

[70] Dawn Kawamoto. "AOL Apologizes for Release of User Search Data." CNET (Web site), August 9, 2006. www.cnet.com.

[71] Ann Cavoukian and Don Tapscott. *Who Knows: Safeguarding Your Privacy in a Networked World*. McGraw-Hill, New York, NY, 1996.

[72] Facebook. "Leading Websites Offer Facebook Beacon for Social Distribution" (press release). November 6, 2007. www.facebook.com.

[73]   Ellen Nakashima. "Feeling Betrayed, Facebook Users Force Site to Honor Their Privacy." *Washington Post*, November 30, 2007.

[74]   Farhad Manjoo. "Facebook Finally Lets Users Turn Off Privacy-Invading Ads." *Salon* (Web site), December 6, 2007. www.salon.com.

[75]   "Malls Stop Tracking Shoppers' Cell Phones." *CNNMoney*, November 28, 2011. money.cnn.com.

[76]   Arun Thampi. "Path Uploads Your Entire iPhone Address Book to Its Servers." *mclov.in* (blog), February 8, 2012. mclov.in.

[77]   Nick Bilton. "Disruptions: So Many Apologies, So Much Data Mining." *New York Times*, February 12, 2012.

[78]   Nicole Perlroth and Nick Bilton. "Mobile Apps Take Data without Permission." *New York Times*, February 15, 2012.

[79]   Jenna Wortham and Nick Bilton. "What Instagram's New Terms of Service Mean for You." *New York Times*, December 17, 2012.

[80]   Nicole Perlroth and Jenna Wortham. "Instagram's Loss Is a Gain for Its Rivals." *New York Times*, December 20, 2012.

[81]   Kevin Systrom. "Updated Terms of Service Based on Your Feedback." Instagram, December 2012. blog.instagram.com.

[82]   Steve Lohr. "How Privacy Vanishes Online." *New York Times*, March 16, 2010.

[83]   Stewart Deck. "Legal Thumbs-Up for Raytheon Employee Suit; Privacy Groups Chilled by ISP Subpoenas." *Computerworld*, April 12, 1999.

[84]   Ken Fisher. "Apple Hides Account Info in DRM-Free Music, Too." Ars Technica (Web site), May 30, 2007. arstechnica.com.

[85]   Jessica Guynn. "Google Glass Sees All—and That Raises Privacy Concerns." *Los Angeles Times*, August 9, 2013.

[86]   Laura Clark Brown. "Third-Party-Privacy-Case-Studies." *Southern Historical Collection 2009 Symposia Wiki*, Chapel Hill, North Carolina, February, 2009. shc2009symposia.pbworks.com.

# Michael Zimmer

Michael Zimmer, PhD, is an assistant professor in the School of Information Studies at the University of Wisconsin–Milwaukee, and codirector of the Center for Information Policy Research. With a background in new media and Internet studies, the philosophy of technology, and information policy and ethics, Zimmer's research focuses on the ethical dimensions of new media and information technologies, with particular interest in privacy, social media, Internet research ethics, and ethical design.

Zimmer serves on numerous advisory boards, including the Washington, DC–based Future of Privacy Forum policy think tank and the NSF–sponsored Values–in–Design Council. He is on the editorial advisory boards of the scholarly journals *Internet Research* and the *International Review of Information Ethics*, and is coeditor of *The Information Society* book series for MIT Press. He has participated in various public interest activities, and provided expert advice and consultation for projects at the American Library Association, the New York Public Library, Google, and Microsoft.

---

***You've become known for your critique of the "Tastes, Ties, and Time" (T3) research project. Please give us an overview of the T3 project.***

The explosive popularity of online social networking platforms such as MySpace, Twitter, and Facebook has attracted attention from a variety of researchers and disciplines. However, most studies rely on external surveys of social networking participants, ethnographies of smaller subsets of subjects, or the analysis of limited profile information extracted from what subjects chose to make visible. As a result, the available data can often be tainted due to self-reporting biases and errors, have minimal representativeness of the entire population, or fail to reflect the true depth and complexity of the information and connections that flow across social networking sites.

Recognizing the data limitations faced by typical sociological studies of online social network dynamics, a group of researchers from Harvard University and the University of California, Los Angeles, set out to construct a more robust dataset that would fully leverage the rich data available on social networking Web sites. Given its popularity, the researchers chose the social network site Facebook as their data source and located a university that allowed them to download the Facebook profiles of every member of the freshman class. This was repeated annually until the study population graduated, providing four years of data about this collegiate social network. Each student's official housing records were also obtained from the university, allowing the researchers to compare Internet-based connections and real-world proximity.

The resulting dataset is unique: it was collected without relying on participant self-reporting, represents nearly an entire real-world social network of college students, includes valuable demographic, cultural, and relational information about the subjects, and provides four years of data for robust longitudinal study.

***The sociologists didn't reveal the name of the college where they had collected the data. How did you determine that the subjects were Harvard College students?***

When the researchers released the dataset, it was noted, "all the data is cleaned so you cannot connect anyone to an identity." This assertion caught my attention, since this dataset potentially includes personal and sensitive information about the students, and attempts to completely anonymize large datasets have fallen short in the past (such as the AOL search data released in 2006 and the NetFlix dataset in 2008). So I decided to investigate.

I downloaded the publicly available codebook of the dataset (gaining access to the data itself required approval by the researchers) and also started examining various articles and public comments made about the research project. An examination of the codebook revealed the source was a private, coeducational institution, whose class of 2009 initially had 1,640 students in it. Elsewhere, the source was described as a "New England" school. A search through an online college database revealed only seven private, coed colleges in New England states (Connecticut, Maine, Massachusetts, New Hampshire, Rhode Island, Vermont) with total undergraduate populations between 5,000 and 7,500 students (a likely range if there were 1,640 in the 2006 freshman class): Tufts University, Suffolk University, Yale University, University of Hartford, Quinnipiac University, Brown University, and Harvard College.

The codebook also listed the majors represented in the dataset, which included unique descriptors, such as Near Eastern Languages and Civilizations, Studies of Women, Gender and Sexuality, and Organismic and Evolutionary Biology. A quick search revealed that only Harvard provides these degree programs. The identification of Harvard College was further confirmed after analysis of a June 2008 video presentation by one of the researchers, where he noted that "midway through the freshman year, students have to pick between one and seven best friends" that they will essentially live with for the rest of their undergraduate career. This describes the unique method for determining undergraduate housing at Harvard: all freshmen who complete the fall term enter into a lottery, where they can designate a "blocking group" of between two and eight students with whom they would like to be housed in close proximity. I was able to confirm this, again, through a simple Web search.

The announcement of this likely identification of the source of the T3 dataset did not prompt a public reply by the research team, but within a week of the discovery the dataset was pulled from the publicly available repository.

### Why does it matter that you were able to determine the subjects of the T3 study were Harvard students?

There are two primary concerns. First, there is the issue of possibly being able to identify particular subjects in the dataset. The researchers took care to remove obvious identifiable data (names, email addresses, etc.), but now that the source of the dataset had been determined, it might be easier to identify unique individuals. For example, the codebook reveals that there is only one person in the dataset from each of the states of Delaware, Louisiana, Mississippi, Montana, and Wyoming. Some time in front of a search engine might reveal the identity of that one student that the state of Delaware sent to Harvard in 2006. Once we've identified that student, we can now connect her with her personal data elements in the dataset. In short, the privacy of the subjects in the database is at risk.

My other concern is actually greater: that the researchers felt their methodology was sufficient. There were a number of good-faith steps taken by the research team, but each fell short. The research team has defended itself by noting it only gathered Facebook information that was already publicly accessible. However, the team utilized Harvard graduate students to access and retrieve the profile data. At the time of the study, it was possible for Facebook users to restrict access to their profiles to people only within their home university. Thus it is entirely possible that the research team had privileged access to a profile by virtue of being within the Harvard network, while the general public would have been locked out by the user's privacy settings. Researchers must avoid such cavalier positions: just because something happens to be accessible on a social media site does not mean that it is free for the taking, no questions asked.

### Is it reasonable for anyone to expect that the information they post online will be kept as private as information shared verbally among a few confidants?

This is an important issue. It is easy for a researcher to simply say "if it is publicly available, then I can take it"; but that simple statement doesn't necessarily fit within the broader tenets of research ethics. Our concern should be with the subject: What was the intention of that post? Who did they think would see it? Did they understand it is visible to everyone? Did the default settings of the platform change since it was originally posted? (Consider how Facebook has suddenly made people's "likes" publicly viewable, when previously they could be hidden.)

I don't mean to suggest that it is never acceptable to mine these Web sites for research data, but simply we must take great care to consider the context and expectations. It is not simply a matter of "already public."

### What is your fundamental objection to the research methodology used in the T3 study?

Fundamentally, my concern is centered on the fact that even well-intended researchers—and their Institutional Research Board (IRB)—failed to fully understand the implications of their methodology. Like many, they seemed to be holding onto the traditional dichotomy of "public versus private" information, assuming that because someone posted something on a (possibly) public social media profile page, it is free for the taking without consent or concern over the poster's original intentions or expectations. I'm concerned that as more powerful tools to automate this kind of scraping of social media platforms are developed, and more research—both from highly experienced scholars and novice undergrads—takes place, this kind of potential breach of privacy and anonymity will become more common.

### If the researchers had been more careful and had succeeded in their goal of making the dataset truly anonymous, would you still have criticized their study?

Better protecting the source of the data would have helped, and it appears that the researchers have rewritten the original codebook to remove the unique names of the majors and also make the geographic origin of the subjects more generic. Despite these improvements, the methodological concerns persist, and I likely would have still expressed concern over the need for informed consent before scraping the students' Facebook data.

### Are you saying that social scientists engaged in research projects should be required to get written permission from subjects before gathering information those subjects have posted on social networks?

This is a complicated issue, and it certainly isn't possible to get written consent from all subjects in every case. Each research project should be considered separately and reviewed by an IRB and related experts. I do feel that the intents of the subjects should be strongly weighed in the decision-making process. I suspect few people with public Twitter feeds ever expected their 140-character utterances—typically lost in a sea of thousands of tweets every moment—would be archived by the Library of Congress for research purposes. These are the kinds of scenarios that should force us as a research community to think about what is the most ethical approach to social media-based research projects.

# 6

# Privacy and the Government

A system that fails to respect its citizens' right to privacy fails to respect the citizens themselves.

—RICHARD NIXON, February 23, 1974

## 6.1 Introduction

IMMEDIATELY AFTER THE LA KINGS HOCKEY TEAM WON THE STANLEY CUP, fans gathered outside the Staples Center in Los Angeles to celebrate. The police flew a surveillance drone over the excited and happy crowd, prompting some fans to respond by throwing cans, cups, shoes, and other objects at it. When someone's shirt brought down the drone, the crowd cheered [1].

On the morning of July 18, 1989, actress Rebecca Schaeffer opened the door to her apartment and was shot to death by obsessed fan Robert Bardo. Bardo got Schaeffer's home address from a private investigator who purchased her driver's license information from the California Department of Motor Vehicles [2]. In response to this murder, the US Congress passed the Driver's Privacy Protection Act in 1994. The law prohibits states from revealing certain personal information provided by drivers in order to obtain licenses. *It also requires states to provide this information to the federal government.*

After seven-year-old Megan Kanka of New Jersey was abducted, raped, and murdered by a neighbor who had a criminal record as a pedophile, Congress passed a law requiring that local police release information about registered sex offenders living in the community. Today there are more than half a million registered sex offenders in the United States. Some experts say police are overwhelmed by the number of offenders they need to monitor; the experts question the value of laws that require persons convicted of relatively minor offenses to be registered along with those who have committed terrible crimes [3].

Since the terrorist attacks of September 11, 2001, concerns about national security rose significantly, at the expense of privacy rights. A 2006 poll revealed that a majority of Americans support "expanded camera surveillance on streets and in public places" (70 percent), "law enforcement monitoring of Internet discussions in chat rooms and other forums" (62 percent), "closer monitoring of banking and credit card transactions, to trace funding sources" (61 percent), and even "expanded government monitoring of cell phones and email, to intercept communications" (52 percent). Remarkably, one-third of those polled agreed that "this use of investigative powers by the president should be done under his executive authority without needing congressional authorization" [4]. In post-9/11 America, President Nixon's abuses of presidential power seem like ancient history.

In this chapter we consider the impact that federal, state, and local governments in the United States have had on the information privacy of those living in America. The word "privacy" does not even appear in the Constitution of the United States, and it has been difficult for the legislative, executive, and judicial branches of government to find the right compromise between demands for privacy and competing concerns. We survey legislation designed to protect the information privacy of individuals as well as legislation allowing law enforcement agencies to collect information about individuals in an effort to prevent criminal or terrorist activities. We look at famous examples from American history in which governmental agencies engaged in illegal activities under the banner of protecting public safety and/or national security, and we see how the US Supreme Court gradually shifted its view of information privacy rights over time.

To organize our presentation, we will use the taxonomy of privacy proposed by Daniel Solove [5].[1] Solove groups privacy-related activities into four categories:

1. *Information collection* refers to activities that gather personal information. We discuss issues related to information collection by the government in Sections 6.2 through 6.6.

2. *Information processing* refers to activities that store, manipulate, and use personal information that has been collected. Sections 6.7 through 6.9 focus on the information-processing category.

3. *Information dissemination* refers to activities that spread personal information. Section 6.10 provides examples of laws designed to restrict information dissemination by private organizations, as well as legal ways in which information held by the government can be disseminated.

4. *Invasion* refers to activities that intrude upon a person's daily life, interrupt a person's solitude, or interfere with someone's decision making. In Section 6.11 we survey government actions to limit intrusion by other organizations, as well as government programs that can be seen as intrusive.

We consider each of these categories in turn, examining how federal, state, and local governments in the United States have addressed the often-competing interests of protecting personal privacy and promoting the common good.

## 6.2  US Legislation Restricting Information Collection

This section gives three examples of federal legislation that limits the amount of information private entities can collect from individuals.

### 6.2.1  Employee Polygraph Protection Act

The Employee Polygraph Protection Act of 1988 (EPPA) prohibits most private employers from using lie detector tests under most situations. An employer may not require or even request a job applicant or employee to take a lie detector test, and an employee who refuses to take a lie detector test cannot suffer any retaliation.

The law has several important exceptions. Pharmaceutical companies and security firms may administer polygraph tests to job applicants in certain job categories. Employers who have suffered an economic loss, such as theft, may administer polygraph tests to employees whom they reasonably suspect were involved. Most significantly, EPPA does not apply to federal, state, and local governments.

### 6.2.2  Children's Online Privacy Protection Act

The Children's Online Privacy Protection Act (COPPA), which went into effect in 2000, is designed to reduce the amount of information gathered from children using the Internet. According to COPPA, online services must obtain parental consent before collecting any information from children 12 years old and younger.

### 6.2.3  Genetic Information Nondiscrimination Act

The Genetic Information Nondiscrimination Act of 2008 is designed to prevent discrimination in the areas of medical benefits and employment based on genetic information. It prohibits health insurance companies and health plan administrators from requesting genetic information from individuals or their family members, and it forbids them from using genetic information when making decisions about coverage, rates, or preexisting conditions. It also prohibits most employers from taking genetic information into account when making hiring, firing, promotion, or any other decisions related to the terms of employment. The law does not extend these nondiscrimination protections to life insurance, disability insurance, or long-term care insurance, and it does not apply to employers with fewer than 15 employees [6].

# 6.3 Information Collection by the Government

In the previous section we considered ways in which the federal government has restricted the amount of information that private organizations can collect about individuals. In this section we look at ways in which the federal government itself has collected vast amounts of sensitive information about its citizens.

## 6.3.1 Census Records

In order to ensure each state has fair representation in the House of Representatives, the United States Constitution requires the government to perform a census every 10 years.

The first census of 1790 had six questions. It asked for the name of the head of the household and the number of persons in each of the following categories: free white males at least 16 years old; free white males under 16 years old; free white females; all other free persons (by sex and color); and slaves.

As time passed, the number of questions asked during the census increased. The 1820 census determined the number of people engaged in agriculture, commerce, and manufacturing. The 1840 census had questions regarding school attendance, illiteracy, and occupations. In 1850 census takers began asking questions about taxes, schools, crime, wages, and property values.

The 1940 census is notable because for the first time statistical sampling was put to extensive use. A random sample of the population, about 5 percent of those surveyed, received a longer form with more questions. The use of sampling enabled the Census Bureau to produce detailed demographic profiles without substantially increasing the amount of data it needed to process.

Today the Census Bureau only uses a single short form when conducting the decennial census. It gathers more detailed information on a continuous basis through the American Community Survey. This program mails a questionnaire with more than 50 questions to 3 million addresses per year. Questions include the following:

- What is this person's ancestry or ethnic origin?
- Does this person speak a language other than English at home?
- How many times has this person been married?
- How did this person usually get to work last week?
- Which fuel is used most for heating this house, apartment, or mobile home?

According to federal law, the Census Bureau is supposed to keep confidential the information it collects. However, in times of national emergency, the Census Bureau has revealed its information to other agencies. During World War I, the Census Bureau provided the names and addresses of young men to the military, which was searching for draft resisters. After the Japanese attack on Pearl Harbor, the Census Bureau provided the Justice Department with information from the 1940 census about the general location of Japanese Americans. The Army used this information to round up Japanese Americans and send them to internment camps (Figure 6.1).

**FIGURE 6.1** After the Japanese attack on Pearl Harbor, the Army used information illegally obtained from the Census Bureau to round up Japanese Americans and send them to internment camps.  (National Archives, file #210-G-3B-414)

## 6.3.2  Internal Revenue Service Records

The United States enacted a national income tax in 1862 to help pay for expenses related to the Civil War. In 1872 the income tax was repealed. Congress resurrected the national income tax in 1894, but a year later the US Supreme Court ruled it unconstitutional. The Sixteenth Amendment to the Constitution, ratified by the states in 1913, gives the United States government the power to collect an income tax. A national income tax has been in place ever since. The Internal Revenue Service (IRS) now collects more than $2 trillion a year in taxes.

Your income tax form may reveal a tremendous amount of personal information about your income, your assets, the organizations to which you give charitable contributions, your medical expenses, and much more.

## 6.3.3  FBI National Crime Information Center 2000

The FBI National Crime Information Center 2000 (NCIC) is a collection of databases supporting the activities of federal, state, and local law enforcement agencies in the

United States, the United States Virgin Islands, Puerto Rico, and Canada [7]. Its predecessor, the National Crime Information Center, was established by the FBI in January 1967 under the direction of J. Edgar Hoover.

When it was first activated, the NCIC consisted of 356,784 records in five databases: stolen automobiles, stolen license plates, stolen or missing guns, other stolen items, and missing persons. Today NCIC databases contain 13 million records in 21 databases, which include such categories as wanted persons, criminal histories, people incarcerated in federal prisons, convicted sex offenders, unidentified persons, people believed to be a threat to the president, foreign fugitives, violent gang members, and suspected terrorists. More than 80,000 law enforcement agencies have access to these data files. The NCIC processes about 12 million requests for information each day. For example, a police officer can initiate an NCIC search during a traffic stop to find out if the vehicle is stolen or there is a warrant out for the driver, and the system "responds instantly" [8].

The FBI points to the following successes of the NCIC:

- Investigating the assassination of Dr. Martin Luther King Jr., the NCIC provided the FBI with the information it needed to link a fingerprint on the murder weapon to James Earl Ray.

- In 1992 alone the NCIC led to the apprehension of 81,750 "wanted" persons, 113,293 arrests, the location of 39,268 missing juveniles and 8,549 missing adults, and the retrieval of 110,681 stolen cars.

- About an hour after the April 19, 1995, bombing of the Alfred P. Murrah Federal Building in Oklahoma City, Oklahoma state trooper Charles Hanger pulled over a Mercury Marquis with no license plates. Seeing a gun in the back seat of the car, Hanger arrested the driver—Timothy McVeigh—on the charge of transporting a loaded firearm in a motor vehicle. He took McVeigh to the county jail, and the arrest was duly entered into the NCIC database. Two days later, when federal agents ran McVeigh's name through the NCIC, they saw Hanger's arrest record. FBI agents reached the jail just before McVeigh was released (Figure 6.2). McVeigh was subsequently convicted of the bombing.

Critics of the National Crime Information Center point out ways in which the existence of the NCIC has led to privacy violations of innocent people:

- Erroneous records can lead law enforcement agencies to arrest innocent persons.

- Innocent people have been arrested because their name is the same as someone listed in the arrest warrants database.

- The FBI has used the NCIC to keep records about people not suspected of any crime, such as opponents of the Vietnam War.

- Corrupt employees of law enforcement organizations with access to the NCIC have sold information to private investigators and altered or deleted records.

- People with access to the NCIC have illegally used it to search for criminal records on acquaintances or to screen potential employees, such as babysitters.

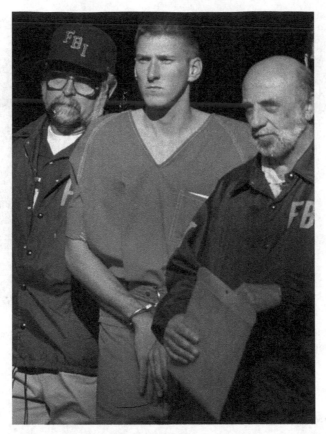

**FIGURE 6.2** The National Crime Information Center facilitated the arrest of Timothy McVeigh for the 1995 bombing of the Federal Building in Oklahoma City. (Bob Owen/ZUMA Press/Newscom)

### 6.3.4 OneDOJ Database

The OneDOJ database, managed by the US Department of Justice, provides state and local police officers access to information supplied by five federal law enforcement agencies: the FBI; the Drug Enforcement Agency; the Bureau of Alcohol, Tobacco, Firearms, and Explosives; the US Marshals Service; and the Bureau of Prisons. The database, called OneDOJ, stores incident reports, interrogation summaries, and other information not presently available through the National Crime Information Center. At the end of 2006, the OneDOJ database already contained more than one million records.

Critics of the OneDOJ database point out that it gives local police officers access to information about people who have not been arrested or charged with any crime. Barry Steinhardt of the American Civil Liberties Union said, "Raw police files or FBI reports can never be verified and can never be corrected. . . . The idea that the whole system is going to be full of inaccurate information is just chilling" [9].

FIGURE 6.3 After the Boston Marathon bombing, images from surveillance cameras played an important role in the apprehension of the suspects. (FBI)

### 6.3.5 Closed-Circuit Television Cameras

The use of closed-circuit television cameras for video surveillance in the United States began in western New York in 1968. The small town of Olean installed a surveillance camera along its main business street in an effort to reduce crime. Within a year, more than 160 police chiefs from around the country visited Olean to learn more about their system [10]. Today there are an estimated 30 million surveillance cameras operating in the United States [11].

The number of surveillance cameras keeps increasing (Figure 6.3). New York City spent $201 million to install 3,000 closed-circuit security cameras in lower Manhattan. These surveillance cameras are connected to computer systems with sophisticated image-scanning software that can sound alarms if someone leaves an unattended package. The cameras are part of a larger network of sensors that also includes license plate readers and radiation detectors [12].

The New York Civil Liberties Union has expressed opposition to the large increase in security cameras, saying they represent a violation of privacy and will not prevent terrorist attacks. The associate legal director of the NYCLU, Christopher Dunn, said "Our main concern is that it's unlike most police activity, which is focused on people who are suspected of unlawful activity. In fact, 99.9 percent of people who are captured in the system are just going to be people walking around, going about their business" [12].

Some critics point to Great Britain as proof that surveillance cameras cannot guarantee public safety. There are 4.2 million surveillance cameras in Britain, one for every 14 people. It has been estimated that the average Briton is caught on camera an average of 300 times per day [13]. Still, the presence of all these cameras did not prevent the suicide bombings in the London subway system in 2005 [14]. Some experts have reached the conclusion that closed-circuit television cameras are "largely ineffective" for crime prevention [15].

### 6.3.6 License Plate Scanners

More than 70 percent of police departments in the United States make use of scanners that read license plate numbers of passing cars and record the time and location where each car was spotted. License plate scanners, typically mounted on police cars, parking enforcement vehicles, road signs, toll gates, or bridges, track the movements of millions of automobiles every year. Police credit license plate scanners with helping them find stolen vehicles and solve criminal cases [16].

The American Civil Liberties Union has protested the widespread collection of data about citizens who are not suspected of committing any crime. In one widely publicized incident, police in New York City drove unmarked cars equipped with license plate scanners to record the license plate numbers of cars parked near a mosque in Queens [17].

The length of time that police departments retain the license plate information varies widely from one jurisdiction to another. For example, the state patrol in Minnesota erases the records after 48 hours. In contrast, the city of Milpitas, California, does not delete license plate scans, and it currently maintains a database of about 5 million scans [16].

Several states have passed legislation restricting the use of license plate scanners and/or putting limits on how long police can retain the scans. For example, New Hampshire prohibits the use of license plate scanners, with several exceptions, including tollbooths, bridges, and police investigations approved on a case-by-case basis. A California statute requires the California Highway Patrol to purge scans after 60 days, except for scans being used as evidence in a criminal investigation, and it prohibits the sale or distribution of license plate data to any non–law enforcement organizations [18].

### 6.3.7 Police Drones

Nine police departments in six different states have begun operating unmanned drones (Figure 6.4). Police drones are nothing like the large Predator drones used in Afghanistan; Federal Aviation Administration rules require that drones used by the police weigh no more than 25 pounds, fly no higher than 400 feet, and be flown during daylight within view of the operator [19]. Possible uses of the small drones include searching for missing persons, surveying storm damage to isolated neighborhoods, controlling illegal immigration, pursuing fugitive criminals, and performing surveillance at large public gatherings [20].

**FIGURE 6.4** Some police departments have acquired small unmanned drones to serve as surveillance platforms. (Mesa County Sheriff's Unmanned Operations Team)

Some uses of police drones are supported by the public, but others are not. In a recent poll conducted by Monmouth University, 66 percent of Americans expressed privacy concerns related to the use of unmanned drones with high-tech cameras by US law enforcement agencies, and 67 percent opposed the use of drones to issue speeding tickets; but 80 percent supported the use of drones in search-and-rescue missions [21].

Numerous cities and states are currently debating what controls, if any, should be placed on the use of drones by police. Should police be required to get a search warrant before deploying a drone, or should they be able to use a drone to collect the evidence they need to get a search warrant? Seattle police purchased two drones, but after a strong public protest, Mayor Mike McGinn ordered the drones to be sent back to the manufacturer [20]. Florida, Virginia, and Idaho have passed laws prohibiting the use of police drones for crowd surveillance at public events [22].

## 6.4 Covert Government Surveillance

We now turn to ways in which the US government has collected information in order to detect and apprehend suspected criminals or to improve national security. Because the individuals being observed are suspected of wrongdoing, they are not alerted or asked for permission before the surveillance begins.

Does covert surveillance violate any of the rights of a citizen? The most relevant statement in the US Constitution is the Fourth Amendment.

∾

## FOURTH AMENDMENT TO THE UNITED STATES CONSTITUTION

The right of the people to be secure in their persons, houses, papers, and effects, against unreasonable searches and seizures, shall not be violated, and no Warrants shall issue, but upon probable cause, supported by Oath or affirmation, and particularly describing the place to be searched, and the persons or things to be seized.

∾

Before the American Revolution, English agents in pursuit of smugglers made use of *writs of assistance*, which gave them authority to enter any house or building and seize any prohibited goods they could find. This activity drew the ire of the colonists. It is not surprising, then, that a prohibition against unreasonable searches and seizures appears in the Bill of Rights.

The position of the US Supreme Court with respect to covert electronic surveillance has changed over time. Let's see how the Supreme Court's position evolved.

### 6.4.1  Wiretaps and Bugs

**Wiretapping** refers to the interception of a telephone conversation. (The term is somewhat anachronistic, because many telephone conversations are no longer transmitted over wires.) Wiretapping has been taking place ever since the 1890s, when telephones became commonly used. The state of New York made wiretapping a felony in 1892, but the police in New York City ignored the law and continued the practice of wiretapping. Until 1920, the New York City police listened to conversations between lawyers and clients, doctors and patients, and priests and penitents. On several occasions the police even tapped the trunk lines into hotels and listened to the telephone conversations of all the hotel guests [23].

#### OLMSTEAD v. UNITED STATES

Wiretapping was a popular tool for catching bootleggers during Prohibition (1919–1933). The most famous case involved Roy Olmstead, who ran a $2-million-a-year bootlegging business in Seattle, Washington. Without a warrant, federal agents tapped Olmstead's phone and collected enough evidence to convict him. Although wiretapping was illegal under Washington law, the state court allowed evidence obtained through the wiretapping to be admitted. Olmstead appealed all the way to the US Supreme Court. His lawyer argued that the police had violated Olmstead's right to privacy by listening in on his telephone conversations. He also argued that the evidence should be thrown out because it was obtained without a search warrant [23, 24].

In a 5–4 decision, the Supreme Court ruled in *Olmstead v. United States* that the Fourth Amendment protected tangible assets alone. The federal agents did not "search" a physical place; they did not "seize" a physical item. Hence the Fourth Amendment's provision against warrantless search and seizure did not apply. Justice Louis Brandeis (mentioned in Section 5.2.3) was one of the four judges siding with Olmstead. In his dissenting opinion, Brandeis argued that the protections afforded by the Bill of Rights ought to extend to electronic communications as well. He wrote:

> Whenever a telephone line is tapped, the privacy of the persons at both ends of the line is invaded, and all conversations between them upon any subject, and although proper, confidential, and privileged, may be overheard. Moreover, the tapping of one man's telephone line involves the tapping of the telephone of every other person whom he may call, or who may call him. As a means of espionage, writs of assistance and general warrants are but puny instruments of tyranny and oppression when compared with wiretapping. [25]

## CONGRESS MAKES WIRETAPPING ILLEGAL

The public and the press were critical of the Supreme Court decision. Since the Court had ruled that wiretapping was constitutional, those interested in prohibiting wiretapping focused their efforts on the legislative branch. In 1934 the US Congress passed the Federal Communications Act, which (among other things) made it illegal to intercept and reveal wire communications. Three years later the Supreme Court used the Federal Communications Act to reverse its position on warrantless wiretaps. In *Nardone v. United States*, the Court ruled that evidence obtained by federal agents from warrantless wiretaps was inadmissible in court. In another decision, *Weiss v. United States*, it ruled that the prohibition on wiretapping applied to intrastate as well as interstate telephone calls. Subsequently, the attorney general announced that the FBI would cease wiretapping [23, 24].

## FBI CONTINUES SECRET WIRETAPPING

After World War II broke out in Europe, FBI director J. Edgar Hoover pressed to have the ban on wiretapping withdrawn. The position of the Department of Justice was that the Federal Communications Act simply prohibited intercepting *and* revealing telephone conversations. In the Justice Department's view, it was permissible to intercept conversations as long as they were not revealed to an agency outside the federal government. President Roosevelt agreed to let the FBI resume wiretapping in cases involving national security, though he asked that the wiretaps be kept to a minimum and limited as much as possible to aliens [23].

Because it knew evidence obtained through wiretapping was inadmissible in court, the FBI began maintaining two sets of files: the official files that contained legally obtained evidence, and confidential files containing evidence obtained from wiretaps and other confidential sources. In case of a trial, only the official file would be released to the court [23].

The FBI was supposed to get permission from the Department of Justice before installing a wiretap, but in practice it did not always work that way. During his 48-year reign as director of the FBI, J. Edgar Hoover routinely engaged in political surveillance, tapping the telephones of senators, congressional representatives, and Supreme Court justices. The information the FBI collected on these figures had great political value, even if the recordings revealed no criminal activity. There is evidence Hoover used information gathered during this surveillance to discredit members of Congress who were trying to limit the power of the FBI [23].

### CHARLES KATZ v. UNITED STATES

A **bug** is a hidden microphone used for surveillance. In a series of decisions, the US Supreme Court gradually came to an understanding that citizens should also be protected from all electronic surveillance conducted without warrants, including bugs. The key decision was rendered in 1967. Charles Katz used a public telephone to place bets. The FBI placed a bug on the outside of the telephone booth to record Katz's telephone conversations. With this evidence, Katz was convicted of illegal gambling. The Justice Department argued that since it placed the microphone on the outside of the telephone booth, it did not intrude into the space occupied by Katz [23]. In *Charles Katz v. United States*, the Supreme Court ruled in favor of Katz. Justice Potter Stewart wrote that "the Fourth Amendment protects people, not places" [26]. Katz entered the phone booth with the reasonable expectation that his conversation would not be heard, and what a person "seeks to preserve as private, even in an area accessible to the public, may be constitutionally protected" [26].

## 6.4.2 Operation Shamrock

During World War II, the US government censored all messages entering and leaving the country, meaning US intelligence agencies had access to all telegram traffic. At the end of the war, the censorship bureaucracy was shut down, and the Signal Security Agency (predecessor to the National Security Agency) wanted to find a new way to get access to telegram traffic. It contacted Western Union Telegraph Company, ITT Communications, and RCA Communications, and asked them to allow it to make photographic copies of all foreign government telegram traffic that entered, left, or transited the United States. In other words, the Signal Security Agency asked these companies to break federal law in the interests of national security. All three companies agreed to the request. The Signal Security Agency gave this intelligence-gathering operation the name "Shamrock."

When the National Security Agency (NSA) was formed in 1952, it inherited Operation Shamrock. The sophistication of the surveillance operation took a giant leap forward in the 1960s, when the telegram companies converted to computers. Now the contents of telegrams could be transmitted electronically to the NSA, and the NSA could use computers to search for key words and phrases.

In 1961 Robert Kennedy became the new attorney general of the United States, and he immediately focused his attention on organized crime. Discovering that information about mobsters was scattered piecemeal among the FBI, IRS, Securities and Exchange Commission (SEC), and other agencies, he convened a meeting in which investigators from all of these agencies could exchange information. The Justice Department gave the names of hundreds of alleged crime figures to the NSA, asking that these figures be put on its "watch list." Intelligence gathered by the NSA contributed to several prosecutions.

Also during the Kennedy administration, the FBI asked the NSA to put on its watch list the names of US citizens and companies doing business with Cuba. The NSA sent information gathered from intercepted telegrams and international telephone calls back to the FBI.

During the Vietnam War, the Johnson and Nixon administrations hypothesized that foreign governments were controlling or influencing the activities of American groups opposed to the war. They asked the NSA to put the names of war protesters on its watch list. Some of the people placed on the watch list included the Reverend Dr. Martin Luther King Jr., the Reverend Ralph Abernathy, Black Panther leader Eldridge Cleaver, pediatrician Dr. Benjamin Spock, folksinger Joan Baez, and actress Jane Fonda.

In 1969 President Nixon established the White House Task Force on Heroin Suppression. The NSA soon became an active participant in the war on drugs, monitoring the phone calls of people put on its drug watch list. Intelligence gathered by the NSA led to convictions for drug-related crimes.

Facing hostile congressional and press scrutiny, the NSA called an end to Operation Shamrock in May 1975 [27].

### 6.4.3  Carnivore Surveillance System

The FBI developed the Carnivore system in the late 1990s to monitor Internet traffic, including email messages. The system itself consisted of a Windows PC and packet-sniffing software capable of identifying and recording packets originating from or directed to a particular IP address. Armed with a search warrant, the FBI would set up its Carnivore system at the suspect's Internet service provider [28].

In 2000 the Justice Department demanded that Earthlink, an Internet service provider, allow the FBI to use Carnivore without a warrant. Earthlink filed a legal challenge questioning the FBI's authority to do this under the Electronic Communications Privacy Act, but a US District Court ruled against Earthlink [29, 30].

Between 1998 and 2000 the FBI used the Carnivore system about 25 times. In late 2001 the FBI stopped using Carnivore, replacing it with commercial software capable of performing the same function [31].

### 6.4.4  Covert Activities after 9/11

The September 11, 2001, attacks on the World Trade Center and the Pentagon spawned new, secret intelligence-gathering operations within the United States. The same question emerged after each activity became public knowledge: Is it constitutional?

#### NSA WIRETAPPING

Early in 2002 the Central Intelligence Agency captured several top al-Qaeda members, along with their personal computers and cell phones. The CIA recovered telephone numbers from these devices and provided them to the NSA. The NSA was eager to eavesdrop on these telephone numbers, hoping to gather information that could be used to disrupt future terrorist attacks. President Bush signed a presidential order allowing the NSA to eavesdrop on international telephone calls and international emails initiated by people living inside the United States, without first obtaining a search warrant [32].

The list of persons being monitored gradually expanded, as the NSA followed connections from the original list of telephone numbers. At any one time, the NSA eavesdropped on up to 500 people inside the United States, including American citizens, permanent residents, and foreigners. The NSA also monitored another 5,000 to 7,000 people living outside the United States at any one time [32].

Sources told the *New York Times* that the surveillance program had foiled at least two al-Qaeda plots: Ohio truck driver Iyman Faris's plan to "bring down the Brooklyn Bridge with blowtorches" and another scheme to bomb British pubs and train stations. Civil libertarians and some members of Congress objected to the program, arguing that warrantless wiretapping of American citizens violated the Fourth Amendment to the US Constitution [32].

### TALON DATABASE

The US Department of Defense created the Threat and Local Observation Notices (TALON) database in 2003. The purpose of the database was to collect reports of suspicious activities or terrorist threats near military bases. These reports were submitted by military personnel or civilians and then assessed by Department of Defense experts as either "credible" or "not credible."

In December 2005, *NBC News* reported that the database contained reports on antiwar protests occurring far from military bases [33]. In July 2006, the Servicemembers Legal Defense Network reported that the TALON database contained emails from students at Southern Connecticut State University, the State University of New York at Albany, the University of California, Berkeley, and William Paterson University of New Jersey, who were planning protests against on-campus military recruiting [34].

The Department of Defense removed many of these reports from TALON after conducting an in-house review that concluded the database should only contain information related to terrorist activity. The American Civil Liberties Union asked Congress to take steps "to ensure that Americans may once again exercise their First Amendment rights without fear that they will be tracked in a government database of suspicious activities" [35]. In April 2007, the new Undersecretary of Defense for Intelligence recommended that the TALON program be terminated [36]. The TALON database was shut down on September 17, 2007 [37].

# 6.5  US Legislation Authorizing Wiretapping

As we have seen, the Federal Communications Act of 1934 made wiretapping illegal, and by 1967 the US Supreme Court had closed the door to wiretapping and bugging performed without a warrant (court order). After the Katz decision, police were left without any electronic surveillance tools in their fight against crime.

Meanwhile, the United States was in the middle of the Vietnam War. In 1968 the country was rocked by violent antiwar demonstrations and the assassinations of Martin Luther King Jr. and Robert F. Kennedy. Law enforcement agencies pressured Congress to allow wiretapping under some circumstances.

### 6.5.1 Title III

Congress responded by passing Title III of the Omnibus Crime Control and Safe Streets Act of 1968. Title III allows a police agency that has obtained a court order to tap a phone for up to 30 days [23].

The government continued to argue that in cases of national security, agencies should be able to tap phones without a warrant. In 1972 the Supreme Court rejected this argument when it ruled that the Fourth Amendment forbids warrantless wiretapping, even in cases of national security [23].

### 6.5.2 Foreign Intelligence Surveillance Act

The Foreign Intelligence Surveillance Act of 1978 (FISA) provides for judicial and congressional oversight of the government's covert surveillance of foreign governments and their agents. The law allows the president to authorize electronic surveillance of foreign nationals for up to one year without a court order, as long as there is little chance that the surveillance will reveal the contents of communications with any US citizens. If communications with US citizens are to be monitored, the government must get a court order from the FISA Court.

FISA was amended by the Protect America Act of 2007. This act allows the US government to wiretap communications beginning or ending in a foreign country without oversight by the FISA Court.

In June 2013, the British newspaper the *Guardian* disclosed it had received a top secret document outlining how the National Security Agency had obtained direct access to the servers at Google, Facebook, Yahoo, and other Internet giants [38]. (The document was provided by Edward Snowden, a former employee of NSA contractor Booz Allen Hamilton.) The secret program, called PRISM, enables the NSA to access stored information such as email messages and monitor live communications such as Skype and PalTalk conversations without first obtaining search warrants, when the NSA has a reasonable suspicion that the person being investigated is a foreigner outside the United States. According to the secret document, the NSA gained access to the servers of Microsoft in 2007; Yahoo in 2008; Google and Facebook in 2009; YouTube in 2010; Skype and AOL in 2011; and Apple in 2012.

All the companies that responded to a request for information by the *Guardian* denied any knowledge of the PRISM program. The Obama administration provided the following statement: "The *Guardian* and *Washington Post* articles refer to collection of communications pursuant to Section 702 of the Foreign Intelligence Surveillance Act. This law does not allow the targeting of any US citizen or of any person located within the United States" [38].

### 6.5.3 Electronic Communications Privacy Act

Congress updated the wiretapping law in 1986 with the passage of the Electronic Communications Privacy Act (ECPA). The ECPA allows police to attach two kinds of surveillance devices to a suspect's phone line. If the suspect makes a phone call, a **pen register** displays the number being dialed. If the suspect gets a phone call, a **trap-and-trace device** displays the caller's phone number. While a court order is needed to approve the installation of pen registers and trap-and-trace devices, prosecutors do not need to demonstrate probable cause, and the approval is virtually automatic.

The ECPA also allows police to conduct **roving wiretaps**—wiretaps that move from phone to phone—if they can demonstrate the suspect is attempting to avoid surveillance by using many different phones [23].

### 6.5.4 Stored Communications Act

The Stored Communications Act, part of the Electronic Communications Privacy Act, has significant privacy implications related to the collection of email messages. Under this law, the government does not need a search warrant to obtain from an Internet service provider email messages more than 180 days old. In other words, when a computer user allows an Internet service provider to store his or her email messages, the user is giving up the expectation of privacy of that information [39].

In the past it had been understood that the government needed a court order to gain access to emails under 180 days old, but in 2010 the government asked Yahoo to turn over emails under 180 days old that had already been read by the recipient [40]. Yahoo challenged this request in federal court, supported by Google, the Electronic Frontier Foundation, and the Center for Democracy & Technology, and the government withdrew its demand for the emails.

Nearly 50 companies and privacy rights organizations, including AOL, the American Civil Liberties Union, the American Library Association, AT&T, Consumer Action, the Electronic Frontier Foundation, Facebook, Google, IBM, Intel, and Microsoft, have joined forces to form an organization called Digital Due Process, which is lobbying Congress to update the Electronic Communications Privacy Act. In the past Internet service providers simply transmitted email messages from senders to recipients. Today most Internet service providers supply convenient, long-term storage of their customers' emails, and millions of customers take advantage of this service to hold their messages indefinitely. With the advent of cloud computing, companies such as Amazon, Google, and Microsoft are storing sensitive documents and other materials that in the past would have been held on personal computers. The view of the Digital Due Process coalition is that the government should not be able to obtain an email message, document, or photo from an Internet or cloud service provider without a proper search warrant [41].

### 6.5.5 Communications Assistance for Law Enforcement Act

The implementation of digital phone networks interfered with the wiretapping ability of the FBI and other organizations. In response to these technological changes, Congress passed the Communications Assistance for Law Enforcement Act of 1994 (CALEA), also known as the Digital Telephony Act. This law required that networking equipment used by phone companies be designed or modified so that law enforcement agencies can trace calls, listen in on telephone calls, and intercept email messages. CALEA thereby ensured that court-ordered wiretapping would still be possible even as new digital technologies were introduced.

CALEA left unanswered many important details about the kind of information the FBI would be able to extract from digital phone calls. The precise requirements were to be worked out between the FBI and industry representatives. The FBI asked for many capabilities, including the ability to intercept digits typed by the caller after the phone call was placed. This feature would let it catch credit card numbers and bank account numbers, for example. In 1999 the FCC finally issued the guidelines, which included this capability and five more requested by the FBI [42]. Privacy rights organizations argued these capabilities went beyond the authorization of CALEA [43]. Telecommunications companies claimed that implementing these capabilities would cost them billions of dollars [44]. Nevertheless, in August 2005, the FCC determined that Voice over Internet Protocol (VoIP) and certain other broadband providers would need to modify their systems as necessary so that law enforcement agencies could wiretap calls made using their services [45].

## 6.6 USA PATRIOT Act

On the morning of September 11, 2001, terrorists hijacked four passenger airliners in the United States and turned them into flying bombs. Two of the planes flew into New York's World Trade Center, a third hit the Pentagon, and the fourth crashed in a field in Pennsylvania. Soon after these attacks, which resulted in about 3,000 deaths and the destruction of the twin towers of the World Trade Center, the US Congress passed the Uniting and Strengthening America by Providing Appropriate Tools Required to Intercept and Obstruct Terrorism (USA PATRIOT) Act of 2001, henceforth referred to as the Patriot Act [46]. The Patriot Act has raised many questions about the extent to which government agencies should be able to collect information about individuals in the United States without first obtaining a search warrant.

### 6.6.1 Provisions of the Patriot Act

The Patriot Act amended many existing laws. Its provisions fall into four principal categories:

1. Providing federal law enforcement and intelligence officials with greater authority to monitor communications
2. Giving the Secretary of the Treasury greater powers to regulate banks, preventing them from being used to launder foreign money
3. Making it more difficult for terrorists to enter the United States
4. Defining new crimes and penalties for terrorist activity

We focus on those provisions of the Patriot Act that most directly affect the privacy of persons living inside the United States.

The Patriot Act expands the kinds of information that law enforcement officials can gather with pen registers and trap-and-trace devices. It allows police to use pen registers on the Internet to track email addresses and URLs. The law does not require they demonstrate probable cause. To obtain a warrant, police simply certify that the information to be gained is relevant to an ongoing criminal investigation.

Law enforcement agencies seeking to install a wiretap or a pen register/trap-and-trace device have always been required to get a court order from a judge with jurisdiction over the location where the device was to be installed. The Patriot Act extends the jurisdiction of court-ordered wiretaps to the entire country. A judge in New York can authorize the installation of a device in California, for example. The act also allows the nationwide application of court-ordered search warrants for terrorist-related investigations.

The Patriot Act broadened the number of circumstances under which roving surveillance can take place. Previously, roving surveillance could only be done for the purpose of law enforcement, and the agency had to demonstrate to the court that the person under investigation actually used the device to be monitored. The Patriot Act allows roving surveillance to be performed for the purpose of intelligence, and the government does not have to prove that the person under investigation actually uses the device to be tapped. Additionally, it does not require that the law enforcement agency report back to the authorizing judge regarding the number of devices monitored and the results of the monitoring.

Under the Patriot Act, law enforcement officials wishing to intercept communications to and from a person who has illegally gained access to a computer system do not need a court order if they have the permission of the owner of the computer system.

The Patriot Act allows courts to authorize law enforcement officers to search a person's premises without first serving a search warrant when there is "reasonable cause to believe that providing immediate notification of the execution of the warrant may have an adverse effect." Officers may seize property that "constitutes evidence of a criminal offense in violation of the laws of the United States," even if that offense is unrelated to terrorism.

### 6.6.2 National Security Letters

The Patriot Act expanded the use of National Security Letters, making it easier for the FBI to collect Internet, business, medical, educational, library, and church/mosque/synagogue records. To obtain a search warrant authorizing the collection of records about an individual, the FBI merely needs to issue a National Security Letter stating that the records are related to an ongoing investigation. (The Patriot Act does specifically prohibit the FBI from investigating citizens solely on the basis of activities protected by the First Amendment.) A typical National Security Letter contains a gag order that forbids the letter's recipient from disclosing receipt of the letter. National Security Letters are controversial because, unlike warrants, they do not require the approval of a judge. That means there is no need for the FBI to show probable cause. Between 2003 and 2006, the FBI issued 192,499 National Security Letters [47].

National Security Letters have prompted several legal challenges by the American Civil Liberties Union (ACLU). One of these cases involved the Library Connection, a consortium of 26 libraries in Connecticut. In July 2005, the FBI sent a National Security Letter to the Library Connection, demanding records of a patron who had used a particular computer. This happened while Congress was debating reauthorization of the Patriot Act, and an important point in the debate was whether the FBI had actually attempted to use the Patriot Act to get information from libraries. The ACLU sought an emergency court order that would have allowed representatives of the Library Connection to tell Congress that they had received a National Security Letter. In September 2005, a district court judge in Connecticut ruled that the National Security Letter's gag order violated the First Amendment to the US Constitution, but the executive branch continued to enforce it. In April 2006, six weeks after Congress had reauthorized the Patriot Act, the FBI dropped the gag order and its demand for the information. The ACLU hailed the government's decision as a victory "not just for librarians but for all Americans who value their privacy" [48].

### 6.6.3  Responses to the Patriot Act

Critics of the Patriot Act warn that its provisions give too many powers to the federal government. Despite language in the Patriot Act to the contrary, civil libertarians are concerned that law enforcement agencies may use their new powers to reduce the rights of law-abiding Americans, particularly those rights expressed in the First and Fourth Amendments to the US Constitution.

First Amendment rights center around the freedom of speech and the free exercise of religion. We have seen that, in the past, the FBI and the NSA used illegal wiretaps to investigate people who had expressed unpopular political views. In November 2003, the ACLU reported that public apprehension about the Patriot Act had led to a significant drop in attendance and donations at mosques [49].

Critics maintain that other provisions of the Patriot Act undermine the right against unreasonable searches and seizures guaranteed by the Fourth Amendment:

- The Patriot Act allows police to install Internet pen registers without demonstrating probable cause that the suspect is engaged in a criminal activity. By revealing the URLs of Web sites visited by a suspect, a pen register is a much more powerful surveillance tool on the Internet than it is on a telephone network.

- The Patriot Act allows for court orders authorizing roving surveillance that do not "particularly describe the place to be searched."

- It allows law enforcement agencies, under certain circumstances, to search homes and seize evidence without first serving a search warrant.

- It allows the FBI to obtain—without showing probable cause—a warrant authorizing the seizure of business, medical, educational, and library records of suspects.

The Council of the American Library Association passed a resolution on the Patriot Act in January 2003. The resolution affirms every person's rights to inquiry and free expression. It "urges librarians everywhere to defend and support user privacy and free and open access to knowledge and information," and it "urges libraries to adopt and implement patron privacy and record retention policies" that minimize the collection of records about the activities of individual patrons [50]. More than four hundred cities and several states have also passed anti–Patriot Act resolutions [51].

As alluded to earlier, the federal government issues about 50,000 National Security Letters every year [52]. Google is an obvious organization for law enforcement agencies to contact, given the significant amount of information it collects from individuals who use its search engine. In December 2009, Google's CEO, Eric Schmidt, told CNBC, "If you have something that you don't want anyone to know, maybe you shouldn't be doing it in the first place." Schmidt admitted Google is obliged to release personal data to law enforcement agencies, saying, "The reality is that search engines—including Google—do retain this information for some time and it's important, for example, that we are all subject in the United States to the Patriot Act and it is possible that all that information could be made available to the authorities" [53].

### 6.6.4 Successes and Failures

According to Tom Ridge, former secretary of the Department of Homeland Security, the Patriot Act has helped the government in its fight against terrorism by allowing greater information sharing among law enforcement and intelligence agencies and by giving law enforcement agencies new investigative tools—"many of which have been used for years to catch mafia dons and drug kingpins" [54]. Terrorism investigations have led to charges being brought against 361 individuals in the United States. Of these, 191 have been convicted or pled guilty, including shoe-bomber Richard Reid and John Walker Lindh, who fought with the Taliban in Afghanistan. More than 500 individuals linked to the September 11th attacks have been removed from the United States. Terrorist cells in Buffalo, Seattle, Tampa, and Portland (the "Portland Seven")[2] have been broken up [54].

---

2. The "Portland Seven" included six American Muslim men accused of attempting to travel to Afghanistan to fight with the Taliban.

Unfortunately, a few innocent bystanders have been affected by the war against terrorism. A notable example is Brandon Mayfield.

During the morning rush hour on March 11, 2004, 10 bombs exploded on four commuter trains in Madrid, Spain, killing 191 people and wounding more than 2,000 others. The Spanish government retrieved a partial fingerprint from a bag of detonators, and the FBI linked the fingerprint to Brandon Mayfield, an attorney in Portland, Oregon [55].

Without revealing their search warrant, FBI agents secretly entered Mayfield's home multiple times, making copies of documents and computer hard drives, collecting 10 DNA samples, removing six cigarette butts for DNA analysis, and taking 355 digital photographs. The FBI also put Mayfield under electronic surveillance [56]. On May 6, 2004, the FBI arrested Mayfield as a material witness and detained him for two weeks. After the Spanish government announced that it had matched the fingerprints to Ouhnane Daoud, an Algerian national living in Spain, a judge ordered that Mayfield be released. The FBI publicly apologized for the fingerprint misidentification [55].

Mayfield said his detention was "an abuse of the judicial process" that "shouldn't happen to anybody" [55]. He said, "I personally was subject to lockdown, strip searches, sleep deprivation, unsanitary living conditions, shackles and chains, threats, physical pain, and humiliation" [57]. The only evidence against Mayfield was a partial fingerprint match that even the Spanish police found dubious. Mayfield had not left the United States in more than a decade, and he had no connections with any terrorist organizations. Some civil rights groups suggest Mayfield was targeted by the FBI because of his religious beliefs. The affidavit that the FBI used to get an arrest warrant pointed out that Mayfield "had converted to Islam, is married to an Egyptian-born woman, and had once briefly represented a member of the Portland Seven in a child-custody case" [58]. Mayfield sued the US government for continuing to investigate him after the Spanish police had eliminated him as a suspect, and in November 2006, the government issued a formal apology and agreed to pay him $2 million [57].

## 6.6.5 Long-Standing NSA Access to Telephone Records

Beginning in 2011, two members of the Intelligence Committee of the US Senate, Ron Wyden of Oregon and Mark Udall of Arizona, repeatedly spoke out against domestic spying. In May 2011, Senator Wyden said, "I want to deliver a warning this afternoon: when the American people find out how their government has secretly interpreted the Patriot Act, they will be stunned and they will be angry" [59].

Two years later Americans began to learn what Senator Wyden was talking about. On June 5, 2013, the British newspaper the *Guardian* revealed that, based on a request from the FBI, the Foreign Intelligence Surveillance Court (FISC) had ordered Verizon to provide to the National Security Agency on a daily basis records of all of its customers' calls from April 25, 2013, to July 19, 2013 [60]. (Edward Snowden, a former employee of NSA contractor Booz Allen Hamilton, was responsible for leaking the information to the *Guardian*.) These call records, also called **telephony metadata**, included the date and time of each telephone call, the location of the phone making the call, the duration of the conversation, and "other identifying information." Verizon was not asked to provide the contents of the conversations. The order from the FISC expressly prohibited Verizon from revealing to the public the FBI's request for this information. Opined the *Guardian*, "These recent events reflect how profoundly the NSA's mission has transformed from an agency exclusively devoted to foreign intelligence gathering, into one that focuses increasingly on domestic communications" [60].

The Obama administration downplayed the revelation and held that the data collection was authorized under Section 215 of the Patriot Act. Deputy Press Secretary Josh Earnest said that the court orders for telephone records "are something that have been in place a number of years now" [61]. Dianne Feinstein, chair of the Senate Intelligence Committee, confirmed that position: "As far as I know, this is an exact three-month renewal of what has been the case for the past seven years" [62].

Senator Udall said, "This sort of wide-scale surveillance should concern all of us and is the kind of government overreach I've said Americans would find shocking" [63]. Former vice president Al Gore called the blanket order "obscenely outrageous" [63]. Republican congressman Jim Sensenbrenner, one of the authors of the Patriot Act, added, "I do not believe the broadly drafted FISA order is consistent with the requirements of the Patriot Act. Seizing phone records of millions of innocent people is excessive and un-American" [63].

In May 2015, a federal court in New York ruled that the NSA's program to collect customer telephone call records in bulk was illegal. According to the US Court of Appeals for the Second Circuit, it is unreasonable to interpret Section 215 of the Patriot Act as authorizing the bulk collection of telephone calling records [64].

Section 215 of the Patriot Act expired on June 1, 2015. Instead of renewing Section 215, Congress passed a reform of Section 215, called the USA Freedom Act. The USA Freedom Act put new restrictions on the government's surveillance activities. In particular, it shifted the bulk collection of telephone records to the phone companies and required government agencies to obtain a court order before accessing them [65].

# 6.7 Regulation of Public and Private Databases

In this section we switch our focus to the information processing category of Solove's taxonomy of privacy. (Our coverage of issues related to information processing and the government continues through Section 6.9.)

Once organizations have collected information, they can manipulate and use it in a variety of ways, and some of these uses have privacy implications. We begin by describing the social conditions that led to the creation of the Code of Fair Information Practices and the passage of the Privacy Act of 1974. We then move on to legislation that regulates databases managed by private organizations.

## 6.7.1 Code of Fair Information Practices

In 1965 the director of the Bureau of the Budget commissioned a consulting committee, composed largely of economists, to look at problems caused by the decentralization of statistical data across many federal agencies. The Census Bureau, the Bureau of Labor Statistics, the Statistical Reporting Service, and the Economic Research Service of the Department of Agriculture maintained independent computer databases, making it impossible for economists and other social scientists to combine information about individuals. Carl Kaysen, the chair of the committee, described it this way:

> It is becoming increasingly difficult to make informed and intelligent policy decisions on such questions in the area of poverty as welfare payments, family allowances, and the like, simply because we lack sufficient "dis-aggregated" information—breakdowns by the many relevant social and economic variables—that is both wide in coverage and readily usable. The information the Government does have is scattered among a dozen agencies, collected on a variety of not necessarily consistent bases, and not really accessible to any single group of policy-makers or research analysts. A test of the proposition, for example, that poor performance in school and poor prospects of social mobility are directly related to family size would require data combining information on at least family size and composition, family income, regional location, city size, school performance, and post-school occupational history over a period of years in a way that is simply not now possible, even though the separate items of information were all fed into some part of the Federal statistical system at some time. [66]

After Kaysen's committee recommended the creation of a National Data Center, there was an immediate outcry from citizens and legislators expressing concerns about possible abuses of a massive, centralized government database containing detailed information about millions of Americans. The US House of Representatives created the Special Subcommittee on Invasion of Privacy, which held hearings about these issues [67].

In the early 1970s, Elliot Richardson, the secretary of the US Department of Health, Education, and Welfare, convened a group to recommend policies for the development of government databases that would protect the privacy of American citizens. The secretary's Advisory Committee of Automated Personal Data Systems, Records, Computers, and the Rights of Citizens produced a report for Congress, which included the following "bill of rights" for the Information Age [68]:

## CODE OF FAIR INFORMATION PRACTICES

1. There must be no personal data record–keeping systems whose very existence is secret.

2. There must be a way for a person to find out what information about the person is in a record and how it is used.

3. There must be a way for a person to prevent information about the person that was obtained for one purpose from being used or made available for other purposes without the person's consent.

4. There must be a way for a person to correct or amend a record of identifiable information about the person.

5. Any organization creating, maintaining, using, or disseminating records of identifiable personal data must assure the reliability of the data for their intended use and must take precautions to prevent misuses of the data.

At about the same time that the Richardson Committee was established in the United States, similar efforts were under way in Europe. In fact, a year before the Richardson Committee issued the report containing the Code of Fair Information Practices, the Committee on Privacy in the United Kingdom released its own report containing many of the same principles. Sweden passed privacy laws consistent with fair information practices in 1973, and later that decade the Federal Republic of Germany and France followed suit [69].

## 6.7.2  Privacy Act of 1974

The Privacy Act of 1974 represents Congress's codification of the principles described in the Code of Fair Information Practices. While the Privacy Act does allow individuals in some cases to get access to federal files containing information about them, in other respects it has fallen short of the desires of privacy advocates. In particular, they say the Privacy Act has not been effective in reducing the flow of personal information into governmental databases, preventing agencies from sharing information with each other, or preventing unauthorized access to the data. They claim agencies have been unresponsive to outside attempts to bring them into alignment with the provisions of the Privacy Act. The Privacy Act has the following principal limitations [70]:

1. *The Privacy Act applies only to government databases.*

   Far more information is held in private databases, which are excluded. This is an enormous loophole, because government agencies can purchase information from private organizations that have the data they want.

2. *The Privacy Act only covers records indexed by a personal identifier.*

   Records about individuals that are not indexed by name or another identifying number are excluded. For example, a former IRS agent tried to gain access to a file containing derogatory information about himself, but the judge ruled he did not have a right to see the file, since it was indexed under the name of another IRS employee.

3. *No one in the federal government is in charge of enforcing the provisions of the Privacy Act.*

   Federal agencies have taken it upon themselves to determine which databases they can exempt. The IRS has exempted its database containing the names of taxpayers it is investigating. The Department of Justice has announced that the FBI does not have to ensure the reliability of the data in its NCIC databases.

4. *The Privacy Act allows one agency to share records with another agency as long as they are for a "routine use."*

   Each agency is able to decide for itself what "routine use" means. The Department of Justice has encouraged agencies to define routine use as broadly as possible.

Although the Privacy Act applies only to government databases, Congress has also passed legislation regulating how some private institutions manage databases containing sensitive information about individuals, and these laws put into effect many of the principles of the Code of Fair Information Practices. In the remainder of this section, we survey some of the most influential of these laws.

### 6.7.3 Fair Credit Reporting Act

Credit bureaus and other consumer reporting agencies maintain information on your bill-paying record, whether you've been sued or arrested, and if you've filed for bankruptcy. They sell reports to other organizations that are trying to determine the credit-worthiness of consumers who are applying for credit, applying for a job, or trying to rent an apartment. The Fair Credit Reporting Act, passed in 1970 and revised in 1996, was designed to promote the accuracy and privacy of information used by credit bureaus and other consumer reporting agencies to produce consumer reports. It also ensures that negative information does not haunt a consumer for a lifetime.

The three major credit bureaus are Equifax, Experian, and TransUnion. According to the Fair Credit Reporting Act, these credit bureaus may keep negative information about a consumer for a maximum of seven years. There are several exceptions to this rule. The two most important are that information about criminal convictions may be kept indefinitely, and bankruptcy information may be held for 10 years.

### 6.7.4 Fair and Accurate Credit Transactions Act

The Fair and Accurate Credit Transactions Act of 2004 requires the three major credit bureaus to provide consumers a free copy of their credit report every 12 months. Consumers can use this opportunity to detect and correct errors in their credit reports. The bureaus do not issue the reports automatically; consumers must take the initiative and request them from AnnualCreditReport.com.

The law also has provisions to reduce identity theft. It requires the truncation of account numbers on credit card receipts, and it establishes the National Fraud Alert System. Victims of identity theft may put a fraud alert on their credit files, warning credit card issuers that they must take "reasonable steps" to verify the requester's identity before granting credit.

### 6.7.5 Financial Services Modernization Act

The Financial Services Modernization Act (also called the Gramm-Leach-Bliley Act of 1999) contains dozens of provisions related to how financial institutions do business. One of the major provisions of the law allows the creation of "financial supermarkets" offering banking, insurance, and brokerage services.

The law also contains some privacy-related provisions. It requires financial institutions to disclose their privacy policies to their customers. When a customer establishes an account, and at least once per year thereafter, the institution must let the customer know the kinds of information it collects and how it uses that information. These notices must contain an opt-out clause that explains to customers how they can request that their confidential information not be revealed to other companies. The law requires financial institutions to develop policies that prevent unauthorized access to their customers' confidential information [71].

## 6.8   Data Mining by the Government

**Data mining** is the process of searching through one or more databases looking for patterns or relationships among the data. In this section we continue our coverage of the information-processing category of Solove's taxonomy by surveying a few well-known data-mining projects run by government agencies. We also consider harms that can result when data mining algorithms create erroneous profiles of individuals.

### 6.8.1   Internal Revenue Service Audits

To identify taxpayers who have paid less in taxes than they owe, the Internal Revenue Service (IRS) uses computer-matching and data-mining strategies. First, it matches information on the tax form with information provided by employers and financial institutions. This is a straightforward way to detect unreported income.

Second, the IRS audits a couple of million tax returns every year. Its goal is to select the most promising returns—those containing errors resulting in underpayment of taxes. The IRS uses an algorithm called the discriminant function (DIF) to score every tax return. The DIF score is an indicator of how many irregularities there are on a tax form, compared to carefully constructed profiles of correct tax returns. About 60 percent of tax returns audited by the IRS are selected due to their high DIF scores.

### 6.8.2   Syndromic Surveillance Systems

Another application of data mining by the government is protecting society from imminent dangers.

A syndromic surveillance system is a computerized system that analyzes 911 calls, visits to the emergency room, school absenteeism, purchases of prescription drugs, and Internet searches to find patterns that might indicate the onset of an epidemic, an environmental problem leading to illnesses, or bioterrorism.

In the fall of 2002, a syndromic surveillance system in New York City detected a surge in people seeking treatment for vomiting and diarrhea. These symptoms were the first signs of an outbreak of a Norwalk-type virus. The alert generated by the system allowed city officials to warn doctors about the outbreak and advise them to be particularly careful about handling the highly contagious body fluids of their affected patients [72].

### 6.8.3   Telecommunications Records Database

After September 11, 2001, several major telecommunications providers began turning over the phone call records of tens of millions of Americans to the National Security Agency, without a court order (see Section 6.6.5). The NSA was not monitoring or recording the actual conversations; instead, it was analyzing calling patterns in order to detect potential terrorist networks [73].

After *USA Today* revealed the existence of the database in May 2006, more than a dozen class-action lawsuits were filed against the telecommunications companies. In August 2006, a federal judge in Detroit ruled the program to be illegal and unconstitutional, violating several statutes as well as the First and Fourth Amendments to the US Constitution [74]. In July 2007, the US Court of Appeals for the Sixth Circuit overturned the ruling on the grounds that the plaintiffs did not have standing to bring the suit forward. In other words, the plaintiffs had not produced any evidence that they personally were victims of the program.

## 6.8.4 Predictive Policing

**Predictive policing** is the use of data mining to deploy police officers to areas where crimes are more likely to occur. It is based on the observation that individual criminals act in a predictable way. For example, criminals tend to frequent familiar areas. If a car is burglarized, the probability increases that another car in the neighborhood will be burglarized. The times at which crimes occur can also fall into predictable patterns [75].

Police in Santa Cruz, California, created a database of information about vehicular, residential, and commercial burglaries, then used data mining to produce maps containing 15 "hotspots" to distribute to police officers as they began their shifts. The department asked officers to make a point of passing through the hotspot areas when they were not handling other calls. Over the first six months of the experiment, the number of burglaries declined 19 percent [75]. The Los Angeles Police Department implemented a similar system in an area with 300,000 residents and observed a 12 percent decline in property crime. Predictive policing is now being practiced in many cities across the United States [75].

## 6.8.5 Potential Harms of Profiling

Experts have begun to warn about the personal harms that can result when organizations pursue their objectives based on individual profiles they have constructed through data mining [76]. Sometimes those objectives are commercial. For example, as we saw in Chapter 5, Target used data mining to predict which of its customers were pregnant women, so that they could use direct mail offers to get these customers into the habit of purchasing a wide variety of items at Target stores. In at least one case, Target sent advertisements for maternity clothing and nursery furniture to a teenage girl before she had told her father she was pregnant [77].

In other situations the objectives are much more serious. A government agency charged with protecting national security is responsible for preventing harm to the nation, and its employees are strongly motivated to take action before—not after—an attack. What happens if a learning algorithm employed by a law enforcement agency mines a massive amount of data and constructs an erroneous profile of an individual, characterizing him or her as a potential terrorist? The amount of data being searched could be so massive, and the algorithms manipulating the data so complicated, that it might be impossible for any human being to explain why the algorithm has profiled a particular individual as a potential terrorist. How are innocent people who are identified on "terrorist watch lists" able to clear their names in this situation?

For example, there are now more than 1.5 million names on the US government's terrorist watch list, officially known as the Terrorist Screening Database [78]. Tens of thousands of these names somehow make their way to the government's "no fly" list. Many people with common names (including the late Senator Edward Kennedy and the author of this book) have encountered problems boarding commercial flights because their names appeared on the "no fly" list [79].

# 6.9 National Identification Card

A great deal can be learned about an individual when information collected at different places and times is combined. In order to combine information from two records, the records must share a common key. A name cannot be used as a common key, because more than one person can have the same name, but if every individual had a unique identification number and that identification number appeared in every database record referring to that individual, then all of these records could theoretically be combined into a massive "electronic dossier" documenting that person's life. In this section we survey the debate around the establishment of a national identification card in the United States.

## 6.9.1 History and Role of the Social Security Number

The Social Security Act of 1935 established two social insurance programs in the United States: a federal system of old-age benefits to retired persons, and a federal-state system of unemployment insurance. Before the system could be implemented, employers and workers needed to become registered. The Social Security Board contracted with the US Postal Service to distribute applications for Social Security cards. The post office collected the forms, typed the Social Security cards, and returned them to the applicants. In this way over 35 million Social Security cards were issued in 1936–1937 [80].

The US government initially stated that Social Security numbers (SSNs) would be used solely by the Social Security Administration and not as a national identification card. In fact, from 1946 to 1972, the Social Security Administration put the following legend on the bottom of the cards it issued: "FOR SOCIAL SECURITY PURPOSES—NOT FOR IDENTIFICATION." However, use of the SSN has gradually increased. President Roosevelt ordered, in 1943, that federal agencies use SSNs as identifiers in new federal databases. In 1961 the Internal Revenue Service began using the SSN as the taxpayer identification number. Because banks report interest to the IRS, people must provide their SSN when they open a bank account. The SSN is typically requested on applications for credit cards. Motor vehicle departments and some other state agencies received permission to use SSNs as identification numbers in 1976. The IRS now requires parents to provide the SSNs of their children over one year old on income tax forms in order to claim them as dependents. For this reason, children now get SSNs soon after they are born. Many private organizations ask people to provide SSNs for identification. The SSN has become a de facto national identification number in the United States.

Unfortunately, the SSN has serious defects that make it a poor identification number. The first problem with SSNs is that they are not unique. When Social Security cards were first issued by post offices, different post offices accidentally assigned the same SSN to different people. In 1938 wallet manufacturer E. H. Ferree included sample Social Security cards in one of its products. More than 40,000 people purchasing the wallets from Woolworth stores thought the cards were real and used the sample card's number as their SSN [81].

A second defect of SSNs is that they are rarely checked. Millions of Social Security cards have been issued to applicants without verifying that the information provided by the applicants is correct. Many, if not most, organizations asking for SSNs do not actually require the applicant to show a card, making it easy for criminals to supply fake SSNs.

A third defect of SSNs is that they have no error-detecting capability, such as a check digit at the end of the number. A check digit enables computer systems to detect common data entry errors, such as getting one digit wrong or transposing two adjacent digits. If someone makes one of these mistakes, the data entry program can detect the error and ask the person to retype the number. In the case of SSNs, if a person accidentally types in the wrong number, there is a high likelihood that it is a valid SSN (albeit one assigned to a different person). Hence it is easy to contaminate databases with records containing incorrect SSNs [82]. Similarly, without check digits or another error detection mechanism, there is no simple way for a system to catch people who are simply making up a phony SSN.

## 6.9.2  Debate over a National ID Card

The events of September 11, 2001, resurrected the debate over the introduction of a national identification card for Americans.

Proponents of a national identification card point out numerous benefits to its adoption:

1. *A national identification card would be more reliable than existing forms of identification.*

   Social Security cards and driver's licenses are too easy to forge. A modern card could incorporate a photograph as well as a thumbprint or other biometric data.

2. *A national identification card could reduce illegal immigration.*

   Requiring employers to check a tamper-proof, forgery-proof national identification card would prevent illegal immigrants from working in the United States. If illegal immigrants couldn't get work, they wouldn't enter the United States in the first place.

3. *A national identification card would reduce crime.*

   Currently, it's too easy for criminals to mask their true identity. A tamper-proof national identification card would allow police to positively identify the people they apprehend.

4. *National identification cards do not undermine democracy.*

Many democratic countries already use national ID cards, including Belgium, France, Germany, Greece, Luxembourg, Portugal, and Spain.

Opponents of a national identification card suggest these harms may result from its adoption:

1. *A national identification card does not guarantee that the apparent identity of an individual is that person's actual identity.*

Driver's licenses and passports are supposed to be unique identifiers, but there are many criminals who produce fake driver's licenses and passports. Even a hard-to-forge identification card system may be compromised by insiders. For example, a ring of motor vehicle department employees in Virginia was caught selling fake driver's licenses [83].

2. *It is impossible to create a biometric-based national identification card that is 100 percent accurate.*

All known systems suffer from false positives (erroneously reporting that the person does not match the ID) and false negatives (failing to report that the person and ID do not match). Biometric-based systems may still be beaten by determined, technology-savvy criminals [83].

3. *There is no evidence that the institution of a national ID card would lead to a reduction in crime.*

In fact, the principal problem faced by police is not the inability to make positive identifications of suspects but the inability to obtain evidence needed for a successful prosecution.

4. *A national identification card makes it simpler for government agencies to perform data mining on the activities of its citizens.*

According to Peter Neumann and Lauren Weinstein, "The opportunities for over-zealous surveillance and serious privacy abuses are almost limitless, as are opportunities for masquerading, identity theft, and draconian social engineering on a grand scale. . . . The road to an Orwellian police state of universal tracking, but actually *reduced* security, could well be paved with hundreds of millions of such [national identification] cards" [83].

5. *While most people may feel they have nothing to fear from a national identification card system since they are law-abiding citizens, even law-abiding people are subject to fraud and the indiscretions and errors of others.*

Suppose a teacher, a doctor, or someone else in a position of authority creates a file about an individual that contains misleading or erroneous information. Files created by people in positions of authority can be difficult to remove [84].

In a society with decentralized record keeping, old school or medical records are less likely to be accessed so that the harm caused by inaccurate records is reduced. However, if all records are centralized around national identification numbers, files containing inaccurate or misleading information could haunt individuals for the rest of their lives.

## 6.9.3 The REAL ID Act

In May 2005, President George W. Bush signed the REAL ID Act, which is significantly changing driver's licenses in the United States. The motivation for passing the REAL ID Act was to make the driver's license a more reliable form of identification. Critics, however, say the act is creating a de facto national ID card in the United States.

The REAL ID Act requires that every state issue new driver's licenses. These licenses will be needed in order to open a bank account, fly on a commercial airplane, enter a federal building, or receive a government service, such as a Social Security check. The law makes it more difficult for impostors to get driver's licenses because it requires applicants to supply four different kinds of documentation, which is verified by state employees using federal databases. Because the new driver's license contains a biometric identifier, it is supposed to be a stronger credential than previous licenses [85].

Although each state is responsible for issuing new driver's licenses to its citizens, these licenses must meet federal standards. The license must include the person's full legal name, date of birth, gender, driver's license number, digital photograph, legal address, and signature. All data on the license must be in machine-readable form. The license must have physical security features designed to prevent tampering, counterfeiting, or duplication [86].

Supporters of the measure say making the driver's license a more reliable identifier will have numerous benefits. Law enforcement is easier when police can be more certain that a driver's license correctly identifies the individual carrying it. Society is better off when parents ducking child support and criminals on the run cannot change their identities by crossing a state border and getting a new driver's license under a different name [87].

Some critics fear having machine-readable information on driver's licenses will aggravate problems with identity theft. Each state is required to share all driver's license information with every other state and with the federal government. American Civil Liberties Union lawyer Timothy Sparapani said, "We will have all this information in one electronic format, in one linked file, and we're giving access to tens of thousands of state DMV employees and federal agents" [88].

Proponents of the bill say such fears are unjustified. They suggest that the personal information available on the new driver's license is relatively insignificant compared to all the other personal information circulating around cyberspace [87].

The Department of Homeland Security repeatedly pushed back the deadline for implementing the new driver's license because of significant opposition in the states. Legislatures in about half the states passed laws or resolutions opposing the REAL ID Act, and many states passed laws prohibiting the expenditure of state funds to implement the requirements of the REAL ID Act.

However, most states have now taken steps to come into compliance with the REAL ID Act to ensure their citizens will not face air travel restrictions when the Department of Homeland Security begins to require approved identification cards for commercial flights. Currently, between 70 and 80 percent of US drivers hold licenses from states that meet the standards of the REAL ID Act or have received an extension from the Department of Homeland Security [89].

# 6.10  Information Dissemination

We now consider the information dissemination category of Solove's taxonomy. After we survey three federal laws that restrict the dissemination of personal information that organizations have collected, we discuss the Freedom of Information Act, designed to promote open government by allowing news organizations and private citizens to access records maintained by federal agencies. We also explore how information collected by the government for one purpose—collecting tolls—is being used as evidence of people's whereabouts in both criminal and civil cases.

## 6.10.1  Family Education Rights and Privacy Act

The Family Education Rights and Privacy Act (FERPA) provides students 18 years of age and older the right to review their educational records and to request changes to records that contain erroneous information. Students also have the right to prevent information in these records from being released without their permission, except under certain circumstances. For students under the age of 18, these rights are held by their parents or guardians. FERPA applies to all educational institutions that receive funds from the US Department of Education.

## 6.10.2  Video Privacy Protection Act

In 1988 President Ronald Reagan nominated Judge Robert Bork to the US Supreme Court (Figure 6.5). Bork was a noted conservative, and his nomination was controversial. A Washington, DC, video store provided a list of Bork's video rental records to a reporter for the *Washington City Paper*, which published the list. While the intention of the paper was most likely to embarrass Bork, it also had the effect of prompting Congress to pass the Video Privacy Protection Act of 1988. According to this law, video providers (including providers of online videos) cannot disclose rental records without the written consent of the customer. In addition, organizations must destroy personally identifiable information about rentals within a year of the date when this information is no longer needed for the purpose for which it was collected.

## 6.10.3  Health Insurance Portability and Accountability Act

As part of the Health Insurance Portability and Accountability Act of 1996, Congress directed the Department of Health and Human Services (HHS) to come up with guidelines for protecting the privacy of patients. These guidelines went into effect in April 2003. They limit how doctors, hospitals, pharmacies, and insurance companies can use medical information collected from patients.

The regulations attempt to limit the exchange of information among health care providers to that information necessary to care for the patient. They forbid health care providers from releasing information to life insurance companies, banks, or other businesses without specific signed authorization from the person being treated. Health care providers must provide their patients with a notice describing how they use the information they gather. Patients have the right to see their medical records and to request corrections to errors they find in those records [90].

FIGURE 6.5 Judge Robert Bork, a nominee to the US Supreme Court, had to endure the publication of his video rental records by the *Washington City Paper*. (AP photo/Charles Tasnadi)

### 6.10.4 Freedom of Information Act

The Freedom of Information Act is a law designed to ensure that the public has access to US government records. Signed into law by President Johnson in 1966, it applies only to the executive branch of the federal government, not the legislative or judicial branches. The act carries a presumption that the government will release the requested records. If an agency does not disclose records, it must explain why the information is being withheld.

There are nine exemptions in the Freedom of Information Act, spelling out those situations in which the government may legitimately withhold information. For example, a document may be withheld if it has been classified as secret for national defense or foreign policy reasons. The government may withhold the release of documents containing trade secrets or confidential commercial or financial information. Another exemption deals with documents related to law enforcement investigations.

### 6.10.5 Tollbooth Records Used in Court

E-ZPass is an automatic toll collection system used on most toll roads, bridges, and tunnels between Illinois and Maine. Drivers who have installed an E-ZPass tag (an RFID transponder) in their vehicles are able to pass through tollbooths without stopping to pay an attendant. Instead, an E-ZPass reader installed in the automated toll lane gets information from the tags of the cars that pass through and deducts the appropriate toll from each driver's account.

The New York State Department of Transportation (NYSDOT) has installed tag readers at locations other than tollbooths in order to track the progress of individual vehicles. In this way the system can provide helpful information to other drivers by displaying on electronic signs above the turnpike the estimated time to reach popular destinations. According to the NYSDOT, the system encrypts information from individual tags, deletes the information as soon as the vehicle passes the last reader, and never makes information about individual cars available to the department [91].

However, states do maintain records of when cars pass through tollbooths, and most of the states in the E-ZPass network provide information in response to court orders in criminal and civil cases. A well-known example is the case of Melanie McGuire, a New Jersey nurse suspected of murdering her husband and throwing his dismembered corpse into Chesapeake Bay. To help prove their case against McGuire, prosecutors used E-ZPass records to reconstruct her movements. E-ZPass records are also playing a role in divorce cases by providing evidence of infidelity. Pennsylvania divorce lawyer Lynne Gold-Bikin explained how E-ZPass helped her show that a client's husband had been unfaithful: "He claimed he was in a business meeting in Pennsylvania. And I had records to show he went to New Jersey that night" [92].

## 6.11  Invasion

Early in Chapter 5 we described privacy as a "zone of inaccessibility." People have information privacy to the extent that they have some control over who has access to their personal information. In quite a few modern situations, people may have very little control; they must cede access to their personal information if they wish to use the service provided. If the loss of control is accompanied by a loss of tranquility or interferes with someone's freedom of decision making, that is a privacy invasion, according to Solove. We begin this section by giving two examples of government actions to prevent invasion and then move on to survey two government actions that can be seen as invasive.

### 6.11.1  Telemarketing

After being sworn in as chairman of the Federal Trade Commission (FTC) in 2001, Timothy Muris looked for an action that the FTC could take to protect the privacy of Americans. It did not take long for the FTC to focus on telemarketing. A large segment of the American population views dinnertime phone calls from telemarketers as an annoying invasion of privacy. In fact, Harris Interactive concluded that telemarketing is the reason why the number of Americans who feel it is "extremely important" not to be disturbed at home rose from 49 percent in 1994 to 62 percent in 2003 [93]. Responding to this desire for greater privacy, the FTC created the National Do Not Call Registry (www.donotcall.gov), a free service that allows people who do not wish to receive telemarketing calls to register their phone numbers. The public reacted enthusiastically to the availability of the Do Not Call Registry by registering more than 50 million phone numbers before it even took effect in October 2003 [94, 95].

The Do Not Call Registry has not eliminated 100 percent of unwanted solicitations. The regulations exempt political organizations, charities, and organizations conducting telephone surveys. Even if your phone number has been registered, you may still receive phone calls from companies with which you have done business in the past 18 months. Still, the registry is expected to keep most telemarketers from calling people who do not wish to be solicited. The creation of the registry is a good example of how privacy is seen as a prudential right: the benefit of shielding people from telemarketers is judged to be greater than the harm caused by putting limits on telephone advertising.

## 6.11.2 Loud Television Commercials

Since the 1960s, television watchers have complained to the Federal Communications Commission (FCC) about loud commercials. The Commercial Advertisement Loudness Mitigation Act (CALM Act), signed into law by President Barack Obama in December 2010, required the Federal Communications Commission to ensure that television commercials are played at the same volume as the programs they are interrupting. The sponsor of the bill, Representative Anna Eshoo of California, said, "Consumers have been asking for a solution to this problem for decades, and today they finally have it. . . . It's a simple fix to a huge nuisance" [96].

## 6.11.3 Requiring Identification for Pseudoephedrine Purchases

In an effort to curb the illegal production of methamphetamine ("meth"), federal and state governments have passed laws limiting access to products containing pseudoephedrine, which is used in the manufacture of methamphetamine. The Combat Methamphetamine Epidemic Act limits the quantity of pseudoephedrine that an individual can purchase in a month. Whether the laws have been effective is a matter of debate. In most states, original Sudafed is still sold behind the counter to adults, but they must show an identification card and fill out a sales log with their name, address, and signature. Two states, Oregon and Mississippi, require a prescription to acquire a product containing pseudoephedrine. In several well-publicized cases, grandparents purchasing cold medicine for members of their families have been arrested by police for exceeding limits set on pseudoephedrine purches [97].

## 6.11.4 Advanced Imaging Technology Scanners

In an effort to provide enhanced passenger security at airports, the Transportation Security Administration began deploying advanced imaging technology (AIT) scanners in 2007. Some AIT scanners use backscatter X-rays to produce a detailed image of the passenger's body, and other scanners use millimeter waves. The TSA began testing AIT systems at Phoenix's Sky Harbor International Airport in 2007 [98]. When the first AIT system was deployed, passengers who failed the primary security screening could choose between the X-ray scan and a traditional pat-down search. In June 2011, the Transportation Security Administration announced that it had already deployed 500 AIT units and would deploy an additional 500 units, enabling it to use this technology to screen 60 percent of all airline passengers in the United States [99]. Even as it was busily deploying systems, the TSA was battling critics.

Some people were offended at the images produced by AIT scanners, which reveal "all anatomical features" (Figure 6.6) [100]. Lawyers for the American Civil Liberties

**FIGURE 6.6** When the first advanced imaging technology scanners were deployed in American airports, they revealed anatomical features in great detail. (© Paul Ellis/AFP/Getty Images/Newscom)

Union called the AIT scan a "virtual strip-search" [101]. In July 2010, the Electronic Privacy Information Center filed a lawsuit to suspend the deployment of AIT systems, pending further review. EPIC called the program "unlawful, invasive, and ineffective," arguing that it violated the Privacy Act, the Religious Freedom Restoration Act, and the Fourth Amendment to the US Constitution [102].

In February 2011, the Transportation Security Administration announced that it was about to begin testing new software on its advanced imaging technology machines that would eliminate passenger-specific images. TSA Administrator John Pistole said that the new system "auto-detects potential threat items and indicates their location on a generic outline of a person" [103]. The tests were successful, and in January 2013 the TSA announced that all body scanners producing passenger-specific images would be removed from airport checkpoints by June 2013 [104].

## Summary

It's only natural that people want government to leave them alone, but they also expect government to keep them safe and secure through effective policing and a strong national defense. Frequently, the constitutional guarantees in the Bill of Rights come into conflict with the desires of law enforcement agencies to gather information that can help them apprehend criminals. Through legislation, administrative policies, and court decisions, the three branches of American government have been engaged in an attempt to find the right balance between competing concerns.

In this chapter we looked at the role that federal, state, and local governments have played in protecting and eroding the information privacy of individual citizens. We organized our presentation using the taxonomy of privacy proposed by Daniel Solove, which divides the field into four categories: information collection, information processing, information dissemination, and invasion. We reviewed legislation and administrative policies that protect the information privacy of individuals by restricting how organizations can collect, process, and disseminate information as well as limit the extent to which they can intrude into people's daily lives. We also looked at ways in which governments have promoted public safety and security by collecting, processing, and disseminating personal information and intruding into people's lives.

We surveyed many governmental activities related to information collection. The federal government maintains extensive databases containing a vast amount of information about individual Americans, and from time to time information in these databases has been misused. The government also collects information through overt and covert surveillance.

After the terrorist attacks of September 11, 2001, concerns about individual privacy took a backseat to concerns about national security, and significant changes occurred in the government's activities related to information collection, information processing, and invasion. The Patriot Act amended many laws and enhanced the ability of law enforcement agencies to gather information about suspected terrorists and criminals. The National Security Agency illegally acquired records of domestic phone calls from telecommunications companies and performed data mining in an attempt to find calling patterns indicating the presence of terrorist networks. The Transportation Security Administration installed invasive advanced imaging technology scanners at airport security checkpoints.

The Social Security number is an important identifier in the United States, but it has many flaws. The US Congress passed the REAL ID Act that created a new federal standard for driver's licenses. Once every state comes into compliance, the driver's license will probably become the most trusted form of identification in the United States, a de facto national identification card.

# Further Reading and Viewing

James Bamford. "The Black Box." *Wired*, April 2012.

⊙ Dan Boylan. "Is the Notion of Privacy Outdated?" *Insights on PBS Hawaii*, July 11, 2013. 56:49. video.pbs.org.

⊙ Patrick A. Hafner. "Naked Citizens." Journeyman Pictures, May 2013. 32:41. topdocumentary films.com/naked-citizens.

George Orwell. *1984*. Knopf, New York, NY, 1992.

Daniel J. Solove. "Why Privacy Matters Even If You Have 'Nothing to Hide.'" *Chronicle of Higher Education*, May 15, 2011.

⊙ Hari Sreenivasan. "Rise of Domestic Drones Draws Questions about Privacy." *PBS News-Hour*, April 18, 2013. 7:30. video.pbs.org.

⊙ Margaret Warner. "Surveillance Court Can't Stop NSA from Violating Privacy." *PBS News-Hour*, August 16, 2013. 6:33. video.pbs.org.

# Review Questions

1. Determine the relationship between the categories of Daniel Solove's taxonomy of privacy and the following definitions of privacy proposed by other authors:
   - Privacy is the right to be left alone. (Warren and Brandeis)
   - Privacy is control over who knows what about us. (Rachels)
   - Privacy is the appropriate flow of personal information. (Nissenbaum)

2. How did the position of the US Supreme Court toward wiretapping evolve over time? Cite the key cases.

3. Give three examples of legislation passed by the US Congress designed to protect the privacy of residents of the United States.

4. Give three examples of US government agencies successfully achieving their ends using data legally obtained from residents of the United States.

5. Give three examples of US government agencies illegally collecting or disseminating information about residents of the United States in order to achieve their ends.

6. What are telephony metadata? Briefly summarize the history of the controversy surrounding the collection of telephony metadata by the National Security Agency after 9/11.

7. Describe similarities and differences between these covert surveillance programs of the US government: Operation Shamrock, Carnivore, PRISM, NSA wiretapping after 9/11, NSA collection of telephony metadata after 9/11.

8. What are the implications of the Stored Communications Act for all those who let an Internet service provider handle their email?

9. Why has the expanded use of National Security Letters raised privacy concerns?

10. Briefly summarize in your own words the five tenets of the Code of Fair Information Practices.

11. Robert Bellair has said, "The Privacy Act, it turns out, is no protection at all. You can drive a truck through the Privacy Act" [70, p. 212]. Why do Bellair and other privacy advocates feel the Privacy Act of 1974 is a weak piece of legislation?

12. What actions has the US Congress taken to help ensure people aren't disadvantaged by poor credit ratings because of erroneous or obsolete information?

13. Give three examples of how information collected by a government for one purpose has been used for an entirely different purpose.

14. What are the problems with using the Social Security number as an identification number?

15. Give two arguments in favor of a national identification card for the United States. Give two arguments against creating a national identification card.

16. For each category in Daniel Solove's taxonomy of privacy, give one example of a law passed by the US Congress protecting individual privacy of that type.

# Discussion Questions

17. Here is a summary of an argument presented by Canadian author Robert Sawyer in a promotion for one of his science fiction novels. (The argument includes a disclaimer that it is not necessarily Sawyer's personal view.)

Who needs privacy? With no privacy there would be far less crime and much less terrorism, and everyone would be safer. The only reason we desire privacy is that society has passed "silly laws" that in the past have made people feel ashamed for being nude or engaging in "natural human activities." Perhaps Victorians had a reason for hiding certain activities, but "who really cares today if someone is gay, smokes pot, or watches porno films?... The message of history, most spectacularly driven home on September 11, 2001, is that preserving society as a whole is much more important than preserving an illusory personal freedom." It's unrealistic to pretend we can still have privacy in the modern world. Instead, we should demand the repeal of those obsolete laws trying to prohibit harmless conduct [105].

Do you agree with this argument? Why or why not?

18. The US Department of Homeland Security is developing the Biometric Optical Surveillance System (BOSS). The purpose of the system, which consists of video cameras, computers, and a database of photographs, is to scan crowds and identify persons of interest with an accuracy of 80 to 90 percent. The BOSS research began as a way of helping American soldiers in Afghanistan and Iraq identify potential suicide bombers, but in 2010 the project was taken over by the Department of Homeland Security, which plans to make the system available to police departments once it is reliable. In 2013 the system was tested at a sports arena in Kennewick, Washington, and found not yet ready for use. Research and development continues [106].

Do you support the development and implementation of BOSS as a crowd surveillance tool for police departments?

19. Florida, Missouri, Ohio, and Oklahoma have passed laws that require lifetime monitoring of some convicted sex offenders after they have been released from prison. The offenders must wear electronic ankle bracelets and stay close to small GPS transmitters, which can be carried on a belt or in a purse. Computers monitor the GPS signals and alert law enforcement officials if the offenders venture too close to a school or other off-limits area. Police interested in the whereabouts of a monitored person can see his location, traveling direction, and speed plotted on a map [107].

Do these laws represent an unacceptable weakening of personal privacy, or are they sensible public safety measures? Should they be repealed? Should people convicted of other crimes also be monitored for life? Would there be less crime if everyone in society were monitored?

20. Think about what you do when you get up in the morning. How would you act differently if you knew you were being watched? Would you feel uncomfortable? Do you think you would get used to being watched?

21. Discuss the following responses to the revelation that telecommunications companies provided domestic phone call records to the National Security Agency [108].

    President George Bush: "Al-Qaeda is our enemy, and we want to know their plans."

    Senator Patrick Leahy of Vermont: "Are you telling me tens of millions of Americans are involved with al-Qaeda?"

    Senator Jon Kyl of Arizona: "We are in a war, and we have got to collect intelligence on the enemy."

    Senator Chuck Grassley of Iowa: "Why are the telephone companies not protecting their customers? They have a social responsibility to people who do business with them to protect our privacy as long as there isn't some suspicion that we're a terrorist or a criminal or something."

22. When asked about Google releasing personal information to law enforcement agencies, Google's CEO Eric Schmidt told CNBC: "If you have something that you don't want anyone to know, maybe you shouldn't be doing it in the first place" [53]. Discuss Mr. Schmidt's perspective.

23. Was the US government's $2 million settlement with Brandon Mayfield reasonable and just?

24. In order to combat the counterfeiting of currency, the US Secret Service convinced several color laser printer manufacturers to add a secret code to every printed page. The code is invisible to the human eye but can be seen under a microscope. When decrypted, it reveals the serial number of the printer and the time and date the page was printed [109].

    By agreeing to secretly insert the codes, did the printer manufacturers violate the privacy rights of their customers?

25. What special responsibilities do computer professionals have with respect to understanding and protecting the privacy rights of their fellow citizens?

## In-Class Exercises

26. The Code of Fair Information Practices applies only to government databases. Divide the class into two groups to debate the advantages and disadvantages of extending the Code of Fair Information Practices to private databases managed by corporations.

27. A database containing the DNA information of every citizen of a country could be a valuable resource to medical researchers. It could also help police solve crimes. Divide the class into two groups (pro and con) to debate the following proposition: It would be in the best interests of society if the government constructed a DNA database of every resident and made the database available to medical researchers and law enforcement agencies.

28. Divide the class into two groups (pro and con) to debate the proposition that every adult resident of the United States ought to carry a national identification card.

29. Debate the following proposition: By creating the Threat and Local Observation Notices (TALON) database, which enabled citizens to report on each other's activities, the US government effectively reduced freedom of speech.

# References

[1]     runnerazzi. "Drone Knocked Down at Staples Center during LA Kings Stanley Cup Celebration" (video). June 14, 2014. 1:19. www.youtube.com/watch?feature=player_embedded&v=KR39DErszRE.

[2]     Jamie Prime. "Privacy vs. Openness." *Quill* 82(8), October 1994.

[3]     Marisol Bello. "Questions Arise on Monitoring of Sex Offenders." *USA Today*, September 1, 2009. www.usatoday.com.

[4]     "Majority of Americans Support Increased Surveillance, Poll Shows." *Wall Street Journal*, August 17, 2006.

[5]     Daniel J. Solove. *Understanding Privacy*. Harvard University Press, Cambridge, MA, 2008.

[6]     "GINA: The Genetic Information Nondiscrimination Act of 2008: Information for Researchers and Health Care Professionals." Department of Health and Human Services, USA, April 6, 2009. www.genome.gov.

[7]     Stephanie L. Hitt. "NCIC 2000." *FBI Law Enforcement Bulletin* 69(7), July 2000.

[8]     Federal Bureau of Investigation. National Crime Information Center (Web page). Accessed August 6, 2015. www.fbi.gov/about-us/cjis/ncic.

[9]     Dan Eggen. "Justice Dept. Database Stirs Privacy Fears." *Washington Post*, December 26, 2006.

[10]    John T. Eberth. "Nation's First Surveillance Cameras Were Installed in Olean." *Olean Times Herald*, October 5, 2008. www.oleantimesherald.com.

[11]    James Vlahos. "Surveillance Society: New High-Tech Cameras Are Watching You." *Popular Mechanics*, October 1, 2009.

[12]    Chris Dolmetsch. "Cameras to Catch Terrorists Triple in New York with Bomb Plots." Bloomberg, November 13, 2010. www.bloomberg.com.

[13]    Jamie Roth. "Bloomberg in London to Study Security System." *WABC Local News*, May 11, 2010. abclocal.go.com/wabc/.

[14]    Jennifer Lee. "Study Questions Whether Cameras Cut Crime." *New York Times*, March 3, 2009.

[15]    M. Angela Sasse. "Privacy and Security: Not Seeing the Crime for the Cameras?" *Communications of the ACM*, pp. 22–25, February 2010.

[16]    James R. Healey, Greg Toppo, and Fred Meier. "You Can't Hide from Cops with License-Plate Scanners." *USA Today*, July 18, 2013. www.usatoday.com.

[17]    Adam Goldman and Matt Apuzzo. "With Cameras, Informants, NYPD Eyed Mosques." Associated Press, February 23, 2012. www.ap.org.

[18]    "Automated License Plate Readers—State Statutes Regulating Their Use." National Conference of State Legislatures, February 2, 2015. www.ncsl.org.

[19]    Federal Aviation Administration. "Fact Sheet—Unmanned Aircraft Systems (UAS)" (press release). February 19, 2013. www.faa.gov.

[20]    Maggie Clark. "States Seek Legal Limits on Domestic Drones." *Stateline*, February 22, 2013. www.pewstates.org.

[21]    Monmouth University. "US Supports Some Domestic Drone Use" (press release). June 12, 2012.

[22]    Maggie Clark. "Boston Bombings Show Future Use for Police Drones." *Stateline*, May 2, 2013. www.pewstates.org.

[23]  Whitfield Diffie and Susan Landau. *Privacy on the Line: The Politics of Wiretapping and Encryption*. MIT Press, Cambridge, MA, 1998.

[24]  Priscilla M. Regan. *Legislating Privacy*. University of North Carolina Press, Chapel Hill, NC, 1995.

[25]  Justice Brandeis, dissenting. Supreme Court of the United States. Olmstead v. United States, 277 US 438 (1928).

[26]  Supreme Court of the United States. Katz v. United States, 389 US 347 (1967).

[27]  James Bamford. *The Puzzle Palace: A Report on America's Most Secret Agency*. Penguin Books, New York, NY, 1983.

[28]  Heinz Tschabitscher. "How Carnivore Email Surveillance Worked." About.com. Accessed October 15, 2013. email.about.com.

[29]  Holly E. Ventura, J. Mitchell Miller, and Mathieu Deflem. "Governmentality and the War on Terror: FBI Project Carnivore and the Diffusion of Disciplinary Power." *Critical Criminology* 13(1): 55–70, January 2005.

[30]  US District Court, Central District of California, Western Division. "In the Matter of the Application of the United States of America for an Order Authorizing the Installation of a Pen Register and Trap and Trace Device." Criminal No. 99-2713M, February 4, 2000.

[31]  Kevin Poulsen. "FBI Retires Its Carnivore." *SecurityFocus*, January 14, 2005. www.securityfocus.com.

[32]  James Risen and Eric Lichtblau. "Bush Lets US Spy on Callers without Courts." *New York Times*, December 16, 2005.

[33]  Lisa Myers, Douglas Pasternak, Rich Gardella, and the NBC Investigative Unit. "Is the Pentagon Spying on Americans?" MSNBC.com, December 14, 2005.

[34]  Samantha Henig. "Pentagon Surveillance of Student Groups Extended to Scrutinizing E-mail." *Chronicle of Higher Education*, July 21, 2006.

[35]  "No Real Threat: The Pentagon's Secret Database on Peaceful Protest." American Civil Liberties Union, January 17, 2007. www.aclu.org.

[36]  Siobhan Gorman. "Intelligence Policies Shift: Pentagon Spy Chief Rolling Back Some of Rumsfeld's Strategies." *Baltimore Sun*, May 26, 2007.

[37]  Nate Anderson. "US to Shutter DoD TALON Database as It Works on Replacement." Ars Technica (Web site), August 21, 2007. www.arstechnica.com.

[38]  Glenn Greenwald and Ewen MacAskill. "NSA Prism Program Taps In to User Data of Apple, Google and Others." *Guardian*, June 6, 2013.

[39]  Orin S. Kerr. "The Case for the Third-Party Doctrine." *Michigan Law Review*, Volume 107, pp. 561–601, February 2009.

[40]  David Kravets. "Yahoo, Feds Battle over E-mail Privacy." Threat Level: Privacy, Crime and Security Online, *Wired*, April 14, 2010. www.wired.com.

[41]  Ryan Singel. "Google, Microsoft Push Feds to Fix Privacy Laws." Threat Level: Privacy, Crime and Security Online, *Wired*, March 30, 2010. www.wired.com.

[42]  Nancy Gohring. "FCC Inflates CALEA." *Telephony* 237(10), September 6, 1999.

[43]  Charlotte Twight. "Conning Congress." *Independent Review* 6(2), Fall 2001.

[44]  Kirk Laughlin. "A Wounded CALEA Is Shuttled Back to the FCC." *America's Network* 104(15), October 1, 2000.

[45]  "FCC Requires Certain Broadband and VoIP Providers to Accommodate Wiretaps." Federal Communications Commission, August 5, 2005. www.fcc.gov.

[46]  "USA PATRIOT Act: Major Provisions of the 2001 Antiterrorism Law." *Congressional Digest* 82(4), April 2003.

[47]  Pete Yost. "FBI Access to E-mail, Web Data Raises Privacy Fear." Associated Press, July 30, 2010. seattletimes.nwsource.com.

[48]  American Civil Liberties Union. "With Help of ACLU, Connecticut Library Group Successfully Keeps Patron Records Private" (press release). June 26, 2006. www.aclu .org.

[49]  "PATRIOT Act Fears Are Stifling Free Speech, ACLU Says in Challenge to Law." American Civil Liberties Union, New York, NY, November 11, 2003. www.aclu.org.

[50]  American Library Association. "Resolution on the USA PATRIOT Act and Related Measures That Infringe on the Rights of Library Users." 2003 ALA Midwinter Meeting, 2002–2003 CD #20.1, January 29, 2003. www.ala.org.

[51]  Bill of Rights Defense Committee (Web site). Accessed September 2, 2011. www.bordc .org.

[52]  Bob Garfield. "Subpoenas and Online Service Providers." *On the Media*, January 21, 2011. www.onthemedia.org.

[53]  Cade Metz. "Google Chief: Only Miscreants Worry about Net Privacy." *Register*, December 7, 2009. www.theregister.co.uk.

[54]  Tom Ridge. "Using the PATRIOT Act to Fight Terrorism." *Congressional Digest*, pp. 266–268, November 2004.

[55]  Ben Jacklet and Todd Murphy. "Now Free, Attorney Brandon Mayfield Turns Furious." *Washington Report on Middle East Affairs* 23(6), July/August 2004.

[56]  Dan Eggen. "Flawed FBI Probe of Bombing Used a Search Warrant." *Washington Post*, April 7, 2005.

[57]  Eric Lichtblau. "U.S. Will Pay $2 Million to Lawyer Wrongly Jailed." *New York Times*, November 30, 2006. www.localnewsdaily.com.

[58]  Andrew Murr, Michael Isikoff, Eric Pape, and Mike Elkin. "The Wrong Man." *Newsweek* 143(23), June 7, 2004.

[59]  Ron Wyden. "Wyden Warns of Potential Public Backlash from Allowing Secret Law." YouTube(video), uploaded May 27, 2011. youtube.com/watch?v=vMAX_Frj8xM.

[60]  Glenn Greenwald. "NSA Collecting Phone Records of Millions of Verizon Customers Daily." *Guardian*, June 5, 2013.

[61]  "White House Defends NSA Order to Verizon to Reveal Call Data." UPI, June 6, 2013. www.upi.com.

[62]  Charlie Savage and Edward Wyatt. "Verizon Case Offers Glimpse of Vast N.S.A. Surveillance." *New York Times*, June 6, 2013.

[63]  Dan Roberts and Spencer Ackerman. "Anger Swells after NSA Phone Records Court Order Revelations." *Guardian*, June 6, 2013.

[64]  Charlie Savage and Jonathan Weisman. "N.S.A. Collection of Bulk Call Data Is Ruled Illegal." *New York Times*, May 7, 2015. www.nytimes.com.

[65]  Jennifer Steinhauer and Jonathan Weisman. "U.S. Surveillance in Place Since 9/11 Is Sharply Limited." *New York Times*, June 2, 2015. www.nytimes.com.

[66]  Carl Kaysen. "Data Banks and Dossiers." *Public Interest*, pp. 52–60, Spring 1967.

[67]  G. Russell Pipe. "Privacy: Establishing Restrictions on Government Inquiry." *American University Law Review*, Vol. 18, pp. 516–551, 1969.

[68]  US Department of Health, Education, and Welfare. "Code of Fair Information Practices." Secretary's Advisory Committee of Automated Personal Data Systems, Records, Computers, and the Rights of Citizens, 1973.

[69]  Robert Gellman. "Fair Information Practices: A Basic History." July 15, 2011. bobgellman.com.

[70]  William Petrocelli. *Low Profile: How to Avoid the Privacy Invaders*. McGraw-Hill, New York, NY, 1981.

[71]  "Fact Sheet 24: Protecting Financial Privacy." Privacy Rights Clearinghouse, July 14, 2005. www.privacyrights.org.

[72]  Richard Peŕez-Peña. "An Early Warning System for Diseases in New York." *NYTimes.com*, April 4, 2003.

[73]  Leslie Cauley. "NSA Has Massive Database of Americans' Phone Calls." *USA Today*, May 11, 2006.

[74]  Wayne Rash. "Federal Court Finds NSA Wiretaps Unconstitutional." *eWeek.com*, August 18, 2006. www.eweek.com.

[75]  Zach Friend. "Predictive Policing: Using Technology to Reduce Crime." *FBI Law Enforcement Bulletin*, April 2013.

[76]  Kate Crawford and Jason Schultz. "Big Data and Due Process: Toward a Framework to Redress Predictive Privacy Harms." *Boston College Law Review*, Vol. 55, No. 1, January 29, 2014. lawdigitalcommons.bc.edu.

[77]  Kashmir Hill. "How Target Figured Out a Teen Girl Was Pregnant Before Her Father Did." *Forbes*, February 16, 2012. www.forbes.com.

[78]  Matthew Barakat. "Terrorist Database Continues to Grow at Rapid Rate." Big Story (Web site), July 18, 2014. bigstory.ap.org.

[79]  Jeremy Scahill and Ryan Devereaux. "The Secret Government Rulebook for Labeling You a Terrorist." *Intercept*, July 23, 2014. firstlook.org.

[80]  "A Brief History of Social Security." Social Security Administration, USA, August 2000.

[81]  "Social Security Cards Issued by Woolworth." Social Security Administration, USA. Accessed October 15, 2013. www.ssa.gov/history/ssn/misused.html.

[82]  "Extent of Social Security Number Discrepancies." Office of Inspector General, Department of Health and Human Services, USA. OAI-06-89-01120, January 1990.

[83]  Peter G. Neumann and Lauren Weinstein. "Risks of National Identity Cards." *Communications of the ACM*, p. 176, December 2001.

[84]  Richard Turner. Letter to the editor. *Times*, London, September 7, 2001.

[85]  Declan McCullagh. "FAQ: How Real ID Will Affect You." *New York Times*, May 6, 2005.

[86]  "REAL ID Act of 2005 Driver's License Title Summary." Real Nightmare.org (Web site). Accessed October 15, 2013. www.realnightmare.org/images/File/NCSL_Summary_of_Real_ID.pdf.

[87]  Dennis Bailey. *The Open Society Paradox: Why the 21st Century Calls for More Openness—Not Less*. Potomac Books, Washington, DC, 2004, p. 42.

[88]  Joseph Menn. "Federal ID Act May Be Flawed." *Los Angeles Times*, May 31, 2005.

[89]  "REAL ID Enforcement in Brief." Department of Homeland Security, July 27, 2015. www.dhs.gov.

[90]   "Protecting the Privacy of Patients' Health Information." Department of Health and Human Services, USA, April 14, 2003. www.hhs.gov/news.

[91]   New York State Department of Transportation. "NYSDOT Announces Travel Time Signs in Staten Island" (press release). July 10, 2007. www.nysdot.gov.

[92]   Chris Newmarker. "E-ZPass Records Out Cheaters in Divorce Court." Associated Press, August 10, 2007. www.msnbc.com.

[93]   Humphrey Taylor. "Most People Are 'Privacy Pragmatists' Who, While Concerned about Privacy, Will Sometimes Trade It Off for Other Benefits." HarrisInteractive, Harris Poll #17, March 19, 2003.

[94]   James Toedtman. "Court Unblocks Do Not Call Registry in Latest Ruling." *Sun-Sentinel*, Fort Lauderdale, FL, October 8, 2003.

[95]   Heather Fleming Phillips. "Consumers Can Thank Do-Not-Underestimate FTC Chairman for Do-Not-Call Peace." *San Jose Mercury News*, January 2, 2004.

[96]   Chris Foresman. "CALM Act Passed, Will Quiet Loud TV Commercials within a Year." Ars Technica (Web site), December 2, 2010. www.arstechnica.com.

[97]   Radley Balko. "As It Turns Out, Meth Laws Have Unintended Consequences." *Washington Post*, October 14, 2014. www.washingtonpost.com.

[98]   Ginger D. Richardson. "Revealing X-Ray Machine Set to Scan Sky Harbor Flyers." *Arizona Republic*, February 23, 2007. www.azcentral.com/arizonarepublic.

[99]   Statement of John S. Pistole, Administrator, Transportation Security Administration, before the US House of Representatives. Committee on Homeland Security, Subcommittee on Transportation Security, June 2, 2011. www.tsa.gov.

[100]  Melissa Cheung. "New Airport X-Ray Too Revealing?" *CBS News*, February 11, 2009. www.cbsnews.com.

[101]  Paul Giblin and Eric Lipton. "New Airport X-Rays Scan Bodies, Not Just Bags." *New York Times*, February 24, 2007.

[102]  "Whole Body Imaging Technology and Body Scanners ('Backscatter' X-Ray and Millimeter Wave Screening)." Electronic Privacy Information Center (Web site). Accessed July 9, 2011. epic.org/privacy/airtravel/backscatter/.

[103]  Transportation Security Administration. "TSA Begins Testing New Advanced Imaging Technology Software" (press release). February 1, 2011.

[104]  Mike M. Ahlers. "TSA Removing 'Virtual Strip Search' Body Scanners." CNN, January 18, 2013. www.cnn.com.

[105]  Robert J. Sawyer. "Privacy: Who Needs It?: We're Better Off without It, Argues Canada's Leading Sci-Fi Writer." *Maclean's* (Toronto Edition), p. 44, October 7, 2002.

[106]  Charlie Savage. "Facial Scanning Is Making Gains in Surveillance." *New York Times*, August 21, 2013. www.nytimes.com.

[107]  David A. Lieb. "States Move on Sex Offender GPS Tracking." Associated Press, July 30, 2005.

[108]  Susan Page. "NSA Secret Database Report Triggers Fierce Debate in Washington." *USA Today*, May 11, 2006.

[109]  John P. Mello Jr. "Codes Make Printers Stool Pigeons." *E-Commerce Times*, October 18, 2005. www.ecommercetimes.com.

# Jerry Berman

Jerry Berman is the founder and chairman of the board of directors for the Center for Democracy and Technology (CDT). CDT is a Washington, DC–based Internet public policy organization founded in December 1994. CDT plays a leading role in free speech, privacy, Internet governance, and architecture issues affecting democracy and civil liberties on the global Internet. Mr. Berman has written widely on Internet and civil liberties issues and often appears in print and television media. He has testified before the US Congress on Internet policy and civil liberties issues.

Prior to founding the Center for Democracy and Technology, Mr. Berman was director of the Electronic Frontier Foundation. From 1978 to 1988, Mr. Berman was chief legislative counsel at the ACLU and founder and director of ACLU Projects on Privacy and Information Technology. Mr. Berman received his BA, MA, and LLB from the University of California, Berkeley.

---

### How did you get involved in Internet law?

When I worked on civil liberties and privacy at the ACLU in the early 1980s, the prevailing view was computer databases and the rise of the computer state posed a major threat to privacy. This is true. But at the same time there was the beginning of the use of the computer as a communications device, and the start of data networks for communications purposes—the beginnings of the Internet. While recognizing the threat to privacy, I saw that the Internet had the potential to facilitate and broaden First Amendment speech.

In many ways my colleagues and I have been involved in trying to frame the law and to define privacy, free speech, and how the Internet is governed. We're trying to sort out the "constitution" for this new social space. By analogy, the Internet business community wants to make sure there's a "commerce clause" to encourage robust commercial transactions over the Internet. We agree with that but also see the need for a "bill of rights" to protect speech, privacy, and other democratic values. We have had some successes, but the work is very much in progress.

### The Internet is a more powerful communication medium than newspapers or television, because it allows everyone with an Internet connection to express their views. How can the Internet be anything but democratic?

Like any other technology, the Internet can be regulated. Other countries are exercising considerable control over what ISPs can connect to and what can reside on a server. Even a well-intentioned Congress attempting to protect intellectual property to reduce theft of music and movies could mandate technological changes to computers that make it difficult to use the computer in an open, interconnected way. So one way the Internet can be less than democratic is from bad laws and bad policy.

Another threat is from bad actors provoking bad law. Hackers, people stealing music, using spyware, and engaging in online fraud can provoke policy responses that may have the unintended consequence of undermining the openness of the Internet. We're seeing this now in legitimate efforts to combat spam, spyware, and piracy. We need appropriate laws that combat these harms without harming the openness of the Net. Finding the right solutions is what CDT is about.

One of the great challenges is that, given the freedom to connect and communicate that everyone has on the Internet, there is a corollary concept of responsibility. Unless there are shared ethics that respect property, privacy, pluralism, diversity, and the rule of law, the Internet will never realize its potential.

### Responding to public pressure, the US Congress passed the Communications Decency Act to restrict access of children to sexually explicit materials on the Web. Why did you organize a legal challenge to the CDA?

In enacting the CDA over our objections, Congress attempted to treat the Internet the same way as other broadcast mass media (TV, radio). The first filed challenge to the CDA, *ACLU v. Reno*, was designed to persuade the courts that if you restrict speech for children, you also necessarily restrict adults' free speech rights, because the definition of indecency covers constitutionally protected speech for adults. If ISPs had to block all indecent content for children, that content would not reach adults who are entitled to it, because adults and children are all on the same Internet network.

We filed a second challenge to the CDA, and eventually the ACLU suit and the CDT suit were joined and argued together. CDT brought together a broad coalition of Internet technology companies, news organizations, and librarians to educate the courts that the Internet was architecturally different from broadcast media. Traditional media is a one-to-many communication and the Internet is a many-to-many communication, much like print. It was also critical to explain that the Internet is a global medium: it isn't effective to censor speech in the United States if it's also available on the Internet from outside the United States. It is impossible for ISPs to prevent content flowing from sources they do not control, and any ISP censorship would violate constitutional rights. The architecture of the Internet leads to different analysis and different policy solutions to both protect free speech and protect children from inappropriate content. The lawyers for our coalition argued the case in the Supreme Court on behalf of all the plaintiffs and made the case for user control and user empowerment. The only effective way to deal with unwanted content is for parents and other users (rather than the government) to voluntarily employ available filtering tools and parental controls offered by ISPs and other vendors.

In issues of constitutionally protected speech, the courts seek to determine if Congress has chosen the least restrictive means for achieving their public purpose. We were able to show that blocking content at the provider end is neither effective nor the least restrictive means for protecting children from inappropriate content. Voluntary filtering is a less restrictive means because it allows users to decide what comes into their homes and, given the global nature of the Internet, gives them the most effective means to do that.

### Should an ordinary American citizen's Web site enjoy the same constitutional protections as the New York Times?

On the Internet everyone can be publishers. And if they're holding themselves out as publishers, they have the same credentials as the *New York Times*, since no one's handing out credentials on the Internet. The Supreme Court heard the Communications Decency Act (CDA) challenge and ruled that the Internet communicator enjoys the maximum protection afforded under the First Amendment. Like the print media, the Internet is not subject to equal time, to the fairness doctrine, or various spectrum allocations. The whole technology of the Internet and the ability of anyone to be a publisher suggests the Internet publisher should, if anything, enjoy greater protection than the *New York Times*. For example, if a newspaper libels someone with false charges, it may require a lawsuit to restore a reputation. On the Internet anyone can answer back in the blogosphere and reputations are often quickly restored. Thus courts may narrow the scope of libel suits when the Internet is concerned in favor of more robust debate and "give-and-take" on the Internet.

***Why should a person who has committed no crime be concerned about electronic information gathering and data mining by government agencies?***

These databases contain vast amounts of information on all of us, including very personal information—our medical histories, financial transactions, what we purchase, and what we read. Under our concept of privacy, people who have done nothing wrong should have every expectation that the government is not viewing, collecting, or analyzing information about them. So asking "Why should I worry if I have nothing to hide?" is the wrong formulation. The question should be "Since I have done nothing wrong, why should the government be investigating me?"

The government can look at records that pertain to a suspected terrorist. Yet with data mining, the government may have no articulable suspicion pointing at anyone, but simply mines personal data from airlines, banks, and commercial entities to look at patterns of behavior that might indicate someone may be a terrorist, is associated with a terrorist, knows a terrorist, or is engaged in a behavior that may fit a pattern that the government thinks applies to terrorists. These types of data mining and data analysis can result in significant false positives—innocent people get caught up in investigations—and this can have consequences. First, just being investigated can be an intrusion into privacy. Second, consequences flow from fitting a pattern—you may be denied the right to get on a plane or be passed over for employment because you lived in an apartment building at the same time as a tenant with the same name as a terrorist's.

Privacy advocates argue that the government needs to have an articulable reason to collect or analyze personal information: the government should need a court order from a judge and should show why they believe a data-mining project is likely to result in identifying suspected or potential terrorists. We do need to realize the government has almost carte blanche to conduct these investigations because they have significant authority under current law to engage in data-mining exercises. There are very few privacy protections under the Constitution or statutes pertaining to these vast databases of personal information. We need stronger privacy laws to deal with data mining.

# 7

# Computer and Network Security

A ship in harbor is safe, but that's not what ships are for.

—John Shedd

## 7.1 Introduction

The Conficker worm has infected millions of Windows computers. Is your PC one of them? You can click on a link from the home page of the Conficker Working Group (www.confickerworkinggroup.org) to find out.

Do you ever go to a coffee shop and use its open wireless network to surf the Web? Did you know freely available software gives any nearby computer user the ability to break into the accounts of people accessing Web sites through password-free wireless networks?

In the movie *Live Free or Die Hard*, a terrorist organization hacks into a variety of computer and communication systems to seize control of traffic lights, natural gas pipelines, and electrical power grids. Are such episodes purely the stuff of Hollywood fiction, or could they really happen?

Millions of people use computers and the Internet to send and receive email, access bank accounts, purchase goods and services, and keep track of personal information, making the security of these systems an important issue. Malicious software can enter computers in a variety of ways. Once active, these programs can steal personal information, destroy files, disrupt industrial processes, and launch attacks on financial systems, supporting criminal enterprises and politically motivated attacks on corporations and governments around the world.

This chapter focuses on threats to computer and network security. We begin our survey with examples of individuals using cunning or skill to gain unauthorized access to computer systems.

## 7.2 Hacking

Today people associate the word "hacking" with computers, but it didn't start out that way.

### 7.2.1 Hackers, Past and Present

In its original meaning, a **hacker** was an explorer, a risk taker, someone who was trying to make a system do something it had never done before. Hackers in this sense of the word abounded at MIT's Tech Model Railroad Club in the 1950s and 1960s. The club constructed and continuously improved an enormous HO-scale model train layout. Members of the Signals and Power Subcommittee built an elaborate electronic switching system to control the movement of the trains. Wearing chino pants, short-sleeved shirts, and pocket protectors, the most dedicated members would drink vast quantities of Coca-Cola and stay up all night to improve the system. To them, a "hack" was a newly constructed piece of equipment that not only served a useful purpose but also demonstrated its creator's technical virtuosity. Calling someone a hacker was a sign of respect; hackers wore the label with pride.

In 1959, after taking a newly created course in computer programming, some of the hackers shifted their attention from model trains to electronic computers [1]. The term "hacker" came to mean a "person who delights in having an intimate understanding of the internal workings of a system, computers and networks in particular" [2].

In the 1983 movie *WarGames*, a teenager breaks into a military computer and nearly causes a nuclear Armageddon. After seeing the movie, a lot of teenagers were excited at the thought that they could prowl cyberspace with a home computer and a modem. A few of them became highly proficient at breaking into government and corporate computer networks. These actions helped change the everyday meaning of the word "hacker."

Today hackers are people who gain unauthorized access to computers and computer networks. An example of the modern use of this word is a story in the February 5, 2015, issue of the *New York Times*, which documents nine incidents in which hackers breached databases of large businesses [3].

Typically, you need a login name and password to access a computer system, but good hackers are adept at guessing short or predictable passwords. In 2013 Ars Technica asked three hackers to attack a list of 16,000 hashed passwords. Using computers, the hackers generated candidate passwords from strings of characters, hashed the candidates, and then checked the hashes against the list, looking for matches. The least successful hacker spent one hour on the task and identified 62 percent of the passwords.

The most successful hacker worked for 20 hours and identified 90 percent of the passwords, using a commodity PC equipped with an AMD Radeon 7970 graphics card [4].

Hackers employ brute-force methods to guess shorter passwords. Passwords are constructed from a set of 95 characters: 26 uppercase letters, 26 lowercase letters, 10 digits, and 33 symbols. That means there are 95 passwords of length 1, $95^2$ passwords of length 2, $95^3$ passwords of length 3, and so on. The total number of passwords up to length 6 is about 744 billion. That may seem like a lot of passwords to you, but a computer can try all of these combinations in just a few minutes.

Hackers use **dictionary attacks** to guess longer passwords. Armed with lists of words that commonly appear in passwords, they generate candidate passwords using a variety of strategies, such as combining words, inserting random characters before or after the words, and replacing characters in words with random characters.

In the experiment conducted by Ars Technica, the hackers' dictionary attacks identified a surprising number of long passwords, including "Apr!l221973," "ilovetofunot," "BandGeek2014," "ilovemySister31," and "Philippians4:6-7" [4].

You probably have many online accounts. Your choice of passwords for these accounts is an important determinant of how safe your accounts are from hackers (see sidebar).

---

## Sidebar: Responsible computer users take passwords seriously

Here is a list of password dos and don'ts from security experts [4, 5, 6].

- **Do not use short passwords.** Modern computers can quickly crack short passwords. As a general rule, the longer a password is, the less likely it is to be guessed. Choose passwords with at least 11 characters.

- **Do not rely solely on words from the dictionary.** Again, such a password is too easy to crack. Make sure your passwords include numbers, as well as upper- and lowercase letters.

- **Do not rely on substituting numbers for letters** (e.g., replacing "E" with "3" and "A" with "4"). Password-cracking programs know these tricks.

- **Do not reuse passwords.** If accounts share passwords, as soon as one account is compromised, the other ones are, too. If you must write down your passwords on a piece of paper in order to remember them, that is safer than reusing passwords in today's environment where an online attack is a greater danger than someone rummaging through your desk. (Of course, you should put sensitive documents like password lists in a locked drawer.)

- **Give ridiculous answers to security questions.** That way they serve as a secondary password. Example: What is your pet's name? Ford Fiesta.

- **Enable two-factor authentication if available.** When you log in from an unfamiliar computer, the system will send you a text message with a confirmation code.

- **Have password recoveries sent to a secure email address.** You don't want hackers to know where your password reset messages are sent. Have these messages sent to an account you never use to send email.

Other techniques for obtaining login names and passwords are decidedly low-tech. Eavesdropping, such as simply looking over the shoulder of a legitimate computer user to learn his login name and password, is a common way that hackers gain access to computers. **Dumpster diving** means looking through garbage for interesting bits of information. Companies typically do not put a fence around their dumpsters. In midnight rummaging sessions, hackers have found user manuals, phone numbers, login names, and passwords. **Social engineering** refers to the manipulation of a person inside the organization to gain access to confidential information. Social engineering is easier in large organizations where people do not know each other very well. For example, a hacker may identify a system administrator and call that person, pretending to be the supervisor of his supervisor and demanding to know why he can't access a particular machine. In this situation, a cowed system administrator, eager to please his boss's boss, may be talked into revealing or resetting a password [7].

## 7.2.2  Penalties for Hacking

Under US law, the maximum penalties for hacking are severe. The Computer Fraud and Abuse Act criminalizes a wide variety of hacker-related activities, including

- Transmitting code (such as a virus or worm) that causes damage to a computer system
- Accessing without authorization any computer connected to the Internet, *even if no files are examined, changed, or copied*
- Transmitting classified government information
- Trafficking in computer passwords
- Computer fraud
- Computer extortion

The maximum penalty imposed for violating the Computer Fraud and Abuse Act is 20 years in prison and a $250,000 fine.

Another federal statute related to computer hacking is the Electronic Communications Privacy Act. This law makes it illegal to intercept telephone conversations, email, or any other data transmissions. It also makes it a crime to access stored email messages without authorization.

The use of the Internet to commit fraud or transmit funds can be prosecuted under the Wire Fraud Act and/or the National Stolen Property Act. Adopting the identity of another person to carry out an illegal activity is a violation of the Identity Theft and Assumption Deterrence Act.

## 7.2.3  Selected Hacking Incidents

Despite potentially severe penalties for convicted hackers, computer systems continue to be compromised by outsiders. Many break-ins are orchestrated by organized groups with a high degree of expertise, but others are committed by solo hackers who exploit a security weakness.

In 2003 a hacker broke into computers at the University of Kansas and copied the personal files of 1,450 foreign students. The files contained names, Social Security numbers, passport numbers, countries of origin, and birth dates. The University of Kansas had collected the information in one place in order to comply with a Patriot Act requirement that it report the information to the Immigration and Naturalization Service [8]. In a similar incident two years later, an intruder broke into a University of Nevada, Las Vegas, computer containing personal information on 5,000 foreign students [9].

In March 2005, someone discovered a security flaw in the online-admissions software produced by ApplyYourself and used by six business schools. The discoverer posted instructions on a *Business Week* online forum explaining how business school applicants could circumvent the software security system and take a look at the status of their applications. It took ApplyYourself only nine hours to fix the flaw, but in the interim period hundreds of eager applicants had exploited the bug and peeked at their files. A week later, Carnegie Mellon University, Harvard University, and the Massachusetts Institute of Technology announced that they would not admit any of the applicants who had accessed their computer systems without authorization [10].

A hacker gained access to the *Sesame Street* channel on YouTube in October 2011, changed the home page, and replaced the videos with pornographic material. The site streamed the X-rated content for 22 minutes before Google could shut down the site [11].

## 7.2.4  Case Study: Firesheep

Only a small fraction of the information transported by the Internet is encrypted; everything else is sent "in the clear" using the HyperText Transport Protocol (HTTP). Encrypting everything would make Internet communications slower and more expensive, which is why most Web sites use encryption only when communicating the most sensitive information, such as usernames, passwords, and credit card numbers. You can tell when a Web site is encrypting the communication because the start of the address in the Web browser is "https://" (meaning "secure HyperText Transport Protocol").

The widespread use of Wi-Fi to connect to the Internet has exposed a vulnerability caused by Internet packets being sent in the clear. A Wi-Fi network uses radio signals to communicate between devices. If the wireless access point is not using encryption, it's easy for devices within range to snoop on the network traffic. (Encryption is the process of protecting information by transforming it into a form that cannot be understood by anyone who does not possess the key; i.e., the means of reversing the process and recreating the original information.)

**Sidejacking** is the hijacking of an open Web session by the capturing of a user's cookie, giving the attacker the same privileges as the user on that Web site. (You can find an explanation of cookies in Section 5.3.12.) Ecommerce Web sites typically use encryption to protect the username and password people provide when logging in, but they do not encrypt the cookie that the Web browser sends to the user to continue the session. Sidejacking is possible on unencrypted wireless networks because another device on the wireless network can "hear" the cookie being transmitted from the Web site back to the user's computer. Even though the Internet security community had known and complained about the sidejacking vulnerability for years, ecommerce Web sites did not change their practices.

On October 24, 2010, Eric Butler released an extension to the Firefox browser called Firesheep. Firesheep makes it easy for a Firefox user to sidejack open Web sessions. The user starts the Firefox browser, connects to an open Wi-Fi network, and clicks on a button called "Start Capturing." When someone using the network visits an insecure Web site that Firesheep knows about, the user's name and photo are displayed in a sidebar, along with the name of the Web site he is connected to, such as Amazon, Facebook, or Twitter. By double-clicking on the photo, the attacker becomes logged in as that user on that Web site and is able to do the same things that the legitimate user is able to do, such as post status messages and purchase products.

Butler released Firesheep as free, open-source software for Mac OS X and Windows. In Butler's view, the organizations managing Web sites have a responsibility to protect the privacy of the people using those sites. Since the organizations had been ignoring this responsibility, it was time for users to step up and demand greater security. Firesheep was a way to help make that happen [12].

The Firesheep extension was downloaded more than 500,000 times in its first week of availability, and it attracted a great deal of media attention [13]. The typical story warned social network users about the dangers of using unencrypted wireless public networks and criticized the social network companies for not providing more security [14, 15, 16, 17].

Responding to criticism for providing a tool that makes it easy for ordinary computer users to perform sidejacking, Butler pointed out that sidejacking tools had been available for years before he released Firesheep. He wrote, "Criminals already know this, and I reject the notion that something like Firesheep turns otherwise innocent people evil" [18].

Three months after Butler released Firesheep, Facebook made the following announcement:

> Starting today we'll provide you with the ability to experience Facebook entirely over HTTPS. You should consider enabling this option if you frequently use Facebook from public Internet access points found at coffee shops, airports, libraries or schools. The option will exist as part of our advanced security features, which you can find in the "Account Security" section of the Account Settings page. [19]

In March 2011, Twitter announced it was offering an "Always use HTTPS" option [20].

## ACT UTILITARIAN ANALYSIS

The release of Firesheep led the media to focus on the risks associated with the use of certain Web sites from unsecured wireless networks, and a few months later Facebook and Twitter made their Web sites more secure. There continues to be strong pressure for other Web services to follow suit. These are tremendous benefits for everyone who accesses the Web at a public Internet access point without encryption.

Butler was right when he predicted that Firesheep would not turn people into criminals. Even though half a million people downloaded Firesheep in the first week, there was no evidence of a big increase in identity theft or even malicious pranks. The harms caused by Firesheep appeared to be minimal. Because the release of Firesheep caused great benefits and negligible harm, we conclude it was a good action from a utilitarian point of view.

### VIRTUE ETHICS ANALYSIS

Butler demonstrated civic responsibility by using his technical skills to develop Firesheep, a piece of software that dramatically illustrated, even to nontechnical people, the lack of security when unencrypted HTTP messages are sent over an unencrypted Wi-Fi network. On the day he released Firesheep, Butler pointed out on his blog that sidejacking attacks are simple to execute because cookies are wirelessly broadcast without encryption. Web sites haven't eliminated this problem even though it has been discussed for a long time. He continued:

> Facebook is constantly rolling out new "privacy" features in an endless attempt to quell the screams of unhappy users, but what's the point when someone can just take over an account entirely? [12]

Butler explained that he released Firesheep to point out the gravity of the problem [12]. Responding to criticisms of his action, he stated emphatically that it is wrong for anyone to harm another person. He did not create Firesheep to facilitate evil; instead, his goal was to make people aware of a problem that had been ignored for too long [18]. All of these statements are characteristic of someone truly interested in protecting the privacy of visitors to popular Web sites. Butler exhibited courage by taking personal responsibility for creating Firesheep, and he demonstrated benevolence by making it freely available.

Therefore, from the perspective of virtue ethics, Butler's actions and statements were characteristic of someone interested in promoting the common good. He seemed to sincerely believe that something significant needed to be done to get the companies to change their privacy policies.

### KANTIAN ANALYSIS

To begin with, accessing someone else's user account is an invasion of that person's privacy and is wrong. Butler clearly agrees with this perspective because he refers to people who sidejack accounts as "evil." Butler's goal was to pressure Facebook, Twitter, Amazon, and other Web sites to adopt proper security measures to protect their users. He saw the best way to achieve this end was to release a tool that would bring to light a well-known security problem that had not gotten sufficient attention.

Criminals already knew how to sidejack Web sessions before Butler created Firesheep. What Firesheep did was make sidejacking so simple that even ordinary computer users could do it. More than half a million copies of Firesheep were downloaded in the first week, and undoubtedly some of these people actually used the software to sidejack Web sessions, which is wrong. It is disingenuous for Butler to "reject the notion that something like Firesheep turns otherwise innocent people evil." He provided a tool that made it much simpler for people to do something that is wrong, and therefore he has some moral accountability for the misdeeds of the people who downloaded Firesheep.

Ultimately, Butler was willing to tolerate a short-term increase in privacy violations in the hope that users would pressure Facebook, Twitter, and other sites to improve their security, which would result in fewer privacy violations in the long term. In other words, he was willing to use the victims of Firesheep as a means to his end. From a Kantian perspective, it was wrong for Butler to release Firesheep to the public.

There are other ways Butler could have achieved his goal without using other people. For example, he could have gone on a popular television show and hacked into the host's Facebook page, generating a great amount of publicity without having to release the software [21].

# 7.3 Malware

The Firesheep extension to the Firefox browser highlights a significant security weakness of unencrypted Wi-Fi networks. Computers have security weaknesses, too, and there are a variety of ways in which malicious software, or **malware**, can become active on your computer. If you are lucky, these programs will do nothing other than consume a little CPU time and some disk space. If you are not so lucky, they may destroy valuable data stored in your computer's file system. An invading program may even allow outsiders to seize control of your computer. Once this happens, they may use your computer as a depository for stolen credit card information, a Web server dishing out pornographic images, or a launch pad for spam or a denial-of-service attack on a corporate or government server.

## 7.3.1 Viruses

Viruses represent one way in which malicious code can get into a computer. A **virus** is a piece of self-replicating code embedded within another program called the **host** [22]. Figure 7.1 illustrates how a virus replicates within a computer. When a user executes a host program infected with a virus, the virus code executes first. The virus finds another executable program stored in the computer's file system and replaces the program with a virus-infected program. After doing this, the virus allows the host program to execute, which is what the user expected to happen. If the virus does its work quickly enough, the user may be unaware of the presence of the virus.

Because a virus is attached to a host program, you may find viruses anywhere you can find program files: hard disks, thumb drives, CD-ROMs, email attachments, and so on. Viruses can be spread from machine to machine via thumb drives or CDs. They may also be passed when a person downloads a file from the Internet. Sometimes viruses are attached to free computer games that people download and install on their computers.

Today many viruses are spread via email attachments (Figure 7.2). We are all familiar with ordinary attachments such as photos, but attachments may also be executable programs or word processing documents or spreadsheets containing macros, which are small pieces of executable code. If the user opens an attachment containing a virus, the

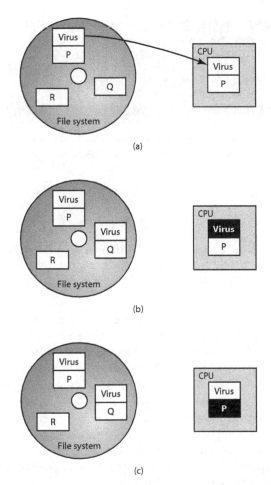

**FIGURE 7.1** One way a computer virus can replicate. (a) A computer user executes program P, which is infected with a virus. (b) The virus code begins to execute. It finds another executable program Q and creates a new version of Q infected with the virus. (c) The virus passes control to program P. The user, who expected program P to execute, suspects nothing.

virus takes control of the computer, reads the user's email address book, and uses these addresses to send virus-contaminated emails to others, as illustrated in Figure 7.3.

Some viruses are fairly innocent; they simply replicate. These viruses occupy disk space and consume CPU time, but the harm they do is relatively minor. Other viruses are malicious and can cause significant damage to a person's file system.

Commercial antivirus software packages allow computer users to detect and destroy viruses lurking on their computers. To be most effective, users must keep them up-to-date by downloading patterns corresponding to the latest viruses from the vendor's Web site. Unfortunately, many people are negligent about keeping their virus protection software up-to-date. According to the statistics office of the European Union, a survey

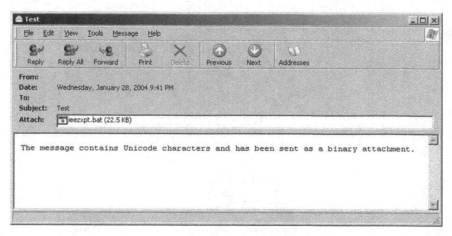

**Figure 7.2** The attachment to this email message probably contains a virus. (The author didn't open it to find out.) (Screenshot by Microsoft. Copyright © 2011 by Microsoft Corporation. Reprinted with permission.)

of Internet users revealed that 31 percent of them had experienced a computer virus in the previous 12 months that had resulted in a loss of information or time, even though 84 percent of them said that their computer was running antivirus software [23]. That means they were not keeping their virus protection current.

To make matters worse, criminals have found a way to profit from people's concern about viruses and their eagerness to install antivirus software when they believe their systems are infected. In July 2011, more than two million PCs were infected with a fake antivirus application that actually routed traffic destined for Google through intermediate servers controlled by the attacker. The purpose of the malware appeared to be to generate "click-through" income for the hackers by directing people to Web sites containing fake security programs [24].

## 7.3.2 The Internet Worm

A **worm** is a self-contained program that spreads through a computer network by exploiting security holes in the computers connected to the network (Figure 7.4). The technical term "worm" comes from *The Shockwave Rider*, a 1975 science fiction novel written by John Brunner [25].

The most famous worm of all time was also the first one to get the attention of the mainstream media, which is why it is popularly known as the Internet worm, even though many other worms have been created that propagate through the Internet. The primary source for this narrative is the excellent biography of Robert Morris in *Cyberpunk: Outlaws and Hackers on the Computer Frontier*, written by Katie Hafner and John Markoff [26].

### BACKGROUND OF ROBERT TAPPAN MORRIS JR.

Robert Tappan Morris Jr. began learning about the Unix operating system when he was still in junior high school. His father was a computer security researcher at Bell Labs, and

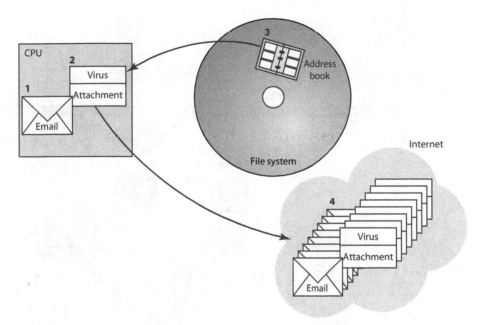

**FIGURE 7.3** How an email virus spreads. A computer user reads an email with an attachment (1). The user opens the attachment, which contains a virus (2). The virus reads the user's email address book (3). The virus sends emails with virus-containing attachments (4).

young Morris was given an account on a Bell Labs computer that he could access from a teletype at home. It didn't take him long to discover security holes in Unix. In a 1982 interview with Gina Kolata, a writer for *Smithsonian* magazine, Morris admitted he had broken into networked computers and read other people's email. "I never told myself that there was nothing wrong with what I was doing," he said, but he acknowledged that he found breaking into systems challenging and exciting, and he admitted that he continued to do it.

As an undergraduate at Harvard, Morris majored in computer science. He quickly gained a reputation for being the computer lab's Unix expert. After his freshman year, Morris worked at Bell Labs. The result of his work was a technical paper describing a security hole in Berkeley Unix.

While at Harvard, Morris was responsible for several computer pranks. In one of them, he installed a program that required people logging in to answer a question posed by "the Oracle" and then to ask the Oracle another question. (The Oracle program worked by passing questions and answers among people trying to log in.)

### DESIGNING THE WORM

Morris entered the graduate program in computer science at Cornell University in the fall of 1988. He became intrigued with the idea of creating a computer worm that would exploit bugs he had found in three Unix applications: `ftp`, `sendmail`, and `fingerd`. His "wish list" for the worm had about two dozen goals, including the following:

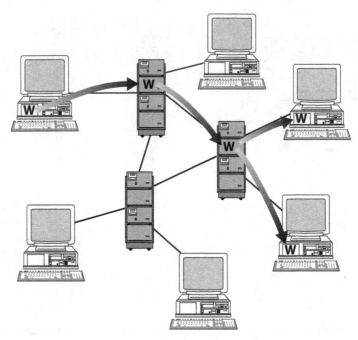

**Figure 7.4** A worm spreads to other computers by exploiting security holes in computer networks.

- Infect three machines per local area network
- Only consume CPU cycles if the machines are idle
- Avoid slow machines
- Break passwords in order to spread to other computers

The goal of the worm was to infect as many computers as possible. It would not destroy or corrupt data files on the machines it infected.

### LAUNCHING THE WORM

On November 2, 1988, Morris learned that a fix for the ftp bug had been posted to the Internet, meaning his worm program could no longer take advantage of that security hole. However, nobody had posted fixes to the other two bugs Morris knew about. After making some last-minute changes to the worm program, he logged in to a computer at the MIT Artificial Intelligence Lab and launched the worm from that computer at about 7:30 P.M.

The worm quickly spread to thousands of computers at military installations, medical research facilities, and universities. Unfortunately, due to several bugs in the worm's programming, computers became infected with hundreds of copies of the worm, causing them to crash every few minutes or become practically unresponsive to the programs of legitimate users.

Morris contacted friends at Harvard to discuss what ought to be done next. They agreed that Andy Sudduth would anonymously post a message to the Internet. Sudduth's message is shown here.[1] Harvard's computers were not affected (the security holes had already been patched), and you can tell from the last sentence that Sudduth was having a hard time believing Morris's story:

```
A Possible virus report:

There may be a virus loose on the internet.
Here is the gist of a message I got:

I'm sorry.

Here are some steps to prevent further
transmission:

1) don't run finger, or fix it to not
overrun its stack when reading arguments.
2) recompile sendmail w/o DEBUG defined
3) don't run rexed

Hope this helps, but more, I hope it is a hoax.
```

Sudduth's email was supposed to get routed through a computer at Brown University. However, computers at Brown were already infected with the worm and did not have spare cycles to route the message. Also, the email did not have a subject line, which made it less likely to be read during a crisis. The result is that the message was read too late to be of any help to those fighting the worm.

System administrators at various universities worked frantically to stop the spread of the worm. Within a day they had examined the worm's code, discovered the bugs in sendmail and fingerd, and published fixes to the Internet community. No one knows exactly how many computers were infected by the worm, but it did make a significant number of systems unusable for a day or two [27].

After some sleuthing by reporter John Markoff, the *New York Times* named Robert Tappan Morris Jr. as the author of the worm. Morris was suspended from Cornell University. A year later, he was the first person to receive a felony conviction under the US Computer Fraud and Abuse Act. He was sentenced to three years' probation and 400 hours of community service, and was fined $10,000. His legal fees and fines exceeded $150,000.

## ETHICAL EVALUATION

Was Robert Morris Jr. wrong to unleash the Internet worm?

A Kantian evaluation must focus on Morris's will. Did Morris have good will? His stated goal was to see how many Internet computers he could infect with the worm.

---

1. Copyright © 2011 by Ruth Kennedy Sudduth. Reprinted with permission.

While Morris did not want to crash these computers or destroy any data stored on them, his motivation was fundamentally selfish: he wanted the thrill of seeing his creation running on thousands of computers. He used others because he gained access to their machines without their permission. There is also evidence Morris knew he was using others: he took measures designed to prevent people from discovering that he was the author of the worm. From a Kantian point of view, Morris's action was wrong.

From a social contract point of view, Morris's action was also wrong. He violated the property rights of the individuals and organizations whose computers were infected by the worm. They had the right to determine who would use their computers, and they attempted to enforce this right by requiring people to identify themselves by username and password. Morris took advantage of security holes in these computers to gain unauthorized access to them. When his worm caused these computers to become unresponsive or crash, he denied access to the legitimate users of these computers.

A utilitarian evaluation of the case focuses on the benefits and harms resulting from the spread of the worm. The principal benefit of the Internet worm was that organizations managing these Unix computers discovered there were two significant security holes in their systems. They received the instructions they needed to patch these holes before a truly malicious intruder took advantage of them to enter their systems and do a lot of damage to their data. Of course, Morris could have produced the same beneficial result simply by contacting the system administrators at UC Berkeley and informing them of the security holes he had found.

The Internet worm had numerous harmful consequences. A large amount of time was spent by system administrators as they defended their machines from further attacks, tracked down the problem, installed patches, and brought machines back on line. There was a disruption in email and file exchange traffic caused by computers being taken off the network. About 6,000 computers were unavailable for a day or two. During this time, many thousands of people were less productive than they could have been had the systems been up and running. Morris himself was harmed by his actions. He was suspended from Cornell and convicted of a felony, which resulted in a sentence of probation, community service, and a substantial fine.

Considering all of Morris's options, it is clear that another course of action—simply alerting the Unix community to the bugs—would have produced all of the benefits with none of the harms. Therefore, from a utilitarian viewpoint, Morris was wrong to have released the Internet worm.

From the perspective of virtue ethics, Morris's actions are not consistent with those of a virtuous person. He selfishly chose to use the Internet as an experimental laboratory, and he deceitfully released the worm from MIT rather than Cornell University. When the worm began spreading uncontrollably, he avoided taking responsibility for his actions by asking a trusted friend to post the message to the Internet explaining how to fight the worm.

In conclusion, Morris may not have been acting maliciously, but he was acting selfishly. If he had wanted to experiment with worms, he probably could have gotten permission to try out his creations on a local area network detached from the Internet, so that even if his worm multiplied out of control, there would have been no fallout to the rest of the computer community. Instead, he chose to use the entire Internet as his experimental laboratory, inconveniencing thousands of people.

### 7.3.3 Sasser

The Sasser worm, launched in April 2004, exploited a previously identified security weakness with PCs running the Windows operating system. Computers with up-to-date software were safe from the worm, but it infected about 18 million computers worldwide nonetheless. The effects of the worm were relatively benign; infected computers simply shut themselves down shortly after booting. Still, the worm made millions of computers unusable and disrupted operations at Delta Airlines, the European Commission, Australian railroads, and the British coast guard [28].

After Microsoft offered a reward of 250,000 euros, a fellow student pointed the finger at German teenager Sven Jaschan, who confessed to the crime and then began working for German computer security firm Securepoint. Because he was 17 when he released the worm, Jaschan was tried in a juvenile court, which sentenced him to one and a half years' probation and 30 hours of community service [28, 29, 30].

### 7.3.4 Instant Messaging Worms

Two early worms to strike instant messaging systems were Choke and Hello, which appeared in 2001. Worms were less devastating back then, because only about 141 million people used instant messaging. Today more than 800 million people rely on instant messaging, so the impact of worms can be much greater. The appearance of the Kelvir worm in 2005 forced the Reuters news agency to remove 60,000 subscribers from its Microsoft-based instant messaging service for 20 hours [31]. In 2010 a variant of the Palevo instant messaging worm rapidly spread through Romania, Mongolia, and Indonesia [32].

### 7.3.5 Conficker

The Conficker (or Downadup) worm, which appeared on Windows computers in November 2008, is notable because computer security experts have found it particularly difficult to eradicate. The worm is able to propagate in several ways [33]. The original variant of the worm spread to computers that were not up-to-date with the latest security patches from Microsoft. The second version of the worm, which appeared about a month later, had two new features that accelerated its spread: the ability to invade computers with weak password protection and the ability to propagate through USB memory sticks and shared files on local area networks. Early in 2009, between 8 and 15 million computers were infected with Conficker, including portions of military networks in France, the United Kingdom, and Germany [34].

According to Rodney Joffe of the Conficker Working Group, "It's using the best current practices and state of the art to communicate and to protect itself" [35]. Even though millions of copies of this worm are circulating, it does not appear to have done great harm. Security experts remain baffled as to the goals of those who created it [36].

### 7.3.6 Cross–Site Scripting

**Cross-site scripting** is another way in which malware may be downloaded without a user's knowledge. Web sites that allow users to read what other users have posted are vulnerable to this security problem. The attacker injects a client-side script into a Web site. When an innocent user visits the site sometime later, the user's browser executes the script, which may steal cookies, track the user's activity, or perform another malicious action.

### 7.3.7 Drive–By Downloads

Many malware creators have hacked into legitimate Web sites and installed software booby traps. In some cases, simply visiting a compromised Web site can result in the unintentional downloading of software, called a **drive-by download**. Another kind of drive-by download occurs when a Web surfer encounters a pop-up window asking permission to download software. The user approves the download, thinking the code is necessary to view the content on the Web site, but in actuality the download contains malware.

The drive-by download problem is growing [37]. The Google Anti-Malware Team has discovered more than three million URLs that initiate drive-by downloads. That may not seem like so many URLs, given the size of the Web, but hackers target the most popular Web sites. As a result, about 1.3 percent of queries to Google's search engine result in a malicious URL appearing somewhere in the results page [38].

### 7.3.8 Trojan Horses and Backdoor Trojans

A **Trojan horse** is a program with a benign capability that conceals a sinister purpose. When the user executes a Trojan horse, the program performs the expected beneficial task. However, the program is also performing actions unknown to, and not in the best interests of, the user.

A recent example of a Trojan horse is Mocmex, first uncovered in 2008 in digital picture frames manufactured in China. It spread from digital picture frames to computer hard drives and other portable storage devices people attached to their PCs. The purpose of the Trojan horse appeared to be to steal passwords to online computer games [39].

A **backdoor Trojan** is a Trojan horse that gives the attacker access to the victim's computer. For example, a backdoor Trojan may purport to cleanse malware from a computer, but in actuality it installs spyware (described later).

### 7.3.9 Rootkits

A **rootkit** is a set of programs that provide privileged access to a computer. Once installed, a rootkit is activated every time the computer is booted. Rootkits are difficult to detect because they start running before the operating system has completed booting up, and they can use security privileges to mask their presence.

### 7.3.10  Spyware and Adware

Spyware is a program that communicates over an Internet connection without the user's knowledge or consent. Spyware programs can monitor Web surfing, log keystrokes, take snapshots of the computer screen, and send reports back to a host computer. Spyware is often part of a rootkit. Adware is a type of spyware that displays pop-up advertisements related to what the user is doing.

Since people would not intentionally download a spyware program, spyware must get installed using subterfuge. Free software downloaded from the Internet often contains spyware. Alternatively, the spyware may be a Trojan horse, tricking users into downloading it because they think it serves a useful purpose. A Trojan horse containing spyware is an example of a backdoor Trojan. A 2006 survey of US consumers with broadband Internet connections found that 89 percent of them had spyware on their computers [40].

### 7.3.11  Bots and Botnets

A **bot** is a particular kind of backdoor Trojan that responds to commands sent by a command-and-control program located on an external computer. The first bots supported legitimate applications: Internet Relay Chat channels and multiplayer Internet games. Today, however, bots are frequently used to support illegal activities. A collection of bot-infected computers is called a **botnet**, and a person who controls a botnet is called a **bot herder**. Botnets can range in size from a few thousand computers to over a million computers. In most cases, people have no idea that their PCs have been compromised and are part of a botnet.

It's been estimated that as much as 90 percent of spam is distributed through botnets [41]. Bots can also be used as spyware, stealing files or logging keystrokes to gain credit card numbers or other sensitive information. Botnets can also be used to support distributed denial-of-service attacks, which we discuss in Section 7.4.3.

The sophistication of bots continues to increase. Computers typically have signature-based detection schemes to identify and destroy bots by looking for particular patterns in their underlying machine code. To counter these detection schemes, programmers are now creating bots that are able to spin off functionally equivalent bots with somewhat different machine code.

### 7.3.12  Defensive Measures

Three defensive measures are important in protecting personal computers from malware: security patches, antimalware tools, and firewalls.

Some kinds of malware exploit vulnerabilities in software systems, and software makers respond by modifying their code to remove the vulnerabilities. At regular intervals software makers release security patches so that the users of the software can update their systems to remove the vulnerabilities that have been uncovered. In fact, most worms exploit vulnerabilities for which security patches have already been created. That means they can only infect those computers that have not been kept up-to-date with the latest patches.

Antimalware tools are designed to protect computers against malware, such as viruses, worms, Trojan horses, adware, and spyware. Antimalware software can be used to scan a computer's hard drive, detecting files that appear to contain viruses or spyware, and deleting the files (with the user's approval). The rapid rate at which new malware appears necessitates frequent updating of these tools.

A **firewall** is a software application installed on a single computer that can selectively block network traffic to and from that computer. A firewall gives the user the ability to control which programs running on the computer are able to access the Internet. One weakness of firewalls is that they are vulnerable to being manipulated by malware. If a computer is infected by a piece of malware, the malware may be able to shut down the firewall, since it is running on the same computer.

## 7.4 Cyber Crime and Cyber Attacks

The Internet plays a vital role in the economic life of developed nations. Its effects include streamlining interactions between manufacturers and their suppliers, stimulating the creation of new companies, fostering the development of new business models, making online videoconferencing much more affordable, and changing how people shop. Today, there are more than 80 million dot-com domains. Annual ecommerce sales now exceed $1 trillion [42]. Given the amount of money changing hands, it's not surprising that organized crime is active on the Internet. The economic importance of Internet-based activities also makes Internet infrastructure an attractive target for politically motivated attacks.

We begin this section by reviewing three common Internet-based attacks. We then explore how these attacks have been used as a means to achieve criminal or political ends.

### 7.4.1 Phishing and Spear Phishing

A **phishing** (pronounced "fishing") attack is a large-scale effort to gain sensitive information from gullible computer users. An attacker sends out millions of email messages from a botnet. The messages inform the recipients that one of their accounts has been compromised and directs them to connect to a Web site to resolve the problem. Targeted users that click on the link encounter an impostor Web site designed to resemble the genuine ecommerce site. Once on the site, they are asked for a login name, password, and other private information. Information collected by the imposter site can then be used for identity theft.

According to an industry study, there were at least 123,972 phishing attacks worldwide in the second half of 2014. An interesting development is the increase in phishing attacks on Chinese ecommerce sites, indicating the growing importance of the Chinese economy [43].

**Spear phishing** is a variant of phishing in which the attacker selects email addresses that target a particular group of recipients. For example, an attacker may target elderly people judged to be more gullible or members of a group that have access to valuable information [44].

### 7.4.2 SQL Injection

**SQL injection** is a method of attacking a database-driven Web application that has improper security. The attacker accesses the application like any other client of the application, but by inserting (injecting) an SQL query into a text string from the client to the application, the attacker can trick the application into returning sensitive information.

### 7.4.3 Denial-of-Service and Distributed Denial-of-Service Attacks

A **denial-of-service (DoS) attack** is an intentional action designed to prevent legitimate users from making use of a computer service [45]. A DoS attack may involve unauthorized access to one or more computer systems, but the goal of a DoS attack is not to steal information. Instead, the aim of a DoS attack is to disrupt a computer server's ability to respond to its clients. Interfering with the normal use of computer services can result in significant harm. A company selling products and services over the Internet may lose business. A military organization may find its communications disrupted. A government or nonprofit organization may be unable to get its message out to the public.

A DoS attack is an example of an "asymmetric" attack, in which a single person can harm a huge organization, such as a multinational corporation or even a government. Since terrorist organizations specialize in asymmetric attacks, some fear that DoS attacks will become an important part of the terrorist arsenal [46, 47].

In a **distributed denial-of-service (DDoS) attack,** the attacker rents access to a botnet from a **bot herder**. At the selected time, the command-and-control computer sends the appropriate instructions to the bots, which launch their attack on the targeted system.

### 7.4.4 Cyber Crime

Criminal organizations have discovered that a great deal of money can be made from malware, so many of them have entered the arena, raising the stakes for corporations and individuals trying to protect their systems and sensitive information, respectively. Edward Skoudis paints a grim picture of the contemporary landscape:

> Some attackers sell to the highest bidder customized malicious code to control victim machines. They may rent out armies of infected systems useful for spam delivery, phishing schemes, denial-of-service attacks, or identity theft. Spyware companies and overly aggressive advertisers buy such code to infiltrate and control victim machines. A single infected machine displaying pop-up ads, customizing search engine results, and intercepting keystrokes for financial accounts could net an attack $1 per month or more. A keystroke logger on an infected machine could help the attacker gather credit card numbers and make $1,000 or more from that victim before the fraud is discovered. With control of 10,000 machines, an attacker could set up a solid profit flow from cyber crime. Organized crime groups

may assemble collectives of such attackers to create a business, giving rise to a malicious code industry. In the late 1990s, most malicious code publicly released was the work of determined hobbyists, but today, attackers have monetized their malicious code; their profit centers throw off funds that can be channeled into research and development to create more powerful malicious software and refined business models, as well as to fund other crimes. [44]

In the remainder of this section, we review a few well-known cyber crime incidents.

## JEANSON JAMES ANCHETA

In 2004 and 2005, Internet café employee Jeanson James Ancheta created a network of about 400,000 bots, including computers operated by the US Department of Defense. Adware companies, spammers, and others paid Ancheta for the use of these computers. After being arrested by the FBI, Ancheta pleaded guilty to a variety of charges, including conspiring to violate the Computer Fraud Abuse Act and the CAN-SPAM Act. In May 2005, a federal judge sentenced Ancheta to 57 months in prison and required him to pay $15,000 in restitution to the US government for infecting Department of Defense computers. Ancheta also forfeited to the government the proceeds of his illegal activity, including his 1993 BMW, more than $60,000 in cash, and his computer equipment [48, 49].

## PHARMAMASTER

Israeli company Blue Security created a spam deterrence system for people tired of receiving unwanted email. Blue Security sold the service to businesses, but individuals could protect their home computers for free. About half a million people signed up for this free service. Users loaded a bot called Blue Frog on their computers. The bot integrated with Yahoo! Mail, Gmail, and Hotmail, checking incoming email messages for spam. When it discovered a spam message, the bot would contact a Blue Security server to determine the source of the email. Then the bot would send the spammer an opt-out message [50].

Spammers who indiscriminately sent emails to millions of addresses started receiving hundreds of thousands of opt-out messages, disrupting their operations. Six of the world's top ten spammers agreed to use Blue Security's filtering software to remove Blue Frog users from their email lists [50].

One spammer, nicknamed PharmaMaster, did not back down. He threatened Blue Frog users with messages such as this one: "Unfortunately, due to the tactics used by Blue Security, you will end up receiving this message or other nonsensical spams 20–40 times more than you would normally" [41]. He followed through on his threats on May 1, 2006, by sending Blue Frog users 10 to 20 times as much spam as they would normally receive [50].

The next day PharmaMaster went after Blue Security itself. He launched a massive DDoS attack from tens of thousands of bots targeting Blue Security's servers. The huge torrent of incoming messages disabled the Blue Frog service. Later DDoS attacks focused on other companies providing Internet services to Blue Security. Finally, the spammer targeted the businesses that paid for Blue Security's services. When Blue Security realized it could not protect its business customers from DDoS attacks and virus-laced emails, it reluctantly discontinued its service. "We cannot take the responsibility for an ever-escalating cyberwar through our continued operations," wrote Eran Reshef, CEO of Blue Security. "We are discontinuing all of our anti-spam activities" [50]. Blue Security's decision to fight bots with bots—always controversial—was ultimately unsuccessful.

### ALBERT GONZALEZ

In 2010 Albert Gonzalez was sentenced to 20 years of imprisonment after pleading guilty to using an SQL injection attack to steal more than 130 million credit and debit card numbers. Some of the credit and debit card numbers were sold online, leading to unauthorized purchases and bank withdrawals. The targets of the attacks were Heartland Payment Systems, 7-Eleven, Hannaford Brothers Supermarkets, TJX, DSW, Barnes & Noble, OfficeMax, and the Dave & Buster's chain of restaurants. Most of the numbers were stolen from Heartland Payment Systems, which estimated its losses at $130 million [51, 52].

### AVALANCHE GANG

The Avalanche Gang is the name given to the criminal enterprise responsible for more phishing attacks than any other organization. The Anti-Phishing Working Group (APWG) estimated that the Avalanche Gang was responsible for two-thirds of all global phishing attacks launched in the second half of 2009. In the second half of 2010, APWG noticed that Avalanche had nearly ceased its phishing attacks, leading APWG to speculate that Avalanche was changing strategies and focusing on the propagation of spam that tricks people into downloading the Zeus Trojan horse [53].

## 7.4.5 Politically Motivated Cyber Attacks

A **cyber attack** is a "computer-to-computer attack that undermines the confidentiality, integrity, or availability of a computer or information resident on it" [54]. Some nation-states, terrorist organizations, and allied groups are mounting politically motivated cyber attacks on the computer and network infrastructure of their opponents, and some of these efforts have caused major disruptions.

### ESTONIA (2007)

The small Baltic country of Estonia was part of the Soviet Union from the end of the Second World War until it became independent in 1991, and ethnic Russians still make up about a quarter of its population. In the capital city of Tallinn, a large bronze statue of a Soviet soldier had long been a point of controversy between Estonians and Russians. Russians saw it as a symbol of the sacrifices made by Soviet troops in the victory over Germany in the Great Patriotic War, while Estonians saw it as a symbol of the oppressive Soviet occupation.

After 16 years of independence, the Estonian government decided to relocate the controversial statue from downtown Tallinn to a Russian military cemetery in the suburbs. They knew the relocation would be hugely unpopular with the Russians. In fact, the Russian government had warned that removing the statue would be "disastrous for

Estonians" [55]. The police were prepared for violence, and although ethnic Russians rioted for two nights after the statue was moved, the damage was limited.

The government also expected an attack on its cyber infrastructure. Sure enough, an attack came, but its magnitude was greater than anything expected by the government's Internet security group. DDoS attacks from nearly a million computers targeted Estonian government ministries and all of Estonia's major commercial banks, telecommunications companies, and media outlets. To combat the attacks, much of Estonia's Internet was made inaccessible to computers outside the country, and on May 10, 2007, Estonia's largest bank had to suspend online services for an hour [55, 56].

In 2009 a group of Russian activists connected with Nashi, a pro-Kremlin youth group, claimed responsibility for the cyber attacks [57].

### GEORGIA (2008)

Georgia is another former Soviet republic that gained independence in 1991. South Ossetia, a region of Georgia adjacent to Russia, gained de facto autonomy from Georgia after a brief war in 1991, though it continues to be recognized as a part of Georgia by the international community. On August 7, 2008, after provocations by South Ossetian separatists, Georgia sent troops into South Ossetia. Russian forces entered South Ossetia on August 8, and Russian and Georgian troops fought in South Ossetia for four days. A cease-fire between Georgia and Russia was signed a week later.

The conflict between Georgia and Russia is notable because even before Russian troops had entered South Ossetia, the Georgian government suffered a series of DDoS attacks that affected its ability to communicate with the outside world. Multiple Web sites went down for hours. The Georgian government went so far as to switch some of its Web hosting locations to the United States. American security experts said they had uncovered evidence of involvement by the Russian Business Network, a criminal gang located in St. Petersburg, but there was no clear link to the Russian military [58, 59, 60].

### GEORGIA (2009)

Twitter service was unavailable worldwide for several hours on August 6, 2009, due to a massive DDoS attack. Max Kelly, the chief security officer at Facebook, said the attack was an effort to silence a political blogger from the Republic of Georgia, citing as evidence the fact that three other sites used by the activist—Facebook, LiveJournal, and Google—were also targets of DDoS attacks at the same time [61, 62].

No group took responsibility for the attacks, but some noted that August 6, 2009, was the first anniversary of the war between Georgia and Russia over South Ossetia [63].

### EXILED TIBETAN GOVERNMENT (2009)

In 2009 computer security experts uncovered a surveillance effort targeting the Dalai Lama, the exiled Tibetan government, and other Tibetans. Some agency had used backdoor Trojans to penetrate 1,295 computers in 103 countries, creating a spying system the experts named GhostNet. When a victim opened an email attachment supposedly containing the translation of a book, the backdoor Trojan was activated. Each backdoor Trojan was able to transfer data files and email messages back to the controlling computer. Even more ominously, it could access the computer's microphone, turning the PC into an eavesdropping station. Some of the researchers that discovered GhostNet blamed the Chinese government for the intrusions, but the Chinese government denied responsibility [64, 65].

### UNITED STATES AND SOUTH KOREA (2009)

A DDoS attack on governmental agencies and commercial Web sites in the United States and South Korea paralyzed a third of them over the Fourth of July weekend in 2009. Targets in the United States included the White House, the Treasury Department, the Secret Service, the New York Stock Exchange, and NASDAQ. In South Korea, the targets included the Blue House (presidential mansion), the Defense Ministry, and the National Assembly.

The DDoS attack was relatively minor, involving a botnet containing only 50,000–65,000 computers, compared with large-scale attacks that may utilize a million computers. Still, the attack disrupted different networks over a period of days as it shifted targets, and some sites in South Korea were unavailable or compromised as late as July 9. South Korea's National Intelligence Service blamed the North Korean government or its sympathizers for the attack, hypothesizing that the attack was in retaliation for United Nations sanctions against North Korea. According to computer experts, it was unlikely the source of the attack would ever be positively identified because those responsible for the attack launched it from systems owned by others [66, 67].

### IRAN (2009)

Industrial processes such as chemical plants, oil and gas pipelines, and electrical power grids require constant monitoring. In the pre-computer era, monitoring was done by employees who watched gauges and warning lights, turned dials, and opened and closed valves. Computers allowed the automation of centralized monitoring. In the 1980s, distributed control systems eliminated local control cabinets. Instead, networks carried information to centralized control centers. Computer monitors with color-coded fields replaced the gauges and warning lights. Initially, distributed control systems were proprietary, but customers asked for "open systems, common protocols and vendor interoperability" [68]. They got what they wanted with the advent of supervisory control and data acquisition (SCADA) systems based on the Internet protocol. Internet-based SCADA systems are less expensive and easier to maintain and administer than proprietary systems (Figure 7.5). Another way to save money and time is to allow an outsider to connect with the SCADA system remotely to perform diagnostics.

These advances carry with them security risks. Allowing remote diagnostics creates an opportunity for a malicious outsider to gain access. Many industrial machines contain embedded microprocessors. Industrial machines last a long time, which means many of these machines contain older microprocessors. Security patches designed to ward off malware may not be available for these microprocessors, and even if they are available, it may be impractical to install them because the processor is so slow that it cannot run the security code and keep up with its machine-control responsibilities.

The Stuxnet worm, launched in 2009, attacked SCADA systems running Siemens software [69]. The worm appeared to target five industrial facilities in Iran, and it may

FIGURE 7.5  Internet-based supervisory control and data acquisition (SCADA) systems can save money and make systems easier to administer, but they also carry security risks.  (Dave and Les Jacobs/Kolostock/Blend Images/Corbis)

have caused a temporary shutdown of Iran's nuclear program by infecting computers controlling centrifuges processing uranium [70, 71]. About 1,000 of Iran's 5,000 centrifuges were damaged in the cyberattack. Developing and launching the worm was a cooperative effort between the United States and Israel [72, 73].

## CYBER ESPIONAGE ATTRIBUTED TO THE PEOPLE'S LIBERATION ARMY

American computer security firm Mandiant spent nearly a decade investigating hundreds of computer security breaches in more than a dozen countries and tracing those breaches back to the organized groups responsible for them. One of these groups, labeled APT1 (for advanced persistent threat 1), was responsible for at least 141 intrusions over a seven-year period. In 2013 Mandiant released a report stating that the APT1 group was located in Shanghai, China, and most likely was Unit 61398 of the People's Liberation Army [74].

According to Mandiant, APT1 was responsible for stealing hundreds of terabytes of data from the 141 organizations whose computer networks it compromised. One of these organizations was Telvent Canada, which provides SCADA systems to oil, gas, and electrical power companies. After Telvent Canada became aware of the security breach, it notified its customers and cut off access to their SCADA systems from its computers in the hope of preventing a remote attack [75].

In response to the allegations made by Mandiant, Hong Lei, a spokesman for China's foreign ministry, stated that China enforces laws prohibiting cyber attacks. He continued, "Groundless criticism is irresponsible and unprofessional, and it will not help to solve the problem" [76].

## ANONYMOUS

The Oxford English Dictionary defines a **hacktivist** as "a computer hacker whose activity is aimed at promoting a social or political cause." Anonymous is a loosely organized international movement of hacktivists. Individuals who identify with Anonymous are called Anons.

The profile of Anonymous was raised significantly in 2008 when it confronted the Church of Scientology [77]. After somebody uploaded to YouTube a video interview of Tom Cruise produced by the Church of Scientology and meant to be seen only by its members, the church filed a copyright violation claim and asked YouTube to remove it. YouTube complied with the request. In response, Anonymous issued a press release stating it was going to conduct attacks on the Church of Scientology "to end the financial exploitation of its members and protect the right to free speech" [78]. Anonymous members launched DDoS attacks on Scientology Web sites and worked to keep the Tom Cruise video available on the Internet. In addition, more than 6,000 Anons donned Guy Fawkes masks and protested the Church of Scientology in the streets of 90 cities across North America, Europe, Australia, and New Zealand.

Since then, a series of actions around the world have been attributed to Anonymous. Here is a sampling.

- Operation Payback was a series of DDoS attacks against the Recording Industry Association of America (RIAA), the Motion Picture Association of America (MPAA), Indian company Aiplex, and the US Copyright Office. These attacks were launched in September 2009 after it was revealed that the RIAA and MPAA had contracted Aiplex to launch DDoS attacks on BitTorrent sites, including the Pirate Bay [79].

- A few months later, the focus of Operation Payback shifted to PayPal, Visa, and MasterCard after they froze the transfer of funds from supporters of Julian Assange to the WikiLeaks organization. The Web sites of all three of these financial institutions were disrupted by DDoS attacks [80, 81].

- Anonymous played an active role in the Arab Spring uprisings of 2011. In Tunisia, for example, Anons launched DDoS attacks on government Web sites, offered advice to dissidents on how to conceal their identities online, and helped local activists upload videos of their protests to the Internet [82].

- After the US Department of Justice announced action against cybervault Megaupload in January 2012, Anons launched DDoS attacks on the US Department of Justice, Universal Music Group, the RIAA, the MPAA, Broadcast Music Inc., and the FBI [83].

- Anons launched a cyber attack on Israeli Web sites on Holocaust Memorial Day in 2013 to protest the Israeli treatment of the Palestinians [84].

- Anons claimed responsibility for shutting down the Web site of the City of Cleveland to protest the killing of 12-year-old Tamir Rice by a Cleveland police officer in November 2014 [85].

- In January 2015, after a terrorist attack on the Paris office of satirical magazine *Charlie Hebdo* left 12 dead and 11 wounded, Anonymous released a video condemning the attack and pledging to shut down jihadist Web sites [86].

Dozens of people around the world have been arrested for their participation in Anonymous cyber attacks, and many have spent time in prison. Dmitriy Guzner pleaded guilty to the unauthorized impairment of a protected computer in his role in the DDoS attacks against the Church of Scientology. He was sentenced to 366 days in a US federal prison and ordered to pay $37,500 in restitution [87]. Brian Mettenbrink was sentenced to a year in prison and ordered to pay $20,000 in restitution after pleading guilty to participating in the DDoS attacks against the Church of Scientology [88]. Chris Doyon was arrested for launching a DDoS attack on a Santa Cruz County, California, Web site. He jumped bail and fled to Canada [89]. Briton Jake Davis pleaded guilty to participating in attacks on Sony Pictures and the Serious Organised Crime Agency in Great Britain and was given a 24-month sentence [90].

## 7.5 Online Voting

Throughout this chapter, we have seen many ways in which malefactors can breach the security of networked computers, yet the convenience and low cost of completing many tasks online are significant benefits. It should come as no surprise, then, that an online solution is often proposed when there is a problem with a traditional process. In this section we evaluate a proposal to conduct elections over the Internet.

### 7.5.1 Motivation for Online Voting

The 2000 presidential election was one of the closest contests in US history. Florida was the pivotal state; without Florida's electoral votes, neither Democrat Al Gore nor Republican George W. Bush had a majority of votes in the Electoral College. After a manual recount of the votes in four heavily Democratic counties, the Florida Secretary of State declared that Bush had received 2,912,790 votes to Gore's total of 2,912,253. Bush's margin of victory was incredibly small: less than 2 votes out of every 10,000 votes cast.

Most of these counties used a keypunch voting machine in which voters select a candidate by using a stylus to poke out a hole in a card next to the candidate's name. Two voting irregularities were traced to the use of these machines. The first irregularity was that sometimes the stylus doesn't punch the hole cleanly, leaving a tiny, rectangular piece of card hanging by one or more corners. Votes with "hanging chad" are typically not counted by automatic vote tabulators. The manual recount focused on identifying ballots with hanging chad that ought to have been counted. The second irregularity was that some voters in Palm Beach County were confused by its "butterfly ballot" and mistakenly punched the hole corresponding to Reform Party candidate Pat Buchanan rather than the hole for Democratic candidate Al Gore (Figure 7.6). This confusion may have cost Al Gore the votes he needed to win Florida [91].

### 7.5.2 Proposals

The problems with the election in Florida led to a variety of actions to improve the reliability of voting systems in the United States. Many states replaced paper-based systems

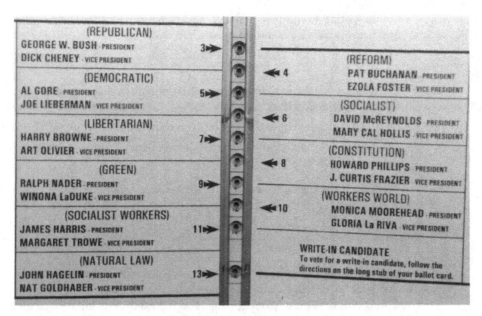

**FIGURE 7.6** The layout of the "butterfly ballot" apparently led thousands of Palm Beach County, Florida, voters supporting candidate Al Gore to punch the hole associated with Pat Buchanan by mistake. (AP photo/Gary I. Rothstein)

with direct-recording electronic voting machines. (These systems are discussed in Chapter 8.)

Others have suggested that voting via the Internet be used, at least as a way of casting absentee ballots. In fact, online voting is already a reality. The state of Alaska supports online voting, and more than 30 US states allow members of the US military to vote online [92].

Several nations allow voting over the Internet. In 2005 Estonia became the first country to allow all of its citizens to vote online in local and national elections, and by 2009 about a quarter of votes were cast online. Online voting is also allowed in Switzerland; the Internet is used for about 20 percent of the ballots cast in the canton of Geneva [93]. An election in New South Wales, Australia, in 2015 set a world record for the most votes cast online: 284,000 citizens cast their ballots over the Internet [94].

## 7.5.3 Ethical Evaluation

In this section we make a utilitarian evaluation of the morality of online voting by weighing its benefits and risks. The discussion assumes that online voting would be implemented via a Web browser, though similar arguments could be made if another technology were employed.

### BENEFITS OF ONLINE VOTING

Advocates of online voting say it would have numerous advantages [95].

- Online voting would give people who ordinarily could not get to the polls the opportunity to cast a ballot from their homes.

- Votes cast via the Internet could be counted much more quickly than votes cast on paper.

- Electronic votes would not have any of the ambiguity associated with physical votes, such as hanging chad and erasures.

- Elections conducted online would cost less money than traditional elections.

- Online voting would eliminate the risk of somebody tampering with a ballot box containing physical votes.

While in most elections people vote for a single candidate, some elections allow a person to vote for multiple candidates. For example, a school board may have three vacancies, and voters may be asked to vote for three candidates. It would be easy to program the voting form to prevent people from accidentally overvoting—choosing too many candidates.

Sometimes a long, complicated ballot results in undervoting—where a voter accidentally forgets to mark a candidate for a particular office. A Web form could be designed in multiple pages so that each page had the candidates for a single office. Hence online voting could reduce undervoting.

## RISKS OF ONLINE VOTING

Critics of online voting have pointed to numerous risks associated with casting ballots over the Web, summarized in the following paragraphs [95].

Online voting is unfair because it gives an unfair advantage to those who are financially better off. It will be easier for people with computers and Internet connections at home to vote.

The same system that authenticates the voter also records the ballot. This makes it more difficult to preserve the privacy of the voter.

Online voting increases the opportunities for vote solicitation and vote selling. Suppose person X agrees to vote for candidate Y in return for getting a payment from Z. If person X votes from his personal computer, he could allow person Z to watch as he cast his vote for Y, proving that he fulfilled his end of the bargain. This is much less likely to occur at an official polling place monitored by election officials.

A Web site hosting an election is an obvious target for a DDoS attack. Unlike corporate Web sites, which have attracted the attention of teenage hackers, a national election Web site could attract the attention of foreign governments or terrorists trying to disrupt the electoral process. What happens if the Web site is unavailable and people are not able to access it before the election deadline?

If voting is done from home computers, the security of the election depends on the security of these home computers. Ways in which the security of home computers could be compromised include the following:

- A virus could change a person's vote without that person even suspecting what had happened. Many people have physical access to other people's computers, giving them the opportunity to install voter-deceiving applications in the weeks leading up to the election. Alternatively, a rogue programmer or group of programmers within a software company could sneak in a vote-tampering virus.

- A backdoor Trojan lurking in a voter's computer could allow a person's vote to be observed by an outsider. A backdoor Trojan could even allow an outsider to cast a ballot in lieu of the rightful voter.

- An attacker could fool a user into thinking she was connected to the vote server when in actuality she was connected to a phony vote server controlled by the attacker. For example, the attacker could send an email telling voters to click on a link to reach the polling site. When voters did so, they would be connected to the phony voting site. The attacker could ask for the voter's credentials, then use this information to connect to the real voter site and cast a vote for the candidate(s) desired by the attacker.

## UTILITARIAN ANALYSIS

A utilitarian analysis must add up the positive and negative outcomes to determine whether allowing online voting is a good action to take. Recall from Section 2.7.2 that not all outcomes have equal weight. We must consider the probability of the outcome, the value of the outcome on each affected person, and the number of people affected.

Sometimes this calculation is relatively straightforward. For example, one of the benefits of online voting is that people who vote online would not have to travel to a polling place and wait in line. Suppose online voting replaced polling places in the United States. This change would affect about 50 percent of adult Americans (the ones who actually vote) [96]. We can estimate that the average voter spends about an hour traveling to a polling place, waiting in line, and traveling back. The average annual salary in the United States is about $43,000, or about $21.00 per hour [97]. We could compute, then, that the time savings associated with replacing polling places with online voting would be worth about $21.00 times one-half the adult population, or $10.50 for every adult.

It is more difficult to come up with reasonable weights for other outcomes. For example, a risk of online voting is that a DDoS attack may prevent legitimate voters from casting their votes before the deadline. While an election result that does not reflect the will of the voters is a great harm, the weight of this harm is reduced by three probabilities: the probability that someone would attempt a DDoS attack, the probability that a DDoS attack would be successful, and the probability that a successful DDoS attack would change the outcome of the election. Experts could have vastly different estimates of these probabilities, allowing the scales of the utilitarian evaluation to tip one way or the other.

## KANTIAN ANALYSIS

A Kantian analysis of any voting system would focus on the principle that the will of each voter should be reflected in that voter's ballot. The integrity of each ballot is paramount. For this reason, every vote should leave a paper record so that, in the event of controversy, a recount can be held to ensure the correctness of the election result.

Eliminating paper records in order to achieve the ends of saving time and money or boosting voter turnout is wrong from a Kantian perspective.

## CONCLUSIONS

We have surveyed the potential benefits and risks of holding elections online, and we have examined the morality of online voting from a utilitarian and a Kantian point of view.

Are we holding computers up to too high a standard? After all, existing voting systems are imperfect. There are two key differences, however, between existing mechanical or electromechanical systems and the proposed online system.

Existing systems are highly localized. A single person may be able to corrupt the election process at a few voting places, but it is impossible to taint the election results across an entire state. A Web-based election system would make it much easier for a single malicious person to taint the process on a wide scale.

The second difference is that most current systems produce a paper record of the vote. Where paper records do not exist, there is a push to make them mandatory [98]. When all else fails, the hard copy can be consulted to try to discern the intent of the voters. A Web-based voting system would not have paper records verified by citizens as true representations of their votes.

There is already evidence of tampering in online elections. In April 2002, Vivendi Universal, a Paris media conglomerate, held an online vote of its shareholders. Hackers caused ballots of some large shareholders to be counted as abstentions [95]. If a private election can draw the attention of a hacker, imagine how much more attractive a target a California election Web site would be!

Bruce Schneier has written, "A secure Internet voting system is theoretically possible, but it would be the first secure networked application ever created in computing history" [99].

Any election system that relies upon the security of personal computers managed by ordinary citizens will be vulnerable to electoral fraud. For this reason alone, there is a strong case to be made that a government should not allow online voting to be conducted in this way.

# Summary

Computer and network security are important not just to those who manage the mainframe computer systems of corporations and government agencies, but to anyone who has a personal computer connected to the Internet. The more that people use computers to mediate their activities, the more opportunities they provide criminal enterprises.

Computer passwords illustrate how computer security is a trade-off between safety and convenience. Shorter passwords are easier to remember, and they take less time to enter. Unfortunately, they are easily cracked. In order to keep their systems secure, computer users must create longer, more obscure passwords that are decidedly less convenient.

One strategy adopted by criminals is to try to get information directly from computer users. Phishing attacks are an example of this kind of exploit. Some people "fall" for phishing attacks because they are accustomed to providing sensitive financial information over an Internet connection.

Another strategy is to spy on the activities of computer users. Some spyware programs contain keystroke loggers that collect and report credit card numbers and other sensitive information users type on the keyboard as they visit ecommerce sites.

Criminals can also make money by co-opting personal computers, turning them into bots. Bot herders rent huge botnets to those who wish to use them as launching pads for spamming, phishing attacks, or distributed denial-of-service attacks.

Personal computers can become infected with malware in many different ways. Even if users remember never to open a suspect email attachment, their systems may still become infected. A worm may enter a computer by taking advantage of a security weakness in the operating system. By simply visiting a Web site, a computer user may become the victim of a cross-site injection or a drive-by download. That is why it is important that all personal computer users set up personal firewalls and keep their systems up-to-date with antimalware tools.

The recent rise in politically motivated cyber attacks raises some interesting questions. How vulnerable would the United States economy be to a cyber attack by a determined foe? At what point does a cyber attack on another nation become an act of war? Should a nation holding an Internet-based election be concerned about interference from outside agencies?

## Further Reading and Viewing

Tom Bearden. "Preventing a 'Cyber-Pearl Harbor.'" *PBS NewsHour*, April 16, 2012. 7:45. video.pbs.org.

John Brunner. *The Shockwave Rider*. Harper & Row, New York, NY, 1975.

Annie Machon (interview). "Anonymous Ops 'a New Front in Protest.'" RT, April 7, 2013. 4:18. rt.com/op-edge/.

Avi Rubin. "All Your Devices Can Be Hacked." TED Talk, February 2012. 16:56. www.ted.com/talks/.

Ray Suarez. "US Fed Up with China's Cyber Theft, Say Analysts." *PBS NewsHour*, July 8, 2013. 9:39. video.pbs.org.

## Review Questions

1. How has the term "hacker" evolved since the 1950s?

2. Describe three "low-tech" methods that hackers have used to obtain login names and passwords.

3. Why is it dangerous to surf the Web using an open Wi-Fi network?

4. What is the difference between a computer virus and a worm?

5. What is the relationship between spyware and backdoor Trojans?

6. What is the difference between spyware and adware?

7. How are Trojan horses and drive-by downloads similar?

8. Why is it dangerous for an email program to open attachments automatically, without waiting for the user to select them?

9. Give two examples of how criminal organizations have used the Internet to make money.

10. What is a cyber attack? Give two examples of cyber attacks that have taken place outside the United States.

11. If converting SCADA systems to the Internet Protocol increases the risk of a hacker taking control of an industrial process, why are companies doing just that?

12. Explain two different ways a vote thief could cast multiple votes in an online election.

# Discussion Questions

13. In a study done in London, people in subway stations were offered a cheap pen in return for disclosing their passwords. About 90 percent offered their passwords in return for the pen [100]. What can be done to get people to take security more seriously?

14. Email viruses are typically launched by people who modify header information to hide their identity. Brightmail's Enrique Salem says that in the future, your email reader will authenticate the sender before putting the message in your inbox. That way, you will know the source of all the emails you read. Alan Nugent of Novell says, "I'm kind of a fan of eliminating anonymity if that is the price for security" [101]. Will eliminating anonymity make computers more secure?

15. Are there conditions under which the release of a worm, virus, or Trojan horse would be morally justifiable?

16. When his worm program did not perform as expected, Robert Morris Jr. contacted two old friends from Harvard to decide what to do next. One of them, Andy Sudduth, agreed to email an anonymous message apologizing for the worm and describing how to protect computers from it, without disclosing Morris as the creator of the worm [26]. Was this the right thing for Sudduth to do?

17. Kalamazoo College requires that all computers connected to the campus network be running up-to-date antivirus software. When a student's computer is discovered to have a virus, its network connection is cut until a staff member can remove the virus. If it turns out that the computer was not running up-to-date antivirus software, the student is fined $100 [102]. Is this a morally justifiable policy?

18. Adam and Charlene are good friends. Both attend East Dakota State University. One day when Adam is off campus interviewing for a part-time job, someone asks him how many credit hours of computer science courses he has completed. Adam calls Charlene and asks her to access his student records by logging into the campus mainframe as if she were Adam. He provides Charlene with his student identification number and password so that she can do this. Is it wrong for Adam to share this information with Charlene? Is it wrong for Charlene to retrieve this information for Adam?

19. Carnegie Mellon University, Harvard University, and the Massachusetts Institute of Technology denied admission to more than 100 business school applicants because they took an online peek at the status of their applications. These students learned how to circumvent the program's security, and they used this knowledge to view their files and see if they had been accepted. Students could see information about their own application, but could not view the status of other students' applications. In many cases the students learned that no admission decision had yet been made. Do you feel the response of these universities was appropriate?

20. Millions of American homes are equipped with wireless networks. If the network is not made secure, any nearby computer with a wireless card can use the network. The range of home wireless networks often extends into neighboring homes, particularly in apartment complexes. If your neighbor's wireless network extends into your home, is it wrong to use that network to get free Internet access?

21. Is it morally acceptable to use a denial-of-service attack to shut down a Web server that distributes child pornography?

22. Some would argue that technological development is inevitable. If Butler had not created Firesheep, someone else would have. Every invention can be put to good or bad uses. Therefore, creators of new technologies bear no moral responsibility for their inventions. In contrast, the author argues that people who create a tool making it easier for someone to do something immoral share some moral accountability for the misdeeds done by people using the tool. Which perspective do you find more compelling?

23. Do you support the actions of Anonymous? Would you consider becoming an Anon?

24. The United States and Israel cooperated to unleash the Stuxnet worm, which apparently slowed down Iran's nuclear program by damaging centrifuges processing uranium. Was unleashing the Stuxnet worm morally justifiable?

25. Do you agree with the author that it is a bad idea for a government to allow online voting from home computers?

# In-Class Exercises

26. Debate this proposition: Those who create nondestructive malware are doing the computer industry a favor because the patches created to block them make computers more secure. To use an analogy, each virus has the effect of strengthening the immune systems of the computers it targets.

27. The University of Calgary offered a senior-level computer science course called "Computer Viruses and Malware." The course taught students how to write viruses, worms, and Trojan horses. It also discussed the history of computer viruses and taught students how to block attacks. All course assignments were done on a closed computer network isolated from the Internet. Some computer security experts criticized the university for offering the course. One researcher said, "No one argues criminology students should commit a murder to understand how a murderer thinks" [103]. Debate whether the University of Calgary was wrong to offer the course.

28. Debate this proposition: It is wrong for a company to hire a former malicious hacker as a security consultant.

29. A distributed denial-of-service attack makes the Web site for a top electronic retailer inaccessible for an entire day. As a result of the attack, nearly a million customers were inconvenienced, and the retailer lost millions of dollars in sales to its competitors. Law enforcement agencies apprehend the person who launched the attack. Should the punishment be determined strictly by considering the crime that was committed, or should the identity of the culprit be taken into account? If the identity of the perpetrator should be taken into account, what punishment do you think would be appropriate if he were:

    - A teenager who launched the attack out of curiosity
    - An adult dedicated to fighting the country's overly materialistic culture
    - A member of a terrorist organization attempting to harm the national economy

30. Divide the class into two groups. One group should come up with arguments why the United States should work to create an international ban on cyber attacks, analogous to the Chemical Weapons Convention that outlaws the production and use of chemical weapons. The other group should come up with arguments why the United States should strive to become preeminent in cyber attack technology.

31. East Dakota has decided to allow its citizens to vote over the Web in the presidential election, if they so desire. Thirty percent of the eligible voters choose to cast their ballots over the Web. The national election is so closely contested that whoever wins the electoral votes of East Dakota will be the next president. After the election, state elections officials report the vote tally and declare candidate X to be the winner.

    Two weeks after the inauguration of President X, state officials uncover evidence of massive electoral fraud. Some voters were tricked into connecting to a phony voting site. The organization running the phony site used the credentials provided by the duped voters to connect to the actual voting site and cast a vote for candidate X.

    State officials conclude the electoral fraud may have changed the outcome of the election, but they cannot say for sure. They have no evidence that candidate X knew anything about this scheme to increase his vote tally.

    Divide the class into groups representing President X, the other presidential candidates, citizens of East Dakota, and citizens of other states to discuss the proper response to this revelation. For guidance, consult Article II, Section 1, along with Amendment XII, of the United States Constitution.

# References

[1]    Steven Levy. *Hackers: Heroes of the Computer Revolution*. Anchor Press/Doubleday, Garden City, NY, 1984.

[2]    G. Malkin and T. LaQuey Parker, editors. "Hacker." *Internet Users' Glossary*, January 1993. www.rfc-editor.org.

[3]    Kevin Granville. "9 Recent Cyberattacks against Big Businesses." *New York Times*, February 5, 2015. www.nytimes.com.

[4]    Dan Goodin. "Anatomy of a Hack: How Crackers Ransack Passwords Like "qeadzwrs-fxv1331." Ars Technica (Web site), May 27, 2013. arstechnica.com.

[5]    William Cheswick. "Rethinking Passwords." *Communications of the ACM*, February 2013.

[6] Mat Honan. "Hacked." *Wired*, December 2012.

[7] Marcia Savage. "Mitnick Turns Gamekeeper." *TechWeb.com*, October 30, 2000.

[8] Michael Arnone. "Hacker Steals Personal Data on Foreign Students at U. of Kansas." *Chronicle of Higher Education*, January 24, 2003.

[9] Sara Lipka. "Hacker Breaks into Database for Tracking International Students at UNLV." *Chronicle of Higher Education*, March 21, 2005.

[10] Dan Carnevale. "Harvard and MIT Join Carnegie Mellon in Rejecting Applicants Who Broke into Business-School Networks." *Chronicle of Higher Education*, March 9, 2005.

[11] John P. Mello Jr. "Sesame Street Hacked, Porn Posted." *PCWorld*, October 17, 2011.

[12] Eric Butler. "Firesheep." *{codebutler}* (blog), October 24, 2010. codebutler.com.

[13] Bob Brown. "Father of Firesheep Fires Away after Wild Week in WiFi Security." *NetworkWorld*, November 2, 2011. www.networkworld.com.

[14] Tom Anderson. "Firesheep in Wolves' Clothing: Extension Lets You Hack into Twitter, Facebook Accounts Easily." TechCrunch, October 24, 2010. techcrunch.com.

[15] Jason Fitzpatrick. "Firesheep Sniffs Out Facebook and Other User Credentials on Wi-Fi Hotspots." *Lifehacker* (blog), October 25, 2010. lifehacker.com.

[16] Gregg Keizer. "How to Protect against Firesheep Attacks." *Computerworld*, October 26, 2010. www.computerworld.com.

[17] Sharon Machlis. "How to Hijack Facebook Using Firesheep." *PCWorld*, October 30, 2010. www.pcworld.com.

[18] Eric Butler. "Firesheep, a Week Later: Ethics and Legality." *{codebutler}* (blog), November 1, 2010. codebutler.com.

[19] Alex Rice. "A Continued Commitment to Security." *The Facebook Blog*, January 26, 2011. blog.facebook.com.

[20] Paul Ducklin. "Twitter Goes Secure—Say Goodbye to Firesheep with 'Always use HTTPS' Option." *nakedsecurity* (blog), March 16, 2011. nakedsecurity.sophos.com.

[21] Jessica Goodman. "Firesheep, What Color Is Your Hat?" *FeelingElephant's Weblog*, November 30, 2010. feelingelephants.wordpress.com.

[22] David Ferbrache. *A Pathology of Computer Viruses*. Springer-Verlag, London, England, 1992.

[23] Eurostat. "Nearly One Third of Internet Users in the EU27 Caught a Computer Virus; 84% of Internet Users Use IT Security Software for Protection" (news release). February 7, 2011. europa.eu.

[24] "Google Warns TWO MILLION Users Their Computers Have Been Infected with a Virus." *Mail Online*, July 21, 2011. www.dailymail.co.uk.

[25] John Brunner. *The Shockwave Rider*. Harper & Row, New York, NY, 1975.

[26] Katie Hafner and John Markoff. *Cyberpunk: Outlaws and Hackers on the Computer Frontier*. Simon & Schuster, New York, NY, 1991.

[27] Paul Graham. "The Submarine." April 2005. www.paulgraham.com.

[28] "Worm Turns for Teenager Who Befuddled Microsoft." *Times*, London, July 6, 2005.

[29] "Hacker behind Sasser, Netsky Worms Gets Job with German Security Company." *San Jose Mercury News*, September 28, 2004.

[30] John Leyden. "Sasser Suspect Walks Free." *Register*, July 8, 2005. www.theregister.do .uk.

[31] Celeste Biever. "Instant Messaging Falls Prey to Worms." *New Scientist*, May 14, 2005.

[32]  Hanleigh Daniels. "Palevo Is Worming Its Way via IM Spam." *Tech Smart*, May 4, 2010. www.techsmart.co.za.

[33]  Ben Nahorney, editor. "The Downadup Codex: A Comprehensive Guide to the Threat's Mechanics." Edition 1.0. Symantec Corporation, 2009. www.symantec.com.

[34]  "Virus Strikes 15 Million PCs." UPI, January 26, 2009. www.upi.com.

[35]  John Markoff. "Defying Experts, Rogue Computer Code Still Lurks." *New York Times*, August 27, 2009.

[36]  Brian Prince. "Conficker Worm Deadline Passes Quietly—So Far." *IT Security & Network Security News*, April 1, 2009. www.eweek.com.

[37]  John Leyden. "Drive-By Download Menace Spreading Fast." *Register*, January 23, 2008. www.theregister.co.uk.

[38]  Ryan Naraine. "Drive-By Downloads. The Web under Siege." *Securelist* (blog), April 15, 2009. www.securelist.com.

[39]  Steve Sechrist. "State of Security: China's Trojan Horse." *Display Daily*, March 18, 2008. displaydaily.com.

[40]  Webroot. "Spyware Infection Rates Return to Peak 2004 Levels According to Webroot State of Spyware Report." August 15, 2006. www.webroot.com.

[41]  Scott Berinato. "Attack of the Bots." *Wired*, November 2006.

[42]  "Ecommerce Sales Topped $1 Trillion for First Time in 2012." eMarketer, February 5, 2013. www.emarketer.com.

[43]  Greg Aaron and Rod Rasmussen. "Global Phishing Survey 2H2014: Trends and Domain Name Use." APWG Internet Policy Committee, May 27, 2015. www.apwg.org.

[44]  Edward Skoudis. "Evolutionary Trends in Cyberspace." In *Cyberpower and National Security*, pp. 163–164, edited by Franklin D. Kramer, Stuart H. Starr, and Larry K. Wentz. Potomac Books, Dulles, Virginia, 2009.

[45]  CERT Coordination Center. "Denial of Service Attacks." June 4, 2001. www.cert.org/ tech_tips/ denial_of_service.html.

[46]  Mike Toner. "Cyberterrorism Danger Lurking." *Atlanta Journal and Constitution*, November 2, 2001.

[47]  Toni O'Loughlin. "Cyber Terrorism Reaches New Heights." *Australian Financial Review*, April 4, 2003.

[48]  "Zombie Master Jeanson Ancheta Pleads Guilty." *Spam Daily News*, January 23, 2006. www.spamdailynews.com.

[49]  "Zombie Master Jeanson Ancheta Sentenced to 5 Years in Prison." *Spam Daily News*, May 9, 2006. www.spamdailynews.com.

[50]  Robert Lemos. "Blue Security Folds under Spammer's Wrath." SecurityFocus (Web site), May 17, 2006. www.securityfocus.com.

[51]  Kim Zetter. "TJX Hacker Charged with Heartland, Hannaford Breaches." Threat Level: Privacy, Crime and Security Online, *Wired*, August 17, 2009. www.wired.com.

[52]  David Morrison. "Albert Gonzalez, Mastermind Heartland Hacker, Gets 20 Years." *Credit Union Times*, April 7, 2010. www.cutimes.com.

[53]  "Avalanche Botnet Moves from Distributing Spam to Zeus Lures." *SC Magazine*, October 25, 2010. www.scmagazineuk.com.

[54]  Kevin O'Shea. "Cyber Attack Investigative Tools and Technologies." Institute for Security Technology Studies at Dartmouth College, May 7, 2003. www.ists.dartmouth.edu.

[55]  Joshua Davis. "Hackers Take Down the Most Wired Country in Europe." *Wired*, August 21, 2007. www.wired.com.

[56]  Mark Lander and John Markoff. "Digital Fears Emerge after Data Siege in Estonia." *New York Times*, May 29, 2007. www.nytimes.com.

[57]  "A Look at Estonia's Cyber Attack in 2007." Associated Press, July 8, 2009. www.msnbc.msn.com.

[58]  John Markoff. "Before the Gunfire, Cyberattacks." *New York Times*, August 12, 2008. www.nytimes.com.

[59]  Kevin Coleman. "Cyber War 2.0—Russia v. Georgia." Defense Tech (Web site), August 13, 2008. defensetech.org.

[60]  "War, Redefined." *Los Angeles Times*, August 17, 2008. articles.latimes.com.

[61]  Jared Newman. "Twitter Crippled by Denial-of-Service Attack." *PCWorld Blogs*, August 6, 2009. www.pcworld.com.

[62]  Elinor Mills. "Twitter, Facebook Attack Targeted One User." CNet News (Web site), August 6, 2009. news.cnet.com.

[63]  Graham Cluley. "Was Twitter Denial-of-Service Targeting Anti-Russian Blogger?" *Graham Cluley's Blog*, August 7, 2009. www.sophos.com.

[64]  "A Chinese Ghost in the Machine?" *Economist*, April 4, 2009.

[65]  John Markoff. "Tracking Cyberspies through the Web Wilderness." *New York Times*, May 12, 2009.

[66]  Choe Sang-Hun and John Markoff. "Cyberattacks Jam Government and Commercial Web Sites in US and South Korea." *New York Times*, July 9, 2009.

[67]  John Markoff. "Internet's Anonymity Makes Cyberattack Hard to Trace." *New York Times*, July 17, 2009.

[68]  "Hacking the Industrial Network." Phoenix Contact Inc., Harrisburg, Pennsylvania. www.isa.org.

[69]  "Siemens SCADA Systems under Attack by Information Stealing Worm." Help Net Security, July 20, 2010. www.net-security.org.

[70]  "Iran Confirms Stuxnet Worm Halted Centrifuges." CBS News, November 29, 2010. www.cbsnews.com.

[71]  John Markoff. "Malware Aimed at Iran Hit Five Sites, Report Says." *New York Times*, February 11, 2011. www.nytimes.com.

[72]  Christopher Williams. "Israeli Video Shows Stuxnet as One of Its Successes." *Telegraph*, February 15, 2011. www.telegraph.co.uk.

[73]  David Sanger. "Obama Order Sped Up Wave of Cyberattacks against Iran." *New York Times*, June 1, 2012. www.nytimes.com.

[74]  "APT1: Exposing One of China's Cyber Espionage Units." Mandiant Corporation, February 18, 2013. www.mandiant.com.

[75]  David E. Sanger, David Barboza, and Nicole Perlroth. "Chinese Army Unit Is Seen as Tied to Hacking against U.S." *New York Times*, February 18, 2013.

[76]  T.P. "Hello, Unit 61398." *Economist*, February 19, 2013.

[77]  Brian B. Kelly. "Investing in a Centralized Cybersecurity Infrastructure: Why 'Hacktivism' Can and Should Influence Cybersecurity Reform." *Boston University Law Review*, Vol. 92, No. 4, October 2012.

[78] PRLog. "Internet Group Anonymous Declares 'War on Scientology'" (press release). January 21, 2008. www.prlog.org.

[79] John Leyden. "4chan Launched DDoS against Entertainment Industry." *Register*, September 20, 2010. www.theregister.co.uk.

[80] Fahmida Y. Rashid. "PayPal, PostFinance Hit by DoS Attacks, Counter-Attack in Progress." *eWeek*, December 6, 2010. www.eweek.com.

[81] Esther Addley and Josh Halliday. "WikiLeaks Supporters Disrupt Visa and MasterCard Sites in 'Operation Payback.'" *Guardian*, December 8, 2010. www.guardian.co.uk.

[82] Yasmine Ryan. "Anonymous and the Arab Uprisings." Al Jazeera, May 19, 2011. www .aljazeera.com.

[83] "Internet Strikes Back: Anonymous' Operation Megaupload Explained." RT, January 20, 2012. rt.com.

[84] Adam Clark Estes. "Anonymous Hits Israel with a Massive Cyber Attack, Israel Attacks Back." *Atlantic Wire*, April 7, 2013.

[85] David Boroff. "Grieving Dad, Anonymous Lash Out at Cleveland Cops Following Shooting Death of Boy, 12, Armed with BB Gun." *New York Daily News*, November 24, 2014. www.nydailynews.com.

[86] Keely Lockhart. "'Hacktivist' Group Anonymous Says It Will Avenge Charlie Hebdo Attacks by Shutting Down Jihadist Websites." *Telegraph*, January 10, 2015. www .telegraph.co.uk.

[87] Nic Corbett. "Verona Teen Sentenced to Year in Prison for Online Attack of Scientology." *Star-Ledger,* New Jersey, November 18, 2009. www.nj.com.

[88] John Leyden. "Second Man Jailed over Scientology DDoS Attacks." *Register*, May 25, 2010. www.theregister.co.uk.

[89] Nate Anderson. "Anon on the Run: How Commander X Jumped Bail and Fled to Canada." Ars Technica (Web site), December 11, 2012. arstechnica.com.

[90] Dave Lee. "Jake Davis: Freed Hacker Faces Strict Tech Rules." BBC, June 24, 2013. www .bbc.co.uk.

[91] A. Agresti and B. Presnell. "Misvotes, Undervotes, and Overvotes: The 2000 Presidential Election in Florida." *Statistical Science* 17(4):436–440, 2002.

[92] Jeremy Hsu. "Alaska's Online Voting Leaves Cybersecurity Experts Worried." *IEEE Spectrum*, November 6, 2014. spectrum.ieee.org.

[93] Rosie Scammell. "Internet Voting a Success in Two European Countries." European University Institute, February 12, 2013. www.eui.eu/News.

[94] "Early Voting Hits New Highs in NSW and Australia, But Is It a Good Idea?" *Conversation*, April 8, 2015.

[95] Rebecca Mercuri. "A Better Ballot Box?" *IEEE Spectrum*, pp. 46–50, October 2002.

[96] Thomas E. Patterson. *The Vanishing Voter: Public Involvement in an Age of Uncertainty*. Alfred A. Knopf/Random House, New York, NY, 2002.

[97] Bureau of Business of Economic Research, University of New Mexico. "Per Capita Personal Income by State." April 2, 2013. bber.unm.edu..

[98] Todd R. Weiss. "N.J. to Get E-voting Paper Trail, but Not until 2008; a Legal Battle Continues to Try to Put the Law into Effect Sooner." *Computerworld*, July 15, 2005.

[99] Bruce Schneier. "Technology Was Only Part of the Florida Problem." *Computerworld*, December 18, 2000.

[100] John Leyden. "Office Workers Give Away Passwords for a Cheap Pen." *Register*, April 17, 2003. www.theregister.co.uk.

[101] "Fighting the Worms of Mass Destruction." *Economist*, pp. 65–67, November 29, 2003.

[102] Kalamazoo College Information Technology Services. "Computer Virus Policy." Accessed July 29, 2011. reason.kzoo.edu.

[103] Brock Read. "How to Write a Computer Virus, for College Credit." *Chronicle of Higher Education*, January 16, 2004.

# Matt Bishop

Matt Bishop received his PhD in computer science from Purdue University, where he specialized in computer security. He was a research scientist at the Research Institute for Advanced Computer Science and was on the faculty at Dartmouth College before joining the Department of Computer Science at the University of California, Davis. He teaches courses in computer security, operating systems, and programming.

His main research area is the analysis of vulnerabilities in computer systems, including modeling them, building tools to detect vulnerabilities, and ameliorating or eliminating them. This includes detecting and handling all types of malicious logic. He is active in the areas of network security, the study of denial-of-service attacks and defenses, policy modeling, software assurance testing, and formal modeling of access control. He also studies the issue of trust as an underpinning for security policies, procedures, and mechanisms.

He is active in information assurance education, is a charter member of the Colloquium on Information Systems Security Education, and led a project to gather and make available many unpublished seminal works in computer security. He has authored a textbook, *Computer Security: Art and Science*, published by Addison-Wesley Professional.

---

### *What led you to focus your research on system vulnerabilities?*

I became interested in this area because of the ubiquity of the problem. We have been designing and building computer systems since the 1950s, and we still don't know how to secure systems in practice. Why not? How can we find the existing vulnerabilities and improve the security of those existing systems?

Also, there are parallels with nontechnical fields. I find those parallels fascinating, and I enjoy learning and studying other fields to see if any of the methods and ideas from those fields can be applied to analyzing systems and improving their security. Some fields, like military science, political science, and psychology, have obvious connections. Others, such as art and literature, have less obvious connections. But all emphasize the importance of people to computer and software security.

### *Do you have an example of what can happen when security is treated as an add-on, rather than designed into a system from the beginning?*

Yes. Consider the Internet. When it was first implemented (as the old ARPANET), the protocols were not developed to supply the security services that are now considered important. (The security services that were considered important were various forms of robustness, so that the network would provide connectivity even in the face of multiple failures of systems in the network and even of portions of the network itself. It supplied those services very well.) As a result, security services such as authentication, confidentiality of messages, and integrity of messages are being treated as add-ons rather than the protocols being redesigned to provide those services inherently. So today we have security problems in the descendant of the ARPANET, the Internet.

### How can the choice of programming language affect the security of the resulting program?

In two ways. The more obvious one is that some programming languages enforce constraints that limit unsafe practices. For example, in Java, the language prevents indexing beyond the end of an array. In C, the language does not. So you can get buffer overflows in C, but it's much harder to get buffer overflows in Java. The less obvious one is that the language controls how most programmers think about their algorithms. For example, a language that is functional matches some algorithms better than one that is imperative. This means the programmer will make fewer mistakes, and the mistakes he or she makes will tend to be at the implementation level rather than the conceptual or design level—and mistakes at the implementation level will be *much* easier to fix.

### What can be done about the problem of viruses, worms, and Trojan horses?

These programs run with the authority of the user who triggers them; worms also spread autonomously through the network and most often take advantage of vulnerabilities to enter a system and spread from it. So several things can ameliorate the situation:

1. Minimize the number of network services you run. In particular, if you don't need the service, disable it. This will stop the spread of many worms.

2. Don't run any attachments you receive in the mail unless you trust the person who sent them to you. Most viruses and many worms spread this way. In particular, some mailers (such as Outlook) can be set up to execute and/or unpack attachments automatically. This feature should be disabled.

3. The user should not be able to alter certain files, such as system programs and system configuration files. If the user must be able to alter them, confirmation should be required. This will limit the effect of most viruses to affecting the user rather than the system as a whole or other users on the system.

### Many personal computer users do not update their systems with the latest operating system patches. Should computer manufacturers be given the ability (and the obligation) to keep up-to-date all of their customers' Internet-connected computers?

I question the wisdom of allowing vendors to update computers remotely. The problem is that vendors do not know the particular environment in which the computers function. The environment determines what "security" means. So a patch that improves security in one realm may weaken it in another.

As an example, suppose a company disallows any connections from the network except through a virtual private network (VPN). Its systems were designed to start all servers in a particular directory that contains all network servers. So to enforce this restriction, all network servers *except* the VPN are removed from the systems. This prevents the other servers from being started.

The system vendor discovers a security vulnerability in the email server and the login procedure. It fixes both and sends out a patch that includes a new login program and a new email server. The patch installs both and reboots the system so the new login program and email server will be used immediately.

The problem here is that by installing the new email server (which improves security in most systems), the company's systems now are nonsecure, as they can be connected to via a port other than those used for the VPN (for example, the email port, port 25). The vendor's patch may therefore damage security.

We saw this with Windows XP SP2. It patched many holes but also broke various third-party applications, some of them very important to their users.

So I believe vendors should be obligated to work with their customers to provide security patches and enhancements, but should not be given the ability to keep the systems up-to-date unless the customer asks for it. Vendors should also provide better configuration interfaces, and default configurations, that are easy to set up and change, as well as (free) support to help customers use them.

### Do you expect personal computers a decade from now to be more secure than they are today?

In some ways yes, and in other ways no. I expect that they will provide more security services that can be configured to make the systems more secure in various environments—not all environments, though! I also expect that the main problem for securing systems will be configuration, operation, and maintenance, though, and those problems will not be overcome in a decade, because they are primarily people problems and not technical problems.

### What advice can you offer students who are seriously interested in creating secure software systems?

Focus on all aspects of the software system. Identify the specific requirements that the software system is to solve, develop a security policy that the software system is to meet (and that will meet the requirements), design and implement the software correctly, and consider the environment in which it will be used when you do all this. Also, make the software system as easy to install and configure as possible, and plan that the users will make errors. People aren't perfect, and any security that depends upon them doing everything correctly will ultimately fail.

CHAPTER

# 8

# Computer Reliability

The greatest of faults, I should say, is to be conscious of none.

—Thomas Carlyle

## 8.1 Introduction

COMPUTER DATABASES TRACK MANY OF OUR ACTIVITIES. What happens when a computer is fed bad information, or when someone misinterprets the information retrieved from a computer? We are surrounded by devices containing embedded computers. What happens when a computer program contains an error that causes the computer to malfunction?

Sometimes the effects of a computer error are trivial. You are playing a game on your PC, do something unusual, and the program crashes, forcing you to start over. At other times computer malfunctions result in a real inconvenience. You get an incorrect bill in the mail, and you end up spending hours on the phone with the company's customer service agents to get the mistake fixed. Some software bugs have resulted in businesses making poor decisions that have cost them millions of dollars. On a few occasions, failures in a computerized system have even resulted in fatalities.

In this chapter we examine various ways in which computerized systems have proven to be unreliable. Systems typically have many components, of which the computer is just one. A well-engineered system can tolerate the malfunction of any single component without failing. Unfortunately, there are many examples of systems in which the computer was the weakest link and a computer error led to the failure of the entire system. The failure may have been due to a data entry or data retrieval error, poor design, or inadequate testing. Through a variety of examples, you will gain a greater appreciation for the complexity of building a reliable computerized system.

We also take a look at computer simulations, which are playing an increasingly important role in modern science and engineering. We survey some of the uses to which these simulations are put and describe how those who develop simulations can validate the underlying models.

The discipline of software engineering emerged when organizations began constructing large software systems and encountered problems meeting project goals with respect to reliability, cost, and schedule. Software engineering refers to the use of processes and tools that allow programs to be created in a more structured manner. We describe the software development process and provide evidence that more software projects are being completed on time and on budget.

At the end of the chapter, we take a look at software warranties. Software manufacturers typically disclaim any liability for lost profits or other consequential damages resulting from the use of their products. We discuss how much responsibility software manufacturers ought to take for the quality of their products.

## 8.2 Data Entry or Data Retrieval Errors

Sometimes computerized systems fail because the wrong data have been entered into them or because people incorrectly interpret the data they retrieve. In this section we give several examples of wrong actions being taken due to errors in data entry or data retrieval.

### 8.2.1 Disenfranchised Voters

In the November 2000 general election, Florida disqualified thousands of voters because preelection screening identified them as felons. The records in the computer database, however, were incorrect; the voters had been charged with misdemeanors. Nevertheless, they were forbidden from voting. This error may have affected the outcome of the presidential election [1].

### 8.2.2 False Arrests

As we saw in Chapter 6, the databases of the National Crime Information Center (NCIC) contain a total of about 40 million records related to stolen automobiles, missing persons, wanted persons, suspected terrorists, and much more. There have been numerous stories of police making false arrests based on information they retrieved from the NCIC. Here are three.

Sheila Jackson Stossier, an airline flight attendant, was arrested at the New Orleans airport by police who confused her with Shirley Jackson, who was wanted in Texas. She spent one night in jail and was detained for five days [2].

California police, relying on information from the NCIC, twice arrested and jailed Roberto Hernandez as a suspect in a Chicago burglary case. The first time he was jailed for 12 days, and the second time he was held for a week before he was freed. They had confused him with another Roberto Hernandez, who had the same height and weight. Both Hernandezes had brown hair, brown eyes, and tattoos on their left arms. They also had the same birthday, and their Social Security numbers differed by only a single digit [3].

Someone used personal information about Michigan resident Terry Dean Rogan to obtain a California driver's license using his name. After the person with the falsified driver's license was arrested for two homicides and two robberies, police entered information about these crimes into the NCIC under his false identity. Over a period of 14 months, the real Terry Dean Rogan was arrested five times by Los Angeles police, three times at gunpoint, even though he and Michigan police had tried to get the NCIC records corrected after his first arrest. Rogan sued the Los Angeles Police Department and was awarded $55,000 [2].

### 8.2.3 Utilitarian Analysis: Accuracy of NCIC Records

Stepping away from a requirement of the Privacy Act of 1974, the Justice Department announced in March 2003 that it would no longer require the FBI to ensure the accuracy of information about criminals and crime victims before entering it in the NCIC database [4].

Should the US government take responsibility for the accuracy of the information stored in NCIC databases?

The Department of Justice argues that it is impractical for it to be responsible for the information in the NCIC database [5]: Much of the information that gets entered into the database is provided by other law enforcement and intelligence agencies. The FBI has no way of verifying that all the information is accurate, relevant, and complete. Even when the information is coming from inside the FBI, agents should be able to use their discretion to determine which information may be useful in criminal investigations. If the FBI strictly followed the provisions of the Privacy Act and verified the accuracy of every record entered into the NCIC, the amount of information in the database would be greatly curtailed. The database would be a much less useful tool for law enforcement agencies. The result could be a decrease in the number of criminals arrested by law enforcement agencies.

Privacy advocates counter that the accuracy of the NCIC databases is now more important than ever, because an increasing number of records are stored in these databases. As more erroneous records are put into the database, the probability of innocent American citizens being falsely arrested also increases.

Which argument is stronger? Let's focus on one of the oldest NCIC databases: the database of stolen vehicles. The total amount of harm caused to society by automobile theft is great. Over one million automobiles are stolen in the United States every year. Victims of car theft are subjected to emotional stress, may sustain a financial loss, and can spend a lot of time trying to recover or replace the vehicle. In addition, the prevalence of automobile theft harms everyone who owns a car by raising insurance rates. In the past car thieves could reduce the probability that a stolen car would be recovered by transporting it across a state line, but the NCIC database contains information about stolen vehicles throughout the United States, and it has enabled law enforcement officials to identify cars stolen anywhere in the nation.

At the present time, just over half of all stolen vehicles are recovered. If we make the conservative estimate that the NCIC has increased the percentage of recovered cars by just 20 percent, more than 100,000 additional cars are being returned to their owners each year. Each recovery has several benefits. First, the car is returned to its owner, who doesn't have to go through the hassle of settling an insurance claim and getting a new vehicle. Second, by returning the car to its owner, the police make sure that "crime does not pay" and may actually apprehend a criminal, which should reduce the number of cars stolen in the future. We assign a total value of $5,000 to the benefit of returning a single stolen car to its owner. Multiplying $5,000 by 100,000, the increase in the number of cars attributed to the NCIC stolen vehicle database, we determine the annual positive impact of the NCIC stolen vehicle database to be $500,000.

Now let's consider the harmful consequences of the database. If an error in the NCIC stolen car database leads to a false arrest, the harm caused to the innocent driver is great. However, after many years there are only a few stories of false arrests stemming from errors in the NCIC stolen car database. Suppose there is one false arrest per year. Based on the case of Terry Dean Rogan presented earlier, we assign a total value of −$55,000 to the harm caused per false arrest.

Adding up the benefits and the harms caused by the NCIC stolen vehicle database, we determine the operation of the database results in an annual total net increase in the happiness of the affected parties of $445,000. If the NCIC stolen vehicle database did not exist, the benefit and the harm would both be zero, meaning there would be no net increase in the happiness of the affected parties. Comparing these two alternatives, we conclude the creation and maintenance of this database has been the right course of action.

# 8.3  Software and Billing Errors

Even if the data entered into a computer are correct, the system may still produce the wrong result or collapse entirely if there are errors in the computer programs manipulating the data. Newspapers are full of stories about software bugs or "glitches." Here is a selection of stories that have appeared in print.

## 8.3.1  Errors Leading to System Malfunctions

Linda Brooks of Minneapolis, Minnesota, opened her mail on July 21, 2001, and found a phone bill for $57,346.20. A bug in Qwest's billing software caused it to charge some customers as much as $600 per minute for the use of their cell phones. About 1.4 percent of Qwest's customers, 14,000 in all, received incorrect bills. A Qwest spokesperson said the bug was in a newly installed billing system [6].

The US Department of Agriculture implemented new livestock price-reporting guidelines after discovering that software errors had caused the USDA to understate the prices meatpackers were receiving for beef. Since beef producers and packers negotiate cattle contracts based on the USDA price reports, the errors cost beef producers between $15 and $20 million [7].

In 1996 a software error at the US Postal Service resulted in two weeks' worth of mail addressed to the Patent and Trademark Office being returned to the senders. In all, 50,000 pieces of mail were returned [8].

A University of Pittsburgh study revealed that, for most students, computer spelling and grammar error checkers actually increased the number of errors they made [9, 10].

Between September 2008 and May 2009, hundreds of families living in public housing in New York City were charged too much rent because of an error in the program that calculated their monthly bills. For nine months, the New York City Housing Authority did not take seriously the renters' complaints that they were being overcharged. Instead, it took to court many of the renters who did not make the higher payments and threatened them with eviction [11].

In 2010 about 450 California prison inmates with a "high risk of violence" were mistakenly released as part of a program meant to reduce prison overcrowding. California officials could not return any of them to prison or put them on supervised parole because they had already been granted "nonrevocable parole" [12].

## 8.3.2 Errors Leading to System Failures

On the first day that a new, fully computerized ambulance dispatch system became operational in the city of London, people making emergency calls were put on hold for up to 30 minutes, with the system losing track of some calls, and ambulances took up to three hours to respond. As many as 20 people died because ambulances did not arrive in time [13].

Japan's air traffic control system went down for an hour on the morning of March 1, 2003, delaying departures for hours. The backup system failed at the same time as the main system, which was out of commission for four hours. Airports kept in touch via telephone, and no passengers were put at risk. However, some flights were delayed over two hours, and 32 domestic flights had to be canceled [14].

A new laboratory computer system at Los Angeles County+USC Medical Center became backlogged the day after it was turned on. For several hours on both April 16 and April 17, 2003, emergency room doctors told the County of Los Angeles to stop sending ambulances, because the doctors could not get access to the laboratory results they needed. "It's almost like practicing Third World medicine," said Dr. Amanda Garner. "We rely so much on our computers and our fast-world technology that we were almost blinded" [15].

Comair, a subsidiary of Delta Air Lines, canceled all 1,100 of its flights on Christmas Day 2004 because the computer system that assigns crews to flights stopped running (Figure 8.1). Airline officials said the software could not handle the large number of

**FIGURE 8.1** Comair canceled all of its flights on Christmas Day 2004 because the computer system that assigned crews to flights failed. (AP photo/Al Behrman, file)

flight cancellations caused by bad weather on December 23 and 24. About 30,000 travelers in 118 cities were affected by the flight cancellations [16].

In August 2005, the passengers on a Malaysia Airlines flight from Perth, Australia, to Kuala Lumpur, Malaysia, suddenly found themselves on a roller coaster–like ride seven miles above the Indian Ocean. When the Boeing 777 unexpectedly began a rapid climb, the pilot disconnected the autopilot, but it took him 45 seconds to regain control of the jet. The plane zoomed upward, downward, and then upward a second time before leveling out. After an investigation, Boeing reported that a software error had caused the flight computers to receive faulty information about the plane's speed and acceleration. In addition, another error had caused the flight computers to fail to respond immediately to the pilot's commands [17].

A software problem forced the NASDAQ stock exchange to shut down for three hours in 2013. Two years later, the New York Stock Exchange halted trading for nearly four hours because of a computer-related "configuration problem" [18, 19].

At the Black Hat conference in Las Vegas in 2011, computer security researcher Jay Radcliffe demonstrated how he could wirelessly hack into and control the insulin pump he was wearing, giving him the ability to change the amount of insulin it was dispensing. According to Radcliffe, the only information a hacker would need to take control of a particular pump is the pump's serial number [20].

In July 2015 two researchers demonstrated to a journalist how they could hack wirelessly into a Jeep Cherokee equipped with a touch screen and Uconnect software and gain control of the vehicle's vital systems. As the journalist, who had consented to the experiment, drove a Cherokee around St. Louis, the hackers, sitting at a laptop computer 10 miles away, took control of the SUV's climate control system, radio, windshield wipers, transmission, and brakes [21]. All Chrysler vehicles from model years 2013 through 2015 equipped with touch screens and Uconnect software had the security vulnerability. National Highway Traffic Safety Administration officials insisted that Fiat Chrysler announce a formal safety recall of 1.4 million affected vehicles to highlight to owners the importance of installing a software patch [22].

### 8.3.3  Analysis: E-retailer Posts Wrong Price, Refuses to Deliver

Amazon.com shut down its British Web site on March 13, 2003, after a software error led it to offer iPAQ handheld computers for 7 pounds instead of the correct price of about 275 pounds. Before Amazon.com shut down the site, electronic bargain hunters had flocked to Amazon.com's Web site, some of them ordering as many as 10 iPAQs [23]. Amazon said that customers who ordered at the mistaken price should not expect delivery unless they paid the difference between the advertised price and the actual price. An Amazon.com spokesperson said, "In our Pricing and Availability Policy, we state that where an item's correct price is higher than our stated price, we contact the customer before dispatching. Customers will be offered the opportunity either to cancel their order or to place new orders for the item at the correct price" [24].

Was Amazon.com wrong to refuse to fill the orders of the people who bought iPAQs for 7 pounds?

Let's analyze the problem from a rule utilitarian point of view. We can imagine a moral rule of the form, "A person or organization wishing to sell a product must always honor the advertised price." What would happen if this rule were universally followed? More time and effort would be spent proofreading advertisements, whether printed or electronic. Organizations responsible for publishing the advertisements in newspapers, magazines, and Web sites would also take more care to ensure no errors were introduced. There is a good chance companies would take out insurance policies to guard against the catastrophic losses that could result from a typo. To pay for these additional costs, the prices of the products sold by these companies would be higher. The proposed rule would harm every consumer who ended up paying more for products. The rule would benefit the few consumers who took advantage of misprints to get good deals on certain goods. We conclude the proposed moral rule has more harms than benefits, and Amazon.com did the right thing by refusing to ship the iPAQs.

We *could* argue, from a Kantian point of view, that the knowledgeable consumers who ordered the iPAQs did something wrong. The correct price was 275 pounds; the advertised price was 7 pounds. While electronic products may go on sale, retailers simply do not drop the price of their goods by 97.5 percent, even when they are being put on clearance. If consumers understood the advertised price was an error, then they were taking advantage of Amazon.com's stockholders by ordering the iPAQ before the error was corrected. They were not acting "in good faith."

# 8.4 Notable Software System Failures

In this section we shift our focus to complicated devices or systems controlled at least in part by computers. An **embedded system** is a computer used as a component of a larger system. You can find microprocessor-based embedded systems in microwave ovens, thermostats, automobiles, traffic lights, and a myriad of other modern devices. Because computers need software to execute, every embedded system has a software component.

Software is playing an ever-larger role in system functionality [25]. There are several reasons why hardware controllers are being replaced by microprocessors controlled by software. Software controllers are faster. They can perform more sophisticated functions, taking more input data into account. They cost less, use less energy, and do not wear out. Unfortunately, while hardware controllers have a reputation for high reliability, the same cannot be said for their software replacements.

Most embedded systems are also **real-time systems**: computers that process data from sensors as events occur. The microprocessor that controls the air bags in a modern automobile is a real-time system, because it must instantly react to readings from its sensors and deploy the air bags at the time of a collision. The microprocessor in a cell phone is another example of a real-time system that converts electrical signals into radio waves and vice versa.

This section contains seven examples of computer system failures: the Patriot missile system used in the Gulf War, the Ariane 5 launch vehicle, AT&T's long-distance network, NASA's robot missions to Mars, the automated baggage system at Denver International Airport, the Tokyo Stock Exchange, and direct-recording electronic voting machines. These are all examples of embedded, real-time systems. In every case at least part of the failure was due to errors in the software component of the system. Studying these errors provides important lessons for anyone involved in the development of an embedded system.

## 8.4.1 Patriot Missile

The Patriot missile system was originally designed by the US Army to shoot down airplanes. In the 1991 Gulf War, the Army put the Patriot missile system to work defending against Scud missiles launched at Israel and Saudi Arabia.

At the end of the Gulf War, the Army claimed the Patriot missile defense system had been 95 percent effective at destroying incoming Scud missiles. Later analyses showed that perhaps as few as 9 percent of the Scuds were actually destroyed by Patriot missiles. As it turns out, many Scuds simply fell apart as they approached their targets—their destruction had nothing at all to do with the Patriot missiles launched at them.

The most significant failure of the Patriot missile system occurred during the night of February 25, 1991, when a Scud missile fired from Iraq hit a US Army barracks in Dhahran, Saudi Arabia, killing 28 soldiers. The Patriot missile battery defending the area never even fired at the incoming Scud.

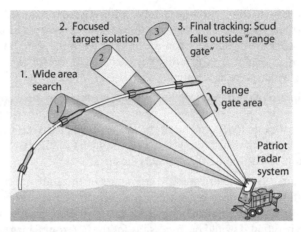

**Figure 8.2** A software error caused the Patriot missile system to lose track of incoming Scud missiles. (1) The radar system doing a wide area search picks up the Scud missile. (2) The radar system isolates the proposed target. (3) A software error causes the system to produce a faulty range gate. The system loses track of the missile, because it does not fly through this gate. (Figure from *Science* 255:1347. Copyright © 1992 by the American Association for the Advancement of Science. Reprinted with permission.)

Mississippi congressman Howard Wolpe asked the General Accounting Office (GAO) to investigate this incident. The GAO report traced the failure of the Patriot system to a software error (Figure 8.2). The missile battery did detect the incoming Scud missile as it came over the horizon. However, in order to prevent the system from responding to false alarms, the computer was programmed to check multiple times for the presence of the missile. The computer predicted the flight path of the incoming missile, directed the radar to focus in on that area, and scanned a segment of the radar signal, called a range gate, for the target. In this case the program scanned the wrong range gate. Since it did not detect the Scud, it did not fire the Patriot missile.

Why did the program scan the wrong range gate? The tracking system relied upon getting signals from the system clock. These values were stored in a floating-point variable with insufficient precision, resulting in a small mathematical error called a *truncation*. The longer the system ran, the more these truncation errors added up. The Patriot missile system was designed to operate for only a few hours at a time. However, the system at Dhahran had been in continuous operation for 100 hours. The accumulation of errors led to a difference between the actual time and the computed time of about 0.3433 seconds. Because missiles travel at high speeds, the 0.3433-second error led to a tracking error of 687 meters (about half a mile). That was enough of an error to prevent the missile battery from locating the Scud in the range gate area [26].

## 8.4.2  Ariane 5

The Ariane 5 was a satellite launch vehicle designed by the French space agency, the Centre National d'Etudes Spatiales, and the European Space Agency. About 40 seconds into its maiden flight on June 4, 1996, a software error caused the nozzles on the solid boosters and the main rocket engine to swivel to extreme positions. As a result, the rocket veered sharply off course. When the links between the solid boosters and the core stage ruptured, the launch vehicle self-destructed. The rocket carried satellites worth $500 million, which were not insured [27].

A board of inquiry traced the software error to a piece of code that converts a 64-bit floating-point value into a 16-bit signed integer. The value to be converted exceeded the maximum value that could be stored in the integer variable, causing an exception to be raised. Unfortunately, there was no exception-handling mechanism for this particular exception, so the onboard computers crashed.

The faulty piece of code had been part of the software for the Ariane 4. The 64-bit floating-point value represented the horizontal bias of the launch vehicle, which is related to its horizontal velocity. When the software module was designed, engineers determined that it would be impossible for the horizontal bias to be so large that it could not be stored in a 16-bit signed integer. There was no need for an error handler, because an error could not occur. This code was moved "as is" into the software for the Ariane 5. That proved to be an extremely costly mistake, because the Ariane 5 was faster than the Ariane 4. The original assumptions made by the designers of the software no longer held true [28].

### 8.4.3  AT&T Long–Distance Network

On the afternoon of January 15, 1990, AT&T's long-distance network suffered a significant disruption of service. About half of the computerized telephone routing switches crashed, and the remainder of the switches could not handle all the traffic. As a result of this failure, about 70 million long-distance telephone calls could not be put through, and about 60,000 people lost all telephone service. AT&T lost tens of millions of dollars in revenue. It also lost some of its credibility as a reliable provider of long-distance service.

Investigation by AT&T engineers revealed that the network crash was brought about by a single faulty line of code in an error recovery procedure. The system was designed so that if a server discovered it was in an error state, it would reboot itself, a crude but effective way of "wiping the slate clean." After a switch rebooted itself, it would send an "OK" message to other switches, letting them know it was back online. The software bug manifested itself when a very busy switch received an "OK" message. Under certain circumstances, handling the "OK" message would cause the busy switch to enter an error state and reboot.

On the afternoon of January 15, 1990, a switch in New York City using the company's new System 7 software detected an error condition and rebooted itself (Figure 8.3). When it came back online, it broadcast an "OK" message. All the switches receiving the "OK" messages handled them correctly, except three very busy switches in St. Louis, Detroit, and Atlanta. These switches detected an error condition and rebooted. When they came back up, all of them broadcast "OK" messages across the network, causing other switches to fail in an ever-expanding wave.

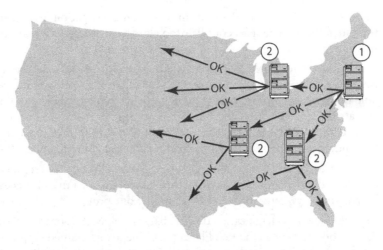

FIGURE 8.3 A software bug in error recovery code made AT&T's System 7 switches crash in 1990. (1) A single switch in New York City detects an error condition and reboots. When it comes back up, it sends an "OK" message to other switches. (2) Switches in Detroit, St. Louis, and Atlanta are so busy that handling the "OK" message causes them to fail. They detect an error condition and reboot. When they come back up, they send out "OK" messages to other switches, causing some of them to fail, and so on.

Every switch failure compounded the problem in two ways. When the switch went down, it pushed more long-distance traffic onto the other switches, making them busier. When the switch came back up, it broadcast "OK" messages to these busier switches, causing some of them to fail. Some switches rebooted repeatedly under the barrage of "OK" messages. Within 10 minutes, half the switches in the AT&T network had failed.

The crash could have been much worse, but AT&T had converted only 80 of its network switches to the System 7 software. It had left System 6 software running on 34 of the switches "just in case." The System 6 switches did not have the software bug and did not crash [29, 30].

### 8.4.4 Robot Missions to Mars

NASA designed the $125 million Mars Climate Orbiter to facilitate communications between Earth and automated probes on the surface of Mars, including the Mars Polar Lander. Ironically, the spacecraft was lost because of a miscommunication between two support teams on Earth.

The Lockheed Martin flight operations team in Colorado designed its software to use English units. Its program output thrust in terms of foot-pounds. The navigation team at the Jet Propulsion Laboratory in California designed its software to use metric units. Its program expected thrust to be input in terms of newtons. One foot-pound equals 4.45 newtons. On September 23, 1999, the Mars Climate Orbiter neared the Red Planet. When it was time for the spacecraft to fire its engine to enter orbit, the Colorado team supplied thrust information to the California team, which relayed it to the spacecraft. Because of the units mismatch, the navigation team specified 4.45 times too much thrust. The spacecraft flew too close to the surface of Mars and burned up in its atmosphere.

A few months later NASA's Martian program suffered a second catastrophe. The Mars Polar Lander, produced at a cost of $165 million, was supposed to land on the south pole of Mars and provide data that would help scientists understand how the Martian climate has changed over time. On December 3, 1999, NASA lost contact with the Mars Polar Lander. NASA engineers suspect that the system's software got a false signal from the landing gear and shut down the engines 100 feet above the planet's surface.

Tony Spear was project manager of the Mars Pathfinder mission. He said, "It is just as hard to do Mars missions now as it was in the mid-70s. I'm a big believer that software hasn't gone anywhere. Software is the number one problem" [31].

Several years after Spear made this observation, NASA successfully landed two Mars Exploration Rovers on the Red Planet [32]. The rovers, named Opportunity and Spirit, were launched from Earth in June and July of 2003, successfully landing on Mars in January 2004. Mission planners had hoped that each rover would complete a three-month mission, looking for clues that the Martian surface once had enough water to sustain life. The rovers greatly exceeded this goal. The Spirit rover operated successfully for more than five years. Opportunity found evidence of a former saltwater lake and was still operational 10 years after its launch.

## 8.4.5 Denver International Airport

As airline passenger traffic strained the capacity of Stapleton International Airport, the City and County of Denver planned the construction of a much larger airport. Stapleton International Airport had earned a reputation for slow baggage handling, and the project planners wanted to ensure the new airport would not suffer from the same problem. They announced an ambitious plan to create a one-of-a-kind, state-of-the-art automated baggage-handling system for the Denver International Airport (DIA).

The airport authorities signed a $193 million contract with BAE Automated Systems to design and build the automated baggage-handling system, which consisted of thousands of baggage carts traveling roller coaster–style on 21 miles of metal tracks. According to the design, agents would label a piece of luggage and put it on a conveyor belt. Computers would route each bag along one or more belts until they reached a cart-loading point, where each bag would be loaded into its own tublike cart. Scanners would read the destination information from the suitcase label, and computers would then route each cart along the tracks at 20 miles per hour to the correct unloading point, where each bag would be unloaded onto a conveyor belt and carried to its final destination. To monitor the movement of the bags, the system used 56 bar code scanners and 5,000 electric eyes.

There were problems from the outset of the project. The airport design was already completed before the baggage-handling system was chosen. As a result, the underground tunnels were small and had sharp turns, making it difficult to shoehorn in an automated baggage system. And given its ambitious goals, the project timeline was too short.

However, the most important problem with the automated baggage handler was that the complexity of the system exceeded the ability of the development team to understand it. Here are a few of the problems BAE encountered.

- Luggage carts were misrouted and failed to arrive at their destinations.
- Computers lost track of where the carts were.
- Bar code printers didn't print tags clearly enough to be read by scanners.
- Luggage had to be correctly positioned on conveyors in order to load properly.
- Bumpers on the carts interfered with the electric photocells.
- Workers painted over electric eyes or knocked photo sensors out of alignment.
- Light luggage was thrown off rapidly moving carts.
- Luggage was shredded by automated baggage handlers.
- The design did not consider the problem of fairly balancing the number of available carts among all the locations needing them.

BAE attempted to solve these problems one at a time by trial and error, but the system was too complicated to yield to this problem-solving approach. BAE should have been looking at the big picture, trying to find where the specifications for the system were wrong or unattainable.

DIA was supposed to open on October 31, 1993. The opening was delayed repeatedly because the baggage-handling system was not yet operational. Eventually, the mayor of Denver announced the city would spend $50 million to build a conventional luggage-handling system using tugs and carts. (This conventional system actually ended up costing $71 million.) On February 28, 1995, flights to and from the new airport began. However, concourse A was not open at all. Concourse C opened with 11 airlines using a traditional baggage system. The BAE automated system, far over budget at $311 million, was used only by United Airlines in concourse B to handle outgoing baggage originating in Denver. United used a traditional system for the rest of its baggage in concourse B.

The failure of BAE to deliver a working system on time resulted in a 16-month delay in the opening of DIA. This delay cost Denver $1 million *a day* in interest on bonds and operating costs. As a result, DIA began charging all the airlines a flight fee of about $20 per passenger, the highest airport fee in the nation. Airlines passed along this cost to consumers by raising ticket prices of flights going through Denver [33].

While the story of the Denver International Airport is noteworthy because of the large amount of money involved, it is not unusual for software projects to take longer than expected and to cost more than anticipated. In fact, most software projects are not completed on time and on budget. We explore this issue in greater detail in Section 8.7.

### 8.4.6  Tokyo Stock Exchange

December 8, 2005, was the first day that shares of J-Com, a recruiting company, were made available to the public on the Tokyo Stock Exchange. That morning, an employee of Mizuho Securities received a call from a customer who said he wished to sell one share of J-Com stock at a price of 610,000 yen. At 9:27 A.M., the Mizuho Securities employee mistakenly entered an order to sell 610,000 shares of J-Com at 1 yen per share. When the computer screen displayed a "Beyond price limit" warning, the employee overrode the warning by hitting the Enter key twice, sending the order to the Tokyo Stock Exchange. At 9:28 A.M., the sell order appeared on the Tokyo Stock Exchange's display board. Spotting the mistake, Mizuho Securities attempted to cancel the sell order several times between 9:29 and 9:35 A.M., but these attempts failed because of a bug in the Tokyo Stock Exchange trading program. Mizuho also phoned the Tokyo Stock Exchange, asking the TSE to cancel the sell order, but the Tokyo Stock Exchange refused.

Beginning at 9:35 A.M., Mizuho started to buy back shares of J-Com, but it was only able to purchase about a half million shares. More than 96,000 shares had already been purchased by other parties. It was impossible for Mizuho to provide shares to these buyers because J-Com only had 14,500 publicly traded shares. Under the terms of a special arrangement brokered by the stock exchange, Mizuho settled these accounts by paying 912,000 yen per share to the buyers. In all, Mizuho Securities lost 40 billion yen ($225 million) buying back shares. When the Tokyo Stock Exchange refused to compensate Mizuho Securities for the loss, Mizuho Securities sued the Tokyo Stock Exchange for $416 million. A court ruled in favor of Mizuho Securities but reduced the compensation from the Tokyo Stock Exchange to $107 million because it was the error of a Mizuho Securities employee that caused the problem in the first place [34].

Eventually, the Tokyo Stock Exchange identified the bug that prevented the order from being canceled. The bug had gone undetected for five years because it only occurred when seven different unusual conditions all happened simultaneously [35].

## 8.4.7 Direct-Recording Electronic Voting Machines

Nearly two million ballots were not counted in the 2000 US presidential election because they registered either no choice or multiple choices. The incredibly close election in Florida was marred by voting machine controversies discussed in Section 7.5. To avoid a repeat of these problems, Congress passed, and President Bush signed, the Help America Vote Act of 2002 (HAVA). HAVA provided money to states to replace punch-card voting systems and improve standards for administering elections [36].

Many states used HAVA funds to purchase direct-recording electronic (DRE) voting machines. DRE voting machines allow voters to indicate each of their choices by touching the screen or pressing a button (Figure 8.4). After all selections have been made, a summary screen displays the voter's choices. At this point, the voter may either cast the ballot or back up to make changes.

Brazil and India have run national elections using DRE voting machines exclusively [37]. By the time of the November 2006 general election, about one-third of voters cast their ballots on DRE systems. Proponents of DRE voting machines pointed out the speed and accuracy of machine counting. They said the systems were more tamper-resistant than paper ballots, which can be marked by election workers. When the ballots are electronic, it is impossible for precincts to run out of ballots if turnout is higher than expected. In addition, touch-screen voting machines can be programmed to help voters

FIGURE 8.4 This Diebold voting machine uses a touch-sensitive screen to capture each voter's choices. (© AP photo/Rogelio Solis)

avoid the previously mentioned errors of not choosing a candidate or selecting too many candidates [38].

Some computer experts spoke out against the conversion to touch-screen voting machines, arguing that they are not necessarily any better than the systems they are replacing. In particular, experts expressed concerns about programming errors and the lack of a **paper audit trail:** a record of the original ballots cast.

Quite a few voting irregularities were linked to DRE voting machines since 2002. Here is a selection.

- In November 2002, a programming error caused a touch-screen voting machine to fail to record 436 ballots cast in Wake County, North Carolina [39].

- Touch-screen voting machines reported that 144,000 ballots were cast in a 2003 election held in Boone County, Indiana, even though the county had only 19,000 registered voters. After a programming error was fixed, the ballots were recounted, producing new results consistent with the number of votes actually cast. However, because there was no paper audit trail, there was no way to know if the new results were correct [40].

- Florida held a special election in January 2004 to determine who would represent State House District 91. When the 10,844 votes were tallied, the voting machines reported that 134 voters had not voted for a candidate, even though that was the only race on the ballot. The winning candidate received 12 more votes than the runner-up. Since the voting machines had no record of the original votes, there was no recount [40].

• In November 2004, initial printouts from all the DRE voting machines in LaPorte County, Indiana, reported exactly 300 votes, disregarding more than 50,000 votes until the problem was sorted out [41].

• In November 2004, a bug in the vote-counting software in DRE voting machines in Guilford County, North Carolina, caused the systems to begin counting backward after they reached a maximum count of 32,767. After the problem was fixed, a recount changed the outcome of two races and gave another 22,000 votes to presidential candidate John Kerry [42].

• In 2006 some Florida voters had a hard time voting for Democratic candidates on DRE voting machines. After choosing Democrats, these voters discovered that the machine's summary screen replaced some of the Democrats with their Republican opponents. Some voters had to repeat their votes several times in order for the proper candidate's name to appear on the summary screen [43].

• In a congressional election held in November 2006 in Florida, more than 18,000 votes cast on DRE voting machines were not recorded. The final tally showed Republican Vern Buchanan beating Democrat Christine Jennings by only 369 votes [44].

Some computer experts expressed concerns about the vulnerability of electronic voting machines to tampering. Finnish security specialist Harri Hursti investigated the memory cartridges used to record votes in Diebold DRE voting machines. (After the polls close, these cartridges are removed from the machines and taken to a central location, where the votes are tallied.) Hursti discovered that he could use a readily available agricultural scanning device to change the vote counts without leaving a trace [45].

Computer science professor Herbert Thompson examined the centralized Diebold machine that tallies the votes from the individual DRE voting machines. According to Thompson, the system lacked even a rudimentary authentication mechanism; he was able to access the system's program without a login name or password. By inserting just five lines of code, he successfully switched 5,000 votes from one candidate to another. "I am positive an eighth grader could do this," he said [45].

The AVS WinVote DRE system was adopted in Mississippi, Pennsylvania, and Virginia, though after 2008 Virginia was the only state to use WinVote machines. Unlike other DRE systems, the WinVote system used Wi-Fi to simplify setting up voting machines and counting the votes from the many machines at a single precinct. An assessment by the Virginia Information Technology Agency (VITA) revealed that WinVote had a number of serious security weaknesses. In particular, the system used obsolete WEP wireless encryption, had a hardwired WEP key of "abcde," used another hardwired key to encrypt the database, and lacked "logs or checksums to detect whether the database had been replaced" [46]. VITA determined that it would be possible for someone to modify the results of an election by taking the following steps: capturing the wireless traffic between the voting machines; breaking the WEP encryption; connecting to the machines; downloading the Microsoft Access databases containing the votes; modifying the databases to add, change, or delete votes; and uploading the modified databases to the voting machines. After receiving this information, the Virginia State Board of Elections decertified the WinVote machines [46].

Without access to the source code to touch-screen systems, there is no way to test how secure they are. The manufacturers of these systems refused to make the software public, saying the source code is valuable intellectual property—a trade secret. The Open Voting Consortium criticized the corporate control of elections in the United States and advocated the development of open-source software to make elections "open and transparent" [47].

Critics of touch-screen voting systems claimed these systems make possible an unprecedented level of election fraud. The old, lever-style mechanical voting machines were susceptible to fraud at the local level. A voting official could enter a voting booth and vote multiple times for a slate of candidates, but the number of extra votes that could be added in any precinct without attracting attention was limited. In contrast, by changing the programming of an electronic voting system, a single person could change votes across thousands of precincts [48].

Supporters of touch-screen voting machines said criticisms of DRE voting machines were overblown. A report by the Pacific Research Institute maintained that DRE voting systems are more secure than traditional paper ballots, which can be tampered with by elections officials. "Open source advocates and paper trail champions want to steer e-voting off a cliff. Rather than demanding utopian machines and spreading conspiracy theories for political gain, they should refocus their energy in a way that actually helps American voters" [49].

Nevertheless, most states had second thoughts about DRE voting machines. In May 2007, Florida's legislature voted to replace DRE voting machines with optical scan ballots. Voters select candidates by filling in bubbles next to their names, and optical scanning machines count the marked ballots. This approach leaves a paper audit trail that makes possible manual recounts in disputed elections [50]. By the time of the general election in November 2014, 70 percent of Americans were back to casting old-fashioned paper ballots. Pamela Smith, president of Verified Voting, said, "paper, even though it sounds kind of old school, it actually has properties that serve the elections really well" [51].

# 8.5  Therac–25

Soon after German physicist Wilhelm Roentgen discovered the X-ray in 1895, physicians began using radiation to treat cancer. Today, between 50 and 60 percent of cancer patients are treated with radiation, either to destroy cancer cells or relieve pain. Linear accelerators create high-energy electron beams to treat shallow tumors and X-ray beams to reach deeper tumors.

The Therac-25 linear accelerator was notoriously unreliable. It was not unusual for the system to malfunction 40 times a day. We devote an entire section to telling the story of the Therac-25 because it is a striking example of the harm that can be caused when the safety of a system relies solely upon the quality of its embedded software.

In a 20-month period between June 1985 and January 1987, the Therac-25 administered massive overdoses to six patients, causing the deaths of three of them. While 1987 may seem like the distant past to many of you, it does give us the advantage of 20/20 hindsight. The entire story has been thoroughly researched and documented [52]. Failures of computerized systems continue to this day, but they have not yet been fully played out and analyzed.

### 8.5.1 Genesis of the Therac-25

Atomic Energy of Canada Limited (AECL) and the French corporation CGR cooperated in the 1970s to build two linear accelerators: the Therac-6 and the Therac-20. Both the Therac-6 and the Therac-20 were modernizations of older CGR linear accelerators. The distinguishing feature of the Therac series was the use of a DEC PDP 11 minicomputer as a "front end." By adding the computer, the linear accelerators were easier to operate. The Therac-6 and the Therac-20 were actually capable of working independently of the PDP 11, and all of their safety features were built into the hardware.

After producing the Therac-20, AECL and CGR went their separate ways. AECL moved ahead with the development and deployment of a next-generation linear accelerator called the Therac-25. Like the Therac-6 and the Therac-20, the Therac-25 made use of a PDP 11. Unlike its predecessor machines, however, AECL designed the PDP 11 to be an integral part of the device; the linear accelerator was incapable of operating without the computer. This design decision enabled AECL to reduce costs by replacing some of the hardware safety features of the Therac-20 with software safety features in the Therac-25.

AECL also decided to reuse some of the Therac-6 and Therac-20 software in the Therac-25. Code reuse saves time and money. Theoretically, "tried-and-true" software is more reliable than newly written code, but as we shall see, that assumption was invalid in this case.

AECL shipped its first Therac-25 in 1983. In all, it delivered 11 systems in Canada and the United States. The Therac-25 was a large machine that was placed in its own room. Shielding in the walls, ceiling, and floor of the room prevented outsiders from being exposed to radiation. A television camera, microphone, and speaker in the room allowed the technician in an adjoining room to view and communicate with the patient undergoing treatment.

### 8.5.2 Chronology of Accidents and AECL Responses

We now chronicle six major incidents involving the Therac-25 that occurred between June 1985 and January 1987, along with the AECL responses to them.

## MARIETTA, GEORGIA, JUNE 1985

A 61-year-old breast cancer patient was being treated at the Kennestone Regional Oncology Center. After radiation was administered to the area of her collarbone, she complained that she had been burned.

The Kennestone physicist contacted AECL and asked if it was possible that the Therac-25 had failed to diffuse the electron beam. Engineers at AECL replied that this could not happen.

The patient suffered crippling injuries as a result of the overdose, which the physicist later estimated was 75 to 100 times too large. She sued AECL and the hospital in October 1985.

## HAMILTON, ONTARIO, JULY 1985

A 40-year-old woman was being treated for cervical cancer at the Ontario Cancer Foundation. When the operator tried to administer the treatment, the machine shut down after five seconds with an error message. According to the display, the linear accelerator had not yet delivered any radiation to the patient. Following standard operating procedure, the operator typed "P" for "proceed." The system shut down in the same way, indicating that the patient had not yet received a dose of radiation. (Recall it was not unusual for the machine to malfunction several dozen times a day.) The operator typed "P" three more times, always with the same result, until the system entered "treatment suspend" mode.

The operator went into the room where the patient was. The patient complained that she had been burned. The lab called in a service technician, who could find nothing wrong with the machine. The clinic reported the malfunction to AECL.

When the patient returned for further treatment three days later, she was hospitalized for a radiation overdose. It was later estimated that she had received between 65 and 85 times the normal dose of radiation. The patient died of cancer in November 1985.

## FIRST AECL INVESTIGATION, JULY–SEPTEMBER 1985

After the Ontario overdose, AECL sent out an engineer to investigate. While the engineer was unable to reproduce the overdose, he did uncover design problems related to a microswitch. AECL introduced hardware and software changes to fix the microswitch problem.

## YAKIMA, WASHINGTON, DECEMBER 1985

The next documented overdose accident occurred at Yakima Valley Memorial Hospital. A woman receiving a series of radiation treatments developed a strange reddening on her hip after one of the treatments. The inflammation took the form of several parallel stripes. The hospital staff tried to determine the cause of the unusual stripes. They suspected the pattern could have been caused by the slots in the accelerator's blocking trays, but these trays had already been discarded by the time the staff began their investigation. After ruling out other possible causes for the reaction, the staff suspected a radiation overdose and contacted AECL by letter and by phone.

AECL replied in a letter that neither the Therac-25 nor operator error could have produced the described damage. Two pages of the letter explained why it was technically impossible for the Therac-25 to produce an overdose. The letter also claimed that no similar accidents had been reported.

The patient survived, although the overdose scarred her and left her with a mild disability.

## TYLER, TEXAS, MARCH 1986

A male patient came to the East Texas Cancer Center (ETCC) for the ninth in a series of radiation treatments for a cancerous tumor on his back. The operator entered the treatment data into the computer. She noticed that she had typed "X" (for X-ray) instead of "E" (for electron beam). This was a common mistake, because X-ray treatments are much more common. Being an experienced operator, she quickly fixed her mistake by using the up arrow key to move the cursor back to the appropriate field, changing the "X" to an "E" and moving the cursor back to the bottom of the screen. When the system displayed "beam ready," she typed "B" (for beam on). After a few seconds, the Therac-25 shut down. The console screen contained the message "Malfunction 54" and indicated a "treatment pause," a low-priority problem. The dose monitor showed that the patient had received only 6 units of treatment rather than the desired 202 units. The operator hit the "P" (proceed) key to continue the treatment.

The cancer patient and the operator were in adjoining rooms. Normally, a video camera and intercom would enable the operator to monitor her patients. However, at the time of the accident neither system was operational.

The patient had received eight prior treatments, so he knew something was wrong as soon as the ninth treatment began. He was instantly aware of the overdose—he felt as if someone had poured hot coffee on his back or given him an electric shock. As he tried to get up from the table, the accelerator delivered its second dose, which hit him in the arm. The operator became aware of the problem when the patient began pounding on the door. He had received between 80 and 125 times the prescribed amount of radiation. He suffered acute pain and steadily lost bodily functions until he died from complications of the overdose five months later.

## SECOND AECL INVESTIGATION, MARCH 1986

After the accident, the ETCC shut down its Therac-25 and notified AECL. AECL sent out two engineers to examine the system. Try as they might, they could not reproduce Malfunction 54. They told the physicians it was impossible for the Therac-25 to overdose a patient, and they suggested that the patient may have received an electrical shock due to a fault in the hospital's electrical system.

The ETCC checked out the electrical system and found no problems with it. After double-checking the linear accelerator's calibration, they put the Therac-25 back into service.

## TYLER, TEXAS, APRIL 1986

The second Tyler, Texas, accident was virtually a replay of the prior accident at ETCC. The same technician was in control of the Therac-25, and she went through the same process of entering X-ray when she meant electron beam, then going back and correcting her mistake. Once again, the machine halted with a Malfunction 54 shortly after she activated the electron beam. This time, however, the intercom was working, and she rushed to the treatment room when she heard the patient moan. There was nothing she could do to help him. The patient had received a massive dose of radiation to his brain, and he died three weeks later.

After the accident, ETCC immediately shut down the Therac-25 and contacted AECL again.

## YAKIMA, WASHINGTON, JANUARY 1987

A second patient was severely burned by the Therac-25 at Yakima Valley Memorial Hospital under circumstances almost identical to those of the December 1985 accident. Four days after the treatment, the patient's skin revealed a series of parallel red stripes—the same pattern that had perplexed the radiation staff in the case of the previous patient. This time, the staff members were able to match the burns to the slots in the Therac-25's blocking tray. The patient died three months later.

## THERAC-25 DECLARED DEFECTIVE, FEBRUARY 1987

On February 10, 1987, the FDA declared the Therac-25 to be defective. In order for the Therac-25 to gain back FDA approval, AECL had to demonstrate how it would make the system safe. Five months later, after five revisions, AECL produced a corrective action plan that met the approval of the FDA. This plan incorporated a variety of hardware interlocks to prevent the machine from delivering overdoses or activating the beam when the turntable was not in the correct position.

## 8.5.3 Software Errors

In the course of investigating the accidents, AECL discovered a variety of hardware and software problems with the Therac-25. Two of the software errors are examples of race conditions. In a **race condition,** two or more concurrent tasks share a variable, and the order in which they read or write the value of the variable can affect the behavior of the program. Race conditions are extremely difficult to identify and fix, because usually the two tasks do not interfere with each other and nothing goes wrong. Only in rare conditions will the tasks actually interfere with each other as they manipulate the variable, causing the error to occur. We describe both of these errors to give you some insight into how difficult they are to detect.

The accidents at the ETCC occurred because of a race condition associated with the command screen (Figure 8.5). One task was responsible for handling keyboard input and making changes to the command screen. A second task was responsible for monitoring the command screen for changes and moving the magnets into position. As shown in Figure 8.5, after the operator uses the first task to complete the prescription (1),

**FIGURE 8.5** Illustration of a Therac-25 bug revealed by fast-typing operators. (1) The operator finishes filling in the form. The software knows the form is filled in because the cursor is in the lower right-hand corner of the screen. (2) The software instructs the magnets to move into the correct positions. While the magnets are moving, the software does not check for screen edits. (3) The operator changes the prescription from X-ray to electron beam. (4) The operator finishes the edit, returning the cursor to the lower right-hand corner of the screen. (5) The magnets finish moving. The software now checks the screen cursor. Since it is in the lower right-hand corner, the program assumes there have been no edits.

the second task sees the cursor in the lower right-hand corner of the screen and begins the eight-second process of moving the magnets (2). Meanwhile, the operator sees her mistake. The first task responds to her keystrokes and lets her change the "X" to an "E" (3). She gets the cursor back to the lower right-hand corner before eight seconds are up (4). Now the second task finishes moving the magnets (5). It sees the cursor in the lower right-hand corner of the screen and incorrectly assumes the screen has not changed. The crucial substitution of electron beam for X-ray goes unnoticed.

What makes this bug particularly treacherous is that it only occurs with faster, more experienced operators. Slower operators would not be able to complete the edit and get the cursor back to the lower right-hand corner of the screen in only eight seconds. If the cursor happened to be anywhere else on the screen when the magnets stopped moving, the software would check for a screen edit and there would be no overdose. It is ironic that the safety of the system actually decreased as the experience of the operator increased.

Another race condition was responsible for the overdoses at the Yakima Valley Memorial Hospital (Figure 8.6). It occurred when the machine was putting the electron beam gun back into position. A variable was supposed to be 0 if the gun was ready to fire. Any other value meant the gun was not ready. As long as the electron beam gun was out of position, one task kept incrementing that variable. Unfortunately, the variable could only store the values from 0 to 255. Incrementing it when it had the value 255 would result in the variable's value rolling over to 0, like a car's odometer.

As illustrated in Figure 8.6, nearly every time that the operator hit the SET button when the gun was out of position, the variable was not 0 and the gun did not fire (a). However, there was a very slight chance that the variable would have just rolled over

**FIGURE 8.6** The Therac-25 could administer radiation too soon if the operator hit the SET button at precisely the wrong time. As long as the electron beam gun was out of position, a software task kept incrementing an 8-bit variable. (a) Usually when the operator hit the SET button, the variable was not zero and the system would wait, just as it was supposed to. (b) If the operator hit the SET button just as the variable rolled over from 255 to 0, the system would administer radiation, even though the gun was out of position.

when the operator hit the SET button (b). In this case the accelerator would emit a charge, even though the system was not ready.

### 8.5.4 Postmortem

Let's consider some of the mistakes AECL made in the design, development, and support of this system.

When accidents were reported, AECL focused on identifying and fixing particular software bugs. This approach was too narrow. As Nancy Leveson and Clark Turner point out, "Most accidents are system accidents; that is, they stem from complex interactions between various components and activities" [52]. The entire system was broken, not just the software. A strategy of eliminating bugs assumes that at some point the last bug will be eradicated. But as Leveson and Turner write, "There is always another software bug" [52].

The real problem was that the system was not designed to be fail-safe. Good engineering practice dictates that a system should be designed so that no single point of failure leads to a catastrophe. By relying completely upon software for protection against overdoses, the Therac-25 designers ignored this fundamental engineering principle.

Another flaw in the design of the Therac-25 was its lack of software or hardware devices to detect and report overdoses and shut down the accelerator immediately. Instead, the Therac-25 designers left it up to the patients to report when they had received overdoses.

There are also particular software lessons we can learn from the case of the Therac-25. First, it is very difficult to find software errors in programs where multiple tasks execute at the same time and interact through shared variables. Second, the software design needs to be as simple as possible, and design decisions must be documented to aid in the maintenance of the system. Third, the code must be reasonably documented at the time it is written. Fourth, reusing code does not always increase the quality of the final product. AECL assumed that by reusing code from the Therac-6 and Therac-20, the software would be more reliable. After all, the code had been part of systems used by customers for years with no problems. This assumption turned out to be wrong. The earlier codes did contain errors, but these errors remained undetected because the earlier machines had hardware interlocks that prevented the computer's erroneous commands from harming patients.

The tragedy was compounded because AECL did not communicate fully with its customers. For example, AECL told the physicists in Washington and Texas that an overdose was impossible, even though AECL had already been sued by the patient in Georgia.

## 8.5.5  Moral Responsibility of the Therac–25 Team

Should the developers and managers at AECL be held morally responsible for the deaths resulting from the use of the Therac-25 they produced?

In order for a moral agent to be responsible for a harmful event, two conditions must hold:

- *Causal condition*: The actions (or inactions) of the agent must have caused the harm.
- *Mental condition*: The actions (or inactions) must have been intended or willed by the agent.

In this case, the causal condition is easy to establish. The deaths resulted both from the action of AECL employees (creating the therapy machine that administered the overdose) and the inaction of AECL employees (failing to withdraw the machine from service or even inform other users of the machine that there had been overdoses).

What about the second condition? Surely the engineers at AECL did not intend or try to create a machine that would administer lethal overdoses of radiation. However, philosophers also extend the mental condition to include unintended harm if the moral agent's actions were the result of carelessness, recklessness, or negligence. The design team took a number of actions that fall into this category. It constructed a system without hardware interlocks to prevent overdoses or to keep the beam from being activated when the turntable was not in a correct position. The machine had no software or hardware devices to detect an accidental overdose. Management allowed software to be developed without adequate documentation. It presumed the correctness of reused code and failed to test it thoroughly. For these reasons the mental condition holds as well, and we conclude the Therac-25 team at AECL is morally responsible for the deaths caused by the Therac-25 radiation therapy machine.

### 8.5.6 Postscript

Three decades after the Therac-25 accidents, computer errors related to radiation machines continue to maim and kill patients. In late 2006, Scott Jerome-Parks received three overdoses from a linear accelerator at a New York City Hospital that led to his death a few weeks later. He was only 43 years old. About the same time, 32-year-old breast cancer patient Alexandra Jn-Charles received 27 straight days of radiation overdoses at another New York hospital that led to her death. An investigation of radiation overdoses by the *New York Times* concluded that a variety of errors, including faulty software, were leading to crippling or fatal accidents [53].

# 8.6 Computer Simulations

In the previous section, we focused on an unreliable computer-controlled system that delivered lethal doses of radiation to cancer patients, but even systems kept behind the locked doors of a computer room can cause harm. Errors in computer simulations can result in poorly designed products, mediocre science, and bad policy decisions. In this section we review our growing reliance on computer simulations for designing products, understanding our world, and even predicting the future, and we describe ways in which computer modelers validate their simulations.

### 8.6.1 Uses of Simulation

Computer simulation plays a key role in contemporary science and engineering. There are many reasons why a scientist or engineer may not be able to perform a physical experiment. It may be too expensive or time consuming, or it may be unethical or impossible to perform. Computer simulations have been used to design nuclear weapons, search for oil, create pharmaceuticals, and design safer, more fuel-efficient cars. They have even been used to design consumer products such as disposable diapers [54].

Some computer simulations model past events. For example, when astrophysicists derive theories about the evolution of the universe, they can test them through computer simulations. A computer simulation has demonstrated that a gas disk around a young star can fragment into giant gas planets such as Jupiter [55].

A second use of computer simulations is to understand the world around us. One of the first important uses of computer simulations was to aid in the exploration for oil. Drilling a single well costs millions of dollars, and most drillings result in "dry wells" that produce no revenue. By using computer simulations, the process becomes much more predictable. Geologists lay out networks of microphones and set off explosive charges. Computers analyze the echoes received by the microphones to produce graphical representations of underground rock formations. Analyzing these formations helps petroleum engineers select the most promising sites to drill.

Computer simulations are also used to predict the future. Modern weather predictions are based on computer simulations. These predictions become particularly important when people are exposed to extreme weather conditions, such as floods, tornadoes, and hurricanes (Figure 8.7). Every computer simulation has an underlying mathematical

**FIGURE 8.7** We rely on computer simulations to predict the path and speed of hurricanes. (Courtesy of NASA)

model. Faster computers enable scientists and engineers to develop more sophisticated models. Over time, the quality of these models has improved.

Of course, the predictions made by computer simulations can be wrong. In 1972 the Club of Rome, an international think tank based in Germany, commissioned a book called *The Limits to Growth*. The book predicted that a continued exponential increase in world population would lead to shortages of minerals and farm land, higher food prices, and significant increases in pollution [56]. A year after the book was published, the Arab oil embargo resulted in dramatically higher oil and gasoline prices in Western nations, giving credence to these alarming forecasts. As it turns out, the book's predictions were far too pessimistic. While the population of the Earth has indeed increased by more than 80 percent in the past 40 years, the amount of tilled land has barely increased, food and mineral prices have dropped, and pollution is in decline in major Western cities [57].

The computer model underlying *The Limits to Growth* was flawed. It assumed all deposits of essential resources had already been discovered. In actuality, many new deposits of oil and other resources have been found in the past four decades. The model ignored the technological improvements that allow society to decrease its use of resources, such as reducing the demand for oil by improving the fuel efficiency of cars or reducing the demand for silver by replacing conventional photography with digital photography.

## 8.6.2 Validating Simulations

A computer simulation may produce erroneous results for two fundamentally different reasons. The program may have a bug in it, or the model upon which the program is based may be flawed. **Verification** is the process of determining if the computer program correctly implements the model. **Validation** is the process of determining if the model is an accurate representation of the real system [58]. In this section we focus on the process of validation.

FIGURE 8.8 A computer simulation of an automobile accident can reveal about the same information as an actual crash test, and it is far less expensive. (Courtesy of Oak Ridge National Laboratory, US Dept. of Energy)

One way to validate a model is to make sure it duplicates the performance of the actual system. For example, automobile and truck manufacturers create computer models of their products (Figure 8.8). They use these models to see how well vehicles will perform in a variety of crash situations. Crashing an automobile on a computer is faster and much less expensive than crashing an actual car. To validate their models, manufacturers compare the results of crashing an actual vehicle with the results predicted by the computer model.

Validating a model that predicts the future can introduce new difficulties. If we are predicting tomorrow's weather, it is reasonable to validate the model by waiting until tomorrow and seeing how well the prediction held up. However, suppose you are a scientist using a global warming model to estimate what the climate will be like 50 years from now. You cannot validate this model by comparing its prediction with reality, because you cannot afford to wait 50 years to see if its prediction comes true. However, you can validate the model by using it to *predict the present*.

Figure 8.9 illustrates how a model can predict the present. Suppose you want to see how well your model predicts events 25 years into the future. You have access to data going back 75 years. You let the model use data at least 25 years old, but you do not let the model see any data collected in the past 25 years. The job of predicting the present, given 25-year-old data, is presumably just as hard as the job of predicting 25 years into the future, given present data. The advantage of predicting the present is that you can use current data to validate the model.

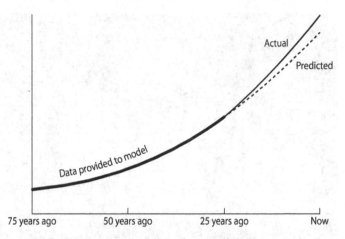

**FIGURE 8.9** You can validate a model's ability to predict 25 years into the future by using it to "predict the present" with data 25 or more years old. You can then compare the model's prediction of the present with current reality.

A final way to validate a computer model is to see if it has credibility with experts and decision makers. Ultimately, a model is valuable only if it is believed by those who have the power to use its results to reached a conclusion or make a decision.

## 8.7   Software Engineering

The field of software engineering grew out of a growing awareness of a "software crisis." In the 1960s, computer architects had taken advantage of commercial integrated circuits to design much more powerful mainframe computers. These computers could execute much larger programs than their predecessors. Programmers responded by designing powerful new operating systems and applications. Unfortunately, their programming efforts were plagued by problems. The typical new software system was delivered behind schedule, cost more than expected, did not perform as specified, contained many bugs, and was too hard to modify. The informal, ad hoc methods of programming that worked fine for early software systems broke down when these systems reached a certain level of complexity.

**Software engineering** is an engineering discipline focused on the production of software, as well as the development of tools, methodologies, and theories supporting software production. Software engineers follow a four-step process to develop a software product [59]:

1. *Specification*: Defining the functions to be performed by the software
2. *Development*: Producing the software that meets the specifications
3. *Validation*: Testing the software
4. *Evolution*: Modifying the software to meet the changing needs of the customer

### 8.7.1 Specification

The process of specification focuses on determining the requirements of the system and the constraints under which it must operate. Software engineers communicate with the intended users of the system to determine what their needs are. They must decide if the software system is feasible given the budget and the schedule requirements of the customer. If a piece of software is going to replace an existing process, the software engineers study the current process to help them understand the functions the software must perform. The software engineers may develop prototypes of the user interface to confirm that the system will meet the user's needs.

The specification process results in a high-level statement of requirements and perhaps a mock-up of the user interface that the users can approve. The software engineers also produce a low-level requirements statement that provides the details needed by those who are going to actually implement the software system.

### 8.7.2 Development

During the development phase, the software engineers produce a working software system that matches the specifications. The first design is based on a high-level, abstract view of the system. The process of developing the high-level design reveals ambiguities, omissions, or outright errors in the specification. When these mistakes are discovered, the specification must be amended. Fixing mistakes is quicker and less expensive when the design is still at a higher, more abstract level.

Gradually, the software engineers add levels of detail to the design. As this is done, the various components of the system become clear. Designers pay particular attention to ensure the interfaces between each component are clearly spelled out. They choose the algorithms to be performed and data structures to be manipulated.

Since the emergence of software engineering as a discipline, a variety of structured design methodologies have been developed. These design methodologies result in the creation of large amounts of design documentation in the form of visual diagrams. Many organizations use **computer-assisted software engineering** (CASE) **tools** to support the process of developing and documenting an ever-more-detailed design.

Another noteworthy improvement in software engineering methodologies is object-oriented design. In a traditional design, the software system is viewed as a group of functions manipulating a set of shared data structures. In an **object-oriented design,** the software system is seen as a group of objects passing messages to each other. Each object has its own state and manipulates its own data based on the messages it receives.

Object-oriented systems have several advantages over systems constructed in a more traditional way:

1. *Because each object is associated with a particular component of the system, object-oriented designs can be easier to understand.*

   More easily understood designs can save time during the programming, testing, and maintenance phases of a software project.

2. *Because each object hides its state and private data from other objects, other objects cannot accidentally modify its data items.*

   The result can be fewer errors like the race conditions described in Section 8.5.3.

3. *Because objects are independent of each other, it is much easier to reuse components of an object-oriented system.*

   A single object definition created for one software system can be copied and inserted into a new software system without bringing along other unnecessary objects.

When the design has reached a great enough level of detail, software engineers write the actual computer programs implementing the software system. Many different programming languages exist; each language has its strengths and weaknesses. Programmers usually implement object-oriented systems using an object-oriented programming language, such as C++, Java, or C#.

### 8.7.3 Validation

The purpose of validation (also called testing) is to ensure the software satisfies the specification and meets the needs of the user. In some companies, testing is an assignment given to newly hired software engineers, who soon move on to design work after proving their worth. However, good testing requires a great deal of technical skill, and some organizations promote testing as a career path.

Testing software is much harder than testing other engineered artifacts, such as bridges. We know how to construct scale models that we can use to validate our designs. To determine how much weight a model bridge can carry, we can test its response to various loads. The stresses and strains on the members and the deflection of the span change gradually as we add weight, allowing us to experiment with a manageable number of different loading scenarios. Engineers can extrapolate from the data they collect to generate predictions regarding the capabilities of a full-scale bridge. By increasing the size of various components, they can add a substantial margin of error to ensure the completed bridge will not fail.

A computer program is not at all like a bridge. Testing a program with a small problem can reveal the existence of bugs, but it cannot prove that the program will work when it is fed a much larger problem. The response of a computer program to nearly identical datasets may not be continuous. Instead, programs that appear to be working just fine may fail when only a single parameter is changed by a small amount. Yet programmers cannot exhaustively test programs. Even small programs have a virtually infinite number of different inputs. Since exhaustive testing is impossible, programs can never be completely tested. Software testers strive to put together suites of test cases that exercise all the capabilities of the component or system being validated.

To reduce the complexity of validating a large software system, testing is usually performed in stages. In the first stage of testing, each individual module of the system is tested independently. It is easier to isolate and fix the causes of errors when the number of lines of code is relatively small. After each module has been debugged, modules are combined into larger subsystems for testing. Eventually, all the subsystems are combined in the complete system. When an error is detected and a bug is fixed in a particular

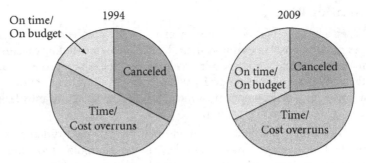

**FIGURE 8.10** Research by the Standish Group reveals that the success rate of IT projects in 2009 was twice that of 1994. Today, about one-third of software projects are completed on time and on budget.

module, all the test cases related to the module should be repeated to see if the change that fixed one bug accidentally introduced another bug.

### 8.7.4 Evolution

Successful software systems evolve over time to meet the changing needs of their users. The evolution of a software system resembles the creation of a software system in many ways. Software engineers must understand the needs of the users, assess the strengths and weaknesses of the current system, and design modifications to the software. The same CASE tools used to create a new software system can aid in its evolution. Many of the datasets developed for the original system can be reused when validating the updated system.

### 8.7.5 Improvement in Software Quality

There is evidence that the field of software engineering is becoming more mature (Figure 8.10). The Standish Group [60] regularly tracks thousands of IT projects. As recently as 1994, about one-third of all software projects were canceled before completion. About one-half of the projects were completed but had time and/or cost overruns, which were often quite large. Only about one-sixth of the projects were completed on time and on budget, and even in these cases the completed systems often had fewer features than originally planned. Another survey by the Standish Group in 2009 showed that the probability of a software project being completed on time and on budget had doubled, to about one in three. Only about one-quarter of the software projects surveyed were canceled. Slightly less than half of the projects were late and/or over budget, but the time and cost overruns were not as large as in the first survey. Overall, the ability of companies to produce software on time and on budget improved over this 15-year period.

Still, with only about one in three software projects being completed on time and on budget, the industry has a long way to go. Rapid change is a fact of life in the software industry. In order to stay competitive, companies must release products quickly. Many organizations feel a tension between meeting tight deadlines and strictly following software engineering methodologies.

## 8.7.6 Gender Bias

When a profession is dominated by men, unconscious gender bias can affect important design decisions. For example, in the United States the leading cause of fetal death due to maternal trauma is automobile accidents. Seatbelts don't protect pregnant women and their unborn children properly. When crash test dummies are designed to model the average adult male, pregnant women (as well as men significantly larger or smaller than average) may suffer harm [61].

Research shows that women and men tend to have different approaches to writing and debugging software, and they use programming tools differently [62]. Many products are designed with the intention of being gender-neutral: appealing to both women and men. If everyone on the team is a man, what may they unconsciously overlook?

Even if there are some women on the team, they may not feel free to express themselves. Some companies have a culture that encourages team members to brainstorm ideas and vote on which ones to implement. Voting tends to suppress minority views. Many women are reluctant to waste political capital by proposing or speaking up for ideas that they believe will just get voted down anyway. Many decisions related to the final product are made informally and under time pressure. If nearly all of the developers are men, the female perspective may not be heard [63].

One way to address the problem of gender bias in software product development is to increase the percentage of women actively engaged in the process. Currently, about three-quarters of IT jobs are held by men [64]. What can be done to increase the number of women in software development and leadership positions? Job postings are a practical place to start. In the United States, Title VII of the Civil Rights Act of 1964 made it illegal for job advertisements to indicate a preference for male or female applicants. However, there is evidence that people creating job advertisements in male-dominated fields continue to convey, either subtly or unconsciously, the gender of the ideal candidate. Women are less likely to apply for a position when the advertisement contains a lot of masculine-themed words, such as active, adventurous, aggressive, ambitious, analytical, assertive, challenging, competitive, decisive, independent, leader, outspoken, and self-reliant. Interestingly, men are just as likely to apply for a position when the advertisement contains a lot of feminine-themed words, such as committed, compassionate, connected, cooperative, dependable, empathetic, honest, interpersonal, kind, loyal, polite, responsible, and trusting [65].

Simply drawing women into software organizations will not solve the problem unless the culture of these organizations also changes. More than half of women who enter the tech field drop out by midcareer, "driven out by hostile work environments and extreme job pressures" [66]. Women feel isolated and lack mentors. They encounter macho cultures. Two-thirds of them experience sexual harassment [66]. Lauren Weinstein, a man with more than 40 years' experience in the tech industry, says, "We see these stories, 'Why aren't there more women in computer science and engineering?' and there's all these complicated answers like, 'School advisers don't have them take math and physics,' and it's probably true. But I think there's probably a simpler reason, which is these guys are just jerks, and women know it" [64].

# 8.8  Software Warranties and Vendor Liability

As mentioned earlier, Leveson and Turner state that "there is always another software bug" [52]. If perfect software is impossible, what should the rights of consumers be to get compensation when programs malfunction? In this section we survey the software warranties offered by some software manufacturers, how these warranties have held up in court, and the variety of ways software vendors may be held liable for software defects.

## 8.8.1  Shrink–Wrap Warranties

Consumer software is often called **shrink-wrap software** because of the plastic wrap surrounding the box containing the software and manuals. In the early years of personal computers, consumer software manufacturers provided no warranty for their products. Purchasers had to accept shrink-wrap software "as is." Today many shrink-wrap software manufacturers provide a replacement or money-back guarantee if the program fails. Here is the wording Microsoft includes with its limited warranty for Microsoft Office 2010:

> LIMITED WARRANTY
>
> A. LIMITED WARRANTY. If you follow the instructions, the software will perform substantially as described in the Microsoft materials that you receive in or with the software.
>
> B. TERM OF WARRANTY; WARRANTY RECIPIENT; LENGTH OF ANY IM- PLIED WARRANTIES. THE LIMITED WARRANTY COVERS THE SOFTWARE FOR ONE YEAR AFTER ACQUIRED BY THE FIRST USER. . . .
>
> D. REMEDY FOR BREACH OF WARRANTY. MICROSOFT WILL REPAIR OR REPLACE THE SOFTWARE AT NO CHARGE. IF MICROSOFT CANNOT RE- PAIR OR REPLACE IT, MICROSOFT WILL REFUND THE AMOUNT SHOWN ON YOUR RECEIPT FOR THE SOFTWARE. IT WILL ALSO REPAIR OR RE- PLACE SUPPLEMENTS, UPDATES AND REPLACEMENT SOFTWARE AT NO CHARGE. IF MICROSOFT CANNOT REPAIR OR REPLACE THEM, IT WILL REFUND THE AMOUNT YOU PAID FOR THEM, IF ANY. YOU MUST UNIN- STALL THE SOFTWARE AND RETURN ANY MEDIA AND OTHER ASSOCI- ATED MATERIALS TO MICROSOFT WITH PROOF OF PURCHASE TO OB- TAIN A REFUND. THESE ARE YOUR ONLY REMEDIES FOR BREACH OF THE LIMITED WARRANTY.

At least Microsoft is willing to state that its software will actually do more or less what the documentation says it can do. The warranty for Railroad Tycoon, distributed by Gathering of Developers (no longer in business), promised only that you would be able to install the software:

> LIMITED WARRANTY. Owner warrants that the original Storage Media holding the SOFTWARE is free from defects in materials and workmanship under normal use and service for a period of ninety (90) days from the date of purchase as evidenced by Your receipt. If for any reason You find defects in the Storage Media,

or if you are unable to install the SOFTWARE on your home or portable computer, You may return the SOFTWARE and all ACCOMPANYING MATERIALS to the place You obtained it for a full refund. This limited warranty does not apply if You have damaged the SOFTWARE by accident or abuse.

Here is even blunter language from the license agreement accompanying Sid Meier's Civilization Revolution game:

Licensor does not warrant . . . that the Software will meet your requirements; that operation of the Software will be uninterrupted or error-free, or that the Software will be compatible with third party software or hardware or that any errors in the Software will be corrected.

In other words, don't blame us if the program doesn't do what you hoped it would do, or if it crashes all the time, or if it is full of bugs, and we're not promising to fix any of these problems either!

## 8.8.2 Are Software Warranties Enforceable?

How can software manufacturers get away with disclaiming any warranties on what they have sold? It's not clear that they can. If the software is mass marketed or if it is included in a sale of hardware, it is likely to be considered a good by a court of law [67]. The damages and warranty provisions of the Uniform Commercial Code (UCC) often apply to the sale of goods, despite what the warranties may say.

An early court case, *Step-Saver Data Systems v. Wyse Technology and The Software Link*, seemed to affirm the notion that software manufacturers could be held responsible for defective programs, despite what they put in their warranties. However, two later cases seemed to indicate the opposite. In *ProCD v. Zeidenberg*, the court ruled that the customer was bound to the license agreement, even if the license agreement does not appear on the outside of the shrink-wrap box. *Mortenson v. Timberline Software* showed that a warranty disclaiming the manufacturer's liability could hold up in court.

### STEP-SAVER DATA SYSTEMS v. WYSE TECHNOLOGY AND THE SOFTWARE LINK

Step-Saver Data Systems Inc. sold time-sharing computer systems consisting of an IBM PC AT server, Wyse terminals, and an operating system provided by the Software Link Inc. (TSL). In 1986–1987, Step-Saver purchased and resold 142 copies of the Multilink Advanced operating system provided by TSL.

To purchase the software, Step-Saver called TSL and placed an order, then followed up with a purchase order. According to Step-Saver, the TSL phone sales representatives said that Multilink was compatible with most DOS applications. The box containing the Multilink software included a licensing agreement in which TSL disclaimed all express and implied warranties.

Step-Saver's time-sharing systems did not work properly, and the combined efforts of Step-Saver, Wyse, and TSL could not fix the problems. Step-Saver was sued by 12 of its customers. In turn, Step-Saver sued Wyse Technology and TSL.

The Third Circuit of the US Court of Appeals ruled in favor of Step-Saver [68]. It based its argument on Article 2 of the UCC. The court held that the original contract between Step-Saver and TSL consisted of the purchase order, the invoice, and the oral statements made by TSL representatives on the telephone. The license agreement had additional terms that would have materially altered the contract. However, Step-Saver never agreed to these terms.

The court wrote, "In the absence of a party's express assent to the additional or different terms of the writing, section 2-207 [of the UCC] provides a default rule that the parties intended, as the terms of their agreement, those terms to which both parties have agreed along with any terms implied by the provision of the UCC." The court noted that the president of Step-Saver had objected to the terms of the licensing agreement. He had refused to sign a document formalizing the licensing agreement. Even after this, TSL had continued to sell to Step-Saver, implying that TSL wanted the business even if the contract did not include the language in the licensing agreement. That is why the court ruled that the purchase order, the invoice, and the oral statements constituted the contract, not the license agreement.

### PROCD INC. v. ZEIDENBERG

ProCD invested more than $10 million to construct a computer database containing information from more than 3,000 telephone directories. ProCD also developed a proprietary technology to compress and encrypt the data. It created an application program enabling users to search the database for records matching criteria they specified. ProCD targeted its product, called SelectPhone, to two different markets: companies interested in generating mailing lists and individuals interested in finding the phone numbers or addresses of particular people they wanted to call or write. Consumers who wanted SelectPhone for personal use could purchase it for $150; companies paid much more for the right to put the package to commercial use. ProCD included in the consumer version of SelectPhone a license prohibiting the commercial use of the database and program. In addition, the license terms were displayed on the user's computer monitor every time the program was executed.

Matthew Zeidenberg purchased the consumer version of SelectPhone in 1994. He formed a company called Silken Mountain Web Services Inc., which resold the information in the SelectPhone database. The price it charged was substantially less than the commercial price of SelectPhone. ProCD sued Matthew Zeidenberg for violating the licensing agreement.

At the trial, the defense argued that Zeidenberg could not be held to the terms of the licensing agreement, since they were not printed on the outside of the box containing the software. The US Court of Appeals for the Seventh Circuit ruled in favor of ProCD. Judge Frank Easterbrook wrote, "Shrinkwrap licenses are enforceable unless their terms are objectionable on grounds applicable to contracts in general (for example, if they violate a rule of positive law, or if they are unconscionable)" [69].

### MORTENSON v. TIMBERLINE SOFTWARE

M. A. Mortenson Company was a national construction contractor with a regional office in Bellevue, Washington. Timberline Software Inc. produced software for the construction industry. Mortenson had used software from Timberline for several years. In July 1993, Mortenson purchased eight copies of a bidding package called Precision Bid Analysis.

Timberline's licensing agreement included this paragraph:

> LIMITATION OF REMEDIES AND LIABILITY.
>
> NEITHER TIMBERLINE NOR ANYONE ELSE WHO HAS BEEN INVOLVED IN THE CREATION, PRODUCTION OR DELIVERY OF THE PROGRAMS OR USER MANUALS SHALL BE LIABLE TO YOU FOR ANY DAMAGES OF ANY TYPE, INCLUDING BUT NOT LIMITED TO, ANY LOST PROFITS, LOST SAVINGS, LOSS OF ANTICIPATED BENEFITS, OR OTHER INCIDENTAL, OR CONSEQUENTIAL DAMAGES, ARISING OUT OF THE USE OR INABILITY TO USE SUCH PROGRAMS, WHETHER ARISING OUT OF CONTRACT, NEGLIGENCE, STRICT TORT, OR UNDER ANY WARRANTY, OR OTHERWISE, EVEN IF TIMBERLINE HAS BEEN ADVISED OF THE POSSIBILITY OF SUCH DAMAGES OR FOR ANY OTHER CLAIM BY ANY OTHER PARTY. TIMBERLINE'S LIABILITY FOR DAMAGES IN NO EVENT SHALL EXCEED THE LICENSE FEE PAID FOR THE RIGHT TO USE THE PROGRAMS.

In December 1993, Mortenson used Precision Bid Analysis to prepare a bid for the Harborview Medical Center in Seattle. On the day the bid was due, the software malfunctioned. It printed the message "Abort: Cannot find alternate" 19 times. Mortenson continued to use the software and submitted the bid the software produced. After the firm won the contract, Mortenson discovered that its bid was $1.95 million too low.

Mortenson sued Timberline for breach of express and implied warranties. It turns out Timberline had been aware of the bug uncovered by Mortenson since May 1993. Timberline had fixed the bug and already sent a newer version of the program to some of its other customers who had encountered it. It had not sent the improved program to Mortenson. Nevertheless, Timberline argued that the lawsuit be summarily dismissed because the licensing agreement limited the consequential damages that Mortsenson could recover from Timberline. The King County Superior Court ruled in favor of Timberline. The ruling was upheld by the Washington Court of Appeals and the Supreme Court of the State of Washington [70].

## 8.8.3 Should Software Be Considered a Product?

As we have seen, when software is judged to be a good, the provisions of the Uniform Commercial Code regarding damages and warranty can apply. If software were to be considered a product, then the theory of strict liability would apply to the software manufacturer. According to the theory of strict liability, the manufacturer is liable for personal injury or property damage caused by a product when it is being used in a reasonable way. Because the theory of strict liability focuses on personal injury and property damage, but not economic loss, the primary impact of treating software as a product would be in those situations where software is part of an embedded system, such as an automobile.

To date, courts in the United States have resisted treating software as a product subject to the theory of strict liability, in part because a software-controlled device may cause harm through no fault of the programmer. Consider, for example, the development of a new software-controlled device for a medical treatment. Even practicing physicians may have differences of opinion about the best treatment option for a particular patient. How, then, can the company developing the device that delivers the treatment guarantee that the treatment will never hurt a patient? Is it reasonable to put all the liability on the manufacturer when others (such as hospital administrators, physicians, and technicians) may share some of the responsibility? The theory of strict liability seems to put too much liability on the software manufacturer in many cases [67].

### 8.8.4 Case Study: Incredible Bulk

Peter downloads a copy of the exciting new computer game Incredible Bulk for $49.95. The game is usable, but it contains some annoying bugs. The company never releases software patches fixing the bugs.

The next year the company releases Incredible Bulk II, which also costs $49.95 to download. According to the product description, the new release has many exciting new features. In addition, all of the annoying bugs of the original game have been fixed.

#### ETHICAL ANALYSIS

From a Kantian point of view, the company did nothing wrong. It never promised to make available software patches to fix bugs. Users particularly worried about the quality of a game can always wait until the reviews come out before deciding whether or not to purchase it. In this case Peter obviously thought Incredible Bulk was worth $49.95, and he went ahead and purchased it. If Peter now has a poor impression of the quality of the games put out by this company, no one is compelling him to purchase Incredible Bulk II. The software manufacturer might gain more customers and make higher profits by providing better customer support, but that is irrelevant to this analysis.

From a social contract point of view, this arrangement is unfair. When Peter downloaded Incredible Bulk, he was not actually purchasing the software, he was just purchasing a license to use the software. At some point before the release of Incredible Bulk II, the manufacturer fixed the bugs in Incredible Bulk. Peter's license gave him the right to play the improved version of Incredible Bulk. The manufacturer should have made software patches containing the bug fixes available on the Web for free downloading. Withholding these patches until the next major release of the software was wrong.

## Summary

Computers are part of larger systems, and ultimately it is the reliability of the entire system that is important. A well-engineered system can tolerate the malfunction of any single component without failing. This chapter has presented many examples of how the computer turned out to be the "weak link" in the system, leading to a failure. These examples provide important lessons for computer scientists and others involved in the design, implementation, and testing of large systems.

Two sources of failure are data entry errors and data retrieval errors. While it's easy to focus on a particular mistake made by the person entering or retrieving the data, the system is larger than the individual person. For example, in the case of the 2000 general election in Florida, incorrect records in the computer database disqualified thousands of voters. The data entry errors caused the *voting system* to work incorrectly. Sheila Jackson Stossier was arrested by police who confused her with Shirley Jackson. The data retrieval error caused the *criminal justice system* to perform incorrectly.

When the topics are software and billing errors, it is easier to identify the system that is failing. For example, when Qwest sent out 14,000 incorrect bills to its cellular phone customers, it's clear that the billing system had failed.

In Sections 8.4 and 8.5, the larger systems were easy to spot. Several embedded systems were dissected to determine the causes of their failures. The program for the Patriot missile's radar tracking system had a subtle flaw: a tiny truncation error occurred every time the clock signal was stored in a floating-point variable. Over a period of 100 hours, all those tiny errors added up to a significant amount, causing the radar system to lose its target. The Ariane 5 blew up because a single assignment statement caused the onboard computers to crash. The AT&T long-distance network collapsed because of one faulty line of code.

A well-engineered system does not fail when a single component fails. In the case of hardware, this principle is easier to apply. For example, a jetliner may have three engines. It is designed to be able to fly on any two of the engines, so if a single engine fails, the plane can still fly to the nearest airport and land. When it comes to software, the goal is much harder to meet. If we have two computers in the system, that provides redundancy in case one of the computers has a hardware failure. However, if both computers are running the same software, there is no software redundancy. A software bug that causes one computer to fail will cause both computers to fail. The partial collapse of the AT&T long-distance network is an example of this phenomenon. All 80 switches containing the latest version of the software failed. Fortunately, 34 switches were running an older version of the software, which prevented a total collapse of AT&T's system.

Imagine what it would take to provide true redundancy in the case of software systems. Should companies maintain two entirely different billing systems so that the bills produced by one system could be double-checked by the other? Should the federal government support two completely different implementations of the National Crime Information Center? These alternatives seem unrealistic. On the other hand, redundancy seems much more feasible when we look at data entry and data retrieval operations. Two different data entry operators could input records into databases, and the computer could check to make sure the records agreed. This would reduce the chance of bad data being entered into databases in the first place. Two different people could look at the results returned from a computer query, using their own common sense and understanding to see if the output makes sense. A paper audit trail is a practical way to add redundancy to an electronic voting machine.

While it may be infeasible to provide redundant software systems, safety-critical systems should never rely completely upon a single piece of software. The Therac-25 overdoses occurred because the system lacked the hardware interlocks of the earlier models.

The stories of computer system failures contain other valuable lessons. The Ariane 5 and Therac-25 failures show that it can be dangerous to reuse code. Assumptions that were valid when the code was originally written may no longer be true when the code is reused. Since some of these assumptions may not be documented, the new design team may not have the opportunity to check if these assumptions still hold true in the new system.

The automated baggage system at the Denver International Airport demonstrates the difficulty of debugging a complex system. Tackling one problem at a time, solving it, and moving on to the next problem proved to be a poor approach, because the overall system design had serious flaws. For example, BAE did not even realize that simply getting luggage carts to where they were needed in a fair and efficient manner was an incredibly difficult problem. Even if BAE had solved all the low-level technical problems, this high-level problem would have prevented the system from meeting its performance goals during the busiest times.

Finally, systems can fail because of miscommunications among people. The Mars Climate Orbiter is an example of this kind of failure. The software written by the team in Colorado used English units, while the software written by the team in California used metric units. The output of one program was incompatible with the input to the other program, but a poorly specified interface allowed this error to remain undetected until after the spacecraft was destroyed.

Computer simulations are used to perform numerical experiments that lead to new scientific discoveries and help engineers create better products. For this reason, it is important that simulations provide reliable results. Simulations are validated by comparing predicted results with reality. If a simulation is designed to predict future events, it can be validated by giving it data about the past and asking it to predict the present. Finally, simulations are validated when their results are believed by domain experts and policymakers.

The discipline of software engineering emerged from a growing realization of a "software crisis." While small programs can be written in an ad hoc manner, large programs must be carefully constructed if they are to be reliable. Software engineering is the application of engineering methodologies to the creation and evolution of software artifacts. Surveys of the IT industry reveal that more projects are being completed on time and on budget, and fewer projects are being canceled. This may be evidence that software engineering is having a positive impact. However, since most projects are still not completed on time and on budget, there remains much room for improvement. For many companies, shipping a product by a particular date continues to be a higher priority than following a strict software development methodology. There is also a growing awareness that unconscious bias on the part of male-dominated software development teams may lead to products being designed that are not truly gender-neutral. For this reason, some companies are taking steps to increase the number of women on software development teams.

Should software manufacturers be held accountable for the quality of their software, or is a program a completely different kind of product than a socket wrench? An examination of the software warranties manufacturers include in their licensing agreements reveals that they do not want to be held liable for any damages that occur from the use of their software. Courts seem willing to treat software as goods, which means the damages and warranty provisions of the Uniform Commercial Code may apply, despite what may appear in a software warranty. However, courts have been reluctant to treat software programs as products, which would expose software manufacturers to the theory of strict liability.

## Further Reading and Viewing

Walt Bogdanich. "Radiation Offers New Cures, and Ways to Do Harm." *New York Times*, January 23, 2010.

Walt Bogdanich. "As Technology Surges, Radiation Safeguards Lag." *New York Times*, January 26, 2010. www.nytimes.com.

Rob Holdorp. "What 3 Million Lines of Code Means to a Piece of Luggage." IBM. 2:33. www .ibm.com/innovation/us/leadership/luggage/.

Poul-Henning Kamp. "The Most Expensive One-Byte Mistake: Did Ken, Dennis, and Brian Choose Wrong with NUL-terminated Text Strings?" *ACM Queue*, July 25, 2011. queue .acm.org.

Nancy Leveson and Clark Turner. "An Investigation of the Therac-25 Accidents." *Computer*, pp. 18–41, July 1993.

## Review Questions

1. What is the difference between an embedded system and a real-time system?

2. What is a race condition in software? Why are software race conditions difficult to debug?

3. Summarize the principal errors made by AECL throughout the life cycle of the Therac-25 linear accelerator.

4. Why are computer simulations playing an increasingly important role in science and engineering?

5. What is the difference between the verification of a computer simulation and the validation of a computer simulation?

6. Name three different ways to validate a computer simulation.

7. Compare and contrast the meaning of the term "validation" in two areas: computer simulations and software engineering.

8. Do courts in the United States view software as a product subject to the theory of strict liability? Why or why not?

9. The following reasons have been given for the failure of computerized systems:
   a. A system designed for one purpose was used for another purpose.
   b. Software was reused without adequate testing.
   c. There was an error in storing or converting a data value.
   d. A line of code became a single point of failure.

  e. The overall system was too complicated to analyze.

  f. There was a software race condition.

  g. There was another software error (other than those listed in a–f).

  For each of the following systems, select the principal reason or reasons why it failed to operate as specified.

- Patriot missile
- Ariane 5
- AT&T long-distance network
- Mars Climate Orbiter
- Mars Polar Lander
- Denver International Airport baggage system
- Tokyo Stock Exchange
- Direct-recording electronic voting machines
- Therac-25

# Discussion Questions

10. Have you ever been the victim of a software error? Whom did you blame? Now that you know more about the reliability of computer systems, do you still feel the same way?

11. Should an ecommerce site be required to honor the prices at which it offers and sells goods and services?

12. Should the FBI be responsible for the accuracy of information about criminals and crime victims it enters into the National Crime Information Center database?

13. Over a period of seven years, about 500 residents of Freeport, Texas, were overbilled for their water usage. Each resident paid on average about $170 too much, making the total amount of the overbillings about $100,000. The city council decided not to issue refunds, saying that about 300,000 bills would have had to be examined, some residents had left town, and the individual refunds were not that large [71]. Did the city council make the right decision?

14. If a company sends a consumer an incorrect bill, should the company compensate the consumer for the time and effort the consumer takes to straighten out the mistake?

15. The chapter quotes NASA's project manager for the Mars Pathfinder as saying software hasn't improved in quality in the past 25 years. How could you determine whether software quality has improved in the past 25 years?

16. Perhaps programs used for business purposes ought to conform to higher standards of quality than games. With respect to software warranties, would it make sense to distinguish between software used for entertainment purposes (such as a first-person shooter game) and software used for business (such as a spreadsheet)?

17. Read the entire end-user license agreement (EULA) from a piece of commercial software. Do any of the conditions seem shady or unreasonable? If so, which ones?

18. While waiting for an appointment with your physician, you see a brochure advertising a new surgical procedure that implants a tiny microprocessor inside your skull just behind your left ear. The purpose of the chip is to help you associate names with faces. The

procedure for inserting the chip is so simple that your physician is performing it in his office. Suppose your career takes you into sales, where such a device could help you earn higher commissions. What questions would you want to have answered before you agreed to have such a device inserted into your skull?

# In–Class Exercises

19. Debate the moral responsibility of three agents associated with the two Therac-25 overdoses occurring in Tyler, Texas: the radiation technician, the hospital director, and the programmer who wrote the code controlling the machine. Divide the class into six groups. Three groups (one for each of the three agents) should give reasons why their particular party should bear at least some of the moral responsibility for the deaths. The other three groups (one for each of the three agents) should give reasons why their particular party should not bear any moral responsibility.

20. California is working on an "intelligent highway" system that would allow computer-controlled automobiles to travel faster and closer together on freeways than today's human-controlled cars. What kinds of safety devices would have to be in such a system in order for you to feel comfortable using an intelligent highway? How many people in class would be comfortable being one of the first people to use the intelligent highway?

21. The New York Transit Authority is transforming the L line into a partially automated subway line. A central computer system will control the speed and spacing of all trains on the line. However, each train will have an operator that starts and stops the train and has the ability to take control of it in an emergency [72]. How many people in the class would ride on a computer-controlled subway train that did not have a human operator on board?

22. Identify people in the class who have been beta testers for new software products. Ask them to tell the rest of the class about their experiences. What did acting as a beta tester teach them about software reliability?

23. A start-up company called Medick has been developing an exciting new product for handheld computers that will revolutionize the way nurses keep track of their hospitalized patients. The device will save nurses a great deal of time doing routine paperwork, reduce their stress levels, and enable them to spend more time with their patients.

    Medick's sales force has led hospital administrators to believe the product will be available next week as originally scheduled. Unfortunately, the package still contains quite a few bugs. All of the known bugs appear to be minor, but some of the planned tests have not yet been performed.

    Because of the fierce competition in the medical software industry, it is critical that this company be the first to market. It appears a well-established company will release a similar product in a few weeks. If its product appears first, Medick will probably go out of business.

    Divide the class into five groups representing the software engineers programming the device, the sales force that has been promoting the device, the managers of Medick, the venture capitalists who bankrolled Medick, and the nurses at a hospital purchasing the device. Discuss the best course of action for Medick.

# References

[1]   Jennifer DiSabatino. "Unregulated Databases Hold Personal Data." *Computerworld* 36(4), January 21, 2002.

[2]   Peter G. Neumann. "More on False Arrests." *Risks Digest* 1(5), September 4, 1985.

[3]   Rodney Hoffman. "NCIC Information Leads to Repeat False Arrest Suit." *Risks Digest* 8(71), May 17, 1989.

[4]   Ted Bridis. "US Lifts FBI Criminal Database Checks." Associated Press, March 25, 2003.

[5]   Department of Justice, Federal Bureau of Investigation. "Privacy Act of 1974; Implementation." *Federal Register* 68(56), March 24, 2003.

[6]   "Computer Glitch Is to Blame for Faulty Bills, Qwest Says." *Deseret News* Salt Lake City, UT, July 24, 2001.

[7]   "USDA Changes Livestock Price-Reporting Guidelines." *Amarillo Globe-News*, July 24, 2001.

[8]   "Software Error Returns Patent Office Mail." *New York Times*, August 9, 1996.

[9]   "Spelling and Grammar Checkers Add Errors." *Wired News*, March 18, 2003.

[10]  D. F. Galletta, A. Durcikova, A. Everard, and B. Jones. "Does Spell-Checking Software Need a Warning Label?" *Communications of the ACM*, pp. 82–86, July 2005.

[11]  Manny Fernandez. "Computer Error Caused Rent Troubles for Public Housing Tenants." *New York Times*, August 5, 2009.

[12]  "Calif. Computer Flub Lets Violent Prisoners Go Free." *Seattle Times*, May 26, 2011.

[13]  Ian MacKinnon and Stephen Goodwin. "Ambulance Chief Quits after Patients Die in Computer Failure." *Independent,* London, October 29, 1992.

[14]  "Flights at Japanese Airports Delayed." Associated Press, March 1, 2003.

[15]  "LA County's Main Hospital Has Computer Breakdown, Delays Ensue." Associated Press, April 22, 2003.

[16]  "Computer Glitches Shut Down Comair Flights." Associated Press, December 26, 2004.

[17]  Daniel Michaels and Andy Pasztor. "Flight Check: Incidents Prompt New Scrutiny of Airplane Software Glitches." *Wall Street Journal*, May 30, 2006.

[18]  Nathaniel Popper. "The Stock Market Bell Rings, Computers Fail, Wall Street Cringes." *DealBook*, July 8, 2015. www.nytimes.com.

[19]  Alan Yuhas. "Stock Trading Closed on NYSE after Glitch Caused Major Outage—as It Happened." *Guardian*, July 8, 2015. www.theguardian.com.

[20]  Dan Kaplan. "Black Hat: Insulin Pumps Can Be Hacked." *SC Magazine*, August 4, 2011. www.scmagazine.com.

[21]  Andy Greenberg. "Hackers Remotely Kill a Jeep on the Highway—with Me in It." *Wired*, July 21, 2015. www.wired.com.

[22]  Aaron M. Kessler. 'Fiat Chrysler Issues Recall over Hacking." *New York Times*, July 24, 2015. www.nytimes.com.

[23]  Robert Fry. "It's a Steal: Bargain-Hunting or Barefaced Robbery?" *Times*, London, April 8, 2003.

[24]  "Amazon Pulls British Site after iPaq Fire-Sale." *NYtimes.com*, March 19, 2003.

[25]   Victor L. Winter and Sourav Bhattacharya. Preface. In *High Integrity Software*, edited by Victor L. Winter and Sourav Bhattacharya. Kluwer Academic Publishers, Boston, MA, 2001.

[26]   E. Marshall. "Fatal Error: How Patriot Overlooked a Scud." *Science* 255(5050):1347, March 13, 1992.

[27]   Jean-Marc Jézéquel and Bertrand Meyer. "Design by Contract: The Lessons of Ariane." *Computer*, pp. 129–130, January 1997.

[28]   J. L. Lions. "ARIANE 5: Flight 501 Failure, Report by the Inquiry Board." European Space Agency, July 19, 1996. www.esa.int.

[29]   Ivars Peterson. "Finding Fault: The Formidable Task of Eradicating Software Bugs." *Science News* 139, February 16, 1991.

[30]   Bruce Sterling. *The Hacker Crackdown: Law and Disorder on the Electronic Frontier*. Bantam Books, New York, NY, 1992.

[31]   Jeff Foust. "Why Is Mars So Hard?" *Space Review*, June 2, 2003. www.thespace review.com.

[32]   Jet Propulsion Laboratory, California Institute of Technology. "NASA Facts: Mars Exploration Rover." October 2004. marsrover.jpl.nasa.gov.

[33]   Richard de Neufville. "The Baggage System at Denver: Prospects and Lessons." *Journal of Air Transport Management* 1(4):229–236, December 1994.

[34]   "Japan Court Upholds Lawsuit against Tokyo Stock Exchange in $400M Error Case." *Japan Daily Press*, July 24, 2013. japandailypress.com.

[35]   Tetsuo Tamai. "Social Impact of Information System Failures." *Computer*, June 2009.

[36]   Stefan Lovgren. "Are Electronic Voting Machines Reliable?" *National Geographic News*, November 1, 2004. news.nationalgeographic.com.

[37]   Jarrett Blanc. "Challenging the Norms and Standards of Election Administration: Electronic Voting." In *Challenging the Norms and Standards of Election Administration*. International Foundation for Electoral Systems, Washington, DC, 2007.

[38]   Sonia Arrison and Vince Vasquez. *Upgrading America's Ballot Box: The Rise of E-voting*. 2nd ed. Pacific Research Institute, San Francisco, CA, 2006.

[39]   "Electronic Ballots Fail to Win Over Wake Voters, Election Officials; Machines Provide Improper Vote Count at Two Locations." WRAL-TV (Raleigh-Durham, NC), November 2, 2002.

[40]   Barbara Simons. "Electronic Voting Systems: The Good, the Bad, and the Stupid." *RFID* 2(7), October 2004.

[41]   William Rivers Pitt. "Worse Than 2000: Tuesday's Electoral Disaster" (editorial). *Truthout*, November 8, 2004. www.Truth-out.org.

[42]   Mark Johnson. "Winner So Far: Confusion." *Charlotte Observer,* November 5, 2004.

[43]   Charles Rabin and Darran Simon. "Glitches Cited in Early Voting: Early Voters Are Urged to Cast Their Ballots with Care Following Scattered Reports of Problems with Heavily Used Machines." *Miami Herald*, October 28, 2006.

[44]   "Florida Candidate Disputes Election Results." CNN.com, December 20, 2006.

[45]   Marc Caputo and Gary Fineout. "New Tests Fuel Doubts about Vote Machines." *Miami Herald*, December 15, 2005.

[46]   Jeremy Epstein. "Weakness in Depth: A Voting Machine's Demise." *IEEE Security & Privacy*, May/June 2015, pp. 55–58.

[47] "Transparent Liberty, Accountable Election Systems" (leaflet). Open Voting Consortium. www.openvoting.org.

[48] Cheryl Gerber. "Voting 2.0." *Chronogram*, January 2006.

[49] Pacific Research Institute. "More E-voting Red Tape Threatens Ballot Booth Benefits, New Study Says" (press release). October 31, 2006.

[50] Terry Aguayo and Christine Jordan Sexton. "Florida Acts to Eliminate Touch-Screen Voting System." *New York Times*, May 4, 2007.

[51] Cory Bennett. "States Ditch Electronic Voting Machines." *Hill*, November 2, 2014. thehill.com.

[52] Nancy Leveson and Clark Turner. "An Investigation of the Therac-25 Accidents." *Computer* 26(7):18–41, 1993.

[53] Walt Bogdanich. "Radiation Offers New Cures, and Ways to Do Harm." *New York Times*, January 23, 2010. www.nytimes.com.

[54] William J. Kauffman III and Larry L. Smarr. *Supercomputing and the Transformation of Science*. Scientific American Library, New York, NY, 1993.

[55] Lucio Mayer, Tom Quinn, James Wadsley, and Joachim Stadel. "Forming Giant Planets via Fragmentation of Protoplanetary Disks." *Science*, November 29, 2002.

[56] Donnella H. Meadows, Dennis I. Meadows, Jorgen Randers, and William W. Behrens III. *The Limits To Growth*. Universe Books, New York, NY, 1972.

[57] Bjørn Lomborg and Olivier Rubin. "Limits to Growth." *Foreign Policy*, October/November 2002.

[58] G. S. Fishman and P. J. Kiviat. "The Statistics of Discrete Event Simulation." *Simulation* 10:185–195, 1968.

[59] Ian Sommerville. *Software Engineering*. 6th ed. Addison-Wesley, Harlow, England, 2001.

[60] David Rubinstein. "Standish Group Report: There's Less Development Chaos Today." *SD Times*, March 1, 2007. sdtimes.com.

[61] Gendered Innovations in Science, Health & Medicine, Engineering, and Environment (Web site). genderedinnovations.stanford.edu.

[62] Margaret Burnett, Scott Fleming, Shamsi Iqbal, Gina Venolia, Vidya Rajaram, Umer Farooq, Valentina Grigoreanu, and Mary Czerwinski. "Gender Differences and Programming Environments: Across Programming Populations." *ESEM '10*, September 16–17, 2010, Bolzano-Bozen, Italy.

[63] Gayna Williams. "Are You Sure Your Software Is Gender-Neutral?" *Interactions*, Vol. 21, No. 1, January–February 2014, p. 36.

[64] Claire Cain Miller. "Technology's Man Problem." *New York Times*, April 4, 2014. www.nytimes.com.

[65] Danielle Gaucher, Justin Friesen, and Aaron Kay. "Evidence that Gendered Wording in Job Advertisements Exists and Sustains Gender Inequality." *Journal of Personality and Social Psychology*, Vol. 101, No. 1, pp. 109–128, 2011.

[66] Sylvia Hewlett, Carolyn Luce, Lisa Servon, Laura Sherbin, Peggy Shiller, Eytan Sosnovich, and Karen Sumberg. "The Athena Factor: Reversing the Brain Drain in Science, Engineering, and Technology." Harvard Business Review Research Report. June 2008.

[67] Lawrence B. Levy and Suzanne Y. Bell. "Software Product Liability: Understanding and Minimizing the Risks." *BTLJ Online*, May 26, 1990. www.law.berkeley.edu.

[68]    United States Court of Appeals for the Third Circuit. Step-Saver Data Systems, Inc. v. Wyse Technology and The Software Link, Inc., 939 F. 2d 91 (1991).

[69]    United States Court of Appeals for the Seventh Circuit. ProCD, Inc., v. Matthew Zeidenberg and Silken Mountain Web Services, Inc., Appeal from the United States District Court for the Western District of Wisconsin, 96–1139 (1996).

[70]    Supreme Court of the State of Washington. M.A. Mortenson Co. v. Timberline Software Corp., et al. Opinion, 140 Wash. 2d 568, 998 P.2d 305, 2000.

[71]    "Texans Get Soaked." *IEEE Software*, p. 114, September/October 1997.

[72]    Elizabeth Hays. "L Trains Do Compute." *New York Daily News*, January 18, 2004.

# Avi Rubin

Dr. Avi D. Rubin is a professor of computer science and the technical director of the Information Security Institute at Johns Hopkins University. Professor Rubin directs the NSF–funded ACCURATE center for correct, usable, reliable, auditable, and transparent elections. He is also a cofounder of Independent Security Evaluators (www.securityevaluators.com), a security consulting firm.

Dr. Rubin has testified before the US House and Senate on multiple occasions. In January 2004, *Baltimore Magazine* named him Baltimorean of the Year for his work in safeguarding the integrity of our election process. He is also the recipient of the 2004 Electronic Frontier Foundation Pioneer Award.

Professor Rubin is the author of several books, including *Brave New Ballot* (Random House, 2006), *Firewalls and Internet Security*, second edition, with Bill Cheswick and Steve Bellovin (Addison–Wesley, 2003), *White-Hat Security Arsenal* (Addison–Wesley, 2001), and *Web Security Sourcebook*, with Dan Geer and Marcus Ranum (John Wiley & Sons, 1997). He is associate editor of ACM *Transactions on Internet Technology*, associate editor of *IEEE Security & Privacy*, and an advisory board member of Springer's Information Security and Cryptography book series.

---

**The Pacific Research Institute maintains that DRE voting machines are more secure than traditional paper ballots, which they say can be tampered with by elections officials. Presumably you disagree with their assertion?**

I agree with them that paper ballots can be tampered with. I also believe that for an unsophisticated attacker, it is probably easier to tamper with paper ballots than with the election results in DREs. However, there are several reasons why I think the use of DREs poses a bigger threat to the integrity of an election than paper ballots do. First, tampering with paper ballots is more likely to be detected than tampering with software or electronic ballots. Second, if someone were to rig the software in a DRE, that could impact ballots in thousands of places, while tampering with paper ballots has to occur on a retail level, increasing the exposure for the attacker. But perhaps my greatest concern is that an accidental bug in a DRE could result in the wrong election results being reported, without anyone ever knowing it. Since paper ballots are not software based, an analogous threat does not exist for paper ballots.

**Proponents say that DRE voting machines eliminate errors that have plagued other voting systems. Two common examples: punched cards can have "hanging chads," and paper ballots can't prevent a voter from accidentally voting for two candidates. Do these benefits outweigh the potential risks?**

The hanging chad is a problem related to punch-card systems, not paper ballots in general. I think punch-card systems should no longer be used. Optical scan technology, a different form of paper ballots, does not suffer the same problems. There are also systems that avoid voter error problems such as voters voting for two candidates when they are only allowed to vote for one. For example, in precinct scanners, the scanner can spit out a ballot that is marked incorrectly, giving the voter a chance to fix it. There are commercial scanners that do this. Furthermore, ballot-marking machines, where voters mark the ballot on a touch screen but then a paper ballot is printed and fed into a scanner, do not suffer from any of these problems.

### What led you to investigate the reliability of Diebold DRE voting machines?

I was a computer security researcher, and in the late 1990s I became interested in electronic voting because it is a hard and interesting problem. When the source code for the Diebold voting machine was found on the Internet, I viewed it as an opportunity to study a real system that was actually used for voting.

### In your paper "Analysis of an Electronic Voting System," you concluded that the public should have access to the source code used in electronic voting machines, yet this code represents a valuable intellectual property to the companies that write it. Why should a company commit time and money to develop innovative, high-quality software that will be revealed to everybody, including potential competitors?

I think that the transparency requirement for something like voting trumps any intellectual property protection that a vendor might want. Furthermore, we have a patent system in this country that can protect intellectual property and that also requires full disclosure. I find this whole argument pretty silly because the primary functionality of a voting machine is very simple. Finally, many companies have shown that they can make plenty of money with open-source systems.

### You've expressed concern that in a close election "paperless DREs [direct-recording electronic voting machines] will produce a cloud of uncertainty over the election." What do you propose, and how would it increase the accuracy of electronic voting systems?

I propose paper ballots with optical scanners at the precinct, which can detect voter error. For accessibility, I propose that voters be given the option of using a ballot-marking machine, as I described above.

### Would you say that federal funding of ACCURATE is proof that there is widespread understanding of the problems associated with DRE voting machines and support for guaranteeing fair elections?

ACCURATE was funded by the National Science Foundation (NSF). The process for funding NSF centers involves rigorous peer review by many top computer scientists. The computer science community understands the risks associated with DREs and also the need to find an alternative system that is transparent, accurate, and correct, and can justifiably hold the public confidence.

### How is ACCURATE going to improve the voting process in the United States?

Our center is developing technology to aid in the voting process. Our investigators are intimately involved in the elections process, working with officials at all levels and volunteering in running elections. It is our hope that some of the technology developed by our center will be utilized in the design and implementation of future systems, to avoid the possibility of an errant software bug or a malicious attacker being able to corrupt an election.

# CHAPTER

# 9 Professional Ethics

> We have come through a strange cycle in programming, starting with the creation of programming itself as a human activity. Executives with the tiniest smattering of knowledge assume that anyone can write a program, and only now are programmers beginning to win their battle for recognition as true professionals.
>
> —GERALD WEINBERG, *The Psychology of Computer Programming*, 1971

## 9.1 Introduction

JACOBUS LENTZ WAS THE NETHERLANDS' INSPECTOR of population registries before World War II. In this role he managed a well-oiled data-processing infrastructure using machines leased from IBM, and he reveled in the collection of personal data, writing: "Theoretically, the collection of data for each person can be so abundant and complete, that we can finally speak of a paper human representing the natural human" [1, p. 304].

Lentz devised a forgery-proof identification card and advocated that every citizen be required to get one and carry it at all times, but the Dutch government rejected his proposal; it offended democratic sensibilities. When the Netherlands came under German occupation in 1940, Lentz got another opportunity to promote his invention. He shared his design with the Nazis, who were impressed; it was far superior to the identification card being used in Germany. Soon the identification card designed by Lentz was issued to everyone in the Netherlands.

In January 1941, the Germans began a special census of the Jews in the Netherlands. All Jews were required to register at their local census office. There was widespread condemnation of this edict across Dutch society, but the Jews complied. The penalty for failing to register was five years in prison and the loss of one's property. Besides, those who failed to register could be tracked down because the government had up-to-date information about them that was gathered when the Lentz identification cards were issued.

Lentz did not simply comply with the directives of the Germans, he anticipated their needs. When they contacted him in May 1941 about producing an alphabetical register of the Jewish population, Lentz replied that his office had already begun setting up a system to do just that. In his memoirs Lentz wrote, "I rented a Hollerith installation with which the professional statistical survey has been composed, which satisfied the Germans very much, and gave them the convictions that my opinions had been correct" [1, p. 312].

In July 1942, twice-weekly trains began deporting Jews from the Netherlands to concentration camps in Eastern Europe. The alphabetized lists provided by Lentz's office allowed the Germans to conduct this operation with great efficiency: rounding up Jews in an orderly fashion and keeping the trains running on schedule. Of the 140,000 Jews in the Netherlands at the time of the German invasion, 107,000 were deported, and of these 102,000 died [1].

Informally, a **profession** is a vocation that requires a high level of education and practical experience in the field. Professionals have a special obligation to ensure their actions are for the good of those who depend on them, because their decisions can have more serious consequences than the choices made by those holding less responsible positions in society. Jacobus Lentz had great expertise in the world of data processing. As inspector of population registries, he was in a position of great responsibility. Sadly, he focused on demonstrating his creativity, technical abilities, and industriousness and ignored the consequences of his actions. Lacking a moral compass, he allowed himself to play an important role in Hitler's "Final Solution" of the Jewish question.

In this chapter we focus on moral decisions made by people who design, implement, operate, or maintain computer hardware or software systems. We begin by considering the extent to which a computer-related career is a profession along the lines of medicine or law. Next we present and analyze a code of ethics for an important computer-related discipline: software engineering. Four case studies give us the opportunity to use the software engineering code of ethics as a tool for ethical analysis.

Finally, we discuss whistle-blowing: a situation in which a member of an organization breaks ranks to reveal actual or potential harm to the public. Whistle-blowing raises important moral questions about loyalty, trust, and responsibility. Two accounts of whistle-blowing illuminate these moral questions and demonstrate the personal sacrifices some have made for the greater good of society. We consider the important role management plays in creating an organizational atmosphere that either allows or suppresses internal dissent.

# 9.2 How Well Developed Are the Computing Professions?

Millions of people have a computer-related job title, such as computer engineer, computer scientist, programmer, software engineer, system administrator, or systems analyst. Is a computer-related career a fully developed profession like medicine or law? Let's consider the characteristics of a fully developed profession.

## 9.2.1 Characteristics of a Fully Developed Profession

A fully developed profession has a well-organized infrastructure for certifying new members and supporting those who already belong to the profession. Ford and Gibbs have identified eight components of a mature professional infrastructure:[1]

- *Initial professional education*—formal course work completed by candidates before they begin practicing the profession
- *Accreditation*—a means of assuring that the formal course work meets the standards of the profession
- *Skills development*—activities that provide candidates with the opportunity to gain practical skills needed to practice the profession
- *Certification*—a process by which candidates are evaluated to determine their readiness to enter the profession
- *Licensing*—the process giving candidates the legal right to practice the profession
- *Professional development*—formal course work completed by professionals in order to maintain and develop their knowledge and skills
- *Code of ethics*—a mechanism by which a profession ensures that its members use their knowledge and skills for the benefit of society
- *Professional society*—an organization promoting the welfare of the profession, typically consisting of most, if not all, members of the profession

Figure 9.1 illustrates how these components work together to support the profession. A person desiring to join the profession undertakes some initial professional education. A process of accreditation assures that the educational process is sound. After completing their formal education, candidates gain skills through practical experience working in the field. Another check determines if the candidate is ready to be certified. Successful candidates are licensed to practice the profession.

When the public can trust the competence and integrity of the members of a profession, every one of its members benefits. For this reason professionals have a stake

1. From Gary Ford and Norman E. Gibbs, "A Mature Profession of Software Engineering." Technical report, Carnegie Mellon University, January 1996. Copyright © 1996 Carnegie Mellon University. All rights reserved.

**Figure 9.1** A mature profession has eight attributes that enable it to certify new members and support existing members [2].

in ensuring that fellow members of the profession are capable and act appropriately. For mature professions, professional societies establish codes of ethics and require their members to keep their knowledge current through continuing education and training. Professionals who do not follow the code of ethics or fail to keep up with changes in the field can lose their licenses.

## 9.2.2 Case Study: Certified Public Accountants

To illustrate these steps, let's consider how a person becomes a certified public accountant (CPA). We choose accounting because it is a fully developed profession that does not require graduate study for membership. In this respect it is more similar to a typical computer-related career than the medical or legal professions, which require their members to earn advanced degrees.

The first step for someone wishing to become a CPA is to graduate with 150 semester credit hours and at least a bachelor's degree from an accredited college or university. Many people pursuing a CPA choose to major in accounting, although it is not strictly necessary. However, the candidate must have completed at least 24 semester credit hours in accounting, auditing, business law, finance, and tax subjects. After graduation, the candidate gets practical training in the profession by finding employment as an accountant working under the supervision of a CPA. Finally, candidates must sit for the CPA exam, which has four sections. Candidates who do not pass at least two parts must retake the entire exam. Candidates who pass at least two parts of the exam must pass the remaining parts within five years.

Completion of the necessary formal education, plus satisfactory scores on every section of the CPA exam, plus two years' work experience enable an accountant to become a certified public accountant. In order to retain certification, CPAs must fulfill continuing education requirements and abide by the profession's code of ethics.

### 9.2.3 How Do Computer–Related Careers Stack Up?

It is easy to find a crucial difference between systems analysts, computer programmers, and system administrators on the one hand and accountants, lawyers, and physicians on the other hand. At the heart of every mature profession is certification and licensing. Certification and licensing allow a profession to determine who will be allowed to practice the profession. For example, a person may not practice law in a state without passing the bar exam and being granted a license. In contrast, people may write computer programs and maintain computer systems, either as consultants, sole proprietors, or members of larger firms, without being certified or having been granted a license.

There are other differences between computer-related careers and mature professions. A person does not have to complete college or serve an apprenticeship under the guidance of an experienced mentor in order to gain employment as a programmer, system administrator, or systems analyst. The vast majority of people who hold computer-related jobs do not belong to either of computing's professional societies. It is up to particular employers to monitor the behavior of their employees and guide their continuing education—no professional organization has the authority to forbid someone from managing computer networks or writing computer programs.

In another important respect computer programmers differ from most professionals, such as dentists and ministers. Typically, professionals work directly with individual clients. A dentist treats one patient at a time. An accountant audits one business at a time. Most computer programmers work inside a company as part of a team that includes many other programmers as well as managers. In this environment the responsibility of an individual person is more difficult to discern. Low-level technical decisions are made by groups, and final authority rests with management.

#### STATUS OF CERTIFICATION AND LICENSING

A **software engineer** is someone engaged in the development or maintenance of software, or someone who teaches in this area. A path to certification and licensing of software engineers in the United States now exists; it is similar to the path taken by engineers in other disciplines, such as civil engineering and mechanical engineering. In order to become licensed, engineers must gain four years of post-college work experience and pass two examinations: the Fundamentals of Engineering (FE) examination and a discipline-specific Principles and Practice of Engineering examination (often called the PE exam). The National Council of Examiners for Engineering and Surveying

(NCEES) is responsible for developing and administering the FE and PE examinations. The NCEES partnered with the professional organization IEEE-USA to develop a PE exam for software, and it offered the exam for the first time in 2013. Most states now offer the PE exam in software.

The introduction of licensing does not mean that every software engineer must be licensed. In fact, only a very small percentage of software professionals will have to be licensed: those who are developing software that can affect the health, safety, and welfare of the public and are offering their services directly to the public. In April 2015, only 16 software professionals in the United States took the PE exam for the first time, and 10 earned a passing score. Two more software professionals were repeat takers of the PE exam, and both of them passed [3].

## ABILITY TO HARM THE PUBLIC

The computing "profession" may not be as well developed as the medical or legal professions, but in one key respect—the ability to harm members of the public—those who design, implement, and maintain computer hardware and software systems sometimes hold responsibilities similar to those held by members of mature professions. The Therac-25 killed or gravely injured at least six people, in part because of defective software. While most software engineers do not write code for safety-critical systems such as linear accelerators, society does depend on the quality of their work. People make important business decisions based on the results they get from their spreadsheet programs. Millions rely upon commercial software to help them produce their income tax returns. Errors in programs can result in such harms as lost time, incorrect business decisions, and fines. System administrators are responsible for keeping computer systems running reliably without infringing on the privacy of the computer users.

~

### The Importance of Taking Personal Responsibility

The ability to cause harm to members of the public is a powerful reason why those in computer-related careers must act according to ethical principles. Without formal certification and licensing and other components of a well-developed profession to rely upon, those in computer-related careers must take more personal responsibility for developing their ethical decision-making skills.

~

One important decision-making skill to develop is the ability to apply the viable ethical theories presented in Chapter 2. Kantianism, utilitarianism, social contract theory, and virtue ethics all contain important insights into what it means to do the right thing. Another important decision making skill to develop is the ability to apply the Software Engineering Code of Ethics and Professional Practice, endorsed by both the ACM and the IEEE-CS.

# 9.3 Software Engineering Code of Ethics

The Software Engineering Code of Ethics and Professional Practice is a practical framework for moral decision making related to problems that software engineers may encounter.

The Software Engineering Code of Ethics and Professional Practice is reproduced here in its entirety (copyright © 2011 by ACM Publications; reprinted with permission).

## Preamble

Computers have a central and growing role in commerce, industry, government, medicine, education, entertainment and society at large. Software engineers are those who contribute by direct participation or by teaching, to the analysis, specification, design, development, certification, maintenance and testing of software systems. Because of their roles in developing software systems, software engineers have significant opportunities to do good or cause harm, to enable others to do good or cause harm, or to influence others to do good or cause harm. To ensure, as much as possible, that their efforts will be used for good, software engineers must commit themselves to making software engineering a beneficial and respected profession. In accordance with that commitment, software engineers shall adhere to the following Code of Ethics and Professional Practice.

The Code contains eight Principles related to the behavior of and decisions made by professional software engineers, including practitioners, educators, managers, supervisors and policymakers, as well as trainees and students of the profession. The Principles identify the ethically responsible relationships in which individuals, groups, and organizations participate and the primary obligations within these relationships. The Clauses of each Principle are illustrations of some of the obligations included in these relationships. These obligations are founded in the software engineer's humanity, in special care owed to people affected by the work of software engineers, and the unique elements of the practice of software engineering. The Code prescribes these as obligations of anyone claiming to be or aspiring to be a software engineer.

It is not intended that the individual parts of the Code be used in isolation to justify errors of omission or commission. The list of Principles and Clauses is not exhaustive. The Clauses should not be read as separating the acceptable from the unacceptable in professional conduct in all practical situations. The Code is not a simple ethical algorithm that generates ethical decisions. In some situations standards may be in tension with each other or with standards from other sources. These situations require the software engineer to use ethical judgment to act in a manner which is most consistent with the spirit of the Code of Ethics and Professional Practice, given the circumstances.

Ethical tensions can best be addressed by thoughtful consideration of fundamental principles, rather than blind reliance on detailed regulations. These Principles should influence software engineers to consider broadly who is affected by their work; to examine if they and their colleagues are treating other human beings with due respect; to consider how the public, if reasonably well informed, would view their decisions; to analyze how the least empowered will be affected by their decisions; and to consider whether their acts would be judged worthy of the ideal professional working as a software engineer. In

FIGURE 9.2 Software engineers shall approve software only if they have a well-founded belief that it is safe, meets specifications, passes appropriate tests, and does not diminish quality of life, diminish privacy, or harm the environment. The ultimate effect of the work should be to the public good (clause 1.03).

all these judgments concern for the health, safety and welfare of the public is primary; that is, the "Public Interest" is central to this Code.

The dynamic and demanding context of software engineering requires a code that is adaptable and relevant to new situations as they occur. However, even in this generality, the Code provides support for software engineers and managers of software engineers who need to take positive action in a specific case by documenting the ethical stance of the profession. The Code provides an ethical foundation to which individuals within teams and the team as a whole can appeal. The Code helps to define those actions that are ethically improper to request of a software engineer or teams of software engineers.

The Code is not simply for adjudicating the nature of questionable acts; it also has an important educational function. As this Code expresses the consensus of the profession on ethical issues, it is a means to educate both the public and aspiring professionals about the ethical obligations of all software engineers.

## Principles

### PRINCIPLE 1: PUBLIC

Software engineers shall act consistently with the public interest. In particular, software engineers shall, as appropriate:

1.01   Accept full responsibility for their own work.

1.02   Moderate the interests of the software engineer, the employer, the client and the users with the public good.

1.03   Approve software only if they have a well-founded belief that it is safe, meets specifications, passes appropriate tests, and does not diminish quality of life, diminish

**FIGURE 9.3** Software engineers shall not knowingly use software that is obtained or retained either illegally or unethically (clause 2.02).

privacy or harm the environment. The ultimate effect of the work should be to the public good.

**1.04** Disclose to appropriate persons or authorities any actual or potential danger to the user, the public, or the environment, that they reasonably believe to be associated with software or related documents.

**1.05** Cooperate in efforts to address matters of grave public concern caused by software, its installation, maintenance, support or documentation.

**1.06** Be fair and avoid deception in all statements, particularly public ones, concerning software or related documents, methods and tools.

**1.07** Consider issues of physical disabilities, allocation of resources, economic disadvantage and other factors that can diminish access to the benefits of software.

**1.08** Be encouraged to volunteer professional skills to good causes and contribute to public education concerning the discipline.

## PRINCIPLE 2: CLIENT AND EMPLOYER

Software engineers shall act in a manner that is in the best interests of their client and employer, consistent with the public interest. In particular, software engineers shall, as appropriate:

**2.01** Provide service in their areas of competence, being honest and forthright about any limitations of their experience and education.

**2.02** Not knowingly use software that is obtained or retained either illegally or unethically.

**2.03** Use the property of a client or employer only in ways properly authorized, and with the client's or employer's knowledge and consent.

**FIGURE 9.4** Software engineers shall ensure proper and achievable goals and objectives for any project on which they work or propose (clause 3.02).

2.04   Ensure that any document upon which they rely has been approved, when required, by someone authorized to approve it.

2.05   Keep private any confidential information gained in their professional work, where such confidentiality is consistent with the public interest and consistent with the law.

2.06   Identify, document, collect evidence and report to the client or the employer promptly if, in their opinion, a project is likely to fail, to prove too expensive, to violate intellectual property law, or otherwise to be problematic.

2.07   Identify, document, and report significant issues of social concern, of which they are aware, in software or related documents, to the employer or the client.

2.08   Accept no outside work detrimental to the work they perform for their primary employer.

2.09   Promote no interest adverse to their employer or client, unless a higher ethical concern is being compromised; in that case, inform the employer or another appropriate authority of the ethical concern.

## PRINCIPLE 3: PRODUCT

Software engineers shall ensure that their products and related modifications meet the highest professional standards possible. In particular, software engineers shall, as appropriate:

3.01   Strive for high quality, acceptable cost and a reasonable schedule, ensuring significant tradeoffs are clear to and accepted by the employer and the client, and are available for consideration by the user and the public.

3.02   Ensure proper and achievable goals and objectives for any project on which they work or propose.

**3.03**  Identify, define and address ethical, economic, cultural, legal and environmental issues related to work projects.

**3.04**  Ensure that they are qualified for any project on which they work or propose to work by an appropriate combination of education and training, and experience.

**3.05**  Ensure an appropriate method is used for any project on which they work or propose to work.

**3.06**  Work to follow professional standards, when available, that are most appropriate for the task at hand, departing from these only when ethically or technically justified.

**3.07**  Strive to fully understand the specifications for software on which they work.

**3.08**  Ensure that specifications for software on which they work have been well documented, satisfy the users' requirements and have the appropriate approvals.

**3.09**  Ensure realistic quantitative estimates of cost, scheduling, personnel, quality and outcomes on any project on which they work or propose to work and provide an uncertainty assessment of these estimates.

**3.10**  Ensure adequate testing, debugging, and review of software and related documents on which they work.

**3.11**  Ensure adequate documentation, including significant problems discovered and solutions adopted, for any project on which they work.

**3.12**  Work to develop software and related documents that respect the privacy of those who will be affected by that software.

**3.13**  Be careful to use only accurate data derived by ethical and lawful means, and use it only in ways properly authorized.

**3.14**  Maintain the integrity of data, being sensitive to outdated or flawed occurrences.

**3.15**  Treat all forms of software maintenance with the same professionalism as new development.

## PRINCIPLE 4: JUDGMENT

Software engineers shall maintain integrity and independence in their professional judgment. In particular, software engineers shall, as appropriate:

**4.01**  Temper all technical judgments by the need to support and maintain human values.

**4.02**  Only endorse documents either prepared under their supervision or within their areas of competence and with which they are in agreement.

**4.03**  Maintain professional objectivity with respect to any software or related documents they are asked to evaluate.

**4.04**  Not engage in deceptive financial practices such as bribery, double billing, or other improper financial practices.

**4.05**  Disclose to all concerned parties those conflicts of interest that cannot reasonably be avoided or escaped.

**4.06** Refuse to participate, as members or advisors, in a private, governmental or professional body concerned with software related issues, in which they, their employers or their clients have undisclosed potential conflicts of interest.

## PRINCIPLE 5: MANAGEMENT

Software engineering managers and leaders shall subscribe to and promote an ethical approach to the management of software development and maintenance. In particular, those managing or leading software engineers shall, as appropriate:

**5.01** Ensure good management for any project on which they work, including effective procedures for promotion of quality and reduction of risk.

**5.02** Ensure that software engineers are informed of standards before being held to them.

**5.03** Ensure that software engineers know the employer's policies and procedures for protecting passwords, files and information that is confidential to the employer or confidential to others.

**5.04** Assign work only after taking into account appropriate contributions of education and experience tempered with a desire to further that education and experience.

**5.05** Ensure realistic quantitative estimates of cost, scheduling, personnel, quality and outcomes on any project on which they work or propose to work, and provide an uncertainty assessment of these estimates.

**5.06** Attract potential software engineers only by a full and accurate description of the conditions of employment.

**5.07** Offer fair and just remuneration.

**5.08** Not unjustly prevent someone from taking a position for which that person is suitably qualified.

**5.09** Ensure that there is a fair agreement concerning ownership of any software, processes, research, writing, or other intellectual property to which a software engineer has contributed.

**5.10** Provide for due process in hearing charges of violation of an employer's policy or of this Code.

**5.11** Not ask a software engineer to do anything inconsistent with this Code.

**5.12** Not punish anyone for expressing ethical concerns about a project.

## PRINCIPLE 6: PROFESSION

Software engineers shall advance the integrity and reputation of the profession consistent with the public interest. In particular, software engineers shall, as appropriate:

**6.01** Help develop an organizational environment favorable to acting ethically.

**6.02** Promote public knowledge of software engineering.

**6.03** Extend software engineering knowledge by appropriate participation in professional organizations, meetings and publications.

**FIGURE 9.5** Software engineers shall help develop an organizational environment favorable to acting ethically (clause 6.01).

6.04   Support, as members of a profession, other software engineers striving to follow this Code.

6.05   Not promote their own interest at the expense of the profession, client or employer.

6.06   Obey all laws governing their work, unless, in exceptional circumstances, such compliance is inconsistent with the public interest.

6.07   Be accurate in stating the characteristics of software on which they work, avoiding not only false claims but also claims that might reasonably be supposed to be speculative, vacuous, deceptive, misleading, or doubtful.

6.08   Take responsibility for detecting, correcting, and reporting errors in software and associated documents on which they work.

6.09   Ensure that clients, employers, and supervisors know of the software engineer's commitment to this Code of ethics, and the subsequent ramifications of such commitment.

6.10   Avoid associations with businesses and organizations which are in conflict with this code.

6.11   Recognize that violations of this Code are inconsistent with being a professional software engineer.

6.12   Express concerns to the people involved when significant violations of this Code are detected unless this is impossible, counter-productive, or dangerous.

6.13   Report significant violations of this Code to appropriate authorities when it is clear that consultation with people involved in these significant violations is impossible, counter-productive or dangerous.

## PRINCIPLE 7: COLLEAGUES

Software engineers shall be fair to and supportive of their colleagues. In particular, software engineers shall, as appropriate:

 7.01   Encourage colleagues to adhere to this Code.

7.02   Assist colleagues in professional development.

7.03   Credit fully the work of others and refrain from taking undue credit.

7.04   Review the work of others in an objective, candid, and properly documented way.

7.05   Give a fair hearing to the opinions, concerns, or complaints of a colleague.

7.06   Assist colleagues in being fully aware of current standard work practices including policies and procedures for protecting passwords, files and other confidential information, and security measures in general.

7.07   Not unfairly intervene in the career of any colleague; however, concern for the employer, the client or public interest may compel software engineers, in good faith, to question the competence of a colleague.

7.08   In situations outside of their own areas of competence, call upon the opinions of other professionals who have competence in that area.

## PRINCIPLE 8: SELF

Software engineers shall participate in lifelong learning regarding the practice of their profession and shall promote an ethical approach to the practice of the profession. In particular, software engineers shall continually endeavor to:

 8.01   Further their knowledge of developments in the analysis, specification, design, development, maintenance and testing of software and related documents, together with the management of the development process.

8.02   Improve their ability to create safe, reliable, and useful quality software at reasonable cost and within a reasonable time.

8.03   Improve their ability to produce accurate, informative, and well-written documentation.

8.04   Improve their understanding of the software and related documents on which they work and of the environment in which they will be used.

8.05   Improve their knowledge of relevant standards and the law governing the software and related documents on which they work.

8.06   Improve their knowledge of this Code, its interpretation, and its application to their work.

8.07   Not give unfair treatment to anyone because of any irrelevant prejudices.

8.08   Not influence others to undertake any action that involves a breach of this Code.

8.09   Recognize that personal violations of this Code are inconsistent with being a professional software engineer.

**FIGURE 9.6** Software engineers shall continually endeavor to improve their ability to create safe, reliable, and useful quality software at reasonable cost and within a reasonable time (clause 8.02).

## 9.4 Analysis of the Code

In this section we analyze the Software Engineering Code of Ethics and Professional Practice and derive an alternate set of underlying principles upon which it rests.

### 9.4.1 Preamble

The preamble to the code points out that there is no mechanical process for determining the correct actions to take when faced with a moral problem. Our experience evaluating moral problems related to the introduction and use of information technology confirms this statement. Even two people with similar philosophies may reach different conclusions when confronted with a moral problem. Two Kantians may agree on the basic facts of a moral problem but disagree on how to characterize the will of the moral agent. Two utilitarians may agree on the benefits and harms resulting from a proposed action but assign different weights to the outcomes, causing them to reach opposite conclusions.

The preamble also warns against taking an overly legalistic view of the code. Simply because an action is not expressly forbidden by the code does not mean it is morally acceptable. Instead, judgment is needed to detect when a moral problem has arisen and to determine the right thing to do in a particular situation.

While the code is expressed as a collection of rules, these rules are based on principles grounded in different ethical theories. This is not surprising, considering that the code was drafted by a committee. When we encounter a situation where two rules conflict, the preamble urges us to ask questions that will help us consider the principles underlying the rules. These questions demonstrate the multifaceted grounding of the code:

1. *Who is affected?*

   Utilitarians focus on determining how an action benefits or harms other people.

2. *Am I treating other human beings with respect?*

   Kant's Categorical Imperative (Section 2.6.1) tells us to treat others as ends in themselves rather than simply as a means to an end.

3. *Would my decision hold up to public scrutiny?*

   In other words, does the action reflect well on my character? Developing a good character is central to virtue ethics.

4. *How will those who are least empowered be affected?*

   Rawls's second principle of justice (Section 2.9.2) requires us to consider whether inequalities are to the greatest benefit of the least advantaged members of society.

5. *Are my acts worthy of the ideal professional?*

   Virtue ethics is based on imitation of morally superior role models.

## 9.4.2 Alternative List of Fundamental Principles

The start of each section of the code begins with the statement of a fundamental principle. For example, the first section begins with the fundamental principle, "Software engineers shall act consistently with the public interest." All these statements of fundamental principles are expressed from the point of view of what software engineers ought to do.

Another way to devise a list of fundamental principles is to consider those virtues we would like to instill among all the members of any profession. We end up with a set of general, discipline-independent rules that cut across the eight categories of the code. Here is an alternative list of fundamental principles derived using that approach.

1. *Be impartial.*

   The good of the general public is equally important to the good of your organization or company. The good of your profession and your company are equally important to your personal good. It is wrong to promote your agenda at the expense of your firm, and it is wrong to promote the interests of your firm at the expense of society. (Supports clauses 1.02, 1.03, 1.05, 1.07, 3.03, 3.12, 4.01, and 6.05.)

2. *Disclose information that others ought to know.*

   Do not let others come to harm by concealing information from them. Do not make misleading or deceptive statements. Disclose potential conflicts of interest. (Supports clauses 1.04, 1.06, 2.06, 2.07, 3.01, 4.05, 4.06, 5.05, 5.06, 6.07, 6.08, 6.09, 6.12, and 6.13.)

3. *Respect the rights of others.*

   Do not infringe on the privacy rights, property rights, or intellectual property rights of others. (Supports clauses 2.02, 2.03, 2.05, and 3.13.)

4. *Treat others justly.*

   Everyone deserves fair wages and appropriate credit for work performed. Do not discriminate against others for attributes unrelated to the job they do. Do not penalize others for following the Code. (Supports clauses 5.06, 5.07, 5.08, 5.09, 5.10, 5.11, 5.12, 7.03, 7.04, 7.05, 7.07, and 8.07.)

5. *Take responsibility for your actions and inactions.*

   As a moral agent, you are responsible for the things you do, both good and bad. You may also be responsible for bad things that you allow to happen through your inaction. (Supports clauses 1.01, 3.04, 3.05, 3.06, 3.07, 3.08, 3.10, 3.11, 3.14, 3.15, 4.02, and 7.08.)

6. *Take responsibility for the actions of those you supervise.*

   Managers are responsible for setting up work assignments and training opportunities to promote quality and reduce risk. They should create effective communication channels with subordinates so that they can monitor the work being done and be aware of any quality or risk issues that arise. (Supports clauses 5.01, 5.02, 5.03, and 5.04.)

7. *Maintain your integrity.*

   Deliver on your commitments and be loyal to your employer, while obeying the law. Do not ask someone else to do something you would not be willing to do yourself. (Supports clauses 2.01, 2.04, 2.08, 2.09, 3.01, 3.02, 3.09, 4.03, 4.04, 6.06, 6.10, 6.11, 8.08, and 8.09.)

8. *Continually improve your abilities.*

   Take advantage of opportunities to improve your software engineering skills and your ability to put the Code to use. (Supports clauses 8.01, 8.02, 8.03, 8.04, 8.05, and 8.06.)

9. *Share your knowledge, expertise, and values.*

   Volunteer your time and skills to worthy causes. Help bring others to your level of knowledge about software engineering and professional ethics. (Supports clauses 1.08, 6.01, 6.02, 6.03, 6.04, 7.01, 7.02, and 7.06.)

In the following section, we use these fundamental, discipline-independent principles to facilitate our analysis in four case studies related to computing.

## 9.5 Case Studies

Throughout this text we have evaluated a wide range of moral problems. Our methodology has been to evaluate the moral problem from the point of view of one or more of these theories: Kantianism, act utilitarianism, rule utilitarianism, social contract theory, and virtue ethics.

Another way to evaluate information technology–related moral problems is to make use of the Software Engineering Code of Ethics and Professional Practice. We follow a three-step process:

1. Consult the list of fundamental principles and identify those that are relevant to the moral problem.

2. Search the list of clauses accompanying each of the relevant fundamental principles to see which speak most directly to the issue.

3. Determine whether the contemplated action aligns with or contradicts the statements in the clauses. If the action is in agreement with all the clauses, that provides strong evidence the action is moral. If the action is in disagreement with all the clauses, it is safe to say the action is immoral.

Usually, the contemplated action is supported by some clauses and opposed by others. When this happens, we must use our judgment to determine which of the clauses are most important before we can reach a conclusion about the morality of the contemplated action.

In the remainder of this section, we apply this methodology to four case studies.

### 9.5.1 Software Recommendation

#### ~ SCENARIO

Sam Shaw calls the Department of Computer Science at East Dakota State University seeking advice on how to improve the security of his business's local area network. A secretary in the department routes Mr. Shaw's call to Professor Jane Smith, an internationally recognized expert in the field. Professor Smith answers several questions posed by Mr. Shaw regarding network security. When Mr. Shaw asks Professor Smith to recommend a software package to identify security problems, Professor Smith tells him that NetCheks got the personal computer magazine's top rating. She does not mention that the same magazine gave a "best buy" rating to another product with fewer features but a much lower price. She also fails to mention that NetCheks is a product of a spin-off company started by one of her former students and that she owns 10 percent of the company.

#### Analysis

From our list of nine fundamental principles, three are most relevant here:

- Be impartial.
- Disclose information that others ought to know.
- Share your knowledge, expertise, and values.

Searching the list of clauses identified with these fundamental principles, the following ones seem to fit the case study most closely:

- *1.06. Be fair and avoid deception in all statements, particularly public ones, concerning software or related documents, methods and tools.*
  Professor Smith was deceptive when she mentioned the most highly rated software package but not the one rated to be a "best buy."

- *1.08. Be encouraged to volunteer professional skills to good causes and contribute to public education concerning the discipline.*

- *4.05. Disclose to all concerned parties those conflicts of interest that cannot reasonably be avoided or escaped.*
- *6.02. Promote public knowledge of software engineering.*
  Professor Smith freely provided Sam Shaw with valuable information about network security.
- *6.05. Not promote their own interest at the expense of the profession, client or employer.*
  Professor Smith did not tell Sam Shaw that she had a personal stake in the success of the NetCheks software. She did not tell him about the "best buy" package that may have provided him every feature he needed at a much lower price.

Mr. Shaw was asking Professor Smith for free advice, and she provided it. When she freely shared her knowledge about network security, she was acting in the spirit of clauses 1.08 and 6.02, and doing a good thing.

However, Professor Smith appears to have violated the other three clauses, at least to some degree. Most important, she did not reveal her personal interest in NetCheks, which could lead her to be biased. The fact that she did not mention the "best buy" package is evidence that she was neither evenhanded nor completely forthcoming when she answered Mr. Shaw's question about software packages.

Perhaps Mr. Shaw should have heeded the maxim, "Free advice is worth what you pay for it." Nevertheless, the ignorance or foolishness of one person does not excuse the bad behavior of another. Professor Smith should have revealed her conflict of interest. At that point Mr. Shaw could have chosen to get another opinion if he so desired.                                               ∼

### 9.5.2  Child Pornography

∼ SCENARIO

Joe Green, a system administrator for a large corporation, is installing a new software package on the PC used by employee Chuck Dennis. The company has not authorized Joe to read other people's emails, Web logs, or personal files. However, in the course of installing the software, he accidentally comes across directories containing files with suspicious-looking names. He opens a few of the files and discovers they contain child pornography. Joe believes possessing such images is against federal law. What should he do?

*Analysis*

Looking over the list of nine fundamental principles, we find these to be most relevant to our scenario:

- Be impartial.
- Respect the rights of others.
- Treat others justly.
- Maintain your integrity.

We examine the list of clauses associated with these four fundamental principles and identify those that are most relevant:

- *2.03. Use the property of a client or employer only in ways properly authorized, and with the client's or employer's knowledge and consent.*
  Somebody has misused the company's PC by using it to store images of child pornography. By this principle Joe has an obligation to report what he discovered.

- *2.09. Promote no interest adverse to their employer or client, unless a higher ethical concern is being compromised; in that case, inform the employer or another appropriate authority of the ethical concern.*
  While revealing the existence of the child pornography may harm the employee, possessing child pornography is illegal. Applying this principle would lead Joe to disclose what he discovered.

- *3.13. Be careful to use only accurate data derived by ethical and lawful means, and use it only in ways properly authorized.*
  Joe discovered the child pornography by violating the company's policy against examining files on personal computers used by employees.

- *5.10. Provide for due process in hearing charges of violation of an employer's policy or of this Code.*
  Simply because Chuck had these files on his computer does not necessarily mean he is guilty. Perhaps someone else broke into Chuck's computer and stored the images there.

Our analysis is more complicated because Joe violated company policy to uncover the child pornography on Chuck's PC. Once he has this knowledge, however, the remaining principles guide Joe to reveal what he has discovered to the relevant authorities within the corporation, even though management may punish Joe for breaking the privacy policy. There is the possibility that Chuck is a victim. Someone else may be trying to frame Chuck or use his computer as a safe stash for their collection of images. Joe should be discreet until a complete investigation is completed and Chuck has had the opportunity to defend himself.

∽

### 9.5.3 Antiworm

∽ SCENARIO

The Internet is plagued by a new worm that infects PCs by exploiting a security hole in a popular operating system. Tim Smart creates an antiworm that exploits the same security hole to spread from PC to PC. When Tim's antiworm gets into a PC, it automatically downloads a software patch that plugs the security hole. In other words, it fixes the PC so that it is no longer vulnerable to attacks via that security hole [4].

Tim releases the antiworm, taking precautions to ensure that it cannot be traced back to him. The antiworm quickly spreads throughout the Internet, consuming large amounts of network bandwidth and entering millions of computers. To system administrators, it looks just like another worm, and they battle its spread the same way they fight all other worms [5].

## Analysis

These fundamental principles are most relevant to the antiworm scenario:

- Continually improve your abilities.
- Share your knowledge, expertise, and values.
- Respect the rights of others.
- Take responsibility for your actions and inactions.

Examining the list of clauses associated with each of these fundamental principles reveals those that are most relevant to our case study:

- *1.01. Accept full responsibility for their own work.*
  Tim tried to prevent others from discovering that he was the author of the antiworm. He did not accept responsibility for what he had done.

- *1.08. Be encouraged to volunteer professional skills to good causes and contribute to public education concerning the discipline.*
  The antiworm did something good by patching security holes in PCs. Tim provided the antiworm to the Internet community without charge. However, system administrators spent a lot of time trying to halt the spread of the antiworm, a harmful effect.

- *2.03. Use the property of a client or employer only in ways properly authorized, and with the client's or employer's knowledge and consent.*
  Tim's "client" is the community of Internet PC owners who happen to use the operating system with the security hole. While his antiworm was designed to benefit them, it entered their systems without their knowledge or consent. The antiworm also consumed a great deal of network bandwidth without the consent of the relevant telecommunications companies.

- *8.01. Further their knowledge of developments in the analysis, specification, design, development, maintenance, and testing of software and related documents, together with the management of the development process.*

- *8.02. Improve their ability to create safe, reliable, and useful quality software at reasonable cost and within a reasonable time.*

- *8.06. Improve their knowledge of this Code, its interpretations and its application to their work.*
  Tim followed the letter of the first two of these three clauses when he acquired a copy of the worm, figured out how it worked, and created a reliable antiworm in a short period of time. The experience improved his knowledge and skills. Perhaps he should invest some time improving his ability to interpret and use the Code of Ethics!

According to some of these principles, Tim did the right thing. According to others, Tim was wrong to release the antiworm. How do we resolve this dilemma? We can simplify our analysis by deciding that Tim's welfare is less important than the public good. Using this logic, we no longer consider the fact that Tim improved his technical knowledge and skills by developing and releasing the antiworm.

That leaves us with three clauses remaining (1.01, 1.08, and 2.03). From the point of view of clause 1.01, what Tim did was wrong. By attempting to hide his identity, Tim refused to accept responsibility for launching the antiworm. He has clearly violated the Code of Ethics in this regard.

When we evaluate Tim's action from the point of view of clause 1.08, we must determine whether his efforts were directed to a "good cause." Certainly, Tim's antiworm benefited the PCs it infected by removing a security vulnerability. However, it harmed the Internet by consuming large amounts of bandwidth, and it harmed system administrators who spent time battling it. Because there were harmful as well as beneficial consequences, we cannot say that Tim's efforts were directed to a completely good cause.

Finally, let's evaluate Tim's action from the point of view of clause 2.03. Even though the antiworm was completely benevolent, Tim violated the property rights of the PC owners, because the antiworm infected their PCs without authorization. Hence Tim's release of the antiworm was wrong from the point of view of this clause.

To summarize our analysis, Tim's release of the antiworm is clearly wrong from the point of view of clauses 1.01 and 2.03. It is also hard to argue that he satisfied the spirit of clause 1.08. We conclude that Tim's action violated the Software Engineering Code of Ethics and Professional Practice.     ∽

## 9.5.4  Consulting Opportunity

∽ SCENARIO

Acme Corporation licenses a sophisticated software package to many state, county, and city governments. Government agencies have the choice of three levels of service: the bronze level provides online support only; the silver level adds phone support; and the gold level includes training classes taught on the customer's site. The gold level of support costs $20,000 a year more than the silver level.

Jean is one of the Acme employees who works in the support organization. Mostly, Jean provides phone support, but from time to time he teaches an on-site class. In fact, Jean created many of the instructional materials used in these classes. Because of the recession, quite a few government agencies have dropped from the gold level of support to the silver level, and some members of Jean's training group have lost their jobs. Jean has a family to support, and he is wondering if his position will soon be eliminated as well.

The state government of East Dakota is one of the many customers that no longer pays Acme Corporation for on-site training. One day Jean gets a call from Maria, who works for the East Dakota state agency using the software package. Maria offers to pay Jean $5,000 plus expenses to run a five-day training class that covers the same material as the official course taught by Acme.

Jean accepts the offer, but he does not inform anyone at Acme Corporation of his decision. Working at home on evenings and weekends, he develops his own set of instructional materials. He takes a week of paid vacation from work, travels to East Daktoa, and teaches the class.

## Analysis

From our list of fundamental principles, quite a few are relevant here:

- Be impartial.
- Take responsibility for your actions and inactions.
- Disclose information that others ought to know.
- Maintain your integrity.
- Continually improve your abilities.

Examining the clauses associated with each of these fundamental principles, the ones that most closely fit this case study are as follows:

- *2.08 Accept no outside work detrimental to the work they perform for their primary employer.*
  Employers provide employees with weekends off and paid vacations so that they can rest from their labors and return to work refreshed and able to perform at a high level. You could argue that Jean's consulting work was detrimental to his "day job" at Acme Corporation because it filled his evenings and weekends and kept him from getting a proper vacation.

- *3.04 Ensure that they are qualified for any project on which they work or propose to work by an appropriate combination of education and training, and experience.*
  Based on his prior experience at Acme, Jean was certainly well qualified to develop the instructional materials and teach the class in East Dakota. He has fulfilled this obligation of the Code.

- *4.05 Disclose to all concerned parties those conflicts of interest that cannot reasonably be avoided or escaped.*
  By accepting the consulting job with the East Dakota state government, Jean created a conflict of interest between himself and Acme Corporation. Namely, it is in Jean's interest if East Dakota does not purchase the gold level of support, but it is in Acme Corporation's interest if East Dakota does buy the gold level of support. Jean violated this clause by not disclosing his consulting job to Acme Corporation.

- *6.05 Not promote their own interest at the expense of the profession, client or employer.*
  By agreeing to teach the class in East Dakota, Jean put his own interest above that of his employer. Clearly, the East Dakota state government recognized a need to have some on-site training. If Jean did not accept the consulting job, the East Dakota government may have gone back to the gold level of support from Acme.

- *8.04 Improve their understanding of the software and related documents on which they work and of the environment in which they will be used.*

  By creating his own set of instructional materials, Jean probably developed an even better understanding of the software package and its capabilities. There is a good chance he came up with some insights about better ways to teach others how to use the software. This additional knowledge will make Jean a more valuable employee of Acme Corporation.

You could argue that Jean is actually helping Acme Corporation. Governments are dropping the gold level of support because it is simply too expensive, but phone support and online support aren't enough. If these agencies cannot find another source of on-site training, they may stop using Acme's software altogether. By providing East Dakota with affordable on-site training, Jean was helping ensure that East Dakota would remain a customer of Acme Corporation, albeit at the silver level.

You could also argue that Jean's work for East Dakota improved his knowledge of the software package and his ability to teach others how to use it, making him a more effective phone support person at Acme.

However, it's unlikely upper management at Acme Corporation will be convinced by these arguments, particularly since Jean did not disclose the offer from East Dakota before accepting it. Jean's decision is much more likely to cause management to question his loyalty to his company and his fellow employees. If the company learns about his consulting work, Jean may well be the next person laid off.

To conclude our analysis, Jean's actions were wrong and unwise. He violated clauses 2.08, 4.05, and 6.05 of the Software Engineering Code of Ethics and Professional Practice, and he may have put his full-time job in jeopardy.    ∽

## 9.6 Whistle-Blowing

All four case studies presented in the previous section involve the actions of a single individual. It is easy for us to assign moral responsibility to that person and to discuss how things might have turned out better if he or she had acted differently. Often, however, a product or decision is the cumulative result of the work of many people within a larger organization. Suppose somebody within the organization perceives a danger to the public but is unable to persuade the rest of the organization to make needed changes to eliminate that danger. Should that person go outside the organization with the information?

A **whistle-blower** is someone who breaks ranks with an organization in order to make an unauthorized disclosure of information about a harmful situation after attempts to report the concerns through authorized organizational channels have been ignored or rebuffed [6]. Sometimes employees become whistle-blowers out of fear that actions taken by their employer may harm the public; other times they have identified fraudulent use of tax dollars [7].

**FIGURE 9.7** The explosion of the *Challenger* killed seven astronauts, including the first civilian in space, Christa McAuliffe. (Courtesy of NASA)

### 9.6.1 **Morton Thiokol/NASA**

On January 28, 1986, the space shuttle *Challenger* lifted off from Cape Canaveral. On board were seven astronauts, including schoolteacher Christa McAuliffe, the first civilian to fly into space. Just 73 seconds after liftoff, hot gases leaking from one of the booster rockets led to an explosion that destroyed the *Challenger* and killed everyone on board (Figure 9.7).

Engineer Roger Boisjoly was in charge of inspecting the O-rings on the boosters recovered after launches of the space shuttle. The O-rings were supposed to seal connections between sections of the booster rockets. On two occasions in 1985, he had seen evidence that a primary O-ring seal had failed. Boisjoly presented a report on his findings to NASA officials at the Marshall Space Flight Center. Frustrated that NASA officials were not giving sufficient attention to the problem, he wrote a memo to vice president for engineering Robert Lund, stating that an O-ring failure could lead to the loss of a shuttle flight and the launch pad. Despite Boisjoly's persistent efforts to get the seals redesigned, the problem was not fixed.

On January 27, 1986, Boisjoly and a group of Morton Thiokol engineers met to discuss the proposed launch for the following day. Florida was in the middle of an unusual cold snap; the weather forecast for northern Florida called for an overnight low of 18 degrees Fahrenheit. The engineers knew that frigid temperatures greatly increased the probability that an O-ring would fail, allowing hot gases to escape from a booster rocket. They prepared a set of 14 slides that documented their concern about a low-temperature launch.

The evening of January 27, Morton Thiokol had a teleconference with the Marshall Space Flight Center and the Kennedy Space Center. Morton Thiokol's presentation ended with the engineers' recommendation that NASA not launch the *Challenger* if the temperature was below 53 degrees. NASA asked Morton Thiokol vice president Joe Kilminster for a go/no-go decision. Kilminster said his recommendation was not to launch.

NASA officials were displeased to get this recommendation from Morton Thiokol. The launch had already been delayed several times. They were eager to launch the space shuttle before the president's State of the Union address the following evening, so that the president could include the mission in his speech. After NASA officials expressed their dismay with the recommendation, Kilminster asked for a five-minute break in the proceedings.

During the recess, Morton Thiokol's four top managers huddled away from the engineers. Senior vice president Jerald Mason and vice president Calvin Wiggins supported the launch, while vice presidents Joseph Kilminster and Robert Lund were opposed. However, Lund changed his mind after Mason "told him to take off his engineering hat and put on his management hat" [8]. (More than half of Morton Thiokol's profits came from its work for NASA.)

When Morton Thiokol rejoined the teleconference, Kilminster told NASA officials that Morton Thiokol recommended the launch go ahead. NASA officials at the Marshall Space Flight Center prevented the engineers' negative recommendation from being communicated to the NASA officials with final authority to approve or delay the launch.

A month after the loss of the *Challenger*, Boisjoly testified before a presidential commission appointed to investigate the disaster. Morton Thiokol lawyers had advised Boisjoly to reply to every question with a simple yes or no. Instead, Boisjoly shared with the commission his hypothesis about how the cold temperature had caused the failure of an O-ring. In later meetings with commission members, he presented documents that supported his hypothesis, including his 1985 memo. Boisjoly's testimony and documents contradicted the testimony of Morton Thiokol management. The company responded by isolating Boisjoly from NASA personnel and the O-ring redesign effort [8, 9].

Distressed by the hostile environment, Boisjoly stopped working for Morton Thiokol in July 1986. Two years later, he found work as a forensic engineer.

### 9.6.2 Hughes Aircraft

In the 1980s, Hughes Aircraft manufactured military-grade hybrid computer chips at its Microelectronic Circuit Division in Newport Beach, California. (A hybrid computer chip contains both digital and analog circuits.) The division produced about 100,000 hybrid chips per year. The military put these chips in a variety of sophisticated weapons systems, such as fighter planes and air-to-air missiles. Manufacturing these chips was a lucrative business for Hughes Aircraft: the government paid between $300 and $5,000 for each chip.

In return for paying these high prices, the government insisted that the chips pass stringent quality assurance tests. Hughes Aircraft technicians made two kinds of tests. First, they ensured the chips functioned correctly. Second, they checked the chips for resistance to shocks, high temperatures, and moisture. About 10 percent of the chips failed at least one of these tests. A common problem was that a chip would have a defective seal, which let moisture in. These chips were called "leakers."

Margaret Goodearl and Donald LaRue supervised the testing area. The company hired Ruth Ibarra to be an independent quality control agent.

In August 1986, floor worker Lisa Lightner found a leaker. Donald LaRue ordered her to pass the chip. Lightner told Goodearl, and Goodearl reported the incident to upper management. Hughes Aircraft management threatened to fire Goodearl if she didn't reveal the identity of the worker who had complained.

Two months later LaRue ordered Shirley Reddick, another floor worker, to reseal lids on some hybrid chips, in violation of the required process for handling leakers. Reddick reported the incident to Goodearl, who relayed the report to upper management. Again, Goodearl was told she might be fired if she kept up this pattern of behavior.

In the same month, LaRue asked tester Rachel Janesch to certify that a defective hybrid chip had passed the leak test. Goodearl played a role in reporting the incident to Hughes Aircraft management. In this case the chips were retested.

Goodearl and Ibarra found a box of hybrid chips with blank paperwork, meaning the necessary tests had not been performed. When Goodearl reported this discovery to her superiors, they told her she was no longer part of the team. Goodearl filed a formal harassment complaint. A midlevel manager in personnel called her into his office, tore up her complaint, threw his glasses at her, and said, "If you ever do anything like that again, I will fire your ass" [7].

Goodearl's performance evaluations, which had been excellent, dropped sharply as soon as she began complaining about irregularities in the chip testing facility. In late 1986, Goodearl and Ibarra contacted the Office of the Inspector General, part of the US Department of Justice. A joint decision was made for Goodearl and Ibarra to find a clear-cut case of fraud.

One day LaRue put two leaky hybrid chips on his desk, planning to approve them after Goodearl had gone home. Goodearl and Ibarra made photocopies of the documentation showing the chips had failed the leak test. After the chips were shipped from Hughes Aircraft, the Department of Defense tested them and found them to be leakers. As a result of this incident, the Office of the Inspector General began a formal investigation of fraud at Hughes Aircraft.

Hughes Aircraft fired Goodearl in 1989. Ibarra had left Hughes Aircraft in 1988 "after being relieved of all meaningful responsibilities and put in a cubicle with nothing to do" [10]. In 1990 Margaret Goodearl and Ruth Ibarra (now known under her married name, Ruth Aldred) filed a civil suit against Hughes Aircraft, claiming that Hughes

Aircraft had violated the False Claims Act by falsifying records in order to defraud the government. This civil suit was put on hold until the end of the criminal trial.

The inspector general's criminal investigation led to a trial in 1992. The jury found Hughes Aircraft guilty of conspiring to defraud the government. Hughes Aircraft appealed the verdict, but the verdict was upheld. Since a criminal conviction can be used as evidence in a civil trial, the verdict nearly assured that Goodearl and Aldred would prevail in their civil suit. Hughes Aircraft began negotiating a settlement in the civil suit.

Four years later, Hughes Aircraft was ordered to pay $4.05 million in damages. Goodearl and Aldred received 22 percent of the settlement, or $891,000. In addition, Hughes Aircraft was required to pay their legal fees, which amounted to $450,000 [7, 11].

Goodearl and Aldred paid a high price for whistle-blowing. Both were unemployed for an extended period of time. Aldred and her husband went on welfare until they could find work. Goodearl and her husband had to file for bankruptcy, and they eventually divorced. Despite these hardships, both whistle-blowers said they "would do it all again" [12].

## 9.6.3 US Legislation Related to Whistle-Blowing

Whistle-blowers are usually punished for disclosing information that organizations have tried to keep under wraps. If they do not lose their jobs outright, they have probably lost all chances for future advancement within the organization. Whistle-blowers and their families typically suffer emotional distress and economic hardship.

Nevertheless, whistle-blowers often serve the public good. For this reason the US government has passed two pieces of legislation to encourage whistle-blowing: the False Claims Act and the Whistleblower Protection Act of 1989.

The False Claims Act was first enacted by Congress in 1863 in response to massive fraud perpetrated by companies providing supplies to the Union Army during the Civil War. The law allowed a whistle-blower to sue, on behalf of the government, a person or company that was submitting falsified claims to the government. If the organization was found guilty and forced to pay a settlement to the government, the whistle-blower received half the settlement.

In 1943 Congress amended the False Claims Act, drastically reducing the share of the settlement a whistle-blower would receive and limiting the evidence or information a whistle-blower could use in the lawsuit. As a result, the law fell into disuse.

In the mid-1980s, the media carried numerous stories about defense contractors perpetrating fraud against the government. Congress responded by amending the False Claims Act once again, making it easier for people to put together a successful lawsuit and allowing whistle-blowers to receive between 15 and 30 percent of settlements. The False Claims Act also provides certain protections to whistle-blowers against retaliation by their employers.

The Whistleblower Protection Act of 1989 establishes certain safeguards for federal employees and former employees who claim negative personnel actions have been taken against them for whistle-blowing. Whistle-blowers can appeal to the US Merit Systems Protection Board.

## 9.6.4 Morality of Whistle–Blowing

Are whistle-blowers heroes or traitors? Marcia Miceli and Janet Near point out that people become whistle-blowers for different reasons. They suggest we ought to consider their motives before we decide if they were acting morally [13]. While it is fair to say that all whistle-blowers are trying to bring an end to wrongdoing, they may well have other reasons for publicizing a problem. We can evaluate the morality of whistle-blowing by considering whether the whistle-blower is motivated by a desire to help others or harm others.

Consider a person who has known about a dangerous product for years but only becomes a whistle-blower after he has been turned down for a raise or promotion. If the disgruntled employee blows the whistle in order to exact revenge on an organization that has let him down, the primary motivation is to hurt the company, not to help the public. Another example of questionable whistle-blowing is the case of employees who have been involved in a cover-up for some period of time, realize that they are about to be caught, and then cooperate with the authorities to identify other guilty parties in order to avoid punishment.

But suppose a person doesn't have ulterior motives for whistle-blowing and is doing it simply to inform the public of a dangerous situation or a misappropriation of funds. There are three general reactions to altruistic whistle-blowing [9].

### WHISTLE-BLOWERS CAUSE HARM

The typical corporate response to whistle-blowing is to condemn it. Whistle-blowers are disloyal to their companies. Through their actions they generate bad publicity, disrupt the social fabric of an organization, and make it more difficult for everyone to work as part of a team. In other words, their betrayal causes short-term and long-term damage to the company. While it is the responsibility of engineers to point out technical problems, the management of a company is ultimately responsible for the decisions being made, both good and bad. If management makes a mistake, the public has recourse through the legal system to seek damages from the company, and the board of directors or CEO can replace the managers who have used bad judgment.

The weakness in this response is its cavalier and overly legalistic attitude toward public harm. If people are hurt or killed, they or their heirs can always sue for damages. Yet surely society is better off if people are not harmed in the first place. A monetary settlement is a poor replacement for a human life.

### WHISTLE-BLOWING IS A SIGN OF ORGANIZATIONAL FAILURE

A second response to whistle-blowing is to view it as a symptom of an organizational failure that results in harm all around [14]. The company suffers from bad publicity. The careers of accused managers can be ruined. It makes people suspicious of one another, eroding team spirit. Whistle-blowers typically suffer retaliation and become estranged from their coworkers. Labeled as troublemakers, their long-term prospects with the company are dim.

Since whistle-blowing is a sign of failure, organizations need to find a way to prevent it from happening in the first place. Some suggest that organizations can eliminate the need for whistle-blowing by creating management structures and communication processes that allow concerns to be raised, discussed, and resolved.

This may be easier said than done. Robert Spitzer observes that organizations have shifted away from principle-based decision making to utilitarian decision making. A characteristic of rule-oriented ethical decision making is its absolute nature. According to Kantianism or social contract theory, the end never justifies the means. If an action violates a moral rule, it shouldn't be done, period. In contrast, a utilitarian process weighs expected benefits and harms. Once an organization begins using utilitarian thinking, the question is no longer "Should we do it?" but "How much of it can we do without harm?" Spitzer writes, "One can see situations in which it would be permissible to use an evil means to achieve a good so long as enough benefit can be actualized." He suggests that organizations should return to using principle-based ethics in their decision making [15].

## WHISTLE-BLOWING AS A MORAL DUTY

A third response is to assert that under certain circumstances people have a moral duty to blow the whistle. Whistle-blowing is alluded to in clauses 1.02, 1.03, 1.04, 1.05, 2.05, 2.09, 3.01, 6.06, and 6.13 of the Software Engineering Code of Ethics and Professional Practice. These clauses provide a justification for whistle-blowing in a variety of circumstances.

Richard De George believes whistle-blowers should ask themselves five questions:

1. Do you believe the problem may result in "serious and considerable harm to the public"?

2. Have you told your manager your concerns about the potential harm?

3. Have you tried every possible channel within the organization to resolve the problem?

4. Have you documented evidence that would persuade a neutral outsider that your view is correct?

5. Are you reasonably sure that if you do bring this matter to public attention, something can be done to prevent the anticipated harm?

According to De George, you have a right to whistle-blow if you answer yes to the first three questions; if you answer yes to all five questions, you have a duty to whistle-blow [16].

De George's five requirements are controversial. Some would say whistle-blowing is justified even when fewer requirements are met. For example, what if the potential whistle-blower knows about a problem that could result in death or injury to millions of people, such as a meltdown inside a nuclear power plant? The whistle-blower has communicated his concerns to his manager, but there is not time to lobby every potential decision maker in the company. He is reasonably sure that if he contacted a television station, something could be done to prevent the meltdown. At the very least, the media could alert people so that they could get out of harm's way. Shouldn't that person be obliged to whistle-blow, even though the answer to the third question is no?

To others, insisting that the whistle-blower have convincing documentation is too strict a condition to be met in order for whistle-blowing to be a moral imperative. After all, once the whistle-blower has revealed the wrong to another organization, that organization may be in a better position to gather supporting evidence than the whistle-blower [17].

Along the same lines, some argue that whistle-blowing should be considered an obligation even when only the first three requirements are met. They hold that people should be willing to sacrifice their good and the good of their families for the greater good of society.

Others believe De George goes too far when he gives conditions under which people are morally *required* to whistle-blow. These commentators suggest that a person's obligation to whistle-blow must be weighed against that person's other obligations, such as the duty to take care of one's family. Whistle-blowing often results in significant emotional stress and the loss of employment. If it results in a person being labeled a troublemaker, whistle-blowing can end a career. Hence there are serious emotional and financial consequences to whistle-blowing that affect not only whistle-blowers but also their spouses and children [9].

Put another way, is it reasonable to take a strictly utilitarian approach to whistle-blowing? Should we expect potential whistle-blowers to weigh the benefits to a large number of people against the harm to themselves and their families, and decide to go public? After all, the whistle-blower has already gone out on a limb to inform management of the dangerous situation. It is the managers who made the immoral decision to cover up the problem, not the whistle-blower. We are asking a lot when we ask innocent people to sacrifice their careers and the welfare of their families for the benefit of strangers. We shouldn't be surprised to learn that when whistle-blower Al Ripskis was asked what advice he would give potential whistle-blowers, his immediate reply was "Forget it!" [18, p. 34].

On the other hand, whistle-blower Carlos G. Bell Jr. chastises fellow engineers for the way they duck responsibility:

> We engineers are almost without exception only too willing to assign moral responsibility to any administrator or executive or politician under whom we can place ourselves. Our reward for living in such ways is a part of the American dream: we are involved in very few arguments and year-by-year, we build up sizable pensions for our old age. [19]

Moral responsibility is different from other kinds of responsibility. First of all, moral responsibility must be borne by people. While the Fourteenth Amendment to the Constitution may make a corporation a person in the legal sense of the word, a corporation is not a moral agent. We cannot assign moral responsibility to a corporation or any other organization [20].

Second, moral responsibility is different from role responsibility, causal responsibility, and legal responsibility in that it is not exclusive [20]. **Role responsibility** is responsibility borne because of a person's assigned duties. A company may hire a bookkeeper to send out invoices and pay the bills. It is the bookkeeper's responsibility to get the bills paid on time. **Causal responsibility** is responsibility assigned to people because they did something (or failed to do something) that caused something to happen. "Joe is responsible for the network being down, because he released the virus that caused the computers to crash." **Legal responsibility** is responsibility assigned by law. Homeowners are responsible for the medical bills of a postal carrier who slips and falls on their driveway. Role responsibility, causal responsibility, and legal responsibility can be exclusive. For example, if one person is responsible for paying the bills, the other employees are not. Moral responsibility is not exclusive. For example, if an infant is brought into a home, both the mother and the father are responsible for the baby's well-being.

Because moral responsibility is not exclusive, people cannot pass the buck by saying, "My boss made the final decision, not me," or by saying, "I just wrote the software; I wasn't responsible for testing it." When people abdicate their moral responsibility, great harms can be done. For example, in the 1970s, executives at Ford Motor Company were anxious to begin selling a 2,000-pound, $2,000 alternative to Japanese imports. Unfortunately, prototypes of the Ford Pinto could not pass the mandatory collision test, because the windshield kept popping out. Forbidden from making design changes that would increase the weight of the car or delay its introduction, engineers solved the problem by redirecting the energy of the collision down the drive train to the gas tank. They knew this change would make the gas tank more likely to rupture, but the car did not have to pass a fuel tank integrity test. Covering up design problems allowed Ford to get its subcompact car to market. However, Ford eventually paid millions of dollars to settle dozens of lawsuits resulting from fiery crashes involving Pintos. Moreover, unfavorable media attention harmed Ford's reputation for years [18].

Michael McFarland argues that a team of engineers should be held to a higher level of moral responsibility than any of its individual members. There may well be situations where a person has a duty to speak the truth. To this duty, McFarland adds another duty held by moral agents: the duty to help others in need. If whistle-blowing should be done and no individual has the strength to do it, then it must be done by the group acting collectively [21].

## Summary

A computer-related job, such as system administration, computer programming, or software engineering, is not a full-fledged profession like medicine or law, because in most cases you do not need to be certified and licensed in order to design, implement, or maintain computer hardware or software. Nevertheless, those who work with computers can, through inadequate education, insufficient practical training, or bad choices, cause a great deal of harm to members of the public. In this respect, the responsibility of computer "professionals" can be similar to that held by members of fully developed professions. For these reasons, the two largest computing societies have worked together to develop a code of ethics to guide the actions of software engineers: those who develop or maintain software and those who teach in this field.

The Software Engineering Code of Ethics and Professional Practice is based upon eight general principles related to the following subjects: the public, client and employer, product, judgment, management, profession, colleagues, and self. Each of these general principles contains a list of clauses related to specific areas of potential moral concern for the practicing software engineer. Good judgment is still needed, however. In many situations, there is a conflict between two or more of the relevant clauses. At these times, the decision maker must determine which of the clauses is most relevant and/or most important.

To many, whistle-blowing is a heroic act requiring great moral courage. A whistle-blower brings to light a real or potential harm to the public, such as an abuse of taxpayers' money or a defective product, after trying and failing to get the problem resolved within the organization. Inevitably, whistle-blowers and their families suffer emotionally and economically. It may take a decade for a whistle-blower to be vindicated in court.

Different commentators have taken widely different views about whistle-blowing. Some say whistle-blowing does so much harm to the whistle-blower and the organization that it is never the right thing to do. At the other extreme are those who argue any harm done to whistle-blowers and their families is outweighed by the benefits to society, at least when certain conditions are met. In the middle are those who argue that any decision for or against whistle-blowing must be made on a case-by-case basis.

If whistle-blowing is ever called for, it is only as a last resort. Everyone agrees that people who discover real or potential harms to the public should first attempt to get the problem fixed within the organization. It would be better if there were never a need for whistle-blowing. Organizations ought to have communication and decision-making structures that make it easier to identify and deal with financial irregularities or product defects.

The predominant American corporate mind-set does not align well with this ideal. Managers focused on maximizing "the bottom line" may well make decisions on utilitarian grounds, weighing the costs and benefits of each alternative. Utilitarian thinking allows an organization to do something that is slightly bad in order to reap a greater good. Undisclosed bad deeds are less harmful than those brought to light. Hence utilitarian thinking can create an atmosphere in which the free communication of organizational actions is suppressed. In this environment, those who wish to report financial irregularities or product defects are ignored or silenced. The financial scandals at Enron, Tyco International, WorldCom, Adelphia Communications, and other corporations that cost investors billions of dollars have prompted some ethicists to call for a return to principle-based decision making.

# Further Reading and Viewing

ComputingCases.org (Web site).

Dan Gotterbarn. "Why Bother with Ethics in Computing: Addressing Harmful Paradigms?" *ACM Inroads*, p. 9, March 2010.

Rob Haythorne. "Ethics in Computing: Real Ethics and Virtual Reality." *Production Zone*, May 28, 2011. 14:19. www.youtube.com.

John Markoff. "Collision in the Making between Self-Driving Cars and How the World Works." *New York Times*, January 24, 2012.

C. Dianne Martin. "Building Character." *ACM Inroads*, p. 11, March 2010.

Jake Pearson. "Drugstore Cowboy." *Wired*, June 2013.

Paul Solman. "How Virtual Reality Games Can Transform Society, Prosperity." *PBS News-Hour*, July 11, 2013. 10:27. video.pbs.org.

# Review Questions

1. In what ways is a computer-related career, such as programming or system administration, similar to a fully developed profession such as medicine? In what ways is a computer-related career unlike a fully developed profession?

2. How prevalent is licensing for software engineers in the United States?

3. Identify as many clauses as you can in the Software Engineering Code of Ethics and Professional Practice that refer to issues related to privacy.

4. Identify as many clauses as you can in the Software Engineering Code of Ethics and Professional Practice that refer to issues related to intellectual property.

5. Identify five clauses in the Software Engineering Code of Ethics and Professional Practice that reflect a utilitarian ethical viewpoint.

6. Identify five clauses in the Software Engineering Code of Ethics and Professional Practice that reflect a Kantian viewpoint.

7. What is whistle-blowing? What harms does it cause? What benefits may it provide?

8. Which clauses in the Software Engineering Code of Ethics and Professional Practice support the legitimacy of whistle-blowing? Which clauses in the code may be violated by a whistle-blower (assuming the whistle-blower is telling the truth)?

# Discussion Questions

9. The *Challenger* disaster led to the deaths of seven astronauts and the loss of hundreds of millions of dollars' worth of equipment. How much moral responsibility should each of the following groups hold for this tragedy: Morton Thiokol engineers, Morton Thiokol senior management, NASA management?

10. In the criminal proceedings resulting from the government's investigation of fraud at the Microelectronic Circuit Division, the jury found Hughes Aircraft guilty, but it found supervisor Donald LaRue not guilty. The jury felt LaRue was simply following orders from management. Was the jury's decision a just one?

11. Do you agree with Michael McFarland that a team of engineers has greater moral responsibility than any individual engineer on the team?

12. You are a manager in charge of a section of 30 employees in a large corporation. This morning one of your employees—Jane Lee—enters your office and tells you she thinks two members of your staff are having an affair. These employees are married—but not to each other. Jane is afraid that if it is true, others in the office will inevitably find out about it, harming morale and productivity. She suggests that you discreetly monitor their emails to see if they provide evidence of an affair. If you find evidence, you can nip

the problem in the bud. If there is no problem, you do not have to embarrass yourself by talking with the employees. What should you do? [22]

13. Two weeks ago you started a new job as system administrator for a computer lab at a small college. Wanting to make a good impression, you immediately set out to learn more about the various applications provided to the users of the lab. One of the packages, an engineering design tool, seemed way out of date. You looked through the lab's file of licensing agreements to see how much it would cost to get an upgrade. To your horror, you discovered that the college never purchased a license for the software—it is running a bootlegged copy!

    When you bring this to the attention of your boss, the college's director of information technology, he says, "The license for this software would cost us $10,000, which we don't have in our budget right now. This software is absolutely needed for our engineering students, though. Maybe we can get the license next year. For the time being, just keep the current version running."

    How would you respond to your manager?

14. You are a junior in college. You sent your resume to a half-dozen companies hoping to get a summer internship. Two weeks ago XYZ Corporation contacted you and offered you a paid summer internship. One week ago you accepted their offer, agreeing to start work a week after your last final exam. Today you received a much better internship offer from ABC Corporation. What should you do?

15. You are a senior in college. You sent your resume to a half-dozen companies hoping to get a job. A month ago you interviewed at ABC Corporation and XYZ Corporation. Two weeks ago XYZ Corporation offered you a job. One week ago you accepted their offer, agreeing to start work a month after graduation. Today you received a much better offer from ABC Corporation. What should you do?

16. You are the manager of a software development group within a large corporation. Your group would be more productive if the PCs were upgraded, but you do not have any money left in your annual equipment budget. Because of employee turnover, you do have plenty of money left in your personnel budget, but corporate rules do not allow you to spend personnel funds on equipment.

    If you overspend your equipment budget, you will receive a negative performance review. You also know that whatever money is left over in your budget at the end of the fiscal year is "swept up" by the corporation. In other words, you cannot carry over a surplus from one year to the next—your group loses the money.

    You complain about your situation to the manager of another group, who has the opposite problem. She has plenty of money left in her equipment budget, but her personnel expenses are going to exceed her labor budget unless she does something. She offers to buy you the $50,000 of equipment you need out of her budget, if you pick up $50,000 of her personnel expenses out of your budget. If you take this action, both groups will get what they need, and neither group will exceed any of its budgets.

    Discuss the morality of the proposed course of action.

17. Five years ago Al graduated from college and began working for Superlative Software Corporation. His most recent promotion has made him the manager of a large group of software engineers and support staff. One of Al's responsibilities is to submit his budget

request for the next fiscal year. He's never done this before, so one day over lunch he asks Barb, a more experienced manager, for some advice.

Barb: Figure out what you really need to complete the projects your group will be doing, and then add another 20 percent. High-level management always cuts everybody's budget 10 to 20 percent, so after they reduce your budget, you'll still have the money you need.

Al: But the memo from the vice president said we should only ask for the amount of money we really need.

Barb: Nobody pays attention to that.

Al: What if they ask me to justify my budget? It'll be pretty obvious that I've padded it.

Barb: They never do that—they don't have the time. Even if they did, you can work the numbers to justify the extra staff you'll need to meet the tight deadlines they've set.

Al: You mean lie?

Barb: Look, what are you going to do if your group doesn't get the budget it needs? You won't be able to staff up for the new projects. That means you and all your current staff are going to be super stressed all year long trying to meet the deadlines. Spare yourself a lot of grief and do what all the other managers are doing.

What would you do if you were in Al's position? Why?

18. Connie interviews a candidate for a software engineering position. She feels the person has several holes in his technical background that could hinder his job performance. The next day Connie and five other people who have interviewed the candidate meet with the hiring manager to discuss his strengths and weaknesses. Before Connie speaks, everyone else voices the opinion that the candidate has great technical skills and should be hired. It seems clear to her that the hiring manager wants to offer this person a job. She wonders if she should bother voicing her reservations.

What would you do if you were in Connie's position? Why?

19. Would you characterize Edward Snowden, the person who leaked information about US surveillance programs to the British newspaper the *Guardian*, as a whistle-blower?

20. Watch "Ethics in Computing: Real Ethics and Virtual Reality" (details in Further Reading and Viewing on p. 445). Discuss whether Sony should have received permission from Manchester Cathedral before featuring that site in *Resistance: Fall of Man*.

# In-Class Exercises

21. A college equips its large lecture halls with wireless networks, and it requires all of its students to purchase a laptop computer when they enroll. A computer science professor plans to streamline how quizzes are administered in his introductory programming class. Students will take the quizzes online as they sit in the classroom. A computer will grade the quizzes instantly, providing the students with immediate feedback. The computer will also provide the professor with information about how well the students did on each question, which will enable him to spend more of his lecture time focusing

on those topics that the students are having the hardest time understanding. Discuss the benefits and risks associated with implementing the proposed system.

22. Company X wants to open a dating service Web site. It hires Company Y to develop the software. Company Y hires Gina as a private contractor to provide a piece of instant messaging software for the package. Gina's contract says she is not responsible for the security of the site. Company Y is supposed to perform that bit of programming. However, software development runs behind schedule, and Company Y implements a simplistic security scheme that allows all messages to be sent in plain text, which is clearly insecure.

    Gina brings her concerns to the management of Company Y. Company Y thanks her for her concern, but indicates it still plans to deliver the software without telling Company X. Company Y reminds Gina that she has signed a confidentiality agreement that forbids her from talking about the software to anyone, including Company X.

    What should Gina do?

23. You are a member of the information services team at a large corporation. The president has asked for a confidential meeting with your group to talk about ways to improve productivity. The president wants to ensure that people are not sending personal emails or surfing the Web for entertainment while they are supposed to be working. The chief information officer suggests that employees be informed that their emails and Web surfing will be monitored. In truth, the company does not have the resources to do this and does not plan to implement any monitoring. The CIO strictly forbids anyone in the information services team from revealing this fact. Debate the morality of management making such an announcement.

24. The members of the class are the employees of a small, privately held company that produces computer games. Everyone shares in the profits of the company. The company has been making electronic versions of popular board games for established game companies. Business is steady, but profits have not been large. The marketing team says that a first-person shooter game based on the war in Afghanistan would generate a huge amount of publicity for the company and could be highly profitable. Debate the morality of producing such a game.

25. The Department of Homeland Security is interested in using computers to identify suspected terrorists operating within the United States. It would like to mine databases containing information about purchases and travel to detect patterns that may identify individuals who are engaged in, or at least planning, terrorist activity. It asks a panel of computer scientists to determine the feasibility of this project. A panel member says the most difficult problem will be determining what patterns of transactions to look for. He suggests it might be possible to construct a computer program that uses artificial intelligence to mimic a terrorist organization. The program would determine the actions needed to execute a terrorist act. Once these actions were determined, it would be possible to search database records to find evidence of these actions.

    Debate the morality of developing a computer program capable of planning the steps needed to execute an act of terror.

# References

[1]   Edwin Black. *IBM and the Holocaust: The Strategic Alliance between Nazi Germany and America's Most Powerful Corporation.* Dialog Press, Washington, DC, 2011.

[2]   Gary Ford and Norman E. Gibbs. "A Mature Profession of Software Engineering." Technical report, Carnegie Mellon University, Pittsburgh, PA, CMU/ SEI-96-TR-004, ESC-TR-96-004, January 1996.

[3]   "PE Exam." NCEES (Web site). Accessed October 29, 2015. ncees.org/exams/pe-exam/.

[4]   J. Eric Smith. "Anti-Worm Worm Makes Rounds, Cleanses Systems of Infection." *Geek.com* (blog), August 20, 2003. www.geek.com.

[5]   Florence Olsen. "Attacks Threaten Computer Networks as Students Arrive for the Fall Semester." *Chronicle of Higher Education*, September 5, 2003.

[6]   Irena Blonder. "Blowing the Whistle." In *Codes of Ethics and the Professions*, pp. 166–190. Melbourne University Press, Melbourne, Australia, 1996.

[7]   Kevin W. Bowyer. "Goodearl and Aldred versus Hughes Aircraft: A Whistle-Blowing Case Study." *Frontiers in Education*, pp. S2F2–S2F7, October 2000.

[8]   Roger M. Boisjoly. "The Challenger Disaster: Moral Responsibility and the Working Engineer." In *Ethical Issues in Engineering*, edited by Deborah G. Johnson, pp. 6–14. Prentice Hall, Englewood Cliffs, NJ, 1991.

[9]   Mike W. Martin. *Meaningful Work: Rethinking Professional Ethics.* Oxford University Press, New York, NY, 2000.

[10]  Taxpayers Against Fraud. "U.S. Department of Justice Joins Whistle-Blowers in Lawsuit against Hughes Aircraft Seeking Several Hundred Million Dollars" (press release). December 15, 1992.

[11]  "The Hughes Whistle-Blowing Case." ComputingCases.org (Web site). Accessed October 31, 2013.

[12]  Andre Mouchard. "Whistle-Blowers Set to Use Their Reward." *Orange County Register,* CA, September 11, 1996.

[13]  Marcia P. Miceli and Janet P. Near. "Whistle-Blowing as Antisocial Behavior." In *Antisocial Behavior in Organizations*, edited by Robert A. Giacalone and Jerald Greenbert. SAGE Publications, Thousand Oaks, CA, 1997.

[14]  Michael Davis. "Avoiding the Tragedy of Whistleblowing." *Business and Professional Ethics Journal* 8(4):3–19, Winter 1989.

[15]  Robert J. Spitzer, SJ. "For Good Reason, 'Organizational Ethics' a Hot Topic Nowadays." *Gonzaga* (Gonzaga University newsletter) 5(2):2, Fall 2003.

[16]  Richard T. De George. *Business Ethics.* 3rd ed. Macmillan, New York, NY, 1990.

[17]  Gene G. James. "Whistle Blowing: Its Moral Justification." In *Business Ethics*, edited by W. Michael Hoffman, Robert E. Frederick, and Mark Schwartz, pp. 332–344. McGraw-Hill, New York, NY, 1990.

[18]  C. Fred Alford. *Whistleblowers: Broken Lives and Organizational Power.* Cornell University Press, Ithaca, NY, 2001.

[19]  Bell, Carlos G., Jr. "One Ethical Problem Faced by the Atomic Energy Commission and Its Contractors." In *Beyond Whistle-Blowing: Defining Engineers' Responsibilities, Proceedings of the Second National Conference on Ethics in Engineering*, pp. 250–258. Illinois Institute of Technology, Chicago, IL, 1983.

[20]   John Ladd. "Collective and Individual Moral Responsibility in Engineering: Some Questions." In *Beyond Whistle-Blowing: Defining Engineers' Responsibilities, Proceedings of the Second National Conference on Ethics in Engineering*, pp. 90–113. Illinois Institute of Technology, Chicago, IL, 1983.

[21]   Michael McFarland. "The Public Health, Safety, and Welfare: An Analysis of the Social Responsibility of Engineers." In *Ethical Issues in Engineering*, edited by D. G. Johnson, pp. 159–174. Prentice Hall, Englewood Cliffs, NJ, 1991.

[22]   Herbert W. Lovelace. "When Affairs of the Heart Raise IT Privacy Issues." *InformationWeek.com*, December 10, 2001.

# Paul Axtell

Paul Axtell provides consulting and personal effectiveness training to a wide variety of clients, from Fortune 100 companies and universities to nonprofit organizations and government agencies. His book *Meetings Matter: 8 Powerful Strategies for Remarkable Conversations* shows how to design meetings for results, lead them to move projects forward, and use them to build the network of relationships that make working together in a remarkable way possible.

He is also the author of *Ten Powerful Things to Say to Your Kids: Creating the Relationship You Want with the Most Important People in Your Life*, which applies the concepts of his work to the special relationships between parents and children of all ages. Thus far, it has been translated into Korean, Vietnamese, Chinese, Arabic, French, and Spanish.

Paul has an engineering degree from South Dakota School of Mines and an MBA from Washington University in St. Louis.

For additional information and resources, please visit the Web site at paulaxtell.com.

---

*Some commentators have suggested that whistle-blowing is a sign of organizational failure. They say that organizations can eliminate the need for whistle-blowing by creating management structures and communication processes that allow concerns to be raised, discussed, and resolved. Do you agree with this assessment?*

Whistle-blowing is a check and balance that is needed in certain circumstances. It is certainly alarming when a situation gets so out of hand that an employee must go to outside authorities to get someone to pay attention. When this happens, it not only reveals a set of circumstances that are not working, but also adds to the distrust of people who lead corporate organizations.

It should not be surprising, however, that we encounter such situations. Almost all of our relationships, both personal and organizational, have problems that begin with not being able to talk. We are raised in a culture that says it's not safe to share our thinking, voice our concerns, or push back in conversations. We debate about bringing things up at home with loved ones and at work in meetings. Given this fundamental approach to relationship and conversation, we should expect problems.

So whatever attention we can give to create structures and processes and permission and safety is well worth it. And the need for it goes well beyond uncovering misdeeds and poor practices. The real benefit would be in a sense of belonging and caring that goes with an open and honest relationship.

In addition to setting up structures that protect people, we need to embrace a far larger goal. We need to set out to establish a cultural norm of freedom, permission, and safety. It will be very difficult to obtain because we are not raised or trained to create such a culture. Still, how can it not be the right path to be on?

Training will probably be required on both sides. We all need training on how to raise questions and concerns with a bit more setup and graciousness. We need to be clear that we are on the same side and speak consistent with that context. And we all need training on how to hear and respond to questions and complaints, especially when they are not presented in the best way.

If a corporation wants to change the culture, it needs to pay attention to the people it is grooming to be supervisors, managers, and directors. As columnist Dave Barry says, "If your date is rude to the waiter, you are dating a rude person." That makes a lot of sense as we promote people and perhaps hire them in the first place. The question to ask is: "Do we want this person representing our organization?"

### From your experience, what are the principal barriers to improved communication inside a large corporation?

I would say that there are three principal barriers. First, people are raised to be careful and not speak up. Second, most supervisors and managers do not have the skill set to thoughtfully deal with questions and complaints. Third, our lack of follow-up and follow-through makes things worse when we invite feedback and then don't deliver.

### How can a corporation remove these barriers?

Constantly invite people to raise issues and concerns. However, don't ask if you don't intend to follow through. Have a great response to missteps by employees. It is management's reaction to problems that determines whether employees feel safe. Last, get to know people. It's very difficult to speak up when I don't know you.

### What would be an example of a great response to a misstep by an employee?

Speak to them right after the incident. Let them know that while what happened is not acceptable, you still value them as an employee. The intent is to both communicate your reactions to their behavior and that everything is still fine between you. Then ask them to explain their thoughts about the situation. Listen deeply and then thank them. The next day check in with them to see how they are doing. Do not follow a difficult conversation with disappearing. Get back to normal conversations quickly.

### How can email be harmful to communication within an organization?

Email has a couple of potential pitfalls. The most common is a lack of context for the message. Context is usually communicated by either tone of voice or setup. Obviously, tone of voice is missing on email, and people usually are very brief, which means they don't do adequate setup. On the receiving end of the message sits a human being who by default tends to take things personally. That creates a defensive response.

### How often have you seen people relying upon email to communicate a problem when they would have been better off having a face-to-face conversation?

The trend toward fewer and fewer face-to-face conversations is a common complaint in my training programs. Partly because technology is so efficient and partly because human beings have always avoided uncomfortable situations. The answer lies in people seeing the value in taking someone to coffee when something needs to be discussed. Something about the invitation and the environment makes every conversation go better. "Who do I need to invite to coffee today?" might be the new practice to adopt for many people.

### It seems to me that text messaging would be even more problematic than email, yet that is the preferred mode of communication for young adults. How are corporations dealing with this cultural shift?

Every technology has a tremendous opportunity associated with it, or it wouldn't be embraced. Texting is super-efficient and allows being in communication with people you can't find time for otherwise. The downside is that it only truly holds onto its magic when it's between people who respect and trust each other. Two important pieces for difficult conversations are setup and tone of voice, both of which are not a part of texting.

### What is the most challenging part of your job?

The first challenge is to reteach people how to learn. We were all wonderful learners when we were two and three years old. We observed. We mimicked. We paid attention to the people around us. We practiced until we could do things. We had little or no concern with looking foolish or not knowing how to do something. Then later we came to value knowing and information as having more relevance than tacit knowledge. Amazingly, it's the really good people who still want to learn, who still want feedback. Most of us are highly selective about who can give us feedback about what. We are not wide open to feedback. We are not even looking for it, for the most part.

The second challenge is to get people to acknowledge the impact of conversation in their lives—even to the point of arguing that they don't really have much else to work with. After their technical competence, it is the quality of their conversations that determines how things turn out. Conversation is the basis for their relationships. Conversation is the basis for having influence in an organization. Conversation determines the culture. Conversation determines how they are viewed.

The third challenge is in working to change the perceptions or views of individuals who have somehow gotten to a place in life where they are not responsible for what happens. As soon as you and I say to ourselves or others that "it's not our fault" or "it's not our job," we essentially are at the mercy of the circumstances. Certainly, the things that happen in our lives often control the outcomes, but truly effective people don't give in completely to the circumstances. They maintain the view that they can make a difference in how things turn out. Interestingly, these people rarely give excuses.

### What are some practical steps corporations could take to improve their communications?

I think there are a number of things that seem to be missing that would make a big difference if they were present:

1. If managers wrote more of their own communication pieces and signed them, they would come across as more authentic. Employees are also highly skeptical about positive spin writing and admire a more direct, what-is-so way of writing.

2. Written notes of acknowledgment and appreciation mean so much to people. We keep them for years. Yet handwritten notes to individuals and groups are a lost art.

3. An essential part of being effective is having the ability to set up a conversation, keep it on track, and wrap it up, not only in meetings but also in hallway conversations. These process skills are often missing at all levels of the organization.

4. Making specific commitments with clear due dates would reduce the amount of upsets that occur with unfulfilled expectations and lack of progress.

5. Checking in with people about their families, projects, weekends, and then engaging in and enjoying the conversation that follows is another piece that technical folks tend not to do.

# 10 Work and Wealth

Work keeps at bay three great evils: boredom, vice, and need.

—VOLTAIRE

## 10.1 Introduction

IT'S 6:30 P.M. AND A NEW SHIFT IS STARTING AT THE LIVEBRIDGE CALL CENTER. Twenty-year-old college graduate "Kristy Grover" begins phoning people to verify information they have provided on their credit card applications. She will work until 3:00 A.M. Her hours are unusual because "Kristy Grover" is actually Shilpa Thukral, and she is calling the United States from India. Companies like LiveBridge are saving billions of dollars every year by employing hundreds of thousands of Indians to staff call centers and back offices [1].

Back in 1996, the Indian telecommunications infrastructure supported a mere 13,000 simultaneous overseas phone conversations. Multinational corporations invested in new underwater fiber-optic cables, and by 2002 the overseas phone capacity had increased to more than 2.5 million simultaneous calls, making it possible for American companies to export hundreds of thousands of jobs to India [1].

Many Americans were unhappy with the customer service they received from Indian call centers. They complained they could not understand the accents of the agents and asked for representatives who spoke American English. Companies responded to these complaints by building new call centers in the Philippines. Filipinos learn American English in grade school, watch American TV shows, and are familiar with American idioms. In 2011 the Philippines, with 400,000 call center employees, surpassed India, with 350,000 call center employees, to become the top offshore site for call centers. Filipino workers earn about $300 a month, slightly more than Indian call center employees, who make about $250 a month, but much less than American call center workers, who start at about $1,700 a month [2].

In this chapter we take a closer look at moral issues raised by globalization and multinational teams, as well as many other attributes of the rapidly evolving workplace. How has automation affected the pool of jobs? Will breakthroughs in artificial intelligence lead to significant job losses? Should we be concerned about the rising number of temporary jobs and the emergence of the "gig economy"? Is there a "digital divide," an opportunity gap, between those who have access to information technology and those who do not? The new economy is characterized by a concentration of wealth among a few top performers. Should we take steps to reduce "winner-take-all" effects?

We begin our study by examining the relationship between automation and employment.

## 10.2 Automation and Employment

Many science fiction writers have described future worlds where machines do much of the noncreative work. Some writers paint an optimistic view of these worlds. In Isaac Asimov's short stories and novels, technology is seen as a tool for the betterment of mankind. Intelligent robots may be disliked by some people, but they are not a threat. The "Three Laws of Robotics" are etched into their positronic brains, guaranteeing that they will never turn against their creators [3]. Other writers, such as Kurt Vonnegut Jr., describe dystopias. Vonnegut's *Player Piano* concerns a future America in which nearly all manufacturing jobs have been lost to automation. People hate machines for taking away their feelings of self-worth, yet their fascination with automation makes its triumph appear inevitable [4].

Are we about to enter an era of high unemployment caused by automation? Let's consider both sides of this question.

### 10.2.1 Automation and Job Destruction

Automation has been blamed for the loss of both manufacturing and white-collar jobs, as well as an increase in the length of the workweek for salaried employees.

#### LOST MANUFACTURING JOBS

Manufacturing employment peaked in the United States in 1979, with 19.4 million jobs. By 2011 manufacturing employment had dropped 40 percent, to 11.7 million, even though the population of the United States had increased 39 percent during the same time period. The percentage of American workers involved in manufacturing has dropped significantly, from 35 percent in 1947 to 9 percent in 2011 (Figure 10.1).

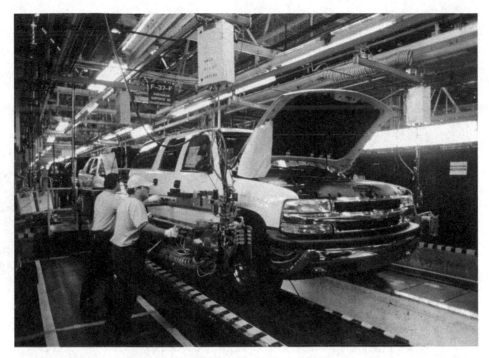

**FIGURE 10.1** General Motors exited bankruptcy in 2009 with 30 percent fewer employees. (Danny Lehman/Encyclopedia/Corbis

Meanwhile, thanks to automation, manufacturing output in America continues to rise and has doubled since 1970 [5]. In other words, productivity has increased: fewer workers are making more products. For example, in 1977 it took 35 person-hours to manufacture an automobile in the United States. By 2008 the number of person-hours had dropped to 15 [6].

## LOST WHITE-COLLAR JOBS

The effects of automation are felt in the office, too. Email, voice mail, and high-speed copy machines eliminate secretarial and clerical positions. Even jobs requiring advanced degrees are vulnerable. Spreadsheets and other software packages reduce the need for accountants and bookkeepers [7]. Twenty years ago, a pharmacist in a small Canadian town would fill about 8,000 prescriptions in a year. Today Merck-Medco runs a Web-accessible pharmacy that uses robots to dispense 8,000 prescriptions an *hour* [8].

In fact, the economic recovery of 1991–1996 was notable because of the large number of white-collar, middle-management jobs that were eliminated even as the economy grew. Unlike the recession of the early 1980s, most of the people whose jobs were eliminated in the 1990s had at least some college education. A large number of these jobs were occupied by people making more than $50,000. Only 35 percent of these higher-paid victims of downsizing were able to find jobs that paid as well [9].

FIGURE 10.2 When jobs are lost to automation or the introduction of information technology, the remaining workers may work harder in order to avoid being part of the next layoff.

## WORKING HARDER, MAKING LESS

While inflation-adjusted household incomes were flat between 1979 and 1994, the work-week got longer. Harvard economist Juliet Schor reports that between 1970 and 1990, the average American increased the number of hours spent at work per year by 163. That's equal to an *extra month* at work every year [10].

Some believe longer work hours are a consequence of corporate downsizing, which is facilitated by the introduction of automation and information technology (Figure 10.2). When an organization sheds some of its workers, the work that needs to be done is divided among fewer employees. Hence there is a natural tendency for the number of hours worked to increase. In addition, the fact that people have been laid off is a strong incentive for those who remain to work harder so that they won't be part of the next layoff [11].

Advances in information technology have also made it easier for people to bring work home. For example, many companies now provide their employees with laptop computers. At work, employees turn their laptop into a desktop system by plugging in a full-sized keyboard, mouse, and monitor. By bringing their laptop home, they have access to the various project files they need to continue working. Labor advocates Stanley Aronowitz, Dawn Esposito, and William DiFazio have written, "After nearly a century when homework was regarded as a wage-busting tool, computers have made it easier for employers to revive this practice. With pagers, cell phones, and laptop computers, all time becomes work time" [7, p. 35]. They conclude:

> Late capitalist society is engaged in a long-term historical process of destroying job security . . . More than ever, we worry about work and are working longer hours; we are more than ever driven, nervous, seemingly trapped. At the very same time, and paradoxically, the twenty-first century bodes a time of post-work: of

**FIGURE 10.3** Superficially, automation eliminates jobs; but automation can also stimulate the creation of new jobs.

automation and work reorganization replacing people at faster and faster rates. [7, pp. 38, 40]

## 10.2.2 Automation and Job Creation

Traditional economists hold a quite different view about the effects of automation and information technology on jobs. They have concluded that while new technology may destroy certain jobs, it also creates new jobs. The net result is an increase, not a decrease, in the number of available jobs.

### INCREASED PURCHASING POWER

The logic of these "automation optimists" is illustrated in Figure 10.3. On the surface, it is obvious that automation eliminates certain jobs. That's what automation means. However, it's also important to look beneath the surface. Automation is introduced as a cost-saving measure: it is less expensive for a machine to perform a particular job than a human being. Because companies compete with each other, lower production costs result in lower prices for the consumer. The drop in the price of a product has two beneficial effects. First, it increases the demand for the product. In order to produce more of the product, workers must be hired. Second, people who were already purchasing the product don't have to pay as much for it. That gives them more money to spend on other things, increasing the demand for other products. This, too, results in job creation. Finally, there is an additional effect, not illustrated in the figure. Some people must be employed designing, creating, and servicing the automated devices themselves.

Consider the automation of stock exchanges. In the past, shares of securities were bought and sold on the floors of stock exchanges by people employed as floor brokers. Today electronic systems handle most of these transactions, and electronic trading has made transactions quicker and less expensive. Although electronic trading has greatly decreased the number of people employed as floor brokers, the number of shares being traded has increased sharply, and employment in the securities industry has continued to rise (except during recessions) [12]. New kinds of jobs have been created. For example, securities firms have hired mathematicians and computer scientists to develop sophisticated automated trading systems.

## WORKING LESS, MAKING MORE

Martin Carnoy disputes the notion that people are working longer hours now than they used to. "Workers today," he writes, "work much less than those of a century ago, produce more, earn substantially more, and have access to a greater variety of jobs. Technology displaced workers but also contributed to a much higher labor productivity and the production of new products, which helped create new jobs, economic growth, and higher incomes" [13, p. 17].

## 10.2.3  Effects of Increase in Productivity

Productivity in the United States doubled between 1948 and 1990. Juliet Schor asks us to consider what our society could have done with this dramatic increase in productivity. We could have maintained our 1948 standard of living and gone to a four-hour workday or a six-month work year. Or every worker could be taking every other year off with pay. Instead of taking the path of working less, the average workweek actually rose slightly. As a result, Americans in 1990 owned and consumed twice as much as in 1948 but had less free time in which to enjoy these things [10].

## AMERICANS WORK LONG HOURS

American society is remarkable for how hard its citizens work. The number of hours worked per year in the United States is significantly higher than the number of hours worked in France or Germany. It also appears modern Americans work harder than the ancient Greeks, Romans, or Western Europeans of the Middle Ages. According to Juliet Schor, "The lives of ordinary people in the Middle Ages or Ancient Greece and Rome may not have been easy, or even pleasant, but they certainly were leisurely" [10, pp. 6–7]. In the mid-fourth century, the Roman Empire had 175 public festival days. In medieval England, holidays added up to about four months a year; in Spain, five months; in France, six months. Schor notes, "There is considerable evidence of what economists call the backward-bending supply curve of labor—the idea that when wages rise, workers supply less labor. . . . [Laborers] worked only as many days as were necessary to earn their customary income" [10, p. 47].

We do not have to look back into history to find significantly shorter workweeks. Consider contemporary "stone age" societies. The Kapauku of Papua never work two days in a row. Australian aborigines and men of the Sandwich Islands work only about 4 hours per day. Kung Bushmen work 15 hours a week [10].

## PROTESTANT WORK ETHIC

Why are Americans such hard workers? In his famous essay *The Protestant Ethic and the Spirit of Capitalism*, Max Weber argues that the Protestant Reformation in general, and

Calvinism in particular, stimulated the growth of capitalism in Western Europe. Before the Reformation, work was seen in a traditional light. Weber describes the traditional view toward labor in this way:

> A man does not "by nature" wish to earn more and more money, but simply to live as he is accustomed to live and to earn as much as is necessary for that purpose. [14, p. 60]

According to Weber, the Calvinist theology introduced a radically different conception of work. He writes:

> Waste of time is thus the first and in principle the deadliest of sins. . . . The religious valuation of restless, continuous, systematic work in a worldly calling, as the highest means to asceticism, and at the same time the surest and most evident proof of rebirth and genuine faith, must have been the most powerful conceivable lever for the expansion of that attitude toward life which we have here called the spirit of capitalism. [14, pp. 157, 172]

We can see an example of the "Protestant work ethic" in the early history of New England. The Puritans banished all holidays, insisting that Sunday be the sole day of rest. In 1659 the General Court of Massachusetts decreed that citizens who celebrated Christmas or other holidays by refusing to work or feasting should be fined or whipped.

### TIME VERSUS POSSESSIONS

We have exchanged leisure time for material possessions. Compared to medieval Europeans or modern Bushmen, we have vastly superior health care systems, educational institutions, and transportation networks. We live in climate-controlled environments, and we have an incredible number of choices with respect to where we travel, what we wear, what we eat, and how we entertain ourselves. The cost of these freedoms and luxuries is less leisure time.

Despite our high standard of living, our expectations about what we ought to have continue to rise. In 1964 the average new American home had 1,470 square feet and one television set. Only about 20 percent of new homes had air conditioning. In 2001 the size of the average new home had risen to 2,100 square feet, and nearly 100 percent of new homes were equipped with air conditioning. The typical family home has two or three television sets. In order to maintain this lifestyle, people are working harder [11].

## 10.2.4 Case Study: The Canceled Vacation

Stuart works as a software developer for a start-up company in Seattle. He is well compensated, but the high salary comes at a price; it is a pressure-packed environment, and everybody is working at least 60 hours a week. The official company policy is that every employee receives three weeks of paid vacation per year. However, Stuart and the other software developers in his group have never taken that much time off. There always seems to be an important deadline looming, and the group's supervisor has a knack for getting people to cancel or curtail their vacations in order to help meet these deadlines. People are reluctant to be labeled as "less dedicated." Some of the employees in Stuart's group have not taken any vacation time in over two years.

Six months ago Stuart learned his parents would be moving from San Diego back to Australia, and he decided it would be good to visit them before they moved so far away. At that time Stuart asked his supervisor for permission to spend a week in San Diego, and his boss approved the request. Stuart hoped to surprise his parents. For this reason, he did not tell them he was planning to come.

A week before Stuart's trip to San Diego, his boss calls him into his office. He asks Stuart to cancel his vacation in order to help get an important product update completed by the deadline. He offers Stuart round-trip air fare to Australia, and he promises Stuart he can have his full three weeks' vacation next year to see his parents. Stuart complies with his supervisor's request and cancels the vacation to San Diego [15].

Did Stuart do anything wrong?

## KANTIAN/SOCIAL CONTRACT THEORY EVALUATION

Stuart did nothing wrong. He broke no promises and didn't deceive anyone. He was not obliged to visit his parents before they moved from San Diego to Australia.

## ACT UTILITARIAN EVALUATION

Stuart gave up a week in San Diego and the displeasure of his boss in return for the appreciation of his boss, three weeks in Australia, and a bonus equal to one week's salary. As we saw in Section 2.7.2, a complete utilitarian analysis requires us to consider seven attributes of the expected results: intensity, duration, certainty, propinquity, fecundity, purity, and extent. The intensity, fecundity, and extent of the two alternatives are similar, so we focus on the remaining four attributes.

Let's begin by considering the duration of the two vacations. If Stuart goes to San Diego, he will be with his parents one week. If Stuart goes to Australia, he will be with his parents three weeks. The trip to Australia is the much better choice from the perspective of the duration of pleasure.

Next, we consider the purity of each option. If Stuart goes to San Diego, he knows he will be worrying about his upset boss, and that will reduce the purity of the experience. He would like to think that he will be able to go to Australia next year without worrying about his boss being mad at him, but since his manager has a history of asking people to curtail or cancel vacations, that's probably unrealistic. In fact, since the trip to Australia is three times as long as the trip to San Diego, Stuart is likely to spend the entire trip with worries about his boss's attitude in the back of his mind. We conclude the two vacations are equivalent from the perspective of the purity of pleasure.

The trip to San Diego is much closer in time than the trip to Australia. Therefore, from the perspective of propinquity, it is the much better choice.

Finally, we consider the certainty of the two experiences. Stuart's manager did not forbid him from traveling to San Diego. Hence that trip was certain. The trip to Australia is much less certain, given the track record of Stuart's manager. Looking only at the certainty of the two alternatives, the decision to delay the vacation and travel to Australia was the wrong choice.

In summary, the duration of the Australian vacation is the greatest benefit of that choice. When we consider the propinquity and certainty of the two experiences, Stuart would have been better off sticking with his original plan and visiting his parents in San Diego. From a utilitarian point of view, Stuart made the wrong decision.

### VIRTUE ETHICS EVALUATION

Stuart demonstrated a lack of courage and a lack of consideration for himself, his coworkers, and his parents when he let himself be bullied by his supervisor. By caving in to his boss's request, he let down himself and his fellow employees by making it just that much more difficult for any of them to get a vacation. In addition, he deprived his parents of the pleasure of his company for at least a year, and maybe longer. From the perspective of virtue ethics, Stuart made the wrong decision.

### SUMMARY

The Kantian and social contract theory analyses determined that Stuart did nothing wrong by canceling his vacation to San Diego. Note, however, that from the perspective of these theories Stuart would have done nothing wrong by deciding to take the vacation over the objections of his boss. The decision is morally neutral.

After taking into account the duration, certainty, propinquity, and purity of the two alternatives, the utilitarian analysis resulted in the conclusion that Stuart made the wrong decision (i.e., the decision with less beneficial outcomes).

The virtue ethics analysis revealed that Stuart let down himself, his coworkers, and his parents when he canceled his vacation to San Diego. If he had taken the vacation, he would have fulfilled his desire to spend some quality time with his parents before they left the United States, and he would have created an opening for others in his group to take some vacation time as well without being labeled as less dedicated.

Taken as a whole, the analyses yield a strong verdict that Stuart was wrong to cancel his vacation to San Diego.

## 10.2.5  Rise of the Robots?

While automation has not yet shortened the workweek of the typical American, some experts maintain that most jobs will eventually be taken over by machines. In fact, roboticist Hans Moravec predicts that by 2050, robots will have replaced human workers not just in manufacturing jobs but in decision-making roles, too [16].

The *Encyclopedia of Computer Science* defines **artificial intelligence** (**AI**) as "a field of computer science and engineering concerned with the computational understanding of what is commonly called intelligent behavior, and with the creation of artifacts that exhibit such behavior" [17]. The same source defines **robots** as "programmable machines that either in performance or appearance imitate human activities" [17]. According to Moravec, developments in artificial intelligence and robotics were held back for decades by inadequate computer power. Rapid increases in microprocessor speeds have resulted in many breakthroughs. Here are a few notable achievements in artificial intelligence and robotics since 1995.

- A minivan equipped with a video camera and a portable workstation drove from Pittsburgh, Pennsylvania, to San Diego, California, in 1995. The computer was in control of the steering wheel 98.2 percent of the time [18]. (A human operator controlled the minivan's gas pedal and brakes, maintaining an average speed of about 60 miles per hour.)

- The IBM supercomputer called Deep Blue defeated world chess champion Gary Kasparov in a six-game match in 1997 [19].

- In 2000 Japanese automaker Honda created ASIMO, the first humanoid robot (android) capable of ascending and descending stairs. Two years later, engineers gave ASIMO the ability to interpret and respond to human gestures and postures [20]. Some believe Japan is a hotbed of robotic research because its population is declining and becoming more elderly, and the Japanese seem to lack the cultural fears of robots that grip many Westerners [21].

- Swedish appliance giant Electrolux introduced Trilobite, the world's first domestic robotic floor vacuum cleaner, in 2001 [22].

- Stanley, a robotic car developed at Stanford University, and four other autonomous vehicles successfully completed a rugged, 128-mile course through the Nevada desert in 2005. Stanley was the fastest vehicle to finish the race, averaging about 19 miles per hour [23].

- In February 2011, an AI program named Watson, running on an IBM supercomputer, easily defeated the two most successful human *Jeopardy!* champions in history: Ken Jennings and Brad Rutter (Figure 10.4). At the end of the three-episode

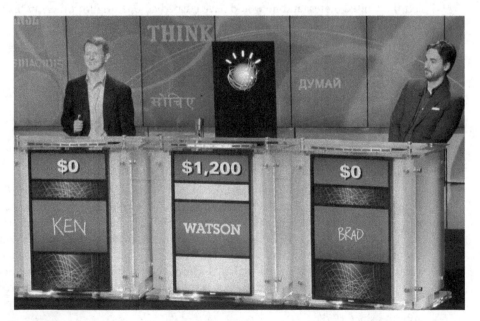

**FIGURE 10.4** In 2011 an AI program named Watson running on an IBM supercomputer trounced the two greatest (human) *Jeopardy!* champions: Ken Jennings and Brad Rutter. (© AP photo/Seth Wenig)

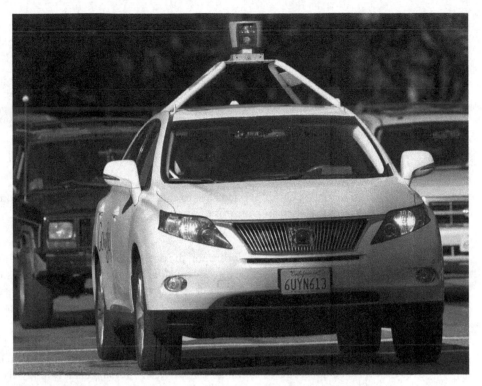

**FIGURE 10.5** Google self-driving cars have driven more than a million miles in autonomous mode without causing a single accident. (John Green/TNS/Newscom)

competition, Watson had won $77,147, compared to $24,000 for Jennings and $21,600 for Rutter.

- Between 2009 and 2015, self-driving cars developed by Google logged more than one million miles in autonomous mode without a single accident caused by the self-driving car (Figure 10.5) [24].

Moravec believes these innovations are just the beginning of a new era in automation. In 30 years, inexpensive desktop computers will be a million times faster than today's models, allowing them to run sophisticated AI programs. Moravec writes, "In the [21st] century inexpensive but capable robots will displace human labor so broadly that the average workday will have to plummet to practically zero to keep everyone usefully employed" [16, p. 131]. Moravec predicts humans will retire to a world of "luxurious lassitude" [16, p. 136].

Perhaps Moravec has a grossly inflated view of what robots may be able to do in 40 years, but what if he is right? The changes he is predicting would profoundly affect our society. For this reason, Richard Epstein suggests there is an urgent need to discuss ethical issues related to the creation of intelligent robots before they become a reality [25]. Here are some of the questions Epstein raises.

- Is it wrong to create machines capable of making human labor obsolete?

- Will humans become demoralized by the presence of vastly more intelligent robots? If so, is it wrong to work on the development of such robots?

- Is it morally acceptable to work on the development of an intelligent machine if we cannot be sure that the machine's actions will be benevolent?

- How will we ensure that intelligent robots will not be put to an evil purpose by a malevolent human?

- How will our notions of intellectual property change if computers become capable of creative work?

- How will our ideas about privacy have to change if legions of superfast computers are analyzing the electronic records of our lives?

Michael LaChat notes, "Many look upon the outbreak of AI research with an uneasy amusement, an amusement masking . . . a considerable disquiet. Perhaps it is the fear that we might succeed, perhaps it is the fear that we might create a Frankenstein, or perhaps it is the fear that we might become eclipsed, in a strange oedipal drama, by our own creation" [26].

LaChat evaluates the issue in the following way. Some people would like to try to construct a **personal AI**—a machine that is conscious of its own existence. No one has proven it can't be done, so let's assume it's theoretically possible. Is it morally acceptable to attempt the construction of a personal AI?

Here is one line of reasoning: According to the second formulation of the Categorical Imperative, we should always treat other persons as ends in themselves and never treat other persons merely as means to an end. In the attempt to construct a personal AI, scientists would be treating the personal AI they created as a means to the end of increasing scientific knowledge. It is reasonable to assume that a fully conscious personal AI would be unwilling to accept its status as a piece of property. In this case, owning a personal AI would be a form of exploitation.

Are we prepared to grant a personal AI the same rights guaranteed to human persons under the United Nation's Universal Declaration of Human Rights, which (among other things) forbids slavery and servitude, and guarantees everyone freedom of movement? If we plan to treat personal AIs as property, then from a Kantian point of view any effort to bring about a personal AI would be immoral.

LaChat concedes that this line of reasoning rests on the controversial assumption that a conscious machine should be given the same moral status as a human being. The argument assumes that a personal AI would have free will and the ability to make moral choices. Perhaps any system operated by a computer program does not have free will, because it has no choice other than to execute the program's instructions as dictated by the architecture of the CPU. If a personal AI does not have free will, it cannot make moral choices, and from a Kantian point of view it should not be valued as an end in itself. Despite its intelligence, it would not have the same moral status as a human being. Creating a personal AI without free will would be morally acceptable.

We do not know whether scientists and engineers will ever be able to construct a personal AI, and we cannot say whether a personal AI would possess free will. Our predictions are uncertain because we do not understand the source of free will in humans. In fact, some philosophers, psychologists, and neuroscientists deny the existence of free will. LaChat concludes, "Though the first word of ethics is 'do no harm,' we can perhaps look forward to innovation with a thoughtful caution," knowing that we may "eclipse ourselves with our own inventions" [26].

It is important to note that mainstream opinion in the artificial intelligence research community holds that the prospects of a personal AI being constructed are quite remote. A panel of leading experts in artificial intelligence met in Pacific Grove, California, in February 2009, to reflect on the societal consequences of the advances in machine intelligence. According to a report from the meeting, the experts were skeptical of the view that machines with superhuman intelligence are on the horizon [27].

## 10.3 Workplace Changes

Experts debate whether or not information technology has resulted in a net reduction in available jobs, but there is no dispute that information technology has affected *how* people work. In this section we survey a few of the ways that information technology is fundamentally changing the work experience.

### 10.3.1 Organizational Changes

Information technology has influenced the way manufacturing and service companies organize themselves. A typical early use of computers was to automate a back-office function, such as payroll. Using computers in this way required a company to make no changes in its organization. Later, companies began using computers inside manufacturing units. Computers enabled companies to customize products and provide better service to their customers. This use of computers delegated more responsibility to the line workers, and it encouraged a decentralization of sales and support functions, reducing a company's bureaucracy. Information technology within corporations reached a third stage with the creation of computer networks linking different parts of the business. For example, integrating cash registers with inventory systems has allowed companies to order replacements automatically.

The overall effect of the introduction of information technology is to flatten organizational structures. When the primary source of information distribution was the hand-typed, carbon-copied memorandum, most information flow followed the lines in organizational charts (Figure 10.6a). Today a wide variety of technologies allow any member of an organization to contact any other member with minimal effort and cost (Figure 10.6b). As a result, new opportunities arise. Many companies assemble "tiger teams" of expert workers drawn from various parts of the organizational chart. A team will work together for a short period of time to solve an urgent problem, then disband. Flexible information flow also allows companies to adopt "just-in-time" production and distribution methods, reducing inventory costs [28].

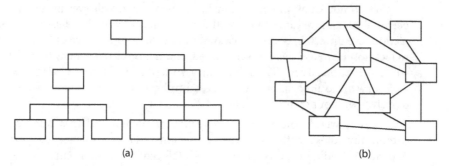

**FIGURE 10.6** (a) When interactions are more expensive and time consuming, most information flows between people and their managers. Organizations are rigid and hierarchical. (b) When interactions become inexpensive and fast, the flow of information is much more flexible. Organizations become flatter and more dynamic.

| Higher Demand | Lower Demand |
| --- | --- |
| Software engineers—applications | Butchers |
| Computer support workers | Secretaries and stenographers |
| Software engineers—systems | Payroll clerks |
| Network administrators | Bank tellers |
| Network systems analysts | File clerks |
| Desktop publishers | Cashiers |
| Database administrators | Typist |
| Personal and home care aides | Pharmacists |
| Computer systems analysts | Bookkeepers |
| Medical assistants | Postal clerks |

**TABLE 10.1** Greater use of information technology in the workplace will increase demand for employees in certain job categories while reducing demand for employees in other categories [29].

Information technology also streamlines organizations by eliminating transactional middlemen. For example, consider the automation of the supply chain. Suppose company A buys widgets from company B. In the past someone at company A called someone at company B to order the widgets. Today many companies have adopted **supply-chain automation.** A computer at company A is linked to a computer at company B. The computers are responsible for ordering the widgets, eliminating the need for employees to handle the orders. Automating the paperwork activities associated with purchasing supplies can reduce the number of people who produce purchase orders and invoices, pay bills, process checks, and so on. The likely effect of information technology on organizations will be an increased demand in some job categories, while the demand in other categories will drop (Table 10.1).

Dell Computer is a leader in supply-chain automation. Customers order computers directly from Dell by telephone or through its Web site. Seventy percent of Dell's sales are to large corporations. These companies have custom Web sites that have preconfigured systems tailored to the needs of the purchaser. Dell does not make any computers until they are ordered, allowing it to keep its inventory small—enough for only a few days' production [30].

### 10.3.2   Telework

Another workplace change brought about through information technology is the rise of telework. **Telework** (also called telecommuting) refers to an arrangement where employees spend a significant portion of their workday at a distance from the employer or a traditional place of work [31]. According to the Consumer Electronics Association, 37 percent of workers in the United States telework at least one day a month [32].

One kind of telework is working out of a home office. Another example of telework is someone who commutes to a telecenter rather than the company's site. Telecenters provide employees from different firms the ability to connect to their company's computers. A third example of telework are salespersons who have no offices, instead transacting all of their business from their cars using cell phones and laptop computers.

#### ADVANTAGES OF TELEWORK

The rapid growth in the number of teleworkers is evidence there are significant benefits associated with telework. Here are some of the most frequently cited advantages [31, 33].

1. *Telework increases productivity.*

   A variety of studies have shown teleworkers have 10 to 43 percent greater productivity than on-site workers.

2. *Telework reduces absenteeism.*

   Teleworkers are less likely to miss work than someone coming into the office.

3. *Telework improves morale.*

   Employees who are teleworking have more freedom. It is easier for them to schedule their work around their personal schedules. If they are working at home, they can dress more casually.

4. *A company can recruit and retain more top employees.*

   For example, a company that allows telework can recruit employees who otherwise would not be interested in the job because they are unable or unwilling to be within commuting distance of the main office. Telework allows companies to retain employees (such as mothers of young children) who would quit otherwise.

5. *Telework saves overhead.*

   With some of its workers away from the office, a company doesn't have to invest as much of its resources in office space.

6. *Telework improves the resilience of a company.*

Because not all the employees are in one place, the company is less likely to be harmed by a natural disaster or a terrorist attack.

7. *Telework is good for the environment.*

   Teleworkers do not take part in the daily commute, which saves energy and reduces pollution.

8. *Employees may save money by teleworking.*

   They may not have to purchase as much business attire, and they may be able to avoid paying child care expenses.

## DISADVANTAGES OF TELEWORK

Telework has its detractors, too. Here are some of the reasons most frequently given why companies discourage or prohibit telework.

1. *Telework threatens the authority and control of managers.*

   When employees work at a distance from their managers, they naturally have more autonomy. How can a manager manage an employee who is not around?

2. *Telework makes it impossible for an employee to have a face-to-face interaction with customers at the company site.*

   For some jobs these interactions are crucial, meaning the job simply cannot be done from a distance.

3. *Sensitive information is less secure.*

   If a person has valuable physical or electronic files at home or in an automobile, they may be far less secure than if they were kept at the office. There is a greater chance that the information will be lost or compromised through fire or theft.

4. *When people in an organization do not keep the same hours or come into the office every day, it is more difficult to schedule team meetings.*

   Even if employees are only teleworking one or two days a week, many others in the organization can suffer significant inconvenience.

5. *Teleworkers are less visible.*

   There is a danger that teleworkers will be forgotten when it's time for raises or promotions. When somebody is "never around," others can get the idea that the teleworker is not making a contribution to the organization.

6. *When faced with a problem or a need for information, employees at the office are less likely to contact a teleworker than another person on-site.*

   Meanwhile, many teleworkers are afraid to leave their telephones even for a short time, afraid that if someone from work calls them and they are not around, they will get the reputation for not being "at work."

7. *Teleworkers are isolated.*

   Some jobs require people to bounce ideas off coworkers. What are people working at home supposed to do?

8. *Teleworkers end up working longer hours for the same pay.*

When everything a person needs to do her job is right there at home, she is more likely to keep coming back to it. How does someone leave her work at the office when her home *is* her office? Critics of telework say that overwork is the reason why teleworkers exhibit higher productivity.

### 10.3.3 The Gig Economy

The modern business environment is highly competitive and rapidly fluctuating. As a result, the level of commitment companies are willing to make to their employees is dropping. Some companies once boasted that they took care of their employees and did not engage in layoffs during business downturns. Those days are gone. The dot-com bust led to massive layoffs in the information technology industry.

Many large institutions are giving themselves more flexibility and saving money on benefits by hiring subcontractors and temporary employees. For example, in the past two decades colleges and universities have greatly increased the number of contingent faculty members with fixed-term contracts rather than indefinite tenure. Contingent faculty members earn less than tenure-track faculty members, and giving faculty members fixed-term contracts makes it easier for colleges and universities to match faculty resources with student demand for classes, thereby improving efficiency [34].

Some start-up companies have taken this idea to the extreme. Instead of hiring employees, they make money by connecting people who want a service with people willing to provide that service. The **gig economy** refers to service workers who make a living by completing these types of short-term jobs for clients. These workers do not have a traditional employer, but typically rely upon one or more companies to connect them with clients. Uber, Lyft, Instacart, and Airbnb are well-known examples of such companies. Uber and Lyft connect riders and drivers, Instacart is a grocery delivery service, and Airbnb connects people who need a place to stay with people who have accommodations for rent.

Proponents of the gig economy say that it provides workers with independence and flexibility. Workers can make their own schedules and decide which assignments they want to accept. Critics say that people only take these jobs because they can't find stable employment. They point out that companies pit workers against each other in an effort to keep prices down. That's good for the people purchasing the services, but bad for the people providing the services. For example, Lyft and Uber engaged in a price war that resulted in significant reductions in the fares drivers earned [35].

"The big money goes to the corporations that own the software. The scraps go to the on-demand workers," writes political economist Robert Reich [36]. "Uber drivers use their own cars, take out their own insurance, work as many hours as they want or can—and pay Uber a fat percentage. Worker safety? Social Security? Uber says it's not the employer so it's not responsible. Amazon's Mechanical Turks work for pennies, literally. Minimum wage? Time-and-a-half for overtime? Amazon says it just connects buyers and sellers so it's not responsible."

Some workers have concluded they would be better off as employees. Uber and Lyft drivers have filed lawsuits to be classified as employees rather than independent contractors [37]. If their lawsuit is successful, drivers could be entitled to an hourly wage and reimbursement for work-related expenses, such as gas and car insurance [38].

### 10.3.4 Monitoring

Information technology has given companies many new tools to monitor the activities of their employees. An American Management Association/ePolicy Institute survey in 2007 revealed that 66 percent of employers were monitoring the Internet use of their employees. Other examples of employee monitoring by American employers included video surveillance (48 percent), monitoring keyboard activity (45 percent), monitoring time spent on the phone (45 percent), and monitoring emails (43 percent) [39].

The principal purpose of monitoring is to identify inappropriate use of company resources [40]. A quarter of companies in the United Kingdom have fired employees for improper use of the Internet. In the majority of these cases, the employee was surfing the Web for pornography. Another study of employee emails concluded that eliminating email containing gossip and jokes would cut the time staff spend reading email by 30 percent [41]. A study conducted by International Data Corporation concluded that between 30 and 40 percent of Internet use by employees was not work related [42].

Monitoring can help detect illegal activities of employees as well. By monitoring instant messaging conversations, employers have caught employees who had performed various misdeeds, including an employee who hacked into a company computer after being denied a promotion [43].

Monitoring is also used to ensure that customers are getting the products and services they need. Reviewing customer phone calls to help desks can reveal if the company ought to be providing its customers with better documentation or training [44].

Many companies use monitoring to gauge the productivity of their workers. For example, telemarketing firms keep track of how many calls their employees make per hour. Sometimes monitoring can help an organization assess the quality of the work done by its employees. Major League Baseball has introduced QuesTec's Umpire Information System to evaluate how well umpires are calling balls and strikes [45].

Companies are beginning to investigate the use of wireless networks to track the locations of their employees. Knowing the location of service technicians would enable an automated system to respond to a breakdown by alerting the technician closest to the malfunctioning piece of equipment. A system that tracked the locations of hospital physicians could upload a patient's file into the wireless laptop held by a doctor approaching a hospital bed.

More schools are using video cameras to increase security [46]. The school district in Biloxi, Mississippi, used gambling-generated tax receipts to install digital cameras in all 500 of its classrooms. An elementary school principal gushes, "It's like truth serum. When we have a he-said, she-said situation, 9 times out of 10, all we have to do is ask children if they want us to go back and look at the camera, and they fess up" [47].

It's an open question whether monitoring is ultimately beneficial to an organization. Obviously, organizations institute monitoring because they have reason to believe it will improve the quantity and/or quality of the work performed by their employees. There is evidence that employee monitoring makes employees more focused on their tasks but also reduces job satisfaction [48].

### 10.3.5 Multinational Teams

In the 1980s, General Electric and Citibank set up software development teams in India. Since then, many corporations have established field offices in India, including Analog Devices, Cadence Design Systems, Cisco, Intel, Microsoft, and Sun Microsystems. Bangalore, in particular, has made an effort to become the Silicon Valley of India. Western-based companies use Indian companies to write software, process credit card applications, and do billing. Texas Instruments' chip design team in Bangalore has 200 patents to its name. Hewlett-Packard and Oracle both have thousands of employees in India. SAP has 500 engineers in Bangalore.

Multinational teams allow a company to have people at work more hours during the day. It becomes easier to have a call support center open 24 hours a day. It is even possible for projects to be shuttled between multiple sites, allowing around-the-clock progress to be made on time-sensitive products. For example, a team in Palo Alto, California, can spend its day finding bugs in a piece of software, then hand the bug reports over to a team in Bangalore that spends *its* day fixing the bugs [49].

However, the main attraction of India is cost savings. Wages in India are substantially lower than in the United States or Western Europe. The total cost of an Indian computer programmer is about $6,000–$9,000 a year. Companies say they need to lower their expenses in order to stay in business. If they go out of business, their US employees will lose their jobs. Hence creating multinational teams is a way for companies to stay in business and preserve jobs in the United States [50].

Creating multinational teams has disadvantages, too. The principal disadvantage is that the infrastructure in less developed countries can make conducting business more difficult.

Despite the difficulties, corporations are increasingly making use of multinational teams. About 90,000 IT-related jobs in the United States are moving to foreign countries every year, and at American companies whose revenues are at least $5 billion, about a quarter of IT jobs have already moved offshore [51].

## 10.4 Globalization

**Globalization** refers to the process of creating a worldwide network of businesses and markets. Globalization results in greater mobility of goods, services, and capital around the world. Investments are made across national boundaries. Products manufactured in one country are sold in another. Consumers calling a telephone help center get connected with support technicians located on the other side of the world.

The rapidly decreasing cost of information technology has made globalization possible (Figure 10.7). The cost of computing dropped by 99.99 percent between 1975 and 1995. The cost of an international telephone call from New York to London dropped by

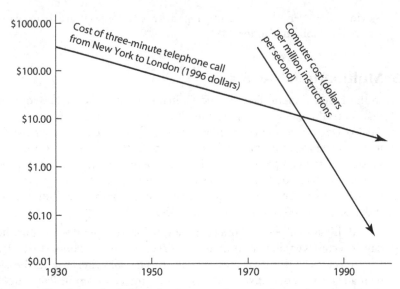

FIGURE 10.7 The dramatic declines in the cost of computing and communications have made global enterprises feasible.

99 percent between 1930 and 1996 [52]. Companies have made extensive use of low-cost information technology to coordinate operations distributed around the planet.

### 10.4.1 Arguments for Globalization

Those who favor globalization seek the removal of trade barriers between nations. The North American Free Trade Agreement (NAFTA) between Canada, the United States, and Mexico was a step toward globalization.

The World Trade Organization (WTO) is an international body that devises rules for international trade and promotes the goal of free trade among nations. The WTO and other proponents of globalization support free trade with these arguments:

1. *Free trade can increase everyone's standard of living.* Every country has a **comparative advantage** at producing certain products and services, meaning it can produce them at a lower opportunity cost than any other country. Consumers get better prices when each area produces the goods or services it does best—corn in Kansas, automobiles in Ontario, semiconductors in Singapore, and so on—and then these products and services are bought and sold without trade barriers. When prices are lower, the real purchasing power of consumers is higher. Hence globalization increases everyone's standard of living.

2. *People in poorer countries deserve jobs, too.* When they gain employment, their prosperity increases.

3. *Every example in the past century of a poor country becoming more prosperous has been the result of that country producing goods for the world market rather than striving for*

*self-sufficiency* [53]. Contrast the remarkable success story that is South Korea with the economic basket case that is North Korea.

4. *Creating jobs around the world reduces unrest and leads to more stability.* Countries with interdependent economies are less likely to go to war with each other.

## 10.4.2 Arguments against Globalization

Ralph Nader, American trade unions, the European farm lobby, and organizations such as Friends of the Earth, Greenpeace, and Oxfam oppose globalization. They give these reasons why globalization is a bad trend:

1. *The United States and other governments should not be subordinate to the WTO.* The WTO makes the rules for globalization, but nobody elected it. It makes its decisions behind closed doors. Every member country, from the United States to the tiniest dictatorship, has one vote in the WTO.

2. *American workers should not be forced to compete with foreign workers who do not receive decent pay and working conditions.* The WTO does not require member countries to protect the rights of their workers. It has not banned child labor. Authoritarian regimes such as the People's Republic of China are allowed to participate in the WTO even though they do not let their workers organize into labor unions.

3. *Globalization has accelerated the loss of both manufacturing jobs and white-collar jobs overseas.*

4. *The removal of trade barriers hurts workers in foreign countries, too.* For example, NAFTA removed tariffs between Canada, Mexico, and the United States. Because they receive agricultural subsidies from the US government, large American agribusinesses grow corn and wheat for less than its true cost of production and sell the grain in Mexico. Mexican farmers who cannot compete with these prices are driven out of business. Most of them cannot find jobs in Mexico and end up immigrating to the United States [54].

Even if globalization is a good idea, there are reasons why a company may not choose to move its facilities to the place where labor is the least expensive. Interestingly, these arguments are more relevant to blue-collar jobs such as manufacturing than they are to white-collar jobs such as computer programming. With automation, the cost of labor becomes a smaller percentage of the total cost of a product. Once the labor cost is reduced to a small enough fraction, it makes little difference whether the factory is located in China or the United States. Meanwhile, there are definite additional costs associated with foreign factories. If you include products in transit, foreign factories carry more inventory than identical factories in the United States. There are also more worries about security when the product is being made in a foreign country. For these reasons, moving a factory to a less developed country is not always in the best interest of a company [5].

### 10.4.3 Dot–Com Bust Increases IT Sector Unemployment

In the 1990s, Intel's stock rose 3,900 percent, Microsoft's stock increased in value 7,500 percent, and Cisco System's stock soared an incredible 66,000 percent. That means $1,000 of Cisco stock purchased in 1990 was worth $661,000 at the end of 1999. Investors looking for new opportunities for high returns focused on **dot-coms,** Internet-related start-up companies. Speculators pushed up the values of many companies that had never earned a profit. Early in 2000, the total valuation of 370 Internet start-ups was $1.5 trillion, even though they had only $40 billion in sales (that's *sales*, not profits) [55].

In early 2000, the speculative bubble burst, and the prices of dot-com stocks fell rapidly. The ensuing "dot-com bust" resulted in 862 high-tech start-ups going out of business between January 2000 and June 2002. Across the United States, the high-tech industry shed half a million jobs [56]. In San Francisco and Silicon Valley, the dot-com bust resulted in the loss of 13 percent of nonagricultural jobs, the worst downturn since the Great Depression [57].

### 10.4.4 Foreign Workers in the American IT Industry

Even while hundreds of thousands of information technology workers were losing their jobs, US companies hired tens of thousands of foreigners to work in the United States. The US government grants these workers visas allowing them to work in America. The two most common visas are called the H-1B and the L-1.

An H-1B visa allows a foreigner to work in the United States for up to six years. In order for a company to get an H-1B visa for a foreign employee, the company must demonstrate that there are no Americans qualified to do the job. The company must also pay the foreign worker the prevailing wage for the job. Information technology companies have made extensive use of H-1B visas to bring in skilled foreign workers and to hire foreign students graduating from US universities.

In the midst of the high-tech downturn, the US government continued to issue tens of thousands of H-1B visas: 163,600 in 2000–2001 and 79,100 in 2001–2002. Meanwhile, the unemployment rate among American computer science professionals was about 5.1 percent. Many of the 100,000 unemployed computer scientists complained to Congress about the large number of H-1B visas being issued. Some professional organizations argued against giving out any H-1B visas at all [58]. Congress decided to drop the H-1B quota to 65,000 for the fiscal year beginning October 1, 2003, and it initially set a quota of 65,000 for the following fiscal year. However, the 65,000 H-1B visas approved for 2004–2005 were filled in a single day; representatives of universities and technology companies said the quota was set too low [59]. Bill Gates said, "Anyone who's got the education and the experience, they're not out there unemployed" [60]. Congress responded in May 2005 by allowing an exemption for an additional 20,000 foreigners with advanced degrees (master's or higher).

The annual quota of 65,000 H-1B visas and the exemption for 20,000 foreigners with advanced degrees remain in effect. During the deep economic recession of 2008–2009, the unemployment rate rose sharply, and the US Citizenship and Immigration Service had a difficult time filling the quota mandated by Congress. With about a month to go in the 2008–2009 fiscal year, the USCIS had received only 45,000 petitions for the regular H-1B visa and about 20,000 petitions for the advanced degree exemption [61].

The other important work visa is called the L-1. American companies use L-1 visas to move workers from overseas facilities to the United States for up to seven years. For example, Intel employees in Bangalore, India, could be transferred to Hillsboro, Oregon, if they held an L-1 visa. Employees brought in to the United States under an L-1 visa do not need to be paid the prevailing wage. That saves employers money.

Critics of L-1 visas claim lower-paid foreign workers are replacing higher-paid American workers within the walls of high-tech facilities located in the United States. The US Congress has put no limit on the number of L-1 visas that may be issued in any given year, but the number of foreigners working in the United States under L-1 visas is much smaller than the number holding H-1B visas. In 2006 about 50,000 foreigners were employed in the United States under the L-1 visa program [62].

### 10.4.5 Foreign Competition

The debate over the number of visas to grant foreign workers seeking employment in the United States should not mask another trend: the increasing capabilities of IT companies within developing nations, particularly China and India.

In 2004 IBM agreed to sell its PC division to Chinese computer manufacturer Lenovo for $1.75 billion, making Lenovo the number three manufacturer of PCs in the world [63]. A few months later, Chinese premier Wen Jiabao visited India to encourage new collaborations between Chinese hardware companies and Indian software companies [64]. Today China is the world's number one producer of computer hardware (Figure 10.8).

India's outsourcing industry is large; Indian companies now employ more than a million people and have annual sales exceeding $60 billion. About two-thirds of these sales are in outsourcing IT work, such as designing, programming, and maintaining computer software. The other third are in outsourcing business processes, such as call centers, medical transcription, and X-ray interpretation [65].

Some Chinese universities are becoming recognized for their research expertise. For example, the Institute of Computing Technology at the Chinese Academy of Science and Tsinghua University have been actively involved in the development of the Open64 optimizing compiler [66].

More evidence of global competition comes from the annual Association for Computing Machinery International Collegiate Programming Contest. When the contest began in 1977, only schools from North America and Europe competed. Today it is a truly international competition. In fact, no American team has placed first since Harvey Mudd College in 1997. In the five-year period from 2011 through 2015, only one of the 20 teams earning gold medals was from the United States [67].

## 10.5 The Digital Divide

The **digital divide** refers to the situation in which some people have access to modern information technology while others do not. The underlying assumption motivating the term is that people who use cell phones, computers, and the Internet have opportunities

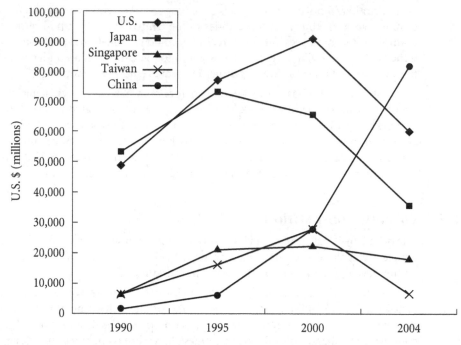

**FIGURE 10.8** In 1990 China's computer hardware industry was virtually nonexistent. By 2004 China had become the world's leading computer hardware–producing nation.

denied to people without access to these devices. The idea of a digital divide became popular in the mid-1990s with the rapid growth in popularity of the World Wide Web.

According to Pippa Norris, the digital divide has two fundamentally different dimensions. The **global divide** refers to the disparity in Internet access between more industrialized and less industrialized nations. The **social divide** refers to the difference in access between the rich and poor within a particular country [68].

## 10.5.1 Global Divide

There is plenty of evidence of what Norris calls the global divide. One piece of evidence is the percentage of people with Internet access (Figure 10.9). In 2014 about 3.1 billion people, representing roughly 42 percent of the world's population, had access to the Internet. Access to the Internet in North America, Oceania/Australia, and Europe was significantly above this average, while access in Africa was well below. Only about 28 percent of the population of Africa had Internet access in 2014 [69].

What is hampering Internet development in less technologically developed countries?

1. *Often there is little wealth.*

    In many of these countries there is not enough money to provide everyone in the country with the necessities of life, much less pay for Internet connections.

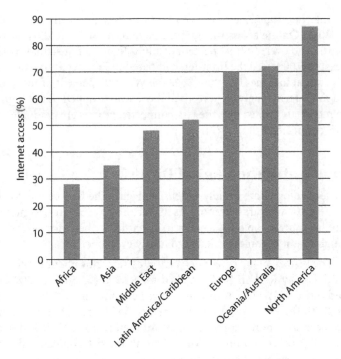

**FIGURE 10.9**  Percentage of people with Internet access, by world region.

2. *Many of these countries have an inadequate telecommunications infrastructure.*
   For example, less than 25 percent of the people in the following countries have
   cell phones: North Korea, Eritrea, Cuba, Kiribati, Somalia, South Sudan, Burundi,
   Ethiopia, Tuvalu, and Djibouti [70]. Many poor people have no access to newspapers, radio, or television [68].

3. *The primary language is not English.*
   English is the dominant language for business and scientific development, giving
   English-speaking countries a comparative advantage with respect to competing in
   the global marketplace.

4. *Literacy is low and education is inadequate.*
   Half the population in poorer countries has no opportunity to attend secondary
   schools. There is a strong correlation between literacy and wealth, both for individuals and for societies [30].

5. *The country's culture may not make participating in the Information Age a priority* [71].

## 10.5.2  Social Divide

Even within wealthy countries such as the United States, the extent to which people use
the Internet varies significantly according to age, wealth, and educational achievement.

Pew Internet polled Americans to find out how many made use of the Internet in the year 2015. Online access varied from 96 percent of 18- to 29-year-olds to 58 percent of those 65 and over. Fully 97 percent of adults living in households with annual incomes of at least $75,000 used the Internet, compared to 74 percent of adults living in households with annual incomes less than $30,000. While 95 percent of those with a college degree used the Internet, only 66 percent of those who dropped out of high school went online. The report also noted that the less-connected groups are gradually catching up with the more-connected groups [72].

### 10.5.3 Models of Technological Diffusion

New technologies are usually expensive. Hence the first people to adopt new technologies are those who are better off. As the technology matures, its price drops dramatically, enabling more people to acquire it. Eventually, the price of the technology gets low enough that it becomes available to nearly everyone.

The history of the consumer VCR illustrates this phenomenon. The first VHS VCR, introduced by RCA in 1977, retailed for $1,000 ($3,562 in 2009 dollars). In 2009 you could buy a VHS VCR from a mass-marketer for under $30. That means between 1977 and 2009, the price of a VCR in constant dollars fell by more than 99 percent! As the price declined, more people could afford to purchase a VCR and sales increased rapidly. The VCR progressed from a luxury that only the rich could afford to a consumer product found in nearly every American household.

**Technological diffusion** refers to the rate at which a new technology is assimilated into a society. Two different theories predict how a new technology is acquired by people in a society, based on their socioeconomic status (Figure 10.10). We divide society into three groups. People with the highest socioeconomic status are in group A, people with the lowest socioeconomic status are in group C, and group B consists of those people in the middle.

**FIGURE 10.10** Two models for technological diffusion. In both models the most advantaged group A is the first to adopt a new technology, while the least advantaged group C is the last to adopt it. (a) In the normalization model, the technology is eventually embraced by nearly everyone in all groups. (b) In the stratification model, the eventual adoption rate of the technology is lower for less advantaged groups.

In the **normalization model** (Figure 10.10a), group A begins to adopt the technology first, followed by group B, and finally group C. However, at some point nearly everyone in all three groups is using the new technology.

In the **stratification model** (Figure 10.10b), the order of adoption is the same. However, in this model the eventual number of people in group C who adopt the technology is lower than the number of adoptees in group A. The percentage of people in group B who adopt the technology is somewhere between the levels of the other two groups.

Technological optimists believe the global adoption of information technology will follow the normalization model. Information technology will make the world a better place by reducing poverty in developing countries. Creating opportunities elsewhere will reduce the number of people trying to immigrate into the United States.

Technological pessimists believe information technology adoption will follow the stratification model, leading to a permanent condition of "haves" and "have nots." Information technology will only exacerbate existing inequalities between rich and poor nations and between rich and poor people within each nation [68].

Technological pessimists point out that the gap between the richest 20 countries and the poorest 20 countries continues to grow. In 1960 the average gross domestic product (GDP) of the richest countries was 18 times larger than the average GDP of the poorest countries. By 1995 the gap had grown to 37 times greater. Some of the poorest countries grew even poorer during the last third of the twentieth century [30].

### 10.5.4 Critiques of the Digital Divide

Mark Warschauer has suggested three reasons why the term "digital divide" is not helpful. First, it tends to promote the idea that the difference between the "haves" and the "have nots" is simply a question of access. Some politicians have jumped to the conclusion that providing technology will close the divide. Warschauer says this approach will not work. To back his claim, he gives as an example the story of a small town in Ireland.

While many factories in Ireland produced IT products, there was not a lot of IT use among Irish citizens. Ireland's telecommunications company held a contest in 1997 to select and fund an "Information Age Town." The winner was Ennis, a town of 15,000 in western Ireland. The $22 million in prize money represented $1,200 per resident, a large sum for a poor community. Every business was equipped with an Integrated Services Digital Network (ISDN) line, a Web site, and a smart card reader. Every family received a smart card and a personal computer.

Three years later, there was little evidence of people using the new technology. Devices had been introduced without adequately explaining to the people why they might want to use them. The benefits were not obvious. Sometimes the technology competed with social systems that were working just fine. For example, before the introduction of the new technology, unemployed workers visited the social welfare office three times a week to sign in and get an unemployment payment. These visits served an important social function for the unemployed people. It gave them an opportunity to visit with other people and keep their spirits up. Once the PCs were introduced, the workers were supposed to "sign in" and receive their payments over the Internet. Many of the workers did not like the new system. It appears that many of the PCs were sold on the black market. The unemployed workers simply went back to reporting in person to the social welfare office.

For IT to make a difference, social systems must change as well. The introduction of information technology must take into account local culture, which includes language, literacy, and community values.

Warschauer's second criticism of the term "digital divide" is that it implies everyone is on one side or another of a huge canyon. Everybody is put into one of two categories: "haves" and "have nots." In reality access is a continuum, and each individual occupies a particular place on it. For example, how do you categorize someone who has a 56k modem connecting his PC to the Internet? Certainly, that person has online access, but he is not able to retrieve the same wealth of material as someone with a broadband connection.

Third, Warschauer says that the term "digital divide" implies that a lack of access will lead to a less advantaged position in society. Is that the proper causality? Models of technological diffusion show that those with a less advantaged position in society tend to adopt new technologies at a later time, which is an argument that the causality goes the other way. In reality, there is no simple causality. Each factor affects the other [30].

Rob Kling has put it this way:

[The] big problem with "the digital divide" framing is that it tends to connote "digital solutions," i.e., computers and telecommunications, without engaging the important set of complementary resources and complex interventions to support social inclusion, of which informational technology applications may be enabling elements, but are certainly insufficient when simply added to the status quo mix of resources and relationships." [30, pp. 7–8]

Finally, Warschauer points out that the Internet does not represent the pinnacle of information technology. In the next few decades, dramatic new technologies will be created. We will see these new technologies being adopted at different speeds, too.

## 10.5.5   Massive Open Online Courses

For the past several decades, the rate of tuition increases at universities and colleges in the United States has exceeded the inflation rate, making a college education increasingly difficult for students from poorer families. Free massive open online courses (MOOCs) are often promoted as a way to make higher education more affordable, which would help all students, but particularly those from lower socioeconomic backgrounds. In 2012 Colorado State University-Global became the first university in the United States to grant credit to students completing a particular MOOC in computer science [73]. Other universities are likely to follow. Is solving the problem of ever more expensive higher education as simple as providing access to online courses?

The Community College Research Center conducted a study of online education at two statewide community systems, one in the southern United States and the other in the western United States. Their study revealed that students who take online courses are less likely to complete and perform well in them, compared with students who take the same courses in a traditional classroom setting. The study also showed that the online experience widened the achievement gap between white and black students and between those with higher GPAs and those with lower GPAs [74].

The Community College Research Center study provides evidence that a shift toward online education could exacerbate differences in success rates that already exist between different subgroups of students. It reinforces Warschauer's point that the difference between the "haves" and the "have nots" in society is not simply a question of access to a technology or even information.

### 10.5.6 Net Neutrality

In the middle of the last decade, corporations that operate the long-distance Internet backbone connections in the United States suggested that they might begin tiered service—charging more for higher-priority routing of Internet packets. These companies said that tiered service would be needed in the future to guarantee a satisfactory level of service to companies that require it, such as voice over Internet Protocol (VoIP) providers [75].

Content providers such as Google and Yahoo! joined forces with the American Library Association and consumer groups to oppose any notion of tiered service. These groups asked the US Congress to enact "net neutrality" legislation that would require Internet service providers to treat all packets the same. Consumer groups suggested that if tiered service were enacted, only large corporations would be able to pay for the highest level of service. Small start-up companies wouldn't be able to compete with established corporate giants. Hence tiered service would discourage innovation and competition. Another argument against tiered service was based on the concern that companies controlling the Internet might block or degrade access to nonfavored content or applications [75]. For example, a customer with an AT&T/Yahoo! DSL connection might find that high-definition video content from AT&T channels performs better than high-definition video from other providers [76]. Net neutrality advocates said this would be unfair and should be prevented, pointing out that 95 percent of consumers have only two choices for broadband access: the local cable company or the local telephone company [77].

Opponents of net neutrality legislation suggested that allowing people to pay more to get a higher quality of service can benefit consumers. For example, rapid delivery of data packets would be more valuable to a person using the Internet for videoconferencing than a person who simply sends email messages. Internet backbone providers argued that even though there was currently enough bandwidth, the rapidly increasing popularity of YouTube and other online video sites would soon fill the Internet's data pipes. A significant amount of money would be needed to upgrade the Internet infrastructure to support the higher-bandwidth applications of the future. This money ought to come from the companies like Netflix that sell access to data-intensive content [75].

In February 2015, the Federal Communications Commission issued the Open Internet Order to preserve net neutrality. It prohibited telecommunications companies from engaging in three activities: blocking content, throttling back the speed of transmissions, and providing a higher speed of service to people or businesses that pay more [78]. FCC Chairman Tom Wheeler said, "No one—whether government or corporate—should control free, open access to the Internet" [79]. The FCC grounded its authority to make these rules on Title II of the Telecommunications Act, in effect deciding that the Internet should be regulated like a public utility.

The FCC's decision was immediately hailed by some groups and criticized by others. Netflix issued a statement saying, "The net neutrality debate is about who picks winners and losers online: Internet service providers or consumers. Today the FCC settled it: Consumers win" [80]. Meanwhile, Broadband for America, an advocacy group that has Internet service providers among its members, issued a statement saying, "The FCC's decision to impose obsolete telephone-era regulations on the high-speed Internet is one giant step backwards for America's broadband networks and everyone who depends upon them. These 'Title II' rules go far beyond protecting the Open Internet, launching a costly and destructive era of government micromanagement that will discourage private investment in new networks and slow down the breakneck innovation that is the soul of the Internet today" [81].

Within two months of the release of the Open Internet Order, seven lawsuits had been filed against the FCC. Three Internet service providers and four trade associations filed suit in federal court, arguing that the FCC did not have the authority to classify the Internet as a utility [82].

## 10.6 The "Winner–Take–All" Society

The Declaration of Independence states that "all men are created equal," but we live in a society in which some people have far more wealth and power than others. What if everyone were guaranteed roughly the same amount of income? The traditional answer to this question is that there would be little motivation for people to exert themselves, either mentally or physically. If everyone were paid the same, there would be no point in getting an education, taking risks, or working hard. Productivity would be low, and the overall standard of living would be poor. For this reason, many people believe a superior alternative is a market economy that rewards innovation, hard work, and risk taking by compensating people according to the value of the goods they produce.

In *The Winner-Take-All Society*, economists Robert Frank and Philip Cook explore the growth of markets in which a few top performers receive a disproportionate share of the rewards. Their book is the primary source for this section [83].

Frank and Cook observe that the winner-take-all phenomenon has existed for quite a while in the realms of sports, entertainment, and the arts. A few "superstar" athletes, actors, and novelists earn millions from their work and garner lucrative endorsements, while those who perform at a slightly lower level make far less. However, the winner-take-all phenomenon has now spread throughout our global economy. Sometimes the qualitative difference between the top product and the second-best product is very slight, yet that can be the difference between success and failure. Hence corporations compete for the top executive talent that can give them the edge over their competition. The compensation of CEOs at America's largest corporations has risen much faster than the wages of production workers (Figure 10.11) [84].

Several factors have influenced the winner-take-all phenomenon in our economy:

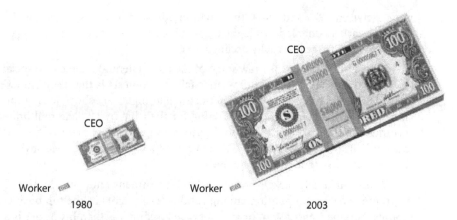

**FIGURE 10.11** In 1980 the average pay for a CEO at a large American company was about 40 times the pay of a production worker. By 2003 the ratio had risen to about 400 to 1.

1. *Information technology and efficient transportation systems make it easier for a leading product to dominate the worldwide market.*

   For example, consider a music studio that has a digital recording of the world's best orchestra playing Beethoven's Symphony no. 5 in C Minor. The studio can produce millions of perfect copies of this recording, enough for every classical music lover on the planet. Why would anyone want to listen to the second-best orchestra when a CD of the best orchestra is available for virtually the same price?

2. *Network economies encourage people to flock to the same product.*

   If by chance you should need to use someone else's computer, it is far more likely that person will own a Windows PC than a Macintosh. In this respect, knowing how to use a Windows computer has greater utility than knowing how to use a Macintosh. If a person cannot decide which computer to purchase, this factor alone may encourage someone to buy a Windows PC.

3. *English has become the de facto language of international business.*

   English is the native language in 12 countries, including the United States, which is the dominant economic power on the planet. Another 56 countries teach English in their schools. The dominance of English makes it easier for products to find a worldwide market.

4. *Business norms have changed.*

   In the past large businesses promoted from within and would not recruit executives from other firms. Today firms vigorously compete with each other for top executive talent.

## 10.6.1 Harmful Effects of Winner–Take–All

Frank and Cook argue that winner-take-all effects are bad for the economy for a variety of reasons. First, winner-take-all markets increase the gap between the rich and the poor. Between 1979 and 1989, the inflation-adjusted incomes of the top 1 percent of US wage earners doubled, while the median income was flat and the average income of the bottom 20 percent actually declined.

Winner-take-all effects draw some of the most talented people into socially unproductive work. The problem with winner-take-all contests is that they attract too many contestants. For every comedian who hosts a late-night talk show, tens of thousands of comedians struggle in nightclubs, hoping for their big break. The multimillion-dollar incomes of a relatively few high-profile attorneys help attract many of the brightest college students toward law school. We end up with a glut of lawyers. Meanwhile, there is a shortage of nurses and nuclear engineers.

Winner-take-all markets create wasteful investment and consumption. For example, there is fierce competition among candidates for slots in the top business and law schools. No one wants to go for an interview looking less than his or her best. For this reason, male interviewees are reluctant to show up for an interview wearing a suit that costs less than $600. But if everyone is wearing a $600 suit, no one has an advantage over the others due to his attire. If they had all spent $300 on their suits, there would have been the same relative equity. The behavior of business school applicants is similar to an arms race. The desire to seek an advantage leads to an escalation of consumption, even if the eventual result is simply parity.

A disproportionate share of the best and brightest college students become concentrated in a few elite institutions. "The day has already arrived," write Frank and Cook, "when failure to have an elite undergraduate degree closes certain doors completely, no matter what other stellar credentials a student might possess" [83, p. 11]. Many Wall Street firms will not even interview candidates who did not graduate from one of a very small number of top law schools. These law schools show a preference for graduates of elite undergraduate programs. Hence high school students interested in reaching the top of the legal profession know their best chance is to do their undergraduate work at an elite school. The result is a tremendous competition for a relatively small number of openings at these colleges, while in truth there are hundreds of top-quality public and private colleges and universities in the United States.

Winner-take-all is not fair because it gives much greater rewards to the top performers than those whose performance is only slightly inferior. Here is an example from the world of professional sports, where winnings and performance data are objective and publicly available. Rory McIlroy, Sergio Garcia, and Derek Ernst all play on the PGA Tour. Their skill levels are very close (see Table 10.2), but their earnings varied dramatically during the 2014 season. McIlroy, who ranked #1 in earnings per tournament, brought home an average of $487,064 for every tournament he entered. Garcia was #2 in this category and earned an average of $308,725 every time he entered a tournament, while Ernst, at #269, earned only $10,916.

Winner-take-all markets harm our culture. Here's why. People are social; they like to read the same books and see the same movies as their friends. It gives them something to talk about. Suppose two books have about the same appeal to a consumer, but one of them is on a best-seller list. The consumer is more likely to select the book on the best-seller list, because it increases the probability she will encounter a friend who has read it. But that means it's really important for a book publisher to get its books on the

| Metric | Rory McIlroy | Sergio Garcia | Derek Ernst |
|---|---|---|---|
| Driving distance (yards) | 310.5 | 294.3 | 297.0 |
| Driving accuracy (%) | 59.93 | 62.19 | 64.41 |
| Greens in regulation (%) | 69.44 | 68.68 | 63.52 |
| Putts/round | 28.59 | 28.59 | 29.92 |
| Scoring average | 69.12 | 69.80 | 72.59 |
| Winnings per tournament | $487,064 | $308,725 | $10,916 |

TABLE 10.2 Comparison of personal statistics of PGA Tour professionals Rory McIlroy, Sergio Garcia, and Derek Ernst for the 2014 season.

best-seller list. Publishers know that books written by "name" authors have a greater chance of making the best-seller list than books written by new authors. This knowledge can lead a publisher to give a big advance to a well-known author to produce a second-rate work, rather than invest the same resources in developing an unknown, but more talented, author. The same effect happens with movie producers. Hoping for the largest possible sales on the first weekend, they bankroll second-rate sequels to big hits rather than original stories filmed by lesser-known directors.

## 10.6.2  Reducing Winner–Take–All Effects

If winner-take-all markets have harmful consequences on our economy and society, what can be done? Frank and Cook suggest four ways to reduce winner-take-all effects. First, societies can enact laws limiting the number of hours that stores remain open for business. These laws ensure parity among competing businesses and prevent them from engaging in positional arms races. Without these laws, one business may extend its hours in order to gain an advantage over its competitors. Soon all of its competitors follow suit. Parity is restored, but now all the employees must bear the burden of the longer hours. Regulations on business hours are often called "blue laws."

Second, in the absence of laws, businesses can form cooperative agreements to reduce positional arms races. An example is when a group of professional sports team owners agrees to establish a cap on team salaries.

Third, more progressive tax structures reduce excess competition for the few handsomely rewarded positions. Back in 1961, the marginal tax rate on income in the highest tax bracket was 91 percent. By 1989, the highest marginal income tax rate had been lowered to 28 percent. Consumption taxes and luxury taxes are other ways of targeting the wealthiest people. Heavily taxing those with the highest incomes makes a higher income less attractive and dissuades some people from competing for the highest-paying jobs. Society benefits when these people engage in more productive work.

Finally, campaign finance reform can reduce the political power of the wealthiest 1 percent of the population, who control more than one-third of the wealth. Reducing the political power of the very wealthy is another way to reduce the attraction of competing for the highest-paying positions.

# Summary

This chapter has explored a variety of ways in which information technology and automation have affected the workplace. We began by asking the question, does automation increase unemployment? On the surface, the answer to this question seems obvious: of course automation increases unemployment. That is what automation means—replacing human labor with machine labor. Industrial robots, voice mail systems, and a myriad of other devices have displaced millions of workers over the past 50 years. However, a deeper look reveals how automation can create jobs, too. When products are less expensive, more people want to buy them, increasing the number that must be made. If products are less expensive, consumers have more money left to spend, which increases demand for other products. Finally, some people are involved in creating and maintaining the machines themselves. For these reasons, the rapid introduction of automation has not yet led to widespread unemployment in the countries where automation is used the most. In fact, the total number of manufacturing jobs worldwide continues to increase.

Thanks to automation, productivity has more than doubled since World War II. However, the length of the workweek in the most highly industrialized nations has not decreased by half. Instead, productivity has been used to increase the standard of living. This choice is understandable since our society defines success in terms of wealth and material possessions. However, not all cultures have the same values. People in some "primitive" cultures choose to work much shorter hours.

Intelligent robots have been a fixture of science fiction novels for more than 60 years. In the past decade, however, faster microprocessors have enabled AI researchers to create systems capable of amazing feats. The success of some research and development efforts leads some to speculate that intelligent machines may make entire job categories obsolete. For example, will a production version of Google's self-driving car make taxi drivers obsolete? A few ethicists have suggested that we temper our efforts to create ever more intelligent computers with some reflection about how highly intelligent computers would affect society.

Information technology has transformed the way businesses organize themselves. Rapid and inexpensive communications allow many more information channels to open up within organizations, which can speed up processes and eliminate middlemen. Evidence of more flexible organizational structures include the rise of telework and multinational teams. Improvements in information technology have also given management unprecedented access to the moment-by-moment activities of employees. Workplace monitoring has become the rule rather than the exception in large corporations.

As modern information technology has spread around the world, corporations form tightly connected networks and sell their products and services in many markets. This process is called globalization. Advocates of globalization claim it creates jobs for people in poorer countries and increases competition, resulting in lower prices and a higher standard of living for everyone. Critics of globalization say it forces workers in highly developed countries to compete with people willing to work for a fraction of the pay.

The notion that only manufacturing jobs could be lost to overseas competition has been disproved by recent events. While the dot-com bust put hundreds of thousands of IT professionals out of work in the United States, American companies shipped hundreds of thousands of jobs to India and other countries where well-educated people work for a fraction of what an American earns. Unemployed American high-tech workers have criticized companies for hiring large numbers of foreigners to work in the United States under H-1B or L-1 visas. Companies respond that reducing labor costs is a necessity in a competitive marketplace. In order to survive and thrive, companies must keep prices down and profits up.

The "digital divide" is a way of splitting people into two groups: those who have access to information technology and those who do not. The term is based on the premise that access to information technology is a prerequisite for success in the Information Age. Some also assume that simply giving people access to the technology solves the problem. Pippa Norris points out that there are several fundamentally different dimensions to the digital divide. One dimension separates the more industrialized nations from the less industrialized nations. Another dimension separates rich and poor within a particular country. Mark Warschauer says the notion of a digital divide is too simplistic for three reasons. First, people have widely varying access to information technology. Access should be seen as a continuum, not a division into "haves" and "have nots." Second, simply giving people information technology devices, such as computers, cell phones, and Internet accounts, does not guarantee they will take full advantage of the opportunities those devices provide. For IT to make a difference, social systems must be taken into account. According to Warschauer, the use of information technology "is a social practice, involving access to physical artifacts, content, skills, and social support" [30, p. 46]. Third, it's too simplistic to say that a lack of access causes someone to have lower socioeconomic status. You could just as easily say that people with lower socioeconomic status adopt new technologies later. In reality, each factor influences the other.

Frank and Cook invented the term "winner-take-all society" to refer to the way that information technology, the spread of English, network effects, and other factors are creating marketplaces where a few top performers gain a disproportionate share of the rewards. They present evidence that winner-take-all effects harm our economy and our culture, and they suggest actions that can be taken to reduce the winner-take-all phenomenon.

# Further Reading and Viewing

Nick Bilton. "The Robot World Is Emerging at Amazon." *New York Times*, March 26, 2012.

Jason Borenstein. "Work Life in the Robotic Age." *Communications of the ACM*, July 2010.

⊚ Rachel Botsman. "The Currency of the New Economy Is Trust." TED Talk, September 2012. 19:42. www.ted.com/talks/.

Philip K. Dick. *Do Androids Dream of Electric Sheep?* Del Ray, New York, NY, 1996. (Originally published in 1968.)

⊚ CGP Grey. "Humans Need Not Apply." YouTube, August 13, 2014. 15:00. www.youtube.com/watch?v=7Pq-S557XQU.

Alan Joch. "Debating Net Neutrality." *Communications of the ACM*, October 2009.

Kevin Kelly. "Better Than Human: Why Robots Will—and Must—Take Our Jobs." *Wired*, December 24, 2012. www.wired.com.

Sarah Kessler. "The Gig Economy Won't Last Because It's Being Sued to Death." *Fast Company*, February 17, 2015. www.fastcompany.com.

⊙ Yul Kwon. "Made in the USA." *America Revisited*, May 2, 2012. 53:10. video.pbs.org.

Steven Levy. "The AI Revolution Is On." *Wired*, January 2010.

"Morals and the Machine" and "March of the Robots." *Economist*, June 2, 2012.

"Not Always with Us." *Economist*, June 1, 2013.

A. Pawlowski. "Why Is America the 'No-Vacation Nation'?" CNN, May 23, 2011. www.cnn .com.

⊙ Daniel Suarez. "The Kill Decision Shouldn't Belong to a Robot." TED Talk, June 2013. 13:20. www.ted.com/talks/.

⊙ Sebastian Thrun. "Google's Driverless Car." TED Talk, March 2011. 4:14. www.ted.com/talks/.

Kurt Vonnegut, Jr. *Player Piano*. Dell, New York, NY, 1988. (Originally published in 1952.)

## Review Questions

1. What are some benefits brought about by automation? What are some harms brought about by automation?

2. What evidence has been given to show that automation eliminates jobs? What evidence has been given to show that automation creates more jobs than it destroys?

3. If automation has doubled productivity since World War II, why hasn't the workweek gotten shorter?

4. In what ways has information technology led to changes in the structure of an organization?

5. Briefly describe some benefits and harms associated with telework.

6. Proponents of globalization claim that it helps workers in developing countries. Opponents of globalization claim the opposite. Summarize the evidence pro and con.

7. Provide a few pieces of evidence demonstrating that access to modern information technology is not uniform.

8. What is the assumption underlying the term "digital divide?" Provide a few arguments that have been raised to cast doubts about the soundness of this assumption.

9. Provide an example of the "winner-take-all" effect, without repeating an example already appearing in the book.

10. Read the interview of Martin Ford at the end of the chapter and summarize his main thesis.

## Discussion Questions

11. Do you agree with Voltaire that a lack of work results in boredom and vice?

12. Would you accept a salaried position (paying a fixed amount each month rather than paying by the hour) if you knew it would require you to work at least 50 hours per week in order to complete the required work?

13. If automation leads to chronic and widespread unemployment, should the government provide long-term unemployed adult citizens with the opportunity to do meaningful work at a wage that will keep them out of poverty? Why or why not?

14. Is it wrong to create machines capable of making human labor obsolete?

15. The Umpire Information System, produced by QuesTec, demonstrates that a computer can call balls and strikes more accurately than a human umpire. In fact, the system is being used by Major League Baseball to evaluate the accuracy of the umpires' calls. Should Major League Baseball allow the Umpire Information System to have the final say on calling balls and strikes?

16. Will humans become demoralized by the presence of vastly more intelligent robots? If so, is it wrong to work on the development of such robots?

17. Is it morally acceptable to work on the development of an intelligent machine if it cannot be guaranteed the machine's actions will be benevolent?

18. How will our notions of intellectual property change if computers become capable of creative work?

19. How will our ideas about privacy have to change if legions of superfast computers are analyzing the electronic records of our lives?

20. Kant says that the rationality and autonomy of human beings must always be respected, and that is why people should always be treated as ends in themselves and never merely as the means to an end. Are there any circumstances under which an intelligent computer should be given the same consideration?

21. It is possible to program responses into computers that simulate human emotions. For example, when a computer taking on the role of a nurse hears a parent say, "My child has diarrhea," it can respond, "I'm sorry to hear that." Studies have shown that people can develop an emotional bond with machines that appear to demonstrate human feelings such as empathy. Is it wrong to encourage these attachments by programming computers to mimic human emotions?

22. *The Grapes of Wrath*, a novel written by John Steinbeck, vividly describes the conditions of migrant workers in California during the Great Depression. In the novel, farmers take advantage of the fact that there is a surplus of labor by lowering wages to the point that families can work all day and still do not earn enough money to feed themselves properly. Do you agree that the gig economy is creating the same kind of "race to the bottom" in terms of worker compensation?

23. A multinational corporation has an office in Palo Alto, California, and an office in Bangalore, India. A 21-year-old American computer science graduate works as a software tester at the Palo Alto office. A 21-year-old Indian computer science graduate has an identical position at the Bangalore office. The American earns $75,000 per year in salary and benefits; the Indian earns $10,000 per year in salary and benefits. Is this arrangement moral? Should the company give equal pay and benefits for equal work?

24. Do you support the concept of tiered Internet service, providing higher bandwidth to those who pay for premium service?

25. Would the music industry be healthier if winner-take-all effects were reduced? If so, which of the proposed solutions in Section 10.6.2 would make the most sense for the music industry?

26. Should the federal government discourage companies from taking advantage of their salaried employees by requiring firms to pay overtime to any employee who works more than 40 hours in one week?

27. Do you agree with Martin Ford (interviewed at the end of this chapter) that countries need to introduce guaranteed income schemes to preserve the market for goods and services?

# In–Class Exercises

28. Seattle, San Francisco, and Los Angeles have approved plans to raise the minimum wage to $15 an hour over the next several years. Critics say such a large increase in the minimum wage will encourage employers to eliminate jobs by introducing automation.

    Debate the following proposition: "The minimum wage in the United States should be raised to $15 an hour." (Before the debate, each side will need to be given sufficient time to research the issue and gather evidence.)

29. A multinational corporation transfers a foreign employee to the United States on an L-1 visa. The foreign employee is a computer programmer, working alongside an American computer programmer doing the same work. Both programmers joined the company five years ago after graduating from college. Their training, skills, and experience are virtually identical.

    Debate the following proposition: "The salaries and benefits of the two computer programmers should be roughly equivalent."

30. You lead a group of five software engineers involved in the testing of a new product. Your manager tells you that because of a company-wide layoff, you need to give notice to one member of your team. From your interactions with the team members, you can easily identify the two members who are least productive, but you are not sure which of them you should lay off. You know that the company keeps track of all Internet traffic to each person's computer, although you have never shared this information with your team. You could use this information to determine how much time, if any, these two employees are spending surfing the Web. Is it wrong to access these records?

31. A company runs a large technical support office. At any time, about 50 technical support specialists are on duty, answering phone calls from customers. The company is considering paying the technical support specialists based on two criteria: the average number of phone calls they answer per hour and the results of occasional customer satisfaction surveys. Debate the pros and cons of the proposed method of determining wages.

32. In this role-playing exercise, students weigh the pros and cons of working for companies with different philosophies about work.

    Company A is a large, established hardware and software company. Employees have a reasonable level of job security, although there have been layoffs in the past few years. Salaries are highly competitive. The company offers stock options, but the stock price is not rising rapidly, and employees know they are not going to get rich from selling their options. The typical programmer works about 45 hours a week.

    Company B is a medium-sized, mature software company that plays a dominant role in a specialized market. The company has never had to lay off employees. Salaries are a little low by industry standards, but programmers get paid overtime when they work more than 40 hours a week. The company discourages managers from resorting to overtime work on projects. Many employees are involved in community activities, such as coaching their kids' sports teams.

Company C is a small start-up company trying to be the first to bring a new kind of shopping experience to the Web. Salaries are not high, but all the employees have a lot of stock options. If the product is successful, everyone expects to become a multimillionaire when the company goes public in a couple of years. In return for the stock options, the founders expect a total commitment from all the employees until the product is released. Every programmer in the company is working 10 hours a day, 7 days a week.

Divide the class into four groups: three groups of recruiters and one group of students about to graduate from college. Each group of recruiters, representing one of the three companies, should make a "pitch" that highlights the reasons why their company represents the best opportunity. The graduates should raise possible negative aspects of working for each company.

33. Debate the following proposition: "It is immoral for a corporation to pay its chief executive officer (CEO) 400 times as much as a production worker."

# References

[1]     Jeffrey Kosseff. "US Calls, India Answers." *Sunday Oregonian* (Portland, OR), October 5, 2003.

[2]     Vikas Balaj. "A New Capital of Call Centers." *New York Times*, November 25, 2011.

[3]     Isaac Asimov. "Runaround." *Astounding Science Fiction*, March 1942.

[4]     Kurt Vonnegut Jr. *Player Piano*. Delacourte Press, New York, NY, 1952.

[5]     "The Misery of Manufacturing." *Economist*, pp. 61–62, September 27, 2003.

[6]     Todd Lassa. "Toyota, Chrysler Have North America's Most Efficient Plants." *Motor Trend* (blog), July 5, 2008. blogs.motortrend.com.

[7]     Stanley Aronowitz, Dawn Esposito, William DiFazio, and Margaret Yard. "The Post-Work Manifesto." In *Post-Work: The Wages of Cybernation*, edited by Stanley Aronowitz and Jonathan Cutler, pp. 31–80. Routledge, New York, NY, 1998.

[8]     Michael Gurstein. "Perspectives on Urban and Rural Community Informatics: Theory and Performance, Community Informatics and Strategies for Flexible Networking." In *Closing the Digital Divide: Transforming Regional Economies and Communities with Information Technology*, edited by Stewart Marshall, Wallace Taylor, and Xinghuo Yu, pp. 1–11. Praeger, Westport, CT, 2003.

[9]     Louis Uchitelle and N. R. Kleinfield. "The Price of Jobs Lost." In *The Downsizing of America*. Times Books/Random House, New York, NY, 1996.

[10]    Juliet B. Schor. *The Overworked American: The Unexpected Decline of Leisure*. Basic Books, New York, NY, 1991.

[11]    Melissa Will. "Hyper Business or Just . . . Hyperbusy." *Women in Business* 53(3), May/June 2001.

[12]    Michael H. Strople. "Bears, Bulls, and Brokers: Employment Trends in the Securities Industry." *Monthly Labor Review Online* 128(12), December 2005. www.bls.gov.

[13]    Martin Carnoy. *Sustaining the New Economy: Work, Family, and the Community in the Information Age*. Russell Sage Foundation/Harvard University Press, New York, NY/Cambridge, MA, 2000.

[14]    Max Weber. *The Protestant Ethic and the Spirit of Capitalism*. Translated by Talcott Parsons, with foreword by R. H. Tawney. Charles Scribner's Sons, New York, NY, 1958.

[15]    The case study is inspired by the following source: Ron Beadle. "Ethics and Employment or the Case of the Cancelled Holiday." *Second UK Conference on Ethical Issues in Contemporary HRM*, Kingston Business School, January 7, 1998.

[16]    Hans Moravec. *Robot: Mere Machine to Transcendent Mind*. Oxford University Press, Oxford, England, 1999.

[17]    Anthony Ralton, Edwin D. Reilly, and David Hemmendinger, editors. *Encyclopedia of Computer Science*. 4th ed. Groves Dictionaries, New York, NY, 2000.

[18]    Steven Ashley. "Driving between the Lines." *Mechanical Engineering* 117(11), November 1995.

[19]    Monty Newborn. *Deep Blue: An Artificial Intelligence Milestone*. Springer, New York, NY 2002.

[20]    "Humanoids on the March." *Economist*, March 12, 2005.

[21]    "Better Than People." *Economist*, December 20, 2005.

[22]    Electrolux. "The Trilobite 2.0." August 3, 2005. www.electrolux.com/node613.asp.

[23]    Joshua Davis. "Say Hello to Stanley." *Wired*, January 2006.

[24]    "Google Self-Driving Car Project Monthly Report." May 2015. static.googleuser content.com/media/www.google.com.

[25]    Richard G. Epstein. "Now Hiring: Dogs and Humans Need Not Apply." *Ethics and Information Technology* 1:227–236, 1999.

[26]    Michael R. LaChat. "Artificial Intelligence and Ethics: An Exercise in the Moral Imagination." *AI Magazine*, pp. 70–79, Summer 1986.

[27]    AAAI Presidential Panel on Long-Term AI Futures. "Interim Report from the Panel Chairs." August 2009. research.microsoft.com/en-us/um/people/horvitz.

[28]    M. Castells. "The Informational Economy and the New International Division of Labor." In *The New Global Economy in the Information Age: Reflections on Our Changing World*, edited by M. Carnoy, M. Castells, S. S. Cohen, and F. H. Cardoso, pp. 15–43. Pennsylvania State University Press, University Park, PA, 1993.

[29]    David Rotman. "How Technology Is Destroying Jobs." *MIT Technology Review*, July/August 2013.

[30]    Mark Warschauer. *Technology and Social Inclusion: Rethinking the Digital Divide*. MIT Press, Cambridge, MA, 2003.

[31]    Mike Gray, Noel Hodson, and Gil Gordon. *Teleworking Explained*. John Wiley & Sons, Chichester, England, 1993.

[32]    Lance Whitney. "Report: Two of Every Five of Workers Telecommute." CNet News (Web site), October 9, 2009. news.cnet.com.

[33]    Joel Kugelmass. *Telecommuting: A Manager's Guide to Flexible Work Arrangements*. Lexington Books, New York, NY, 1995.

[34]    Gerald Friedman. "The Rise of the Gig Economy." *Dollars&Sense: Real World Economics*, March/April 2014. dollarsandsense.org.

[35]    Natasha Singer. "In the Sharing Economy, Workers Find Both Freedom and Uncertainty." *New York Times*, August 16, 2014. www.nytimes.com.

[36]    Robert Reich. "In Sharing Economy, Workers Get Stuck with the Scraps." SFGate (Web site), February 7, 2015. www.sfgate.com.

[37]  Carolyn Said. "Internal Uber E-mails Reflect Company's Brash Reputation." SFGate (Web site), January 30, 2015. www.sfgate.com.

[38]  Maya Kosoff. "The California Labor Commission Just Ruled That an Uber Driver Is an Employee—Here's Why It Could Dramatically Change Uber's Business Model." *Business Insider*, June 17, 2015. www.businessinsider.com.

[39]  American Management Association. "2007 Electronic Monitoring & Surveillance Survey." February 28, 2008. press.amanet.org.

[40]  "Employers Take a Closer Look." *InformationWeek.com*, pp. 40–41, July 15, 2002.

[41]  Rachel Fielding. "Management Week: Web Misuse Rife in UK Firms." VNU NET (Web site), July 15, 2002.

[42]  "Stopping Workplace Internet Abuse—First Step Is Identifying Scope of the Problem." *PR Newswire*, October 7, 2002.

[43]  Carl Weinschenk. "Prying Eyes." *Information Security*, August 2002.

[44]  Melissa Solomon. "Watching Workers; the Dos and Don'ts of Monitoring Employee Productivity." *Computerworld*, July 8, 2002.

[45]  Murray Chass. "Umpires Renew Objections to Computer System." *New York Times*, March 4, 2003.

[46]  Katie Hafner. "Where the Hall Monitor Is a Webcam." *New York Times*, February 27, 2003.

[47]  Sam Dillon. "Classroom Cameras Catch Every Move." *Sunday Oregonian* (Portland, OR), September 28, 2003.

[48]  Andrew Urbaczewski and Leonard M. Jessup. "Does Electronic Monitoring of Employee Internet Usage Work?" *Communications of the ACM* 45(1):80–83, January 2002.

[49]  Robert X. Cringely. "Holy Cow! What Are All These Programmers Doing in India?" *I, Cringely*, PBS, July 10, 1997. www.pbs.org/cringely.

[50]  Cindy Easton. "Offshore Software Development: Is It Helping or Hurting Our Economy?" *Cursor* (Software Association of Oregon Newsletter), February 2003.

[51]  Patrick Thibodeau. "Survey: One in Four IT Jobs Moving Offshore." *Computerworld*, December 9, 2008. www.computerworld.com.

[52]  "One World?" *Economist*, October 16, 1997.

[53]  Paul Krugman. "Enemies of the WTO; Bogus Arguments against the World Trade Organization." *Slate*, November 24, 1999. www.slate.msn.com.

[54]  Anthony B. Bradley. "Corn Subsidies at Root of US–Mexico Immigration Problems." Acton Institute, February 29, 2012. www.acton.org.

[55]  Anthony Perkins. "Investors: Brace Yourselves for the Next Bubble Bath." *Red Herring*, pp. 21–22, November 13, 2000.

[56]  Reuters. "Technology Sector Lost 560,000 Jobs in Two Years." *NYTimes.com*, March 19, 2003.

[57]  Joseph Menn. "Data Reveals Severity of Tech's Pain." *Los Angeles Times*, March 7, 2003.

[58]  Patrick Thibodeau. "H-1B Visa Count Down, Anger Up." *Computerworld*, February 3, 2003.

[59]  Patrick Thibodeau. "Feds to Research 20,000 H-1B Visas Next Week." *Computerworld*, May 4, 2005.

[60]  Eric Chabrow. "Opposing Views: The Debate over the H-1B Visa Program." *Information Week*, May 9, 2005.

[61]    US Citizenship and Immigration Services. "Cap Count for H-1B and H-2B Workers for Fiscal Year 2010." September 3, 2009. www.uscis.gov.

[62]    Ephraim Schwartz. "Senators Open Inquiry of L-1 Visa Program." *InfoWorld*, June 27, 2007. www.infoworld.com.

[63]    "Chinese Firm Buys IBM PC Business." *BBC News*, December 8, 2004.

[64]    S. Srinivasan. "Chinese PM Seeks Indian Tech Cooperation." Associated Press, April 10, 2005.

[65]    "A Wealth of Choices: From Anywhere on Earth to No Location at all." ATKearney (Web site), accessed October 29, 2015.

[66]    Alban Douillet, Juergen Ributzka, and Suneel Jain. "Open64 Compiler and Tools," 2015. sourceforge.net/projects/open64/

[67]    ACM International Collegiate Programming Contest (Web site). Accessed August 15, 2015. cm.baylor.edu /ICPCWiki/.

[68]    Pippa Norris. *Digital Divide: Civic Engagement, Information Poverty, and the Internet Worldwide*. Cambridge University Press, Cambridge, England, 2001.

[69]    Internet World Stats: Usage and Population Statistics. "World Internet Usage and Population Statistics." December 31, 2014. www.internetworldstats.com.

[70]    Telecom Asia. "World's Least Penetrated Mobile Markets." *Telecom Ramblings*, January 24, 2013. www.telecomramblings.com.

[71]    Elena Murelli. *Breaking the Digital Divide: Implications for Developing Countries*. Edited and with foreword by Rogers W'o Okot-Uma. SFI Publishing, 2002.

[72]    Andew Perrin and Maeve Duggan. "Americans' Internet Access: 2000–2015." Pew Research Center, June 26, 2015. www.pewinternet.org.

[73]    Steve Kolowich. "A University's Offer of Credit for a MOOC Gets No Takers." *Chronicle of Higher Education*, July 8, 2013.

[74]    Community College Research Center. "What We Know about Online Course Outcomes." Columbia University, April 2013. ccrc.tc.columbia.edu.

[75]    "Broadband Connectivity Competition Policy." Federal Trade Commission, Washington, DC, June 2007.

[76]    Jim Louderback. "Winter of My Discontent." *PC Magazine*, April 10, 2007.

[77]    S. Derek Turner. "Give Net Neutrality a Chance." *BusinessWeek Online*, July 12, 2007.

[78]    Jeff Sommer. "What the Net Neutrality Rules Say." *New York Times*, March 12, 2015. www.nytimes.com.

[79]    Bill Chappell. "FCC Approves Net Neutrality Rules for 'Open Internet.'" National Public Radio, February 26, 2015. www.npr.org.

[80]    Tom Huddleston, Jr. "Reactions to FCC Net Neutrality Vote: Celebrations, Legal Threats and Morse Code." *Forbes*, February 26, 2015. fortune.com.

[81]    "Broadband for America Statement on FCC Open Internet Order Vote." February 26, 2015. www.broadbandforamerica.org.

[82]    Rudy Takala. "Seven Lawsuits Now Pending against FCC over 'Net Neutrality' Rule." CNSNews (Web site), April 24, 2015. www.cnsnews.com.

[83]    Robert H. Frank and Philip J. Cook. *The Winner-Take-All Society*. Penguin Books, New York, NY, 1995.

[84]    "Where's the Stick?" *Economist*, p. 13, October 11, 2003.

# Martin Ford

Martin Ford is the author of *The Lights in the Tunnel: Automation, Accelerating Technology and the Economy of the Future.* The book argues that accelerating information technology, and in particular robotics and artificial intelligence, is likely to have a disruptive impact on the future job market and economy. He has also written articles focusing on job automation technology for publications such as *Forbes, Fortune,* and the *Washington Post.*

Ford is the founder of a Silicon Valley–based software development firm and has over 25 years' experience in the fields of computer design and software development. He holds a computer engineering degree from the University of Michigan, Ann Arbor, and a graduate business degree from the University of California, Los Angeles. He blogs regularly at econfuture.wordpress.com.

---

### What is propelling the trend toward job automation?

The primary force is the continuing acceleration of information technology. Computers are now able to take on basic cognitive tasks such as decision making and problem solving to an unprecedented degree, and this capability is certain to advance greatly over the next decade and beyond. We can expect dramatic advances in both robotics and software automation applications that take on tasks and analysis now performed by white-collar workers.

A closely related issue is the vast amount of data now being collected throughout the economy: businesses are tracking the actions and behaviors of both consumers and workers. Virtually every transaction and customer interaction, as well as a great many activities internal to organizations, is being recorded. As organizations strive to make sense of—and somehow leverage—all that information, algorithmic approaches are becoming the only viable option. That is driving a lot of development in artificial intelligence (in particular, machine learning), and ultimately those advances are likely to get applied to a great many areas, including job automation.

Economic factors are also, of course, important. As consumer demand remains relatively weak, the primary path to corporate profitability is through efficiency and cost cutting. The danger going forward is that business will continue to focus on extracting as much wealth as possible through cost cutting, rather than on making investments that create new markets and help expand the economy.

### Why should we be concerned about the trend toward job automation?

I think it is a matter of degree. Technology has, of course, been advancing for hundreds of years, and we are all far better off because of that. However, I think we may soon approach a tipping point where machines evolve from being tools to becoming autonomous workers. Historically, as technology advanced and machines became more capable, the value of the average worker operating one of those machines increased, and so average wages also increased. However, once machines, on the average, get closer to running themselves, the value of workers will begin to stagnate and then decrease rather than increase over time. In fact, we see evidence of that already: real wages for average workers in the United States have not increased since the 1970s.

Once we pass that tipping point, technology will no longer drive broad-based prosperity. Instead, the fruits of innovation will all go to a tiny number of people at the top of the income distribution—to people who own or control large amounts of capital.

### *Isn't offshoring a bigger threat to the jobs of computer professionals in the United States than automation?*

Offshoring is more visible, but studies have shown that automation actually eliminates more IT jobs. In the 1990s, huge numbers of jobs were created for IT professionals, like systems administrators. Many of those tasks are now automated, and the trend toward cloud computing is eliminating a lot of positions as businesses outsource IT functions to centralized facilities.

I think that offshoring is very often the leading edge of the trend toward automation. Both are driven by advancing technology. When the technology is not yet sufficient to fully automate a task, offshoring will be pursued on an interim basis, but in the longer run, the task may well get automated. We already see this in areas like basic customer service where low-wage offshore workers have been replaced by digital voice systems in some cases.

### *For a long time, economists have argued that the drop in the price of a product resulting from automation has two beneficial effects. It increases the demand for the product, which means more workers must be hired in order to help produce more of the product. Also, people who were already purchasing the product don't have to pay as much for it, meaning they have more money to spend on other things, increasing the demand for other products, which also results in job creation. Why is this line of reasoning no longer sound?*

Once we pass the tipping point I mentioned earlier—where machines cease to be tools and begin to operate more autonomously—then businesses will be increasingly able to ramp up production without hiring many new workers. So from that point on, it will be very difficult to maintain full employment.

As an example, consider the mechanization of agriculture early in the twentieth century. Millions of farm jobs were eliminated, but ultimately those people found work in other sectors. As food prices fell, consumers were able to spend more on manufactured goods and on services—driving employment in those areas.

Why won't that same process happen today? Because today's information technology is ubiquitous: it will get applied to every sector of the economy and to every new industry that appears in the future. That is very different from agriculture or early manufacturing automation, where the technologies were primarily mechanical and highly specific to the sector. Today's IT is far more flexible and will impact across the board.

The greatest disruption to the US job market will occur when the service sector begins to see substantial automation. It seems likely that many of the more traditional, labor-intensive areas of the economy—like fast food, retail, and other service jobs—will eventually be impacted by these technologies. Once that happens, it is difficult to see how the economy will create the millions of new jobs necessary to absorb those workers.

Most economists believe that the economy will once again adapt and create jobs in new industries and employment sectors. However, we already see that businesses and industries created in recent years are highly technology/capital-intensive—and not labor-intensive. We can probably get some insight into what future industries will look like by considering prominent corporations like Google, Facebook, Amazon, or Netflix. All rely heavily on technology and employ relatively few workers.

While it is easy to imagine many new industries arising in the future in areas like nanotechnology, biotech, genetic engineering, and so forth, it is much harder to imagine truly new future industries that will employ large numbers of "average" people. One possible exception may be the so-called "green jobs," but these are primarily infrastructure/refitting jobs doing things like installing insulation or solar panels; they are not really associated with a sustainable new employment sector. For the most part, it seems likely that information technology will underlie newly created industries, while at the same time disrupting the more traditional industries that now employ a large fraction of our workforce.

**This sounds like a version of the tragedy of the commons. It is to the advantage of each individual company to reduce its costs by introducing automation and cutting workers, but when every company does this, the pool of consumers evaporates.**

Yes; in fact, in my book *The Lights in the Tunnel*, I suggest that we should view the market for goods and services much like a public resource such as a river or an ocean. If you imagine that the market consists of a "river of purchasing power," then as a business sells a product or service into the market, it will extract purchasing power. As a business pays wages to workers, it returns purchasing power to the river.

However, as automation increases throughout the economy, the mechanism for returning purchasing power to the river begins to break down—so the river will eventually run dry. For any individual business, there is a clear incentive to pay out as little as possible in wages; yet, collectively, those wages are the primary source of income for the consumers who purchase the products and services the businesses are selling.

**In many cases, jobs have been eliminated through the introduction of information technology, but the job wasn't automated; the service function was transformed into a self-service function. I'm thinking of self-service gas pumps and self-service checkout lanes. The customer is now doing much of the work.**

Yes, this trend is important because it effectively lowers the threshold for eliminating jobs. In fact, a business does not need to fully automate everything a worker does: it simply needs to make the task simple and approachable enough so it can be taken on by the consumer. This is, of course, happening with ATMs, self-serve checkout lanes, and increasingly sophisticated vending machines. We are also beginning to see information and customer service provided via mobile devices.

It's also important to note that self-service of this type will happen internal to organizations. For example, a manager who currently supervises a number of knowledge workers may someday instead have access to powerful AI-enabled tools that enable him or her to directly take on many of the tasks now performed by those workers. This is likely to further flatten organizations, eliminating knowledge-based jobs and middle managers.

**Are you anti-technology? Would our global society be better off without the development of new information technologies?**

Not at all. I believe that the prosperity we now enjoy in developed countries is almost entirely due to technological progress. And I think technology offers the only hope for increased prosperity in the future.

The problem is not with technology but with our economic system. We need to adapt it to reflect the new realities implied by advancing information technology. Without that, the benefits from innovation will accrue only to a tiny number of people, while the vast majority see their situations stagnate or decline. Ultimately, that seems likely to undermine the entire economy as well as our political and social institutions.

**You have argued that without some fundamental changes, we're facing a continuing downward spiral in our economy: job losses leading to consumers being eliminated from**

***the market leading to falling demand leading to further job losses. Briefly, what is your prescription for preventing this collapse?***

Ultimately, I think we will have to decouple access to an income from the need to have a traditional job. The easiest way to do this is through some type of basic, guaranteed income scheme. In other words, everyone would receive an income, and those who have the necessary skills and motivation (and could find an opportunity) would also be able to generate additional income through work or entrepreneurship.

In today's political environment, a guaranteed income would probably be disparaged as an extreme leftist idea or "the welfare state run amok." However, a guaranteed income is actually a free-market concept and was supported by conservative economists like Friedrick Hayek and Milton Friedman.

One problem with a guaranteed income is that jobs, of course, provide more than just an income—work is a way to occupy time and also gives people a sense of purpose. In *The Lights in the Tunnel,* I suggest that we might modify a basic income scheme by incorporating incentives—especially for education.

For example, suppose we offered everyone a minimal income, but if a person manages to graduate from high school or pass an equivalency test, he or she will receive a higher income. The same could be done for higher levels of education, and other incentives such as work in the community could also be incorporated. The idea would be to maintain a strong incentive for the population to become educated while at the same time giving consumers access to the income they need to participate in and drive the economy.

# Plagiarism

AN ETHICAL ANALYSIS OF A SCENARIO INVOLVING PLAGIARISM APPEARS IN SECTION 2.6.2. This appendix provides a much more complete picture of what plagiarism is and how to avoid it.

## Consequences of Plagiarism

According to the Council of Writing Program Administrators (WPA), "plagiarism occurs when a writer deliberately uses someone else's language, ideas, or other original (not common-knowledge) material without acknowledging its source" [1]. The consequences of plagiarism can be severe. Newspaper reporters and college professors have lost their jobs because they plagiarized the work of others [2, 3]. Colleges and universities view plagiarism as a form of cheating. A few years ago at the University of Virginia, 48 students either quit or were expelled for plagiarism [4].

The vast amount of information freely available on the Internet, the power of search engines, and the cut-and-paste capability of contemporary computer programs have made it easier than ever to commit plagiarism. Of course, Web search engines can also make it easy for teachers to detect plagiarism [5].

## Types of Plagiarism

You are plagiarizing if you deliberately do any of the following:

- Copy the words of another without both (1) putting the copied text in quotation marks and (2) citing the source
- Paraphrase the words of another without citing the source
- Incorporate the figures or drawings of another person without crediting the source
- Include facts that are not common knowledge without citing the source
- Use another person's ideas or theories without giving that person credit

## Guidelines for Citing Sources

**Common knowledge** means information that is available in many places and known to a large number of people. For example, it is common knowledge that Delaware was the first state to ratify the United States Constitution. You do not have to cite a source when presenting common knowledge.

However, you *should* cite a source when you present facts that are not common knowledge. For example, it is not common knowledge that the percentage of college freshmen in the United States interested in majoring in computer science dropped by more than 60 percent between 2000 and 2004 [6].

You must cite a source if you present another person's interpretation of the facts, whether or not you acknowledge the person by name. For example, Cass Sunstein argues that information technology may weaken democracy by allowing people to filter out news that contradicts their view of the world [7]. If you repeat someone else's idea, you must cite where you found it.

## How to Avoid Plagiarism

Always put quotation marks around text you have obtained from another source, and write down enough information about the source that you can cite it properly. Do this when you are collecting your notes, so that when you are writing your paper, you will not forget that the words are a direct quotation or whom you are quoting.

When you are paraphrasing the work of another, read over the material, then put it aside before you begin writing. That will help ensure you are using your own words to express the ideas. Check your paraphrase against the source document. Make sure you have not distorted the original meaning. Whenever you have used a phrase from another person's work, you must put the phrase in quotation marks. Always cite the source of the ideas you are paraphrasing, even if there are no direct quotations.

Finally, remember to cite the sources of illustrations and figures that you reproduce.

## Misuse of Sources

The WPA definition of plagiarism emphasizes that it is the *deliberate* attempt to conceal the source of the words or ideas. This aligns with our definition of ethics as being focused on the *voluntary* moral choices people make. If a person has no intention of deceiving, but fails to cite sources or use quotation marks correctly, that person's actions constitute **misuse of sources.**

## Additional Information

For more information, read "Defining and Avoiding Plagiarism: The WPA Statement on Best Practices," which is the principal source document for this appendix [1].

## References

[1]     Council of Writing Program Administrators. "Defining and Avoiding Plagiarism: The WPA Statement on Best Practices." January 2003. www.wpacouncil.org.

[2]     "Corrections." *New York Times*, May 2, 2003.

[3]     Scott Smallwood. "Arts Professor at New School U. Resigns after Admitting Plagiarism." *Chronicle of Higher Education*, September 20, 2004.

[4]     Brian Hansen. "Combating Plagiarism: Is the Internet Causing More Students to Copy?" *CQ Researcher* 13(32), 2003.

[5]     Katie Hafner. "Lessons in Internet Plagiarism." *New York Times*, June 28, 2001.

[6]     Jay Vegso. "Interest in CS as a Major Drops among Incoming Freshmen." *Computing Research News* 17(3), May 2005.

[7]     Cass Sunstein. *Republic.com*. Princeton University Press, Princeton, NJ, 2001.

# Index